To
Doris Whyde —
Thank you for your
interest
John ate
10 July 1983

Other Books by Author

Collectible Boy Dolls

Collectible Dolls in National Costume

The Collectible Dionne Quintuplets

Collectible Black Dolls

Collectible Patsy Dolls and Patsy-Types

Collectible Sonja Henie

Tammy and Dolls You Love to Dress

Collecting Modern Dolls (Editor)

Effanbee: A Collector's Encyclopedia Volume III—1950-1983

The Encyclopedia of Celebrity Dolls

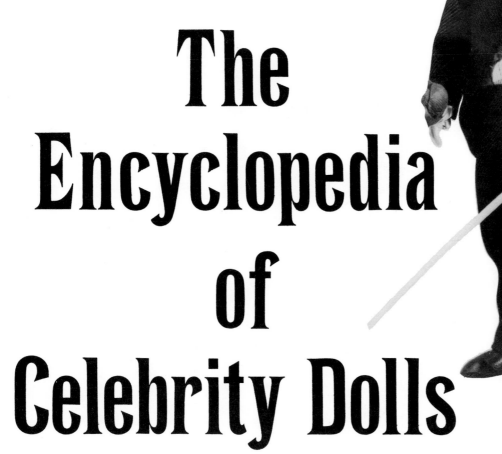

by John Axe

Additional Copies of this Book may be Purchased at $27.50
from
HOBBY HOUSE PRESS, INC.
900 Frederick Street
Cumberland, Maryland 21502
or from your favorite bookstore or dealer.
Please add $2.25 per copy postage.

OPPOSITE PAGE: JOHN BUNNY by Louis Amberg and Son, 1914. *Irene Trittschuh Collection.*

ISBN: 0-87588-186-6

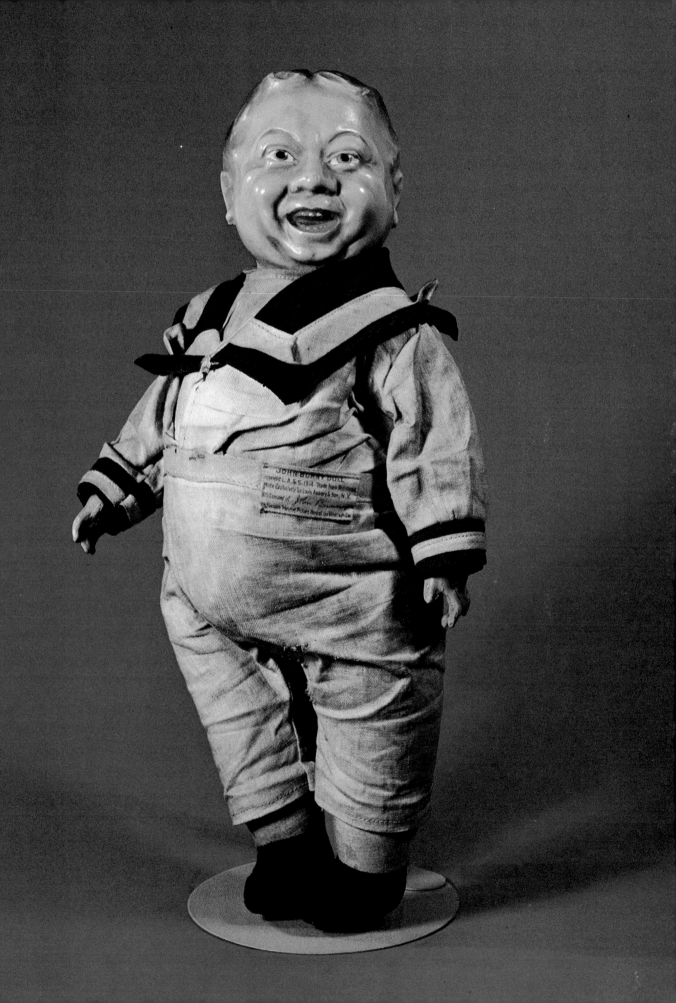

PRINCESS CHARLOTTE by Ann Parker. See page 84.

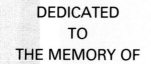

DEDICATED
TO
THE MEMORY OF
my sister
Susan P. Axe
(February 21, 1950—July 4, 1981)

HAROLD LLOYD, maker unknown, circa late 1920s. *Ralph Griffith.*

W.C. FIELDS by Effanbee, 1938. *Beulah Franklin Collection. Photograph by Carole Bowling.*

RIGHT: SHIRLEY TEMPLE baby by Ideal, 1935. 16in (40.6cm). *Betty Shriver Collection.*

BELOW LEFT: SHIRLEY TEMPLE Texas Ranger by Ideal, 1936. 16in (40.6cm). *Mandeville-Barkel Collection. Photograph by Chip Barkel.*

BELOW RIGHT: SHIRLEY TEMPLE from *The Blue Bird* by Ideal, 1940. 18in (45.7cm). *Mandeville-Barkel Collection. Photograph by Chip Barkel.*

Acknowledgements

I could not have completed this project without the cooperation of the following individuals and organizations:

For permitting me to photograph dolls from their collections: Margaret Ashbrook, Lois Barrett, Frances Benson, Kay Bransky, Peter Bransky, Shirley Buchholz, Rosemarye Bunting, Janet Butler, Jean Canaday, Celina Carroll, Penny Caswell, Connie Chase, Barbara DeVault, Dolls & Stuff—Ginny's Antiques, Peggy Fesperman, Fran's Dolls, Patricia Gardner, Ralph Griffith, Phyllis Houston, Lee Jenkins, Joyce Kintner, Bobby Lodwick, Wanda Lodwick, Marge Meisinger, Ursula Mertz, Jeanne Niswonger, Billie Jo Phillips, Jean Pritchard, Emilie Marie Reynolds, Mary Lee Ruddell, Betty Shriver, Patricia Slabe, Ted Tarr, Edna Tinker, and Irene Trittschuh;

For providing research material: Javier Barragán, Kay Bransky, Shirley Buchholz, Marceil Drake, Patricia Gardner, Sally Hile, Virginia Ann Heyerdahl, Andrea Jones, Cookie Mullins, Bernadine O'Donnell, Dori O'Melia, Fay Rodolfos, Jimmy Rodolfos, Mary Stuecher, and Alma Wolfe;

For sending me photographs of their dolls: Chip Barkel, Alma Boudreaux Cansler, Dorothy S. Coleman, Mary K. Dahl, Ruth E. Fisher, Rosemary Dent, Beulah Franklin, Patricia Gardner, Betty Kilgore, Glenn Mandeville, Ted Menten, Sandy Rankow, Fay Rodolfos, Jimmy Rodolfos, Patricia N. Schoonmaker, and Shelia Wallace;

Companies who aided me with photographs or information: Alexander Doll Company; Columbia Pictures; Dolls by Al Trattner; Effanbee Doll Corporation; House of Nisbet; Ideal Toy Corp.; Kenner Products; Knickerbocker Toy Co., Inc.; LJN Toys; Mego Corp.; Montgomery Ward; Paramount Pictures; Pittsburgh Doll Company; Playthings; and United States Historical Society;

For valuable photographs: The Margaret Woodbury Strong Museum;

Reference librarians and libraries: Cleveland Public Library; Library of Congress, Washington, D.C.; Maag Library of Youngstown State University; and Public Library of Youngstown and Mahoning County, whose reference librarians were the most helpful of all;

For her time and generosity: Anne Shirley Lederer;

For her doll and for her daughter: Ruby K. Arnold;

For technical assistance: Bette Ann Axe, Patricia Axe, and C. Kenneth Clark, Jr.;

For their work in the production of this book: The Staff at Hobby House Press, Inc.;

For her sharp eye, for her dedication and for her interest: Editor Donna H. Felger;

For his confidence in me and in this project: Publisher Gary R. Ruddell.

I will always be grateful for their help.

All photographs by John Axe unless otherwise credited.

ABOVE: DIONNE QUINTUPLETS by Madame Alexander, 1936. 7in (17.8cm). *Rodolfos Collection. Photograph by Fay Rodolfos.*

RIGHT: DEANNA DURBIN by Ideal, 1939. 17½in (44.5cm). *Jean Canaday Collection.*

OPPOSITE PAGE: SHIRLEY TEMPLE from *Heidi,* 1937. *Patricia Slabe Collection.*

BOTTOM LEFT: BABY SANDY by Ralph A. Freundlich, Inc., 1939. *Mandeville-Barkel Collection. Photograph by Chip Barkel.*

BOTTOM RIGHT PRINCESS ELIZABETH by Madame Alexander, circa 1939. 17in (43.2cm). *Patricia Slabe Collection.*

Table
of Contents

LEFT: CARMEN MIRANDA by Madame Alexander, circa 1941. *Mandeville-Barkel Collection. Photograph by Chip Barkel.*

RIGHT: MARGARET O'BRIEN by Madame Alexander, 1946. All-composition. 18in (45.7cm). *Mandeville-Barkel Collection. Photograph by Chip Barkel.*

BELOW LEFT: MARGARET O'BRIEN by Madame Alexander, 1947. Hard Plastic. 18in (45.7cm). *Mandeville-Barkel Collection. Photograph by Chip Barkel.*

BELOW RIGHT: QUEEN ELIZABETH II and PRINCE PHILIP by Madame Alexander, circa 1953. 18in (45.7cm). *Mandeville-Barkel Collection. Photograph by Chip Barkel.*

OPPOSITE PAGE: KING GEORGE VI by Farnell's Alpha Toys, late 1930s.

How To Use This Book

This book is an encyclopedia of all celebrities who have been made in doll form and all dolls of celebrities. It provides historical perspective, facts both pertinent and interesting about the persons who have had dolls manufactured to represent them, and is a complete record of the dolls themselves.

All celebrity dolls are not portraits. Some of them are difficult to identify. Many of the dolls of entertainment personalities, for example, are based on a character the celebrity played, rather than being a rendition of the person's usual physical appearance. Such dolls were neither sold nor advertised using the celebrity's name. Yet all are described in this encyclopedia, as are all dolls sold as portraits of celebrities.

The Reader will find the extensive Index and the Introduction to the book helpful. All dolls and all celebrities are cross-indexed and are listed in the Index under the name of the person and the name (or names) of the doll. The Encyclopedia section is listed in strict alphabetical order under the name of the celebrity. The doll, or dolls, that represent the celebrity are listed after the celebrity's biography. Names of celebrities and/or dolls are *not* misspelled. For celebrities, the most common spellings are used, and common alternatives are cited; for dolls, the name from original advertising or from original packages is used. For example, under ELIZABETH OF YORK, the Peggy Nisbet doll is ELYSABETH OF YORK.

The names of all celebrity entries are printed in dark, bold type (i.e., **JUDY GARLAND**); the names of all dolls listed under the celebrity are printed in capitals (i.e., DOROTHY). For ease in identification, the names of films are printed in italics (i.e., *The Wizard of Oz*); plays, television shows and songs are printed with quotation marks around them (i.e., "The Wiz," "The Wizard of Odds" and "Over the Rainbow").

The sizes given for a doll may vary from other sources. If the accompanying illustration was photographed by the author, the size of the doll was established from an accurate measurement. If a doll is pictured from catalog illustration and/or doll company photographs, the sizes given in the catalog are used.

Values are not given for the dolls in this book. These prices change too frequently for them to have been included in an encyclopedia. The author recommends *The Blue Book of Dolls and Values* by Jan Foulke, published by Hobby House Press, Inc., as the best source for doll values. This price guide is updated on a regular schedule.

This encyclopedia is to be *used and enjoyed* by the Collector. Do not hesitate to make notations in your own book. The Reader may also find the extensive Bibliography useful for further study.

Part One
Defining Celebrity Dolls

This book is an encyclopedia of all the celebrity dolls that have been commercially made through the beginning of 1982. It is as accurate as possible and all known celebrity dolls are cited. However, I have no doubt unintentionally omitted some dolls. New dolls will be manufactured as I write these words. Other dolls I did not locate that represent celebrities will appear. Some unidentified dolls will be identified. And there will be some disagreement about my choices.

I have deliberately omitted many dolls that some collectors consider "celebrity dolls." The reason for this is that I can find no proof for the identity of the dolls. It is not my purpose to discredit the writers of some books on dolls and to dispute their findings, nor do I wish to set myself up as the final authority on what is or what is not a celebrity doll. The field of celebrity dolls is an ambiguous category, but I have attempted to define the issue and to clarify much misinformation. The following points out why the encyclopedia section of this book lists and shows many celebrity dolls and omits what some collectors might consider a celebrity doll.

The dictionaries, *Webster's International* among them, define a celebrity as "1.) State of being celebrated; renown; 2.) A celebrated person." Therefore a "celebrity" is a famous or well-known person. A *celebrity doll* then would have to be a doll made to represent a famous or well-known person. I have considered all dolls that are called "celebrity dolls" and my criteria for inclusion in this book is that the dolls had to have been sold as representing a famous individual. I qualify the word "sold" as meaning "sold commercially," because it would be nearly impossible to cite all the dolls that were ever made to represent a famous individual.

Some dolls are very popular among doll collectors and have great fame as dolls; however, they do not represent famous or well-known persons. As example of this is KEWPIE by Rose O'Neill which she stated was inspired by her little baby brother. Rose O'Neill's little brother was never famous. GLADDIE by Helen Jensen, which is usually considered a girl doll, was designed by using the creator's young son as a model. Helen Jensen's son was not famous.

Other dolls seem like they were famous persons because they were so popular as both dolls and "personalities." Some dolls of this type are BETTY BOOP, who was a cartoon character in drawings and animated films; CHARLIE McCARTHY appeared on radio shows and in the movies, but he was a ventriloquist's dummy whose voice was supplied by his creator, Edgar Bergen; HOWDY DOODY was a puppet who was operated by strings and whose voice was supplied by Bob Smith for television shows.

Many dolls are given the names of celebrities, but they were not supposed to represent any person and they are not celebrity dolls. Doll collectors like their dolls to be "someone" and many times this is a selling feature as it is easier to sell a thing that has a name rather than one which is an abstract item, such as a "doll" and nothing more. This is the reason why many dolls of the 19th century have names like "Jenny Lind" if their hairdo looks like that of the famous Swedish singer or "Mary Todd Lincoln" if the doll's hair is in the style of the mid 1800s. In recent times this violation of identity has reached comical proportions which will be cited later.

There are also many wonderful and interesting collectibles that do, indeed, represent a famous person but they are not dolls. The *Glossary* of the United Federation of Doll Clubs, Inc. defines a *doll* as "A child's plaything in human form." This is also my criteria in establishing what a celebrity doll is. The *Glossary* also excludes toys and novelties, religious and ceremonial figures such as creche figures and Indian religious images, artist's and store mannequins, puppets, marionettes, lead and wooden soldiers and modern versions of toys and figures. (Some puppets and marionettes are shown in the encyclopedia section if they are based on *real* people. This is to establish their identity.)

Many toys have also been made of famous animals. During the 1920s toys of the German shepherd or police dog, Strongheart, were advertised as reproductions of the "famous moving picture actor" and that "old and young alike consider 'Strongheart' their favorite actor and await each new film with eager anticipation." The world would be very boring without dogs in it, and although they seem to have many human qualities and some dogs and other animals are quite celebrated, they are not "persons."

There are many dolls that are considered by some collectors to be celebrity dolls, but they were not

Illustration 1. 13in (33cm) *Kewpie* by Effanbee, No. 9713, 1948. All-composition and fully-jointed. Yellow painted hair; painted black eyes. The doll is not marked; the box tells that this is "The original Rose O'Neill 'Kewpie' Doll // a Cameo Doll Product."

LEFT: MARY HARTLINE by Ideal, 1952.

BELOW RIGHT: SHIRLEY TEMPLE by Ideal, 1957. 15in (38.1cm) and 17in (43.2cm).

BELOW LEFT: ELVIS PRESLEY, 1957. *Mandeville-Barkel Collection. Photograph by Chip Barkel.*

BOTTOM: LAURENCE HARVEY as Romeo and SUSAN SHENTALL as Juliet by Madame Alexander, 1955. *Patricia Gardner Collection.*

LEFT: JACQUELINE KENNEDY by Madame Alexander, 1962. 10in (25.4cm). *Ted Menten Collection. Photograph by Ted Menten.*

RIGHT: JACQUELINE KENNEDY by Madame Alexander, 1962. 21in (53.3cm). *Ted Menten Collection. Photograph by Ted Menten.*

BELOW LEFT: JENNY LIND by Madame Alexander, 1969. 10½in (26.7cm). *Ted Menten Collection. Photograph by Ted Menten.*

BELOW RIGHT: JENNY LIND by Madame Alexander, 1970-1971. Holding the "Listening Cat." *Ted Menten Collection. Photograph by Ted Menten.*

Illustration 2. *Stronheart*, the celebrated dog of the movies, who was quite a gifted "actor," although not a person, during the early 1920s. 4in (10.2cm) high; 6¾in (17.2cm) long from the nose to the end of the tail. Papier-mâché with simulated fur covering in black and white. Glass eyes. *Shirley Buchholz Collection.*

Illustration 4. 4¾in (12.2cm) Martin Landau as "Official Space: 1999 Parachutist" by ATV Licensing Ltd., No. 6347, 1976. The plastic toy is part of a series of various television and comic personalities in a similar guise.

Illustration 3. 10in (25.4cm) *Benji* by R. Dakin & Co., circa 1980. Stuffed plush, wearing a cotton cap. Benji is indeed a famous dog and the star of movies and television programs but he is not a person, hence not a celebrity.

Illustration 5. 5½in (14cm) BORIS KARLOFF as *The Mummy* by Vic's Novelty Manufacturing Co., 1979. This is not a doll. It is a soft vinyl figure with painted features and "mummy wrappings" molded onto the body. Copyright by Universal City Studios. Made in North Hollywood, California.

advertised or sold as such and were usually not meant to represent a celebrated individual. This is the area that is the most difficult to define.

The figures and dolls of Santa Claus and Father Christmas are examples of "mythical" persons in doll form. The legend of Santa Claus is based on the life of St. Nicholas, a 4th century bishop of Asia Minor. St. Nicholas was the patron saint of boys and sailors in Greece and Sicily. He was also called St. Nicholas of Bari because some relics of St. Nicholas were stolen and taken there in Italy. In the northern countries, particularly in the Netherlands, the feast day of St. Nicholas, December 6, was a children's holiday. In Germany St. Nicholas became the gift-bearing Father Christmas. This present-giving event became incorporated into the modern-day visit of Santa Claus who waits until December 25 to make his appearance. This later tradition developed when the English settlers in the Dutch colony of New York adopted St. Nicholas for children and turned him into Santa. Our modern concept of Santa derives from the poem "A Visit from St. Nicholas" written by Clement Clarke Moore in 1823, which makes the saint the "jolly old elf" that he is now.

Other mythical or fictional persons have been made as dolls. An example of this is Paul Bunyan, the giant hero of "tall tales" that were popular with lumbermen from Michigan to the West Coast in the last century. The

Illustration 6. 4½in (11.5cm) PRESIDENT JIMMY CARTER as "Jimmy the Walking Peanut" by B.J. Wolfe Ent., circa 1977. This is a plastic wind-up walking toy, not a doll. (There is a vulgar plastic novelty doll of President Carter that was manufactured commercially.) Made in Japan.

Illustration 7. 12½in (31.8cm) COLONEL HARLAND SANDERS by Ron Starling Plastics, Ltd., 1965. One-piece plastic with a slot in the back so it can be used as a bank. Colonel Sanders was a celebrated individual, and a doll was made of him. This item fits nicely into a collection of celebrity memorabilia or advertising collectibles, but it is not a doll. Made in London, Ontario.

Illustration 8. 9in (22.9cm) *Santa Claus.* All-composition; only the right arm is jointed. No marks.

ABOVE LEFT: KAREN DOTRICE as Jane, JULIE ANDREWS as Mary Poppins and MATTHEW GARBER as Michael from *Mary Poppins* by Horsman, 1966. *Jean Canaday Collection.*

ABOVE RIGHT: CHRISTOPHER ROBIN MILNE with Winnie the Pooh by Horsman, 1964. *Jean Canaday Collection.*

LORI MARTIN by Ideal, 1961. *Barbara DeVault Collection.*

DIANA ROSS by Ideal, 1969. *Jean Canaday Collection.*

Small set of dolls from THE SOUND OF MUSIC by Madame Alexander, 1971-1973.

LAUREL AND HARDY by Berman & Anderson, Inc., 1975. *Jean Canaday Collection.*

dolls of Snow White can not be considered celebrity dolls either, although Snow White was the subject of a movie. The dolls are either fictional characters or cartoon characters. Edgar Rice Burrough's Tarzan was played in the movies by 16 different actors, beginning with Elmo Lincoln in 1918 and most recently by Miles O'Keefe in 1981. There have been several different dolls of Tarzan, but none of them look like any of the screen Tarzans, although the manufacture of a Tarzan doll often coincided with the release of a Tarzan film.

Illustration 9. 12½in (31.8cm) *Snow White* by Knickerbocker Toy, 1937. All-composition and fully-jointed. Painted black hair and painted brown eyes. The yellow dress has a blue velvet bodice. Head marked: "KNICKERBOCK-ER TOY // WALT DISNEY." This is not a celebrity doll. She is a storybook character or a cartoon character.

Illustration 10. 9in (22.9cm) *Tarzan and the Giant Ape* by Mattel, No. 2029, 1977. All-vinyl and fully-jointed. Molded and painted hair; painted eyes. The vinyl ape is 8in (20.3cm). Copyright by Edgar Rice Burroughs, Inc. This is the Mattel *Big Jim* doll with a different head.

Illustration 11. 7¾in (19.8cm) *Tarzan* by Mego, No. 51305, 1973. Vinyl and plastic and fully-jointed. The vinyl head has painted black hair and painted black eyes. Head marked: "© ERB INC. 1972." Made in Hong Kong. This *Tarzan* is wearing his loincloth over a beige body suit. The doll does not resemble any of the actors who played Tarzan.

Because of a popular movie countless dolls have been made to cash in on the publicity engendered by this or to deliberately look like a current film favorite. As time passes, the dolls receive a new identity because their original carton or identifying data were lost and the popularity of the screen character continues. ONCLE JUPP from Germany *(Illustration 12)* could certainly be transformed into a W.C. Fields doll if he lost the sticker on his foot. In 1966 the film *One Million B.C.* was re-made with the popular star Raquel Welch. The original film was in 1940; the new picture was titled *One Million Years B.C.* Mego Corp. issued a set of dolls after the release of the second film and called the set "One Million B.C." The dolls are all "prehistoric" types, but their names are not the same as the names of the characters in either film. (See *Illustration 13*.)

Illustration 12. This character resembles W. C. Fields but it is not he. This is 8in (20.3cm) *Oncle Jupp* by Trollydoll, No. 927, late 1950s. Papier-mâché head and hands; wire and styrofoam body. Painted features. Made in Western Germany. *Fran's Dolls.*

Illustration 13. Five characters by Mego in a set called *One Million B.C.* These are not celebrity dolls as none of their names are the same as the characters in the 1940 film *One Million B.C.* or the 1966 British film *One Million Years B.C.* The dolls date from the 1970s and all are fully-jointed vinyl with rooted hair. From left to right the dolls are: *Zon,* who is 6¼in (15.9cm), No. 62600/4; *Grok,* No. 62600/3, who has a painted beard; *Orm,* No. 62600/5, also with a painted beard; *Trag,* No. 62600/1; and *Mada,* No. 62600/2. The larger figures are all 7¾in (19.8cm). A vinyl "Tribal Lair" (tree house) was also available for the dolls.

LEFT: QUEEN ELIZABETH II and PRINCE PHILIP by Peggy Nisbet, late 1970s. *Shirley Buchholz Collection.*

Ann Parker Dolls, late 1970s. From left to right: GEORGE WASHINGTON, MARTHA WASHINGTON, HENRY VIII, QUEEN VICTORIA, DUKE OF WELLINGTON and BEATRIX POTTER. *Shirley Buchholz Collection.*

ABOVE: JOE NAMATH by Mego, 1970. *Lee Jenkins Collection.*

TOP RIGHT: CHERYL LADD by Mattel, 1978.

RIGHT: LOIS CHILES by Mego, 1979.

Illustration 14. Lassie and Her Friends by Gabriel, No. 36561, 1976. The boy is all-vinyl and fully-jointed and is 8½in (21.6cm). Lassie is plastic and is jointed at the legs and head and is 10in (25.4cm) long. The puppy and the basket are vinyl. Copyright by Lassie Television, Inc. Made in Hong Kong. This set was made long after Tommy Rettig played Jeff on "Lassie" (1954 to 1957) or Jon Provost essayed the role of Timmy (1957 to 1964) and is not a portrait of either boy. Even several different dogs played Lassie while the series was on television from September 1954 to September 1971.

The same confusion occurs with personalities or shows from television. An example of television characters who have been made into dolls, but who do not really represent any certain actor are the dolls of Lassie's "Friend" and THE INCREDIBLE HULK. Several different boys played Lassie's master and the "Hulk" is based on the comic books and not on the character in the TV programs. (*Illustrations 14* and *15*.)

The dolls from two companies cause a great deal of confusion for collectors who want to identify them. One of these is Molly-'es. Recently an abundance of unmarked dolls attributed to Molly-'es are appearing that now are sold under such names as Kathryn Grayson, Betty Grable, Mamie Eisenhower, Marlene Dietrich, Irene Dunn, Gene Tierney and Judy Garland. The dolls have no characteristics of these ladies except for hair coloring. None of the dolls have been found in original packages or with identifying tags or markings and must be considered speculation, wishful thinking or identity-establishing in retrospect. It seems unlikely that Mollye Goldman could have produced these dolls for the commercial market without paying royalties to a movie studio or to the star who it is now claimed that the doll represents. No original advertising has been found to justify these claims either.

Another vague and confusing area in deciding if a doll is a celebrity or not is with the dolls of Madame Alexander. It is a well-established fact now that Madame Alexander's LITTLE COLONEL doll was a knock-off on the popularity of Ideal's SHIRLEY TEMPLE, and not based on "the books" of the Little Colonel as was advertised during the mid 1930s. The Ideal Novelty and Toy Company successfully obtained a court injunction against the Alexander LITTLE COLONEL dolls, so the courts must have decided that there was a copyright infringement. It was no coincidence that Madame Alexander released many "storybook" characters as dolls at the same time a film version of a book containing these characters was released. This can be seen clearly with the "Little Women" dolls of 1933, ALICE IN WONDERLAND of 1935, DAVID COPPERFIELD of 1935 and many others.

Illustration 15. 12in (30.5cm) *The Incredible Hulk* by Mego, No. 81304, 1978. All-vinyl and fully-jointed. Green skin tones; painted features. Back marked: "©1978 // MARVEL COMICS GROUP // ALL RIGHTS RESERVED // MADE IN HONG KONG." The small packaged *Hulk* is a one-piece vinyl construction from Vic's Novelty Manufacturing, #HK3, copyright 1978 by Marvel Comics Group. *Jean Canaday Collection*. The Hulk dolls are all copyrighted by Marvel Comics and although the tie-in to the TV show is obvious, the dolls look like the comic strip character and not like Lou Ferigno who plays him on the CBS-TV series.

Illustration 16. The character *Jor-el*, the father of Superman by Mego. In the film *Superman* (1978) Jor-el was played by Marlon Brando, which caused some doll dealers to advertise this doll as Marlon Brando. Indeed it is not and does not at all resemble Brando. The doll represents *Jor-el* from the comic books rather than from the film. 12¼in (31.2cm) *Jor-el* has a vinyl head with painted gray hair and painted brown eyes. Head marked: "© D C COMICS INC. // 1977." Back marked: "© 1978 MEGO CORP // MADE IN HONG KONG." The Mego number is 87003/1. This doll is part of a set that also includes *Superman, Lex Luthor* and *General Zod of the Phantom Zone.* It is no coincidence that the dolls came out at the time the movie was in general release. SEE: SUPERMAN.

Illustration 17. Not all dolls that were made with a series of characters from a movie or television show represent real persons. I can find no reference to any person having played the role of Chopper on "Starsky and Hutch." On the original boxes *Chopper* is shown as a cartoon; the other characters from "Starsky and Hutch" are depicted with accompanying photographs of the actors. 7½in (19.1cm) *Chopper* from "Starsky and Hutch" by Mego, No. 62800/5. All-vinyl and fully-jointed with painted hair and features. Copyright 1976 by Spelling Goldberg Productions. Made in Hong Kong.

LEFT: SHAUN CASSIDY by Kenner, 1978; PARKER STEVENSON by Kenner, 1978; JOHN TRAVOLTA by Chemtoy, 1977.

BELOW: Characters from SPACE ACADEMY by Aviva Toy Company, 1978.

RIGHT: MARK HAMILL by Kenner, 1978; GIL GERARD by Mego, 1979; HARRISON FORD by Kenner, 1979.

LINCOLN TATE as Custer by Gabriel, 1981.

BELOW: JOHN SCHNEIDER and TOM WOPAT by Mego, 1981.

HARRY HAMLIN as Perseus, riding Pegasus, by Mattel, 1981.

BELOW: MAE WEST and JOHN WAYNE, both by Effanbee 1982.

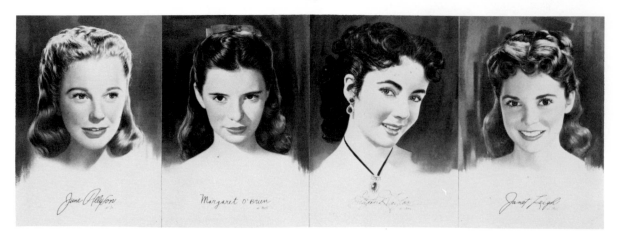

Collectors like their dolls to be "somebody" so they are receptive to erroneous information about the identity of a doll. A case in point is the KAREN BALLERINA of Alexander in composition in 1946. This doll, and other similar later Alexander dolls in hard plastic, have been erroneously transformed into "Karen (sic) Booth, the Prima Ballerina." Karin Booth was given an MGM studio contract in the late 1940s, but she only appeared in two Margaret O'Brien films and later in very minor parts at other studios in such productions as *Jungle Man-Eaters* (1954). In *The Unfinished Dance,* 1947, (a year after the KAREN BALLERINA of Alexander) Karin Booth, for the only time, played a ballerina (not a *prima ballerina,* which means *first lady of dance*) to very poor reviews. Yet the tale persists that there is a "Karen Booth" doll. (Note the spelling of Karen and Karin.) The same problem arises with such dolls as "Arlene Dahl," "Hedy Lamarr" and "Kathryn Grayson," to name a few. This sounds much better than just a "lady doll." Interviews with Madame Alexander herself are of no help here either, as it is reported that she has been known to offer conflicting evidence to different interviewers. Many Alexander dolls have been given a name which coincides with that of a popular celebrity. The most obvious is the black doll called LESLIE which appeared at the time black singer Leslie Uggams was quite popular. (See LESLIE UGGAMS in the listing section.)

The "Little Women" dolls of 1949 were used as premiums in a contest that promoted the MGM film. They can not be considered "celebrity dolls." The same molds were used in the previous year and in the following years by the Alexander Doll Company, and the other dolls had no tie-in to the film, although they are also "Little Women." Madame Alexander had been producing "Little Women" dolls since 1933, and they were always advertised as "based on Louisa May Alcott's book," as was the set from 1949. It is also no coincidence that David O. Selznick released his film *Little Women* in 1933, but the set of dolls from that year did not tie into the film in any way, except to be released in time to earn the extra publicity. The labels on the dolls' dresses cite the book by Louisa May Alcott, and it is obvious that the dolls do not represent any actresses from either film version of *Little Women*. Some collectors like to think that the "Little Women" dolls in hard plastic and/or vinyl produced from 1948 to today represent June Allyson (Jo), Janet Leigh (Meg), Elizabeth Taylor (Amy) and Margaret O'Brien (Beth), who played the *Little Women* in the 1949 MGM film, but there is no basis for this belief. The dolls are just as desirable for what they truly are.

Illustration 18. The above portraits of June Allyson, Margaret O'Brien, Elizabeth Taylor and Janet Leigh, the stars of *Little Women,* were a premium promotional item from MGM in 1949. Both June Allyson and Elizabeth Taylor wore wigs for their parts in the film and did not look like they do here. *Mary Steucher Collection.*

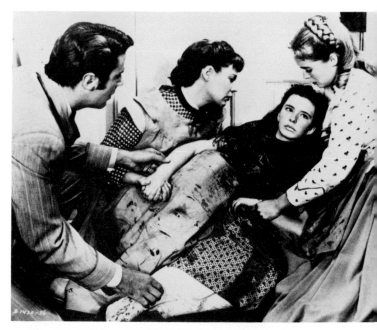

Illustration 19. Peter Lawford, June Allyson, Margaret O'Brien and Janet Leigh in *Little Women,* 1949.

Illustration 20. 14in (35.6cm) *Meg* of "Little Women" by Madame Alexander, 1949-1950. All-hard plastic and fully-jointed. Dark blonde wig; blue sleep eyes with lashes. The doll is not marked. This is the so-called "Margaret mold." *Fran's Dolls.*

Illustration 23. 14in (35.6cm) *Amy* of "Little Women" by Madame Alexander, 1949-1950. The all-hard plastic and fully-jointed doll is not marked. Blue sleep eyes with lashes. Note the looped curls on the blonde wig. This is the so-called "Margaret mold." *Fran's Dolls.*

Illustration 21. 14in (35.6cm) *Jo* of "Little Women" by Madame Alexander, 1948-1949. All-hard plastic and fully-jointed. Light brown floss wig. Brown sleep eyes with lashes. This face is considered the "Maggie mold." Doll not marked. *Fran's Dolls.*

Illustration 22. 14in (35.6cm) *Beth* of "Little Women" by Madame Alexander, circa 1949. All-hard plastic and fully-jointed. Brown floss wig; brown sleep eyes with lashes. The doll is not marked. Note the clover leaf wrist tag. It is marked: "LITTLE WOMEN. BETH" in script. This head is the "Maggie mold." *Fran's Dolls.*

Illustration 24. 14in (35.6cm) *Marme* of "Little Women" by Madame Alexander, 1951-1952. All-hard plastic and fully-jointed. Dark brown wig; blue sleep eyes with lashes. The doll is not marked. The wrist tag is for Madame Alexander's "fashion academy award," *NOT* the Academy Award, as has been stated in describing these doll tags. *Fran's Dolls.*

TOP LEFT: CHARLES LINDBERGH, JR., an artist's original by Alice McKee Cumming, late 1920s. *Jean Pritchard Collection.*

TOP RIGHT: JOHN F. KENNEDY, JACQUELINE KENNEDY, CAROLINE KENNEDY and JOHN-JONN KENNEDY, artist's originals designed by Lita Wilson and executed by Muriel B. Kramer in porcelain, 1965. *Shirley Buchholz Collection.*

LEFT: RUDOLPH VALENTINO, an artist's original in porcelain by Linda Steele, 1982. 15½in (39.4cm).

OPPOSITE PAGE: EMMETT KELLY by Baby Barry Toy, late 1950s.

In 1953 Madame Alexander created a group of 36 dolls called the "Recessional." These dolls were based on the participants in the Coronation of Queen Elizabeth II in that year. They are not considered here because they were a one-shot production made for exhibition and publicity only. The dolls have been pictured in several doll books that feature Alexander dolls. They were never accessible to any private collector and are now housed in the Brooklyn Children's Museum.

There are all sorts of dolls that have acquired new names since the time that they were first produced. Again, the new identity is based on wishful thinking by buyers and sellers. Into this group of dolls fall the ones that look like a celebrity doll or like a certain celebrity and for lack of a better name have assumed the new identity. These dolls could be classified as look-alikes, as for the most part they were manufactured to tie-in to the popularity of another doll. Also shown in the encyclopedia section of this book along with certain celebrity dolls there are many dolls that are look-alikes or tie-ins. The more popular a doll was, the more likely it was that dolls would be produced to look like the higher priced doll. The best examples of the newly-acquired identities are all the "unmarked Dionne Quintuplet" dolls.

Americans have always admired famous persons, and some celebrities have become "cult figures." We have no princesses, kings or queens so we invented our own. In the 19th century Americans admired the wealthy like Carnegie and Rockefeller because they started small, made their money turn into more money, took advantage of their opportunities and made it big. The most admired have also been the socially prominent, sports stars, military men, heroes, and movie, radio and television stars. The most admired of all were the Hollywood film stars in the period between the two world wars. All of these people are the ones of whom celebrity dolls have been made. The most popular of all were the movie stars. They were the most recognizable, the most famous and the best known. They were seen in their films and in magazine pictures and were always marketable, whether to advertise a product or to be created in toy likenesses for children. The further back in time some of the film stars are, the more confusion there is in identifying dolls that seem to look like them.

Illustration 25. 11in (27.9cm) skating doll by Arranbee, early 1940s. Although called "Sonja Henie," this doll was never meant to be she. All-composition and fully-jointed. Blonde mohair wig; blue sleep eyes with lashes and eye shadow. The skating costume is white velvet lined with red flannel. The blades are missing from the skates. The doll is unmarked and the costume is not tagged.

Illustration 26. 18in (45.7cm) *Nancy Lee* by Arranbee, circa early 1940s. All-composition and fully-jointed. Blonde mohair wig; blue sleep eyes with lashes; closed mouth. All-original velveteen skating costume with paper label on front which gives the doll's identity. Head marked: "R & B." Paper label: "NANCY LEE // AN // R & B // QUALITY DOLL." This is the doll that is erroneously credited as an "R & B Sonja Henie." R & B (Arranbee) *never* made a Sonja Henie doll. *Joyce Kintner. Photograph by Jane Buchholz.*

Illustration 27. 11in (27.9cm) unmarked doll by Dream World, late 1940s. This doll is an example of wishful thinking. We always called her "Merle Oberon" because of her black mohair wig and painted blue eyes. She was originally a bride.

Illustration 29. 11in (27.9cm) Carmen Miranda-type or Brazil by Dream World, late 1940s. All-composition and fully-jointed. Painted blue eyes. Note the poor quality construction in the seam of the left arm; however, these dolls never seem to flake or peel off their paint layers. Unmarked. There *never* was a doll that was sold as the popular film star Carmen Miranda although many dolls were made dressed in the costumes she wore in her films. Alexander even called its doll of this type "Carmen." SEE: CARMEN MIRANDA.

Illustration 28. Leslie Howard and Merle Oberon in *The Scarlet Pimpernel,* 1934.

Illustration 31. Carmen Miranda wearing one of her typical high head-dresses, circa 1940.

Illustration 30. 11in (27.9cm) Dream World doll dressed in a Brazilian costume.

Illustration 33. Canadian Mountie by Reliable.

Illustration 32. 17½in (44.5cm) *Canadian Mountie* by Reliable, circa 1940s. Composition head with painted brown hair and painted brown eyes. Composition half arms; stuffed cloth body. Head marked: "RELIABLE // MADE IN // CANADA." The epaulets are printed: "R.C.M.P." This doll resembles Nelson Eddy, but it is not meant to be he, although Nelson Eddy wore a similar costume in the film *Rose Marie* (1936). Reliable made other men dolls using this same mold.

Illustration 34. Nelson Eddy from *Rose Marie*, 1936.

Illustration 35. This boy doll is often described as being Prince Charles of England as a little boy. There is no evidence for such a supposition, although the facial modeling does suggest a resemblance to Charles. The doll is about 27in (68.6cm) with a composition head, stuffed cloth body and early vinyl arms and legs, which dates it about 1950. Painted brown hair and blue sleep eyes with lashes. The head is marked: "A X." A similar doll was also made with a vinyl head.

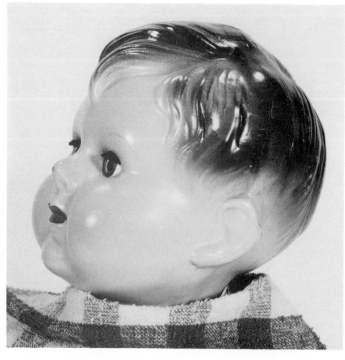

One sees dolls of Jeanette MacDonald all over the place. They have blue eyes; they have brown eyes. They have hair of every shade and color from snow white to jet black. Most of the so-called Jeanette MacDonald dolls are ones that originally had other identities. My favorite in recent times was one that was dressed in a Russian costume and was meant to be a doll in a Russian costume. Someone had a vague recollection of Jeanette MacDonald in a film with a Russian setting and thought the doll was from the film. Actually they were thinking of Nelson Eddy, her frequent co-star, who was in *Balalaika*. The problem is that the lady in that film was Ilona Massey and not Jeanette MacDonald. But Jeanette MacDonald is better remembered today than Ilona Massey, hence the doll becomes an "authentic Jeanette MacDonald - rare," rather than a doll dressed in a Russian peasant costume when offered for sale.

Jackie Cooper is another case in point. There is a doll called PUGGY which bears some resemblance to little Jackie Cooper, so the doll is usually called "Jackie Cooper" now. In 1928 Effanbee made a doll of SKIPPY based on the cartoon character by P.L. Crosby. In 1931 a film was made of *Skippy* starring Jackie Cooper. Now one sees the doll advertised as "Jackie Cooper" rather than SKIPPY, even though the doll is a good likeness of the Crosby creation and bears only slight resemblance to Jackie Cooper. There is *no* Jackie Cooper doll at all.

No matter. There was never a doll of Robert Redford, Martha Mitchell or David Carradine. But *Illustrations 37, 38* and *39* show why the confusion occurs and why dolls are being offered for sale under these names. The dolls are still very collectible even if they are not dolls of some famous individual.

Illustration 36. Unidentified doll who has been given an identity by collectors. 11¼in (28.6cm) "Haley Mills" by Remco. Vinyl head and arms; plastic legs and torso. Rooted blonde hair; blue sleep eyes with molded lashes. Head marked: "4 // REMCO IND. INC // ©1968." *Phyllis Houston Collection.*

Illustration 37. 10in (25.4cm) *The Sundown Kid* by Marx Toys, No. 1711, 1970s. This doll, part of "The Ready Gang," looks very much like Robert Redford from his role as the Sundance Kid in *Butch Cassidy and the Sundance Kid* (1969). The doll has no marks; the original box has no dates. Copyright by Louis Marx Co., Inc., Girard, Pennsylvania. Made in Hong Kong.

Illustration 38. 7in (17.8cm) *Twister* by Deluxe Reading Corporation, 1965. One-piece vinyl body with wire inside the legs and arms. Vinyl head with painted features and a blonde mohair wig. The gown and the necklace are original. The body has no marks; the head is marked: "6 3 // DELUX READING COR //© 1965." *Shirley Buchholz Collection.* Even when a doll can be identified by recent catalogs, some people persist in giving them the name of a real person whom they may slightly resemble to make them more desirable. This doll is interesting because she represents a dancer who did the twist, a popular dance of the 1960s. She has been offered for sale by more than one individual as Martha Mitchell, the wife of the Attorney-General under President Nixon, because there is some resemblance. (John Mitchell was publicly unknown until he became Attorney-General in 1969.)

Illustration 39. 8½in (21.6cm) *Kung Fu* by Durham Industries, Inc., No. 3010, 1970s. All-vinyl and fully-jointed. Painted hair and features. The doll resembles Bruce Lee who played in a series of Kung Fu movies that were filmed in Hong Kong, but there is nothing about the doll, nor the way it was advertised to suggest that it was Bruce Lee rather than anyone else. It also resembles David Carradine who was the star of the TV series "Kung Fu" from 1972 to 1975. *Bobby Lodwick Collection.*

One type of celebrity doll that is not classified in this book is the Artist's Doll. Many of these dolls certainly represent famous or well-known persons, but they were not produced commercially in large numbers and this type of collectible is outside the scope of this study. The artists' originals oftentimes look more like the real person they are supposed to represent than the commercial dolls do and the detail, modeling and execution is far more realistic and life-like than the commercial dolls. With the recent increased interest in doll collecting, there are more doll artists than ever before and more persons who collect artists' dolls. The dolls are produced in limited numbers, even though the doll is sometimes a "Convention Souvenir" that had a production of about 2000. They are still rather scarce in general when compared with many of the commercial dolls that were produced in the millions, even though frequently less of the later dolls have survived. Some examples of the artists' dolls are shown here for comparative purposes.

Many "celebrity dolls" are not included in this book because they do not exist, although legend says that they do. (One still sees "Wants" for the Barbie Benton doll.) Others are not included because they were not produced commercially as children's playthings. And others are omitted because only a single doll of the celebrity is known to exist. (An example of this is General Audrey W. and Harriet St. John Simpson Arlington, shown in *The Collector's Encyclopedia of Dolls* by Dorothy S., Elizabeth A. and Evelyn J. Coleman, Crown Publishers, 1968, page 149.)

Illustration 42. 14in (35.6cm) (in seated position) JOHN MUIR by artist Cecilia Rothman, 1976. Porcelain head, hands and feet; cloth body with wire armatures inside. John Muir, one of the first conservationists, was born in Scotland in 1838. He came to the United States as a boy and later settled in California. He died in 1914. Muir Woods National Monument in California was named for him in recognition of his efforts as a crusader for the establishment of national parks in the United States. The boulder on which the figure is seated is also cast from ceramic porcelain. *Shirley Buchholz Collection.*

OPPOSITE PAGE: Illustration 40. 31in (78.7cm) CHARLES LINDBERGH, JR., an artist's original, designed and made by Alice McKee Cumming. Papier-mâché socket head; silk body that seems to be stuffed with horse hair. Painted blue eyes; painted light brown hair. The flyer's suit is khaki; the hat is leather. The wear and aging indicate that the doll dates from the late 1920s or the early 1930s. *Jean Pritchard Collection.*

LEFT: Illustration 41. MARIE ANTOINETTE AND HER CHILDREN, artist's dolls by Shelia Wallace, 1978. Marie Antoinette is 23in (58.4cm), including her hat. The heads and hands are of bleached beeswax; the bodies are stuffed cloth. The hair and the eyelashes are implanted. Shelia Wallace dolls are individually modeled, not cast, and each is an original. Shelia is widely recognized for her authentic and detailed costumes. The grouping of the Queen of France and her children shows them in about 1786. The little girl is the Princess Marie-Thérèse, Madame Royale (1778-1851); the older boy is the dauphin Louis (1781-1789); the baby is Louis-Charles (born 1785), considered Louis XVII after the execution of Louis XVI in 1793. Louis-Charles died in prison at age ten, two years after the execution of Marie Antoinette in 1793. *Shelia Wallace. Photograph by Shelia Wallace.*

26

Illustration 43. 9¾in (24.9cm) OSCEOLA, THE SEMINOLE INDIAN CHIEF, an artist's original doll by Zanthos Kontis of Pittsburgh, 1954. Osceola is made of fired clay and has a moveable head and arms. The features are painted and the clothing is authentic. This was the souvenir doll for the 5th UFDC National Convention in Miami, Florida, in 1954. *Shirley Buchholz Collection.*
Osceola was born in Georgia in about 1804 of an English father and a Seminole mother. He led the Seminole Indians in their resistance against the American government who intended to expel them from Georgia and Florida in the 1830s. After a two year war the Seminoles retreated to the Everglade swamps in Florida where they continued their war into the 1840s. Under a flag of truce Osceola met with the American army in 1837. He was taken prisoner and was held in Charleston, South Carolina, where he died on June 30, 1838. The Seminoles were not as active in their battle to keep their ancestral lands after the death of Osceola.

Illustration 44. 19in (48.3cm) EDGAR RED CLOUD OF THE SIOUX, an artist's original by June Goodnow. Porcelain head and hands; cloth body; mohair wig. The tanned buckskin clothing is beaded. *Shirley Buchholz Collection.*

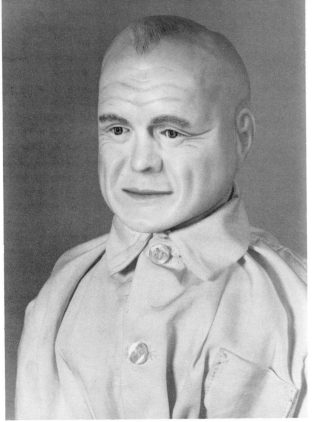

Illustration 45. 19in (48.3cm) Astronaut JOHN GLENN of Ohio by doll artist Rosamond McCall. Porcelain head, hands and feet; cloth body. Painted hair and features. *Shirley Buchholz Collection.*
In 1962 John Glenn was the first man to orbit the earth. He has been a U.S. Senator from Ohio since 1975.

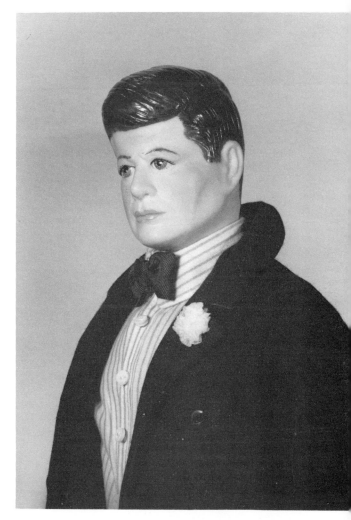

Illustration 46. 17in (43.2cm) PRESIDENT JOHN F. KENNEDY designed by doll artist Lita Wilson and executed by Muriel B. Kramer, 1964. Porcelain head, hands and legs; cloth body. Painted hair and features. *Shirley Buchholz Collection.*
Kennedy was President of the United States from 1961 to 1963.

Illustration 47. 16¾in (42.6cm) CORETTA KING, the widow of Dr. Martin Luther King, Jr., an artist's original by Grace Herold. Porcelain head, hands and legs; cloth body. The hair and the facial features are painted. *Shirley Buchholz Collection.*

Mrs. King continued her husband's work for social justice after his assassination on April 4, 1968.

Illustration 48. 18¾in (47.7cm) GERALD FORD, an artist's original by Faith Wick, 1978. Porcelain head and hands, stuffed body with wire armatures for posing. Painted blonde hair on a head that is mostly "bald;" painted blue eyes. The costume is labeled: "FAITH WICK ORIGINALS." Head marked: "100/15 // FW."

Gerald Ford was President of the United States from 1974 to 1977.

Illustration 50. 17in (43.2cm) *Father Christmas,* the UFDC Convention Souvenir doll in Washington, D.C., 1980. Porcelain shoulder plate head, hands and black boots. The body is stuffed cloth. The hair, moustache and beard are painted white; the painted eyes are blue and are intaglio. The back of the head is incised in script: "FATHER CHRISTMAS // BEVERLY WALTER // 1980." Dressed by Joyce Kintner.

Illustration 49. GERALD FORD by Faith Wick.

Illustration 51. 14½in (36.9cm) NELLIE BLY, an artist's doll by Lita Wilson, executed by Muriel Kramer, 1981. Porcelain head, lower arms and lower legs; stuffed cloth body. Painted light brown hair; painted blue eyes. This was the Souvenir Doll for the Pittsburgh Doll Club Region 13 Convention in May of 1981. The doll was presented completed as shown here. The shoulder plate is marked in script: "NELLIE BLY // LW // PGH. REG. 5/81 // MURIEL // KRAMER."

As a reporter for the New York *World*, Nellie Bly traveled around the world in 1889-1890 in 72 days, 6 hours and 11 minutes, beating the record of fiction's Phileas Fogg.

Illustration 52. NELLIE BLY.

Illustration 53. 20½in (52.1cm) CHARLES A. LINDBERGH, JR. by NIADA artist Faith Wick, 1981. This was the Souvenir Doll for the 1981 UFDC National Convention in St. Louis, Missouri. The porcelain head has painted light brown hair, blue eyes and molded teeth in the smiling mouth. It is incised on the shoulder plate: "F.W." It has printed information that tells that this example was Number 1025 of 1200 and that it was designed by Faith Wick and executed by Viv (Vivian Mertins). The body is stuffed cloth with wire armatures for posing. (See *Illustration 40* for an earlier artist's version of Lindbergh and LINDBERGH in the encyclopedia section for a commercial doll.)

Illustration 54. Faith Wick's CHARLES A. LINDBERGH, JR.

In admitting that I may have inadvertently excluded some celebrity dolls, here I offer SALLY STARR (*Illustration 55*). She probably was a celebrity. I have heard that she was a local television personality on the East Coast, but I have no evidence of Sally's existence. I have also seen other dolls with "Sally Starr" written or embossed on her cowgirl skirt.

Illustration 55. 10in (25.4cm) *Sally Starr*, manufacturer unknown, 1960s. All-vinyl and fully-jointed, including a twist waist. Platinum rooted hair; blue sleep eyes with molded lashes. Head marked: "(P)" The cowgirl shirt and skirt are felt; the name and the trim is printed. *Kay Bransky Collection*.

My own candidate for a celebrity doll, where no justification permits the inclusion, is seen in *Illustrations 56* and *57*. This little boy is a very special doll because of the artistry of his execution. He certainly looks like Felipe de Borbón, even if he is not! I wonder if the artist had the Crown Prince of Spain in mind when the doll was made?

Hundreds and hundreds of different celebrity dolls have been made. Most of them are from the 20th century, so the encyclopedia concentrates on this time period. Most dolls are fascinating whether they are celebrity dolls or not, and to borrow the title of Genevieve Angione's and Judith Whorton's book, "All Dolls Are Collectible" anyhow.

OPPOSITE PAGE:
Illustration 57. "Teta Ling" boy.

Illustration 56. 10⅝in (27cm) carved wooden boy imported from the Philippines, 1970s. The doll is hand-sculpted from the wood of the langset tree. He has inset glass eyes and real hair lashes. Only the arms are jointed. The hair is carved and painted blonde. This is reputed to be a "Teta Ling Doll made by Julia Casos."

Illustration 58. Felipe de Borbón, the Prince of Asturias, on a Spanish postage stamp, 1977. The crown prince of Spain was born in December of 1968.

Part Two
Celebrity Dolls From A to Z

A

AARON, HENRY ("HANK"). Professional baseball player. Born February 5, 1934, in Mobile, Alabama. "Hammerin' Hank" Aaron began his career as a semi-professional baseball player and then from 1954 to 1974 played for the Milwaukee Braves, who later became the Atlanta Braves. After 1975 he played for the Milwaukee Brewers. On April 8, 1974, Hank broke Babe Ruth's record for career home runs by hitting his 715th home run. He was elected into Baseball's Hall of Fame in 1982.
DOLLS:
　1. HANK AARON. Sports Spec. Corp., 1974. 7¾in (19.8cm). *Illustration 59.*

Illustration 59. 7¾in (19.8cm) HENRY "HANK" ARRON "nodder," Souvenir Mascot, 1974. Composition with painted features. Embossed on the bottom of the base: "©1974 SPORTS SPEC. CORP. LA-CAL. 90024." The box tells that "extra dolls can be ordered from Milwaukee Brewer Promotions, Milwaukee County Stadium, Milw., Wisc. 53214."

ADAMS, ABIGAIL (SMITH). Wife of John Adams, the second President of the United States (1797-1801). Born 1744; died 1818. Today Abigail Adams is considered a pioneer in the feminist movement because of her letters. Her son, John Quincy Adams, was the 6th President of the United States.
DOLLS:
　1. ABIGAIL ADAMS. Peggy Nisbet, No. P728, circa 1976. Plastic "collectors' doll." John Adams, No. P727, is the companion doll. Made in England. About 7½in (19.1cm).
　2. ABIGAIL ADAMS. Madame Alexander, No. 1502, 1976-1978. Plastic and vinyl; part of the first First Ladies Series of six dolls. 14in (35.6cm).
　3. ABIGAIL ADAMS. Crafted Heirlooms, designed by Sandy Williams, 1981. Made in Cumberland, Maryland. 12in (30.5cm). *Illustration 60.*
SEE: FIRST LADIES.

Illustration 60. 12in (30.5cm) ABIGAIL ADAMS from The First Ladies Collection, designed by Sandy Williams, 1981. All-cloth, hand screened in white bleached muslin. Abigail is portrayed in a blue Canton crepe gown. (MARTHA WASHINGTON and MARTHA RANDOLPH are part of a set of three.) Made in Cumberland, Maryland, by Crafted Heirlooms.

ADAMS, JOHN. Second President of the United States. Born October 30, 1735; died July 4, 1826, the 50th Anniversary of the signing of the Declaration of Independence and the same day Thomas Jefferson died. John Adams was one of the "radical" American patriots who helped the United States gain its freedom from Great Britain. He was married to Abigail Smith Adams for more than 50 years. Their son, John Qunicy Adams, served a single term as President.
DOLLS:
1. JOHN ADAMS. Peggy Nisbet, No. P727, circa 1976. Plastic "collectors' doll." Abigail Adams, No. P728, is the companion doll Made in England. About 8in (20.3cm).

ADAMS, LOUISA (CATHERINE JOHNSON). Wife of the 6th President of the United States, John Quincy Adams (1825-1829). Born 1775; died 1852. Louisa married John Quincy Adams in London, England, in 1797 just before he departed to begin his position as a minister to Prussia.
DOLLS:
1. LOUISA ADAMS. Madame Alexander, No. 1506, 1976-1978. Plastic and vinyl; part of the First Ladies Series of six dolls. 14in (25.6cm).
SEE: FIRST LADIES.

PRINCE ALBERT. The Prince Consort of Victoria, Queen of England and Empress of India. Born 1819; died 1861. Albert, the son of Ernest I of Saxe-Coburg-Gotha, was selected to become the husband of his young cousin, Queen Victoria, in 1840. Although he sired the Queen's nine children, it was reputed that she loved him far more than he did she. Victoria survived Albert by 40 years.
DOLLS:
1. PRINCE ALBERT. Peggy Nisbet, No. P624, circa 1960s. Plastic "collector's doll." Queen Victoria in State Robes, No. P708, is the companion doll. Made in England. About 8in (20.3cm).
2. PRINCE ALBERT. Peggy Nisbet, No. LE99, 1982. Plastic "collectors' doll." Part of a Limited Edition of 500 sets, called "Royal Victorian Christening." The set also includes Queen Victoria, No. LE98, and Nanny holding the future King Edward VII, No. LE100. Made in England. About 8in (20.3cm).

KING ALBERT I OF BELGIUM. Born 1875; died 1934. Albert led resistance to the German invasion of Belgium in World War I and won great popularity with his democratic ways. He married Queen Elizabeth of Belgium in 1900. He died in a rock-climbing accident.
DOLLS:
1. KING ALBERT I OF BELGIUM. Plaster of paris head with brown molded hair and moustache; blue painted eyes; stuffed cloth body; molded hands and high, black laced boots; wears a dark uniform. Unmarked. 1918.

ALDA, ALAN. Motion picture and TV actor. Born January 28, 1936, in New York, New York. Alan Alda played leading men in movies after 1963; since September 1972 he has played Captain Benjamin Franklin ("Hawkeye") Pierce in "M*A*S*H" on CBS-TV.

DOLLS:
1. M*A*S*H. F.W.Woolworth Co., No. 3008, circa 1976. Plastic and vinyl. A M*A*S*H "Nurse" (LORETTA SWIT) was issued as a companion doll. Made in Hong Kong. 8½in (20.6cm). *Illustration 61*.
2. HAWKEYE. CAPT. BENJAMIN FRANKLIN PIERCE. Tristar International, Ltd., Series No. 4100, 1982. All-vinyl and fully-jointed with painted features and clothing. Made in Hong Kong. 3¾in (9.6cm).
SEE: M*A*S*H.

Illustration 61. 8½in (20.6cm) ALAN ALDA as *Hawkeye* from "M*A*S*H" distributued by F.W. Woolworth Co., circa 1976. All-vinyl and fully-jointed. Painted and molded black hair. Copyright by Aspen Productions and Twentieth Century-Fox Film Corporation. Made in Hong Kong. (See LORETTA SWIT, a companion doll.)

ALDEN, JOHN (or ALDIN). Settler in the Pilgrim colony of Plymouth. Born circa 1599; died 1687.His legendary romance with fellow colonist Priscilla Mullens was made immortal by the poet Henry Wadsworth Longfellow in *The Courtship of Miles Standish* in 1858. At the time of his death, John Alden was the last male survivor of the Mayflower Company.
DOLLS:
1. JOHN ALDEN. Vogue, circa 1953. Hard plastic Ginny doll with a wig. (Name of doll not confirmed.) Made in USA. 7½in (19.1cm).

ALDEN, PRISCILLA MULLENS (MULLINS). Sailed on the Mayflower and settled in the Pilgrim colony of Plymouth in 1620. Priscilla Mullens Alden is remembered chiefly because of Longfellow's poem which tells of her courtship by Captain Miles Standish and her marriage to John Alden, who wooed her first for Standish, in 1623. The story is not based on historical evidence.

DOLLS:
1. PRISCILLA. Madame Alexander, late 1930s. Composition "Little Betty" doll with moveable arms and legs. 7in (17.8cm).
2. PRISCILLA. Madame Alexander, No. 789, 1965; No. 729, 1966-1970. Hard plastic with "bending knees." 8in (20.3cm).
3. PRISCILLA ALDEN. Plastic Molded Arts, 1951. Cheaply constructed plastic doll with jointed arms and sleep eyes. Made in USA. 6in (15.2cm).

QUEEN ALEXANDRA. Princess of Denmark and Consort of King Edward VII of England. Born 1844; died 1925. She married Edward, the then Prince of Wales, in 1863. Her beauty and her gracious manners made her a great favorite with the public. She bore her husband six children, one of whom later became King George V.

DOLLS:
1. QUEEN ALEXANDRA. Peggy Nisbet, No. P612, circa 1960s. Plastic "collectors' doll," wearing State Robes. King Edward VII, No. P611, is the companion doll. Made in England. About 7½in (19.1cm).

TSARITSA ALEXANDRA (ALEKSANDRA FEODOR-OVNA). Empress of Russia and Consort of Nicholas II. Born 1872; executed 1918. Alexandra's ruling of Russia while her husband was at the front in World War I is in a large part responsible for the collapse of the monarchy in 1917. Most of Alexandra's neuroses concerned her young son, the Tsarevich Aleksei, who suffered from hemophilia, and her association with the debauched "holy man" Rasputin, who attempted to heal him. She was put to death with her husband and her five children at Ekaterinburg during the night of July 16-17, 1918.

DOLLS:
1. TSARITSA ALEXANDRA, EMPRESS OF RUSSIA. Peggy Nisbet, No. P791, circa 1960s. Plastic "collectors' doll." Tsar Nicholas II, No. P792, is the companion doll. Made in England. About 7½in (19.1cm).

PRINCESS ALEXANDRIA. English royalty. Born December 25, 1936. Alexandria, the sister of Edward, the Duke of Kent, is the daughter of George, the Duke of Kent (born December 20, 1902; killed in action August 15, 1942), who was a son of King George V (reigned 1910-1936). This makes Alexandria an aunt of Queen Elizabeth II. In 1963 Alexandria married the Honorable Angus Ogilvy.

DOLLS:
1. PRINCESS ALEXANDRIA. Chad Valley, circa 1941. Stiffened felt with a velveteen torso. Set-in glass eyes; mohair wig. Part of a series with Edward, the Duke of Kent, Princesses Elizabeth and Margaret Rose. Made in England. About 17in (43.2cm).

ALFONSO XIII. King of Spain from 1886 to 1931. Born 1886; died 1941. Alfonso was proclaimed King immediately upon his birth as his father Alfonso XII had already died. His mother, Maria Cristina, acted as regent until 1902 when he was 16, the year he married

Princess Victoria Eugénie of Battenberg (Queen Ena). In April of 1931 Alfonso was forced to abdicate his throne and leave Spain. His grandson became King Juan Carlos of Spain in 1975.

DOLLS:
1. KING ALFONSO XIII. Peggy Nisbet, No. P794, circa 1960s. Plastic "collectors' doll." Queen Ena of Spain, No. P793, is the companion doll. Made in England. About 8in (20.3cm).

ALI, MUHAMMAD (CASSIUS CLAY). American prizefighter and actor. Born 1942 in Louisville, Kentucky. He was the heavyweight gold medalist at the Rome Olympics in 1960 and later three times world heavyweight champion. Ali adopted his Arabic name when he converted to the Muslim religion. He portrayed himself in the film biogrpahy *The Greatest* (1977).

DOLLS:
1. MUHAMMAD ALI, THE CHAMP. Mego Corp., No. 61701, 1976. Made in Hong Kong. 9¼in (23.6cm). *Illustration 62.*

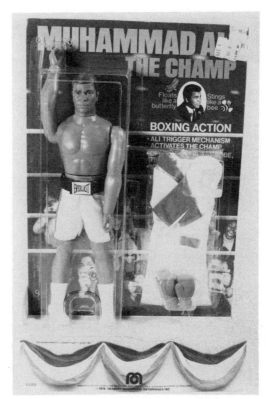

Illustration 62. 9¼in (23.6cm) MUHAMMAD ALI *the Champ* by Mego Corp., No. 61701, 1976. All-vinyl and fully-jointed. Painted hair and features. "Boxing action" is provided by a trigger mechanism. Copyright by Muhammad Enterprises Inc. Made in Hong Kong.

ALLEN, KAREN. Actress. Born October 5, 1951, in Maryland. By the 1980s Karen Allen had become one of the most versatile actresses in films, most of which were highly successful. In *Raiders of the Lost Ark* she played Marion Ravenwood.

DOLLS:
1. MARION RAVENWOOD. Kenner, Series No. 46010, 1982. All-vinyl and fully-jointed. Painted features and clothing with a cloth skirt like Marion wore in the "Well of the Souls" sequence in *Raiders*

of the Lost Ark. The doll is packaged with a small vinyl monkey. Copyright by Lucasfilm Ltd. About 4in (10.2cm).

SEE: RAIDERS OF THE LOST ARK.

ANDERSON, LONI. Actress. Born on August 5, ?. Loni Anderson began her acting career as a brunette. After she "went blonde" she became popular. Since September of 1978 she has played Jennifer Marlowe, the receptionist, on "WKRP in Cincinnati" on CBS-TV. In 1980 she also played Jayne Mansfield in a TV-movie about the life of the famous star of the 1950s.
DOLLS:
  1. LONI ANDERSON. Ideal, No. 1272-4, 1981. 11½in (29.2cm). *Illustration 63.*

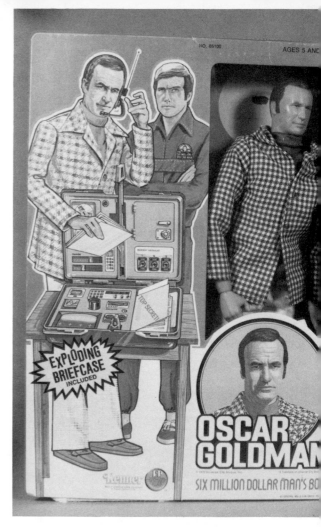

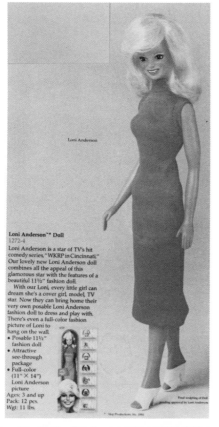

Illustration 63. 11½in (29.2cm) LONI ANDERSON by Ideal, No. 1272-4, 1981. All-vinyl and fully-jointed. Rooted blonde hair; painted brown eyes. This is an advertisement from the 1981 Ideal catalog. The doll did not appear on the market as of this writing. The catalog stated that "final sculpting of the doll pending approval by Loni Anderson."

ANDERSON, RICHARD. Motion picture and television actor. Born August 8, 1926. Richard Anderson played second leads and supporting parts in films since 1950. He was a regular in several TV series after 1961, the best known part being that of Oscar Goldman in "The Six Million Dollar Man" and "The Bionic Woman" during the 1970s.
DOLLS:
  1. OSCAR GOLDMAN. Kenner, No. 65100, 1977. (Companion dolls are Lee Majors and Lindsay Wagner.) Made in Hong Kong. 13in (33cm). *Illustrations 64* and *65.*

Illustration 64. 13in (33cm) RICHARD ANDERSON as *Oscar Goldman* from "The Six Million Dollar Man" by Kenner, No. 65100, 1977. All-vinyl and fully-jointed. Painted hair and eyes. Back marked: "©1977 GENERAL MILLS FUN // GROUP INC. BY ITS DIVISION // KENNER PRODUCTS CINCINNATI // OHIO 45202 CAT. NO. 65100 // MADE IN HONG KONG." Copyright 1973 by Universal City Studios, Inc. *Shirley Buchholz Collection.*

Illustration 65. RICHARD ANDERSON by Kenner.

PRINCE ANDREW. Third child of Queen Elizabeth II of England. Born February 19, 1960. Prince Andrew is said to be very athletic and very amorous.

DOLLS:
1. H.R.H. PRINCE ANDREW. Peggy Nisbet, No. P413, circa 1970s. Plastic "collectors' doll." H.R.H. Prince Edward, No. P414, is a companion doll. Made in England. About 8in (20.3cm).
2. H.R.H. PRINCE ANDREW IN NAVAL UNIFORM. Peggy Nisbet, No. P427, early 1980s. Plastic "collectors' doll." Made in England. About 8in (20.3cm).

ANDREWS, JULIE. Actress and singer. Born Julia Elizabeth Welles, October 1, 1935, in England. Julie Andrews began performing as a child of 12. In 1955 she created the musical role of Eliza Doolittle in *My Fair Lady* on Broadway. She won an Academy Award for her film debut, playing the lead in Walt Disney's *Mary Poppins* of 1964. In 1965 she was tremendously popular playing Maria von Trapp in *The Sound of Music,* one of the most commercially successful musical films ever made. Her career has been in the decline ever since.

DOLLS:
1. MARY POPPINS. Horsman, 1964. Plastic and vinyl with rooted black hair and painted blue eyes. Made in USA. 11½in (29.2cm).
2. MARY POPPINS. Horsman, 1964. Plastic and vinyl walker. Made in USA. 35in (88.9cm) *Illustrations 69* and *70.*
3. MARY POPPINS. 1965. Same doll as No. 1 by Horsman with two extra outfits. 11½in (29.2cm). *Illustrations 67* and *68.*
4. MARY POPPINS. Horsman, 1965. Plastic and vinyl. 16in (40.6cm).
5. MARIA from THE SOUND OF MUSIC. Part of the all-8in (20.3cm) Set. Madame Alexander, No. 1006, 1965. Hard plastic. Made in USA.
6. MARIA from THE SOUND OF MUSIC. Large Sound of Music set. Madame Alexander, 1965-1966. Plastic and vinyl with the "Polly face." 17in (43.2cm). Note: The six children that match this set came in two different versions. (See listing under SOUND OF MUSIC.)
7. MARIA from THE SOUND OF MUSIC. Large Sound of Music Set. Madame Alexander, 1965 to 1970. Plastic and vinyl with the "Elise face." Made in USA. 17in (43.2cm). *Illustration 73.* Note: The six children that match this doll in a set came in two different versions. (See listing under SOUND OF MUSIC.)
8. MARY POPPINS. Horsman, 1966. 27½in (69.9cm). Made in USA. *Illustration 71.*
9. MARY POPPINS. Horsman, 1966. Set with Jane and Michael. This is the same Mary Poppins as No. 1 and No. 2. 11½in (29.2cm). *Illustration 66.*
10. MARY POPPINS. Gund Mfg. Co., 1966. Made in Japan. 11½in (29.2cm). *Illustration 72.*
11. MARIA from THE SOUND OF MUSIC. Small set. Madame Alexander, No. 1206, 1971 to 1973. Hard plastic and vinyl using the "Nancy Drew face." 12in (30.5cm). *Illustration 74.*
12. MARY POPPINS. Horsman, No. 928, 1973. This is basically the same doll as No. 1 by Horsman, wearing the blue coat, except that the umbrella is cardboard instead of cloth and vinyl. Designed by Irene Szor; made in USA. 11½in (29.2cm). *Illustration 75.*
13. MARY POPPINS. Horsman, No. 1098, 1981. Made in USA. 8½in (21.6cm). *Illustration 76.*

SEE: THE SOUND OF MUSIC.

Illustration 66. 8¼in (21cm) KAREN DOTRICE as *Jane*; 8¼in (21cm) MATTHEW GARBER as *Michael* and 11½in (29.2cm) JULIE ANDREWS as *Mary Poppins* by Horsman, 1964. The children are all-vinyl and fully-jointed with rooted blonde hair and painted blue eyes. Karen is marked on the head: "7 // HORSMAN DOLLS INC. // 6681." Matthew is marked on the head: "©11 // HORSMAN DOLLS INC. // 6682." Julie Andrews is described in *Illustration 68. Jean Canaday Collection.*

Illustration 67. 11½in (29.2cm) JULIE ANDREWS as *Mary Poppins* by Horsman, 1964. *Sears 1965 Christmas Book.* Made in USA.

Illustration 68. 11½in (29.2cm) JULIE ANDREWS as *Mary Poppins* by Horsman, 1964. Vinyl head and arms; plastic body and legs. Rooted dark brown hair; painted blue eyes. These two dolls are dressed in the extra costumes that came with the doll seen in *Illustration 67*. Made in USA. Head marked: "H."

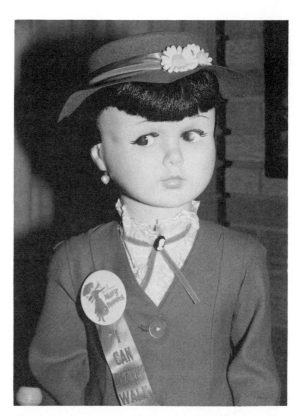

Illustration 70. 35in (88.9cm) *Mary Poppins. Betty Shriver Collection.*

Illustration 69. 35in (88.9cm) JULIE ANDREWS as *Mary Poppins* by Horsman, 1964. Vinyl head with rooted black hair and painted blue eyes with attached lashes. Plastic fully-jointed body. This doll is a "walker." No markings. Made in USA. *Betty Shriver Collection.*

Illustration 71. 27½in (69.9cm) JULIE ANDREWS as *Mary Poppins* by Horsman, 1966. All-vinyl and fully-jointed. Rooted dark brown hair; bright blue sleep eyes with lashes. Disproportionately chubby body. Head marked: "HORSMAN DOLL INC. // ©1966 // 66271." Made in USA. *Wanda Lodwick Collection.*

Illustration 72. 11½in (29.2cm) JULIE ANDREWS as *Mary Poppins* by Gund Mfg. Co., 1966. Silk head; vinyl lower arms; body of stuffed cloth with wire inside for posing. Brown yarn hair; painted **blue eyes** with brown eye shadow. The skirt is lavender; the coat is dark blue flannel. The hat and umbrella are missing. The coat is labeled, and the item carries the Walt Disney copyright. Made in Japan.

Illustration 74. 12in (30.5cm) JULIE ANDREWS as *Maria* from *The Sound of Music* by Madame Alexander, No. 1206, 1971. Vinyl head; hard plastic body; fully-jointed. Rooted blonde hair; blue sleep eyes with molded lashes. Head marked: "ALEXANDER // 19 © 63."

Illustration 73. 17in (43.2cm) JULIE ANDREWS as *Maria* from *The Sound of Music* by Madame Alexander, No. 1706, 1967-1970. Vinyl with rooted blonde hair; blue sleep eyes with lashes. Head marked: "ALEXANDER // 19©66." *Jean Canaday Collection.*

Illustration 75. 11½in (29.2cm) JULIE ANDREWS as *Mary Poppins* by Horsman, No. 928, 1973. Vinyl head and arms; plastic torso and legs. Rooted dark brown hair, painted blue eyes. Designed by Irene Szor; made in USA. Head marked: "H."

Illustration 76. 8½in (21.6cm) JULIE ANDREWS as *Mary Poppins*, one of "Walt Disney's Classics," by Horsman, No. 1098, 1981. Vinyl head and arms; plastic torso and legs. Fully-jointed. Rooted dark brown hair; painted blue eyes. White blouse, lavender skirt, dark blue flannel coat. Head marked: "HORSMAN DOLLS INC. // 19 © 81." Made in USA. *Marge Meisinger Collection.*

ANNE OF CLEVES. Fourth Queen Consort of King Henry VIII of England. Born September 22, 1515; died July 16, 1557. Anne's marriage to Henry VIII was a political arrangement to consolidate England's relations with the German Lutherans. Henry became enthused about Anne because of artist Hans Holbein's flattering portrait of her, but when he saw her for himself on January 1, 1540, he was supposed to have described her as "no better than a Flanders mare." They were married five days later, and the marriage was annulled after six months because Henry found his bride so repulsive. Anne stayed in England where she was awarded a pension, and was reported to be happier than ever and wearing a new dress every day.

DOLLS:
1. ANNE OF CLEVES. Peggy Nisbet, No. P605, late 1970s. Plastic "collectors' doll," part of a series of Henry VIII and his six wives in the "Portrait Series." Made in England. About 7½in (19.1cm).
2. ANNE OF CLEVES. Peggy Nisbet, No. H222, late 1970s. Plastic "collectors' doll," part of a series of Henry VIII and his six wives in "The Tudor Period" series. Made in England. About 7½in (19.1cm).
3. ANNE OF CLEVES. Peggy Nisbet, No. M934, late 1970s. Plastic "collectors' doll," part of the series "Inch-to-the-foot Miniatures (Historical Series)" of Henry VIII and his six wives. Made in England.

PRINCESS ANNE. Daughter of Queen Elizabeth II of England. Born August 15, 1950. The second child and only daughter of Queen Elizabeth and Prince Phillip is famous for her horse riding ability. Princess Anne was the first member of a royal family ever to compete in an Olympic event. At the Summer Olympics in Montreal in 1976 she placed 24th out of 30 in the equestrian event with her skittish horse, Goodwill. In November of 1973 the Princess married Lieutenant Mark Phillips of the Queen's Dragoon Guards in Westminister Abbey.

DOLLS:
1. PRINCESS ANNE. Madame Alexander, No. 396, 1957. Hard plastic with bending knees. Prince Charles, No. 395 is a companion doll. 8in (20.3cm).
2. PRINCESS ANNE. Chelsea Art, 1957. Prince Charles is a companion doll. Made in England. 8¾in (22.3cm). *Illustration 77.*
3. PRINCESS ANNE. Peggy Nisbet, No. P405, 1973. Plastic "collectors' doll," dressed in a copy of the Princess' wedding dress. Made in England. About 7½in (19.1cm).
4. H.R.H. PRINCESS ANNE (IN FORMAL RIDING DRESS). Peggy Nisbet, No. P412, 1970s. Plastic "collectors' doll." Made in England. About 7½in (19.1cm).

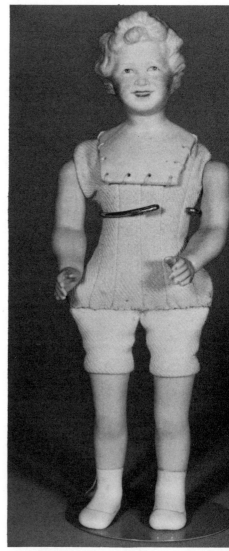

Illustration 77. 8 ¾in (22.3cm) PRINCESS ANNE by Chelsea Art, 1957. Bisque shoulder plate head, arms and lower legs; cloth body. Painted hair and features with smiling mouth. Marked on back of shoulder plate: "MADE FOR // DOLL MAKERS // BY CHELSEA ART // 1957." Prince Charles, *Illustration 190* is a companion doll. Made in England. *Shirley Buchholz Collection.*

Queen Anne

QUEEN ANNE. Queen of Great Britain and Ireland from 1702 to 1714. Born February 6, 1665; died August 1, 1714. Anne was the second daughter of James II and became Queen when William III, the husband of James' first daughter, Mary, died. Anne was married to Prince George of Denmark. All of the children born of this union died before Anne, so she was succeeded by George Louis, the Elector of Hanover, a distant relative. Queen Anne was supposed to have become very fat from having 17 children, and it is reputed that her coffin is as wide as it is long.

DOLLS:
1. QUEEN ANNE. Ann Parker, 1977. Plastic "collectors' doll," affixed to a wooden base. Made in England. 11in (27.9cm) *Illustrations 78* and *79.*
2. QUEEN ANNE. Peggy Nisbet, No. P450, late 1970s. Plastic "collectors' doll." Prince George of Denmark, No. P451, is a companion doll. Made in England. About 7½in (19.1cm). *Illustration 80.*

Illustration 79. 11in (27.9cm) QUEEN ANNE by Ann Parker, late 1970s. All-hard plastic and affixed to a wooden base. Reddish-brown mohair wig; painted blue eyes. The costume is purple and white with an inset panel of gold and aqua. Made in England. *Shirley Buchholz Collection.*

Illustration 78. Front cover of Ann Parker Dolls catalog.

Illustration 80. About 7½in (19.1cm) QUEEN ANNE, No. P450, and PRINCE GEORGE OF DENMARK, No. P451, by Peggy Nisbet, 1970s. All-hard plastic and jointed only at the arms. Mohair wigs and painted features. Made in England. *Photograph Courtesy of House of Nisbet.*

ANNIE. Broadway play and musical motion picture based on the popular comic strip. "Little Orphan Annie" began as a comic strip in 1924 in *The New York News* and *The Chicago Tribune* and later in most American newspapers and was drawn by Harold Gray. On April 6, 1931, "Little Orphan Annie" debuted on radio on ABC's Blue Network as a six-a-week juvenile adventure serial. Shirley Bell and later Janice Gilbert played Annie. "Annie" was sponsored by Ovaltine chocolate-flavored mix. Ovaltine was one of the great premium give-away dispensers. For a dime and/or the aluminum strip from inside an Ovaltine container listeners could send for decoders and shake-up mugs. Around 1940 Ovaltine abandoned its sponsorship of "Little Orphan Annie" and she disappeared from the air by 1943. On the radio shows Annie solved exciting mysteries and lived through various harrowing adventures. In 1977 "Annie" became a musical play on Broadway. ANDREA McARDLE played Annie and she won a Tony nomination for her musical role. The play won the Tony Award for Musical of the Year, as did Dorothy Louden as Actress in a Musical, the producers for the Musical Play of the Year, Thomas Meehan for Best Book of the Year, the songwriters for Scoring, Costume Designs, and Peter Gennaro for Choreography. The Broadway play is still running. The

Illustration 80-A. The stars of the film *Annie* by Knickerbocker Toy Co., Inc., 1982. From left to right: ALBERT FINNEY as *Daddy Warbucks*, No. 3869; GOEFFREY HOLDER as *Punjab*, No. 3866; AILEEN QUINN as *Annie*, No. 3856, CAROL BURNETT as *Miss Hannigan*, No. 3867 and TONI ANN GISONDI as *Molly*, No. 3868. The adults are 7in (17.8cm); the girls are 6in (15.2cm). From *The World of Annie* (catalog) by Knickerbocker.

film *Annie* went into general release on June 1, 1982. It is the most expensive musical production ever produced by Columbia Pictures, and it takes place in "hard times." *Annie* is about a poor New York City waif who was rescued from a Charles Dickens-type orphanage by rich Daddy Warbucks who took Annie and her dog, Sandy, to live with him in a fabulous mansion. In 1982 the Knickerbocker Toy Co., Inc. launched a two million dollar advertising campaign to promote a line of toys and dolls called "The World of Annie." The stars from the film who are made in doll form are AILEEN QUINN as Annie, ALBERT FINNEY as Daddy Warbucks, GOEFFREY HOLDER as Punjab, CAROL BURNETT as Miss Hannigan and TONI ANN GISONDI as Molly. See entries under each celebrity and *Illustration 80-A.*

ANSARA, MICHAEL. Film and TV actor. Born April 15, 1922, in Lowell, Massachusetts. Ansara unually plays heavies, ethnic types and Indians. He played Cochise on the TV series "Broken Arrow" from September 1956 to September 1960 and Deputy United States Marshall Sam Buckhart in another western series, "Law of the Plainsman" from October 1959 to September 1962. In 1958 he married actress Barbara Eden.

DOLLS:
1. COCHISE AND HIS PINTO WARHORSE FROM BROKEN ARROW. Hartland Plastics, Inc., No. 816, circa 1958. Plastic and painted figure with moveable arms. Made in Hartland, Wisconsin. Doll is about 8in (20.3cm).
2. KLINGON COMMANDER from STAR TREK. Mego, No. 51200/6, 1974. Vinyl with painted hair and painted features. Made in Hong Kong. 8in (20.3cm).

SEE: STAR TREK.

ANTHONY, SUSAN B (ROWNELL). Pioneer leader in the women's suffrage movement. Born February 15, 1820; died March 13, 1906. Susan B. Anthony was a school teacher, an organizer of temperance societies and after 1854 she devoted her life to the anti-slavery movement and woman's rights. Her work helped to bring about the 19th Amendment to the United States Constitution in 1920 which gave full voting rights to women. She was arrested, tried and convicted because of staging demonstrations in 1872 and for the rest of her life worked with national organizations to seek equality for women. She was the first woman to have her portrait on an American coin, the unsuccessful dollar coin of 1976 that was rejected by the public because it is too similar to a quarter.

DOLLS:
1. SUSAN B. ANTHONY. Hallmark, No. 400DT113-8, 1979. Made in Taiwan. 7in (17.8cm). *Illustration 81*.
2. SUSAN B. ANTHONY COMMEMORATIVE DOLL. Effanbee Limited Edition Doll Club, 1980. Included a Susan B. Anthony dollar coin in a souvenir case. 15in (38.1cm). *Illustration 82*.

Illustration 81. 7in (17.8cm) SUSAN B. ANTHONY by Hallmark, No. 400DT113-8, 1979. All-cloth. Sewn body joints with printed features and clothing. Made in Taiwan. *Shirley Buchholz Collection.*

ANTONIUS, MARCUS (MARC, or MARK ANTONY.) Roman political leader and general. Born circa 82BC; died 30BC. Antony was a very handsome man, a good soldier and a brilliant politician; however, he was not able to combat the schemes of Octavian, who later became the Emperor Augustus. He is most famous for his alliance with the Egyptian Queen Cleopatra, whom he married in about 37BC. On August 1, 30BC, Antony received a false report of Cleopatra's death and he committed suicide. Antony's romance with Cleopatra inspired a play by William Shakespeare and many motion pictures.

DOLLS:
1. ANTONY. Madame Alexander, No. 1310, 1980. *Illustration 212.* Hard plastic with a vinyl head. Cleopatra, No. 1315, is a companion doll. 12in (30.5cm).

ARNESS, JAMES. Film and TV actor. Born James Aurness, May 26, 1923. Because of his huge size (6 foot, 6 inches), the young Arness had troubles breaking into the movies. In 1950 he played the monster called *The Thing.* His greatest fame came from portraying Marshall Matt Dillon on "Gunsmoke" for 20 years on television—September 1955 to September 1975. Three years after "Gunsmoke," the longest running dramatic series ever on television ended, Arness played Zeb Macahan on "How the West was Won."

DOLLS:
1. MARSHALL MATT DILLON OF "GUNSMOKE." Hartland Plastics, Inc., No. 822, circa 1958. Plastic painted figure with moveable arms. About 8in (21.6cm). Came with a plastic buckskin horse. Made in Hartland, Wisconsin.

Illustration 82. 15in (38.1cm) SUSAN B. AN-THONY Commemorative Doll by Effanbee, 1980. All-vinyl and fully-jointed. Root-ed dark brown hair; fixed brown glass eyes. Head inscribed: "S.B. ANTHONY // LIMITED EDITION // EFFANBEE." Back: "SUSAN B. ANTHONY // EFFANBEE DOLL // LTD. EDITION // 19 © 80." The dress is made of moire taffeta and is gray. *Jean Pritchard Collection.*

Illustration 83. 9¾in (24.9cm) JAMES ARNESS as *Zeb Macahan* from "How the West Was Won" by Mattel, No. 2367, 1978. All-vinyl and fully-jointed. Painted yellow hair, brown moustache and blue eyes. Head not marked. Back marked: "©1971 MATTEL, INC. // HONG KONG US & // FOREIGN PATENTED." (This is the *Big Jim* body by Mattel.) Copyright by MGM, Inc. *Shirley Buchholz Collection.*

2. THE THING. Mego, 1970s. Vinyl with painted hair and features. Made in Hong Kong. 8in (21.6cm).
3. HOW THE WEST WAS WON, ZEB MACAHAN. Mattel, Inc., No. 2367, 1978. 9¾in (24.9cm). *Illustrations 83* and *84*. Ivan Naranjo as Lone Wolf is a companion doll.

Illustration 84. JAMES ARNESS by Mattel. *Shirley Buchholz Collection.*

AUSTEN, JANE. English novelist. Born December 16, 1775; died July 18, 1817. Jane Austen's novels of social criticism are masterpieces. During her own lifetime Jane Austen enjoyed critical success, but her books were considered "old fashioned" for almost another one hundred years until her work was re-appraised in this century. She is now considered one of the greatest novelists of all time. Her best loved work is *Sense and Sensibility* (1811) and *Pride and Prejudice* (1813).

DOLLS:
1. JANE AUSTEN. Ann Parker, 1970s. Plastic "collectors' doll," affixed to a wooden base. Made in England. 11in (27.9cm).

AUTRY, GENE. Actor, singing "cowboy," songwriter, producer, bussinessman, baseball team owner. Born September 29, 1907. Beginning in the early 1930s Gene Autry had his own radio show and was making his first recordings. His first western film was made in 1934; his last was in 1953. Autry wrote about 200 popular songs, including "Here Comes Santa Claus." His most popular recording was "Rudolph, the Red-Nosed Reindeer." In 1978 he published his autobiography, *Back in the Saddle Again,* which was the title of his theme song.

DOLLS:
1. GENE AUTRY. Ralph A. Freundlich, Inc., 1939. Details unknown.
2. GENE AUTRY. Terri Lee, 1950s. All-hard plastic with painted features, dressed in two different cowboy outfits. Made in USA. 16in (40.6cm). *Illustration 85*.
3. GENE AUTRY. National Mask and Puppet Corp., 1950s. Hand puppet with a rubber head with molded hat, rubber hands and feet and a cloth body. 10in (25.4cm).

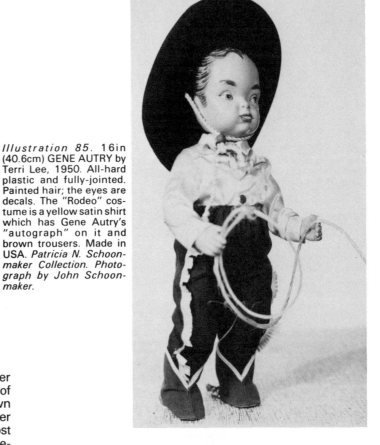

Illustration 85. 16in (40.6cm) GENE AUTRY by Terri Lee, 1950. All-hard plastic and fully-jointed. Painted hair; the eyes are decals. The "Rodeo" costume is a yellow satin shirt which has Gene Autry's "autograph" on it and brown trousers. Made in USA. *Patricia N. Schoonmaker Collection. Photograph by John Schoonmaker.*

B

BABY JANE. SEE: QUIGLEY, JUANITA.

BABY PEGGY (MONTGOMERY). Child performer. Born 1917. Baby Peggy entered films at age three, starring in numerous two-reelers and many features. She was the Shirley Temple of the 1920s. Baby Peggy's popularity declined as she neared her teen years, but she continued in the movies under her full name until the mid 1930s. Her first husband was Gordon "Freckles" Ayres, one of the "Our Gang" members.

DOLLS:
1. BABY PEGGY. Louis Amberg & Son, 1923. Composition shoulder plate; composition lower arms and legs; stuffed cloth body. Painted brown hair; painted brown eyes; open-closed mouth with painted teeth. 20in (50.8cm).

2. BABY PEGGY. Louis Amberg & Son, circa 1923. All-bisque with jointed arms and legs. 4⅜in (11.1cm). *Illustration 87.*
3. BABY PEGGY. Louis Amberg & Son, circa 1923. All-bisque with jointed arms only. Painted hair and features. 6in (15.2cm).
4. BABY PEGGY. Manufacturer unknown, circa 1924. All-celluloid. 5⅜in (13.6cm). *Illustration 88.*
5. BABY PEGGY. Manufacturer unknown, 1924. Bisque head with jointed kid body. "Sober face." 18in (45.7cm). *Illustration 89.*
6. BABY PEGGY. Manufacturer unknown, 1924. Bisque head with brown sleep eyes. Jointed kid body. The head is marked: "19 © 24 // N-Y // Germany, 50 // 983/2." She has a "smiling face." About 19in (48.3cm).

Illustration 88. 5⅜in (13.6cm) BABY PEGGY, circa 1924. All-celluloid. Molded hair, clothing, shoes and socks. Gold colored strips are glued to the head to form a hat. The hair is painted dark brown, the eyes black, the socks pink and the shoes gold. No markings. There are slits around the arms as if she once wore some sort of sash.

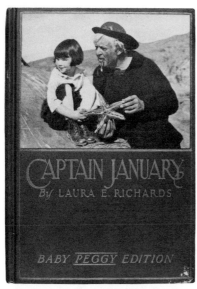

Illustration 86. Baby Peggy Edition of *Captain January,* L.C. Page & Company, Boston, 1924.

Illustration 87. 4⅜in (11.1cm) BABY PEGGY by Louis Amberg and Son, circa 1923. All-bisque with jointed arm and legs. Painted hair and features; painted shoes and socks. The crocheted dress is a replacement. There was originally a paper label on the front telling that this doll was "Baby Peggy." *Patricia N. Schoonmaker Collection. Photograph by John Schoonmaker.*

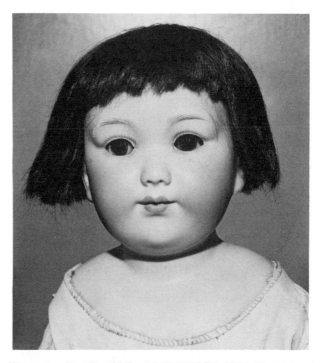

Illustration 89. 18in (45.7cm) BABY PEGGY, 1924. Bisque head with brown sleep glass eyes. The body is of kid and is jointed. The head is marked: "19 © 24 // N-Y // GERMANY, 50 // 982/2." *Courtesy of Patricia Schoonmaker. Photograph by John Schoonmaker.*

BABY SANDY (HENVILLE). Child performer. Born Sandra Henville on January 14, 1938. Universal featured Sandy in some films in the late 1930s and the early 1940s, such as *Sandy is a Lady, Sandy Steps Out* and *Sandy Gets Her Man*. Her career lasted from ages one to four. Today Sandy is a legal secretary and she has no memory of her screen career.

DOLLS:
1. BABY SANDY. Ralph A. Freundlich, Inc., 1939. 7½in (19.1cm). *Illustration 91*.
2. BABY SANDY. Ralph A. Freundlich, Inc., 1939. 11⅛in (28.2cm). *Illustrations 92* and *93*.
3. BABY SANDY. Ralph A. Freundlich, Inc., 1939. 16½in (41.9cm). *Illustrations 93* and *94*.
4. BABY SANDY. Ralph A. Freundlich, Inc., 1940. 16½in (41.9cm). This is the same doll as the above with a blonde mohair wig. *Illustration 95*.

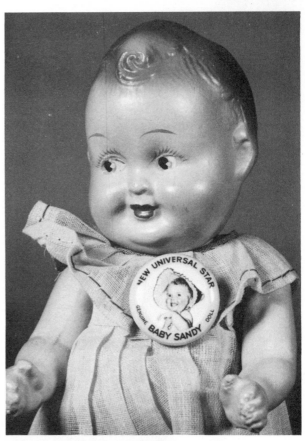

Illustration 91. 7½in (19.1cm) BABY SANDY by Ralph A. Freundlich, Inc., 1939. All-composition and fully-jointed. Painted, molded yellow hair; painted blue eyes. The simple cotton dress is pink. Head marked: "BABY SANDY." *Marge Meisinger Collection.*

Illustration 90. Baby Sandy with a Freundlich doll of Baby Sandy, 1939. Note that the shoes match the sunsuit.

Illustration 92. 11⅛in (28.2cm) BABY SANDY by Ralph A. Freundlich, Inc., 1939. All-composition and fully-jointed. Painted yellow hair; blue tin sleep eyes; open mouth with two upper teeth and a felt tongue. The dress has been replaced. Head marked: "BABY SANDY."

Illustration 94. 16½in (41.9cm) BABY SANDY by Ralph A. Freundlich, Inc., 1939. All-composition and fully-jointed. Painted yellow hair; green sleep eyes with lashes; open mouth with a felt tongue and two teeth. Clothing replaced. Head marked: "BABY SANDY." *Betty Shriver Collection.*

Illustration 93. 16½in (41.9cm) and 11⅛in (28.2cm) BABY SANDY by Ralph A. Freundlich, Inc., 1939. Both toddlers are all-composition and fully-jointed. Molded hair; blue tin sleep eyes with lashes. Heads marked: "BABY SANDY." Neither the costumes nor the shoes are original. *Jean Canaday Collection.*

Bring the Sensational "Baby

A DOLL
plus A PERSONALITY

Sandra Henville (*Baby Sandy*), lovable two-year-old screen star, who, literally over night, made motion picture history by captivating the hearts of millions of children and grown-ups in the screen classics, "East Side of Heaven," "Unexpected Father" and "Little Accident."

Next Picture
"Sandy Is A Lady"
to be released
latter part of April, 1940

A NATURAL

Obviously a natural, this irresistible infant now reproduced in amazingly realistic doll form and backed by powerful screen, radio and magazine publicity is a precedent smashing Freundlich value that will instantly start your doll sales soaring to new record highs.

●

COPYRIGHT NOTICE!

We have been granted exclusive permission to manufacture the Baby Sandy Doll and will vigorously protect our rights against infringers.

Licensed by
MITCHELL J. HAMILBURG
for UNIVERSAL PICTURES

RALPH A.
The World's Largest
Sales Rooms 200 5TH AVE
NEW YORK

Illustration 95. **BABY SANDY** doll with a wig by Ralph A. Freundlich. Advertisement from *Playthings*, April 1940.

BACH, CATHERINE. Actress. Born Catherine Ann Bachman in Warren, Ohio, on March 1, 1954. Catherine Bach has played long legged, high heeled and shorts wearing Daisy Duke on "The Dukes of Hazzard" since the TV show debuted on January 26, 1979.

DOLLS:
1. DAISY DUKE. Mego, No. 09050/3, 1981. Made in Hong Kong. 7¾in (19.8cm). *Illustration 97*.
2. DAISY. Mego, No. 09010/3, 1982. All-vinyl and fully-jointed with painted hair, features and clothing. Copyright by Warner Bros., Inc. Made in Hong Kong. 3¾in (9.6cm).
3. DAISY WITH JEEP. Mego, No. 09062, 1982. Same doll as No. 2 above. Comes packaged with a plastic "free-wheeling jeep." Copyright by Warner Bros., Inc.

Illustration 96. "The Dukes of Hazzard" on one of their three *TV Guide* covers, July 12-18, 1980. From left to right: John Schneider, Catherine Bach, Tom Wopat.

Illustration 97. 7 ¾in (19.8cm) CATHERINE BACH as *Daisy Duke* from "The Dukes of Hazzard" by Mego, No. 09050/3, 1981. All-vinyl and fully-jointed. Rooted long brown hair; painted blue eyes. Head marked: " © WARNER BROS., // INC. 1980." Back marked: "©WARNER BROS INC 1980 // MADE IN HONG KONG."

BADEN-POWELL, ROBERT STEPHENSON SMYTH, FIRST BARON BADEN-POWELL OF GILWELL. English founder of the Boy Scouts. Born February 22, 1857, in London, England; died January 8, 1941 in Kenya, East Africa. Baden-Powell founded the Boy Scouts in 1907. He and his sister, Agnes, founded the Girl Guides in 1910. (In the United States the Girl Guides were called the Girl Scouts after 1912.) In 1916 Baden-Powell founded a junior division of the Boy Scouts, called the Wolf Cubs. (In the United States the Wolf Cubs are called the Cub Scouts.) He also wrote books on Scouting. Baden-Powell was already a national hero in Britain before the time of the Scout movement because of his participation in the Boer War in South Africa from 1899-1902. He and his wife retired to Kenya in 1938.

DOLLS:
1. LORD BADEN POWELL. Peggy Nisbet, No. P827, early 1980s. Plastic "collectors' doll." Lady Baden Powell, No. P828, is a companion doll. Made in England. About 8in (20.3cm).

BADEN-POWELL, LADY OLAVE ST. CLAIR SOAMES. Born February 2, 1889; died 1977. Lady Baden-Powell worked with Agnes Baden-Powell, the sister of her husband, to promote the Girl Guide movement. She toured the world several times with her husband to review Scouts and Guides. After Lord Baden-Powell died in East Africa in 1941, Lady Olave returned to England and worked to promote home front unity during World War II.

DOLLS:
1. LADY BADEN POWELL. Peggy Nisbet, No. P828, early 1980s. Plastic "collectors' doll." Lord Baden-Powell, No. P827, is a companion doll. Made in England. About 7½in (19.1cm).

BAIN, BARBARA. Actress. Born Millie Fogel in Chicago, Illinois, on September 13, 1934. Barbara Bain and her husband, Martin Landeau, appeared on "Mission: Impossible" from 1966 until the end of the 1969 season when they both left over contract disputes. The pair later starred in "Space: 1999" when it began in 1975.

Illustration 98. Barbara Bain and Martin Landau in "Space: 1999."

DOLLS:
1. SPACE: 1999 DOCTOR RUSSEL. Mattel, Inc., No. 9544, 1975. Made in Taiwan. 8½in (21.6cm). *Illustrations 99* and *100*.

SEE: SPACE: 1999.

Illustration 99. 8½in (21.6cm) BARBARA BAIN as *Doctor Russel* from "Space: 1999" by Mattel, No. 9544, 1975. All-vinyl and fully-jointed. Painted yellow hair and painted blue eyes. Copyright 1973 by ATV Licensing Limited; Copyright 1975 by Mattel, Inc. Made in Taiwan. *Shirley Buchholz Collection.*

Illustration 100. BARBARA BAIN by Mattel. *Shirley Buchholz Collection.*

BAKER, KENNY. Actor. Born August 24, 1934, in Birmingham, England. Kenny Baker is a dwarf who played the robot Artoo-Detoo (R2-D2) in *Star Wars,* 1977, and *The Empire Strikes Back,* 1980.

DOLLS:
1. STAR WARS R2-D2. Kenner, No. 38200, 1977. Vinyl "action figure." Made in Taiwan. 2¼in (5.8cm).
2. STAR WARS THE EMPIRE STRIKES BACK R2-D2. Kenner, 1980. Vinyl "action figure." 2¼in (5.8cm). Made in Hong Kong.
3. STAR WARS R2-D2. Kenner, 1977. Plastic walking robot. 7½in (19.1cm).
4. STARS WARS RADIO-CONTROLLED R2-D2. Kenner, No. 38430, 1977. Battery-operated plastic walking robot. 8in (20.3cm).
5. ARTOO-DETOO (R2-D2) WITH SENSORSCOPE. Kenner, Series No. 69570, 1982. Vinyl and plastic figure. Copyright by Lucasfilm Ltd. Made in Hong Kong. 2½in (6.4cm).

SEE: STAR WARS.

BARNUM, P.T. (PHINEAS TAYLOR). American circus proprietor. Born July 5, 1810; died April 7, 1891. P.T. Barnum began his career in 1835 with the purchase and exhibition of Joice Heath, a black slave who was supposed to have been George Washington's nurse and who was claimed to be over 160 years old. From 1841 to 1865 Barnum toured the world with Charles Stratton, billed as General Tom Thumb, the world's smallest man. He engaged Jenny Lind, the celebrated Swedish singer, for her American tour. In 1871, Barnum began his circus, "The Greatest Show on Earth." He claimed, "There's a sucker born every minute," and wrote several instruction manuals on how to become rich. As he lay

Illustration 101. P.T. Barnum and General Tom Thumb (Charles Stratton).

dying, his last request was to see the day's circus receipts.

DOLLS:
1. P.T. BARNUM. Hallmark, No. 400DT113-9, 1979. Made in Taiwan. 6¾in (17.2cm). Illustration 102.

Illustration 102. 6 ¾in (17.2cm) P.T. BARNUM by Hallmark, No. 400DT113-9, 1979. All-cloth with printed clothing and features. Sewn body joints. Copyright by Hallmark Cards, Inc., August 1979. Made in Taiwan.

BARTON, CLARA (CLARISSA). Founder of the American Red Cross. Born December 25, 1821; died April 12, 1912. In 1869, Clara Barton went to Europe for a vacation but when the Franco-Prussian War began, she went to work with the International Red Cross. When she returned to America, she founded the American Red Cross and was its president from 1881 to 1904.

Illustration 103. 6 ¾in (17.2cm) CLARA BARTON by Hallmark, No. 400DT114-4, 1979. All-cloth with printed clothing and features. Sewn body joints. Copyright by Hallmark Cards, Inc., August 1979. Made in Taiwan.

DOLLS:
1. CLARA BARTON. Hallmark, No. 400DT114-4, August 1979. Made in Taiwan. 6¾in (17.2cm). *Illustration 103*.

BEATLES, THE. The four Beatles, all born in Liverpool, England, influenced an entire generation with their music, fashions (including haircuts), life-styles and ideologies. The Beatles were GEORGE HARRISON, JOHN LENNON, PAUL McCARTNEY and RINGO STARR. (See entries under these listings.) In 1964 the Beatles came to America and appeared on "The Ed Sullivan Show" after gaining success in Europe. In 1963 the Beatles had recorded three Number One recordings— "She Loves You," "From Me to You" and "I Want to Hold Your Hand." In 1964 they recorded four more million sellers, seven long playing records and one double long playing record. During 1964 because of the Beatles, British rock groups dominated American popular music. By March 24, 1964, for the first time, every top ten record in the United States was by a British group. As a group, the Beatles appeared in several films. Lennon and McCartney composed hundreds of songs, many of which are held in high regard by music experts. The group disbanded in 1971 because of artistic differences after selling over 400 million records.

DOLLS:
1. THE BOB'N HEAD BEATLES. Car Mascots, Inc., 1964. Papier-mâché and plaster "nodders." Ringo, 7in (17.8cm); others 7¾in (19.8cm). Made in Japan. (See Paul McCartney.)
2. THE BOB'N HEAD BEATLES. Same as the above in all-plastic, 1964. 4in (10.2cm).
3. THE OFFICIAL BEATLES. Remco, 1964. Vinyl and plastic. Made in USA. Paul is 4⅞in (12.2cm); the others are 4½in (11.5cm). *Illustration 106.* (See each Beatle for full description.)
4. THE BEATLES. Pelham Puppets, 1965. Made in England. About 13in (33cm). *Illustration 107.*

Illustration 104. The Beatles, circa 1964. From left to right: Paul McCartney, Ringo Starr, George Harrison and John Lennon.

Illustration 105. Beatles bubble gum cards, circa **1965**. Copyright by T.C.G. and printed in the USA. Beatles cards came in three series and included **165** different cards. The signatures are facsimiles of the autographs of the Beatles, although they often appear in flea markets now billed as "signed." *Peter Bransky Collection.*

Illustration 106. THE BEATLES by Remco, 1964. From left to right: *RINGO STARR, JOHN LENNON, GEORGE HARRISON, PAUL McCARTNEY. Fran's Dolls.*

Illustration 108. 12in (30.5cm) JOSEPHINE, No. 1335, and NAPOLEON, No. 1330, by Madame Alexander, 1980. Vinyl heads with rooted hair; hard plastic bodies. *Alexander Doll Company, Inc. catalog, 1981.*

Illustration 107. THE BEATLES. About 13in (33cm) strung marionettes by Pelham, 1965. Composition heads and hands; wooden feet; jointed wooden segments for bodies. Black fur wigs; painted features. The *Sears 1965 Christmas Catalog* described these simply as "Pop Singers," but they certainly represent the Beatles, from left to right: *PAUL McCARTNEY, GEORGE HARRISON, JOHN LENNON and RINGO STARR.* Stamped on the wooden cross bars at the ends of the strings: "MADE IN ENGLAND" and "PELHAM PUPPETS." *Peter Bransky Collection.*

BEAUHARNAIS, JOSEPHINE (DE). Empress of France. Born Marie Josèphe Rose Tascher de la Pagerie on June 23, 1763; died May 29, 1814. When Napoleon had himself crowned Emperor in 1804 and crowned her as Empress, the 41 year old Josephine (Napoleon was 34 at the time) tried to look as young and innocent as possible to spite her envious detractors. Napoleon divorced her in 1810 "for reasons of state." She continued her lavish life style at her home near Paris, France, her debts paid for by Napoleon.

DOLLS:
1. JOSEPHINE BEAUHARNAIS. Peggy Nisbet, No. P461, circa 1970s. Plastic "collectors' doll." Napoleon Bonaparte, No. P460 is the companion doll. Made in England. About 7½in (19.1cm).
2. JOSEPHINE. Madame Alexander, No. 1335, 1980. Plastic and vinyl. Napoleon, No. 1330, is the companion doll. 12in (30.5cm). *Illustrations 108* and *109*.

Illustration 109. 12in (30.5cm) JOSEPHINE by Madame Alexander, No. 1335, 1980. Vinyl head; hard plastic body. Rooted dark brown hair; blue sleep eyes with molded lashes. White satin gown with cream overskirt. Head marked: "ALEXANDER // 19©76." Dress tag: "Josephine (in script) // by Madame Alexander // NEW YORK, U.S.A." *Shirley Buchholz Collection.*

BEERY, CAROL ANN. Child performer. Born circa 1921. Carol Ann Beery was adopted by actor Wallace Beery and she played in one of his films, *China Seas*, 1935.

DOLLS:

1. CAROL ANN BEERY. American Character Doll Co, 1935. All-composition and fully-jointed with painted hair or wigs, using the *Sally* doll. Sizes of 13in (33cm), 16½in (41.9cm) and 19½in (49.6cm). *Illustrations 110 and 111*.

Illustration 110. Advertisement for CAROL ANN BEERY, a "Hollywood 'Two-Some' Doll" by American Character from *Playthings*, October 1935.

Illustration 111. 13in (33cm) CAROL ANN BEERY by American Character, 1935. All-composition and fully-jointed. Blonde mohair wig over molded hair in the "Patsy style." Brown glass sleep eyes with lashes. Back marked: "PETITE." The costume may be original. *Marge Meisinger Collection.*

BELL, MARILYN. Swimming champion. Born 1938. Marilyn Bell won the 25 mile championship race for men and women in Atlantic City, New Jersey, when she was 16. That same year, 1954, she became the first person to swim across Lake Ontario.

DOLLS:

1. MARILYN BELL. D and C Company, 1954. Vinyl head with rooted blonde hair; rubber body. Blue sleep eyes; open mouth with teeth. Made in Canada. 15in (38.1cm).

BENEDICT, DIRK. Actor. Born Dirk Niewoehner March 1, 1946. Dirk Benedict began acting in films in juvenile roles. He played Lt. Starbuck on the ABC-TV show "Battlestar Galactica," which ran for a single season beginning in September 1978.

DOLLS:

1. BATTLESTAR GALACTICA. LT. STARBUCK. Mattel, No. 2871, 1978. Lorne Greene as Commander Adama, No. 2868, is part of the series of six figures. Made in Hong Kong. 4in (10.2cm). *Illustrations 113 and 114*.

Illustration 112. Dirk Benedict on a notebook cover. Copyright 1978 by Pro Arts, Inc., Medina, Ohio.

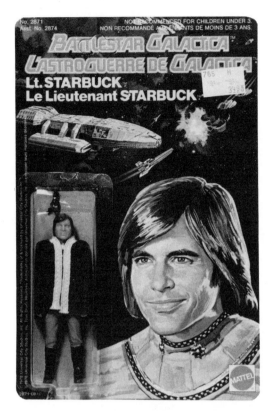

Illustration 113. 4in (10.2cm) DIRK BENEDICT as *Lt. Starbuck* from "Battlestar Galactica" by Mattel, No. 2871, 1978. (This is a package from Canada.) All-vinyl with painted hair and clothing with a cloth cape. (Note that the features are left blank.) Copyright by Universal City Studios, Inc. Made in Hong Kong. LORNE GREENE as *Commander Adama* is a companion doll.

Illustration 114. DIRK BENEDICT.

BERENGER, TOM. Actor. Tom Berenger received good notices in a wide range of roles. In *Butch and Sundance: The Early Days* he was Butch Cassidy in his youth, a part that Paul Newman played in *Butch Cassidy and the Sundance Kid* in 1969, ten years earlier, in which Butch was older.

DOLLS:
1. BUTCH CASSIDY. Kenner, No. 53010, 1979. Made in Hong Kong. 4in (10.2cm). *Illustration 115.*

Illustration 115. 4in (10.2cm) TOM BERENGER as *Butch Cassidy* from *Butch and Sundance: The Early Days* by Kenner, No. 53010, 1979. All-vinyl and fully-jointed with painted features and clothing. Copyright by Twentieth Century-Fox Film Corporation. Made in Hong Kong.

BERENSON, MARISA. Actress. Born February 15, 1948, in New York, New York. After a successful modeling career, the active jet-setter entered films. Her maternal grandmother was the noted dress designer Elsa Shiaparelli.

DOLLS:
1. CONTESSA DI BARRY LYNDON. Furga, 1979. Dressed in the role from the film *Barry Lyndon,* 1975. Soft vinyl with dark brown rooted hair; brown glass sleep eyes with lashes. Made in Italy. 18in (45.7cm).

BEST, JAMES. Actor. Born July 26, 1926. Best began his career as a model and a stage actor. He made his film debut in 1949 and played mostly supporting roles. He appeared on many television shows and was a regular in two series. He was on "The Andy Griffith

Show" on CBS-TV from October 1960 to September 1968 and he began playing Sheriff Rosco P. Coltrane on "The Dukes of Hazzard" on CBS-TV in January 1979.

DOLLS:
1. ROSCO. Mego, No. 09010/5, 1982. All-vinyl and fully-jointed. Painted hair and features. Copyright by Warner Bros., Inc. Made in Hong Kong. 3¾in (9.6cm).

SEE: DUKES OF HAZZARD, THE.

BILLY THE KID. Born William Bonney in 1859; died 1881. Billy was a legendary outlaw and cattle rustler in New Mexico. He was shot by a sheriff at the age of 22.

DOLLS:
1. BILLY THE KID. Durham Inc., Inc., 1975. Plastic with molded and painted clothing. Made in Hong Kong. 8in (20.3cm).

THE BLACK HOLE. A science fiction film released by Buena Vista (Walt Disney Productions) in December of 1979. This was the first Disney film with a PG (Parental Guidance) rating. Dolls were made of MAXIMILIAN SCHELL, ANTHONY PERKINS, ROBERT FORSTER, JOSEPH BOTTOMS, YVETTE MIMIEUX and ERNEST BORGNINE in two sizes. See listings under each celebrity.

Illustration 116. 3¾in (9.6cm) "Action figures" from *The Black Hole* by Mego. From left to right: JOSEPH BOTTOMS as *Charles Pizer*, YVETTE MIMIEUX as *Dr. Kate McRae*, ERNEST BORGNINE as *Harry Booth*, ANTHONY PERKINS as *Dr. Alex Durant*, ROBERT FORSTER as *Captain Dan Holland* and MAXIMILIAN SCHELL as *Dr. Hans Reinhardt.*

BLAKE, ROBERT. See GUBITOSI, MICKEY.

BLISS, BETTY TAYLOR. Daughter of President Zachary Taylor. President Taylor was elected in 1849 and died the following year. His daughter acted as "First Lady," because Mrs. Taylor preferred to remain in New Orleans.

DOLLS:
1. BETTY TAYLOR BLISS. Madame Alexander, No. 1512, 1976. Plastic and vinyl; part of the First Ladies Series of six dolls. 14in (35.6cm).

SEE: FIRST LADIES, THE.

BLOCKER, DAN. Actor. Born 1928; died 1972. Dan Blocker is most known for his role of Hoss on NBC-TV's "Bonanza" from September 1959 through the 1971-1972 season. Dan Blocker died unexpectedly before the 1972-1973 season began. "Bonanza" ended its series run on January 16, 1973.

DOLLS:
1. HOSS OF THE CARTWRIGHT FAMILY. Fully-jointed "action figure" by American Character, 1965. Plastic. Molded and painted features and clothing. 8in (20.3cm). Lorne Greene as Ben Cartwright and Michael Landon as Little Joe Cartwright are companion dolls. *Illustration 117.*

Illustration 117. 8in (20.3cm) "Action figures" of the characters from "Bonanza" by American Character, 1965. Plastic with molded and painted features and clothing. From left to right they are: MICHAEL LANDON as *Little Joe Cartwright*, DAN BLOCKER as *Hoss Cartwright* and LORNE GREENE as *Ben Cartwright. Sears 1967 Christmas Book.*

BOLEYN, ANNE. Queen Consort of Henry VIII. Born circa 1507; died 1536. Henry VIII divorced Queen Katharine of Aragon to marry Anne in 1533. Anne was the mother of Queen Elizabeth I. She fell out of favor with Henry and was accused of adultery, for which she was beheaded. Henry married four more wives.

DOLLS:
1. ANNE BOLEYN. Peggy Nisbet, No. P603, 1970s. Plastic "collectors' doll," part of a series of Henry VIII and his six wives, "Portrait Series." Costume from contemporary portraits in the National Portrait Gallery, London. Made in England. About 7½in (19.1cm).
2. ANNE BOLEYN. Peggy Nisbet, No. H217, 1970s. Plastic "collectors' doll," part of a series of Henry VIII and his six wives, "Standard Series." Accurate reproduction of clothing worn by Anne. Made in England. About 7½in (19.1cm).

3. ANNE BOLEYN.   Peggy Nisbet, No. M932, 1979.
   Inch-to-the-foot miniature plastic "collectors'
   doll," part of a series of Henry VIII and his six
   wives. Made in England.
4. ANNE BOLEYN.   Ann Parker, 1977. Plastic "collectors' doll" affixed to a wooden base. Made in
   England. 11in (27.9cm). *Illustration 118*.

Illustration 119. Ray Bolger and Judy Garland in *The Wizard of Oz*, 1939.

Illustration 118. 11in (27.9cm) ANNE BOLEYN by Ann Parker, late 1970s. All-hard plastic and affixed to a wooden base. Brown mohair wig; painted brown eyes. The costume is black and gold with fur trim at the sleeves. Made in England. *Shirley Buchholz Collection.*

BOLGER, RAY.   Actor, dancer. Born January 10, 1904, in Dorchester, Massachusetts. Bolger made his dancing debut in 1922 with a touring company. His best known film role was that of the Scarecrow companion to Dorothy in *The Wizard of Oz* in 1939.

DOLLS:
1. SCARECROW from THE WIZARD OF OZ.   Mego, No. 51500/4, 1974. Made in Hong Kong. 8in (20.3cm). *Illustrationm 120*.
2. SCARECROW from THE WIZARD OF OZ. Mego, No. 59039, 1974. Vinyl head; cloth body. Copyright 1974 by MGM, Inc. Made in Hong Kong. 15in (38.1cm).

SEE: WIZARD OF OZ, THE.

Illustration 120. 8in (20.3cm) RAY BOLGER as the *Scarecrow* from the 1939 film *The Wizard of Oz* by Mego, No. 51500/4, 1974. All-vinyl and fully-jointed. Rooted hair; painted features. Copyright by Metro-Goldwyn-Mayer, Inc. Made in Hong Kong. *Shirley Buchholz Collection.*

BONAPARTE, NAPOLEON. (NAPOLEON I.)

French emperor. Born 1769; died 1821. From his birth on the Island of Corsica to his death on the Island of Saint Helena, Napoleon always lived a very full life. The French Revolution of 1793 and his own determination made him a brigadier general, a First Consul of France, Consul for life in 1802, a self-proclaimed Emperor of France in 1802 and King of Italy in 1805. He annulled his marriage to the Empress Josephine in 1810 and married Archduchess Marie Louise of Austria, who bore him a son. Napoleon set out to conquer all of Europe and placed various members of his family on the thrones of several countries. In 1814 after his defeat at Leipzig he was exiled to the Island of Elba. He escaped in 1815 and was defeated again at the Battle of Waterloo. The British held him under arrest at Saint Helena, where he died of cancer. Napoleon's body was returned to Paris, France, in 1840 and is entombed under the dome of the Invalides. In spite of his failings, Napoleon will always be remembered as one of the greatest of France's citizens.

DOLLS:

1. NAPOLEON. From Monaco, 1950. All-felt with embroidered features. 10in (25.4cm). *Illustration 121.*

2. NAPOLEON BONAPARTE. Peggy Nisbet, No. P460, 1970s. Plastic "collectors' doll." Josephine Beauharnais, No. P461 is the companion doll. Made in England. About 7½in (19.1cm). *Illustration 122.*

3. NAPOLEON. Madame Alexander, No. 1330, 1980. Plastic and vinyl. 12in (30.5cm). Josephine, No. 1335, is the companion doll. *Illustration 123.*

Illustration 122. About 8in (20.3cm) NAPOLEON BONAPARTE, No. P460, and JOSEPHINE BEAUHARNAIS, No. P461, by Peggy Nisbet, 1970s. All-hard plastic; jointed only at the arms. Mohair wigs; painted features. Made in England. *Photograph Courtesy of House of Nisbet.*

Illustration 121. 10in (25.4cm) NAPOLEON BONAPARTE from Monaco, 1950. All-felt with felt clothing. Embroidered facial features and yarn hair. The paper tag tells that he is one of "Les Poupees d'Art de Monaco." *Shirley Buchholz Collection. Photograph by Jane Buchholz.*

Illustration 123. 12in (30.5cm) NAPOLEON by Madame Alexander, No. 1330, 1981. Vinyl head with rooted dark brown hair; brown sleep eyes with molded lashes. Hard plastic body.

BOND, WARD. Actor. Born April 9, 1903; died 1960. Bond was a football player for UCLA when John Ford cast him in the film *Salute* in 1929. He played supporting roles in some 200 films, most of them westerns and many of them with John Wayne. He was Major Seth Adams on television's "Wagon Train" from 1957 to 1961.

DOLLS:
1. MAJOR SETH ADAMS OF "WAGON TRAIN." Hartland Plastics, No. 824, 1958. Plastic figure with moveable arms; includes an "action horse." Made in Hartland, Wisconsin. About 8in (20.3cm).

BONO, SONNY. Singer and actor. Born Salvatore Philip Bono, February 16, 1935. Sonny and his wife, Cher, first appeared on television on "Shindig" in 1964 singing their own recordings. The couple starred on "The Sonny and Cher Comedy Hour" from August 1971 until May 1974 when they were divorced. They each had their own shows, which failed, so they reteamed professionally for another show from February 1976 until August 1977. In the meantime Cher had been married to Greg Allman for five days.

DOLLS:
1. SONNY. Mego, No. 62401, 1976. Companion doll to Cher, No. 62400. 12in (30.5cm). *Illustrations 124* and *125.*

Illustration 125. 12in (30.5cm) SONNY BONO by Mego, No. 62401, 1976. All-vinyl and fully-jointed. Painted hair and features. Marked on the neck: " ©MEGO CORP. 1976." *Wanda Lodwick Collection.*

BOOKE, SORRELL. Actor. Born on January 4, 1930. Booke has played many character parts on the stage and on the screen. Since January 26, 1979, he has played conniving Boss Hogg who controls a southern town on "The Dukes of Hazzard" on CBS-TV. In real life Sorrell Booke is a highly educated gentleman who speaks five languages without an accent, including Southern. For the TV show pudgy Booke performs all his own stunts and pratfalls.

DOLLS:
1. BOSS HOGG. Mego, No. 09050/4, 1981. Made in Hong Kong. 7¾in (19.8cm). *Illustration 126*.
2. BOSS HOGG. Kenner, No. 09010/4, 1982. All-vinyl and fully-jointed. Painted features and clothing; removable hat. Copyrighted by Warner Bros., Inc. Made in Hong Kong. 3¾in (9.6cm).
3. BOSS HOGG WITH CADDY. Mego, No. 09064, 1982. Same doll as No. 2 above. Comes packaged with a white plastic Cadillac convertible. Copyright by Warner Bros., Inc.

SEE: THE DUKES OF HAZZARD.

Illustration 124. SONNY and CHER by Mego. *Wanda Lodwick Collection.*

Illustration 126. 7¾in (19.8cm) SORRELL BOOKE as *Boss Hogg* from "The Dukes of Hazzard" by Mego, No. 09050/4, 1981. All-vinyl and fully-jointed. The vinyl head has painted brown hair and painted brown eyes. Note the big belly, like the *Wizard of Oz* doll (FRANK MORGAN). Head marked: " ©WARNER BROS. // INC. 1980." The hat is white vinyl. Made in Hong Kong.

BOONE, DANIEL. American frontiersman. Born 1734 near Reading, Pennsylvania; died 1820 in Missouri. Daniel Boone was one of the first settlers of the American "West," founding Boonesboro in present-day Kentucky in 1775. His bravery and his accomplishments have become legends from the many books, movies and television shows based on his life.

DOLLS:
1. DANIEL BOONE. Manufacturer unknown, late 1950s. Pressed plastic face mask; plush body. 20in (50.8cm).
2. DANIEL BOONE. Louis Marx & Co., 1964. All-rigid vinyl and fully-jointed with vinyl clothing. 12in (30.5cm).
3. DANIEL BOONE. S.S. Kresge Company, 1976. Vinyl and plastic. Part of a series. Made in Hong Kong. 7½in (19.1cm). *Illustration 127.* (Note: The last three lines of the biography on the box are in error. *The Last of the Mohicans* was a fiction written by James Fenimore Cooper.)

NOTE: Other marked and unmarked dolls represent Daniel Boone. None are top-quality collectibles.
SEE: FESS PARKER.

Illustration 128. Debby Boone.

Illustration 127. 7½in (19.1cm) DANIEL BOONE manufactured for the S.S. Kresge Company, 1976. Vinyl head with painted hair and features. Fully-jointed plastic body with swivel waist. Marked on back: "MADE IN // HONG KONG." *Shirley Buchholz Collection.*

BOONE, DEBBY. Singer. Born Deborah Ann Boone September 22, 1956. Debby is the daughter of singer and actor Pat Boone and Shirley Foley, the daughter of country and western singer Red Foley. Debby's most popular recording was "You Light Up My Life." Debby married Gabriel Ferrer, the son of actor Jose Ferrer and singer Rosemary Clooney.

DOLLS:
1. DEBBY BOONE. Mattel, No. 2843, 1978. Made in Taiwan. 11½in (29.2cm). *Illustrations 129* and *130.*

Illustration 129. 11½in (29.2cm) DEBBY BOONE by Mattel, No. 2843, 1978. All-vinyl and fully-jointed with a twist waist. (The body is a *Barbie* mold.) Rooted blonde hair and painted greenish-blue eyes. Head marked: "©RESI, INC. 1978 // TAIWAN." Lower back marked: "©MATTEL, INC. 1966 // TAIWAN." *Penny Caswell Collection.*

Illustration 130. DEBBY BOONE by Mattel. *Penny Caswell Collection.*

BOONE, RICHARD. Actor. Born June 18, 1916, in Los Angeles, California; died in 1981. Richard Boone entered films in 1951 and usually played "heavies." He was also successful on television in such series as "Medic," "Have Gun, Will Travel," and "The Richard Boone Show."

DOLLS:
1. PALADIN of "HAVE GUN, WILL TRAVEL." Hartland Plastics, Inc., No. 766, 1958. Plastic and jointed at the arms. Made in Hartland, Wisconsin. About 8in (20.3cm).

BORGNINE, ERNEST. Actor. Born Ermes Effron Borgnine on January 24, 1917, in Hamden, Connecticut. Borgnine made his film debut in 1951 and won an Academy Award for his portrayal of the lonely butcher *Marty* in 1955. He played the lead in ABC-TV's "McHale's Navy" from 1962 to 1966.

DOLLS:
1. HARRY BOOTH from THE BLACK HOLE. Mego, No. 95010/6, 1979. Made in Hong Kong. 3¾in (9.6cm). *Illustration 131*.
2. HARRY BOOTH from THE BLACK HOLE. Mego, 1979. Vinyl and plastic. Copyright by Walt Disney Productions. 12½in (31.8cm).
SEE: THE BLACK HOLE.

Illustration 131. 3¾in (9.6cm) ERNEST BORGNINE as *Harry Booth* from *The Black Hole* by Mego, No. 95010/6, 1979. All-vinyl and fully-jointed with painted features and clothing. Copyright by Walt Disney Productions. Made in Hong Kong.

BOTTOMS, JOSEPH. Actor. Born April 22, 1954. Joseph Bottoms' two brothers, Sam and Timothy were also juvenile actors.

DOLLS:
1. CHARLES PIZER from THE BLACK HOLE. Mego, No. 95010/3, 1979. Made in Hong Kong. 3¾in (9.6cm). *Illustration 132*.
2. CHARLES PIZER from THE BLACK HOLE. Mego, No. 95005/6, 1979. Made in Hong Kong. 12½in (31.8cm). *Illustration 133 and 134*.
SEE: THE BLACK HOLE.

Illustration 132. 3¾in (9.6cm) JOSEPH BOTTOMS as *Charles Pizer*, 1st Officer from *The Black Hole*, by Mego, No. 95010/3, 1979. All-vinyl and fully-jointed with painted features and clothing. Copyright by Walt Disney Productions. Made in Hong Kong.

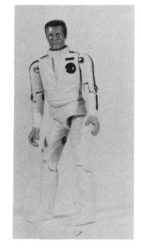

Illustration 133. 12½in (31.8cm) JOSEPH BOTTOMS as *Charles Pizer* from *The Black Hole* by Mego, No. 95005/6, 1979. Vinyl head with painted brown hair and eyes. Fully-jointed vinyl body. Head marked: "©WALT DISNEY // PRODUCTIONS 1979." Back marked: " © MEGO CORP. 1977 // MADE IN HONG KONG." In the film, Pizer is the "Palomino's young brash, 1st officer and right hand to Captain Holland."

Illustration 134. 12½in (31.8cm) JOSEPH BOTTOMS by Mego.

Illustration 135. William Boyd in a 1930s western *North of the Rio Grande.*

Illustration 136. 5¼in (13.4cm) FANNY BRICE as *Baby Snooks,* date and maker unknown. All-cloth with wire inside arms and legs. Facial features painted. Fanny Brice in the sailor suit has pink skin tones; Fanny in the dress has white skin tones. The clothing is sewn in place. *Rosemarye Bunting Collection.*

BOWIE, JIM. Frontiersman. Born 1799; died 1836. Legend says that the bowie knife was named after Jim Bowie. He was a hero of the Texas Revolution who died at the Alamo during the War with Mexico.

DOLLS:
1. JIM BOWIE. Hartland Plastics, No. 817, 1958. Plastic with jointed arms; includes a plastic horse, "Blaze." Made in Hartland, Wisconsin. About 8in (20.3cm).

BOYD, WILLIAM (BILL). Actor; producer. Born June 5, 1898, in Cambridge, Ohio; died 1972. Boyd's first role was in Cecile B. DeMille's *Why Change Your Wife?* in 1920. In 1935 Boyd was chosen to play the lead in *Hop-a-long Cassidy* (later called Hopalong). Boyd starred in 54 Hopalong Cassidy films until 1943 when he series was dropped. He then produced 12 more episodes. Boyd later acquired the rights to the character of Hopalong Cassidy and made a fortune showing the 66 films on television and marketing Hopalong Cassidy merchandise. He filmed a new series of Hopalong Cassidy adventures that ran from June 1949 to December 1951 on NBC-TV. During the television phase of his career, Boyd thought that he *was* Hopalong Cassidy and wanted to be treated accordingly as a great western hero.

DOLLS:
1. HOPALONG CASSIDY. Ideal, 1949. Vinyl head with painted adult features resembling William Boyd. Stuffed cloth body. Unmarked. Came in sizes of 18in (45.7cm) and 21in (53.3cm).
2. HOPALONG CASSIDY. Ideal, 1949. Same as above with styled features. 25in (63.5cm).
NOTE: Various other dolls were made and dressed in "Hopalong Cassidy" clothing. They do not represent William Boyd.

BRICE, FANNY. Comedienne and singer. Born Fanny Borach, October 29, 1891, in New York, New York, died 1951. Fanny Brice got her first big break in the 1910 Ziegfeld Follies. She appeared in some films after 1928. Fanny Brice is best known as radio's "Baby Snooks," which she played from 1938 to 1951. Barbra Streisand played Fanny Brice in *Funny Girl* (1968) and *Funny Lady* (1975).

DOLLS:
1. FANNY BRICE AS BABY SNOOKS. Date and maker unknown. All-cloth. 5¼in (13.4cm). *Illustrations 136, 137* and *138.*
2. FANNY BRICE AS BABY SNOOKS. Ideal, 1939. 12in (30.5cm). *Illustrations 139* and *140.*

Illustration 137. 5¼in (13.4cm) FANNY BRICE. *Rosemarye Bunting Collection.*

Illustration 138. 5¼in (13.4cm) FANNY BRICE. *Rosemarye Bunting Collection.*

Illustration 140. Ideal's FANNY BRICE as *Baby Snooks,* a "Flexy Doll," to show the body construction. On the left is Edgar Bergen's *Mortimer Sneerd,* also from about 1939 with the same type of flexible wire tubing for the arms and legs. *Patricia N. Schoonmaker Collection. Photograph by John Schoonmaker.*

BRONTË, CHARLOTTE. English novelist and poet. Born 1816; died 1855. Charlotte and her sisters, Emily and Jane, lived in a remote parsonage in Yorkshire, England, causing them to adopt an imaginative world and to write imaginative literature. Charlotte's great masterpiece is *Jane Eyre,* published in 1847.

DOLLS:
1. CHARLOTTE BRONTË. Peggy Nisbet, No. P820, 1970s. Made in England. About 7½in (19.1cm). *Illustration 141.*
2. CHARLOTTE BRONTË. Ann Parker, 1979. Plastic "collectors' doll," affixed to a wooden stand. Made in England. 11in (27.9cm).

Illustration 139. 12in (30.5cm) FANNY BRICE as *Baby Snooks* by Ideal, 1939. Composition head and hands; wooden torso and feet; "flexy" wire arms and legs. Designed by Joseph Kallus. Painted light brown hair; painted blue eyes; open-closed mouth with painted lower teeth. The original costumes came in various shades and patterns. This one is dark blue and red. Head marked: "IDEAL DOLL."

Illustration 141. About 7½in (19.1cm) CHARLOTTE BRONTË by Peggy Nisbet, No. P820, 1970s. All-hard plastic; jointed only at the arms. Mohair wig; painted features. Made in England. *Photograph Courtesy of House of Nisbet.*

BROOKE, LADY DAISEY. (COUNTESS OF WARWICK.) Mistress of King Edward VII. Born December 10, 1861; died July 26, 1938. The Countess of Warwick was King Edward's mistress until she became active in socialist causes in the 1890s.

DOLLS:
1. COUNTESS OF WARWICK (LADY BROOKE). Peggy Nisbet, No. P786, 1970s. Plastic "collectors' doll," part of the series of the mistresses of King Edward VII. The other dolls are Hon. Alice Keppel, No. P787, and Lillie Langtry, No. P788. Made in England. About 7½in (19.1cm).

BROWN, GEORG STANFORD. Actor. Born June 24, 1943. Georg Stanford Brown is best known for playing Officer Terry Webster on "The Rookies" on ABC-TV from September 1972 to July 1976. He has turned to directing television shows.

DOLLS:
1. TERRY WEBSTER OF THE ROOKIES. L.J.N. Toys, Ltd., No. 6101, 1976. All-vinyl and fully-jointed. Copyright by Spelling-Goldberg Productions. Part of a series. Made in Hong Kong. 7½in (19.1cm).
SEE: THE ROOKIES.

BROWN, PETER. Actor. Born October 5, ?. Peter Brown played juvenile parts in films and later on television. His most enduring television roles were as Deputy Johnny McKay on "The Lawman" from October 1958 to October 1962 and as Chad Cooper on "Laredo" from September 1965 to September 1967.

DOLLS:
1. JOHNNY MCKAY FROM "LAWMAN." Hartland Plastics, No. 768, 1958. Made in Hartland, Wisconsin. 7⅝in (19.4cm). *Illustration 142*.

BUCK ROGERS IN THE 25TH CENTURY. Television show on NBC-TV from September 1979 to September 1980. Twenty-two episodes. The program was based on the 1929 science fiction comic strip and followed Buck's adventures when he returned to New Chicago on Earth in the year 2491 after having been frozen in space for 504 years. The dolls are based on this television series. They came in two sizes. The characters are GIL GERARD as *Buck*, ERIN GRAY (small size only) as *Wilma Deering*, FELIX SILLA as *Twiki*, TIM O'CONNOR as *Dr. Huer*, JOSEPH WISEMAN as *Draco*, HENRY SILVA as *Killer Kane*, DUKE BUTLER as *Tiger Man*, and PAMELA HENSLEY as *Ardella* (small size only). A *Draconian Guard* also comes with the small set. A revised version of the show, called "Buck Rogers," was on from January to September of 1981. The only characters retained for the new series were Buck, Wilma and the robot Twiki.

Illustration 143. Painting that was used with all Buck Rogers toys, dolls, puzzles, games and other tie-ins. At the left is FELIX SILLA as *Twiki*, behind ERIN GRAY as *Wilma Deering*. GIL GERARD as *Buck* is in the foreground.

Illustration 142. 7⅝in (19.4cm) PETER BROWN as *Johnny McKay* in "Lawman" by Hartland Plastics, Inc., No. 768, 1958. All-plastic with jointed arms only. The hat and the gun are separate. Marked on the right arm: "©HARTLAND // PLASTICS, INC." Copyright by Warner Brothers Pictures, Inc. Made in Hartland, Wisconsin.

Illustration 144. Small BUCK ROGERS figures by Mego with *Draconian Marauder* in the background. The dolls, from left to right: FELIX SILLA as *Twiki*, GIL GERARD as *Buck Rogers*, TIM O'CONNOR as *Dr. Huer*, JOSEPH WISEMAN as *Draco* (behind Heur), HENRY SILVA as *Killer Kane, Draconian Guard*, ERIN GRAY as *Wilma Deering* and DUKE BUTLER as *Tiger Man. Bobby Lodwick Collection*.

Illustration 145. 3¾in (9.6cm) *Draconian Guard* from ''Buck Rogers in the 25th Century'' by Mego, No. 85000/6, 1979. All-vinyl and fully-jointed. Painted features and molded helmet; painted clothing. Coypright by Robert C. Dille. Made in Hong Kong. This doll is part of the small set of *Buck Rogers* dolls, but it does not represent a celebrity, as do the others.

BULLOCH, JEREMY. Actor. Jeremy Bulloch played the robot Boba Fett in the sequel to *Star Wars, The Empire Strikes Back,* in 1980.

DOLLS:
1. BOBA FETT. Kenner, No. 39140, 1979. Fully-jointed figure of plastic. 13¼in (33.7cm).
2. BOBA FETT. Kenner, Series No. 38899, 1980. Fully-jointed figure of plastic. 3¾in (9.6cm).

SEE: STAR WARS.

BUNNY, JOHN. Actor. Born September 21, 1863, in New York, New York; died 1915. After years in the theater John Bunny joined the Vitagraph Company in 1910 to make movies. Weighing at least 300 pounds, Bunny became a leading comic of the silent screen. He made more than 200 short comedies and a number of dramatic appearances during his five years in films. Most of John Bunny's comedy material pertained to his immense size or his extramarital escapades which constantly annoyed equally homely Flora Finch, who played his fierce wife.

DOLLS:
1. JOHN BUNNY. Louis Amberg & Son, 1914. 13½in (34.3cm). *Illustration 147.*

Illustration 146. John Bunny, circa 1914.

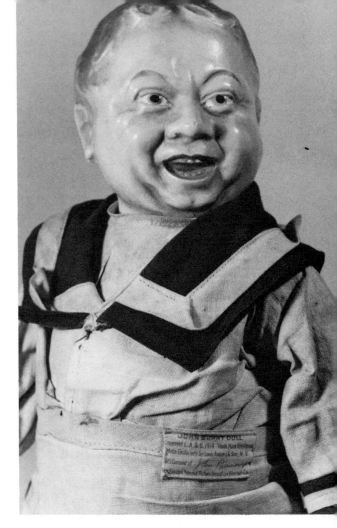

Illustration 147. 13½in (34.3cm) JOHN BUNNY by Louis Amberg and Son, 1914. Composition head with painted reddish hair and blue eyes; open-closed mouth with painted teeth. The head is marked, but most of the markings are below the wire that holds it on the all-cloth body. Visible is: "©14." The cloth label on the sailor suit reads:
JOHN BUNNY DOLL
COPYRIGHT L.A. & S. 1914 TRADEMARK REGISTERED
MADE EXCLUSIVELY BY LOUIS AMBERG & SON, N.Y.
WITH CONSENT OF JOHN BUNNY (Name in script)
THE FAMOUS MOTION PICTURE HERO OF THE VITAGRAPH CO.
The sailor suit is less common than the soldier suit. *Irene Trittschuh Collection.*

BURKE, BILLIE. Actress. Born Mary William Ethelbert Appleton Burke in Washington D.C., August 7, 1885; died 1970. Billie Burke made her stage debut in London, England, in 1903 and became the "toast of New York" after her Broadway debut in 1907. She was married to producer Florenz Ziegfeld from 1914 until his death in 1932. She entered films in 1916 in leading lady roles. After 1931, attempting to help her financially ruined husband, she adopted a new screen image—that of a feather-brained comedienne.

DOLLS:
1. GLINDA, THE GOOD WITCH FROM THE WIZARD OF OZ. Mego, No. 51500/5, 1974. Made in Hong Kong. 7½in (19.1cm). *Illustration 148.*

Illustration 148. 7½in (19.1cm) BILLIE BURKE as *Glinda, the Good Witch* from the 1939 film *The Wizard of Oz* by Mego, No. 51500/5, 1974. All-vinyl and fully-jointed. Rooted red hair; painted blue eyes. Head marked: "©MGM // INC." Made in Hong Kong. *Shirley Buchholz Collection.*

BURNETT, CAROL Actress, comedienne, singer. Born April 26, 1933, in San Antonio, Texas. Carol Burnett is one of America's most versatile and beloved actresses. She appeared in revues in New York, New York, before gaining national prominence on Garry Moore's variety shows on television. Her greatest popularity came with her own television show. She appeared in plays on Broadway, in television specials and in some movies. Her prime-time television series shows were "Stanley" on NBC from September 1956 to March 1957; "Pantomine Quiz" on ABC during 1958 and 1959; "The Garry Moore Show" on CBS from 1959 to 1962 (Emmy Award in 1962); "The Entertainers" on CBS from September 1964 to March 1965; and "The Carol Burnett Show" on CBS from September 1967 to August 1978 (Emmys in 1972, 1974, 1975). She also won an Emmy for "Julie and Carol at Carnegie Hall" in 1963. In 1969 she won a special Tony Award for her contribution to the theater. In the film *Annie* she played Daddy Warbuck's secretary, Miss Hannigan.

DOLLS:
1. MISS HANNIGAN. Knickerbocker Toy Co., Inc., No. 3867, 1982. All-vinyl and fully-jointed. Rooted brown hair; painted features. Copyright by Columbia Pictures Industries, Inc. 7in (17.8cm).
SEE: ANNIE.

BURNEY, FANNY (FRANCES). English novelist. Born 1752; died 1840. Fanny Burney's novels dealt with society and home life. She is also famous for her amusing diary, which she kept until she died at age 88.
DOLLS:
1. FANNY BURNEY. Ann Parker, 1979. Plastic "collectors' doll," affixed to a wooden base. Made in England. 11in (27.9cm).

BURNS, ROBBIE (ROBERT). Scottish poet. Born 1759; died 1796. Burns was a great humorist and he depicted the simple rural life that he knew in verse, combining Scottish and English romanticism. His lyrics, such as "Auld Lang Syne" and "Comin thro' the Rye" are the most popular in the English language. Burns was never financially successful during his 37 years so he accepted the patronage of several women.
DOLLS:
1. ROBBIE BURNS. Peggy Nisbet, No. P618, 1970s. Plastic "collectors' doll." Made in England. 8in (20.3cm).

BUTLER, DUKE. Actor. Duke Butler played Tiger Man in many of the early episodes of "Buck Rogers in the 25th Century" on NBC-TV beginning in September 1979.
DOLLS:
1. TIGER MAN. Mego, No. 85000/3, 1979. Made in Hong Kong. 3¾in (9.6cm). *Illustration 149.*
2. TIGER MAN. Mego, No. 85001/2, 1979. Vinyl and plastic. Copyright by Robert C. Dille. Made in Hong Kong. 12½in (31.8cm).
SEE: BUCK ROGERS IN THE 25TH CENTURY.

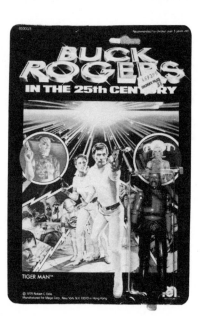

Illustration 149. 3¾in (9.6cm) DUKE BUTLER as *Tiger Man* from "Buck Rogers in the 25th Century" by Mego, No. 85000/3, 1979. All-vinyl and fully-jointed. Painted features and clothing. Copyright by Robert C. Dille. Made in Hong Kong.

CALAMITY JANE (MARTHA JANE CANARY). American frontier character. Born circa 1852; died 1903. Calamity Jane lived in Deadwood, South Dakota, and later went into show business.
DOLLS:
1. CALAMITY JANE. Azark-Hamway, 1973. Vinyl with rooted hair. Made in Hong Kong. 11½in (29.2cm).
2. CALAMITY JANE. Excel Toy Corp., 1974. Vinyl with molded hair. Made in Hong Kong. 9¼in (23.6cm).

CALHOUN, RORY. Actor. Born Francis Timothy Durgin on August 8, 1922, in Los Angeles, California, Rory Calhoun drifted into films in the mid 1940s and played mostly in Westerns and action pictures. From September 1958 to September 1960 he played Bill Longley on "The Texan" for CBS-TV.

DOLLS:
1. THE TEXAN. Hand puppet produced by Tops in Toys in 1960. (See: Anderton, *More Twentieth Century Dolls,* page 1034.)

CAMERON, JOANNA. Actress. Born September 20, ?. JoAnna Cameron began her role in the CBS-TV show "Isis" in 1975, playing the part of Andrea Thomas, a schoolteacher, and Isis, the Egyptian Goddess of Fertility. This was a children's show so Isis was a "dedicated foe of evil, defender of the weak and a champion of truth and justice."

DOLLS:
1. ISIS. Mego, No. 51345, 1976. Made in Hong Kong. 8in (20.3cm). *Illustration 150.*

Illustration 150. About 8in (20.3cm) JOANNA CAMERON as *Isis* by Mego, No. 51345, 1976. All-vinyl and fully-jointed. Rooted black hair; painted blue eyes. Copyright by Filmation Assoc. Made in Hong Kong.

CANTINFLAS. Actor. Born Mario Moreno Reyes on August 12, 1911, in Mexico City, Mexico. Cantinflas began in show business as a dancer and singer, later became a circus clown and acrobat and then became famous as a comic bullfighter. He entered Mexican films in 1936 and became one of the most popular comedians in the Spanish-speaking world. He became internationally famous after appearing in *Around the World in 80 Days* in 1956. Because of his sudden fame he was starred in *Pepe* in 1960 with Dan Dailey and Shirley Jones and 35 guest stars. The film was a failure and is considered a "bomb." He returned to Mexico.

DOLLS:
1. PEPE. Papier-mâché nodder from an unknown manufacturer, circa 1960. Painted features. 5in (12.7cm).
2. CANTINFLAS. Made in Mexico, circa 1960. Plastic with wire inside the limbs for bending in different positions. 7½in (19.1cm).

CANTOR, EDDIE. Comic actor, singer. Born Edward Israel Iskowitz in New York, New York, on January 31, 1892; died 1964. Eddie Cantor became popular in burlesque and vaudeville and was on Broadway by World War I. During the 1930s he was acclaimed for his radio show. An unsuccessful film, *The Eddie Cantor Story,* starring Keefe Brasselle, was made of his life in which Brasselle imitated Cantor's "banjo eyes."

DOLLS:
1. EDDIE CANTOR. A. Ponnock, 1938. All-rubber. About 8in (20.3cm). *Illustration 152.*
2. EDDIE CANTOR. A. Ponnock, 1938. Composition head, hands and feet with molded shoes; cloth body. 20in (50.8cm). Not marked.

Illustration 151. Eddie Cantor in *Strike Me Pink,* 1935.

Illustration 152. 8in (20.3cm) EDDIE CANTOR by A. Ponnock, 1938. From an ad in *Playthings,* October 1938. All-rubber, probably jointed at the head, and painted in "No injurious colors." Eddie Cantor planned to turn all royalties from the doll over to "selected boys' camps." In the same issue of *Playthings,* an article states that "Mr. Ponnock has offered to match personally every dollar of royalty paid to Mr. Cantor for the same purpose—making a double contribution to the worthy work of sending underprivileged youngsters to the country each summer."

CARNEY, AUGUSTUS. Actor. Deceased. Augustus Carney was one of the most popular American comics in films in the period between 1909 and 1913. His popularity was at its peak from 1911 to 1912, during which time he played a rural character called Alkali Ike in a series of slapstick comedies for the Essanay Film Company, which was located in Chicago, Illinois. Carney quit the movies in 1915 and was soon forgotten.

DOLLS:
1. ALKALI IKE. Particulars not known. *Illustration 153.*

Illustration 153. AUGUSTUS CARNEY as *Alkali Ike* from an advertisement in *Playthings,* November 1913. In 1914 these dolls were supposed to have been sold in great quantities. All that is presently known about the doll is what appears in this ad.

CARON, LESLIE. Actress, dancer. Born July 1, 1931, near Paris, France. Miss Caron began studying ballet at the age of 10 and at 16 was dancing in the Ballet des Champs Elysées. Gene Kelly saw her there and signed her for the film *An American in Paris* (1951). Leslie Caron had a brillant career in musicals and dramatic films and won the British Film Academy Award for *Lili* in 1953 and *The L-Shaped Room* in 1962, but by the late 1970s she was playing character parts.

DOLLS:
1. LESLIE CARON AS "GIGI." Old Cottage Dolls, late 1950s. Plastic. Made in England. 10in (25.4cm).

CARR, CHARMAINE. Actress. Charmaine Carr played Liesl in *The Sound of Music* in 1965.
DOLLS:
1. LIESL. Madame Alexander, No. 1005, 1965. All-hard plastic with blonde wig. 8in (20.3cm).

2. LIESL. Madame Alexander, No. 1405, 1965-1970. Vinyl head with rooted blonde hair; plastic body. 14in (35.6cm) *Illustration 154.*
3. LIESL. Madame Alexander, 1966. Same doll as No. 2, dressed in a sailor school outfit.
4. LIESL. Madame Alexander, No. 1105, 1971-1973. All-hard plastic with blonde wig. 9in (22.9cm). *Illustrationm 155.*
SEE: THE SOUND OF MUSIC.

Illustration 154. 14in (35.6cm) CHARMAINE CARR as *Liesl* from *The Sound of Music* by Madame Alexander, No. 1405, 1965-1970. Vinyl with rooted blonde hair; blue sleep eyes. Head marked: "ALEXANDER // 19 © 65." *Jean Canaday Collection.*

Illustration 155. 9in (22.9cm) CHARMAINE CARR as *Liesl* from *The Sound of Music* by Madame Alexander, No. 1105, 1971. All-hard plastic and fully-jointed, including bending knees. Blonde wig; blue sleep eyes with molded lashes and blue eye shadow. Back marked: "MME // ALEXANDER."

CARRILLO, LEO. Actor. Born in Los Angeles, California, August 6, 1880; died 1961. Carrillo was a comedian who specialized in dialects in vaudeville, on the legitimate stage and then in movies by the late 1920s. In the early 1950s he played Pancho, the sidekick of Duncan Renaldo, who was "The Cisco Kid," on a half-hour television show.

DOLLS:
1. PANCHO.   Cloth with a painted mask face, maker unknown, 1950s. 16in (40.6cm)

CARROLL, DIAHANN.   Actress, singer. Born in New York, New York, July 17, 1935. At the age of ten Diahann Carroll received a scholarship from the Metropolitan Opera to study music. She later performed in nightclubs, on TV and in films. She was the first black performer who was the star of a regular television series, NBC-TV's "Julia," from 1968 to 1971.

DOLLS:
1. JULIA.   Mattel, No. 1127, 1969. Made in Japan. 12in (30.5cm). *Illustrations 156* and *157.*
2. TALKING JULIA.   Mattel, No 1128, 1969. Same as the non-talking doll with a pull-string mechanism to make her "talk." 12in (30.5cm).

Illustration 157. DIAHANN CARROLL by Mattel. *Shirley Buchholz Collection.*

CARROTT, RIC.   Young actor who played on many television series. He was Chris Gentry on "Space Academy" from September 1977 to September 1978.

DOLLS:
1. CHRIS GENTRY.   Aviva Toy Company, No. 100, 1978. Made in Hong Kong. 8½in (21.6cm). *Illustration 158.*
SEE: SPACE ACADEMY.

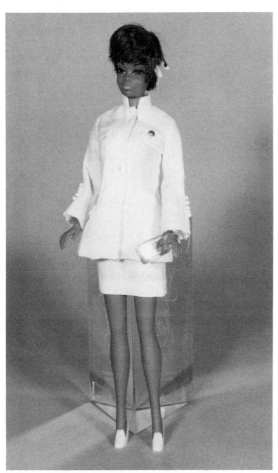

Illustration 156. 12in (30.5cm) DIAHANN CARROLL as *Julia* by Mattel, No. 1127, 1969. All-vinyl and fully-jointed. Rooted black hair and painted brown eyes with long lashes. Hip marked: "© 1966 // MATTEL INC. // U.S. PATENTED // U.S. PAT. PEND. // MADE IN // JAPAN." Arm tag: "Copyright © by // Savannah Productions, Inc. // Made in Japan // ©1968 Mattel Inc." *Shirley Buchholz Collection.*

Illustration 158. 8½in (21.6cm) RIC CARROTT as *Chris Gentry* from "Space Academy" by Aviva Toy Company for F.W. Woolworth Co., No. 100, 1978. All-vinyl and fully-jointed. Painted blonde hair and painted blue eyes. Lower back marked: "©1978 // FILMATION ASSOCIATES // ALL RIGHTS RESERVED // MADE IN HONG KONG // PAT. PEND." *Penny Caswell Collection.*

CARSON, KIT. American frontiersman. Born 1809; died 1868. Kit Carson was a noted Indian fighter and guide for expeditions into the West in the 1840s.
DOLLS:
1. KIT CARSON. Azark-Hamway, 1973. All-vinyl and fully-jointed. Painted hair and features. Made in Hong Kong. 12in (30.5cm).

CARTER, AMY. Daughter of President Jimmy Carter. Born October 19, 1967.
DOLLS:
1. AMY CARTER. Lim Co., Style No. S-1 and S-2, 1978. Made in Korea. 20½in (52.1cm). *Illustrations 159* and *160*.

Illustration 159. AMY CARTER by Lim Co.

Illustration 160. 20½in (52.1cm) AMY CARTER, "an original Tom McPartland's...Love Doll" from the Lim Co., Style No. S-1, 1978. All-cloth; painted blue eyes; yellow acrylic yarn hair; dress sewn to doll. The flowered dress is blue on this doll. Style No. S-2 is red. Made in Korea. The doll's white felt glasses are missing.

CARTER, JIMMY. The 39th President of the United States (1977-1981). Born October 1, 1924 in Plains, Georgia. Carter's Presidency will be remembered as the one during which 52 Americans were held hostage in Iran. In 1980 he became one of the few incumbent American Presidents not to be re-elected when he lost to Ronald Reagan.
DOLLS:
1. JIMMY CARTER. Kasia, 1977. Lithographed cloth; body stuffed with beans. 15in (38.1cm).
2. JIMMIE. Hollywood Creations, 1980. All-plastic. Painted hair and features. An "adult novelty doll." Made in Hong Kong.

CARTER, LYNDA. Actress and singer. Born July 24, 1951. Lynda Carter was a Miss USA and a Miss World and later played "Wonder Woman" on television, beginning in December of 1976. She has also appeared on TV Specials as a singer and dancer.
DOLLS:
1. LYNDA CARTER AS WONDER WOMAN. Mego, No. 73500/1, 1976. Made in Hong Kong. 12½in (31.2cm). *Illustration 162* and *163*.
NOTE: There are three other dolls from this series, but they do not seem to represent the characters from the TV show, although Lynda Carter's picture is on each package. They are Nubia, Mego, No. 73500/4; Queen Hippolyte, Mego, No. 73500/5; and Steve Trevor. All are 12in (31.2cm) and are all-vinyl and fully-jointed. All are made in Hong Kong and are copyrighted by D. C. Comics.

Illustration 161. Lynda Carter as Yoeman Diana Prince, "Wonder Woman."

Illustration 162. 12½in (31.2cm) LYNDA CARTER as *Wonderwoman* by Mego, No. 73500/1, 1976. All-vinyl and fully-jointed. Rooted long black hair; painted blue eyes with long lashes. Head marked: " © D.C. COMICS // INC. 1976." Made in Hong Kong. *Shirley Buchholz Collection*.

Illustration 163. LYNDA CARTER by Mego. *Shirley Buchholz Collection.*

CARTWRIGHT, ANGELA. Child actress. Born September 9, 1952. On television Angela Cartwright played Linda Williams in the situation comedies "The Danny Thomas Show" (Fall 1957 to 1965) and "Danny Thomas in Make Room for Granddaddy" (September 1970 to September 1971). Between these two she was in the science fiction adventure "Lost in Space" (September 1965 to September 1968). She also appeared in a few motion pictures, most notably *The Sound of Music,* 1965.

DOLLS:
1. LINDA WILLIAMS. Plastic Molded Arts Corp. for General Foods Corp. 1959. 14½in (36.9cm). *Illustration 164.*
2. LINDA WILLIAMS. Natural Doll Company, Inc., 1963. Plastic and vinyl with rooted dark brown hair. Came in sizes of at least 14in (35.6cm) and 30in (76.2cm). The larger doll "walked and talked." (Burdick: *Child Star Dolls and Toys,* 1977.)
3. BRIGITTA. Madame Alexander, No. 1003, 1965. All-hard plastic with a dark brown wig. 8in (20.3cm).
4. BRIGITTA. Madame Alexander, No. 1403, 1965-1970. Plastic and vinyl with rooted dark brown hair. 14in (35.6cm). *Illustration 167.*
5. BRIGITTA. Madame Alexander, 1966. All-hard plastic with a dark brown wig. Dressed in Tyrolean outfit. 12in (30.5cm)
6. BRIGITTA. Madame Alexander, 1966. All-hard plastic with a dark brown wig. This is the same as the above doll except that she is dressed in the sailor school dress. 12in (30.5cm). *Illustrations 165 and 166.*
7. BRIGITTA. Madame Alexander, No. 1103, 1971-1973. All-hard plastic with a dark brown wig. 9in (22.9cm). *Illustration 168.*

SEE: SOUND OF MUSIC, THE.

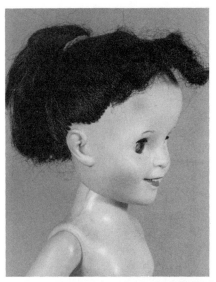

Illustration 164. 14½in (36.9cm) ANGELA CARTWRIGHT as *Linda Williams* by Plastic Molded Arts Corp. for General Foods Corp., 1959. This doll was a premium and cost $2.00 plus two Post Toasties box tops. All-vinyl and fully-jointed. Rooted brown hair; blue sleep eyes with lashes; painted teeth in a smiling mouth. The body, arms and legs are similar to the Ideal *Shirley Temple* doll of the late 1950s; they are identical to that of the *Ginny Tiu* doll. Head marked: "LINDA WILLIAMS." *Wanda Lodwick Collection.*

Illustration 165. 12in (30.5cm) ANGELA CARTWRIGHT as *Brigitta* from *The Sound of Music* by Madame Alexander, 1966. All-hard plastic and fully-jointed. Dark brown wig; blue sleep eyes with lashes. This doll is from the Sound of Music set that was all dressed in similar outfits and is the only one that is hard plastic from the group. *Ted Menten Collection. Photograph by Ted Menten.*

Illustration 166. Brigitta in sailor outfit. This is considered the "Lissy face" by Madame Alexander collectors. *Ted Menten Collection. Photograph by Ted Menten.*

Illustration 168. 9in (22.9cm) ANGELA CARTWRIGHT as *Brigitta* from *The Sound of Music* by Madame Alexander, No. 1103, 1971. All-hard plastic and fully-jointed, including bending knees. Dark brown wig; blue sleep eyes with molded lashes and blue eye shadow. Back marked: "MME // ALEXANDER."

CARVER, GEORGE WASHINGTON. Agricultural chemist. Born circa 1864 near Carthage, Missouri; died 1943. George Washington Carver worked most of his life to improve the economy of the South, teaching soil improvement and crop diversity. He discovered many uses for peanuts, soybeans and sweet potatoes.

DOLLS:
1. GEORGE WASHINGTON CARVER. Hallmark, No. 400DT113-7, 1979. Made in Taiwan. 7in (17.8cm). *Illustration 169.*

Illustration 167. 14in (35.6cm) ANGELA CARTWRIGHT as *Brigitta* from *The Sound of Music* by Madame Alexander, No. 1403, 1965-1970. Vinyl with rooted dark brown hair; brown sleep eyes with lashes. Head marked: "ALEXANDER // 19©64." *Fran's Dolls.*

Illustration 169. 7in (17.8cm) GEORGE WASHINGTON CARVER by Hallmark, No. 400DT113-7, 1979. All-cloth with printed features and clothing. Sewn body joints. Made in Taiwan. *Shirley Buchholz Collection.*

CASANOVA, GIOVANNI JACOPO. Celebrated lover. Born in Italy on April 2, 1725; died June 4, 1798. Casanova, whose name has become synonomous with sexual conquest, only made love to about 132 women. This is just a fraction of the sex partners claimed by such as Sarah Berhnardt and Elvis Presley. Casanova had sexual relations with boys, girls, nuns, his own daughter, young women, old women, deformed persons and a great variety of others. (For his adventures consult *The Intimate Sex Lives of Famous People* by Irving Wallace, Amy Wallace, David Wallechinsky and Sylvia Wallace; Delacorte Press, 1981.) Casanova began life as the illegitimate son of a Venetian actress and ended his life as a librarian in a castle in Bohemia.

DOLLS:

1. CASANOVA.   Anili, 1981. Designed by Lenci; made in Italy. 23in (43.2cm) *Illustration 170.*

Illustration 171. Shaun Cassidy as Joe Hardy from "The Hardy Boys Mysteries."

Illustration 170. 23in (43.2cm) CASANOVA by Anili, 1981. Stiffened felt and fully-jointed. Blonde synthetic wig; painted blue eyes. Designed by Lenci and made in Italy. *Pittsburgh Doll Company.*

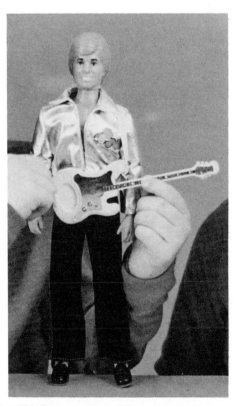

Illustration 172. The *Joe Hardy* (SHAUN CASSIDY) doll from the 1978 Kenner catalog. This doll was never for sale in any store or from any catalog. All of the 1978 Christmas catalogs, including J.C. Penney Company, Inc., Montgomery Ward & Co., Inc., Sears, Roebuck and Co., and Spiegel showed this doll in their advertisements. Each catalog shows the doll in a different pose, so dolls must have been made rather than the catalogs using Kenner photos. The only Shaun Cassidy doll ever for sale was the one pictured in *Illustrations 173* and *174*. During 1978 newspaper articles reported that "Shaun Cassidy was suing Kenner" over the manufacture of the dolls, presumably because of royalty rights. The Parker Stevenson doll from the Hardy Boys was availabale long before the Shaun Cassidy doll was, although the two are a set. (Note: This is not the same modeling used for PARKER STEVENSON as *Frank Hardy*.)

CASSIDY, SHAUN   Singer, actor. Born September 27, 1958. Shaun Cassidy began his show business career as a rock musician, performing shirtless to attract attention. He played young detective Joe Hardy on "The Hardy Boys Mysteries" from January of 1977 until the fall of 1978 on ABC-TV. During the fall of 1980 he starred on NBC-TV's "Breaking Away," which had high critical acclaim but poor viewership so the show was cancelled. Shaun is the son of actress, singer Shirley Jones and actor, singer Jack Cassidy. His half-brother, David Cassidy, was a "teenage idol" in the early 1970s and his younger brother, Patrick, is also in show business.

DOLLS:

1. SHAUN CASSIDY as JOE HARDY.   Kenner, No. 45000, 1978. Made in Hong Kong. 12in (30.5cm). *Illustrations 173* and *174* for the two commercial versions of the doll.

Illustration 173. 12in (30.5cm) SHAUN CASSIDY as *Joe Hardy* from "The Hardy Boys" by Kenner, No. 45000, 1978. All-vinyl and fully-jointed. The doll came in two versions. One has painted yellow hair, light brown eyes and black eyebrows. The other has painted reddish brown hair with painted reddish brown eyebrows and darker brown eyes. Both dolls wear a red shirt and black pants. The guitar has a red lens insert so that "secret messages" can be written with a combination of blue and red pencils and only the blue part can be read through the guitar. Head marked: "©1978 U.C.S.I." The torso is marked: " © G.M.F.I.G.I. 1978 KENNER PROD. // CINCINNATI, OHIO 45202 // MADE IN HONG KONG." Copyright by Universal City Studios, Inc. PARKER STEVENSON as *Frank Hardy* is a companion doll.

Illustration 174. Kenner's SHAUN CASSIDY with painted yellow hair. Like all Kenner dolls, the facial modeling and the body construction are quality craftsmanship.

Illustration 175. Shaun Cassidy from "Breaking Away," 1980.

CASSIDY, TED. Actor. Born in Pittsburgh, Pennsylvania, in 1932; died January 16, 1979. From September of 1964 to September of 1966 Cassidy played the seven foot tall butler Lurch on ABC-TV's "The Addams Family." During the 1968-1969 television he was Injun Joe on "The New Adventures of Huck Finn." He played Bigfoot on "The Six Million Dollar Man" in the 1970s. He also appeared in films in character parts.
DOLLS:
1. LURCH OF THE ADDAMS FAMILY. Remco, 1964. Vinyl with a jointed head. Rooted hair; painted clothing. Copyright by Filmways T.V. Prod., Inc. Marked: "L6" on neck. 5¾in (14.7cm).
2. ADDAMS FAMILY. Hand puppet. Ideal, 1966.

COUNTESS OF CASTLEMAINE. See VILLIERS, BARBARA.

CATHERINE OF ARAGON. Queen of England. Born in Castile on December 16, 1485; died 1536 in England. Catherine was the daughter of Isabella of Castile and Ferdinand of Aragón and the first wife of Henry VIII of England. She was married to Prince Arthur, Henry's brother, in 1501. Arthur died the following year without consumating the marriage or receiving the Spanish dowry for Catherine. She was then married to Henry from 1509 to 1533. Henry had become infatuated with Anne Boleyn and had married her four months before his marriage to Catherine was officially annulled. The Pope refused to go along with the King's plan, which led to the English Reformation and Henry proclaiming himself the head of the Church of England. Catherine never accepted the decision that her marriage was invalid. Her daughter became Queen Mary I, known as "Bloody Mary" because she returned her mother's religion to England and persecuted Protestants.
DOLLS:
1. CATHERINE OF ARAGON. Peggy Nisbet, No. P602, 1970s. Plastic "collectors' doll," part of a series of Henry VIII and his six wives, "Henry VIII, Portrait Series." Costume from contemporary portraits in the National Gallery, London, England. Made in England. About 7½in (19.1cm).
2. CATHERINE OF ARAGON. Peggy Nisbet, No. H219, 1970s. Plastic "collectors' doll," part of a

series of Henry VIII and his six wives, "Henry VIII, Standard Series." Costume is an accurate reproduction of the clothing worn by the Queen. Made in England. About 7½in (19.1cm).

3. CATHERINE OF ARAGON. Peggy Nisbet, No. M931, 1979. Plastic "collectors' doll," part of a series of Henry VIII and his six wives, "Henry VIII, Historical Series." Made in England. Inch-to-the-foot miniatures.

4. CATHERINE OF ARAGON. Peggy Nisbet, No. LE92, 1980. Plastic "collectors' doll," part of a series including Henry VIII (LE91) and Cardinal Wolsey (No. LE93). Made in England. About 7½in (19.1cm).

CATHERINE OF BRAGANZA. Consort of Charles II of England. (Reigned 1660 to 1685.) Born 1638; died 1705. Catherine's dowry included the ports of Bombay and Tangier, as she was the daughter of King John IV of Portugal, who claimed them. In 1678 the conspirator Titus Oates invented the story of a plot to poison the King and claimed that Queen Catherine was involved. Charles protected her honor.

DOLLS:
1. QUEEN CATHERINE OF BRAGANZA. Peggy Nisbet, No. H286, 1970s. Plastic "collectors' doll." Made in England. About 7½in (19.1cm).

CAVELL, EDITH. British nurse. Born 1865; died 1915. Edith Cavell was a nurse in a hospital in Brussels, Belgium, during World War I. The Germans shot her for aiding in the escape of wounded French and English soldiers.

DOLLS:
1. EDITH CAVELL. Ann Parker, 1970s. Plastic "collectors' doll," attached to a wooden base. Made in England. 11in (27.9cm).

CHAMBERLAIN, RICHARD. Actor. Born George Richard Chamberlain on March 31, 1935, in Beverly Hills, California. Chamberlain entered films in 1960 but achieved his greatest fame playing Dr. Kildare on television in "Dr. Kildare" from September 1961 to August 1966. He later tried to erase this clean-cut image by acting on the British stage in Shakespearean roles and by tackling character parts. He also sang on TV and made recordings.

DOLLS:
1. DR. KILDARE. Manufacturer unknown, early 1960s. 23½in (59.7cm). *Illustration 177*.
2. DR. KILDARE. Manufacturer unknown, early 1960s. 11¾in (29.9cm). *Illustrations 178* and *179*.
3. DR. KILDARE. Bobble-head doll of unknown manufacture, early 1960s. 6¾in (17.2cm). *Illustration 180*.
NOTE: For each Dr. Kildare doll there was a comparable Dr. Ben Casey doll. See Vincent Edwards.

Illustration 176. Richard Chamberlain, 1964.

ABOVE LEFT: Illustration 177. 23½in (59.7cm) RICHARD CHAMBERLAIN as *Dr. Kildare*, manufacturer unknown, early 1960s. Vinyl head and arms; plastic torso and legs. Painted light brown molded hair; blue sleep eyes with lashes. No marks. The doll was originally dressed in a simple white doctor outfit. An attached pin read: "DR. KILDARE IS A DOLL." The same doll represented Vincent Edwards as *Dr. Ben Casey*. The only difference was a pin that stated: "I'VE GOT A CASE ON BEN CASEY."

ABOVE RIGHT: Illustration 178. 11¾in (29.9cm) RICHARD CHAMBERLAIN as *Dr. Kildare*, early 1960s. All-vinyl and fully-jointed. Painted light brown hair; painted brown eyes. This crudely made doll of unknown manufacture is like the VINCENT EDWARDS as Ben Casey doll, *Illustration 307*. On the pocket of the shirt is printed: "DR. KILDARE // (Medical Insignia) // BLAIR GENERAL HOSPITAL." (Blair General was the name of the hospital on the television series.)

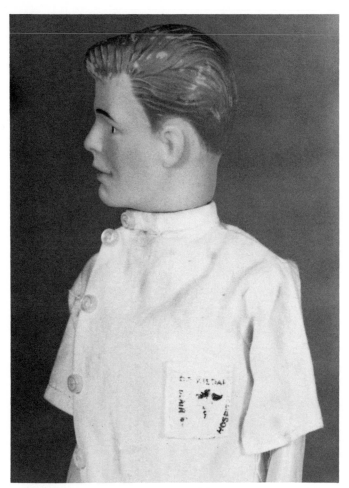

Illustration 179. RICHARD CHAMBERLAIN as *Dr. Kildare,* maker unknown.

Illustration 180. 6¾in (17.2cm) RICHARD CHAMBERLAIN as *Dr. Kildare,* circa early 1960s. Papier-mâché "bobble head." The head has a wire spring attachment inside to make it "bobble" when moved. Painted features. No marks except for the name on the front. *Shirley Buchholz Collection.*

CHANEY, LON. Actor. Born Alonso Chaney on April 1, 1883; died 1930. As the son of deaf-mute parents, Chaney learned to communicate with facial expressions and pantomine. He went on the stage when he was 17 and entered films in 1912. Between 1913 and 1930 he played more than 150 roles, most of them bizarre, earning him the name "The Man of a Thousand Faces." This was also the title of a biographical film in 1957 starring James Cagney. His horror films, like *The Phantom of the Opera* in 1925, are his best remembered.

DOLLS:
1. PHANTOM OF THE OPERA. Remco, No. 772, 1980. Made in Hong Kong, 4in (10.2cm). *Illustration 181.*

Illustration 181. 4in (10.2cm) LON CHANEY as the *Phantom of the Opera* by Remco, No. 772, 1981. All-vinyl and fully-jointed. Painted hair and features; painted clothing with a vinyl opera cape. Copyright 1980 by Universal City Studios, Inc. Made in Hong Kong.

CHANEY, LON, JR. Actor. Born Creighton Chaney, February 10, 1906; died 1973. The son of actor Lon Chaney began his screen career in 1932 using his real name. He changed his name to Lon Chaney, Jr. in 1935. During the 1940s he played many monsters in horror films, including Frankenstein's monster, Dracula, the Mummy and the Wolf Man several times.

DOLLS:
1, THE WOLF MAN. Remco, No. 1902, 1974. All-vinyl and fully jointed. Copyright by Universal City Studios, Inc. Made in Hong Kong. 8in (20.3cm).
2. THE WOLF MAN. Remco, No. 754, 1980. Same doll as No. 1.
3. THE WOLF MAN. Remco, 1980. All-vinyl and fully jointed. Copyright by Universal City Studios, Inc. Made in Hong Kong. 4in (10.2cm).

CHANNING, CAROL. Comic actress. Born January 31, 1921. Carol Channing is a large-eyed, very blonded entertainer on the stage, nightclubs, TV and sometimes in the movies. Her best known portrayal on Broadway was in Anita Loos's "Gentlemen Prefer Blondes" in which she sang her theme song, "Diamonds Are a Girl's Best Friend," in her raspy voice. She was nominated for an Academy Award for the film *Thoroughly Modern Millie* (1967).

DOLLS:
1. CAROL CHANNING. Manufacturer unknown, about 1961. Plastic and vinyl with rooted orange-blonde hair; painted eyes. The doll was an antihistamine premium. Head marked: "AE." 11½in (29.2cm).
2. HELLO DOLLY. Nasco, 1961. Plastic with a vinyl head. Rooted white hair; blue sleep eyes with lashes; eye shadow; high heeled feet. Head marked: "1373 // K // 1961. 24in (61cm).

CHAPLIN, CHARLIE (SIR CHARLES SPENCER CHAPLIN). Actor, director, producer, screenwriter, composer. Born April 16, 1889, in London, England; died 1977. As a young boy Charlie Chaplin and his half-brother, Sydney, roamed the streets of London as urchins because of their mother's nervous breakdown. The boys were found dancing in the streets for pennies and were placed in an orphanage. By the time Charlie was eight he was dancing on the London stage and appearing in plays. In December of 1913 Charlie joined the Keystone Studio in the United States and made his first film, *Making a Living,* which was not a success. He made 35 films during his year with Keystone for a weekly salary of $175. Then he signed with Essanay, located in Chicago, Illinois, at $1,250 a week in 1915, also receiving $10,000 bonus for doing so. In April of 1915 he made *The Tramp,* his first masterpiece, which became his most identified screen character. By 1916 he signed with Mutual, where he was given a salary of $10,000 a week plus a bonus of $150,000. In 1918 Charlie signed a contract with First National for more than a million dollars for eight two-reel films. In 1921 at First National he made his first feature-length film, *The Kid,* which was considered a masterpiece and became a box office success second only to *The Birth of a Nation.* During the 1930s, after the advent of sound in films, Chaplin made two silent features which were hits. He knew that his genius was best seen in pantomine. His last film venture was *A Countess from Hong Kong* in 1966, in which he directed Sophia Loren. It was a critical and a commercial disaster. In 1975 the former street urchin from London was made a Knight by Queen Elizabeth. He died in Switzerland, a self-imposed exile from the United States since 1952 because of his sexual indiscretions and his affiliations with alleged communist-front organizations.

DOLLS:
1. CHARLIE CHAPLIN. Louis Amberg and Son, 1915. 14½in (36.9cm). *Illustrations 183* and *184.*
2. CHARLIE CHAPLIN. Louis Amberg and Son, circa 1915. All-cloth with painted features and similar clothing to the composition head version. Marked with tag on the foot. 17in (43.2cm).

3. CHARLIE CHAPLIN. Dean's Rag Dolls, 1920. Pressed cloth face; one-piece construction; printed clothing. Made in England. 11½in (29.2cm).
4. CHARLIE CHAPLIN AS THE TRAMP. Kenner, 1973. Lithographed cloth with a walking mechanism. 14in (35.6cm).
5. CHARLIE CHAPLIN AS THE TRAMP IN *CITY LIGHTS.* Peggy Nisbet, No. P755, 1970s. Plastic "collectors' doll." Made in England. About 7½in (19.1cm).
6. CHARLIE CHAPLIN. Cadeaux, 1972. Made in USA. 19in (48.3cm). *Illustration 185.*
7. CHARLIE CHAPLIN. Late 1970s. Porcelain head, hands and feet; cloth body. Made in Taiwan. 23in (58.4cm). *Illustration 186.*
8. CHARLIE CHAPLIN. Circa 1980. Porcelain head, hands and feet; cloth body. Made in Taiwan. 18in (45.7cm). *Illustration 187.*
9. CHARLIE CHAPLIN. Dean's Childsplay Toys Ltd., No. 280900, 1982. All-cloth. Printed features and clothing. Legs are joined together. Separate hat. This is a reproduction of the doll from 1920 (No. 3 above). Made in Pontnewynydd, Pontypool, Gwent, Great Britain. 11in (27.9cm).

NOTE: Many other dolls were made of Charlie Chaplin, including CHARLOT from France, the name by which he was known there.

Illustration 182. Charlie Chaplin and Jackie Coogan in *The Kid,* 1921.

Chaplin, Charlie

Illustration 185. 19in (48.3cm) CHARLIE CHAPLIN by Cadeaux, No. 3211, 1972. Vinyl head, hands and feet; cloth body; wooden cane molded to left hand. Molded black hat and painted black hair and eyes. Head marked: "BUBBLES INC. // © 1972." The original box tells that Cadeaux is a Milton Bradley Company. Copyright by Bubbles, Inc. Made in USA.

Illustration 184. Amberg's CHARLIE CHAPLIN. *Coleman Collection. Photograph by Ann Coleman.*

OPPOSITE PAGE: *Illustration 183.* 14½" (36.9cm) CHARLIE CHAPLIN by Louis Amberg and Son, 1915. Composition head and hands; straw-filled cloth body with pin and disk joints. Deeply molded hair and painted features. Label sewn to right sleeve: "CHARLIE CHAPLIN DOLL // WORLD'S GREATEST COMEDIAN // MADE EXCLUSIVELY BY LOUIS AMBERG & SON, N.Y. // BY SPECIAL ARRANGEMENT WITH ESSANAY FILM CO." In 1915 the Charlie Chaplin dolls by Amberg retailed for 65¢ and $1.00, which would imply that there were two different sizes. *Coleman Collection. Photograph by Ann Coleman.*

Illustration 186. 23in (58.4cm) CHARLIE CHAPLIN from Taiwan, late 1970s. Unglazed porcelain head, hands and feet; stuffed cloth body. Painted features. The opening in the hands is for the doll to hold a nickel-plated cane. The suit is a velveteen material with a cotton shirt. The only marking is a gold sticker on the left foot: "MADE IN TAIWAN."

Illustration 187. 18in (45.7cm) CHARLIE CHAPLIN from Taiwan, circa 1980. Porcelain head, hands and feet; stuffed cloth body. Black synthetic wig; painted features. The doll wears a black velveteen suit.

Illustration 188. King Charles II, "the Merry Monarch," and three of his favorite mistresses, a Special Collectors' Set, limited to the sale of 500 sets by Peggy Nisbet, 1970s. From left to right: NELL GWYN, No. LE84; COUNTESS OF CASTLEMAINE, No. LE85; KING CHARLES II, No. LE83; and the DUCHESS OF PORTSMOUTH, No. LE86. About 7½in (19.1cm) each. All-hard plastic; jointed only at the arms. Mohair wigs and painted features. Made in England. Photograph Courtesy of House of Nisbet.

CHAPMAN, BEN. Character actor who played Gill-Man, *The Creature from the Black Lagoon* in the 1954 film. The movie was a horror story of the discovery of a pre-historic monster living near the Amazon River. It was originally shown in 3D.
DOLLS:
1. THE CREATURE FROM THE BLACK LAGOON. Remco, 1980. All-vinyl and fully-jointed. Copyright by Universal City Studios, Inc. Made in Hong Kong. 4in (10.2cm).

CHARLES II. King of England from 1660 to 1685. Born 1630; died 1685. Charles II was the king of the Restoration Period in England, after 11 years of Civil War and a Dictatorship under the Cromwells. He married Catherine of Braganza in 1662. The Queen never had any children, but Charles had at least 14 children by various mistresses such as Nell Gwyn, an orange seller. As there was no legitimate issue, his brother James, the Duke of York, succeeded him as James II. The Great Plague of London of 1665 and the Great Fire of 1666 occurred during his reign.
DOLLS:
1. KING CHARLES II. Peggy Nisbet, No. P639, 1970s. Plastic "collectors' doll." Made in England. About 8in (20.3cm).
2. KING CHARLES II. Peggy Nisbet No. LE83, 1970s. "Special Collectors' Set." Made in England. About 8in (20.3cm). *Illustration 188.*

PRINCE CHARLES. The 21st Prince of Wales. Born November 14, 1948. Prince Charles is the son of Queen Elizabeth II and Prince Philip, the Duke of Edinburgh. He was invested as the Prince of Wales on July 1, 1969. After a career of serving in each of the British armed forces and representing Great Britain in state visits, he married Lady Diana Spencer on July 29, 1981, in an elaborate ceremony, an event that was well publicized because of the interest engendered by the public.
DOLLS:
1. PRINCE CHARLES. Madame Alexander, No. 395 (with jointed knees) and No. 397, 1957. All-hard plastic and fully-jointed. Blonde wig; blue sleep eyes with molded lashes. Princess Anne, No. 396 is a companion doll. 8in (20.3cm).
2. PRINCE CHARLES. Chelsea Art, 1957. Made in England. 9in (22.9cm). *Illustration 190.*
3. H.R.H. PRINCE CHARLES. PRINCE OF WALES. Peggy Nisbet, No. P409, early 1970s. Plastic "collectors' doll," dressed as "Trooping the Colour." Made in England. About 8in (20.3cm).
4. H.R.H. PRINCE CHARLES. PRINCE OF WALES. Peggy Nisbet, No. P402, early 1970s. Plastic "collectors' doll," dressed as "Order of the Garter." Made in England. About 8in (20.3cm).
5. H.R.H. PRINCE CHARLES. Peggy Nisbet, No. P411, late 1970s. Plastic "collectors' doll," dressed in "State Robes." Made in England. About 8in (20.3cm).
6. H.R.H. PRINCE CHARLES. Peggy Nisbet, No. P423, 1970s. Made in England. About 8in (20.3cm). *Illustration 191.*
7. PRINCE AND PRINCESS OF WALES. Peggy Nisbet, Limited Edition Collectors' Set No. 19, for the Royal Wedding, 1981. Plastic. Made in England. About 8in (20.3cm). (Set limited to 4000.)

Illustration 189. Prince Charles, from an English calendar, 1954.

8. PRINCE CHARLES. Dean's Rag Book Co., Ltd., 1981. Four-color, uncut, cloth doll sheet of Prince Charles and Lady Diana made for the Royal Wedding of July 29, 1981. Made in Sussex, England. 16in (40.6cm).

9. H.R.H. PRINCE CHARLES AS COLONEL IN CHIEF. Peggy Nisbet, No. P426, 1981. Plastic "collectors' doll." Dressed as "The Gordon Highlanders." Lady Diana Spencer (The Princess of Wales), No. P428, is a companion doll. Made in England. About 8in (20.3cm).

10. THE PRINCE OF WALES. (ROYAL WEDDING). Peggy Nisbet, No. P1004, 1982. Plastic "collectors' doll." The Princess of Wales, No. P1005, is a companion doll. Made in England. About 8in (20.3cm).

Illustration 191. About **8in** (20.3cm) PRINCE CHARLES by Peggy Nisbet, no. **P423**, 1970s. All-hard plastic; jointed only at the arms. Painted hair and features. Made in England. *Photograph Courtesy of House of Nisbet.*

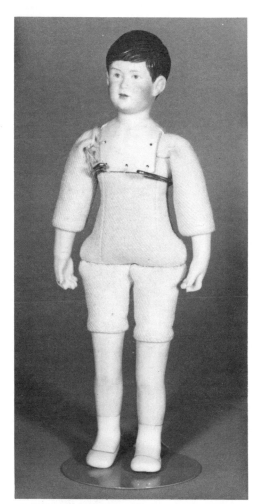

Illustration 190. 9in (22.9cm) PRINCE CHARLES by Chelsea Art, 1957. Bisque shoulder plate head, lower arms and legs. Painted hair and features. Marked on back of shoulder plate: "MADE FOR // DOLL MAKERS // CHELSEA ART // 1957." PRINCESS ANNE, *Illustration 77*, is a companion doll. Made in England. *Shirley Buchholz Collection.*

Illustration 192. Prince Charles and Lady Diana on the cover of *People Weekly*, August 1981. Most magazines carried a picture of this couple during the summer of 1981.

CHARLIE'S ANGELS. An hour long detective drama that was on ABC-TV from September 22, 1976, through re-runs during the 1981 season. The main ingredient of this show was the sex appeal of the actresses who played the "Angels." Dolls were made of four of the women who played these detectives. *Sabrina* (KATE JACKSON) was the leader; *Jill* (FARRAH FAWCETT-MAJORS) was the athletic type; *Kelly* (JACLYN SMITH) was a former showgirl who had "been around;" *Kris* (CHERYL LADD) was Jill's younger sister, who replaced Farrah when she left the show over contract disputes after the first season. Kate Jackson also left the show before its run ended. See listings under the celebrity names for the various dolls.

PRINCESS CHARLOTTE. Daughter of George IV of England; wife of Prince Leopold of Belgium. Born 1796; died 1817. Princess Charlotte would have become Queen of England had she not died before her father, who was king from 1820 to 1830. She would also have been Queen of Belgium, as her husband Leopold was king from 1831 to 1865. It was Leopold who helped raise the future Queen Victoria, his niece, and who arranged her marriage with his nephew, Albert.

DOLLS:
1. PRINCESS CHARLOTTE. Ann Parker, 1970s. Plastic "collectors' doll," affixed to a wooden base. Made in England. 11in (27.9cm). *Illustrations 195* and *196*.

Illustration 195. 11in (27.9cm) PRINCESS CHARLOTTE by Ann Parker, late 1970s. All-hard plastic and affixed to a wooden base. Blonde mohair wig; painted gray eyes. The costume is white with silver trim. Made in England. *Shirley Buchholz Collection.*

Illustration 193. Jaclyn Smith, Farrah Fawcett-Majors and Kate Jackson, the first team of "Charlie's Angels."

Illustration 194. CHARLIE'S ANGELS set. 8½in (21.6cm) KATE JACKSON, FARRAH FAWCETT-MAJORS and JACLYN SMITH by Hasbro, No. 4864, 1977. Copyright by Spelling Goldberg Productions. Made in Hong Kong.

Illustration 196. PRINCESS CHARLOTTE by Ann Parker. *Shirley Buchholz Collection.*

QUEEN CHARLOTTE. Queen of England. Born 1744; died 1818. Charlotte married King George III of England in 1761. He reigned from 1760 until his death in 1820. They had 15 children. After 1811 George was not able to reign. (It is in dispute whether or not he became insane.) Charlotte controlled the government with her eldest son acting as Prince-Regent. King George and Queen Charlotte were the last king and queen of the 13 colonies that became the United States of America in 1776.

DOLLS:
1. QUEEN CHARLOTTE. Peggy Nisbet, No. P707, 1970s. Plastic "collectors' doll." King George III in State Robes, No. P706, is the companion doll. Made in England. About 7½in (19.1cm).

CHASE, DUANE. Duane Chase was the boy who played Kurt in *The Sound of Music,* 1965.
DOLLS:
1. KURT from THE SOUND OF MUSIC. Madame Alexander, 1966. Vinyl with rooted blonde hair and blue sleep eyes. Marked on the head: "ALEXANDER // 19 © 62." 12in (30.5cm). This is the only Kurt doll from the various sets of dolls from *The Sound of Music,* and he wears the blue sailor outfit.
SEE: THE SOUND OF MUSIC.

CHENNAULT, GENERAL CLAIRE LEE. United States general. Born 1890; died 1958. Chennault formed the American volunteer group, the Flying Tigers, in China in 1941 during the time the Japanese were determined to occupy the country. From 1942 to 1945 he headed the United States Air Task Force in China, whose goal it was to bomb the Japanese homeland from bases in China.

DOLLS:
1. GEN. CLAIRE L. CHENNAULT. Excel Toy Corp., No. 507, 1974. Made in Hong Kong. 9¾in (24.9cm). *Illustration 197.*

Illustration 197. 9¾in (24.9cm) GENERAL CLAIRE L. CHENNAULT by Excel Toy Corp., No. 507 1974. All-vinyl and fully-jointed; painted black hair. Marked on lower back: " © EXCEL TOY CORP. // MADE IN HONG KONG."

CHER. Singer, actress. Born Cherilyn Sarkisian (or Sakisian, or Cherilyn La Piere) on May 20, 1946, in El Centro, California. Cher came to prominence singing with her husband, Sonny Bono, on the TV program "Shindig" in 1964. Their big hit recording "I've Got You, Babe" became their theme song. Cher was also on television in "The Sonny and Cher Comedy Hour" from August 1971 to May 1974, "Cher" from February 1975 to January 1976, and again on "The Sonny and Cher Comedy Hour" from February 1976 to August 1977. During the "Cher" period she divorced Sonny and married rock musician Gregg Allman briefly. Cher later became a singer with her new group, Black Rose, and changed her image to "Punk" for this hard rock band. During this time she was romantically involved with Gene Simmons of the group KISS. Neither venture was a success.

DOLLS:
1. CHER. Mego, No. 62400, 1976. Sonny (see SONNY BONO) is companion doll. 12¼in (31.2cm). *Illustration 198.*
2. GROWING HAIR CHER. Mego, No. 62402, 12¼in (31.2cm), 1976. *Illustrations 199* and *200.*
3. CHER. Mego, No. 62403, 1981. 12in (30.5cm). *Illustration 201.*

Illustration 199. 12¼in (31.2cm) CHER with "Growing Hair" by Mego, No. 62402, 1976. All-vinyl and fully-jointed. Rooted long black hair with key wind in the back to make the hair shorter; painted eyes with very long attached lashes; dark skin tones. Head marked: "MEGO CORP // 19 © 75." *Wanda Lodwick Collection.*

Illustration 200. Growing Hair CHER. *Wanda Lodwick Collection.*

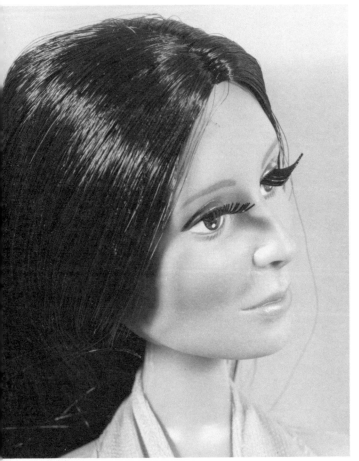

Illustration 198. 12¼in (31.2cm) CHER by Mego, No. 62400, 1976. All-vinyl and fully-jointed, including waist and wrists. Rooted black hair; painted eyes with very long attached lashes; dark skin tones. This is the first version of Cher by Mego. The doll also had an extensive wardrobe, sold separately. *Wanda Lodwick Collection.*

Illustration 201. 12in (30.5cm) CHER by Mego, No. 62403, 1981. Vinyl head with rooted long black hair; very thin and cheaply made five-piece plastic body. Head marked: "3906 // AF // MEGO CORP // 19 © 76." This version of Cher wears nothing except a blue nylon stretch swimsuit and is similar to FARRAH, *Illustration 331.*

CHIANG KAI-SHEK. Chinese soldier and statesman. Born October 31, 1887; died April 5, 1975. Chiang fought against the Manchu Dynasty of China in 1911 and then joined Sun Yat-Sen, the leader of the Revolutionary Army, in 1925. He established himself as the Chinese head of state from 1928 to 1949, trying to unify the nation under one rule. During World War II he was fighting both the Japanese invaders and the Chinese Communists. He was defeated by the Communists in 1949 and resumed the Presidency of China in exile on Taiwan until his death.

DOLLS:
1. GENERAL CHIANG KAI-SHEK. Maker unknown, circa 1944. 18in (45.7cm). *Illustration 202.*

Illustration 202. 18in (45.7cm) GENERAL CHIANG KAI-SHEK, circa 1944. Head, gloved hands and shoes are of composition. The body is stuffed and covered with paper that has Chinese writing on it, so the doll was no doubt made in China during the years of World War II, as it shows Chiang in his army uniform. The facial features are painted with oil paints. No markings. *Peggy Fesperman Collection.*

CHILES, LOIS. American actress. Born 1950. Lois Chiles appeared in the films *The Way We Were* (1973) and *The Great Gatsby* (1974) among others. In *Moonraker* (1979) she was Holly Goodhead, a space scientist who eventually fell under the charms of James Bond, played by Roger Moore.

DOLLS:
1. HOLLY. Mego, No. 96003, 1979. Made in Hong Kong. 12½in (31.8cm). *Illustrations 203* and *204.*

Illustration 203. 12½in (31.8cm) LOIS CHILES as *Holly* from *Moonraker* by Mego, No. 96003, 1979. All-vinyl and fully-jointed. Rooted dark brown hair; painted brown eyes. Head marked: "© 1979 EON // PRODUCTIONS LTD." Made in Hong Kong.

Illustration 204. LOIS CHILES by Mego.

CHIPS. CHiPs is an acronym for California Highway Patrol. When the television show began in September of 1977, it featured Jon Baker (LARRY WILCOX) and Francis "Ponch" Poncherello (ERIK ESTRADA) as two young bachelors whose adventures helped fight crime while they led active social lives at the same time. Jon and Ponch were patrolmen who worked from motorcycles. In the summer of 1981 Erik Estrada announced that he would not return to the show unless his contract could be improved. The producers announced that he would be replaced by Bruce Jenner, which helped encourage a settlement, after Jenner appeared on four shows. 8in (20.3cm) dolls were made of ERIK ESTRADA, LARRY WILCOX and ROBERT PINE as *Sarge*. These dolls are also in a 3¾in (9.6cm) size. In addition there are also CHiPs dolls of the characters "Wheels Willy" and "Jimmy Squeeks" (*Illustrations 205* and *206*) in the smaller size.

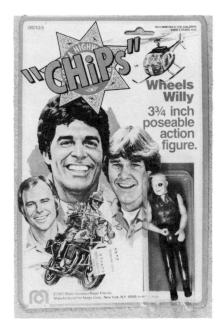

Illustration 205. 3¾in (9.6cm) *Wheels Willy* from "CHiPs" by Mego, No. 08010/5, 1981. All-vinyl and fully-jointed. Painted eye patch and painted clothing. Copyright 1977 by Metro-Goldwyn-Mayer Film Co. Made in Hong Kong. In the photo on the card, from left to right, Robert Pine, Erik Estrada and Larry Wilcox.

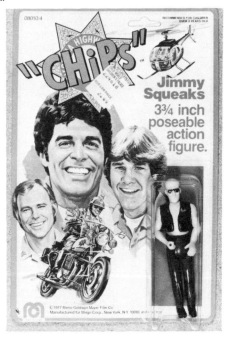

Illustration 206. 3¾in (9.6cm) *Jimmy Squeaks* from "CHiPs" by Mego, No. 08010/4, 1981. All-vinyl and fully-jointed. Painted and molded sun glasses; painted clothing. Copyright 1977 by Metro-Goldwyn-Mayer Film Co. Made in Hong Kong.

CHOU EN-LAI. Chinese communist leader. Born 1898; died January 6, 1976. Chou became a communist while living in France from 1920 to 1924. He participated in the Revolution in China and succeeded Mao Tse-tung as the political commissar of the Red Army in 1932. At the end of World War II he was the chief negotiator of the Chinese Communist party with the United States against Japan. Chou was the Premier of the People's Republic of China from 1949 until his death in 1976.

During the 1970s it was he who normalized relations with the West because of the growing Soviet threat to China.

DOLLS:
1. CHOU EN-LAI. All-vinyl; jointed only at the neck. 5½in (14cm). (See: Patrician Smith: *Doll Values*, 1980.)

CHRISTOPHER, WILLIAM. Actor. Born October 20, 1932. Christopher has appeared in many films and television shows. He was in "Gomer Pyle. U.S.M.C." on CBS-TV from September 1964 to September 1969. On "M*A*S*H" on CBS-TV he has played Father John Francis Mulcahy since September 1972.

DOLLS:
1. FATHER MULCAHY. (CAPTAIN FRANCIS JOHN PATRICK MULCAHY). Tristar International, Ltd., Series No. 4100, 1982. All-vinyl and fully-jointed. Painted features and clothing. Made in Hong Kong. 3¾in (9.6cm).

SEE: M*A*S*H.

CHURCHILL, LADY RANDOLPH (JEANETTE JEROME). American-born wife of Lord Randolph Henry Spencer Churchill and mother of Winston Churchill. Born 1854; died 1921. Jennie married Lord Randolph in April of 1874, and her famous son was born prematurely the following November.

DOLLS:
1. LADY RANDOLPH CHURCHILL. Peggy Nisbet, No. H592, 1970s. Plastic "collectors' doll." Made in England. About 7½in (19.1cm).
2. LADY RANDOLPH CHURCHILL. Ann Parker, 1970s. Made in England. 11in (27.9cm). *Illustration 207*.

Illustration 207. 11in (27.9cm) LADY RANDOLPH CHURCHILL (JENNIE JEROME) by Ann Parker, late 1970s. All-hard plastic and affixed to a base. Brown mohair wig; painted brown eyes. The costume is purple rayon. Made in England. *Shirley Buchholz Collection*.

CHURCHILL, WINSTON (SIR WINSTON). British statesman. Born November 30, 1874; died January 24, 1965. Churchill was first elected to Parliament in 1900. In 1940, seven months after the outbreak of World War II, he became Prime Minister. He was the symbol of British resistance to Nazi Germany, offering England "blood, toil, tears and sweat" and promising to "wage war by sea, land and air, with all our might and with all the strength God can give us." Churchill was the author of histories, biographies and memoirs. In 1953 he was awarded the Nobel Prize in Literature and was knighted by Queen Elizabeth.

DOLLS:
1. SIR WINSTON CHURCHILL IN ROBES OF THE ORDER OF THE GARTER. Peggy Nisbet, No. P615, 1970s. Plastic "collectors' doll." Made in England. About 7½in (19.1cm).
2. SIR WINSTON CHURCHILL (KARSH PORTRAIT). Peggy Nisbet, No. P796, 1970s. Plastic "collectors' doll." Made in England. About 7½in (19.1cm).

CLARK, DAVE. English musician and drummer of THE DAVE CLARK FIVE. Born in London, England, on December 15, 1942. In the early 1960s Dave Clark entered movies playing small parts. He organized the group The Dave Clark Five because he needed the money to get to Holland to play on his soccer team, as did Mike Smith, Lenny Davidson, Rick Huxley and Denis Payton, the other members of the new group who were also on the team. As The Dave Clark Five the group performed from 1963 to 1970 when Dave Clark disbanded it to study drama and become involved in film production.

DOLLS:
1. THE DAVE CLARK FIVE. Remco, No. 1808, 1964. 5in (12.7cm). *Illustration 208.*
SEE: THE DAVE CLARK FIVE.

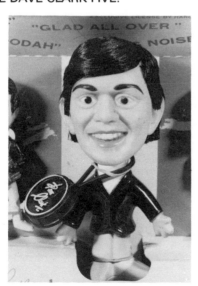

Illustration 208. 5in (12.7cm) DAVE CLARK by Remco, No. 1808, 1964. Vinyl head with rooted black hair and painted black eyes; one-piece plastic body. Head marked: "DAVE CLARK // 19©64 // REMCO IND. INC." Back marked: "DAVE // CLARK // 5 // ©1964 REMCO IND." This is part of a set of the DAVE CLARK FIVE. See that listing.

CLARK, DICK. TV host, producer, actor. Born November 30, 1929. Dick Clark began "American Bandstand" as a local show in Philadelphia, Pennsylvania. In November of 1981 Bandstand celebrated its 30th anniversary. In 1957 the show became a late afternoon entry on ABC-TV and from October to December of 1957 it was an evening program also. Dick Clark was responsible for promoting the careers of many "teenage idols," the most prominent of whom were Frankie Avalon and Fabian. He has produced many musical specials for television and a number of low-budget movies. During the 1960s he also acted in several films.

DOLLS:
1. DICK CLARK. Juro, 1958. 26½in (67.3cm). *Illustrations 209* and *210.*

Illustration 209. 26½in (67.3cm) DICK CLARK by Juro, 1958. Vinyl head and hands; cloth body. Painted dark brown hair; painted brown eyes; molded teeth. Head marked: "JURO." The original box cites that this is "another Juro Celebrity Doll" and includes an autograph pen. The original price sticker was for $7.98. *Jean Canaday Collection.*

Illustration 210. DICK CLARK by Juro. *Jean Canaday Collection.*

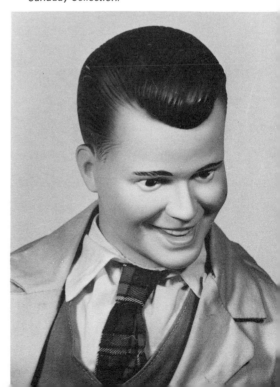

CLASH OF THE TITANS. A British action-adventure film released in June of 1981. *Clash of the Titans* is a film based on Ancient Greek mythology. The plot relates the adventures of Perseus, a son of the god Zeus by one of his many extra-maritial affairs, and his life as a beastslayer and a rescurer of fair maidens. Perseus was played by Harry Hamlin, Zeus by Sir Laurence Olivier and Andromeda, the rescued maiden, by Judi Bowker. The film was noted for its melodramatic special effects and for the notable actors who played small parts. Maggie Smith, Claire Bloom, Burgess Meredith and Flora Robson were cast in minor roles. Mattel made a set of dolls and figures of some of the film characters. HARRY HAMLIN came packaged alone or with the winged horse *Pegasus,* who was also sold separately. There are dolls of TIM PIGOT-SMITH as *Thallo* and NEIL McCARTHY as *Calibos.* Another figure represents *Charon, the Devil's Boatman* and a 14⅜in (36.5cm) figure is the monster *Kraken.* See listings under HAMLIN, PIGOT-SMITH and McCARTHY.

CLEOPATRA. Queen of Ancient Egypt. Born 69BC; died 30BC. Cleopatra is one of the greatest romantic figures in history. Her family, the XXXI Dynasty of Ancient Egypt, was from Macedonia (Greece) and they ruled Egypt from 304BC to the death of Cleopatra. Cleopatra was not beautiful, but she will always be remembered as being fabulously alluring. After the death of her first two husbands, who were also her brothers because of family custom, she married Julius Caesar and then Marc Antony. Antony committed suicide when the Roman forces of Octavian (later the Emperor Augustus) defeated him and Cleopatra at Actium in 31BC. When Cleopatra saw that she could not influence her adversaries, she let a poisonous asp bite her. Cleopatra was the subject of many plays and films, the most famous of which is the Elizabeth Taylor version of 1963.

DOLLS:
1. CLEOPATRA. Effanbee, No. 1158, 1978. All-vinyl and fully-jointed. Rooted black hair; blue sleep eyes with lashes; heavy eye make-up. 11in (27.9cm). *Illustration 211.*
2. CLEOPATRA. Madame Alexander, No. 1315, 1980. 12in (30.5cm). *Illustrations 212* and *213.*

Illustration 212. 12in (30.5cm) CLEOPATRA, No. 1315, and ANTONY, No. 1310, by Madame Alexander, 1980. Vinyl heads with rooted hair; plastic bodies. *Alexander Doll Company, Inc.* catalog, 1980.

Illustration 213. 12in (30.5cm) CLEOPATRA by Madame Alexander, No. 1315, 1981. Vinyl head with rooted black hair and brown sleep eyes with molded lashes. Hard plastic body.

Illustration 211. 11in (27.9cm) CLEOPATRA by Effanbee, No. 1158, 1978. All-vinyl and fully-jointed. Rooted black hair; blue sleep eyes with molded lashes; heavy eye makeup. Head marked: "EFFANBEE // © 1975 // 1176." (In the 1979 Effanbee catalog this doll was *Miss Ancient Egypt,* No. 1116.)

COBB, JOE. Child performer in films. Born November 17, 1917. Joe Cobb played the chubby and good-natured Fatty in 86 "Our Gang" comedies during the 1920s.
DOLLS: SEE: OUR GANG.

COCHISE. Apache Indian leader. Born circa 1812; died June 9, 1874. Cochise led the Indians in war against the white settlers who entered their territory in the Southwest from 1861 to 1872.

DOLLS:
1. COCHISE. Mego, No. 1361, 1973. Made in Hong Kong. 7½in (19.1cm) *Illustration 214*.
2. COCHISE. Excel Toy Corp., 1974. Vinyl and plastic. Made in Hong Kong. 9¼in (23.6cm).
3. COCHISE. Carolina Enterprises, Inc., 1978. All-vinyl 4¼in (10.9cm).

Illustration 214. 7½in (19.1cm) COCHISE of the "World's Greatest Super-Heroes" series made for K Mart by Mego, No. 1361, 1973. The vinyl head has painted black hair and eyes; the body is fully jointed. Made in Hong Kong.

COCHRAN, DEWEES. Doll designer. Dewees Cochran is best known for the portrait dolls that she designed for Effanbee during the 1930s. Her "American Children" dolls were featured on the cover of *Life* in 1939. She trained in art as a young girl and later studied in Europe. Her design studio was located in Vermont until 1960, when she moved to California. In 1977 Mrs. Cochran designed the Effanbee Limited Edition Doll, which was a "self-portrait" from the "Turn of the Century."

DOLLS:
1. THE DEWEES COCHRAN SELF-PORTRAIT DOLL. Effanbee, 1977. 16½in (41.9cm). *Illustration 215*.

Illustration 215. 16½in (41.9cm) DEWEES COCHRAN Self-Portrait by Effanbee Limited Doll Club, 1977. All-vinyl and fully-jointed. Rooted blonde hair; blue sleep eyes with lashes. She is dressed in a white organdy party dress and wears a white cameo at her neck. Head marked: "EFFANBEE // LTD. // © 1977." Back marked: "EFFANBEE // LIMITED EDITION // 19 © 77 // DEWEES COCHRAN."

CODY, BUFFALO BILL (WILLIAM FREDERICK CODY). American plainsman. Born 1846; died 1917. Buffalo Bill organized Buffalo Bill's Wild West Show in 1883 and traveled with it for many years. His most famous protégée was Annie Oakley.

DOLLS:
1. BUFFALO BILL, PONY EXPRESS RIDER. Hartland Plastics, No. 819, 1958. Plastic with a plastic horse. Made in Hartland, Wisconsin. About 8in (20.3cm).
2. BUFFALO BILL CODY. Mego, No. 1363, 1973. Vinyl and plastic. Made in Hong Kong for S.S. Kresge Company. 7½in (19.1cm).
3. BUFFALO BILL CODY. Excel Toy Corp., 1974. Vinyl and plastic. Made in Hong Kong. 9¼in (23.6cm).
4. BUFFALO BILL CODY. Carolina Enterprises, Inc., 1978. Vinyl and plastic. Made in Hong Kong. 4¼in (10.9cm).
SEE: THE LONE RANGER.

COLEMAN, JAMES. James Coleman played Officer T.J. McCabe on ABC-TV's "S.W.A.T." from February 1975 to July 1976.

DOLLS:
1. McCABE from S.W.A.T. L.J.N. Toys, Ltd., No. 6600, 1975. Made in Hong Kong. 7½in (19.1cm). *Illustration 216*.
2. McCABE from S.W.A.T. L.J.N. Toys, Ltd., No. 6850, 1976. Made in Hong Kong. 7½in (19.1cm). *Illustrations 217* and *218*.
SEE: S.W.A.T.

Illustration 216. 7½in (19.1cm) JAMES COLEMAN as *McCabe* from "S.W.A.T." by L.J.N. Toys Ltd., No. 6600, 1975. All-vinyl and fully-jointed and very crudely and cheaply made in Hong Kong. Copyright by Spelling-Goldberg Productions. The close-up photograph is of Robert Urich.

COLLINS, DOROTHY. Singer. Born Marjorie Chandler in Windsor, Ontario, Canada, on November 18, 1926. Blonde Dorothy Collins was tremendously popular as one of the four lead singers on television's "Your Hit Parade" from 1950 to 1959. In 1971 she was in the play "Follies."

DOLLS:

1. DOROTHY COLLINS. Star Doll Company, 1954. All-hard plastic and fully-jointed. Yellow saran wig; blue sleep eyes with lashes; open mouth with teeth. The arm tag called the doll "The Dorothy Collins Walking Doll." Head marked: "14." Back marked: "MADE IN USA." 14in (25.6cm). (This doll looks very much like the Lu Ann Simms doll, which see.)

Illustration 217. 7½in (19.1cm) JAMES COLEMAN as *McCabe* from "S.W.A.T." by L.J.N. Toys Ltd., No. 6850, 1976. All-vinyl and somewhat better modeling than the 1975 version of the same doll. (The clothing is identical.) Copyright 1975 by Spelling-Goldberg Productions. Made in Hong Kong. The close-up photograph is of Steve Forrest.

COLLINS, STEPHEN. Actor. Born October 1, 1947. Stephen Collins always wanted to be an actor. As a youngster he was in high school plays; later in college productions; then appeared in several plays on Broadway; following this he guest-starred in many television programs; by the late 1970s he was in major films. In July of 1978, after an extensive talent search, Stephen was chosen to play Decker in *Star Trek: The Motion Picture.*

DOLLS:

1. DECKER. Mego, No. 91200/3, 1979. Made in Hong Kong. 3¾in (9.6cm). *Illustration 220.*
2. DECKER. Mego, No. 91210/3, 1979. Made in Hong. 12in (30.5cm). *Illustrations 221* and *222.*

SEE: STAR TREK.

Illustration 218. JAMES COLEMAN by L.J.N. in the 1976 version.

Illustration 219. Stephen Collins.

Collins, Stephen

Illustration 220. 3¾in (9.6cm) STEPHEN COLLINS as *Decker* from *Star Trek: The Motion Picture* by Mego, No. 91200/3, 1979. All-vinyl with painted features and clothing. Copyright by Paramount Pictures Corporation. Made in Hong Kong.

Illustration 222. 12in (30.5cm) STEPHEN COLLINS by Mego.

Illustration 221. 12in (30.5cm) STEPHEN COLLINS as *Decker* from *Star Trek: The Motion Picture* by Mego, No. 91210/3, 1979. Vinyl head with painted brown hair and blue eyes. Fully-jointed body. Head marked: " © PPCo." Back marked: " © MEGO CORP. 1977 // MADE IN HONG KONG." Copyright by Paramount Pictures Corporation. In the film, Decker is "the young, aggressive Executive Officer, second in command to Capt. Kirk. His vast knowledge of the remodeled Enterprise and its technology threaten Kirk's authority."

CONNERY, SEAN. Actor. Born Thomas Connery on August 25, 1930, in Edinburgh, Scotland. Connery was employed in a variety of occupations until 1951 when he took a chorus part in the London stage production of "South Pacific." He had also become involved with body building, and his splendid physique and his sexy good looks let him be chosen for the part of Ian Flemming's James Bond in 1962. The first of the Bond films, *Dr. No*, was an immediate success, and he repeated the part in several other productions and became closely identified with the part. He later tried to shake off this image and appeared in numerous other film roles, none of them as successful.

DOLLS:
  1. SEAN CONNERY as JAMES BOND, AGENT 007. Gilbert, No. 16101, 1965. 12¼in (31.2cm). *Illustrations 224* and *225*.
SEE: JAMES BOND

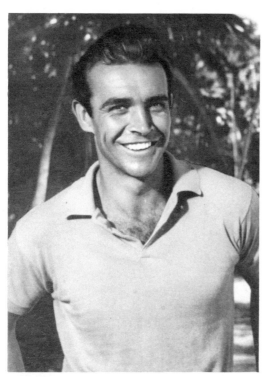

Illustration 223. Sean Connery from a Spanish postcard, early 1960s.

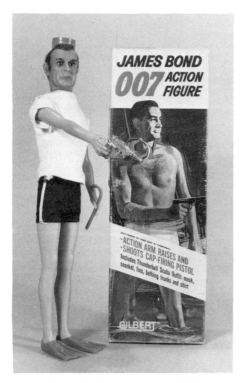

Illustration 224. 12¼in (31.2cm) SEAN CONNERY as *James Bond, Agent 007,* in *Thunderball* by Gilbert, No. 16101, 1965. Soft vinyl head with painted brown hair and painted black eyes. The body is plastic with vinyl arms and is a mold from the Ideal Toy Corp. that was used for the *Ted* doll, part of the *Tammy* series of the early 1960s. The head is not marked. Marked on the back: "© IDEAL TOY CORP. // B 12½ // 2." The original price of the doll was $3.75. Copyright by Gilrose Productions, Ltd. and Eon Productions, Ltd.

Illustration 225. SEAN CONNERY as *James Bond* by Gilbert in an original suit. *Wanda Lodwick Collection.*

CONWAY, PAT. Actor. Pat Conway played the part of Sheriff Clay Hollister on ABC-TV's "Tombstone Territory" from October 1957 to October 1959.
DOLLS:
1. SHERIFF CLAY HOLLISTER of "TOMBSTONE TERRITORY." Hartland Plastics, Inc., No. 763, 1958. Plastic with moveable arms. Made in Hartland, Wisconsin. About 8in (20.3cm).

COOGAN, JACKIE. Actor. Born Jack Coogan on October 24, 1914, in Los Angeles, California. His first screen role was in *Skinner's Baby* in 1917. Charlie Chaplin saw his act in an Annette Kellerman show when Coogan was four and used him in a two-reel comedy and in his first feature-length film, *The Kid.* Jackie became an international celebrity after playing the bright-eyed ragamuffin. During the 1920s Jackie Coogan was among the highest paid persons in the world. For switching from First National to Metro he got a bonus of a half million dollars and a two year contract that called for one million dollars and a percentage of the profits. By 1935 Jackie Coogan was almost forgotten as his roles dwindled along with his cuteness. That year he was supposed to receive the four million dollars he had earned as a child. By 1937, when he married Betty Grable, he was desperate for money so he brought a suit in court for his earnings. His mother and his stepfather were determined that they would keep it. By the time the case was settled, Jackie's share was only $126,000 out of all the millions he had earned. This abuse led to the passage of California's Child Actors Bill, known as the Coogan Act. In the 1960s Jackie was a television actor. He was in "McKeever and the Colonel" from September

1962 to June 1963, and he played the ghoolish Uncle Fester on "The Addams Family" from September of 1964 to September of 1966. He also played character parts in many films as an adult.

DOLLS:
1. JACKIE COOGAN. Horsman, 1921. 13½in (34.3cm). *Illustrations 226* and *227*.
2. COOGAN KID. Dean's Rag Dolls, circa 1921. All-cloth with lithographed features. Made in England.
3. UNCLE FESTER of THE ADDAMS FAMILY. Remco, 1964. vinyl head with painted features; plastic body. Copyright by Filmways T.V. Prod. Inc. 5in (12.7cm).
4. THE ADDAMS FAMILY. Hand puppet. Ideal, 1964.

Illustration 226. 13½in (34.3cm) JACKIE COOGAN as *The Kid* by Horsman, 1921. Composition shoulder plate head and arms; cloth body. Painted, molded reddish brown hair; painted brown eyes. The original costume is an orange shirt, gray pants, brown shoes and a black and white check hat. Head marked: "E.I.H.Co. // 19 © 21." The pin is original. The pants are labeled: "JACKIE COOGAN KID // LICENSED BY JACKIE COOGAN // PATENT PENDING." *Jean Pritchard Collection.*

Illustration 227. 13½in (34.3cm) JACKIE COOGAN by Horsman, 1921. This doll is like the one in *Illustration 226,* except that the turtle neck shirt is aqua.

COOK, FREDERICK ALBERT. Arctic explorer. Born 1865; died 1940. Cook claimed that he scaled Mt. McKinley in 1906 and reached the North Pole in 1908. Explorer Robert E. Peary accused him of fraud, and he was stripped of his honors. Later Cook was involved in an oil field swindle and was imprisoned from 1925 to 1930.

DOLLS:
1. COOK. Advertised in *Playthings,* September 1909. Probably a jointed doll with a bisque head and a composition body. Dressed in Eskimo clothing. Sold by the Strobel & Wilken Co. of New York.

COOK, JAMES. English explorer and navigator. Born 1728; died 1779. Cook circumnavigated the globe from 1768 to 1771, exploring Australia and New Zealand. The purpose of his expedition of 1772 to 1775 was to discredit the rumor of a great southern continent in the Pacific Ocean. In 1778 he rediscovered the Sandwich Islands (Hawaii), where he was killed by Hawaiian natives.

DOLLS:
1. CAPTAIN JAMES COOK. Peggy Nisbet, No. P798, 1970s. Plastic "collectors' doll." Made in England. About 8in (20.3cm).

CORBY, ELLEN. Actress. Born Ellen Hansen on June 3, 1913. After working for 12 years as a script girl, Ellen Corby became a character actress in the 1940s. She was nominated for an Academy Award for her part as the lovelorn aunt in *I Remember Mama* (1948). She was Esther (Grandma) Walton on "The Waltons" from the beginning of the show in September 1972. She was not seen during the 1977-1978 season until the last episode because she had suffered a stroke. Ellen Corby was far from being fully recovered so the scene was brief.

DOLLS:
1. GRANDMA and GRANDPA from THE WALTONS. Mego, 1975. Will Geer as Grandpa is part of the packaged set. 8in (20.3cm). *Illustration 228.*

Illustration 228. 8in (20.3cm) ELLEN CORBY as *Grandma Esther Walton* from "The Waltons" by Mego, 1974. All-vinyl and fully-jointed. Rooted white hair and painted gray eyes. Head marked: "© 1974 // LORIMAR INC." *Penny Caswell Collection.*

COREY, JEFF. Character actor. Born August 10, 1914. During the 1940s Corey played a wide range of character roles in films. During the 1950s he concentrated on running an acting school. He returned to films in the 1960s, again in character parts.

DOLLS:

1. SHERIFF RAY BLEDSOE from BUTCH AND SUNDANCE, THE EARLY DAYS. Kenner, No. 53040, 1979. Made in Hong Kong. 4in (10.2cm). *Illustration 229.*

Illustration 229. 4in (10.2cm) JEFF COREY as *Sheriff Ray Bledsoe* from *Butch and Sundance: The Early Days* by Kenner, No. 53040, 1979. All-vinyl and fully-jointed. Painted hair and features. Copyright by Twentieth Century-Fox Film Corporation. Made in Hong Kong.

CRABBE, (LARRY) BUSTER. Actor. Born Clarence Linden Crabbe on February 17, 1907. Buster Crabbe grew up in Hawaii where he became an excellent swimmer. He entered the Olympics in 1932 and won a gold medal, breaking the previous record of Johnny Weissmuller. Like Weissmuller, he headed for Hollywood and played Tarzan. He starred in many action-adventure pictures. He was in the serials of Buck Rogers, Flash Gordon and Billy the Kid. During the 1950s he was on television as "Captain Gallant of the French Foreign Legion." Later he became involved in the swimming pool business.

DOLLS

1. FLASH GORDON. Mattel, No. 1525, 1980. Made in Hong Kong. 4in (10.2cm). *Illustration 231*.

Illustration 230. Charles Middleton as Ming the Merciless and Buster Crabbe as Flash Gordon in *Flash Gordon's Trip to Mars,* 1938.

Illustraiton 231. 4in (10.2cm) BUSTER CRABBE as *Flash Gordon* by Mattel, No. 1525, 1980. All-vinyl and fully-jointed. Painted yellow hair and painted features. Copyright 1979 by King Features Syndicate, Inc. Made in Hong Kong.

CRAIG, YVONNE. Actress, dancer. Born May 16, 1941. Yvonne Craig played Barbara Gordon—Batgirl on "Batman" during 1967 and 1968.

DOLLS:

1. BATGIRL. Mego, No. 1343, 1974. All-vinyl and fully-jointed. Made in Hong Kong. 7½in (19.1cm).

CRAVEN, GEMMA. Actress. Born 1950. Gemma Craven was the lovely young actress chosen to play Cinderella in the musical film *The Slipper and the Rose,* British 1976. Everyone in the film, including Richard Chamberlain as the Prince, sang and danced.

DOLLS:

1. CINDERELLA. Dinky Toys, 1976. Made in England. *Illustration 232.*

Illustration 232. GEMMA CRAVEN in Cinderella's Coach from *The Slipper and the Rose* by Dinkey Toys, 1976. A small plastic doll is seated inside the metal and plastic coach that measures 9½in (24.2cm) long and is 2½in (6.4cm) high. Copyright by Paradine Co-Productions Limited. Made in England.

CREWS, LAURA HOPE. Actress. Born December 12, 1879; died 1942. From the ages of four to seven Laura Hope Crews acted on the stage. She returned at age 19 and played leading ladies on Broadway. In films her most typical parts were as mothers and aunts. Her best known portrayal was as the silly Aunt Pittypat in *Gone With the Wind* in 1939.

DOLLS:
1. AUNT PITTYPAT. Madame Alexander, No. 435, 1957. All-hard plastic; jointed-knee walker. Back marked: "ALEX." 8in (20.3cm).

CRISCOULA, PETER GEORGE JOHN. (PETER of KISS). Rock musician. Born December 20, 1947, in Brooklyn, New York. Peter left the group KISS and performed as himself in 1980.

DOLLS:
1. PETER of KISS. Mego, No. 88000/3, 1978. Made in Hong Kong. 12½in (31.8cm). *Illustration 233.*
SEE: KISS.

Illustration 233. 12½in (31.8cm) PETER GEORGE JOHN CRISCOULA, *Peter of KISS*, by Mego, No. 88000/3, 1978. All-vinyl and fully-jointed. Rooted hair and painted features and makeup. Head marked: " © 1978 AUCOIN // MGMT. INC." Back marked: "© MEGO CORP. 1977 // MADE IN HONG KONG." Copyright by Aucoin Management, Inc. by agreement with KISS, a partnership. *Penny Caswell Collection.*

Illustration 234. 11½in (29.2cm) DAVY CROCKETT by Marx Toys, circa 1964. Very heavy vinyl. Jointed only at head, shoulders, elbows and wrists. Painted hair and features. Marked: "LOUIS MARX & CO., INC." on right foot; "MARX TOYS" on back. *Phyllis Houston Collection.*

CROCKETT, DAVY. American frontiersman. Born 1786; died 1836. Davy Crockett was a United States Representative from Tennessee from 1827 to 1831 and from 1833 to 1835. He was known for his humor and his tall tales. He died defending the Alamo during the War with Mexico. His exploits, real and legendary, were popularized with the episodes of "Davy Crockett" on the "Walt Disney" television program on ABC-TV in December of 1954 and January and February of 1955. Davy Crockett became a national fad.

DOLLS:
1. DAVY CROCKETT. Madame Alexander, 1955. All-hard plastic. Red fur wig. Wears yellow fleece "coonskin cap with a tail." 8in (20.3cm).

2. DAVY CROCKETT. Vogue, 1955. All-hard plastic "Ginny" doll dressed as a boy and wearing a coonskin cap. Identified by a gold sticker on the costume. 8in (20.3cm).
3. DAVY CROCKETT. Marx Toys, circa 1964. 11½in (29.2cm). *Illustration 234.*
4. DAVY CROCKETT. Mego, No. 1362, 1973. All-vinyl and fully-jointed. Made in Hong Kong. 7½in (19.1cm).
5. DAVY CROCKETT. Excel Toy Corp., No. 100, 1973. Made in Hong Kong. 9¼in (23.6cm). *Illustration 235.*
6. DAVY CROCKETT. Carolina Enterprises, Inc., 1978. All-vinyl. 4¼in (10.9cm).
7. DAVY CROCKETT. Effanbee, No. 1154, 1977. All-vinyl and fully-jointed. Rooted brown hair; brown sleep eyes with lashes. 11in (27.9cm).
8. DAVY CROCKETT. Hallmark, No. 400DT11402, 1979. Made in Taiwan. 6¾in (17.2cm). *Illustration 236.*
SEE: FESS PARKER.

Illustration 235. 9¼in (23.6cm) DAVY CROCKETT from the "Legends of the West" series by Excel Toy Corp., No. 100, 1973. All-vinyl with painted hair and eyes. Fully-jointed with extra joints at the elbows, knees and wrists. Head marked: " © EXCEL TOY CORP. // HONG KONG."

CULP, ROBERT. Actor. Born August 16, 1930. Culp entered the entertainment profession by acting on Broadway. He then appeared in motion pictures and became a star from his television series shows. On television he was the star of "Trackdown" on CBS from October 1957 to February 1959; "I Spy" with Bill Cosby on NBC from September 1965 to September 1968; and with William Katt as "The Greatest American Hero," playing Bill, the FBI agent, since March 14, 1981, on ABC.

DOLLS:
1. BILL. Mego, No. 22010, 1982. All-vinyl and fully-jointed. Painted hair, features and clothing. Comes in a set called "The Greatest American Hero Free-Wheeling Convertible Bug With Ralph and Bill." Copyright by Stephen J. Connell Productions.* 3¾in (9.6cm).
2. BILL. Mego, Series No. 22001, 1982. All-vinyl and fully-jointed. Painted hair and features. Copyright by Stephen J. Connell Productions.* 8in (20.3cm).

SEE: GREATEST AMERICAN HERO, THE.
*So stated in the Mego catalog. The television show is produced by Stephen J. Cannell Productions.

CUSTER, GEORGE ARMSTRONG. American army officer. Born 1839; died 1876. As a youthful general during the Civil War, Custer came to military prominence. In 1876 at the junction of the Little Horn and the Big Horn Rivers in Montana, Custer made his "last stand" against the Sioux. He and 200 of his men were killed by the Indians. The site is now a National Monument. Elizabeth Bacon Custer (1842-1933) devoted most of her life to upholding her husband's memory.

DOLLS:
1. GENERAL CUSTER AND HIS FAVORITE MOUNT "BUGLER." Hartland Plastics, No. 814, 1958. Plastic with jointed arms; carries an American flag. Made in Hartland, Wisconsin. About 8in (20.3cm).
2. GENERAL CUSTER. Louis Marx and Co., Inc., 1968. Solid, heavy vinyl; fully-jointed. Painted features and clothing with long blonde hair. Made in USA. 11½in (29.2cm).
3. GENERAL CUSTER. Peggy Nisbet, No. P823, early 1980s. Plastic "collectors' doll." Made in England. About 8in (20.3cm).

SEE: THE LONE RANGER.

D

DAFOE, ALLAN ROY. Canadian country doctor in Callander, Ontario, Canada; personal physician of the Dionne Quintuplets. Born May 29, 1883; died 1943. Shortly after he delivered the world's first set of surviving quintuplets on May 28, 1934, Dr. Dafoe became as internationally famous as the Quints themselves. Because of his quarrels with the Dionne parents, Dafoe resigned his position as the Quints' personal physician on February 14, 1942. The cause of much of this was the lucrative product endorsements from which Dafoe earned an undisclosed sum of money, his exclusive rights with the Quints and the legal battles

Illustration 236. 6¾in (17.2cm) DAVY CROCKETT by Hallmark, No. 400DT114-2, 1979. All-cloth with printed clothing and features. Copyright by Hallmark Cards, August 1979. Made in Taiwan.

with Oliva and Elzire Dionne to have the Quints returned to their custody.

DOLLS:
1. DOCTOR DOLL FOR THE QUINTS. Madame Alexander, 1936. 14½in (36.9cm). *Illustration 237*.

Illustration 237. 14½in (36.9cm) DR. DAFOE, the *Doctor Doll for the Quints*, by Madame Alexander, 1936. All-composition and fully-jointed. Gray mohair wig; painted blue eyes; dimple in chin. The doll is not marked. The original outfit is a doctor's smock over a one-piece pants and shirt combination and is labeled only "Madame / Alexander / New York." *Ruby K. Arnold Collection. Photo by Phyllis Houston.* This doll was *never* advertised as Dr. Dafoe, but all doll buyers knew whom the doll represented. It also tied into the publicity of the 1936 film *The Country Doctor*, a fiction about the Quints.

DALTON, ARLENE. Television personality. Arlene Dalton played the "Story Princess" on "Howdy Doody." The program began on NBC-TV on December 27, 1947, and continued until September 24, 1960.

DOLLS:
1. STORY PRINCESS. Madame Alexander, No. 1560, 1954. All-hard plastic and fully-jointed. "Margaret face." 15in (38.1cm).
2. STORY PRINCESS. Madame Alexander, No. 1860, 1954. All-hard plastic and fully-jointed. "Cissy face." 18in (45.7cm).
3. STORY PRINCESS. Madame Alexander, No. 1549, 1955. All-hard plastic and fully-jointed. "Cissy face." 15in (38.1cm).
4. STORY PRINCESS. Madame Alexander, No. 892, 1956. All-hard plastic and fully-jointed. 8in (20.3cm).
5. STORY PRINCESS. Madame Alexander, No. 1592, 1956. All-hard plastic and fully-jointed. "Cissy face." 15in (38.1cm).
6. STORY PRINCESS. Madame Alexander, No. 1892, 1956. All-hard plastic and fully-jointed. "Cissy face." 18in (45.7cm).

NOTE: All the Story Princess dolls are labeled as such on the long gown. The "Cissy face" dolls are marked on the head: "ALEX."

DANIELS, ANTHONY Actor. Anthony Daniels played the tall, verbose robot C-3PO (See Threepio) in the films *Star Wars* (1977) and *The Empire Strikes Back* (1980).

DOLLS:
1. C-3PO (SEE THREEPIO). Kenner, No. 38220, 1978. 3¾in (12.2cm).
2. C-3PO (SEE THREEPIO). Kenner, No. 38620, 1978. 12in (30.5cm).
3. SEE-THREEPIO (C-3PO) WITH REMOVABLE LIMBS. Kenner, Series No. 69570, 1982. All-plastic and fully-jointed. Comes with a carrying basket. Copyright by Lucasfilm Ltd. Made in Hong Kong. 3¾in (9.6cm).

SEE: STAR WARS.

DANIELS, MICKEY. Child actor. Born 1916. Mickey Daniels played mischievous Freckles in the "Our Gang" comedies beginning in 1922. In the late 1960s he was a supervisor for an iron ore mine in Tasmania.

DOLLS: SEE: OUR GANG.

DARE, VIRGINIA. American colonial child. Born August 18, 1587, on Roanoke Island, Virginia (now North Carolina); died circa 1587. Virginia Dare was not the first white child born in the New World. This distinction belongs to Snorri, a child of the Vikings born in Newfoundland in about 1001. Virginia Dare was the first English baby born in America. She was the grandchild of John White, the founder of the colony. She is known to have lived at least nine days, when White left for England for more supplies. When he returned in 1591 he found no traces of the settlers and their disappearance has always been a mystery.

DOLLS:
1. VIRGINIA DARE. Madame Alexander, 1940. All-composition and fully-jointed. Painted blue eyes. 9in (22.9cm).
2. VIRGINIA DARE. Maker unknown, circa 1950. All-cloth. Made in USA. 7¾in (19.8cm). *Illustration 238*.

Illustration 238. 7¾in (19.8cm) VIRGINIA DARE, maker unknown, circa 1950. All-cloth except for composition arms. The molded cloth face has painted features with blue eyes; yellow yarn wig. The tag also includes: "DESIGN PATENT NO. 128,796 // MADE IN AMERICA. A-MERICA'S FIRST WHITE CHILD." (Refer to biography of Virginia Dare. She was the first English child, *not* the first white child.) *Pat Geikler Collection.*

Illustration 239. THE DAVE CLARK FIVE by Remco, No. 1808, 1964. 5in (12.7cm) Dave Clark (center) has a vinyl head with rooted black hair and painted black eyes. The body is one-piece and is plastic. Head marked: "DAVE CLARK // 19 © 64 // REMCO IND. INC." Back marked: "DAVE // CLARK // 5 // © REMCO IND." At the left of Dave Clark are Rick Huxley and Mike Smith; to the right of Dave are Lenny Davidson and Denis Payton. These four 3in (7.6cm) figures are plastic and are not marked except for the name tags attached to the legs.

THE DAVE CLARK FIVE. The five members of the band joined together in 1964 to finance their way to a soccer game in Holland, in which they were all on the English team. If there had been no Beatles, there probably would not have been The Dave Clark Five. Their style and act was similar. The members of the group were DAVE CLARK on drums, RICK HUXLEY and LENNY DAVIDSON on guitar, DENIS PAYTON on sax and MIKE SMITH as the lead singer. The Dave Clark Five toured the United States in the Spring of 1964, arriving months before the Beatles. Like the Beatles, they were introduced to the American public on "The Ed Sullivan Show," on which they appeared 32 times. The biggest song hits of the Dave Clark Five were "Glad All Over" and "Because" in 1964 and "I Like It Like That" and "Over and Over" in 1965. The group disbanded in 1970.
DOLLS:
1. THE DAVE CLARK FIVE. Remco, No. 1808, 1964. 5in (12.7cm) and 3in (7.6cm). *Illustration 239*.

DAVID. Second King of Israel. Born in the 11th century BC. David ruled from about 1013 to 973 BC and was the symbol of the ideal king in the Jewish tradition. It was David who united the tribes of Israel into one nation, completed the conquest of the Promised Land and established Jerusalem as the capital of the united kingdom.
DOLLS:
1. DAVID. Madame Alexander, 1954. All-hard plastic and fully-jointed. Caracul wig; sleep eyes with lashes. 8in (20.3cm).

DAVID, JACKIE. Child actor. Jackie David was one of the original members of the "Our Gang" series beginning in 1922. He was the brother-in-law of actor Harold Lloyd.
DOLLS: SEE: OUR GANG

DAVIDSON, LENNY. One of the members of the rock and roll group THE DAVE CLARK FIVE. He played guitar.
SEE: THE DAVE CLARK FIVE and *Illustration 239*.

DAVIS, GAIL. Actress. Born Betty Jeanne Grayson on October 5, 1925. Gail Davis played the lead in the ABC-TV show "Annie Oakley" from 1953 to 1958. The setting of the series was the town of Diablo in the 1860s, where Annie, a woman rancher and sharpshooter, attempted to maintain law and order. Annie's horse was Buttercup on the show. (The television series had almost no relation to the life of the real Annie Oakley.)

DOLLS:
1. ANNIE OAKLEY AND HER HORSE TARGET. Hartland Plastics, No. 823, circa 1958. Plastic doll and horse. Doll about 8in (20.3cm). The original advertising stated: "We have used Gail Davis as a model for this figure and it is perfectly executed." Made in Hartland, Wisconsin.

DAVIS, SPENCER. Musician and singer. Born July 17, 1942, in England. In 1963 Spencer Davis formed The Spencer Davis Group, a rock band in the tradition of the Beatles. During the 1960s the group had some hit records. The real talent of the group was 16 year old Stevie Winwood who did vocals and played guitar and keyboards. Winwood left The Spencer David Group in 1967 to form the more successful group Traffic. There was a constant shuffling of group members and styles in The Spencer Davis Group and about a dozen different performers were in it at one time or another. After Winwood left The Spencer Davis Group, it wasted away.
DOLLS:
1. SPENCER DAVIS. A "Show Biz Baby" by Hasbro, No. 8813, 1968. All-vinyl with a jointed head. Rooted blonde hair; painted features. Attached to a 33 1/3 rpm record. Made in Hong Kong. 4in (10.2cm).

DAWBER, PAM. Actress. Born in Detroit, Michigan, on October 18, 1951. Pam Dawber began playing the girl who befriended Mork from the distant planet Ork on ABC-TV's "Mork and Mindy" in September of 1978.
DOLLS:
1. PAM DAWBER AS MINDY from MORK AND MINDY. Mattel, No. 1277, 1979. Made in Taiwan. 8¾in (22.3cm). *Illustrations 240* and *241*.
SEE: ROBIN WILLIAMS.

Illustration 240. 8¾in (22.3cm) PAM DAWBER as *Mindy* from "Mork and Mindy" by Mattel, No. 1277, 1979. All-vinyl and fully-jointed. Rooted long brown hair; painted blue eyes. Head marked: "TAIWAN // © 1979 PPC." Lower back marked: " © 1973 // MATTEL, INC. // TAIWAN." Copyright by Paramount Pictures Corporation. *Penny Caswell Collection.*

Illustration 241. PAM DAWBER by Mattel. *Penny Caswell Collection.*

DEADWOOD DICK. (NAT LOVE or RICHARD W. CLARKE). American frontiersman who became famous because of "dime novels" in the 19th century. According to the information on the box from the Excel doll, Deadwood Dick was born a black slave in Tennessee in 1854. When he was 15 he went to Kansas and was adopted by an Indian tribe. He was the most famous of the thousands of black cowboys and was friends with legendary heroes such as the James Brothers and Billy the Kid. Other sources cite Richard W. Clarke (1845-1930), an Englishman who came to the gold diggings of the Black Hills and later became a scout, as being Deadwood Dick.
DOLLS:
1. DEADWOOD DICK: Excel Toy Corp., No. 200, 1973. Fully-jointed vinyl figure with "authentic costume." Made in Hong Kong. 9½in (24.2cm).

De CARLO, YVONNE. Actress. Born Peggy Yvonne Middleton in Vancouver, British Columbia, Canada, on September 1, 1922. Yvonne De Carlo was a dancer since childhood and entered films in 1942. In 1945 she was starred in the role *Salome—Where She Danced* and became typecast as an exotic Arabian Nights beauty in scores of adventure films. She played Lily Munster on the CBS-TV comedy-horror series "The Munsters" from September 1964 to September 1966. In 1971 she was on Broadway in the musical "Follies."
DOLLS:
1. LILY MUNSTER. Remco, No. 1822, 1964. Vinyl with a jointed head. Rooted black hair and painted features. Copyright by Karo-Vue Productions. 4¾in (12.2cm).

DeHAVILLAND, OLIVIA. Actress. Born July 1, 1916, in Tokyo, Japan, of British parents. Olivia De Havilland came to California with her mother and her sister, Joan Fontaine, after her parents' divorce. In 1933, while in college, she appeared in "A Midsummer Night's Dream" and was cast in the film in 1935. Her early roles for Warner Brothers were in action films, many of them opposite Errol Flynn. She was cast as the demure Melanie in *Gone With the Wind* (1939) and was perfect for the part. In 1946 she won the Academy Award for *To*

Each His Own and another in 1949 for *The Heiress.* Her most recent film assignments were in horror movies.

DOLLS:

1. MELANIE. Madame Alexander, No. 2235, 1961. All-hard plastic and fully-jointed "Portrait Doll," using the "Cissy mold." Dark brown wig; blue sleep eyes with lashes. 21in (53.3cm).
2. MELANIE. Madame Alexander, No. 2181, 1968. 21in (53.3cm). *Illustrations 242* and *243.*
3. MELANIE. Madame Alexander, No. 2193, 1969. "Portrait Doll," using the "Jacqueline face." 21in (53.3cm).
4. MELANIE. Madame Alexander, No. 2196, 1970. Similar to the 1969 Portrait Doll. 21in (53.3cm).
5. MELANIE. Madame Alexander, No. 2162, 1971. Similar to the 1969 Portrait Doll. 21in (53.3cm).

NOTE: Madame Alexander made other dolls called Melanie, but they are blondes and can not be considered as the Melanie from *Gone With the Wind.*

Illustration 242. 21in (53.3cm) OLIVIA DeHAVIL-LAND as *Melanie* by Madame Alexander, No. 2181, 1968. All-vinyl. Dark wig; brown sleep eyes with lashes. This doll is the "Jacqueline" face. *Ted Menten Collection. Photograph by Ted Menten.*

Illustration 243. Melanie by Madame Alexander *Ted Menten Collection. Photograph by Ted Menten.*

De KEROUALLE, LOUISE (DUCHESS OF PORT-SMITH). Mistress of King Charles II of England (ruled 1660 to 1685). The Duchess and the King had a son, Charles Lennox, the Duke of Richmond, one of Charles' acknowledged 14 illegitimate offspring.

DOLLS:

1. DUCHESS OF PORTSMITH. Peggy Nisbet, No. LE83, 1970s. Plastic. Part of the "Special Collectors' Set King Charles II, 'the Merry Monarch' and three of his favorite mistresses." Made in England. About 7½in (19.1cm). See *Illustration 188.*

DENNEHY, BRIAN. Actor who played O.C. "Camilla" Hanks in the film *Butch and Sundance: The Early Days,* 1979.

DOLLS:

1. O.C. HANKS. Kenner, No. 53030, 1979. Made in Hong Kong. 4in (10.2cm). *Illustration 244.*

Illustration 244. 4in (10.2cm) BRIAN DENNEHY as *O.C. Camilla Hanks* from *Butch and Sundance: The Early Days* by Kenner, No. 53030, 1979. All-vinyl and fully-jointed. Painted hair; hat molded to head; painted features. Copyright by Twentieth Century-Fox Film Corporation. Made in Hong Kong.

De VOS, CORNELIS, DAUGHTER OF. Child who appears in the painting "The Artist's Daughter." Dutch artist Cornelis De Vos painted his oil portrait in about 1627. It is now in Chateworth Settlement in England.

DOLLS:

1. THE ARTIST'S DAUGHTER. Doll Classics by Al Trattner, 1982. Made in Delaware. 12in (30.5cm). *Illustration 244-A.*

Illustration 244-A. 12in (30.5cm) DAUGHTER of artist Cornelis DE VOS by Doll Classics by Al Trattner, 1982. All-bisque and fully-jointed. Reddish hair; brown glass eyes; pierced nostrils. Note the straps on the costume at the arms. In the 17th century these straps were attached to the back of a little girl's dress so her governess could support her as she walked on her high heeled shoes. A limited edition of 1500 dolls. Made in Delaware. Based on the painting "The Artist's Daughter" by Cornelis De Vos. Head marked: "Doll Classics // by // Al Trattner // © 1982 // DMS // SCD // 1-82." *Photograph Courtesy of Al Trattner.*

DEWEY, GEORGE. American admiral. Born 1837; died 1917. In 1898 Dewey was considered a great hero for annihilating the Spanish fleet in the Battle of Manila Bay during the three month Spanish-American War. Because of the resulting enthusiasm for America's most popular war, Dewey was briefly touted as Presidential material.

DOLLS:
1. GEORGE DEWEY. Manufacturer unknown, circa 1910. 15½in (39.4cm). *Illustration 245.*
SEE: SPANISH-AMERICAN WAR HEROES.

DEY, SUSAN. Actress. Born September 10, 1952. Susan Dey gained prominence by playing teenage Laurie Partridge on ABC-TV's "The Partridge Family" from September 1970 to September 1974. This situation comedy featured Shirley Jones and her step-son, David Cassidy, and told of the exploits of a family of traveling rock musicians and singers. The group had hit records, and the series was based on a real-life family of singers, the Cowsills. Susan Dey was also on the mini-series "Loves Me, Loves Me Not" in the Spring of 1977.

DOLLS:
1. LAURIE PARTRIDGE. Remco, 1973. 19in (48.3cm). *Illustration 246.*

Illustration 245. 15½in (39.4cm) GEORGE DEWEY, manufacturer unknown, circa 1910. Bisque head on a jointed composition body. Painted hair and moustache; glass eyes. Part of a series of six different officers from the Spanish-American War. *Courtesy of the Margaret Woodbury Strong Museum.*

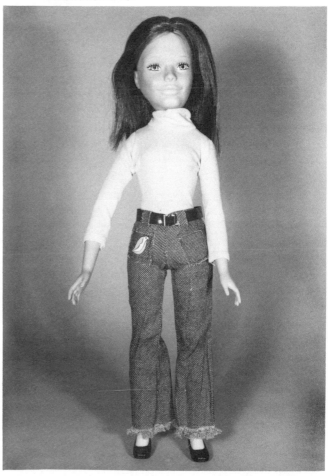

Illustration 246. 19in (48.3cm) SUSAN DEY as *Laurie Patridge* from "The Partridge Family" by Remco, 1973. Vinyl head, arms and legs; plastic torso. Rooted long brown hair; painted eyes and lashes. Head marked: "© 1973 // REMCO IND. INC. // HARRISON, N.J. // ITEM NO. 3461." *Shirley Buchholz Collection.*

PRINCESS DIANA. The Princess of Wales. Born July 1, 1961. On television on July 29, 1981, an estimated 750 million persons around the world watched Lady Diana Spencer marry Charles, the Prince of Wales in St. Paul's Cathedral in London, England. This was the first wedding of a Prince of Wales since 1863. Lady Diana married the Prince after a five-month engagement and after years of speculation by the public about whom would become his Princess. Lady Diana was *the* celebrity of 1981. Famous celebrities have become princesses, but future Princess Lady Diana became a famous and widely admired celebrity. She brought out the romanticism in human nature and proved that a future queen of the United Kingdom could be informal and still have style and class. Diana very quickly became widely imitated—her hairdo, her clothes and ruffled collars became fashion trendsetters at once. After the wedding the newlyweds set off on the royal yacht *Britannia* to be alone (with a crew of 276) for their honeymoon. Within weeks it was announced that in June 1982 bells would peal, cannons would roar and bonfires would burn to greet the arrival of a royal baby.

DOLLS:
1. LADY DIANA SPENCER. Peggy Nisbet, No. P428, 1981. Prince Charles in Uniform of Colonel-in-Chief, No. P426, was used as a companion doll. Made in England. 7½in (19.1cm). *Illustration 246-B*.
2. LADY DIANA SPENCER. Dean's Rag Book Co., Ltd., 1981. All-cloth with printed features. Prince Charles was part of the set. Made in Rye, Sussex, England. 16in (40.6cm).
3. PRINCE AND PRINCESS OF WALES. THE MARRIAGE OF THE CENTURY. Peggy Nisbet Limited Edition Collectors' Set No. 19, for the Royal Wedding, No. 1005, 1981-1982. Limited to 4000 sets. Plastic. Made in England.
4. A ROYAL BRIDE—DIANA, PRINCESS OF WALES. Effanbee Limited Edition Doll Club, 1982. 18in (45.7cm). *Illustration 246-C*.

NOTE: Peggy Nisbet also made a set of dolls called Elder and Younger Bridesmaids, No. P430 and P431, to go with Doll No. 3. and Prince Charles. 7½in (19.1cm). *Illustration 246-D.* There is also a doll of The Archbishop of Canterbury (see RUNCIE) in 8in (20.3cm) to go with this set.

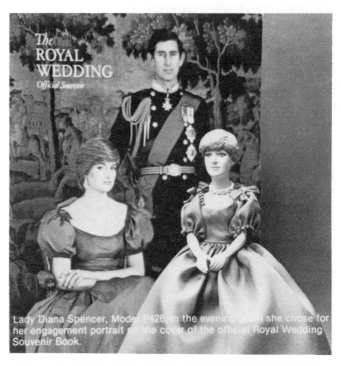

Lady Diana Spencer, Model P428, in the evening gown she chose for her engagement portrait on the cover of the official Royal Wedding Souvenir Book.

Illustration 246-B. 7½in (21.6cm) LADY DIANA SPENCER by Peggy Nisbet, No. P428, 1981. Plastic with painted features and vinyl hair. Jointed at the arms. Lady Diana is wearing "the evening gown she chose for her engagement portrait on the cover of the official Royal Wedding Souvenir Book." The gown is green. Made in England. *From Peggy Nisbet folder, July 1981*.

Illustration 246-C. 18in (45.7cm) DIANA, THE PRINCESS OF WALES by Effanbee for the Limited Edition Doll Club, 1982 presentation. All-vinyl and fully-jointed. Brown wig; painted blue eyes. Candlelight ecru gown of silk-like fabric, long veil of bridal tulle. The bouquet is ribbons and white roses. Head marked: "EFFANBEE // LIMITED EDITION © 1982 // PRINCESS DIANA." Back marked: "EFFANBEE // LIMITED EDITION © 1982 // PRINCESS DIANA." From *Effanbee Limited Edition Doll Club* advertising page.

Illustration 246-A. Prince Charles and Lady Diana on a 25p British stamp, 29 July 1981.

Illustration 246-D. 7½in (19.1cm) "Elder and Younger Royal Bridesmaids" from the wedding party of Lady Diana Spencer on July 29, 1981, by Peggy Nisbet, No. P430 and No. P431, 1982. Plastic with jointed arms. Painted features. The bridesmaid on the left has a blonde mohair wig; the lady on the right has a dark mohair wig. Made in England. *Photograph Courtesy of House of Nisbet.*

DICKINSON, ANGIE. Actress. Born Angeline Brown September 30, 1931, in Kulm, North Dakota. Angie Dickinson began in films as a starlet in 1954 and played small parts for years. Her most famous part was as Sgt. Suzanne "Pepper" Martin on NBC-TV's "Police Woman" from September 1974 to August 1978. In the series Angie Dickinson posed as an undercover cop in all sorts of guises, from prostitutes to gun molls.

DOLLS:

1. ANGIE DICKINSON AS "POLICE WOMAN." Horsman, No. 8000, 1976. 9in (22.9cm). *Illustration 247.*

Illustratin 247. 9in (22.9cm) ANGIE DICKINSON as "Police Woman" by Horsman, No. 8000, 1976. All-vinyl and fully-jointed. Rooted blonde hair; painted brown eyes. Head marked: "HORSMAN DOLLS INC. // U // L CPT // 19 © 76." Copyright by Columbia Pictures Television.

DIONNE QUINTUPLETS (YVONNE, ANNETTE, CECILE, EMILIE and MARIE). During the 1930s the Dionne Quintuplets were the most famous children in the world. They were born near Corbeil, Ontario, Canada, on May 28, 1934. Emilie died August 6, 1954; Marie died February 24, 1970; the three surviving Quintuplets live near Montreal, Quebec, Canada. Because of the Dionne Quintuplets, the most famous citizens Canada ever had, many other people also became popular magazine and newspaper copy from 1934 until the early 1940s. Among these were Dr. Allan Roy Dafoe, the doctor who delivered the world's first set of quintuplets who lived beyond a few days; Yvonne Leroux and the other nurses who attended the babies; and parents Oliva and Elzire Dionne. In September of 1934 the babies were placed in a special nursery and were raised as wards of the government of Canada. By the summer of 1938 an average weekday brought 3,000 visitors to the nursery to view the Quintuplets, and daily reports were issued to news services about the girls' antics. In 1944 the Quintuplets were reunited with their family in a mansion built with their earnings from product endorsements. After Emilie's death from suffocation during an epileptic seizure in 1954 the Quints became permanently estranged from their parents, returning to Corbeil only once for the funeral of their father, who died on November 15, 1979. Marie, Annette and Cecile were married for a time; Yvonne never married. The Dionne Quintuplets are still the only set of identical quintuplets ever recorded in the history of the world.

ONLY MADAME ALEXANDER WAS EVER AUTHORIZED TO MAKE DIONNE QUINTUPLET DOLLS. During 1936 Madame Alexander ads in *Playthings* constantly pointed out that "Alexander Dionne Quintuplet Dolls are the *only* quintuplet dolls" and threatened to bring suit in court against all infringers. The guardians for the Dionnes had registered the name "Quintuplets" as a trademark in 1936. Madame Alexander registered "Quins," "Quinties," "Quintuplets," "Quints," and "Five Little Babies" as trademarks for dolls in the United States. There are at least 35 different sets of Dionne Quintuplet dolls by Madame Alexander, many of which were sold in various outfits. Other companies made "Quintuplet Dolls," but they were NEVER advertised as the Dionnes. The Dionne Quintuplet dolls are listed by sizes, with the years of the first issue given. Dionne-type and Dionne-knock-off dolls are shown in the accompanying *Illustrations 261* through *272.* The most commonly seen Dionne-type dolls were made by Superior, circa 1935, marked "SUPERIOR," and were made in the United States in the 7in (17.8cm) size. Others were "Tinyette Quints" by Effanbee, 1935, marked "EFFANBEE // BABY TINYETTE," 6½in (16.5cm) and "Five Baby Dolls and Nurse" by Ralph A. Freundlich, Inc., 1935, 7in (17.8cm) babies with a 9½in (24.2cm) nurse. Many kinds of Quintuplet dolls also came from Japan in the late 1930s and again after World War II. Several examples of these are also illustrated. (*Illustrations 268* through *279.*)

MADAME ALEXNADER DIONNE QUINTUPLET DOLLS: (Listed by size with the first year of issue given. All the dolls, unless noted, are all-composition and fully-jointed.)

Babies:

1. 7in (17.8cm). Painted straight hair; painted brown eyes. Marked on heads: "DIONNE // ALEXANDER." 1935. *Illustration 249*.

2. 7in (17.8cm). Mohair wig over molded, straight hair; painted brown eyes. Marked like No. 1. Circa 1936.

3. 7in (17.8cm). Molded curly hair; painted brown eyes. Head and back marked: "ALEXANDER." 1936. *Illustrations 250, 251,* and *253*.

4. 10in (25.4cm). Painted straight hair; closed mouth; brown sleep eyes with lashes. Head marked: ""DIONNE" // ALEXANDER." Back marked: "MADAME // ALEXANDER." 1935. *Illustration 252*.

5. 11½in (29.2cm). Painted curly hair; open mouth; brown sleep eyes with lashes; cloth body. Head marked: "ALEXANDER." 1936.

6. 16½in (41.9cm). Painted straight hair; closed mouth; brown sleep eyes with lashes; cloth body. Head marked: ""DIONNE" // ALEXANDER." 1935.

7. 17½in (44.5cm). Painted curly hair; closed mouth; brown sleep eyes with lashes; cloth body. Head marked: "ALEXANDER." 1936.

8. 23in (58.4cm). Painted straight hair; open mouth with teeth; brown sleep eyes with lashes; cloth body. Head marked: ""DIONNE" // ALEXANDER." 1935.

Illustration 249. 7in (17.8cm) DIONNE QUINTUPLET curved leg babies with the molded straight hair by Madame Alexander, 1935. Each quint wears a diaper, undershirt and a bib with her name embroidered on it. The furniture is also from 1935 and is rather plain white, painted wood and was sold with a set of babies and a nurse in a cardboard room called the "Dionne Quintuplet's Home." The furniture is unmarked. It was made for Alexander by S.B. Novelties of New York. The dolls are marked on the heads: "DIONNE // ALEXANDER." The backs are marked: "ALEXANDER."

Illustration 248. The Dionne Quintuplets from a 1936 calendar. The picture was taken in 1935 when the Quints were a year old.

Illustration 252. 10in (25.4cm) YVONNE DIONNE curved-leg baby by Madame Alexander, 1935. All-composition and fully-jointed. Molded and painted straight brown hair; brown sleep eyes with lashes. She wears a white organdy dress over a white cotton slip and flannel diaper. The bib with her name is trimmed in pink, as are the knitted botties. The box is "025 EMILIE," a factory or department store mix-up. Head marked: "DIONNE" // ALEXANDER." Back marked: "MADAME ALEXANDER." *Wanda Lodwick Collection.*

Illustration 250. 7in (17.8cm) DIONNE QUINTUPLETS by Madame Alexander, about 1936. All-composition and fully-jointed. Painted and molded curly hair; painted brown eyes. Heads and backs marked: "ALEXANDER." This set is still in mint condition, and nothing has ever been removed from the original suitcase of brown leatherette. The dolls wear cotton sunsuits with matching bonnets in orchid, aqua, yellow, blue and pink. In that same order, the dolls would represent Emilie, Cecile, Annette, Marie and Yvonne. Grouped around the dolls are white slips and underpants of organdy. On the lid are attached sleeveless white organdy dresses with matching hats trimmed in the same colors as mentioned above. Only the sunsuits on the dolls are labeled: "GENUINE // DIONNE QUINTUPLET DOLLS // ALL RIGHTS RESERVED // MADAME ALEXANDER—N.Y." The suitcase has a lace-trimmed cloth lining and is not marked. It has two keys for the lock. *Jean Pritchard Collection.*

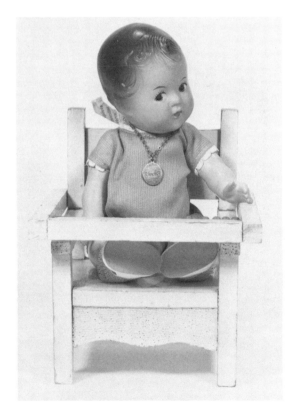

Illustration 251. 7in (17.8cm) DIONNE QUINTUPLET babies with the curly, molded hair in the "Quint-o-Bile" by Madame Alexander, late 1936. *Patricia Gardner Collection. Photograph by Patricia Gardner.*

Illustration 253. 7½in (19.1cm) EMILIE DIONNE baby by Madame Alexander, 1936. All-composition and fully-jointed. Curly molded and sprayed hair; painted brown eyes. Marked on the head and back: "ALEXANDER." The lavender pique sunsuit is labeled. The locket on a chain is a gold colored metal and is embossed: "EMELIE." (sic). These disks on the chain are rather rare; the pin is more common. The "low chair" is an original from a set that was sold with the Quintuplet dolls. (The matching bonnet was removed to show the modeling of the hair.)

Illustration 254. 7½in (19.1cm) DIONNE QUINTUPLET toddlers by Madame Alexander, circa 1936. All-composition and fully-jointed. Dark red mohair wigs over unpainted molded hair; painted brown eyes. Each doll in this set came in a separate box, and three of the original boxes are with the dolls. Heads marked: ""DIONNE // ALEXANDER." Backs marked: "ALEXANDER." *Wanda Lodwick Collection.*

Illustration 255. 7½in (19.1cm) DIONNE QUINT toddler by Madame Alexander, circa 1937. All-composition and fully-jointed with straight legs. Molded, painted curly brown hair; painted brown eyes. The yellow organdy dress and bonnet appear to have been made for a Quint-type doll as they are definitely not Alexander clothing. The shoes are original. Head and back marked: "ALEXANDER."

Toddlers:

9. 7½in (19.1cm). Mohair wig over molded straight hair; painted brown eyes. Head marked: "DIONNE // ALEXANDER." Back marked: "ALEXANDER." 1936.

10. 7½in (19.1cm). Curly, painted hair; painted brown eyes; Head and back marked: "ALEXANDER." 1936. *Illustrations 254, 255* and *256.*

11. 11½in (29.2cm). Mohair wig over molded, straight hair; closed mouth; brown sleep eyes with lashes. Head marked: ""DIONNE" // ALEXANDER." 1936.

12. 11½in (29.2cm). Curly, painted hair; brown sleep eyes with lashes; closed mouth. Head marked: "ALEXANDER." 1936.

13. 11½in (29.2cm). Curly, painted hair; brown sleep eyes with lashes; open mouth with teeth. Head and back marked: "ALEXANDER." 1936-1938.

14. 11½in (29.2cm). Curly, painted hair; brown sleep eyes with lashes; open mouth with teeth. Head marked: "ALEXANDER." Back marked: "MADAME // ALEXANDER." 1936-1938.

15. 11½in (29.2cm). (Can be 11¼in (28.6cm).) Curly, painted hair, brown sleep eyes with lashes; open mouth with teeth; chubby legs. Marked like No. 14. 1936-1938.

16. 11½in (29.2cm). Human hair wig over plain head; brown sleep eyes with lashes; closed mouth. Head marked: ""DIONNE" // ALEXANDER." Back marked: "MADAME // ALEXANDER." 1936.

17. 11½in (29.2cm). Human hair wig over plain head; brown sleep eyes with lashes; open mouth with teeth. Head marked: ""DIONNE // ALEXANDER." Back marked: "ALEXANDER." 1936.

18. 11½in (29.2cm) Straight painted hair; brown sleep eyes with lashes; closed mouth. Head marked: ""DIONNE" // ALEXANDER." Back marked: "MADAME // ALEXANDER." 1936-1938.

19. 14½in (36.9cm). Curly molded hair; brown sleep eyes with lashes; closed mouth. Head and back marked: "ALEXANDER." 1936.

20. 14½in (36.9cm). Human hair wig over plain head; brown sleep eyes with lashes; open mouth. Back marked: "ALEXANDER." 1936.

21. 14½in (36.9cm). Human hair wig over plain head; brown sleep eyes with lashes; closed mouth. Head and back marked: "ALEXANDER." 1936.

22. 17in (43.2cm). Curly painted hair; brown sleep eyes with lashes; closed mouth. Head and back marked: "ALEXANDER." 1937-1938.

23. 17in (43.2cm). Human hair wig over plain head; brown sleep eyes with lashes; closed mouth. Back marked: "ALEXANDER." 1937-1938.

24. 17in (43.2cm). Human hair wig over plain head; brown sleep eyes with lashes; open mouth with teeth. Back marked: "ALEXANDER." 1937-1938. *Illustration 257.*

25. 19½in (49.6cm). Human hair wig over molded straight hair; brown sleep eyes with lashes; closed mouth. Head and back marked: "ALEXANDER." 1937-1938. *Illustration 258.*

26. 19½in (49.6cm). Curly molded hair; brown sleep eyes with lashes; open mouth. Head and back marked: "ALEXANDER." 1937-1938.

27. 19½in (49.6cm). Curly molded hair; brown sleep eyes with lashes; closed mouth. Head and back marked: "ALEXANDER." 1937-1938.

Illustration 256. 7½in (19.1cm) DIONNE QUINT toddler by Madame Alexander, circa 1937. This is the same doll as in *Illustration 255*, but here she is wearing an original labeled outfit. The suit is unusual in two ways; it is cherry red, rather than the usual pink found on Dionne outfits for Yvonne, and this tiny checked pattern is rarely seen.

Illustration 257. 17in (43.2cm) YVONNE of the DIONNE QUIN-TUPLETS by Madame Alexander, circa 1937. All-composition and fully-jointed. Dark brown human hair wig; brown sleep eyes with lashes; open mouth with teeth. The labeled dress is of dotted swiss to which is attached Yvonne's name pin. The body is marked: "ALEXANDER." *Lois Barrett Collection.*

Girls: (All girls have stuffed cloth bodies.)

28. 13½in (34.3cm). Human hair wig over plain head; brown sleep eyes with lashes; closed mouth. Head marked: ""DIONNE" // ALEXANDER." 1938-1939.

29. 13½in (34.3cm). Human hair wig over plain head; brown sleep eyes with lashes; open mouth with teeth. long, thin legs. Head marked: "DIONNE // ALEXANDER." 1938-1939.

30. 17in (43.2cm). Human hair wig over plain head; brown sleep eyes with lashes; open mouth with teeth. No markings. 1938-1939.

31. 17½in (44.5cm). Human hair wig over plain head; brown sleep eyes with lashes; closed mouth; stuffed cloth body with cry box. Head marked: "ALEXANDER." *Illustration 259.*

32. 19½in (49.6cm). Human hair wig over plain head; brown sleep eyes with lashes, closed mouth; long, thin legs. Head marked: "DIONNE // ALEXANDER." 1938-1939.

All-cloth babies:

All-cloth with molded felt mask face with painted features; stockinette body and limbs. Human hair wig or mohair wig. The painted eyes are brown. Doll not marked, but clothing labeled. Circa 1936.

33. 10½in (26.7cm). Fits the above general description.

34. 17in (43.2cm). Fits the above general description.

35. 21in (53.3cm). Fits the above general description.

Illustration 258. 19½in (49.6cm) CECILE DIONNE by Madame Alexander, circa late 1930s. All-composition and fully-jointed. Brown molded hair; brown sleep eyes with lashes; closed mouth. The original costume is pale green organdy; the name pin is attached to the collar of the dress. The shoes and socks are replaced. Head and back marked: "ALEXANDER." *Barbara DeVault Collection.*

Illustration 259. 17½in (44.5cm) YVONNE DIONNE girl by Madame Alexander, circa 1939. Dark brown human hair wig; brown sleep eyes with lashes; closed mouth. Composition shoulder plate head, arms and legs; tightly stuffed cloth body with a cryer inside. Head marked: "ALEXANDER." *Rodolfos Collection.*

Illustration 260. Ad from Wards Fall-Winter 1936-1937 catalog showing toddlers dresses endorsed by the Dionne Quintuplets. There were also doll dresses based on the same designs. *Marceil Drake Collection.*

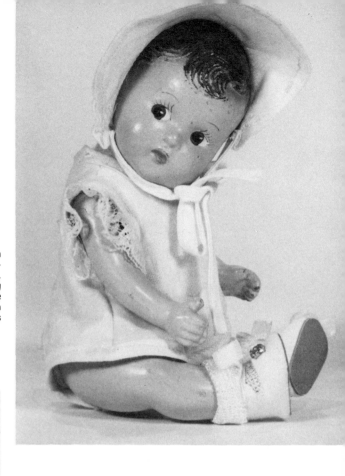

Illustration 263. 7in (17.8cm) Dionne Quint-type baby, maker unknown, late 1930s. The modeling is like the Quint-types made by Superior. Painted brown hair and eyes. The doll is redressed.

Illustration 261. 6½in (16.5cm) *Tinyette Quints* by Effanbee, 1935. All-composition and fully-jointed. Painted brown hair; painted blue eyes. Marked on the head: "EFFANBEE." Back marked: "EFFANBEE // BABY TINYETTE." The diapers are original.

Illustration 262. 7¼in (18.5cm) Dionne Quint-type baby by Hollywood Doll, circa late 1930s. All-composition and fully-jointed. Painted brown hair and painted blue eyes. Back marked: "HOLLYWOOD // DOLL."

Illustration 264. 7in (17.8cm) Dionne Quint-type, maker unknown, late 1930s—early 1940s. All-composition with a one-piece head and body and jointed at the arms and legs. Painted brown hair; painted blue eyes. The original costume is white with red print.

Dionne Quintuplets

Illustration 265. 7in (17.8cm) Dionne Quint-type baby, maker unknown, late 1930s. The modeling is like the Quint-types made by Superior. All-composition and fully-jointed. Painted black hair; painted brown eyes. The dress and bonnet are pink.

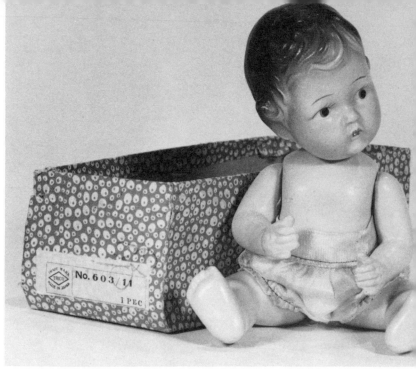

Illustration 268. 6½in (16.5cm) Dionne Quint-type made in Japan by Truco, No. 603/11, circa late 1930s. The doll is made of a papier-mâché over plaster type of composition, and the head has painted brown hair and painted blue eyes. The back is marked: "JAPAN." The box is original.

Illustration 266. 7in (17.8cm) Dionne Quint-type baby, maker unknown. The modeling is like the Quint-types made by Superior in the late 1930s. All-composition and fully-jointed. Painted black hair; painted blue eyes. The organdy dress and hat are pink.

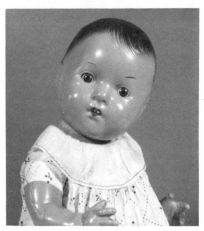

Illustration 267. 15in (39.4cm) Dionne Quint-type toddler, reputedly made in Canada, late 1930s. All-composition and fully-jointed. The doll is very similar to the Alexander baby. It has straight molded dark brown hair, brown tin sleep eyes with painted lashes only and a closed mouth with two painted teeth. There are no markings. (Compare the head with *Illustration 252.*)

Illustration 269. 7in (17.8cm) Dionne-type toddlers from Japan, circa late 1930s. Papier-mâché type of composition over plaster; fully-jointed. Painted brown hair; painted blue eyes; open-closed mouths. Stamped on the backs and on the original panties: "JAPAN." *Jean Canaday Collection.*

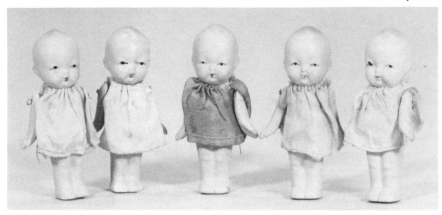

Illustration 272. 2⅝in (6.7cm) *"Quintuplets"* from Japan, late 1940s. Painted bisque with jointed arms only. The dresses are various pastel shades. Backs marked vertically: "MADE IN // OCCUPIED // JAPAN."

Illustration 270. 9in (22.9cm) Dionne-type toddler from Japan, circa late 1930s. Papier-mâché type of composition over plaster; fully-jointed. Painted brown hair; open-closed mouth. Marked on back: "JAPAN." *Jean Canaday Collection.*

Illustration 273. 2⅝in (6.7cm) *"Quintuplets"* made in Japan by the House of Seco Service, No. 4324, 1940s. Brightly painted heavy bisque with moveable arms only. The lid of the box has a cellophane window. The dolls are sewn into their community bunting.

Illustration 271. 3½in (8.9cm) DIONNE QUINTUPLETS, euphemistically referred to here as *"America's 5 Sweethearts,"* Transo-Company, Inc., No. 155, 1936. All-painted bisque with jointed arms and legs. Painted black hair and painted black eyes. All five Quints wear pink dresses. Backs marked: "JAPAN // T.CO. N.Y." The original box also tells that this set is "a Gold Medal Toy" and that the Transogram Company was located in New York, New York. *Betty Shriver Collection.*

Illustration 274. 2¾in (7.1cm) *"Quintuplets,"* probably 1940s. Painted bisque with jointed arms and curved legs. The hair is a reddish color. The simple dresses are different colors. The backs are marked: "JAPAN // Ⓔ."

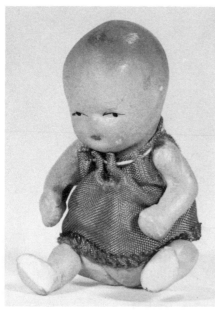

Illustration 275. Close-up of curved leg, painted bisque Quint from Japan.

Illustration 278. 5¾in (14.7cm) Dionne Quint-type baby from Japan, circa 1930s. All-painted bisque and fully-jointed with curved legs. Painted dark brown hair; painted black eyes. Back incised: "MADE IN // JAPAN // S1419."

Illustration 276. 2⅞in (7.3cm) "Quintuplets" marked on the backs: "JAPAN." Painted bisque with moveable arms. The hair is yellow and the dresses are various pastel shades. These little dolls are similar to ones that were made during the 1920s, but these probably date from the 1940s.

Illustration 277. 2½in (6.4cm) painted bisque "Quintuplets" stamped on the bottoms: "MADE IN // JAPAN." The bisque is a very thin type, although the dolls are painted crudely. The dresses are various bright colors.

Illustration 279. Figurine that represents the Dionne Quintuplets, probably late 1930s. This piece, measuring 3in (7.6cm) by 5in (12.7cm) is unusual in that the black haired little girls resemble the Dionnes more than most of the quintuplet dolls that came from Japan, and the girls are also older than most items of this sort show them to be. Another unusual feature is that it is made of celluloid that is molded over a plaster foundation. The back of the log on which the quintuplets are sitting is marked: "MADE IN JAPAN."

DOHERTY, DENNY. Singer. Denny Doherty was one of the original members of the Mamas and the Papas singing group of the 1960s. He provided vocal harmonies with John Phillips, Michelle Phillips and Cass Elliott until 1968.

DOLLS:
1. DENNY of THE MAMAS AND THE PAPAS, A SHOW BIZ BABY. Hasbro, No. 8806, 1967. All-vinyl with painted features; brown rooted hair; open mouth with molded teeth. Made in Hong Kong. 4in (10.2cm). Came attached to a 33 1/3 rpm record.

SEE: THE MAMAS AND THE PAPAS.

DOLENZ, MICKY (MICKEY BRADDOCK). Actor, singer. Born March 8, 1945. Micky Dolenz was child actor Mickey Braddock when he played Corky on television's "Circus Boy" from September 1956 to September 1958. Later he was Micky Dolenz of "The Monkees," a situation comedy on NBC-TV from September 1966 to August 1968. The Monkees also performed as a group with Micky singing and playing drums, and recorded a number of successful hit records. Micky also appeared in the film *Head* in 1968.

DOLLS:
1. MICKY OF THE MONKEES, A SHOW BIZ BABY. Hasbro, No. 8803, 1967. All-vinyl with painted features. Jointed at the head. Brown rooted hair; open mouth with molded teeth. Made in Hong Kong. 4⅛in (10.5cm). Came attached to a 33 1/3 rpm record.
2. MICKEY (sic) OF THE MONKEES. Remco, 1970. Made in Hong Kong. 5in (12.7cm). *Illustration 281.*
3. MONKEES hand puppet. See THE MONKEES.

SEE: THE MONKEES.

DOOHAN, JAMES. Actor. Born in Vancouver, British Columbia, Canada, on March 3 ?. James Doohan spoke with an authentic Scottish accent for his part of Lt. Commander Montgomery "Scotty" Scott on the "Star Trek" television series from September 1966 to September 1969 and for *Star Trek The Motion Picture* in 1979. He also did guest appearances in a wide variety of parts on some 350 different television shows. Because of his daring aviation maneuvers during World War II, he was known as "the craziest pilot in the Canadian Air Force."

DOLLS:
1. MR. SCOTT (SCOTTIE) (sic). Mego, No. 51200/5, 1974. 8in (20.3cm). Made in Hong Kong. *Illustration 282.*
2. SCOTTY FROM STAR TREK. Mego, No. 91200/5, 1979. 3¾in (9.6cm). Made in Hong Kong. *Illustration 283.*

SEE: STAR TREK.

Illustration 282. 8in (20.3cm) JAMES DOOHAN as *Mr. Scott (Scottie)* from "Star Trek" by Mego, No. 51200/5, 1974. All-vinyl and fully-jointed. Painted hair and features. Copyright by Paramount Pictures Corporation. Made in Hong Kong. *Penny Caswell Collection.*

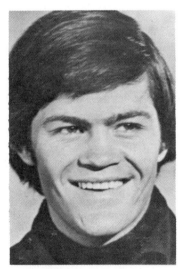

Illustration 280. Micky Dolenz from the Monkee's first album cover, 1966.

Illustration 281. 5in (12.7cm) finger puppet of MICKY DOLENZ of the Monkees by Remco, 1970. Vinyl head; plastic arms and chest section. The cloth pants with yellow vinyl boots are for finger operation. Rooted curly brown hair; painted brown eyes. Back marked: "© 1970 // REMCO IND. INC. // HARRISON N.J. // PAT. PEND. // HONG KONG." Copyright by Columbia Pictures Industries Inc. *Shirley Buchholz Collection.*

Illustration 283. 3¾in (9.6cm) JAMES DOOHAN as *Scotty* from *Star Trek: The Motion Picture* by Mego, No. 91200/5, 1979. All-vinyl and fully-jointed. Painted features and clothing. Copyright by Paramount Pictures Corporation. Made in Hong Kong.

DOTRICE, KAREN. British child actress. Born 1955. Karen Dotrice played Jane in *Mary Poppins*, 1964.

DOLLS:

1. JANE from MARY POPPINS set. Horsman, 1966. All-vinyl and fully-jointed with rooted blonde hair and blue painted eyes. 8¼in (21cm). See *Illustration 66*.

DOUGLAS, DONNA. Actress. Born Doris Smith on September 26, 1933 or 1939. Donna Douglas played Elly May Clampett on "The Beverly Hillbillies" on CBS-TV from September 1962 to 1971. This was one of TV's longest-running situation comedies and was about a family from the Ozarks who struck it rich in oil and moved to a mansion in Beverly Hills, never changing their folksy ways. Elly May had an enormous collection of dogs and other pets.

DOLLS:

1. ELLY MAY CLAMPETT. Unique, 1960s. 12in (30.5cm). *Illustration 284*.

Illustration 284. 12in (30.5cm) DONNA DOUGLAS as *Elly May Clampett* from "The Beverly Hillbillies" by Unique, 1960s. Vinyl head and arms; plastic torso and legs. Fully-jointed. Rooted blonde hair; painted blue eyes. Head marked: " © UNIQUE."

DRAEGER, JUSTIN and JASON. The Draeger twins were babies who took turns playing Joey Stivic on TV's "All in the Family." Joey was the son of Mike and Gloria (Rob Reiner and Sally Struthers) and the grandson of Archie Bunker (Carroll O'Connor). Little Joey was seen from the end of 1975 to 1978, when he moved to California from Queens (New York) with his parents. (The actors who played his parents left the show at the end of the 1978 season.)

DOLLS:

1. JOEY STIVIC, ARCHIE BUNKER'S GRANDSON. Ideal, No. 1380-5, 1976. Made in USA. 14in (35.6cm). *Illustration 285*.

Illustration 285. 14in (35.6cm) JASON and JUSTIN DRAEGER as *Archie Bunker's Grandson, Joey Stivic,* on "All in the Family" by Ideal, No. 1380-5, 1976. All-vinyl with a jointed head and a one-piece body. Rooted blonde hair; painted blue eyes. The doll is an open-mouth nurser and is "anatomically correct." Head marked: "IDEAL TOY CORP. // 13-14-R-253." Back marked: " © 1976 // TANDEM PRD'S INC. // ALL RIGHTS RESERVED // IDEAL 5-58." Made in USA.

DRAGON, DARYL. Musician and singer. Born August 27, 1942. Daryl Dragon is half of the husband and wife pop-rock singing duo The Captain and Tennille. They came to fame with their hit record "Love Will Keep Us Together" and parlayed this into a TV show—"The Captain and Tennille," from September 1976 to March 1977. "The Captain" hardly ever said a word on the show, including during comedy sketches. He wore an ever-present captain's hat, perhaps to conceal thinning hair. Daryl Dragon is a master at keyboard instruments and is the son of concert conductor Carmen Dragon.

DOLLS:

1. DARYL DRAGON. Mego, No. 75001, 1977. Made in Hong Kong. 12½in (31.8cm). *Illustrations 286* and *287*. Toni Tennille is the companion doll.
SEE: TONI TENNILLE.

Illustration 286. 12½in (31.8cm) DARYL DRAGON, *the Captain* of The Captain and Tennille by Mego, No. 75001, 1977. All-vinyl and fully-jointed. Painted hair and eyes. No marks on head. Copyright 1977 by Moonlight & Magnolias, Inc. Made in Hong Kong. TONI TENNILLE is a companion doll. *Shirley Buchholz Collection.*

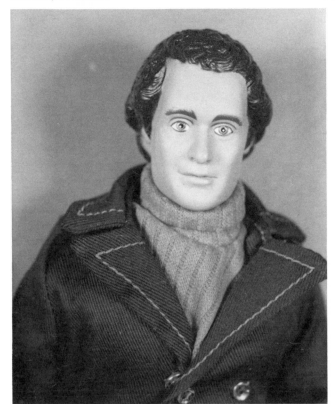

Illustration 287. DARYL DRAGON by Mego. *Shirley Buchholz Collection.*

DRAKE, DEBBIE. Debbie Drake was a television personality who hosted a weight-reducing show that combined dance steps with exercise movements. Debbie demonstrated the advantages of all this on syndicated shows after 1961.

DOLLS:
1. DEBBIE DRAKE. Valentine Dolls, 1963. Vinyl head; plastic body with extra joints for "posing." White rooted hair; black painted eyes. Not marked. 11½in (29.2cm).

DRAKE, LADY ELIZABETH. Elizabeth Drake was the daughter of Sir John Sydenham and the wife of Sir Francis Drake, whom she married in 1569.

DOLLS:
1. LADY ELIZABETH DRAKE. Peggy Nisbet, No. P655, 1970s. Plastic with painted features. Made in England. About 7½in (19.1cm). Sir Francis Drake, No. P622, is the companion doll.

DRAKE, SIR FRANCIS. Born circa 1540; died 1596. Sir Francis Drake was a navigator and pirate who sailed for Queen Elizabeth I of England. In 1578 he piloted *The Golden Hind* around the world and during this voyage claimed the Oregon Country for England. In 1588 his light ships helped to defeat the Invincible Spanish Armada of Philip II, which was attempting to conquer England and dethrone Queen Elizabeth.

DOLLS:
1. SIR FRANCIS DRAKE. Peggy Nisbet, No. P622, 1970s. Plastic "collectors' doll" with painted features. Made in England. About 8in (20.3cm). Lady Elizabeth Drake, No. P655, is the companion doll.

MADAME DU BARRY. (COMTESSE JEANNE DU BARRY). Madame Du Barry, born 1743; died 1793, was the last mistress of King Louis XV of France. She came from a humble background and elevated her status with her beauty and a secession of wealthy lovers. Although she did not seek political influence, she was known for her extravagant living at the French Court. Madame Du Barry was guillotined during the French Revolution.

DOLLS:
1. MADAME DU BARRY. Peggy Nisbet, No. H271, 1970s. Plastic "collectors' doll" with a white wig and painted features. Made in England. About 7½in (19.1cm).
2. MADAME DU BARRY. Effanbee, No. 1535, 1977-1978. All-vinyl and fully-jointed. Rooted blonde hair; blue sleep eyes. Wears blue taffeta dress with organdy overskirt. 15in (38.1cm).

DUKE, PATTY (PATTY DUKE ASTIN). Actress. Born Anna Marie Duke on December 14, 1946. Patty Duke became a professional actress at age seven and at twelve played the young Helen Keller in the stage production "The Miracle Worker" in 1959. When the film version of the play was cast in 1962 the producers would consider no one else for the part of Helen Keller, although by that time Patty Duke was a bit too old for the role. Her performance was so compelling that she became the youngest person (at the time) to receive a Best Supporting Actress Academy Award. As a teenager she was the star of "The Patty Duke Show" on ABC-TV from September 1963 to August 1966, playing Patty Lane, an American, and Cathy Lane, her intellectual Scottish cousin. She later appeared in many TV and film dramas and won high critical acclaim. In 1980 she again starred in a movie for television of "The Miracle Worker," this time playing Helen Keller's teacher, Annie Sullivan. After a relationship with Desi Arnaz, Jr. and two stormy marriages, she married actor John Astin and added his name to her professional billing.

DOLLS:
1. PATTY DUKE. Horsman, 1965. 12½in (31.8cm). *Illustration 288*.

Illustration 288. 12½in (31.8cm) PATTY DUKE with her telephone by Horsman, 1965. Vinyl head with rooted blonde hair and painted blue eyes. Plastic torso; vinyl arms and legs with wire inside for posing. Head marked: "H."

THE DUKES OF HAZZARD. Television situation comedy set in rural Georgia. The Duke cousins are JOHN SCHNEIDER as Bo Duke, TOM WOPAT as Luke Duke and CATHERINE BACH as Daisy Duke. DENVER PYLE plays Uncle Jesse Duke. SORRELL BOOKE plays conniving Boss Hogg, who constantly attempts to land the Duke boys in jail on trumped-up charges. Other characters on the show are JAMES BEST as Hogg's corrupt sheriff, Rosco P. Coltrane; BEN JONES as Cooter Davenport, the garage mechanic; and RICK HURST as Reserve Deputy Cletus Hogg. Car chases are the main attraction on the series. The show premiered on January 26, 1979. See listings under each actor and *Illustrations 288-A* and *288-B*.

Illustration 289. "The Dukes of Hazzard" from the cover of *TV Guide,* March 7-13, 1981. Back row: Tom Wopat, John Schneider and Catherine Bach. In front: Sorrell Booke.

Illustration 288-A. The stars of CBS-TV's "The Dukes of Hazzard" by Mego. From left to right: TOM WOPAT as *Luke,* CATHERINE BACH as *Daisy,* JOHN SCHNEIDER as *Bo* and SORRELL BOOKE as *Boss Hogg.* 8in (20.3cm) See listings under each celebrity. Copyright by Warner Bros., Inc. From *Soar with the Eagles* (Mego catalog), 1982.

Illustration 290. 3¾in (9.6cm) TOM WOPAT as *Luke* and JOHN SCHNEIDER as *Bo* from "The Dukes of Hazzard" by Mego, NO. 09060, 1981. *Luke* has painted brown hair; *Bo* has painted yellow hair. Molded clothing. The set also included an orange car, "The General Lee," which is of vinyl and is 10½in (26.7cm) long. Backs of the dolls marked: "©WB 1980 // MADE IN HONG KONG." The car was made in USA.

Illustration 288-B. The cast of television's "The Dukes of Hazzard" by Mego. 3¾in (9.6cm). From left to right: BEN JONES as *Cooter,* DENVER PYLE as *Uncle Jesse,* CATHERINE BACH as *Daisy,* TOM WOPAT as *Luke,* JOHN SCHNEIDER as *Bo,* SORRELL BOOKE as *Boss Hogg,* RICK HURST as *Cletus* and JAMES BEST as *Sheriff Rosco Coltrane.* See listings under each celebrity. In the background is "Cooter's Garage Playset," No. 09066 by Mego. Copyright by Warner Bros., Inc. From *Soar with the Eagles* (Mego catalog), 1982.

DUPREZ, JUNE. Actress. Born in London, England, on May 14, 1918. June Duprez played exotic roles in British and American films like *The Thief of Bagdad*, 1940.

DOLLS:
1. JUNE DUPREZ. Molly-'es, 1940. All-composition and fully-jointed. Wears costume from *The Thief of Bagdad.* 15in (38.1cm).
2. JUNE DUPREZ. Molly-'es, 1940. All-composition and fully-jointed. Wears costume for *The Thief of Bagdad.* 21in (53.3cm).

DURANT, DON. Actor. Don Durant played the title role in the CBS-TV series "Johnny Ringo" from October 1959 to September 1960. Johnny Ringo was a gun-fighter-turned-lawman, supposedly based on a real character from the 1880s.

DOLLS:
1. JOHNNY RINGO. Hand puppet based on the television series. (Johana Gast Anderton: *More Twentieth Century Dolls*, page 1034.)

DURBIN, DEANNA. Actress, singer. Born Edna Mae Durbin in Winnipeg, Manitoba, Canada, on December 4, 1921. At the age of 14, Deanna Durbin was placed under an MGM contract and appeared with Judy Garland in a musical short *Every Sunday*, 1936. The studio dropped Deanna and promoted Judy. Universal signed Durbin and placed her in a series of musicals that made her internationally famous and one of the leading box-office attractions of the late 1930s and early 1940s. In 1938 she shared a special Juvenile Academy Award with Mickey Rooney. In 1948, at which time she was Hollywood's highest paid woman star, she suddenly retired from films and has since lived near Paris, France, with her third husband, director Charles David. Deanna Durbin never grants interviews and makes a point of having nothing to do with the motion picture industry that made her a star.

DOLLS:
1. DEANNA DURBIN. Ideal, 1938. 21in (53.3cm) *Illustrations 295* and *296*.
2. DEANNA DURBIN. Ideal, 1938. 25in (63.5cm). *Illustrations 292* and *298*.
3. *DEANNA DURBIN. Ideal, 1939. 14½in (36.9cm). Illustration 292.*
4. DEANNA DURBIN. Ideal, 1939. 17½in (44.5cm). *Illustrations 293* and *294*.

Illustration 292. DEANNA DURBIN by Ideal, circa 1939. From left to right: 25in (63.5cm), 21in (53.3cm) and 14½in (36.9cm). All-composition and fully-jointed. Sleep eyes with lashes; open mouths with teeth; dark brown human hair wigs. The heads are all marked: "DEANNA DURBIN // IDEAL DOLL." The backs are marked, respectively: "IDEAL DOLL // 25", "IDEAL DOLL" and "15 // IDEAL DOLL." The smallest doll is not dressed in an original costume. *Wanda Lodwick Collection.*

Illustration 293. 17½in (44.5cm) DEANNA DURBIN by Ideal, 1939. All-composition and fully-jointed. Dark brown human hair wig; blue sleep eyes with lashes and eye shadow; open mouth with six teeth and a tongue. The costume is replaced and the pin is a reproduction. Head marked: "DEANNA DURBIN // IDEAL DOLL." Back marked: "DEANNA DURBIN // IDEAL DOLL // 8 r ."

Illustration 291. Thurston Hall, Nella Walker and Deanna Durbin from *Three Smart Girls Grow Up*, 1940.

OPPOSITE PAGE: Illustration 294. 17½in (44.5cm) DEANNA DURBIN by Ideal, 1939. All-composition and fully-jointed. Dark brown human hair wig; green sleep eyes with lashes; open mouth with teeth and tongue. Everything is all-original. The pins came with the dolls; the photograph of Deanna Durbin was packaged in the box. The dress is a cotton print. Head marked: "DEANNA DURBIN // IDEAL DOLL." Back marked: "IDEAL DOLL." *Jean Canaday Collection.*

Illustration 295. 21in (53.3cm) DEANNA DURBIN by Ideal, circa 1939. All-composition and fully-jointed. Dark brown human hair wig; green sleep eyes with lashes and eye shadow; open mouth with teeth and a tongue; painted red fingernails. Note the white organdy bodice that is over the usual flowered dress. Head marked: "DEANNA DURBIN // IDEAL DOLL." Back marked: "IDEAL DOLL." *Lois Barrett Collection.*

Illustration 298. 25in (63.5cm) DEANNA DURBIN by Ideal, circa 1939. All-composition and fully-jointed. Dark brown human hair wig; green "flirty eyes;" open mouth with teeth and tongue. Head marked: "DEANNA DURBIN // IDEAL DOLL." Back marked: "IDEAL DOLL // 25." *Barbara DeVault Collection.*

Illustration 297. Original box from DEANNA DURBIN in *Lois Barrett Collection.*

Illustration 296. 21in (53.3cm) DEANNA DURBIN from *Lois Barrett Collection.* Note the original set of the hair with the original hair ribbons.

Illustration 299. Deanna Durbin, 1941.

E

EARHART, AMELIA. American aviator. Born 1898; died 1937. In 1928 Amelia Earhart was the first woman to fly the Atlantic as a passenger, and in 1932 she was the first woman to fly the same route solo. In 1937 during a round-the-world flight attempt she was lost in the Pacific. Although the Japanese have been blamed for her death, her whereabouts were never known. She had married George Palmer Putnam in 1931.

DOLLS:

1. AMELIA EARHART. Lenci, 1920s. All-felt with painted features and a mohair wig. Made in Italy. 16in (40.6cm).
2. AMELIA EARHART. Hallmark, No. 400DT113-6, 1979. Made in Taiwan. 7in (17.8cm). *Illustration 300.*

Illustration 300. 7in (17.8cm) AMELIA EARHART by Hallmark, No. 400DT113-6, 1979. All-cloth. Sewn body joints; printed features and clothing. Made in Taiwan. *Shirley Buchholz Collection.*

EARP, WYATT. United States law officer. Born in Monmouth, Illinois, March 19, 1848; died January 13, 1929. The famous gunfighter was involved with his brothers and Doc Holliday in the controversial shootout at the OK Corral in Tombstone, Arizona, in 1881.

1. WYATT EARP AND HIS HORSE, TOMBSTONE. Hartland Plastics, Inc., No. 809, 1958. Plastic. Made in Hartland, Wisconsin. 8in (20.3cm).
2. WYATT EARP. Mego, No. 1360, 1973. All-vinyl and fully-jointed. Made in Hong Kong. 7½in (19.1cm).
3. WYATT EARP. Excel Toy Corp., 1974. All-vinyl and fully-jointed. Made in Hong Kong. 9¼in (23.6cm).
4. WYATT EARP. Durham Ind., Inc., 1975. All-vinyl and fully-jointed with molded clothing, except for removable hat. Made in Hong Kong. 8in (20.3cm).
5. WYATT EARP. Carolina Enterprises, Inc., 1978. All-vinyl and fully-jointed. Molded clothing. Made in Hong Kong. 4¼in (10.9cm).

EDEN, BARBARA. Actress. Born Barbara Huffman on August 23, 1934. Eden began her career as an all-American cheerleader and a pop singer. She appeared in films after 1956. In 1958 she played Loco Jones in the syndicated TV series "How to Marry a Millionaire." From September 1965 to September 1970 she was the lead on NBC-TV's "I Dream of Jeannie." On January 16, 1981, she debuted with a new show, "Harper Valley P.T.A." based on her 1978 movie which was based on the hit song sung by Jeannie C. Riley in 1968.

DOLLS:

1. JEANNIE. Remco, circa 1966. Made in Hong Kong. 6½in (16.5cm). *Illustration 301.*
2. JEANNIE. Libby, 1966. 20in (50.8cm). *Illustrations 302* and *303.*

Illustration 301. 6½in (16.5cm) BARBARA EDEN as "I Dream of Jeannie" by Remco, circa 1966. All-vinyl and fully-jointed. Rooted blonde hair; painted black eyes. Holes in feet to attach to stand. Back marked: "© REMCO TOYS INC. // MADE IN HONG KONG."

Illustration 302. 20in (50.8cm) BARBARA EDEN as *Jeannie* from "I Dream of Jeannie" by Libby, 1966. All-vinyl and fully-jointed. Rooted blonde hair; blue sleep eyes with heavy painted lashes. The feet are arched for the high-heeled vinyl shoes. Head marked: " © 1966 // LIBBY." *Wanda Lodwick Collection.*

Illustration 303. 20in (50.8cm) BARBARA EDEN. *Wanda Lodwick Collection.*

EDWARD VI. King of England from 1547 to 1553. Born 1537; died 1553. Edward was the son of Henry VIII and Jane Seymour, the king's third wife who died shortly after Edward was born. Edward, a frail, sickly youth succeeded Henry as King of England and died when he was 16.

DOLLS:
1. KING EDWARD VI. Peggy Nisbet, No.P420, late 1970s. All-plastic "collectors' doll." Made in England. About 8in (20.3cm).

EDWARD VII. King of England, 1901 to 1910. Born 1841; died 1910. Edward was the eldest son of Queen Victoria and was the Prince of Wales for 60 years. Victoria denied Edward any part in her government but after he became king, he was known as a "peacemaker" because of the foreign alliances he brought about. Edward was married to Queen Alexandra who tollerated his romances with the Countess of Warwick, Lilly Langtry and the Hon. Alice Keppel, among others.

DOLLS:
1. KING EDWARD VII. Peggy Nisbet, No. P611, 1970s. All-plastic "collectors' doll." Made in England. About 8in (20.3cm). Queen Alexandra, No. P612, is a companion doll.
2. ROYAL VICTORIAN CHRISTENING. Peggy Nisbet Special Collectors' Set No. 20, a limited edition of 500 sets, 1982. Plastic dolls. Edward is a baby of about 2in (5.1cm), in the arms of Nanny Holding The Future King, No. LE100. Companion dolls are Queen Victoria, No. LE98, and Prince Albert, No. LE99. Made in England.

EDWARD VIII. King of England from January to December 1936. Born June 23, 1894; died May 28, 1972. Edward became king when his father, George V, died. Shortly after his accession he announced his intention of marrying Mrs. Wallis Warfield Spencer Simpson, a twice-divorced American, whose two former husbands were still alive. In a great romantic move, Edward abdicated the throne so that he could marry Mrs. Simpson. His brother became George VI, and Edward was given the title Duke of Windsor. Edward lived mostly in France after his marriage, as his wife could not be "received" by his family. He was also governor of the Bahamas from 1940 to 1945.

DOLLS:
1. KING EDWARD VIII, DUKE OF WINDSOR. Peggy Nisbet, No. P711, 1970s. All-plastic "collectors' doll." Made in England. About 8in (20.3cm). King George V, No. P709, and Queen Mary, No. P710, his parents, are part of the set called "The House of Windsor, Portrait Series."
2. KING EDWARD VIII, DUKE OF WINDSOR. Peggy Nisbet, No. P418, 1970s. All-plastic "collectors' doll." Made in England. About 8in (20.3cm). Mrs. Wallis Simpson, Duchess of Windsor, No. P419, is a companion doll.

PRINCE EDWARD, THE DUKE OF KENT. Born Edward George Nicholas Paul Patrick Windsor on October 9, 1935. Edward's father was George, the Duke of Kent, the son of King George V. This makes Prince Edward a first cousin to Queen Elizabeth II.

DOLLS:
1. PRINCE EDWARD, THE DUKE OF KENT. Chad Valley, 1938. Made in England. 16in (40.6cm). *Illustration 304.*

Illustration 304. 16in (40.6cm) PRINCE ED-WARD, THE DUKE OF KENT by Chad Valley, 1953. Pressed felt head with inset blue glass eyes; blonde mohair wig. The body is fully-jointed of stuffed cotton velvet. He is marked with a label attached to the sole of the right foot. Made in England. *Shirley Buchholz Collection.* NOTE: This doll was originally produced in 1938. The doll pictured was manufactured by special request in 1953.

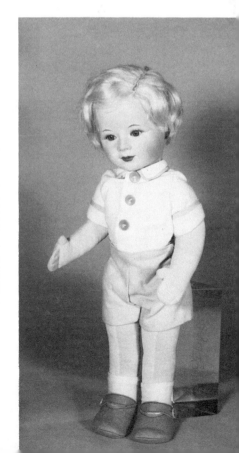

Illustration 305. Chad Valley label on right foot of the DUKE OF KENT. *Shirley Buchholz Collection.*

PRINCE EDWARD.   Born 1964. Edward is the fourth child of Queen Elizabeth II and Prince Philip of England. He is said to be "quieter" than his brother, Andrew, and he is "an accomplished fly-fisher."

DOLLS:
  1. PRINCE EDWARD.   Peggy Nisbet, No. P414, 1970s. Plastic "collectors' doll." Made in England. About 7in (17.8cm). Prince Andrew, No. P413, is a companion doll.

EDWARDS, VINCENT.   Actor. Born July 9, 1928. Vincent Edwards debuted in the Broadway musical "High Button Shoes" in 1947 and entered films in 1951. His greatest popularity as an actor came when he played brooding Doctor "Ben Casey" on the ABC-TV series from October 1961 to March 1966. He also appeared in nightclubs as a singer.

DOLLS:
  1. DR. BEN CASEY.   Manufacturer unknown, early 1960s. This is the same doll as Dr. Kildare (*Illustration 177*) except for the attached pin stating: "I'VE GOT A CASE ON BEN CASEY."
  2. DR. BEN CASEY.   Maker unknown, 1960s, 11½in (29.2cm). *Illustration 307.*
  3. DR. BEN CASEY.   Bobble-head of unknown manufacture, 1960s. Papier-mâché. Painted features. No marks. 6¾in (17.2cm).

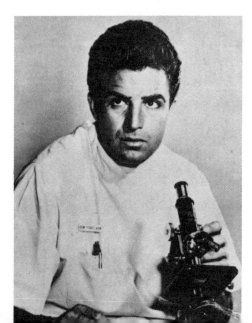

Illustration 306. Vincent Edwards as Ben Casey from a photo comic book, K. K. Publications, Poughkeepsie, New York, 1962.

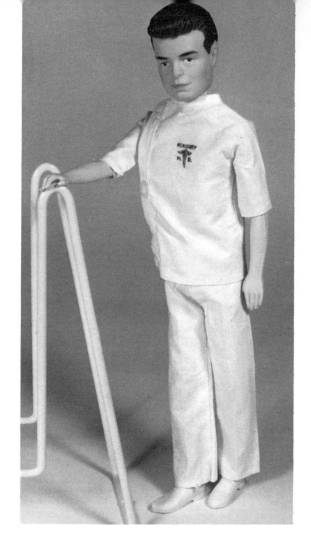

Illustration 307. 11½in (29.2cm) VINCENT EDWARDS as *Dr. Ben Casey*, manufacturer unknown, 1960s. Soft vinyl head with painted hair and features. Plastic fully-jointed body. (The construction is rather crude; this is similar to the Dr. Kildare doll, *Illustration 178 and 179*.) No marks. Shirt reads: "BEN CASEY // (Medical insignia) // M.D." *Lee Jenkins Collection.*

EISENHOWER, DWIGHT.   American general and President of the United States. Born October 14, 1890; died March 28, 1969. During World War II Eisenhower commanded the Allied forces in North Africa. In 1943 he was appointed supreme commander of the Allied Expeditionary Force. In 1944 he was made a "five-star general." He was appointed supreme commander of Allied Forces in Europe (NATO) in 1950. In 1953 he began a two-term presidency. During his administration a truce was arranged in Korea (1953); Federal troops were sent to Little Rock, Arkansas, (1957) to enforce school desegregation; and the "Eisenhower Doctrine" was formed (1957) to defend Middle Eastern nations from Communism. Eisenhower was a conservative Republican president, and his nickname was "Ike."

DOLLS:
  1. DWIGHT D. EISENHOWER.   Marx, 1970s. All-vinyl with painted features. Fully-jointed. Cloth clothing. Made in Hong Kong. 11in (27.9cm).
  2. GEN. DWIGHT D. EISENHOWER.   Excel Toy Corp., 1974. All-vinyl and fully-jointed. Made in Hong Kong. 9¾in (24.9cm).
  3. DWIGHT EISENHOWER.   Peggy Nisbet, No. P735, 1970s. Plastic "collectors' doll." Made in England. About 8in (20.3cm).

ELIZABETH (ELISABETH), EMPRESS OF AUSTRIA. Born in Munich, Bavaria (now part of Germany) on December 24, 1837; died September 10, 1898. Elizabeth was the most beautiful princess in Europe in 1853. Francis Joseph, the Emperor of Austria, fell in love with her when they met and they were married in Vienna, Austria, on April 24, 1854. Elizabeth, called "Sissi," was not popular in Austria because of her disregard for court etiquette and convention but she was widely admired in Hungary, which joined Austria in 1867. Her only son, Crown Prince Rudolf, committed suicide in 1889 in the hunting lodge of Mayerling and she never fully recovered from the shock. Her nephew, Francis Ferdinand, became the Crown Prince and his assassination at Sarajevo, Bosnia, on June 28, 1914, was the immediate cause of World War I. Empress Elizabeth was killed by an anarchist, Luigi Luccheni, while on a visit to Geneva, Switzerland, in 1898. She was the subject of the "Sissi" series of films in the late 1950s. This series starred Romy Schneider and was very popular in the German-speaking world. The classic film *Mayerling* (1937) is about the love affair Elizabeth's son, Rudolf, had with a commoner. The film was remade in 1969.

DOLLS:
1. EMPRESS OF AUSTRIA. Peggy Nisbet, No. P466, 1982. Made in England. About 7½in (19.1cm). *Illustration 307-A*.

Illustration 307-A. 7½in (19.1cm) EMPRESS ELIZABETH OF AUSTRIA by Peggy Nisbet, No. P466, 1982. All-plastic with jointed arms. Dark mohair wig; painted eyes. White gown. Made in England. *Photograph Courtesy of House of Nisbet*.

ELIZABETH I. Queen of England from 1558 to 1603. Born 1533; died 1603. Queen Elizabeth, the greatest monarch England ever had, set her country on its course and caused it to become the most powerful nation on earth. She was the daughter of Henry VIII and his second wife, Anne Boleyn, and was declared illegiti-

mate after her mother's execution. She became Queen after the deaths of her father, her half-brother, Edward VI, and her half-sister, Mary I. She took England through the period that produced such men as William Shakespeare, Spencer, Francis Bacon and Walter Ralegh. England became a first-rate power because of events engineered by Elizabeth. She re-established the Anglican Church and adopted harsh measures against Catholics; she aided other Protestants in Europe, especially the Dutch who were waging a war of independence against Spain, which gave her allies; she financed pirates, such as Sir Francis Drake, who robbed the wealth of the Spanish ships coming from the New World; she had her cousin Mary, Queen of Scots, executed because Mary was the pawn of a plan to have herself seated on the throne of England. All of this caused Philip II of Spain, whose offer of marriage Elizabeth had refused, to send the Spanish Armada to England in 1588 to conquer England and Elizabeth. The Armada failed, Spain's power was broken and England controlled the seas with its navy. Elizabeth was vain and fickle and bestowed favors on her "favorites," such as the Earl of Essex and the Earl of Leicester. She was also immensely courageous.

DOLLS:
1. QUEEN ELIZABETH I. Robin and Nell Dale, 1977. Made in England, 7⅞in (20cm). *Illustration 308*.
2. QUEEN ELIZABETH I. Peggy Nisbet, No. H214, 1970s. Plastic "collectors' doll." Made in England. About 7½in (19.1cm).
3. QUEEN ELIZABETH I. Peggy Nisbet "Portrait Series," No. P600, 1970s. Plastic "collectors' doll." Made in England. About 7½in (19.1cm).
4. QUEEN ELIZABETH I. Ann Parker, 1979. Made in England. 11in (27.9cm). *Illustrations 309* and *310*.

NOTE: There are many other commercially made "souvenir dolls" of Queen Elizabeth I.

Illustration 308. 7⅞in (20cm) QUEEN ELIZABETH I by Robin and Nell Dale, 1977. The figure is a turned wooden dowel with jointed arms. The skin tones are natural wood; the clothing is painted. These dolls are from the Silver Jubilee Collection, Bank House Farm, Holme Mills, Holme, Carnforth, Lancashire, England. Marked on the bottom: "QUEEN ELIZABETH I BY ROBIN AND NELL DALE // ENGLAND // SILVER // JUBILEE // 1977. *Rosemarye Bunting Collection*.

Illustration 309. 11in (27.9cm) QUEEN ELIZABETH I by Ann Parker, late 1970s. All-hard plastic and affixed to a wooden base. Orange mohair wig; painted brown eyes. Made in England. *Shirley Buchholz Collection.*

ELIZABETH II. Queen of England since 1952. Born 1926. Elizabeth is the eldest daughter of King George VI and Lady Elizabeth Bowes, now the Queen Mother. As Princesses, Elizabeth and her sister, Margaret Rose, took part in the Coronation of their parents in 1937. The little princesses were rather popular in the English-speaking world during the late 1930s, as they were pretty and charming. Elizabeth married Prince Philip Mountbatten of Greece in 1947, which created another surge of her popularity because of the attending publicity. (The Mountbattans are a family of German origin.) In 1953 Elizabeth was crowned Queen of Great Britain and her husband was given the title Duke of Edinburgh. The couple have four children, Prince Charles, the Prince of Wales; Princess Anne; Prince Andrew; and Prince Edward. Elizabeth II is fond of horse racing, and she raises Pembroke Welsh Corgi dogs.

DOLLS OF PRINCESS ELIZABETH:

All-composition and fully-jointed by Madame Alexander:

1. 1937. Closed mouth with crown in hair. Shown in *Playthings* ad in September of 1937 in four sizes. Only the 13in (33cm) size is known. *Illustrations 311* and *312.*

2. 7½in (19.1cm). Circa 1938. Blonde mohair wig over molded hair; blue painted eyes. Tagged gown. Head marked: "'DIONNE' // ALEXANDER." Back marked: "ALEXANDER." The head and the torso are from the mold of the Dionne Quint toddler by Alexander.

3. through 11.
    1938 to about 1941. Open mouth with teeth. Various tagged costumes. The heads are marked: "PRINCESS ELIZABETH." and "ALEXANDER" or "ALEXANDER DOLL CO." The sizes are 13in (33cm), 14in (35.6cm), 15in (38.1cm), 16in (40.6cm), 17in (43.2cm), 18in (45.7cm), 20in (50.8cm), 24in (61cm) and 27in (68.6cm). *Illustrations 313, 314* and *315.*

Illustration 310. QUEEN ELIZABETH I by Ann Parker. *Shirley Buchholz Collection.*

Illustration 311. 13in (33cm) PRINCESS ELIZABETH by Madame Alexander, 1937. All-composition and fully-jointed. Blonde human hair wig; blue tin sleep eyes; dimples in the cheeks. The metal crown is set with "jewels." The gown is lavender taffeta with rosebuds applied to the front and is tagged "PRINCESS ELIZABETH." The doll is not marked. (This head is considered the "Betty" mold and was also used for *Betty* and the *Little Colonel.*)

Illustration 312. 13in (33cm) PRINCESS ELIZABETH by Madame Alexander.

12. and 13.
Schoenau & Hoffmeister, circa 1938. Bisque head with glass sleep eyes, smiling mouth with teeth. Fully-jointed composition body. Made in Germany. 16in (40.6cm) and 21in (53.3cm). *Illustration 316.*

14. Jumeau. 1938. Bisque socket head with glass flirty eyes, closed mouth. Fully-jointed composition body. Head marked: "UNIS // FRANCE // 71 149 // 306 // JUMEAU // 1938 // PARIS." 19in (48.3cm).

15. Chad Valley. 1938. Felt head; velvet body. Made in England. 18in (45.7cm). *Illustrations 317* and *318.*

16. Liberty of London. Circa 1938. All-cloth with stitched and painted features. This is a "Coronation Group" and includes dolls fo George VI, Queen Elizabeth (the Queen Mother) and Princess Margaret Rose. Made in England. 6in (15.2cm).

17. Tower Treasures, Ltd., 1979. Bisque head and limbs; leather and/or calico bodies. Painted features; synthetic blonde wig. Made in England. 15in (38.1cm).

Illustration 313. 16in (40.6cm) PRINCESS ELIZABETH by Madame Alexander, circa 1938. All-composition and fully-jointed. Blonde mohair wig; blue sleep eyes with lashes. The crown and necklace are probably new additions to the doll. Head marked: "PRINCESS ELIZABETH // ALEXANDER DOLL CO." *Fran's Dolls.*

Illustration 314. 18in (45.7cm) PRINCESS ELIZABETH by Madame Alexander, circa 1938. All-composition and fully-jointed. Blonde human hair wig; brown sleep eyes with lashes. The dress is tagged: "PRINCESS ELIZABETH." Head marked: "PRINCESS ELIZABETH // ALEXANDER." *Fran's Dolls.*

Illustration 315. 17in (43.2cm) PRINCESS ELIZABETH by Madame Alexander, circa 1939. All-composition and fully-jointed. Blonde human hair wig; green sleep eyes with lashes; open mouth with teeth. The original, tagged costume is one of the more rare ones. It is a white cotton shirt attached to pale yellow serge jodhpurs with a heel strap under each foot; black velvet riding jacket; black felt hat; black leatherette boots with a side snap. Head marked: "PRINCESS ELIZABETH // ALEXANDER DOLL CO." Back marked: "17." A reverse 17 appears at the top of each arm at the joints. *Patricia Slabe Collection.*

Illustration 317. 18in (45.7cm) PRINCESS ELIZABETH by Chad Valley, 1938. Head of molded felt with painted features; blonde mohair wig. Fully-jointed body of stuffed velvet. Turquoise wool coat has a label reading "Made in England." Floral dress and matching underwear. The cardboard tag carries the following information: "This model was manufactured by the CHAD VALLEY CO. LTD. by appointment. Toy makers to her Majesty the Queen. Harborne, Birmingham, England. Specially for the export trade and has been shipped to you in a British ship under the protection of the British Navy." The box covered with pictures of animals is the original carton. *Sandy Rankow Collection. Photograph by Sandy Rankow.*

Illustration 318. Chad Valley PRINCESS ELIZABETH. *Sandy Rankow Collection. Photograph by Sandy Rankow.*

DOLLS OF QUEEN ELIZABETH II:

1. Chelsea Art, 1953.   Ceramic shoulder head on a cloth body. Molded and painted features with blue eyes and brown hair. Dressed in Uniform of the Grenadier Guards. Made in England. 14in (35.6cm).

The following are all-hard plastic by Madame Alexander:

2. 1953, No. 2025.   Wears white brocade court gown and blue Sash of the Garter. 18in (45.7cm).
3. 1953, No 2020A.   Walking doll dressed the same as No. 2053. 18in (45.7cm).
4. 1954, No. 2030A.   Walking doll dressed in white court gown, blue Sash of the Garter and a white "ermine" cape. 18in (45.7cm).
5. 1954, No. 0030A.   A "Miniature Portrait" that matches No. 2030A of 1954. The set was called "Me and My Shadow." 7½in (19.1cm).
6. 1955, No. 499. Same as above. 7½in (19.1cm).
7. 1955, No. 2099.   Wears a court gown of white brocade with garter sash and star. This is the *Cissy* doll. 20in (50.8cm).
8. 1956, No. 2042.   A repeat of No. 2099 from 1955. 20in (50.8cm).
9. 1957, No. 2171.   Same as the above.
10. 1961, No. 2230.   Same as the above in white. 21in (53.3cm).
11. 1962, No. 2180.   Wears court gown of gold brocade decorated with the sash of the Order of the Bath. *Cissy* doll used again. 21in (53.3cm).
12. 1963, No. 1780.   Wears the same costume as the above. The *Elise* doll was used this year. 18in (45.7cm).

NOTE: Alexander produced other dolls that look like a queen. For example, the 1960 *Cissette,* No. 842, was called "Debutante" in Alexander's 1960 catalog; No. 742 *Cissette,* 1959, was called "Queen."

13. Robin and Nell Dale, 1977. Made in England. 6½in (16.5cm). *Illustration 319.*

The following are by Peggy Nisbet and are all-plastic "collectors' dolls." Made in England during the 1970s. Each is about 7½in (19.1cm).

14. No. P400.   Dressed in State Robes.
15. No. P401.   Dressed in Garter Robes.
16. No. P406.   Dressed in Thistle Robes.
17. No. P408.   Dressed in a riding habit with the jacket of an Officer of the Regiment of the Guards, which the Queen wears at the Annual Ceremony of Trooping the Colour on her "official birthday," June 14.

NOTE: There are many other commercially made "souvenir dolls" of Queen Elizabeth II.

OPPOSITE PAGE: Illustration 316. 21in (53.3cm) PRINCESS ELIZABETH by Schoenau & Hoffmeister, circa 1938. Bisque head with open crown; five-piece jointed composition toddler body. Blonde mohair wig; blue glass sleep eyes; open mouth with four teeth. Head marked: "PORZELLANFABRIK // BURGGRUB // PRINCESS ELIZABETH // 5 // MADE IN GERMANY." The costume may be original. The china tea set is decorated with pictures of Princess Elizabeth and her sister, Princess Margaret Rose, and is from Germany. *Wanda Lodwick Collection.*

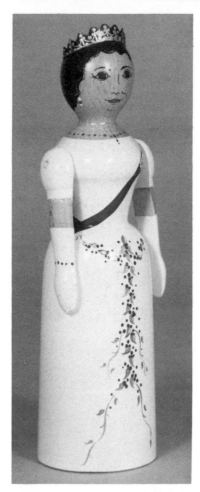

Illustration 319. 6½in (16.5cm) QUEEN ELIZABETH II by Robin and Nell Dale, 1977. The figure is a turned wooden dowel with jointed arms. The skin tones are natural wood; the clothing is painted on. These dolls are from the Silver Jubilee Collection, Bank House Farm, Holme Mills, Holme, Carnforth, Lancashire, England. Marked on the bottom: "QUEEN ELIZABETH II BY ROBIN & NELL DALE // ENGLAND // SILVER // JUBILEE // 1977." *Rosemarye Bunting Collection.*

QUEEN ELIZABETH, THE QUEEN MOTHER. Queen of Great Britain. Born Lady Elizabeth Bowes in 1900. She was crowned Queen Consort of her husband King George VI in 1937. The QEW (Queen Elizabeth Way) of Canada was named in her honor. The "Queen Mum," as she is affectionately known, is the mother of Queen Elizabeth II and Princess Margaret Rose.

DOLLS:

1. QUEEN ELIZABETH. Liberty of London, circa 1938. All-cloth with stitched and painted features. Part of the "Coronation Group" that includes King George VI, Princess Elizabeth and Princess Margaret Rose. Made in England. About 7½in (19.1cm).

2. H.R.H. QUEEN ELIZABETH THE QUEEN MOTHER. Peggy Nisbet, No. P404, 1970s. All-plastic "collectors' doll." Part of "The Royal Family Portrait Series" that includes H.M. Queen Elizabeth II, wearing the Order of the Thistle, No. P406; H.R.H. Prince Charles, Prince of Wales, No. P402, H.R.H. Prince Philip, No. P408, and H.M. Queen Elizabeth II, No. P401, all wearing the Order of the Garter. Made in England. About 7½in (19.1cm).

3. QUEEN ELIZABETH THE QUEEN MOTHER. Peggy Nisbet, No. P713, 1970s. All-plastic "collectors' doll," wearing State Robes. Made in England. About 7½in (19.1cm). King George VI, No. P712, is a companion doll.

4. H.M. QUEEN ELIZABETH, THE QUEEN MOTHER. Tower Treasures Ltd., 1980. Made in England. About 7½in (19.1cm). *Illustration 320.*

5. H.M. QUEEN ELIZABETH, THE QUEEN MOTHER IN 80th BIRTHDAY STATE DRESS. Peggy Nisbet, No. P425, early 1980s. Plastic "collectors' doll." Made in England. About 7½in (19.1cm).

Illustration 320. 8½in (21.6cm) H.M. QUEEN ELIZABETH, THE QUEEN MOTHER by Tower Treasures, Ltd., 1980. English bone china bisque head and limbs on a white simulated leather body. Limited edition of 790 models for the Queen Mother's 80th birthday in 1980. Made in England. *Photo Courtesy of House of Nisbet.*

ELIZABETH OF YORK. Queen of England; Consort of Henry VII. Born February 11, 1465; died February 11, 1503. On January 18, 1486, Elizabeth married Henry Tudor. She was the daughter of King Edward IV and the sister of the "little princes" who disappeared from the Tower in 1483 after the death of Edward IV. After the disappearance of the young princes, Henry VII met Richard III in the Battle of Bosworth. Richard III was no doubt responsible for the deaths of his nephews, the princes, and he had seized the throne of their father, Edward IV. Richard III was killed at Bosworth and Henry VII claimed the throne of England by title of inheritance and by the judgment of God in battle. He was crowned in 1485. He then married Elizabeth of York, uniting the two houses who had claim to the throne of England. A son, Arthur, was born nine months later. His name was chosen because he would one day be king and would be named after a famous British king from whom he claimed descent. Arthur did not live to be crowned, but Elizabeth's second son became King Henry VIII, inheriting the Tudor and York claims to the throne.

DOLLS:
1. ELYSABETH OF YORK.   Peggy Nisbet, No. P652, early 1980s. Plastic "collectors' doll." Made in England. About 7½in (19.1cm).

ELLIOTT, CASS (MAMA CASS). Singer. Born Cassandra Elliott on September 19, 1941; died July 29, 1974. Mama Cass was a rather plump singer who was part of the Mamas and the Papas pop-rock group from 1963 to 1967. From 1967 until her death she was a successful solo act. At the time she died it was reported that Cass Elliott choked to death on a sandwich.

DOLLS:
1. CASS OF THE MAMAS AND THE PAPAS, one of the "Show Biz Babies" by Hasbro, No. 8809, 1967. Made in Hong Kong. 4¼in (10.9cm). *Illustration 321* and *322.*
SEE: THE MAMAS AND THE PAPAS.

Illustration 321. 4¼in (10.9cm) MAMA CASS ELLIOT of the Mamas and the Papas, a Show Biz Baby by Hasbro, No. 8809, 1967. All-vinyl; jointed only at the head; wired vinyl poseable body. Rooted dark blonde hair; painted green eyes; open-closed mouth with painted teeth. Attached to record cover. Copyright by Hassenfeld Bros. Inc. (Hasbro). Back marked: "©1967 // HASBRO // HONG KONG." *Wanda Lodwick Collection.*

Illustration 322. 4¼in (10.2cm) MAMA CASS ELLIOT by Hasbro.

ELSSLER, FANNY. Ballet and folk dancer. Born 1810 in Austria; died 1884. Fanny Elssler made her debut in 1833 and was very popular in Paris, France, London, England, and the United States until she retired in 1851.

DOLLS:
1. FANNY ELSSLER.   Made in Germany, circa 1844. China head with a cloth body. Dressed as a ballerina. (This is a supposition. See: *A Treasury of Beautiful Dolls* by John Noble, Weathervane Books, 1971, pages 42 and 47.)

QUEEN ENA (VICTORIA EUGENIE). Queen of Spain. Born 1887; died 1969. Ena, the daughter of Prince Henry and Princess Beatrice of Battenburg, was 19 years old when she married 16 year old King Alfonso XIII of Spain. The couple's first son was born with hemophylia, a disease transmitted by his great grand-mother, Queen Victoria, as was his cousin, the Tsarevich Aleksei of Russia. The couple's second son was born a deaf mute. The Royal Family of Spain was forced into exile in 1931, after which time the King and the Queen lived apart. Queen Ena's grandson, Juan Carlos, is now King of Spain.

DOLLS:
1. QUEEN ENA OF SPAIN.   Peggy Nisbet, No. P793, 1970s. Plastic "collectors' doll." Made in England. 7½in (19.1cm). King Alfonso XIII, No. P794, is a companion doll.

ERVING, JULIUS ("DR. J."). Basketball player. Born February 22, 1950. Dr. J. was an American Basketball Association leading scorer in 1973, 1974 and 1976. In 1977 and 1978 he was an all-star player for the National Basketball Association.

DOLLS:
1. JULIUS (DR. J.) ERVING. Shindana, No. 9025, 1977. Made in Hong Kong. 9½in (24.2cm). *Illustration 323*.

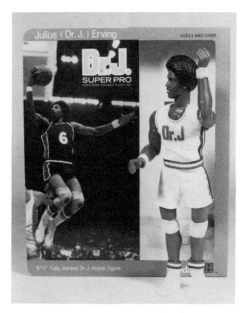

Illustration 323. 9½in (24.2cm) JULIUS (DR. J.) ERVING by Shindana, No. 9025, 1977. All-vinyl and fully-jointed, including twist waist. Painted black hair and eyes. Basketball included. Copyright 1976 by Shindana Toys, Inc. Made in Hong Kong.

Illustration 324. 3¾in (9.6cm) ERIK ESTRADA as *Ponch* from "CHiPs" by Mego, No. 08010/1, 1981. All-vinyl and fully-jointed. Painted features and clothing. Copyright 1977 by Metro-Goldwyn-Mayer Film Co. Made in Hong Kong.

ESTRADA, ERIK. Actor. Born March 16, 1949, in New York, New York. Estrada's fame comes from his role as Officer Francis "Ponch" Poncherello as NBC-TV's "CHiPs" (began September 1977), his semi-nude posters, and his much-publicized and scandal-tainted divorce from Joyce Miller in 1980.

DOLLS:
1. PONCH. Mego, No. 08010/1, 1981. Made in Hong Kong. 3¾in (9.6cm). *Illustration 324*.
2. PONCH. Mego, No. 07500/2, 1981. Made in Hong Kong. 8in (20.3cm). *Illustration 325*.

SEE: CHiPs.

Illustration 325. 8in (20.3cm) ERIK ESTRADA as *Ponch* from "CHiPs" by Mego, No. 87500/2, 1980. All-vinyl and fully-jointed with painted black hair. Copyright 1977 by M.G.M., Inc. Made in Hong Kong.

EVANS, DALE. Actress, singer. Born Frances Octavia Smith on October 31, 1912. Dale Evans broke into show business as a radio and nightclub singer in the 1940s. In 1947 she married her leading man, cowboy star Roy Rogers. The couple continued to film westerns and later starred in "The Roy Rogers" show on NBC-TV from December 1951 to June 1957 and "The Roy Rogers and Dale Evans Show" on ABC-TV from September to December 1962. Dale Evans rode her horse, Buttermilk, in the first series which was a western-adventure program. The second series was a variety program in which Dale and Buttermilk sometimes performed horse acts. "The Queen of the Cowgirls" also wrote several books of a devotional nature.

DOLLS:
1. DALE EVANS. Dolls of Hollywood, 1948. All-cloth with painted features and yarn wig. Roy Rogers is a companion doll. 17in (43.2cm).
2. DALE EVANS. Duchess Doll Corp., 1948. All-plastic and fully-jointed. Sleep eyes; mohair wig. Roy Rogers is a companion doll. 7in (17.8cm).
3. DALE EVANS*. Madame Alexander, circa 1947. All-composition and fully-jointed. "Margaret face" with brown sleep eyes and a mohair wig. Head marked: "MME ALEXANDER." 14½in (36.9cm).

4. DALE EVANS*. Madame Alexander, circa 1951. All-hard plastic and fully-jointed. "Maggie face" with blue sleep eyes and a saran wig. 14½in (36.9cm).
5. DALE EVANS. Zany Toys, Inc., 1957. Hand puppet with a vinyl head. Roy Rogers is a companion doll.
6. DALE EVANS. Nancy Ann Storybook Dolls, Inc., 1955. All-plastic and fully-jointed. Sleep eyes; synthetic wig. Roy Rogers is a companion doll. 8in (20.3cm).
7. DALE EVANS, QUEEN OF THE WEST, AND HER FAVORITE HORSE, "BUTTERMILK." Hartland Plastics, Inc, No. 802, circa 1958. All-plastic. About 8in (20.3cm).
*Not confirmed. See *More Twentieth Century Dolls* by Johana Gast Anderton, Athena Publishing Company, 1974, page 1027.

EVANS MAURICE. Actor. Born June 3, 1901, in England. Evans began his career as a boy singer and made his professional stage debut in 1926. In 1935 he began a long career on the Broadway stage, interpreting the plays of Shakespeare and Shaw. Evans was in films after 1930, playing parts that were not of the same stature as his stage roles. He played the role of Maurice in many episodes of ABC-TV's "Bewitched" from 1964 to 1972. He was Dr. Zaius in *Planet of the Apes* in 1968 and *Beneath the Planet of the Apes* in 1970.

DOLLS:
1. PLANET OF THE APES DR. ZAIUS. Mego, No. 1962, 1974. All-vinyl and fully-jointed with painted features. Made in Hong Kong. 8in (20.3cm).
SEE: PLANET OF THE APES.

F

FAIRBURN, BRUCE. Actor. Born February 19, 1947. Bruce Fairburn played Officer Chris Owens on ABC-TV's "The Rookies" from 1974 to 1976. He was a new recruit who replaced Willie (Michael Ontkean), who was on the show when it began in September 1972 through the 1973-1974 season.

DOLLS:
1. CHRIS from THE ROOKIES. L.J.N. Toys Ltd., No. 6101, 1976. All-vinyl and fully-jointed. Painted hair and features. Copyright 1973 by Spelling-Goldberg Productions. Made in Hong Kong. 7½in (19.1cm).
SEE: THE ROOKIES.

FARGAS, ANTONIO. Actor. Antonio Fargas was the flamboyant informant who worked for the principals on ABC-TV's "Starsky and Hutch," which ran from September 1975 through the summer of 1979. Fargas played a similar part, "more man than you'll ever *be* and more woman than you'll ever *get*," in some films.

DOLLS:
1. HUGGY BEAR from STARSKY AND HUTCH. Mego, No. 62800/3, 1976. Made in Hong Kong. 7½in (19.1cm). *Illustration 326.*
SEE: STARSKY AND HUTCH.

Illustration 326. 7½in (19.1cm) ANTONIA FARGAS as *Huggy Bear* from "Starsky and Hutch" by Mego, No. 62800/3, 1976. All-vinyl and fully-jointed. Painted hair and features. Copyright by Spelling Goldberg Productions. Made in Hong Kong.

FARR, JAMIE. Actor. Born Jameel Joseph Farah in Toledo, Ohio, on July 1, 1934. Farr entered films in the 1950s and also appeared on many television programs. His first series show was "The Chicago Teddy Bears" on CBS-TV from September to December 1971. In September 1973 he joined the cast of CBS-TV's "M*A*S*H" to play Corporal Maxwell Klinger. Klinger began on the series as an aide to the doctors in the operating room. He wanted so desperately to get out of the army that he dressed in a bizarre variety of women's clothing, hoping to be discharged as mentally unfit. This ploy was dropped when he became the aide to the medical chief.

DOLLS:
1. KLINGER. (CORP. MAX Q. KLINGER). Tristar International, Ltd., Series No. 4100, 1982. All-vinyl and fully jointed. Painted hair and clothing. Made in Hong Kong. 3¾in (9.6cm).
SEE: M*A*S*H.

FARRELL, MIKE. Actor. Born February 6, 1939. Farrell began his acting career in films and became a star playing B.J. Hunnicut on "M*A*S*H" on CBS-TV beginning in September 1975. B.J. replaced Wayne Rogers as Hawkeye's co-conspirator when Rogers left the show in the summer of 1975 over a contract dispute. Farrell had previously played on "The Interns" on CBS-TV from September 1970 to September 1971 and "The Man and the City" on ABC-TV from September 1971 to September 1972.

DOLLS:
1. B.J. (CAPT. B.J. HUNNICUT). Tristar International, Ltd., Series No. 4100, 1982. All-vinyl and fully-jointed. Painted features and clothing. Made in Hong Kong. 3¾in (9.6cm).
SEE: M*A*S*H.

FAWCETT, FARRAH (FARRAH FAWCETT-MA-JORS).

Actress. Born February 2, 1946. Farrah became a popular pin-up of the 1970s through TV commercials, magazine covers, posters and as a one-season star as Jill on ABC-TV's "Charlie's Angels" during the 1976-1977 season. She left the series to become a "movie star." She had entered films in 1969, but even after her popularity on TV she never made it. She hyphenated her name and added Majors to it during the time she was married to actor Lee Majors.

DOLLS:

1. FARRAH FAWCETT-MAJORS AS JILL FROM CHARLIE'S ANGELS. Hasbro, No. 4863, 1977. Made in Hong Kong. 8½in (21.6cm). *Illustration 328*.
2. FARRAH. Mego, No. 77000, 1977. Made in Hong Kong. 12¼in (31.2cm). *Illustrations 329* and *330*.
3. FARRAH. Mego, No. 08888, 1981. Made in Hong Kong. 12in (30.5cm). *Illustration 331*.

Illustration 329. 12¼in (31.2cm) FARRAH FAWCETT-MAJORS by Mego, No. 77000, 1977. All-vinyl and fully-jointed, including wrists and waist. Rooted blonde hair; painted green eyes with long attached lashes; dark skin tones. (The body is the same as the CHER doll.) Copyright by Farrah. Made in Hong Kong. *Wanda Lodwick Collection.*

Illustration 327. Farrah Fawcett-Majors.

Illustration 328. 8½in (21.6cm) FARRAH FAWCETT-MAJORS as *Jill* from "Charlie's Angels" by Hasbro, No. 4863, 1977. All-vinyl and fully-jointed. Rooted platinum hair; painted blue eyes. Copyright by Spelling Goldberg Productions. Made in Hong Kong. *Shirley Buchholz Collection.*

Illustration 330. FARRAH FAWCETT-MAJORS by Mego, 1977. *Wanda Lodwick Collection.*

Illustration 331. 12in (30.5cm) FARRAH by Mego, No. 08888, 1981. Vinyl head with rooted blonde hair; painted green eyes with long lashes; very thin and cheaply made five-piece plastic body. Head marked: "© FARRAH." Back marked: "HONG KONG." This version of Farrah Fawcett (-Majors) wears nothing except a bright yellow stretch swimsuit and is similar to CHER, *Illustration 201.*

FERNANDEL. Actor. Born Fernand Joseph Désiré Contandin on May 8, 1903, in Marseille, France; died 1971. Fernandel began performing while still a child and turned professional in 1922, appearing in vaudeville, operettas and music hall revues. He made his film debut in France in 1930. He played many serious parts but was in more than 100 comedies, which made him France's top funny man for four decades. His long, horse-like face also made him an audience favorite in England and the United States. He died of lung cancer during the production of his last film.
DOLLS:
1. FERNANDEL. Puppet on strings, made in France. Composition head, hands and feet; key-wind music box that played the "Third Man Theme." A paper tag gives this information: "Fernandel, Agent de Police. Exclusivité des Poupées. Paris. J.C. Déposé. Reproduction interdité."

FIELD, SALLY. Actress. Born November 6, 1946. Sally Field was first popular as a cute, pug-nosed juvenile lead in several successful TV series. They were "Gidget" on ABC-TV from September 1965 to September 1966, "The Flying Nun" on ABC-TV from September 1967 to January 1970, as Clementine Hale on "Alias Smith and Jones" on ABC-TV from January 1971 to January 1973, and "The Girl with Something Extra" on NBC-TV from September 1973 to May 1974. In 1977 she starred in a dramatic role, *Sybil*, a four-hour TV movie, in which she played a mentally disturbed woman who had 16 distinct personalities. For this she won an

Emmy Award. For the film *Norma Rae*, another dramatic part in 1979, she won the Best Actress Award at the Cannes Film Festival and the Academy Award.
DOLLS:
1. GIDGET. Madame Alexander, No. 1415, 1966. All-vinyl and fully-jointed. Rooted dark brown hair. 14in (35.6cm). Dressed in a pinchecked jumper.
2. GIDGET. Madame Alexander, No. 1420, 1966. Same as the above, wearing a cotton formal.
3. GIDGET. Madame Alexander, No. 1421, 1966. Same as the above, wearing a sailor dress and hat.
4. THE FLYING NUN. Hasbro, 1967. All-vinyl and fully-jointed. Rooted brown hair; painted eyes; open-closed mouth with one painted tooth. Trademark of Screen Gems, Inc. Made in Hong Kong. 4¼in (10.9cm).
5. THE FLYING NUN. Hasbro, No. 9200, 1967. Made in Hong Kong. 10½in (26.7cm). *Illustrations 332 and 333.*

Illustration 332. 10½in (26.7cm) SALLY FIELD as "The Flying Nun" by Hasbro, No. 9200, 1967. All-vinyl and fully-jointed. Rooted brown hair; painted brown eyes. Trademark of Screen Gems, Inc.; Hassenfeld Bros. Inc. is the authorized user. Made in Hong Kong. *Shirley Buchholz Collection.*

Illustration 333. SALLY FIELD by Hasbro. *Shirley Buchholz Collection.*

FIELDS, W. C. Actor and screenwriter. Born William Claude Dunkenfield in 1879; died 1946. When he was 11, W.C. Fields ran away from home. He lived as a street urchin and was often involved in fights. He claimed this is what gave him his large bulbous nose. His bitter childhood experiences became the basis for his skeptical view of life both on and off the screen in later years. He began his professional career as a juggler at age 14 and by the age 20 was a vaudeville headliner. In 1905 he starred in his first Broadway play, and he entered films in 1915. His first smash movie was *Sally of the Sawdust* in 1925. With sound films Fields became a top comedy star because of his raspy voice and his droll manner of speaking. His greatest role was his only serious part, that of Mr. Micawber in *David Copperfield* in 1935. Fields disliked and mistrusted children, dogs, banks, executives and authority symbols because of attitudes he formed as a youngster, and he used these as foils for his comedy material. He seemed to work hard to become hated, but even today audiences love his style. Fields was portrayed by Rod Steiger in a perfectly awful screen biography *W.C. Fields and Me* in 1976.

DOLLS:

1. W.C. FIELDS. Effanbee 1938. Composition head, hands and shoes; cloth body. Ventriloquist mouth with painted teeth; painted blue eyes; painted light-colored hair. Wears top-hat and suit. 17½in (44.5cm).

NOTE: This doll is often cited as having been produced in 1929; it did not appear until 1938.

2. W.C. FIELDS. Knickerbocker, 1972. Made in Taiwan. 16in (40.6cm). *Illustration 335*.

3. W.C. FIELDS. Peggy Nisbet, No. P759, 1970s. Made in England. About 7½in (19.1cm). *Illustration 336*.

4. W.C. FIELDS. Effanbee, 1980. 15½in (39.4cm). *Illustration 337* and *338*.

5. W.C. FIELDS. Juro (Goldberger), 1980. 30in (76.2cm). *Illustrations 339* and *340*.

Illustration 335. 16in (40.6cm) "Talking" W.C. FIELDS by Knickerbocker, circa 1972. All-cloth with printed features and clothing. Arms and legs jointed. Tag: "DOLLS OF DISTINCTION // © KNICKERBOCKER // MADE IN TAIWAN." *Rosemarye Bunting Collection.*

Illustration 334. W.C. Fields in his only serious role, that of Mr. Micawber in *David Copperfield*, 1935.

Illustration 336. About 7½in (19.1cm) W.C. FIELDS as *Micawber* in *David Copperfield* by Peggy Nisbet, No. P759, 1970s. All-hard plastic and jointed only at the arms. Painted hair and features. Copyright 1935 by MGM; renewed by MGM 1962. Made in England. *Photograph Courtesy of House of Nisbet.*

Illustration 337. 15½in (39.4cm) W.C. FIELDS Centennial Doll by Effanbee, 1980. All-vinyl and fully-jointed with reddish hair and painted blue eyes. This is an unusually high quality doll in modeling, construction and clothing. Head marked: "W. C. FIELDS // EFFANBEE // 19 © 80." Back marked: "W.C. FIELDS // EFFANBEE // © 1979 // W.C. FIELDS PROD. INC." Made in USA.

Illustration 338. W.C. FIELDS Centennial doll by Effanbee.

Illustration 339. 30in (76.2cm) W.C. FIELDS ventriloquist doll by Juro, a Division of Goldberger Doll Mfg. Co., Inc. (EEGEE Co.), 1980. Vinyl head and hands; painted reddish blonde hair; painted blue eyes; painted teeth. Stuffed cloth body. Head marked: W.C. FIELDS © 1980 // W.C. FIELDS PRODUCTIONS, INC. // EEGEE CO."

Illustration 340. W. C. FIELDS by Juro (Eegee).

FILLMORE, ABIGAIL. First Lady. Born Abigail Powers on March 13, 1798; died 1853. When President Zachary Taylor died in 1850 his Vice President, Millard Fillmore, became President for the remainder of the term (1853). Mrs. Fillmore is credited with installing the first bathtub and the first library in the White House. Abigail Fillmore became chilled when she attended the inauguration of President Pierce on March 4, 1953. She then became ill and died a few weeks later.

DOLLS:
1. ABIGAIL FILLMORE. Madame Alexander, No. 1514, 1982. Vinyl and plastic and fully-jointed. Rooted dark hair in two long curls. She wears a gown that is trimmed with multiple bows and braid, and she has a flowered tiara in her hair. Part of the third six Firsts Ladies Series. 14in (35.6cm).
SEE: FIRST LADIES, THE.

FINDLAY, JANE. First lady of the United States for a month in 1841. President William Henry Harrison— "Old Tippecanoe"—was inaugurated as President on March 4, 1841. He caught pneumonia at the long ceremony and died on April 4, 1841. His wife was too ill to act as First Lady, and his daughter-in-law was asked to fill the office. She, in turn, asked her aunt, Jane Findlay, to accept the assignment. Mrs. Findlay was never recognized as much of a celebrity in her own time.

DOLLS:
1. JANE FINDLAY. Madame Alexander, No. 1509, 1979. Part of the second six First Ladies Series. 14in (35.6cm).
SEE: FIRST LADIES, THE.

FINE, LARRY. Comedian. Born 1911; died 1974. In 1928 Larry Fine joined with brothers Moe Howard and Shemp Howard to form The Three Stooges. The trio played in vaudeville, on Broadway, and by 1930 in feature films. By 1934 Shemp had left the act and was replaced by his brother, Curly. Moe, Curly and Larry appeared in about 200 two-reel comedies from 1934 to 1958. This was the longest running comedy series in the history of sound films. The comedy routines of The Three Stooges dealt with their brutal treatment of each other, such as gouging eyes. By 1959 The Three Stooges were "Curly Joe" De Rita, Moe Howard and Larry Fine. These three made several feature films, a result of the renewed popularity of The Three Stooges from television appearances and the release on TV of their old short films.

DOLLS:
1. LARRY. Hand puppet by unknown maker, circa 1960s. Vinyl head with cloth glove for body. Painted hair and features. 10in (25.4cm).
NOTE: Hand puppets were no doubt made of two other Stooges.

FINNEY, ALBERT. Actor. Born May 9, 1936, in England. Finney trained for the stage at the Royal Academy of Dramatic Art. During the late 1950s he appeared in Shakespearean roles, but later he also tackled modern parts. After 1960 he starred in several well-received films, and gained international prominence with his portrayal of *Tom Jones* (1963). In recent films Finney has essayed character parts, such as Daddy Warbucks in *Annie* (1982).

DOLLS:
1. DADDY WARBUCKS. Knickerbocker Toy Co., Inc., No. 3869, 1982. All-vinyl and fully-jointed. Bald head and painted features. Copyright by Columbia Pictures Industries, Inc. 7in (17.8cm).
SEE: ANNIE

THE FIRST LADIES. The First Ladies are the women who act as hostess for the different American Presidents. Many were the wives of the Presidents, others were relatives. Several different doll companies have manufactured sets of dolls that represent these ladies. The most prominent dolls and the most desirable collectibles are those produced by Madame Alexander and the Limited Edition set from Crafted Heirlooms.

The Madame Alexander First Ladies from 1976 are: MARTHA WASHINGTON, ABIGAIL ADAMS, MARTHA RANDOLPH, DOLLEY MADISON, ELIZABETH MONROE, and LOUISA ADAMS. *Illustration 341*. Madame Alexander began the "Second Six First Ladies" in 1979. They are: SARAH JACKSON, ANGELICA VAN BUREN, JANE FINDLAY, JULIA TYLER, SARAH POLK and BETTY TAYLOR BLISS. *Illustration 342*. In 1982 Madame Alexander introduced the "Third Six First Ladies." They are ABIGAIL FILLMORE, JANE PIERCE, HARRIET LANE, MARY TODD LINCOLN, MARTHA JOHNSON PATTERSON and JULIA GRANT. *Illustration 342-A*.

The First Ladies Collection from Crafted Heirlooms are MARTHA WASHINGTON, ABIGAIL ADAMS and MARTHA RANDOLPH.

See entries under the names of each of these ladies.

Illustration 341. The "First Six FIRST LADIES" by Madame Alexander, 1976. 14in (35.6cm) each. Vinyl and plastic and fully-jointed. Back row, from left to right: ABIGAIL ADAMS, No. 1502; MARTHA WASHINGTON, No. 1501; ELIZABETH MONROE, No. 1505. Front row, from left to right: LOUISA ADAMS, No. 1506; MARTHA RANDOLPH, No. 1503; DOLLEY MADISON, No. 1504. *Alexander Doll Company, Inc.* catalog, 1978.

Illustration 342. 14in (35.6cm) "Second Six First Ladies" by Madame Alexander, 1979. Top row, left to right: SARAH POLK, No. 1511; SARAH JACKSON, No. 1507; ANGELICA VAN BUREN, No. 1508. Front row, left to right: JANE FINDLAY, No. 1509; JULIA TYLER, No. 1510; BETTY TAYLOR BLISS, No. 1512. *Alexander Doll Company, Inc.* catalog, 1979.

Illustration 342-A. The "Third Six FIRST LADIES" by Madame Alexander, 1982. 14in (35.6cm) each. Vinyl and plastic and fully-jointed with rooted hair. Back row, from left to right: JANE PIERCE, No. 1515; ABIGAIL FILLMORE, No. 1514; MARY TODD LINCOLN, No. 1517. Front row, from left to right: MARTHA JOHNSON PATTERSON, No. 1518; HARRIET LANE, No. 1516; JULIA GRANT, No. 1519. 1982 Alexander catalog.

FISCHER QUINTUPLETS (JAMES ANDREW, MARY MAGDALLENE, MARY MARGARET, MARY ANNE and MARY CATHERINE FISCHER). Born September 14, 1963, to Mr. and Mrs. Andrew Fischer of Aberdeen, South Dakota. These Quints were the first surviving set born in the United States and were four girls and a boy. The babies were called Jimmy, Maggie, Margie, Annie and Cathy. Their parents signed a contract with the Curtis Publishing Company for the rights of the children to be a featured exclusive in its magazines, like *The Saturday Evening Post*, and they appeared on calendars by Brown and Bigelow and on some other advertising, but the babies never engendered any real interest from the public. Shortly after the time of their birth there were surviving quintuplets and even sextuplets all over the world, and this was no longer the "miracle" it had been with the Dionnes in the 1930s.

Several sets of dolls were made to take advantage of the Fischer Quints, but none of them were ever sold as "Fischer Quintuplets."

DOLLS:
1. QUINTUPLETS.   Maker unknown, 1963. Made in Hong Kong. 1¾in (4.5cm). *Illustration 345*.
2. QUINTUPLETS—BABY DARLINGS.   Maker unknown, 1963. Made in Hong Kong. 2½in (6.4cm). *Illustration 344.*
3. ORIGINAL QUINTUPLETS.   Madame Alexander, 1964. 7¼in (18.5cm). *Illustrations 346* and *347.*
4. QUINTUPLETS.   Maker unknown, circa 1964. Made in Hong Kong. 3½in (8.9cm). *Illustration 348.*
5. QUINT-TOTS.   Maker unknown; made for Grant's circa 1964. 7½in (19cm). *Illustration 349.*
6. QUINTUPLETS.   Allied Doll & Toy Corp., circa 1964. 8in (20.3cm). *Illustration 350* and *351.*

Illustration 343. The Fischer Quintuplets. The painting, "Five Going on Four," was a 1967 Brown & Bigelow calendar by artist Clair Fry. *Alma Boudreaux Cansler Collection. Photograph by Alma Boudreaux Cansler.*

Illustration 344. 2½in (6.4cm) (FISCHER) QUINTUPLETS—*Baby Darlings,* maker unknown, circa 1963. One-piece plastic with painted fatures. The blankets are lavender, navy, pink, red and blue. Marked on the backs: "MADE IN HONG KONG." *Alma Boudreaux Cansler Collection. Photograph by Alma Boudreaux Cansler.*

Illustration 345. 1¾in (4.5cm) (FISCHER) QUINTUPLETS, maker unknown, circa 1963. Plastic with jointed arms and legs. Painted hair and features. These babies were sold nude in a plastic bag marked: "QUINTUPLETS." Marked on the backs: "MADE IN HONG KONG." *Alma Boudreaux Cansler Collection. Photograph by Alma Boudreaux Cansler.*

Illustration 347. An "Original Quintuplet," called the FISCHER QUINTUPLETS by collectors. The dolls came in sets that had four pink baby bottles and one blue bottle, using the same boy-girl ratio as the Fischer Quints.

BELOW: Illustration 346. 7¼in (18.5cm) QUINTUPLETS (called the FISCHER QUINTUPLETS) by Madame Alexander, 1964. Hard plastic heads with sprayed brown hair and blue sleep eyes with molded lashes. Jointed vinyl bodies. These dolls are never marked. The original sweaters are labeled: "MFR of the // 'ORIGINAL QUINTU-PLETS' // by MADAME ALEXANDER." The white cotton nightgowns hanging in the center rear have the same labels. The two different pillow and blanket sets in the boxes were also sold for the "Original Quintuplets." They were boxed in sets of six, to be sold individually in retail stores.

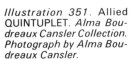

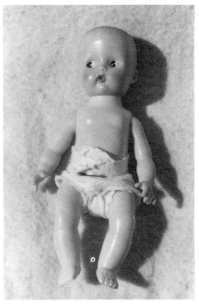

Illustration 348. 3½in (8.9cm) (FISCHER) QUINTUPLET, maker unknown, circa 1964. Made of cheap, thin plastic. Only the arms are jointed. Blue sleep eyes. Four of the babies are dressed in pink blankets; one is in blue. Marked on the back: "MADE IN HONG KONG." *Alma Boudreaux Cansler Collection. Photograph by Alma Boudreaux Cansler.*

Illustration 351. Allied QUINTUPLET. *Alma Boudreaux Cansler Collection. Photograph by Alma Boudreaux Cansler.*

Illustration 349. 7½in (19.1cm) (FISCHER) QUINTUPLETS made for Grant's, maker unknown, 1963 or 1964. Fully-jointed. Vinyl head with painted molded brown hair; blue sleep eyes; nurser mouth. Plastic body that is jointed. Four are girls dressed in pink blankets with a pink satin bow; the boy is dressed in a blue blanket with a blue satin bow. No markings. *Alma Boudreaux Cansler Collection. Photograph by Alma Boudreaux Cansler.*

FISHER, CARRIE. Actress. Born October 21, 1956. Carrie Fisher is the daughter of actress Debbie Reynolds and singer, actor Eddie Fisher. At age 12 she performed in her mother's Las Vegas nightclub act. When she was 15 she dropped out of school to spend more time on her show business career. Her first Broadway part was in the chorus of her mother's show "Irene" in 1973. Her first film role was as a sex-pot who seduced Warren Beatty in *Shampoo* (1975). In 1977 George Lucas selected her to play Princess Leia Organa in *Star Wars*, and she repeated the role in the 1980 sequel *The Empire Strikes Back*.

DOLLS:
1. PRINCESS LEIA ORGANA. Kenner, No. 38190, 1978. All-vinyl and fully-jointed. Painted features. Made in Hong Kong. 3½in (8.9cm).
2. PRINCESS LEIA ORGANA. Kenner, No. 38070, 1978. Made in Hong Kong. 11½in (29.2cm). *Illustration 353*.
3. PRINCESS LEIA ORGANA. Kenner, 1979. Wears Bespin gown. 3½in (8.9cm).
4. LEIA ORGANA. Kenner, 1981. Wears Hoth outfit. 3½in (8.9cm).

SEE: STAR WARS.

Illustration 350. 8in (20.3cm) (FISCHER) QUINTUPLETS by Allied Doll & Toy Corp., 1963 or 1964. Fully-jointed. Head and arms of vinyl; torso and legs of plastic. Painted molded brown hair; painted side-glancing eyes; nurser mouth. The original outfits are for four girls with pink flannel diapers and blankets and a boy with a blue diaper and blanket. The girls have blue-topped bottles; the boy has a pink-topped bottle. Heads marked: "805 // 5." (These dolls also came with no markings.) *Alma Boudreaux Cansler Collection. Photograph by Alma Boudreaux Cansler.*

Illustration 352. Carrie Fisher as Princess Leia Organa and Mark Hamill as Luke Skywalker in *Star Wars*, 1977.

Illustration 353. 11½in (29.2cm) CARRIE FISHER as *Princess Leia Organa* from *Star Wars* by Kenner, No. 38070, 1978. All-vinyl and fully-jointed. Rooted dark brown hair; painted brown eyes. Copyright 1977 by Twentieth Century-Fox Film Corporation and copyright 1978 by General Mills Fun Group, Inc. Head marked: "© G.M.F.G.I. 1978." Made in Hong Kong.

FLASH GORDON. American comic strip hero involved in science fiction adventures. Buster Crabbe starred in a series of Flash Gordon films in the 1930s. They were: *Flash Gordon,* a serial in 1936, in which Flash and his friends saved the Earth from colliding with another planet at the cost of being stranded in space at the mercy of the wicked Emperor Ming; *Flash Gordon's Trip to Mars,* a serial in 1938 with a feature version *Mars Attacks the World*; and *Flash Gordon Conquers the Universe,* a serial in 1940. A softcore satire of the Flash Gordon films, called *Flesh Gordon,* appeared in 1974. In 1980 Sam J. Jones was *Flash Gordon* in an updated version of the original adventure.

There are two sets of Flash Gordon dolls. The first, by Mego, is a series of four dolls from 1976. These are based on the comic strip and look like the drawings, rather than any film version. The characters are *Flash Gordon, Ming, the Merciless, Dr. Zarkov* and *Dale Arden. (Illustrations 354 through 358.)* In 1980 Mattel released a series of dolls based on the "TV Spectaculars." At the time it appeared as if the dolls were from the films of the 1930s, which were popular on television. In late 1982 the animated film *Flash Gordon—The Greatest Adventure of All* was shown on television. This movie was made in 1979 and withheld because of the 1980 film release *Flash Gordon*. The Mattel dolls are from the animated film *Flash Gordon—The Greatest Adventure of All*, although they resemble the stars of the 1930s Flash Gordon films.

The Mattel dolls are cited as BUSTER CRABBE as *Flash,* ROBERT MIDDLETON as *Ming,* JAMES PIERCE as *Thun,* FRANK SHANNON as *Dr. Zarkov,* JOHN LIPSON as *Vultan,* and *Captain Arak, Beastman* and *Lizard Woman*. See entries under the celebrity names and *Illustrations 359* through *362.*

Illustration 354. 9½in (24.2cm) *Flash Gordon* by Mego, No. 74400/1, 1976. All-vinyl and fully-jointed. Painted yellow hair; painted blue eyes. Head marked: "©KING FEATURES // SYN INC 1976." Back marked: " ©1976 MEGO CORP. // MADE IN HONG KONG."

Illustration 355. *Flash Gordon* by Mego.

Illustration 356. 9½in (24.2cm) *Ming the Merciless* by Mego, No. 74400/2, 1976. All-vinyl and fully-jointed. Painted black hair, beard, moustache and eyes. Copyright 1976 King Features Syndicate, Inc. Made in Hong Kong.

Illustration 357. 9½in (24.2cm) *Dr. Zarkov* by Mego, No. 74400/3, 1976. All-vinyl and fully-jointed. Painted brown hair, moustache, beard and eyes. Copyright 1976 by King Features Syndicate, Inc. Made in Hong Kong.

Illustration 358. 9½in (24.2cm) *Dale Arden* by Mego, No. 74400/4, 1976. All-vinyl and fully-jointed. Rooted black hair; painted green eyes with blue eye shadow. The high heeled boots are molded as part of the leg. Copyright by King Features Syndicate, Inc. Made in Hong Kong.

Illustration 359. 4in (10.2cm) *Flash Gordon* from the 1982 film *Flash Gordon—The Greatest Adventure of All* by Mattel, No. 1525, 1980. All-vinyl with painted features and clothing. Copyright 1979 by King Features Syndicate, Inc. Made in Hong Kong.

Illustration 360. 4in (10.2cm) *Captain Arak* from *Flash Gordon* by Mattel, No. 1531, 1980. All-vinyl and fully-jointed with painted features and clothing. Copyright 1979 by King Features Syndicate, Inc. Made in Hong Kong.

Illustration 361. 4in (10.2cm) *Beastman* from *Flash Gordon* by Mattel, No. 1530, 1980. All-vinyl and fully-jointed. Painted features and clothing. Copyright 1979 by King Features Syndicate, Inc. Made in Hong Kong.

Illustration 362. 4in (10.2cm) *Lizard Woman* from *Flash Gordon* by Mattel, No. 1527, 1980. All-vinyl and fully-jointed with painted features. Copyright 1979 by King Features Syndicate, Inc. Made in Hong Kong.

FLEMING, MARY. Mary Fleming was a Lady-in-Waiting to Mary, Queen of Scots while she was the Queen of France (1558-1560). When Mary's husband, Francis II, died, Mary and the four ladies-in-waiting who accompanied her to France returned to Scotland.

DOLLS:
1. MARY FLEMING. Peggy Nisbet, No. H248, 1970s. Plastic "collectors' doll." Made in England. About 7½in (19.1cm). Mary Seaton, No. H247, is a companion doll.

FLICKER, TED (THEODORE J.). Writer, director, producer, actor. Born June 6, 1930. Multi-talented Ted Flicker has been involved with many phases of the production of films and television programs. On television he was the director of many series episodes but did not appear as a regular as an actor. In the 1981 film *The Legend of the Lone Ranger* he was Buffalo Bill Cody.

DOLLS:
1. BUFFALO BILL CODY from THE LEGEND OF THE LONE RANGER. Gabriel, No. 31634, 1981. All-vinyl and fully-jointed. Painted hair, features and clothing. Copyright 1980 by Lone Ranger Television, Inc. Made in Hong Kong. 4in (10.2cm).
SEE: THE LONE RANGER.

FORD, HARRISON. Actor. Born July 13, 1942. Ford began acting in college and performed in summer stock. He played small parts in several films of the late 1960s and did minor roles on many television shows, such as "Gunsmoke." He then became a carpenter. Ford returned to the screen in 1973 in George Lucas' *American Graffiti*. His greatest popularity came from three other George Lucas films. He was Han Solo, the captain of a pirate starship, in *Star Wars* in 1977 and *The Empire Strikes Back* in 1980 and Indiana Jones in *Raiders of the Lost Ark* in 1981.

DOLLS:
1. HAN SOLO. Kenner, No. 38260, 1978. All-vinyl and fully-jointed with painted features and clothing. Made in Hong Kong. 3¾in (9.6cm).
2. HAN SOLO. Kenner, No. 39170, 1979. Painted brown eyes. Made in Hong Kong. 12in (30.5cm). *Illustrations 363* and *364*.
3. HAN SOLO. Kenner, No. 39790, 1980. Hoth Outfit. Made in Hong Kong. 3¾in (9.6cm). *Illustration 365*.
4. HAN SOLO. Kenner, 1981. Wears Bespin Outfit. 3¾in (9.6cm).
5. INDIANA JONES. Kenner, No. 46000, 1981. This is the same doll as No. 2 with painted blue eyes instead of brown. 12in (30.5cm). *Illustration 366*.
6. INDIANA JONES. Kenner, Series No. 46010, 1982. All-vinyl and fully-jointed with painted features and clothing. Copyright by Lucasfilm Ltd. About 4¾in (12.2cm).
7. INDIANA JONES IN ARAB DISGUISE with MAP ROOM. Kenner, No. 46020, 1982. All-vinyl and fully-jointed with painted hair and features. Dressed in cloth robe. Copyright by Lucasfilm Ltd. about 4¾in (12.2cm).
SEE: STAR WARS and RAIDERS OF THE LOST ARK.

Illustration 363. 12in (30.5cm) HARRISON FORD as *Han Solo* from *Star Wars* by Kenner, No. 39170, 1979. All-vinyl and fully-jointed. Painted reddish hair and painted light brown eyes. Head marked: "©G.M.F.G.I. 1979." Back marked: "©G.M.F.G.I. 1978 KENNER PROD. // CINCINNATI, OHIO 45212 // MADE IN HONG KONG." Copyright 1977 by Twentieth Century-Fox Film Corporation.

Illustration 364. 12in (30.5cm) HARRISON FORD by Kenner.

Illustration 366. 12in (30.5cm) HARRISON FORD as *Indiana Jones* from *Raiders of the Lost Ark* by Kenner, 1981. Copyright by Lucasfilm Ltd. This advertisement is from *Playthings*, September 1981. The doll shown is no doubt a prototype.

FORREST, STEVE. Actor. Born William Forrest Andrews on September 29, 1924. Forrest is the younger brother of star Dana Andrews. He entered films in the early 1950s. He has played leads, second leads and supporting parts in a variety of roles. On television he was John Mannering, "The Baron," on ABC from January 1966 to July 1966 and Lt. Dan "Hondo" Harrelson in "S.W.A.T." from February 1975 to July 1976 on ABC.

DOLLS:
1. HONDO from S.W.A.T. L.J.N. Toys Ltd., No. 6600, 1975. Made in Hong Kong. 7½in (19.1cm).
2. HONDO from S.W.A.T. L.J.N. Toys Ltd., No. 6850, 1976. Made in Hong Kong. 7½in (19.1cm). *Illustration 367.*

SEE: S.W.A.T.

Illustration 365. 3¾in (9.6cm) HARRISON FORD as *Han Solo* in Hoth Outfit from *The Empire Strikes Back* (Star Wars Set #3) by Kenner, No. 39790, 1980. All-vinyl with painted features and clothing. Copyright 1977 by Twentieth Century-Fox Film Corporation. Made in Hong Kong.

Illustration 367. 7½in (19.1cm) STEVE FORREST as *Hondo* from "S.W.A.T." by L.J.N. Toys, No. 6850, 1976. (The same mold from 1975 is No. 6600.) All-vinyl and fully-jointed with painted hair and features. Copyright 1975 by Spelling-Goldberg Productions. The close-up photograph on the original box is of Steve Forrest.

FORSTER, ROBERT. Actor. Born July 13, 1941. Forster is a virile leading man type. In his first film, *Reflections in a Golden Eye,* he terrorized Elizabeth Taylor and was infatuated with by Marlon Brando. On television he played "Banyon" on NBC from September 1972 to 1973 and "Nakia" on ABC from September to December of 1974. In 1979's *The Black Hole* he was Captain Dan Holland, the commander pilot of the *Palomino.*

DOLLS:
1. CAPTAIN DAN HOLLAND OF THE BLACK HOLE. Mego, No. 95010, 1979. All-vinyl and fully-jointed with painted features and clothing. Copyright by Walt Disney Productions. Made in Hong Kong. 3¾in (9.6cm).
2. CAPTAIN DAN HOLLAND OF THE BLACK HOLE. Mego, No. 95005/5, 1979. Vinyl and plastic with painted features. Copyright by Walt Disney Productions. Made in Hong Kong. 12½in (31.8cm).

SEE: THE BLACK HOLE.

FOXX, REDD. Comedian. Born John Elroy Sanford on December 9, 1922. Since 1941 Redd Foxx has been a nightclub comedian. He also achieved fame and notoriety for his "party records." On television he was Fred Sanford on NBC-TV's "Sanford and Son" from January of 1972 to September of 1977, in which he played an elderly Los Angeles, California, junk dealer. He left the series to do a comedy-variety show with a black orientation, "Redd Foxx," which lasted briefly, from September 1977 to January 1978.

DOLLS:
1. REDD FOXX. Shindana, 1976. 16in (40.6cm). *Illustrations 368* and *369*.

Illustration 368. 16in (40.6cm) REDD FOXX, a two-sided cloth doll by Shindana, 1976. Printed features and clothing. Tag: " © 1976 // REDD FOXX ENTERPRISES // SHINDANA TOYS, INC."

Illustration 369.

FRANCIS, ANNE. Actress. Born September 16, 1930. Anne Francis began as a successful model and cover girl at the age of five. She played child roles on radio programs and was signed by MGM for films in 1947. She was always a second rank leading lady, even though she was capable of essaying a wide variety of parts. She was also a frequent star on television. Her first part in this medium was as the "Bonny Maid" who did floor covering commercials for the children's show "Versatile Varieties" during the 1949-1950 season on NBC. She was sexy private detective "Honey West" on ABC-TV from September 1965 to September 1966. During the 1971-1972 season she was Terri Dowling on CBS-TV's "My Three Sons."

DOLLS:
1. HONEY WEST. Gilbert, No. 16114, 1965. Made in Hong Kong. 11¾in (29.9cm). *Illustration 370.*

Illustration 370. 11¾in (29.9cm) ANNE FRANCIS as *Honey West* by Gilbert, No. 16114, 1965. Soft vinyl head; heavy vinyl arms; plastic legs and torso. Rooted blonde hair; painted eyes; painted "beauty spot" near mouth. Head marked: "K73." Honey West's leopard is plastic with flocked "fur" covering and is fully-jointed. It is not marked. Copyright by Four Star Television and A.C. Gilbert Co. Made in Hong Kong, Japan and USA. *Lee Jenkins Collection.*

FRANKLIN, BENJAMIN. American statesman, printer, scientist and writer. Born 1706; died 1790. Franklin was one of the most active patriots in America during the colonial period. He was a printer in Boston, Massachusetts, and Philadelphia, Pennsylvania. His yearly magazine, *Poor Richard's Almanack,* published from 1732 to 1757, was filled with his wit and common sense philosophy. ("Where there is marriage without love, there will be love without marriage.") In 1751 he helped to establish the University of Pennsylvania. He experimented with electricity, designed better carriage wheels, described the causes of weather conditions, crossbred better plants, improved sailing techniques, invented bifocal eye glasses, designed a portable fireplace called the Franklin stove, and invented a reading chair that kept the flies away from his book. (The chair was a rocker with a flap attached to the top that moved when rocked.) He was Deputy Postmaster General of the colonies (1753-1774). During the French and Indian War he tried to create a union of all the colonies at the Albany Congress (1754). He helped to draft the Declaration of Independence, which he signed in 1776. In 1781 he was chosen to lead the American peace delegation in Paris, France, after the Revolution was won. He was in his late 70s, but he was very popular with the French ladies. In 1787 he helped to form the Federal Constitution. His autobiography is a must for any student of American history.

DOLLS:
1. BENJAMIN FRANKLIN. Peggy Nisbet, No. P729, late 1970s. Plastic "collectors' doll." Made in England. About 8in (20.3cm).
2. BENJAMIN FRANKLIN. Manufactured for the S.S. Kresge Company as part of the "Heroes of the American Revolution" series, 1976. Made in Hong Kong. 7½in (19.1cm). *Illustration 371.*
3. BENJAMIN FRANKLIN. Hallmark, No. 250DT900-3, 1979. Made in Taiwan. 7in (17.8cm). *Illustration 372.*

4. BENJAMIN FRANKLIN. Made for Franklin Life Insurance Company as an advertising item, early 1980s. All-cloth with printed features and clothing. 12in (30.5cm).
5. BENJAMIN FRANKLIN. United States Historical Society, 1982. Fired porcelain head and hands; porcelain elastic body. Painted features; gray wig. Authentic portrait, attached to a wooden base. 11in (27.9cm). *Illustration 372-A.*

Illustration 372. 7in (17.8cm) BENJAMIN FRANKLIN by Hallmark, No. 250DT900-3, 1979. All-cloth. Sewn body joints with printed features and clothing. Made in Taiwan. *Shirley Buchholz Collection.*

Illustration 372-A. 11in (27.9cm) BENJAMIN FRANKLIN by United States Historical Society, 1982. Porcelain head and hands; porcelain elastic body. Painted features; gray wig. Worsted wool coat and trousers and velvet vest lined with satin; cotton cambric scarf, shirt and stockings; handmade kid leather shoes. Pewter buckles and buttons; sterling silver spectacles; silver headed walking stick. The mahogany base includes a brass identification plate. Limited edition of 2,500.

Illustration 371. 7½in (19.1cm) BENJAMIN FRANKLIN manufactured for the S.S. Kresge Company, 1976. Vinyl head with painted hair and features. Fully-jointed plastic body with swivel waist. Marked on back: "MADE IN // HONG KONG." *Shirley Buchholz Collection.*

FREDERICK III. Kaiser (Emperor) of Germany; King of Prussia. Born 1831; died 1888. Frederick, the son of William I and the father of William II (the Kaiser of World War I), ruled from March to June of 1888, only 98 days. In 1858 he had married Victoria, the daughter of Queen Victoria of England.

DOLLS:
1. KAISER FREDERICK III. Peggy Nisbet, No. P790, 1970s. Plastic "collectors' doll." Made in England. About 8in (20.3cm). Victoria, Empress of Germany, No. P789, is a companion doll.

FREEMAN, PAUL. British actor. In the film *Raiders of the Lost Ark* (1981) Paul Freeman was Belloq.

DOLLS:
1. BELLOQ. Kenner, 1982. All-vinyl and fully-jointed. Copyright by Lucasfilm Ltd. This character was offered as a free premium from Kenner with three proofs of purchase of "The Adventures of Indiana Jones" from *The Raiders of the Lost Ark* dolls, in an offer expiring March 31, 1983. About 4¾in (12.2cm).
SEE: RAIDERS OF THE LOST ARK.

FREHLEY, PAUL DANIEL (ACE). One of the four musicians of the rock group KISS. Born April 27, 1951. To illustrate the immense popularity of the bizarre group KISS, in April of 1980 *16 Magazine* carried Ace's "Vital Stats."

DOLLS:
1. ACE OF KISS. Mego, No. 88000 /4, 1978. Made in Hong Kong. 12½in (31.8cm). *Illustration 373.*
SEE: KISS.

FRY, ELIZABETH. English reformer. Born 1780; died 1845. Elizabeth Fry was a Quaker who believed, as do all Quakers, that all people are equal. She spent a good part of her life trying to bring reforms to prisons and lunatic asylums in England and France. She was also an ordained minister, an unusual status for a lady in her time.

DOLLS:
1. ELIZABETH FRY. Ann Parker, 1970s. All-plastic "collectors' doll," affixed to a wooden base. Made in England. 11in (27.9cm).

G

GABLE, CLARK. Actor. Born William Clark Gable in Cadiz, Ohio, February 1, 1901 (?); died 1960. Gable wanted to become an actor from the time he was a young boy. His first break came when he met actress Josephine Dillon, who married him in 1924. (If Gable's birthdate is accurate, Dillon would have been 14 years older than he.) Through Dillon, Gable obtained small parts in silent films in the mid-1920s. By 1928 Gable left Josephine Dillon, as she was not able to promote his career. He went to Broadway and appeared in some stage productions. His next break came in 1931 when he got the part of a villian in a William Boyd western film. He was then signed by MGM and promoted as a "promising new star." Gable appeared in pictures with Joan Crawford, Jean Harlow, Greta Garbo and others and became a top moneymaker for MGM. He won an Academy Award for *It Happened One Night,* a loan-out assignment for Columbia Pictures in 1934. The most important role of Clark Gable's career was playing Rhett Butler in *Gone With the Wind* in 1939, a part for which he was perfect. After World War II Clark Gable returned to the screen from the Air Force, and although he was heavier and much older looking his popularity on the screen lasted until his death. His last film was *The Misfits*, released in 1961. (This was also Marilyn Monroe's last completed picture.) Of his five wives, the

Illustration 373. 12½in (31.8cm) PAUL DANIEL FREHLEY, ACE of KISS, by Mego, No. 88000/4, 1978. All-vinyl and fully-jointed. Rooted hair and painted features and makeup. Head marked: "©1978 AUCOIN // MGMT. INC." Back marked: "© MEGO CORP. 1977 // MADE IN HONG KONG." *Penny Caswell Collection.*

Illustration 374. About 8in (20.3cm) CLARK GABLE as *Rhett Butler* in *Gone With the Wind,* No. P750, and VIVIEN LEIGH as *Scarlett O'Hara* in *Gone With the Wind,* No. P751, by Peggy Nisbet, 1970s. All-hard plastic and jointed only at the arms. Made in England. Copyright 1939 by Selznick; renewed 1967 by MGM. *Peggy Nisbet Silver Jubilee Edition Collectors Reference Book* (1977).

happiest marriage was said to have been with Carole Lombard. A son, John Clark, was born to his last wife, Kay, shortly after "The King" died.

DOLLS:
1. CLARK GABLE AS RHETT BUTLER IN *GONE WITH THE WIND.* Peggy Nisbet, No. P750, 1970s. Vivien Leigh, No. P750 is the companion doll. Made in England. About 7½in (19.1cm). *Illustration 374.*
2. RHETT. Madame Alexander, No. 1380, 1981. Scarlett, No. 1385, is the companion doll. 12in (30.5cm). *Illustration 375.*

Illussration 375. 12in (30.5cm) CLARK GABLE as *Rhett* from *Gone With the Wind* by Madame Alexander, No. 1380, 1981. Vinyl head with rooted dark brown hair; brown sleep eyes with molded lashes; painted moustache. Fully-jointed hard plastic body.

GARBER, MATTHEW. Child actor. Matthew Garber appeared in three Walt Disney films. They were *The Three Lives of Thomasina* in 1963, *Mary Poppins* in 1964 and *The Gnome-Mobile* in 1967. In *Mary Poppins* he was Michael.

DOLLS:
1. MICHAEL from *Mary Poppins.* Horsman, 1964. All-vinyl and fully-jointed. Rooted blonde hair; painted blue eyes. Came in a set with Mary Poppins and Jane. 8¼in (21cm). See *Illustration 66.*

GARBO, GRETA. Actress. Born Greta Louisa Gustafsson on September 18, 1905, in Sweden. Garbo's film career began when she appeared in a short film for a department store in Stockholm in 1921. She later won a scholarship to the Royal Dramatic Theater training school. While at the school she came to the attention of the noted director Mauritz Stiller who cast her in her first important film, *The Story of Gösta Berling,* 1924, which was a critical success. In 1925 Stiller was invited to Hollywood to work for Louis B. Mayer at MGM. The condition of Stiller's acceptance was that his protégé would also receive a contract. Garbo was big, clumsy, timid and plain. But when she was put in front of a camera she came alive, looked beautiful and gave many interesting performances in silent films. Garbo became a superstar. Her career also soared in sound films in spite of her heavy accent, and she was considered the greatest actress in the movies by the critics and by the

public, especially in Europe. In 1941 Garbo suddenly retired from films, which helped to further promote the "air of mystery" that always surrounded her. She now lives in New York, New York, and still works hard to protect her "privacy" and refuses all offers for screen assignments. Garbo is one of the greatest legends of the movies.

DOLLS:
1. GRETA GARBO AS MARGURITE GAUTIER IN *CAMILLE* by Peggy Nisbet, No. P753, 1970s. Made in England. 7½in (19.1cm). *Illustration 377.*

Illustration 376. Greta Garbo and Robert Taylor in *Camille*, 1936.

Illustration 377. 7½in (19.1cm) GRETA GARBO as *Marguerite Gautier* in *Camille* by Peggy Nisbet, No. P753, 1970s. All-hard plastic; jointed only at the arms. Painted blue eyes; brown mohair wig. Copyright 1936 and 1963 by MGM. Made in England.

GARLAND, JUDY. Actress, singer. Born Frances Gumm on June 10, 1922; died 1969. Judy Garland's first performances were on the vaudeville stage. At age 13 Louis B. Mayer of MGM signed her to a contract when he heard her sing. Her first screen role was in a short, *Every Sunday*, featuring Deanna Durbin. In 1939 she won a special Academy Award for the greatest performance of her juvenile career, that of Dorothy in *The Wizard of Oz*. The role was originally intended for Shirley Temple, but nobody could have sung "Over the Rainbow" better than Judy Garland, and the part of Dorothy was perfect for her. During her teen years Garland was in nine films with Mickey Rooney, another top juvenile star. During this time she began gaining weight and allegedly the studio assigned a doctor to give her pills to control the problem. Before long she was depending on pills for most bodily functions. The most successful film of her young adult years was *Meet Me in St. Louis* in 1944. In 1950 MGM fired her because she would not show up for work. She returned to the screen in 1954 and gave her finest performance of all in *A Star is Born*. During the 1960s she appeared on her own television program, sometimes visibly suffering the effects of too much alcohol. Yet when she sang she was

as good as ever. By 1968 she was performing in a nightclub in London, England. Audiences tossed garbage on stage because she was not able to sing properly or remember any of her lines. Judy Garland had a miserable personal life compounded by five husbands, nervous breakdowns, suicide attempts, lawsuits, counter-law-suits, pills and booze. Her death was attributed to "an accidental overdose of sleeping pills." Yet she will always be a show business legend because of her enormous talent.

DOLLS:
1. DOROTHY from *The Wizard of Oz*. Ideal, circa 1939. Made in USA. 15½in (39.4cm). *Illustrations 378* and *379*.
2. JUDY GARLAND "teen." Ideal, circa 1941. Made in USA. 21in (53.3cm). *Illustrations 380* and *381*.
3. DOROTHY from *The Wizard of Oz*. Mego, No. 51500 /1, 1974 / Made in Hong Kong. 7¾in (19.8cm). *Illustration 382*.
4. DOROTHY from THE WIZARD OF OZ. Mego, No. 59036, 1974. Vinyl head; cloth body. Copyright 1974 by MGM, Inc. Made in Hong Kong. 15in (38.1cm).
5. JUDY GARLAND IN *MEET ME IN ST. LOUIS*. Peggy Nisbet, No. P754, 1970s. Plastic "collectors' doll." Copyright 1944 by Lowe's; renewed 1971 by MGM. Made in England. About 7½in (19.1cm).

SEE: THE WIZARD OF OZ.

Illustration 378. 15½in (39.4cm) JUDY GARLAND as *Dorothy* from *The Wizard of Oz* by Ideal, circa 1939. All-composition and fully-jointed. Dark brown human hair wig; brown sleep eyes with lashes; open mouth with teeth and tongue. Head marked: "IDEAL DOLL // MADE IN USA." Back marked: "USA // 16." The doll is all-original, but the basket with Dorothy's dog, Toto, is an addition. *Rosemary Dent Collection. Photograph by Maury S. Saunders.*

Illustration 379. JUDY GARLAND as *Dorothy*. This is a similar doll to the one in the full view. *Emilie Marie Reynolds Collection.*

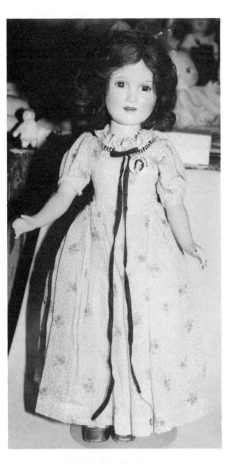

LEFT: Illustration 380. 21in (53.3cm) JUDY GARLAND "teen" by Ideal, circa 1941. All-composition and fully-jointed. Dark brown human hair wig; brown sleep eyes with lashes; open mouth with teeth and a felt tongue. The dress is pink; the pin, showing a photograph of Judy Garland, is original to the doll. Head marked: "IDEAL DOLL // MADE IN U.S.A." Back marked: "IDEAL DOLL // I**S** * ." (NOTE: This doll is very similar to the Deanna Durbin doll and an unnamed "teen" doll from Ideal at the same time.) *Frances Benson Collection.* * a backwards "21."

RIGHT: Illustration 382. 7¾in (19.8cm) JUDY GARLAND as *Dorothy* from *The Wizard of Oz* carrying Toto in a basket by Mego, No. 51500/1, 1974. All-vinyl and fully-jointed, including waist. Rooted dark brown hair; painted brown eyes. Head marked: "© 1974 MGM // INC." Back marked: " © MEGO CORP. // MCMLXXII // MADE IN // HONG KONG." 1½in (3.8cm) Toto is marked on the bottom: "MGM INC. © ." Dorothy wears a blue and white check dress and red shoes like she did in the film.

GARNER, JAMES. Actor. Born James Baumgarner on April 7, 1928. Garner began his show business career in 1954 when a friend gave him a role in the Broadway play "The Caine Mutiny Court-Martial." He soon landed parts in films and on television because of his good looks. By the late 1960s he was one of the top box office stars in Hollywood. He played Bret Maverick on ABC-TV's "Maverick" from 1957 to 1960, when he walked out on his contract, demanding a larger salary. He was on "Nichols," another western from September of 1971 to August of 1972 on NBC-TV and "The Rockford Files" as private investigator Jim Rockford from September of 1974 to July of 1980 on NBC-TV. On December 1, 1981 James Garner returned to television in a weekly series, reprising his original TV role as "Bret Maverick" on NBC.

DOLLS:
1. JAMES GARNER AS BRET MAVERICK. Hartland Plastics, Inc., No. 762, circa 1958. Plastic, jointed at the arms. Made in Hartland, Wisconsin. 8in (20.3cm).

Illustration 381. JUDY GARLAND "teen." *Frances Benson Collection.*

Illustration 383. James Garner as Bret Maverick from the TV show "Maverick," circa 1957.

GEER, WILL. Actor. Born March 9, 1902; died 1978. Will Geer appeared on Broadway during the 1920s and was in films during the 1930s and 1940s. From 1951 to 1962 he was unable to find work as an actor because he had been "blacklisted" for alleged "Communist activities." He came back as a character actor in films and later on TV. His most memorable part was that of Zeb (Grandpa) Walton on "The Waltons" on CBS-TV from September of 1972 until his death.

DOLLS:
1. GRANDPA ZEB WALTON. Mego, 1975. Came as a set with Grandma Walton. 8in (20.3cm). *Illustration 384.*

SEE: THE WALTONS.

Illustration 386. BOBBIE GENTRY by Hasbro. *Wanda Lodwick Collection.*

Illustration 384. 8in (20.3cm) WILL GEER as *Grandpa Zeb Walton* from "The Waltons" by Mego, 1975. All-vinyl and fully-jointed. Painted gray hair and painted gray eyes. Head marked: " © 1974 LORIMAR // PROD. INC." *Penny Caswell Collection.*

GENTRY, BOBBIE. Singer, songwriter. Born July 27, 1944, in Mississippi. In 1967 Bobbie Gentry wrote and recorded her hit record "Ode to Billy Joe." The song won three Grammy Awards and was made into a film in 1976 starring Robbie Benson. (Billie Joe McAllister jumped off the Tallahatchie Bridge because of a homosexual relationship.)

DOLLS:
1. BOBBIE GENTRY, one of the SHOW BIZ BABIES. Hasbro, No. 8814, 1967. Made in Hong Kong. 4¼in (10.9cm). *Illustrations 385* and *386.*

GEORGE III. King of Great Britain and Ireland, 1760-1820. Born 1738; died 1820. George's wanting to personally rule the Empire and the growing ascendency of Parliament led to the American Revolution in which Britain lost the American colonies. The Industrial Revolution also developed during his reign. In 1811 he was forced to turn the throne over to his son, George IV, because of his alleged insanity.

DOLLS:
1. KING GEORGE III. Peggy Nisbet, No. P706, 1970s. Plastic "collectors' doll." Made in England. About 8in (20.3cm). Queen Charlotte, No. P707 is a companion doll.

GEORGE V. King of England from 1910 to 1936. Born 1865; died 1936. George was the second son of Edward VII whom he succeeded. He was king during World War I, and it was he who gave up all German titles inherited from Victoria and Albert and changed the family name from Saxe-Coburg-Gotha to Windsor. His sons became King Edward VIII and King George VI. His granddaughter is Elizabeth II.

DOLLS:
1. KING GEORGE V. Peggy Nisbet, No. P709, 1970s. Plastic "collector's doll." Prince Edward VIII, the Duke of Windsor, No. P711 and Queen Mary, No. P710, are companion dolls in a set called "The House of Windsor." Made in England. About 8in (20.3cm).

Illustration 385. 4¼in (10.9cm) BOBBIE GENTRY, a Show Biz Baby by Hasbro, No. 8814, 1967. All-vinyl; jointed only at the head; wired vinyl poseable body. Rooted dark brown hair; painted brown eyes. Attached to a record cover. Back marked: " © 1967 // HASBRO // HONG KONG." *Wanda Lodwick Collection.*

GEORGE VI. King of Great Britain from 1936 to 1952. Born 1895; died 1952. George became king when his brother, Edward VIII, gave up the throne to marry the twice-divorced Mrs. Wallis Warfield Simpson. During World War II he visited bombed areas and toured the theaters of war. Winston Churchill personally resisted the King's efforts to be among the first to land on the beaches of Normandy on D-Day, June 6, 1944, during the largest land invasion in history. George was succeeded by his eldest daughter, Elizabeth.

DOLLS:

1. to 4.

GEORGE VI. J.K. Farnell Co., Ltd., 1937. Felt head; cloth jointed body. Painted features. The doll came dressed four different ways: Coronation Robes, Colonel of the Grenadier Guards, Royal Highlander and Marshal of the Royal Air Force. Made in England by Farnell's Alpha Toys. 13½in (34.3cm). *Illustrations 387, 388* and *389*.

5. H.R.H. KING GEORGE VI. Liberty of London, circa 1938. All-cloth with stitched and painted features. 9½in (24.2cm). Came as a set called the "Coronation Group" and included Queen Elizabeth, Princess Elizabeth and Princess Margaret Rose. Made in England.

6. KING GEORGE VI. Peggy Nisbet, No. P712, 1970s. Plastic "collectors' doll." Queen Elizabeth, No. P713, is a companion doll. Made in England. About 8in (20.3cm).

Illustration 387. 15in (38.1cm) (including hat) H.M. KING GEORGE VI by Farnell Alpha Toys, late 1930s. Felt head; cloth jointed body with slim proportions. Painted blue eyes. King George, dressed as a Colonel of the Grenadiers, is wearing a black fur guardsman's hat, a scarlet jacket and navy blue trousers. A paper tag is attached to the right arm. A cloth tag on the left foot cites: "FARNELL // ALPHA TOYS // MADE IN ENGLAND." *Shirley Buchholz Collection. Photograph by Jane Buchholz.*

Illustration 388. 13½in (34.3cm) H.M. KING GEORGE VI dressed as a Marshall of the Royal Air Force by Farnell's Alpha Toys, late 1930s. Felt head; cloth jointed body. Painted blue eyes. The suit is navy blue; the hat is black "fur." The sword and the plume in the hat are missing.

PRINCE GEORGE. Prince of Denmark; Consort of Queen Anne of Great Britain and Ireland from 1683 to 1708. Born 1653; died 1708. The second son of King Frederick III and the brother of King Christian V of Denmark, he married Anne of England in an unpopular political move. Anne and her husband were a happy couple, and she honored him with the titles Earl of Kendal and Duke of Cumberland in 1689.

DOLLS:
1. PRINCE GEORGE OF DENMARK. Peggy Nisbet, No. P451, 1970s. Plastic "collectors' doll." Queen Anne, No. P450, is a companion doll. Made in England. About 8in (20.3cm).

GERARD, GIL. Actor. Born in Little Rock, Arkansas, in 1940. Gil Gerard was on the serial "The Doctors" and the TV Pilot "Ransom for Alice" in 1977. He played the part of Buck Rogers on NBC-TVs "Buck Rogers in the 25th Century" from September 1979 to September 1980. A revised version of the show entitled "Buck Rogers" ran from January 1981 through repeats in the summer of 1981 with Gil Gerard again as Buck.

DOLLS:
1. BUCK ROGERS. Mego, No. 85000/1, 1979. Made in Hong Kong. 3¾in (9.6cm). Illustration 390.
2. BUCK ROGERS. Mego, No. 85001/1, 1979. Made in Hong Kong. 12½in (31.8cm). Illustrations 391 and 392.

SEE: BUCK ROGERS IN THE 25TH CENTURY.

Illustration 391. 12½in (31.8cm) GIL GERARD as *Buck Rogers* from "Buck Rogers in the 25th Century" by Mego, No. 85001/1, 1979. All-vinyl and fully-jointed, including waist. Painted black hair and painted blue eyes; dark skin tones; very muscular body. Head marked: "© 1978 ROBERT // C. DILLE." Back marked: "© 1978 MEGO CORP. // MADE IN HONG KONG."

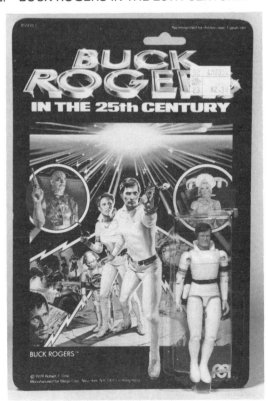

Illustration 390. 3¾in (9.6cm) GIL GERARD as *Buck Rogers* from "Buck Rogers in the 25th Century" by Mego, No. 85000/1, 1979. All-vinyl and fully-jointed. Painted features and clothing. Copyright by Robert C. Dille. Made in Hong Kong.

OPPOSITE PAGE: Illustration 389. KING GEORGE VI by Farnell's Alpha Toys dressed in the Royal Air Force uniform.

Illustration 392. GIL GERARD by Mego in the 12½in (31.8cm) size.

GERONIMO. Indian chief. Born circa 1829; died 1909. Geronimo was a chief of the Chiricahua tribe of the Apache Indians. This group terrorized the Arizona Territory by brutal raids in the 1880s.

DOLLS:
1. GERONIMO. Louis Marx & Co., 1972. All-heavy vinyl with molded and painted hair, features and clothing. Fully-jointed. Came with a wide assortment of accessories such as ceremonial dress, masks, quiver, saddle bag, drum, knives and other equipment and sold for $3.44. 11½in (29.2cm).

GIBB, ANDY. Singer. Born in Manchester, England, on March 5, 1958. Andy Gibb became a teen disco singing idol in the late 1970s. His hit songs were "Shadow Dancing," "I Just Want to Be Your Everything" and "Love is Thicker Than Water." Tight-panted Andy is the younger brother of the Bee Gees, an English rock group. The Bee Gees (Brothers Gibb) are Barry, Maurice and Robin.

DOLLS:
1. ANDY GIBB. Ideal, No. 2L-1219, 1979. Made in Hong Kong. 7¼in (18.5cm). *Illustration 394*.

Illustration 393. Andy Gibb on a notebook cover. Copyright 1978 by Stigwood Group, Ltd.

GIBBS, MARLA. Actress. Born June 14, 1946. Marla Gibbs played Florence Johnston, the acid-tongued maid on CBS-TV's "The Jeffersons," which began in January of 1975. In 1980 she left the series to appear on a short-lived show of her own, playing the same character. In October of 1981 she returned to "The Jeffersons."

DOLLS:
1. MARLA GIBBS. Shindana, No. 1048, 1978. Made in Hong Kong. 15in (38.1cm). *Illustrations 395* and *396*.

Illustration 394. 7¼in (18.5cm) ANDY GIBB by Ideal, No. 2L-1219, 1979. All-vinyl and fully-jointed. Rooted blonde hair; painted blue eyes. The plastic stand is finger operated so Andy can go "disco dancing." Head marked: "©1979 // S.G.L. IDEAL // H-3177 // HONG KONG." Back marked above jointed waist: "ANDY GIBB TM // IDEAL TOY CORP. // HONG KONG." Copyright by Stigwood Group, Ltd.

Illustration 395. 15in (38.1cm) MARLA GIBBS as the maid *Florence* from "The Jeffersons" by Shindana Toys, No. 1048, 1978. All-vinyl with rooted black hair and painted brown eyes. Fully-jointed. The original carton includes an extra outfit that is a gown. Copyright by Marla Gibbs Enterprises, Inc. and Shindana Toys, Inc. Made in Hong Kong.

Illustration 396. MARLA GIBBS by Shindana.

GILBERT, MELISSA. Actress. Born May 8, 1964. Melissa Gilbert has played Laura Ingalls in "Little House on the Prairie" since the show debuted on NBC-TV in September of 1974. In 1979 she tackled the role of Helen Keller in a new version of *The Miracle Worker*, a presentation made especially for television.

DOLLS:

1. LAURA from "Little House on the Prairie." Knicker-bocker, Asst. No. 9361—No. 0405, 1978. Made in Taiwan. 12in (30.5cm). *Illustration 397.* Carrie, Asst. No. 9361—No. 0404, is a companion doll.

Illustration 397. 12in (30.5cm) MELISSA GILBERT as *Laura* from "Little House on the Prairie" by Knickerbocker, Asst. No. 9361—No. 0405, 1978. Vinyl head and lower arms; stuffed cloth body. Rooted dark blonde hair in braids; painted green eyes. Head marked: "© ED FRIENDLY PRODS. INC. // LIC JLM // MADE IN TAIWAN T-1." The costume is tagged: "Little House on the Prairie." *Penny Caswell Collection.*

GILBERT, RUTH. Character actress. Ruth Gilbert was a star of early television. From August to September of 1949 she was the lead in "Ruthie on the Telephone" for CBS-TV. From 1952 to 1955 she played Max, Milton Berle's secretary on "The Milton Berle Show" on NBC-TV. Max's secret love was Francis, an NBC stagehand.

DOLLS:

1. to 4.

MAXINE. Roberta Doll Co., 1954. All-hard plastic and fully-jointed. A wallking doll. Dressed in velvet jumper and white blouse. Blonde saran hair; blue sleep eyes with lashes. The doll came with a small steno pad and a pencil. Sizes of 14in (35.6cm), 16in (40.6cm), 19in (48.3cm) and 22in (55.9cm).

GISH, DOROTHY and LILLIAN. Actresses. Dorothy was born in 1898; died 1968. A stage actress since she was four years old, Dorothy Gish shared her personal and professional life with her sister, Lillian. The sisters made their screen debut in film pioneer D.W. Griffith's *An Uneasy Enemy* in 1912. Dorothy appeared in many silent films, and her talents were best seen in light comedy. She had some parts in talking pictures, the last of which was in *The Cardinal* in 1963. Lillian was born in 1896, and she became a stage actress at the age of five. She is known as "The First Lady of the Silent Screen." She has been a movie star for almost 70 years. Lillian excelled in dramatic parts and usually played a fragile heroine, beginning her film career under the guidance of Griffith. After the advent of sound in films, Lillian returned to the stage and has appeared in movies less frequently since. Her last film was *A Wedding* in 1978.

DOLLS:

Dorothy S. Coleman reported in *Lenci Dolls, Fabulous Figures in Felt* (Hobby House Press, 1977), page 67, that a pair of 24in (61cm) felt dolls by Lenci of Italy resemble the Gish sisters. From the photograph of the dolls they do seem to look like Dorothy and Lillian, but other Lenci dolls from the 1920s also have the same expression and appearance. Mrs. Coleman said of her research on the Lenci dolls that in regard to them being the Gish sisters "...no information has been found to verify this assumption."

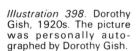

Illustration 398. Dorothy Gish, 1920s. The picture was personally autographed by Dorothy Gish.

GISONDI, TONI ANN. Child actress. Toni Ann Gisondi played Molly, Annie's friend in the orphanage, in the film *Annie* (1982).

DOLLS:
1. MOLLY. Knickerbocker Toy Co., Inc., No. 3868, 1982. All-vinyl and fully-jointed. Rooted brown hair; painted features. Copyright by Columbia Pictures Industries, Inc. 6in (15.2cm).

SEE: ANNIE.

GLASER, PAUL MICHAEL. Actor. Born Paul Manfred Glaser on March 25, 1943. Paul Michael Glaser began his acting career by appearing in small parts like his movie role in *Butterflies Are Free* in 1972. He was also in the serials "Love is a Many Splendored Thing" and "Love of Life" on television. He is best known as Detective Dave Starsky from "Starsky and Hutch" on ABC-TV from September 1975 to August 1979.

DOLLS:
1. STARSKY. Mego, No. 62800 /2, 1976. Made in Hong Kong. 7½in (19.1cm). *Illustration 400*.

SEE: STARSKY AND HUTCH.

Illustration 399. Paul Michael Glaser.

Illustration 400. 7½in (19.1cm) PAUL MICHAEL GLASER as *Starsky* from "Starsky and Hutch" by Mego, No. 62800/1, 1976. All-vinyl and fully-jointed. Painted black hair; painted features. Copyright by Spelling-Goldberg Productions. Made in Hong Kong.

GOLDWATER, BARRY. Politician. Born January 1, 1909, in Phoenix, Arizona. Goldwater is a highly respected conservative Repulican leader. He was the United States Senator from Arizona from 1952 to 1964 and again since 1969. In 1964 he was the Republican Presidential Candidate. He urged a more aggressive stance against Communism and a drastic reduction of Federal power. He lost to Lyndon B. Johnson.

DOLLS:
1. SENATOR BARRY M. GOLDWATER. Remco, No. 1816, 1964. Made in USA. 5¾in (14.7cm). *Illustration 401*. Lyndon B. Johnson, No. 1815, is a companion doll.

Illustration 401. 5¾in (14.7cm) BARRY GOLDWATER by Remco, No. 1816, 1964. All-vinyl with a jointed head and a one-piece body. Attached plastic glasses. The features and clothing are painted. This was a tie-in for the 1964 presidential elections in which the Senator was the Republican candidate. LYNDON B. JOHNSON is of the same concept. Marked on neck: "REMCO IND. INC. // © 1964." Made in USA. *Shirley Buchholz Collection.*

GORSHIN, FRANK. Impressionist, actor. Born April 5, 1934. Gorshin began his show business career as a comic impressionist and later turned to dramatic acting, specializing in villian roles. He was the Riddler on the ABC-TV fantasy adventure "Batman," which ran from January 1966 to March 1968.

DOLLS:
1. RIDDLER. Mego, No. 1352, 1974. All-vinyl and fully-jointed. Made in Hong Kong. Part of the "Arch-Enemy" series from "Batman." 7½in (19.1cm). Other dolls in the series are Batman, Robin, Joker, Penguin and Mr. Mxyzptlk. These dolls probably should be considered Comic Book dolls rather than Celebrity Dolls, but the characters are from the TV shows.

GRANDY, FRED. Actor. Born June 29, (?) in Sioux City, Iowa. Grandy appeared in many films and television shows beginning in the 1970s. For a time he was a boyfriend of Carol on "Maude" on CBS-TV. In 1977 he was in the pilot film "Duffy." He was a regular on "The Monster Squad" on NBC-TV from September 1976 to September 1977. After appearing in two pilot films for "The Love Boat" in early 1977, Grandy continued his regular part as Burl "Gopher" Smith beginning in September 1977. In May 1979 he was in the miniseries "Blind Ambition."

DOLLS:
1. "GOPHER" from THE LOVE BOAT. Mego, No. 23005 /5, 1982. All-vinyl and fully-jointed. Painted hair, features and molded clothing. Copyright by Aaron Spelling Productions, Inc. Made in Hong Kong. 3¾in (9.6cm).
SEE: LOVE BOAT, THE.

GRANT, JULIA. First Lady. Born Julia Boggs Dent, January 26, 1826; died December 14, 1902. Ulysses S. Grant's military victories during the Civil War assured him of two terms as President (1869-1877). As the White House hostess, Mrs. Grant spent much of her time receiving groups of Union veterans. After leaving the White House, the Grants made a two years' trip around the world.

DOLLS:
1. JULIA GRANT. Madame Alexander, No. 1519, 1982. Vinyl and plastic and fully-jointed. Rooted blonde hair with thick braids on top. Dressed in a white and silver brocaded coat-style gown. Part of the third six First Ladies Series. 14in (35.6cm).
SEE: FIRST LADIES, THE.

GRANT, ULYSSES S. Commander-in-Chief of the Union Army in the Civil War, 18th President of the United States. Born Hiram Ulyssess Grant in 1822; died 1885. Grant always went by the name Ulysses and when a congressman from Ohio appointed him to West Point, he filled in the name Simpson as his middle name on the application, thinking that his mother's maiden name was his middle name. Grant was considered brutal during the Civil War, because he believed that the most important military objective should be to destroy the enemy armies. He was the successful Republican Candidate for President in 1868 and 1872. Grant is considered the worst of all United States Presidents. He was honest but he was naïve, and his Administration was filled with disreputable politicians and financiers.

DOLLS:
1. GEN. ULYSSES S. GRANT. Excel Toy Corp., 1974. All-vinyl and fully-jointed with painted hair and features. Made in Hong Kong. 9¾in (24.9cm).

GRAY, ERIN. Actress. Erin Gray played Colonel Wilma Deering, Commander of the Third Force of the Earth Directory, on "Buck Rogers in the 25th Century" on NBC-TV from September 1979 to September 1980. Other than Gil Gerard as Buck and Felix Silla as Twiki, she was the only original cast member in the revamped show "Buck Rogers" from January 1981 through summer reruns of 1981.

DOLLS:
1. WILMA DEERING. Mego, No. 85000 /3, 1979. All-vinyl and fully-jointed with painted features and clothing. Copyright by Robert C. Dille. Made in Hong Kong. 3¾in (9.6cm).
SEE: BUCK ROGERS IN THE 25TH CENTURY.

THE GREATEST AMERICAN HERO. Television series on ABC. The show had a two-hour premiere on March 18, 1981. It is a spoof of the super-hero genre, for which the copyright holders of "Superman" filed suit and apparently lost their case. The premise of the show is that Ralph Hinkley, played by WILLIAM KATT, is a mild-mannered teacher who had a close encounter with aliens from outer space. Ralph was given a red suit and cape that allowed him to fly and to have super-strength with which to combat assorted criminal types. Ralph is aided by Bill Maxwell, an FBI agent, played by ROBERT CULP, and his level-headed girlfriend, Pam, played by CONNIE SELLECCA. See entries under each celebrity and *Illustration 402-A*.

Illustration 402-A. The stars of television's "The Greatest American Hero" by Mego, Series No. 2201, 1982. From left to right: CONNIE SELLECCA as *Pam*, ROBERT CULP as *Bill* and WILLIAM KATT as *Ralph*. 8in (20.3cm). Copyright by Stephen J. Connell Productions.* From *Soar with the Eagles* (Mego catalog), 1982.

*So stated in the Mego catalog. The television show is produced by Stephen J. Cannell Productions.

GREENBUSCH, LINDSAY and SIDNEY. Child actresses. The identical twin girls were born on May 25, 1970. They have taken turns playing Carrie Ingalls in NBC-TV's "Little House on the Prairie" since the show began in September 1974. (Initially this was because of laws that prevent babies from "working" too long in front of the cameras and hot lights.)

DOLLS:
1. CARRIE from "Little House on the Prairie." Knickerbocker, Asst. No. 9361—No. 0404, 1978. Made in Taiwan. 12in (30.5cm). *Illustration 402.* Laura, Asst. No. 9361—No. 0405 is a companion doll.

Illustration 402. 12in (30.5cm) LINDSAY and/or SIDNEY GREEN-BUSCH (twins) as *Carrie* from "Little House on the Prairie" by Knickerbocker, Asst. No. 9361—No. 0404, 1978. Vinyl head and lower arms; stuffed cloth body. Painted blue eyes; long rooted auburn hair. Head marked: "©1978 ED FRIENDLY PRODS. INC. // LIC JLM // MADE IN TAIWAN T-2." The costume is tagged: "Little House on the Prairie." *Penny Caswell Collection.*

GREENE, ERIC. Child actor. Eric Greene played Loki, the boy who was an alien ally, on "Space Academy" on CBS-TV from September 1977 to September 1979.
DOLLS:
1. LOKI from "Space Academy." Aviva Toy Company, No. 110, 1978. Made in Hong Kong. 6¼in (15.9cm). *Illustration 403*.
SEE: SPACE ACADEMY.

GREENE, LORNE. Actor. Born February 12, 1915, in Canada. After graduating from college, Lorne Greene went into radio and became a newscaster. In the 1950s he came to the United States and appeared in plays, television shows and movies. On television he achieved fame as Ben Cartwright in the long-running NBC-TV western "Bonanza" which lasted from September 1959 to January 1973. He was a private detective on "Griff" on ABC-TV from September 1973 to January 1974. Then he was Commander Adama on "Battlestar Galactica" from September 1978 to August 1979 and repeated the same part on "Galactica 1980" which only lasted three episodes in January and February of 1980. In the fall of 1981 he began a new series on ABC-TV, "Code Red."
DOLLS:
1. BEN CARTWRIGHT. American Character, 1965. Fully-jointed "action figure" of plastic. Molded and painted clothing and features. 8in (20.3cm). Dan Blocker as Hoss Cartwright and Michael Landon as Little Joe Cartwright are companion dolls. (See DAN BLOCKER.)
2. COMMANDER ADAMA FROM BATTLESTAR GALACTICA. Mattel, No. 2868, 1978. Made in Hong Kong. 4in (10.2cm). *Illustration 404.* Dirk Benedict as Lt. Starbuck, No. 2871, is a companion doll in the series.

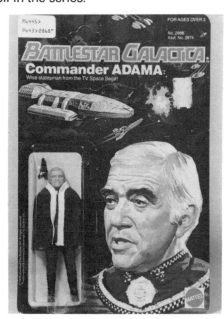

Illustration 404. 4in (10.2cm) LORNE GREENE as *Commander Adama* from "Battlestar Galactica" by Mattel, No. 2868, 1978. All-vinyl and fully-jointed. Painted hair and clothing with a cloth cape. Note that the features are left blank. Copyright by Universal City Studios, Inc. Made in Hong Kong.

LEFT: Illustration 403. 6¼in (15.9cm) ERIC GREENE as *Loki* from "Space Academy" by Aviva Toy Company for F. W. Woolworth Co., No. 110, 1978. All-vinyl and fully-jointed. Painted black hair and eyes. Lower back marked: " © 1978 // FILMATION ASSOCIATES // ALL RIGHTS RESERVED // MADE IN HONG KONG // PAT. PEND." *Penny Caswell Collection.*

GREY, LADY JANE. Candidate for the throne of England. Born 1537; died 1554. Edward VI, the son of Henry VIII, was persuaded by the Duke of Northumberland, Lady Jane Grey's father-in-law, to name her as his successor. This was to cover the confusion of Henry's many marriages and the legitimacy of his heirs. Lady Jane Grey was a great-niece of Henry and would have been first in line for the throne if Henry's daughters, Mary and Elizabeth, could be considered illigimate and unable to inherit the throne. Against her judgment, Lady Jane Grey was proclaimed Queen in 1553 but after nine days, Mary I, Henry's eldest daughter, seized the throne. Lady Jane Grey was beheaded at age 17.

DOLLS:
1. LADY JANE GREY. Peggy Nisbet, No. H216, 1970s. Plastic "collectors' doll." Made in England. About 7½in (19.1cm).
2. LADY JANE GREY. Tower Treasures Ltd., late 1970s. Bisque head and limbs; simulated leather stuffed body. Mohair wig; painted features. Made in England in a "Limited Edition." 8in (20.3cm).

GUBITOSI, MICKEY. (BOBBY BLAKE. ROBERT BLAKE). Born Michael Gubitosi on September 18, 1933. During the 1930s and 1940s he was a child actor in the "Our Gang" comedies. By the late 1940s, under the name Bobby Blake, he was the Indian lad, Little Beaver, in the Red Ryder western films and also played in other features. In 1956 he returned to the screen as an adult under the name Robert Blake. His best adult role was as a brutal murderer in the film *In Cold Blood*. On television he was the off-beat detective "Baretta" on ABC-TV from January 1975 to June 1978. Since then he often appears on "Tonight" (The Johnny Carson Show).

DOLLS:
1. MICKEY. Mego, No. 61600 /5, 1975. 6in (15.2cm). *Illustration 405*.
SEE: OUR GANG.

GUINNESS (SIR) ALEC. Actor. Born April 2, 1914, in London, England. After 1934 he was in stage productions. Since 1946 in films he has been known for the wide variety of roles he essays and the disguises he uses. He won the Best Actor Academy Award for his part in *The Bridge on the River Kwai*, 1957. In *Star Wars*, 1977, and *The Empire Strikes Back*, 1980, he was Ben Kenobi (Obi-Wan Kenobi). Alec Guinness was knighted in 1959 by Queen Elizabeth for his acting achievements.

DOLLS:
1. BEN (OBI-WAN) KENOBI. Kenner, No. 38250, 1978. All-vinyl and fully-jointed with painted features and clothing. Made in Hong Kong. 3½in (8.3cm).
2. BEN (OBI-WAN) KENOBI. Kenner, No. 39340, 1980. 12in (30.5cm). *Illustration 407*.
SEE: STAR WARS.

Illustration 406. Alec Guiness as Ben (Obi-Wan) Kenobi in *Star Wars, 1977.*

Illustration 405. 6in (15.2cm) MICKEY GUBITOSI (ROBERT BLAKE) as *Mickey* from *Our Gang* by Mego, No. 61600/5, 1975. All-vinyl and fully-jointed. Painted hair and features. Copyright by Metro-Goldwyn-Mayer, Inc. *Jean Canaday Collection.*

Illustration 407. 12in (30.5cm) ALEC GUINESS as *Ben (Obi-Wan) Kenobi* from *Star Wars* by Kenner, No. 39340, 1980. All-vinyl and fully-jointed. Painted hair and features. *Bobby Lodwick Collection.*

GWYN, NELL. (or GWYNN). English actress. Born Eleanor Gwyn in 1650; died 1687. After 1669 she was the mistress of King Charles II. She bore Charles two sons.

DOLLS:
1. NELL GWYN. Peggy Nisbet, No. H275, 1970s. Plastic "collectors' doll." Made in England. About 7½in (19.1cm).
2. NELL GWYN. Peggy Nisbet, No. LE84, 1970s. Special Collectors' Set that includes Countess of Castlemaine, No. LE85; King Charles II, No. LE83; Duchess of Portsmouth, No. LE86. The set is called "King Charles II, 'the Merry Monarch,' and three of his favorite mistresses." Made in England. About 7½in (19.1cm).
3. NELL GWYN. Ann Parker, late 1970s. Plastic "collectors' doll," affixed to a wooden base. Made in England. 11in (27.9cm).

GWYNNE, FRED. Actor. Born July 10, 1926. Fred Gwynne played Officer Francis Muldoon on "Car 54, Where Are You?" on NBC-TV from September 1961 to September 1963. He was later cast as Herman Munster, a Frankenstein-type, who worked for a funeral home on "The Munsters" on CBS-TV from September 1964 to September 1966.

DOLLS:
1. HERMAN MUNSTER. Mattel, 1964. Cloth with a vinyl head and hands. Molded and painted features. Copyright by Karo-Vue Productions. Pull ring makes the doll "talk." 21in (53.3cm).
2. HERMAN MUNSTER. Remco, No. 1820, 1964. Vinyl head with painted features; plastic body with molded and painted clothing. Copyright by Karo-Vue Productions. 6½in (16.5cm).

SEE: THE MUNSTERS.

H

HAGGERTY, DAN. Actor, animal trainer. Born November 19, 1941. Athletic Dan Haggerty played the lead in the 1974 film *The Life and Times of Grizzly Adams.* It was a nature tale of a mountain man who was wrongly accused of murder, so he left civilization to live with a bear in the rugged north country. The film was the

Illustration 408. 9½in (24.2cm) DAN HAGGERTY as *Grizzly Adams* from "The Life and Times of Grizzly Adams" by Mattel, No. 2377, 1978. All-vinyl and fully-jointed. Painted yellow hair and beard; painted brown eyes. The body is the *Big Jim* body by Mattel. No marks on head. Back marked: " ©1971 MATTEL, INC. // HONG KONG US & // FOREIGN PATENTED." Copyright 1978 by Schick Sunn Classic Productions, Inc. *Shirley Buchholz Collection.*

basis for a television series of the same name with the same actors that was on NBC-TV from February 1977 to July 1978, with one last episode on December 19, 1978.

DOLLS:
1. GRIZZLY ADAMS. Mattel, No. 2377, 1978. 9½in (24.2cm). *Illustrations 408* and *409*. Don Shanks as Nakoma, No. 2381, is a companion doll.

Illustration 409. DAN HAGGERTY by Mattel. *Shirley Buchholz Collection.*

HALE, NATHAN. American patriot. Born 1755; died 1776. Nathan Hale was hanged by the British as a spy during the American Revolution. He is remembered for his reputed last words, "I regret that I have but one life to lose for my country."

DOLLS:
1. NATHAN HALE. Made for S.S. Kresge Company, 1976. A "Hero of the American Revolution." Made in Hong Kong. 7½in (19.1cm). *Illustration 410.*

Illustration 410. 7½in (19.1cm) NATHAN HALE manufactured for the S.S. Kresge Company, 1976. Vinyl head with painted hair and features. Fully-jointed plastic body with a swivel waist. Marked on the back: "MADE IN // HONG KONG." *Shirley Buchholz Collection.*

HALELOKE. Singer. From 1950 to 1955 Haleloke, a shy exotic Hawaiian singer, was featured on the television program "Arthur Godfrey and His Friends" on CBS-TV. Beginning in 1953 Godfrey began firing his "friends" off the show, starting with Julius LaRosa, whom Godfrey said lost his "humility." When Haleloke was fired, she was replaced by Japanese singer Miyoshi Umeki. From that point on, the once-popular show began to decline steadily in the ratings.

DOLLS:
1. HALELOKE. Cast Distributing Corp., 1954. Made in USA. 18in (45.7cm). *Illustration 412.*

Illustration 411. Arm tag from Haleloke doll. Arthur Godfrey is in the upper right. *Fran's Dolls.*

Illustration 412. 18in (45.7cm) HALELOKE by Cast Distributing Corp., 1954. All-hard plastic and fully-jointed walker. Black saran wig; blue sleep eyes; open mouth with teeth. The trunk set includes extra hawaiian costumes. Back marked: "MADE IN U.S.A." The paper tag tells that Cast Distributing Corp. was located at 200 Fifth Avenue, New York. *Fran's Dolls.*

HALEY, JACK. Actor. Born 1899; died 1979. Haley was a comedian of vaudeville, stage and screen. He will be forever remembered as the Tin Man in *The Wizard of Oz*, 1939. After a long absence from the screen, Jack Haley returned to appear in *Norwood*, 1970, which was directed by his son Jack Haley, Jr., who produced the MGM compilation film *That's Entertainment*, 1974.

DOLLS:
1. TIN WOODSMAN FROM THE WIZARD OF OZ. Mego, No. 51500/2, 1974. Made in Hong Kong. 8½in (21.6cm). *Illustrations 413 and 414*.

Illustration 413. 8½in (21.6cm) JACK HALEY as the *Tin Woodsman* from the 1939 film *The Wizard of Oz* by Mego, No. 51500/2, 1974. All-vinyl and fully-jointed. Painted features. Head marked: "© 1974 MGM // INC." Made in Hong Kong. *Shirley Buchholz Collection.*

2. TIN WOODSMAN from THE WIZARD OF OZ. Mego, No. 59037, 1974. Vinyl head; cloth body. Copyright 1974 by MGM, Inc. Made in Hong Kong. 17in (43.2cm).
SEE: WIZARD OF OZ, THE.

HALL, ADRIAN. Adrian Hall was the boy who played Jeremy in the 1968 musical film *Chitty Chitty Bang Bang*. The movie, starring Dick Van Dyke and Sally Ann Howes, was a children's musical about a flying car. Although the story was written by Ian Flemming, the creator of James Bond, it was a failure, mostly because of a poor musical score and disasterous special effects.

DOLLS:
1. JEREMY in CHITTY CHITTY BANG BANG set. Mattel, 1968. Included Dick Van Dyke as Mr. Potts, Sally Ann Howes as Truly Scrumptious and Heather Ripley as Jemima. All-vinyl with a jointed head. Rooted blonde hair. Made in Hong Kong. 1¼in (3.2cm).

HALSEY, WILLIAM American admiral. Born 1882; died 1959. During World War II Halsey commanded the navy in the South Pacific. He was promoted to Admiral of the Fleet in 1945, and he retired in 1947.

DOLLS:
1. ADM. WILLIAM F. HALSEY, JR. Excel Toy Corp., 1974. All-vinyl and fully-jointed. Made in Hong Kong. 9¾in (24.9cm).

HAMER, RUSTY. Child actor. Born Russell Hamer on February 15, 1947. Rusty Hamer was Russell (Rusty) Williams, the son of Danny Williams, played by Danny Thomas on two comedy series on ABC-TV. The first was "Make Room for Daddy" from September 1953 to September 1964; the second was "Make Room for Granddaddy" from September 1970 to September 1971. There were 336 episodes of the first show and only 24 of the second. Rusty Hamer is now unemployed and lives in Louisiana.

DOLLS:
1. RUSTY. Effanbee, circa 1955. All-vinyl and fully-jointed. Painted hair; blue sleep eyes with lashes. Dressed in bibbed overalls. 20in (50.8cm).

HAMILL, DOROTHY. Skater. Born 1956. Dorothy Hamill won the Gold Medal in Women's Singles in Figure Skating in the Winter Olympics at Innsbruck, Austria, in 1976 for the United States. She turned professional afterwards and appeared in specials on ABC-TV. In commercials on television she touted a brand of shampoo that was to give one the "short and sassy look" like her own hairdo. In 1976 she also became a headliner with the Ice Capades, a skating revue. In 1982 she married Dean Martin's son, Dean Paul Martin.

DOLLS:
1. DOROTHY HAMILL. Ideal, No. 1290-6, 1977. Made in Hong Kong. 11½in (29.2cm). *Illustration 415*.

Illustration 414. JACK HALEY by Mego. *Shirley Buchholz Collection.*

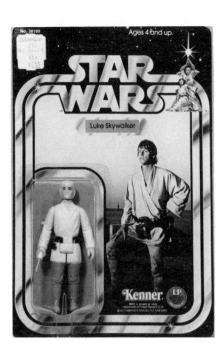

Illustration 415. 11½in (29.2cm) DOROTHY HAMILL by Ideal, No. 1290-6, 1977. Vinyl and plastic. Rooted dark brown hair; painted blue eyes. The plastic "Ice Skating Rink" can be moved around on a smooth surface causing the doll to "spin and skate." Head marked: " © 1977 D.H. // IDEAL // H-282 // HONG KONG P." Marked vertically on the hip: "©1975 IDEAL // US. PAT. NO. 3903640 // HOLLIS N.Y. 11423 // HONG KONG P." Copyright by Dorothy Hamill and Ideal Toy Corp.

HAMILL, MARK.   Actor. Born September 25, 1951. In 1970 Mark Hamill made his professional debut on "The Bill Cosby Show." He was a guest star on numerous television shows, playing juveniles. He also played in several TV movies and had a regular part on the soap opera "General Hospital." He was Doobie in the critically-acclaimed, but short-lived comedy series, "The Texas Wheelers" on ABC-TV in September and October of 1974 and June and July of 1975. Mark Hamill was the top-billed star in the two highest box-office grossing films in motion picture history. This was as Luke Skywalker in *Star Wars* in 1977 and *The Empire Strikes Back* in 1980. His hobby is collecting antique toys.

DOLLS:
1. LUKE SKYWALKER.   Kenner, No. 38180, 1978. Made in Taiwan. 3¾in (9.6cm). *Illustration 416*.
2. LUKE SKYWALKER.   Kenner, No. 38080, 1978. Made in Hong Kong. 12in (30.5cm). *Illustration 417*.
3. LUKE SKYWALKER IN BESPIN FATIGUES.   Made in Hong Kong. Kenner, No. 39780, 1979. 3¾in (9.6cm). *Illustration 418*.
4. LUKE SKYWALKER: X-WING PILOT.   Kenner, No. 39060, 1980. Made in Hong Kong. 3⅞in (9.8cm). *Illustration 419*.
SEE: STAR WARS.

RIGHT: Illustration 417. 12in (30.5cm) MARK HAMILL as *Luke Skywalker* from *Star Wars* by Kenner, No. 38080, 1978. All-vinyl and fully-jointed. Painted yellow hair and painted blue eyes. Head marked: " © G.M.F.G.I. 1978." Back marked: " © G.M.F.G.I. 1978 KENNER PROD. // CINCINNATI, OHIO 45202 // MADE IN HONG KONG." Copyright 1977 by Twentieth Century-Fox Film Corporation.

Illustration 416. 3¾in (9.6cm) MARK HAMILL as *Luke Skywalker* from *Star Wars* by Kenner, No. 38180, 1978. All-vinyl with painted hair and features. Copyright 1977 by Twentieth Century-Fox Film Corporation. Made in Taiwan.

Illustration 418. 3¾in (9.6cm) MARK HAMILL as *Luke Skywalker* in "Bespin Fatigues" from *Star Wars—The Empire Strikes Back* by Kenner, No. 39780, 1979. All-vinyl and fully-jointed. Painted yellow hair and features; painted clothing. Copyright 1977 by Twentieth Century-Fox Film Corporation; Copyright 1980 by Lucasfilm Ltd. Made in Hong Kong.

Illustration 419. 3⅞in (9.8cm) MARK HAMILL as *Luke Skywalker: X-Wing Pilot* from *Star Wars—The Empire Strikes Back* by Kenner, No. 39060, 1980. This is from Set No. 3 of the Star Wars figures. All-vinyl with painted features and clothing. Copyright 1977 by Twentieth Century-Fox Film Corporation; copyright 1980 by Lucasfilm Ltd. Made in Hong Kong.

HAMILTON, BERNIE. Actor. Since 1950 Bernie Hamilton has played black character parts in motion pictures. From September 1975 until August 1979 he was gruff Captain Harold Dobey on "Starsky and Hutch" on ABC-TV.
DOLLS:
  1. DOBEY. Mego, No. 62800 /4, 1976. Made in Hong Kong. 7½in (19.1cm). *Illustration 420.*
SEE: STARSKY AND HUTCH.

Illustration 420. 7½in (19.1cm) BERNIE HAMILTON as *Dobey* from "Starsky and Hutch" by Mego, No. 62800/4. All-vinyl and fully-jointed with painted hair and features. Copyright 1976 by Spelling-Goldberg Productions. Made in Hong Kong.

HAMILTON, EMMA, LADY. English beauty. Born circa 1765; died 1815. Emma was the mistress and later the wife of Sir William Hamilton. While he was ambassador to Naples she had great influence on the Queen of Naples. After 1798 she became the mistress of Horatio Nelson, whose daughter she bore in 1801. When Nelson died he stated in his will that Emma was his "bequest to the nation."
DOLLS:
  1. LADY HAMILTON. Madame Alexander, No. 2175, 1957. Cissy doll in a formal gown with a large picture hat. All-hard plastic. 20in (50.8cm).
  2. LADY HAMILTON. Madame Alexander, No. 1282, 1968. Jacqueline doll in a formal gown with a picture hat. Plastic and vinyl. Rooted blonde hair. 21in (53.3cm).
  3. LADY HAMILTON. Peggy Nisbet, No. P463, 1970s. All-plastic "collectors' doll." Made in England. About 7½in (19.1cm). Lord Nelson, No. P642, is a companion doll.

HAMILTON, MARGARET. Actress. Born December 9, 1902, in Cleveland, Ohio. Margaret Hamilton played a wide variety of screen roles after 1933, appearing as gossips, spinsters, housekeepers and the like. The role that she will always be identified with is that as The Wicked Witch of the West in *The Wizard of Oz* in 1939. In recent times she was Cora, who promoted Maxwell House Coffee in television commercials.
DOLLS:
  1. THE WICKED WITCH OF THE WEST. Mego, No. 51500/6, 1974. Made in Hong Kong. 7¾in (19.8cm). *Illustration 421.*
SEE: THE WIZARD OF OZ.

Illustration 421. 7¾in (19.8cm) MARGARET HAMILTON as *The Wicked Witch of the West* from the 1939 film *The Wizard of Oz* by Mego, No. 51500/6, 1974. All-vinyl and fully-jointed. Rooted black hair; green tinted face color; painted features. Copyright 1974 by Metro-Goldwyn-Mayer, Inc. Made in Hong Kong. *Shirley Buchholz Collection.*

HAMLIN, HARRY. Actor. Born in Pasadena, California, in 1952. Harry Hamlin entered films in the 1970s. In *The Clash of the Titans* he was Perseus, the hero son of Zeus and Danaë. It was Perseus who, according to ancient Greek mythology, slayed the Gorgon Monster Medusa, changed King Atlas, who held the world on his shoulders into stone by displaying the severed head of Medusa in front of him, rescued the beautiful Andromeda from the Sea Monster, and later used the Medusa head to dispatch his enemies at his wedding feast when he married Andromeda.

DOLLS:
1. PERSEUS.   Mattel, No. 3268, 1981. Made in the Phillipines. 4in (10.2cm). *Illustration 422.*
2. PERSEUS AND PEGASUS.   Mattel, 1981. A set that includes both Perseus and Pegasus, the winged horse. These are the same figures as the ones that were packaged individually. Made in USA. 4in (10.2cm). *Illustration 423.*

SEE: CLASH OF THE TITANS.

Illustration 422. 4in (10.2cm) HARRY HAMLIN as *Perseus* from *Clash of the Titans* by Mattel, No. 3268, 1981. All-vinyl and fully-jointed. Painted brown hair; painted clothing. Copyright 1980 by Metro-Goldwyn-Mayer Film Co. Made in the Philippines. Back marked: "©1980 MGM INC. // PHILIPPINES."

Illustration 423. 4in (10.2cm) HARRY HAMLIN from *Clash of the Titans* with the winged horse *Pegasus* by Mattel. Pegasus is 6in (15.2cm) tall and is No. 3293, 1981. The horse is not marked. It is copyrighted 1980 by Metro-Goldwyn-Mayer Film Co. Made in USA.

HAMMOND, NICHOLAS.   Actor. As a child performer Nicholas Hammond played Frederich in *The Sound of Music* in 1965. As an adult he essayed the dual role of Peter Parker and Spider-Man in "The Amazing Spider-Man" on CBS-TV. The series was 12 episodes that was shown on an irregular basis during 1978 and 1979. In the six-hour television mini series "The Manions of America," in 1981, Hammond again had a dual role, playing two Irish brothers.

DOLLS:
1. FREDERICH from THE SOUND OF MUSIC. Madame Alexander, No. 1001, 1965. All-hard plastic and fully-jointed. Blonde wig. This is from the all-8in (20.3cm) set.
2. FREDERICH from THE SOUND OF MUSIC. Madame Alexander, No. 1107, 1965-1966. Plastic and vinyl with rooted blonde hair. From the large set of Sound of Music dolls. 11in (27.9cm). *Illustration 424.*
3. FREDERICH from THE SOUND OF MUSIC. Madame Alexander, No. 0807, 1971. All-hard plastic, with or without bending knees. 7½in (19.1cm). *Illustration 425.*

SEE: THE SOUND OF MUSIC.

During 1978 and 1979 many different versions of Spider-Man dolls were manufactured by different companies such as Mego, Remco and Knickerbocker. These are copyrighted by Marvel Comics, but their popularity coincided with the television shows in which Nicholas Hammond played Spider-Man. *Illustration 426* is an example.

Illustration 424. 11in (27.9cm) NICHOLAS HAMMOND as *Frederich* from *The Sound of Music* by Madame Alexander, No. 1107, 1966. Vinyl and plastic. Rooted blonde hair; black sleep eyes with lashes. Head marked: "ALEXANDER // 19©65." *Jean Canaday Collection.*

Illustration 425. 7½in (19.1cm) NICHOLAS HAMMOND as *Frederich* from *The Sound of Music* by Madame Alexander, No. 0807, 1971. All-hard plastic and fully-jointed. Blonde wig; blue sleep eyes with molded lashes. Back marked: "ALEX."

Illustration 426. 7⅞in (20cm) *Spider-Man* by Mego, No. 51306, 1978. All-vinyl and fully-jointed. The head is a molded Spider-man hood. Head marked: "© MARVEL 1972." Back Marked: "© MEGO CORP. // REG. U.S. PAT. OFF. // PAT. PENDING // HONG KONG // MCMLXXI." This body is a stock Mego mold used for many different dolls of this general size. *Bobby Lodwick Collection.* Nicholas Hammond played Spider-man on television in a live-action series, but the doll should be considered a comic character because of the copyright information. Animated versions of the Spider-man story were also shown on television.

HAPPY DAYS. The television situation comedy "Happy Days," which began on ABC-TV in January of 1974 on a regular basis, was a nostalgic backward glance at the Eisenhower era of the 1950s. Ron Howard as Richie Cunningham, the main character when the show began, was a shy teenager with an assortment of buddies and relatives. In 1976 Mego Corp. made a set of dolls based on some of the show's characters. They are RON HOWARD as *Richie,* ANSON WILLIAMS as *Potsie,* HENRY WINKLER as *Fonzie* and DONNY MOST as *Ralph Malph.* See listings under each celebrity.

HARDY, OLIVER. Actor. Born Oliver Norvell Hardy, Jr. in Georgia in 1892; died 1957. Hardy began in show business at age eight, singing in minstrel shows in the South. He left the University of Georgia in 1910 to operate a movie theater. In 1913 he joined the Lubin Company in Jacksonville, Florida, to film short comedies. He continued in minor roles until 1926 when he teamed with Stan Laurel to form the most successful screen comedy team of all time. Hardy was "the fat one" and his characterizations usually made the most of his portly figure. He also appeared in many other films without Laurel from 1914 to 1950.

DOLLS: SEE LAUREL AND HARDY.

HARLOW, JEAN. Actress. Born Harlean Carpentier on March 3, 1911; died 1937. When she was 16 Jean Harlow eloped with a young businessman and settled in Hollywood where she found work in silent films as an extra. In 1929 she obtained a divorce and committed herself to a film career. She was not an important player until after 1932 when she obtained an MGM contract. Her screen persona was changed from a flashy, tarty, bleached blonde to a light comedy performer, and she became a superstar. Successful film assignments followed, but her private life was a chaotic series of affairs and marriages. In 1937 she became ill during the filming of *Saratoga* and died of cerebral edema at age 26 before filming was completed. (A double finished her part.) In 1965 two tasteless films were released that purported to be biographies of her short and sensational life. Harlow was played in these movies by Carroll Baker and Carol Lynley.

DOLLS:
1. JEAN HARLOW IN *BOMBSHELL*. Peggy Nisbet, No. P752, 1970s. Plastic "collectors' doll." Copyright 1933 by MGM; renewed 1960 by MGM. Made in England. About 7½in (19.1cm).

HARPER, RON. Actor. Born January 12, 1936. Ron Harper appeared on television shows in several different roles. He was in two soap operas, "Love of Life" and "Where the Heart Is." On "Planet of the Apes," which only lasted from September to December of 1974 on CBS-TV he was astronaut Alan Virdon. On the children's show "Land of the Lost," on NBC—TV from September 1974 to September 1977 he was Jack Marshall.

DOLLS:
1. ALAN VERDON (sic). Mego, No. 50900/0, 1975. Made in Hong Kong. 7¾in (19.8cm). *Illustration 427*.
SEE: PLANET OF THE APES.

Illustration 427. 7¾in (19.8cm) RON HARPER as *Alan Verdon* (sic) from "Planet of the Apes" by Mego, No. 50900/0, 1975. All-vinyl and fully-jointed. Painted yellow hair and painted blue eyes. Head marked: "©1974 20th CEN-// TURY-FOX FILM CORP." Made in Hong Kong.

HARRIS, JONATHAN. Actor. Born circa 1919. Harris is a veteran character actor who has been in films since the 1950s. In "Space Academy," on CBS-TV from September 1977 to September 1979 on Saturday mornings he was 300-year-old Professor Isaac Gampu who led a group of youthful space explorers, each of whom had some exceptional talent. The program was a children's show.

DOLLS:
1. PROFESSOR ISAAC GAMPU. Aviva Toy Company, No. 199, 1978. Made in Hong Kong. 8½in (21.6cm). *Illustration 428*.
SEE: SPACE ACADEMY.

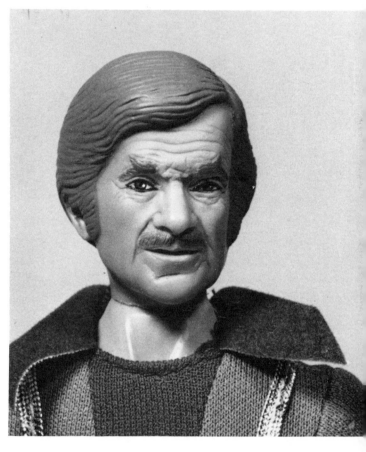

Illustration 428. 8½in (21.6cm) JONATHAN HARRIS as *Professor Isaac Gampu* from "Space Academy" by Aviva Toy Company for F. W. Woolworth Co., No. 100, 1978. All-vinyl and fully-jointed. Painted gray hair and painted blue eyes. Lower back marked: "© 1978 // FILMATION ASSOCI-ATES // ALL RIGHTS RESERVED // MADE IN HONG KONG // PAT. PEND." *Penny Caswell Collection.*

HARRISON, GEORGE. Musician, singer, actor. Born February 25, 1943, in Liverpool, England. When the Beatles were formed in the early 1960s Harrison played guitar and provided vocals. He found his interests drifting away from the group even before its celebrated 1971 breakup. He added to his stature as a solo artist with several record albums, the most successful of which was the concert he organized for the benefit of stricken Bangladesh in 1971. In recent years he has devoted more and more time to his spiritual obsessions.

DOLLS:
1. BOB'N HEAD BEATLES; GEORGE HARRISON. Car Mascots, Inc., 1964. Papier-mâché and plaster "nodder." Made in Japan.
2. BOB'N HEAD BEATLES; GEORGE HARRISON. Same as the above in all-plastic. 4in (10.2cm).

3. GEORGE HARRISON. Remco, No. 1800, 1964. Made in USA. 4½in (11.5cm). *Illustration 429*.
4. GEORGE HARRISON. Pelham Puppets, 1965. Made in England. About 13in (33cm). *Illustration 430*.
SEE: THE BEATLES.

Illustration 429. 4½in (11.5cm) GEORGE HARRISON by Remco, No. 1800, 1964. Vinyl head; rooted black hair; painted eyes; open mouth with molded teeth; one-piece vinyl body. Holds a vinyl guitar. Back marked: "THE // BEATLES // INC." Copyright 1964 by Nems Ent., Ltd.; Licensed by Seltaeb Inc. Made in USA.

Illustration 430. About 13in (33cm) GEORGE HARRISON of the Beatles by Pelham, 1965. Composition head and hands; wooden feet; jointed wooden segments form body. Black "fur" wig; painted features. This is part of a set described simply as "Pop Singers" in the *Sears 1965 Christmas Book*. Stamped on cross bar: "MADE IN ENGLAND" and "PELHAM PUPPETS." *Peter Bransky Collection*.

HARRISON, REX. Actor. Born Reginald Carey Harrison on March 5, 1908, in England. In 1930 he first appeared on the stage and in British films. During World War II he served as a flight lieutenant in the RAF and returned to the movies in 1945. His acting career on both sides of the Atlantic achieved its highest success with his stage role as Professor Henry Higgins in "My Fair Lady" on Broadway during the mid 1950s. He won an Academy Award for the film version of the play in 1964. In 1967 he had the title role in the musical film *Doctor Doolittle,* a part that was far less successful. Harrison was married six times and was involved in many love affairs, the most scandalous of which purportedly led to the suicide of actress Carole Landis in 1948. For this reason he has been known as "Sexy Rexy" by gossip columnists.

DOLLS:
1. DOCTOR DOOLITTLE. Mattel, No. 3579, 1967. 6in (15.2cm). Came packaged with the Pushmi-Pullyu and Polynesia, the Parrot. Made in Japan. 6in (15.2cm). *Illustration 431*.
2. DOCTOR DOOLITTLE. Mattel, No. 3575, 1967. Made in Japan. 6in (15.2cm). Came packaged with Polynesia, the Parrot. *Illustration 432*.

Illustration 431. 6in (15.2cm) REX HARRISON from *Doctor Doolittle* by Mattel, No. 3579, 1967. All-vinyl and fully-jointed with painted hair and features. The furry Pushmi-Pullyu is 5in by 6in (12.7cm by 15.2cm). Polynesia, the parrot, is made of a pipe-cleaner type of material. Copyright by Twentieth Century-Fox Film Corporation and Apjac Productions, Inc. Made in Japan.

Illustration 432. 6in (15.2cm) REX HARRISON as *Doctor Doolittle* by Mattel, No. 3575, 1967. All-vinyl and fully-jointed with painted hair and features. This is the same doll and parrot as in *Illustration 431*. *Shirley Buchholz Collection*.

Illustration 433. 13in (33cm) REX HARRISON as *Doctor Doolittle*, a talking puppet, by Mattel, No. 5365, 1967. Vinyl head with painted dark brown hair and blue eyes; open-closed mouth with molded and painted teeth. The cloth body portion has a box set inside with a pull ring for "talking." The head is the same as the Talking Doctor Doolittle doll. Copyright by Twentieth Century-Fox Film Corporation and Apjac. Made in Hong Kong.

3. DOCTOR DOOLITTLE. Mattel, No. 3565, 1967. Talking hand puppet. Made in Hong Kong. 13in (33cm). *Illustration 433.*
4. DOCTOR DOOLITTLE. Mattel, No. 5349, 1967. 22in (55.9cm). *Illustration 434.*

Illustration 435. 15in (38.1cm) MARY HARTLINE by Ideal, 1952. All-hard plastic and fully-jointed. Blonde nylon wig; blue sleep eyes with lashes and eye shadow. Both majorette dresses are red cotton trimmed in white. The doll on the left is holding her original baton and her box is pictured in *Illustration 436.* Heads marked: "P-91 // IDEAL DOLL // MADE IN U.S.A." Backs marked: "IDEAL DOLL // P-91." Copyright by M.H.E. (Mary Hartline Enterprises). These dolls are the standard Toni doll with the addition of eye shadow and a different hairstyle.

Illustration 434. 22in (55.9cm) REX HARRISON as *Doctor Doolittle* by Mattel, No. 5349, 1967. Vinyl head with painted hair and features. Cloth body with a talking mechanism inside that is operated with a pull string. The felt top hat is missing. Tag marked: " © MCMLXVII // TWENTIETH CENTURY-FOX // FILM COR-PORATION AND APJAC //©1967 MATTEL INC." *Wanda Lodwick Collection.*

HARTLINE, MARY. Television personality. Born circa 1926. Mary Hartline was the "Queen of the Super Circus" on the ABC-TV show "Super Circus" on Sunday evenings from January 1949 to June 1956. The program featured circus variety acts, and Mary acted as the bandleader. She later married millionaire Woolworth Donahue and retired to Palm Beach, Florida. She is now a widow and retains her membership in the American Federation of Musicians, but she refuses to acknowledge any correspondence inquiring about her present life.

DOLLS:
1. MARY HARTLINE. Ideal, 1952. Came in red, white and green dresses. Made in USA. 15in (38.1cm). *Illustration 435.*
2. MARY HARTLINE. Ideal, 1952. 22½in (57.2cm). *Illustration 437.*
3. MARY HARTLINE. Probably by Duchess, early 1950s. 7¼in (18.5cm). *Illustration 438,* on the left.
4. MARY HARTLINE. Ideal, 1952. 7¾in (19.8cm). *Illustration 438,* on the right.

Illustration 436. Original box for the Mary Hartline doll in *Illustration 435* holding the baton. Mary Hartline is shown with her doll likeness.

Illustration 437. 22½in (57.2cm) MARY HARTLINE by Ideal, 1952. All-hard plastic and fully-jointed. The head is unusual for this type of doll and is a socket head. Blonde nylon wig; blue sleep eyes with lashes. The red majorette dress is a shiny rayon. Head marked: "IDEAL DOLL." Body marked: "IDEAL DOLL // P-94." The body is the regular P-94 mold for Toni dolls.

Illustration 438. MARY HARTLINE, early 1950s. On the left: 7¼in (18.5cm) hard plastic jointed at the arms and head. Blonde nylon wig; blue sleep eyes. Back marked: "THIS IS AN ORIGINAL // LINGERIE LOU // DOLL." On the right: 7¾in (19.8cm) all-hard plastic, jointed at the arms and head. Blonde nylon wig; yellow sleep eyes. Back marked in script: "IDEAL." It is difficult to see in the photo, but each doll has a different leg and painted boot construction.

HARVEY, LAURENCE. Actor. Born Larushka Mischa Skikne in Yomishkis, Lithuania, on October 1, 1928; died 1973. As a child, Harvey escaped from Lithuania to South Africa with his Jewish parents. At 15 he made his stage debut and in 1946 went to England to enroll in the Royal Academy of Dramatic Art. He made his first screen appearence in 1948 and played youthful parts, like his role in the Italian-British production *Giulietta e Romeo/Romeo and Juliet* as Romeo in 1954. As an adult he specialized in performances as ruthless and ambitious young men. He died of cancer before his last films were released.

DOLLS:
 1. ROMEO. Madame Alexander, No. 474, 1955. Juliet is a companion doll. 7¾in (19.8cm). *Illustration 439.*

Illustration 439. 7¾in (19.8cm) LAURENCE HARVEY as *Romeo* from *Romeo and Juliet* by Madame Alexander, No. 474, 1955. All-hard plastic and fully-jointed. Straight-leg walker. Red caracul wig; blue sleep eyes with molded lashes. Back marked: "ALEX." Purple body suit and black felt jacket trimmed in gold. Costume tagged: "ALEXANDERKINS." *Patricia Gardner Collection.*

Madame Alexander

presents

Romeo and Juliet

Inspired by "Romeo and Juliet" starring Susan Shentall and Laurence Harvey. Color by Technicolor. Released thru United Artists.

Illustration 440. Original tag from Madame Alexander's *Romeo and Juliet* dolls. *Ted Menten Collection.*

HAY, WILL. Actor. Born 1888 in England; died 1949. Hay was a popular music hall comic in England after 1909. During the 1930s and the 1940s he was a top draw in British film comedies. (Will Hay is not to be confused with Will Hays, the grim policeman of Hollywood morals who headed the Hays Office after 1922 to insure that film productions did not include anything that might be construed as "indecent.")
DOLLS:
1. WILL HAY. Dean's Rag Book Company, 1938. All-cloth; jointed. Wears an academic gown and carries a cane and a book. Made in England.

HAYES, GEORGE "GABBY." Actor. Born May 7, 1885; died 1969. Gabby Hayes played "sidekicks" in more than 200 western films. He was a comic support for William Boyd, Roy Rogers and others. From May to July 1956 he was the host and storyteller of "The Gabby Hayes Show" on ABC-TV.
DOLLS:
1. GABBY HAYES. Hand puppet by Zany Toys, Inc., 1952. Vinyl head with painted features; cloth body.

HAYWORTH, RITA. Actress. Born Margarita Carmen Cansino in New York, New York, October 17, 1918. Hayworth was the daughter of Spanish-born dancer Eduardo Cansino and his partner, Volga Haworth. She began dancing professionally at age 12 and after 1935 played bit parts in numerous Hollywood films. In 1937 she married Ed Judson, an older businessman who got her a seven-year contract with Columbia Pictures. With the art of cosmetics she was transformed into a red-headed sophisticate. During World War II she was a favorite pinup of American servicemen, and her picture decorated the test atomic bomb dropped at Bikini in 1946. Rita Hayworth was dubbed the "Love Goddess," and she proved it in many films of the 1940s. In May of 1949 she was married to Prince Aly Khan and was a princess for two years. After her divorce she returned to Columbia to restore her contract, but she was never the draw she had been before. Her last movies were routine films shot in Europe. By th 1970s Rita Hayworth was suffering from premature senility and could no longer perform.
DOLLS:
1. CARMEN, INSPIRED BY RITA HAYWORTH IN "THE LOVES OF CARMEN." Uneeda, 1948. All-composition and fully-jointed. Red mohair wig; blue sleep eyes with lashes. Wears a "Spanish gypsy" gown. The doll is not marked; a cardboard tag carries the descriptive information. 14in (35.6cm).

HEGYES, ROBERT. Actor. Born May 7, 1951. Hegyes played Juan Epstein, the Puertorican-Jewish boy on "Welcome Back, Kotter" on ABC-TV from September 1975 to August 1979.
DOLLS:
1. EPSTEIN. Mattel, No. 9774, 1976. Made in Taiwan. 9¼in (23.6cm). *Illustration 441*.
SEE: WELCOME BACK, KOTTER.

Illustration 441. 9¼in (23.6cm) ROBERT HEYGES as *Epstein* from "Welcome Back, Kotter" by Mattel, No. 9774, 1976. All-vinyl and fully-jointed with painted hair and features. Copyright by the Wolper Organization, Inc. and the Komack Company, Inc. Made in Taiwan. *Shirley Buchholz Collection.*

HENIE, SONJA. Skater, actress. Born in Oslo, Norway, on April 8, 1912; died October 12, 1969. By the time she was five years old Sonja Henie was an accomplished skier and dancer; at the age of six she learned to skate; at the age of ten she won the national figure skating championship of Norway; by the time she was 24 she had won the world's championship in figure skating ten consecutive times—an unequaled record—and had placed first in figure skating at three Olympic Games, those of 1928, 1932 and 1936. Then she signed a movie contract and became one of the highest salaried film performers of all time. She only appeared in 12 feature-length motion pictures, but she was always the top-billed star. (This does not include a part in a Norwegian film early in her career.) Her first Hollywood production was *One In a Million*, which indeed she was. Sonja Henie also toured with her "Hollywood Ice Revue" from 1937 to 1953. In 1969 she was traveling on an ambulance plane from Paris, France to Oslo. Sonja Henie died of leukemia before the plane landed in Norway.

Illustration 442. Sonja Henie, *Screen Life*, November 1940.

Illustration 444. 14in (35.6cm) SONJA HENIE by Madame Alexander, circa 1939. All-composition and fully-jointed. Blonde human hair wig; brown sleep eyes with lashes and eye shadow. It is doubtful if the extras came with the doll originally. Head marked: "MADAME ALEXANDER // SONJA // HENIE." *Wanda Lodwick Collection.*

DOLLS of SONJA HENIE:
NOTE: ONLY MADAME ALEXANDER EVER MADE SONJA HENIE DOLLS.
Other skating dolls were not advertised, sold or represented as being Sonja Henie dolls. They must be considered "skating dolls" if they can not be identified, or Sonja-Henie types. R & B *never* made a Sonja Henie doll. The so-called "closed-mouth Sonja Henie" by R & B is *Nancy Lee.* See *Illustration 25* and *26*.

1. 7in (17.8cm). All-composition with jointed arms and legs. Blonde mohair wig; painted blue eyes. This is the "Tiny Betty" doll. Wears a labeled white taffeta dress trimmed with marabou feathers. 1939. Back marked: "MME // ALEXANDER."

The following are unmarked or marked on the heads as described in the illustrations:

2. 13½in (34.2cm). All-composition and fully-jointed with a swivel waist. 1939. *Illustration 443*.
3. 14in (35.6cm); 14¼in (36.3cm); 14½in (36.9cm); or 14¾in (37.6cm). All-composition and fully-jointed. 1939. *Illustrations 444, 445, 446* and *447*.
4. 17½in (44.5cm); 17¾in (45.1cm); 18in (45.7cm); or 18½in (47cm). All-composition and fully-jointed. 1939. *Illustrations 448* and *449*.
5. 21in (53.3cm). All-composition and fully-jointed. Circa 1940. *Illustrations 450* and *451*.
6. 15in (38.1cm). Vinyl head; hard plastic, fully-jointed body. Blonde wig; blue sleep eyes with lashes. Head marked: "ALEXANDER." 1951.
7. 18in (45.7cm). Vinyl head; hard plastic, fully-jointed body. 1951. *Illustration 452*.
8. 21in (53.3cm). Vinyl head; hard plastic, fully-jointed body. Blonde wig; blue sleep eyes with lashes. Head marked: "ALEXANDER." 1951.

Illustration 443. 13½in (34.3cm) SONJA HENIE by Madame Alexander, 1939. All-composition and fully-jointed. This is the *Wendy Ann* body with the swivel waist. Blonde human hair wig; brown sleep eyes with lashes and eye shadow; open mouth with teeth. The costume is replaced. Head not marked. Back marked: "WENDY ANN // MME. ALEXANDER // NEW YORK." Right leg at top: "R." Left leg at top: "L."

Illustration 445. 14in (35.6cm) SONJA HENIE by Madame Alexander, circa 1939. All-composition and fully-jointed. Blonde human hair wig; brown sleep eyes with lashes and eye shadow. The satin dress is pink. She carries her one original skate in her left hand; the ones that she wears are replacements. Marked on head: "MADAME ALEXANDER // SONJA // HENIE." *Fran's Dolls.*

Illustration 447. The Sonja Henie doll from *Illustration 446*, wearing an original ski outfit. The ski costumes were part of the extra clothing that came in a suitcase set with some of the Sonja Henie dolls. The pants are beige; the jacket and the hat that is trimmed with marabou feathers are red. The skis and poles are reproductions.

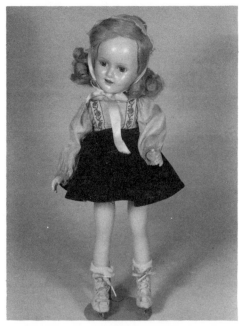

Illustration 448. 17½in (44.5cm) SONJA HENIE by Madame Alexander, 1939. All-composition and fully-jointed. Blonde human hair wig; brown sleep eyes with lashes and eye shadow; open mouth with teeth. The black skirt is velveteen. (There should be a matching cap; the one on the doll is a replacement.) This version was advertised in *Sears Christmas Book, 1939.* for $4.69. Head marked: "MADAME ALEXANDER // SONJA // HENIE." *Fran's Dolls.*

Illustration 446. 14½in (36.8cm) SONJA HENIE by Madame Alexander, circa 1940. All-composition and fully-jointed. Blonde mohair wig; brown sleep eyes with lashes and eye shadow; open mouth with teeth. The original dress is yellow taffeta with sprigs of red flowers. The shoes are replaced. Head marked: MADAME ALEXANDER // SONJA // HENIE."

Illustration 451. 21in (53.3cm) SONJA HENIE by Madame Alexander, circa 1940. All-composition and fully-jointed. Blonde mohair wig; brown sleep eyes with lashes and eye shadow. Marked on head: "MADAME ALEXANDER // SONJA // HENIE." The skating costume is yellow wool and has an attached hood. *Fran's Dolls.*

Illustration 449. 18½in (47cm) SONJA HENIE by Madame Alexander, 1939. All-composition and fully-jointed. Blonde mohair wig. The original skating dress with marabou feather trim is labeled: "MADAME ALEXANDER // NEW YORK // ALL RIGHTS RESERVED." The skates are old but are probably replacements. *Wanda Lodwick Collection.*

BELOW, CENTER: Illustration 452. 18in (45.7cm) SONJA HENIE by Madame Alexander, 1951. Vinyl head with glued-on blonde synthetic wig; blue sleep eyes with lashes. The body is fully-jointed hard plastic. The head is marked: "A L E X A N D E R." The dress is labeled only "MADAME ALEXANDER (in script) // NEW YORK // ALL RIGHTS RESERVED." It is pale blue satin with applied rhinestones on the bodice. The shoe skates do not appear to be original. The original boxes for these later versions of Sonja Henie dolls, which are actually the Madelaine doll from the same time period, have been reported to be stamped: "SONJA HENIE." The original wrist tags read only: "SONJA." *Jeanne Niswonger Collection.*

Illustration 450. 21in (53.3cm) SONJA HENIE by Madame Alexander, circa 1940. All-composition and fully-jointed. Blonde human hair wig; brown sleep eyes with lashes; open mouth with teeth. The metal barrettes in the hair were original on the Sonja Henie dolls. The skating costume is pale blue taffeta trimmed with marabou feathers. The headpiece is also of marabou feathers, and the undergarments are the same material as the dress. The doll is not marked. *Patricia Slabe Collection.*

ABOVE, RIGHT: Illustration 453. 8½in (21cm) Sonja Henie-look-alike commercially made in Norway by Ronnaig Pettersen, circa late 1930s. Felt mask face with painted features; blonde mohair wig. The body is wired covered with cloth, and the wool suit and the cotton blouse are sewn in place. The original paper tag on the arm identifies the maker.

HENRY VIII. King of England from 1509 to 1547. Born 1491; died 1547. Much of Henry VIII's life revolved around his six marriages. His wives were Catherine of Aragon, Anne Boleyn, Jane Seymour, Anne of Cleves, Catherine Howard and Catherine Parr. Henry's queens ended up this way: divorced, beheaded, died; divorced, beheaded, survived. While he was married to Catherine of Aragon, the mother of the future Queen Mary, England prospered under Henry's chief minister, Thomas Wolsey, and his court was a center of learning. The pope bestowed the title "Defender of the Faith" on Henry for his treatise against Martin Luther, but when he wanted to divorce Catherine to marry Anne Boleyn, the pope refused to grant permission. Henry married Anne anyhow and when the Pope excommunicated him Henry, became the supreme head of the English church. The marriage to Anne, the mother of the future Queen Elizabeth, did not last long and she was accused of adultery and beheaded. Ten days later Henry married Jane Seymour. Queen Jane died giving birth to the future Edward VI. Henry then married Anne of Cleves. He could not stand her, so he divorced her and had

Thomas Cromwell, his chief minister who arranged the match, beheaded. He then married Catherine Howard, who suffered the same fate as Anne Boleyn. Catherine Parr became his final queen. Henry was immensely popular as king despite his personal ambitions, and during his time England moved towards Protestantism and went through a period of peace and prosperity.

DOLLS:
1. HENRY VIII. Peggy Nisbet, No. H218, 1970s. All-plastic "collectors' doll." Made in England. About 8in (20.3cm). Companion dolls are Henry's six wives in the "Standard Series," which means that all the faces on the ladies are alike and only the costumes differ.
2. HENRY VIII. Peggy Nisbet, No. P653, 1970s. All-plastic "collectors' doll." Made in England. About 8in (20.3cm). Companion dolls are Henry's six wives in the "Portrait Series," which are individual portraits of Henry's queens modeled from paintings of the ladies.
3. HENRY VIII. Peggy Nisbet, No. M930. Inch-to-the-foot miniature, 1970s. All-plastic "collectors' doll." Made in England. This is the "Historical Series," and includes Henry's six wives.
4. HENRY VIII. Ann Parker, 1970s. Made in England. *Illustration 454*.
5. HENRY VIII. Peggy Nisbet, No. LE91, 1980. All-plastic "collectors' doll." Made in England. About 8in (20.3cm). This is a "Special Collectors' Set," No. 17, which was a limited edition of 500 sets. Companion dolls are Catherine of Aragon, No. LE92 and Cardinal Wolsey, No. LE93.

HENRY, PATRICK. Born 1736; died 1799. American patriot and orator. During the 1770s Patrick Henry spurred revolt in the southern colonies with his oratory, such as the phrase, "Give me liberty or give me death." After the Revolution he fought to have the Bill of Rights, the first ten amendments, added to the Constitution.

DOLLS:
1. PATRICK HENRY. Made for S.S. Kresge Company, 1976. A "Hero of the American Revolution." Made in Hong Kong. 7½in (19.1cm). *Illustration 455*.

Illustration 454. 11¼in (28.6cm) HENRY VIII by Ann Parker, late 1970s. All-hard plastic and permanently affixed to a wooden base. The facial features are painted. The moustache is mohair. Tagged with an Ann Parker label. Made in England. *Shirley Buchholz Collection*.

Illustration 455. 7½in (19.1cm) PATRICK HENRY manufactured for the S.S. Kresge Company, 1976. Vinyl head with painted hair and features. Fully-jointed plastic body with a swivel waist. Marked on the back: "MADE IN // HONG KONG." *Shirley Buchholz Collection*.

HENSLEY, PAMELA. Actress. Born Pamela Gail Hensley on October 3, 1950. Pamela Hensley played many roles in television programs. On December 21, 1975, she married Dr. Kiley (played by James Brolin) on "Marcus Welby, M.D." Then she was in "Kingston: Confidential" on NBC-TV from March to August of 1977. In "Buck Rogers in the 25th Century" she was sexy and wicked Princess Ardella during the 1979-1980 season.

DOLLS:
1. ARDELLA. Mego, No. 85000/7, 1979. Made in Hong Kong. 3¾in (9.6cm). *Illustration 456.*
SEE: BUCK ROGERS IN THE 25TH CENTURY.

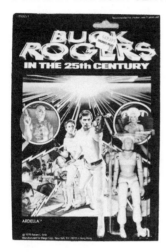

Illustration 456. 3¾in (9.6cm) PAMELA HENSLEY as *Ardella* from "Buck Rogers in the 25th Century" by Mego, No. 85000/7, 1979. All-vinyl and fully-jointed. Painted features with molded hat; painted clothing. Copyright by Robert C. Dille. Made in Hong Kong.

HENVILLE, SANDRA. SEE: BABY SANDY.

HIAWATHA. Legendary Indian leader. Around 1450 Hiawatha was supposed to have been the chief of the Onondaga tribe. By Indian tradition he formed the League of Five Nations, known as the Iroquois. Hiawatha taught the Iroquois agriculture, navigation, medicine and the arts, using his magic powers. He was the subject of the well-known poem by Longfellow.

DOLLS:
1. HIAWATHA. Madame Alexander, No. 720, 1967-1969. All-hard plastic and fully-jointed. Black synthetic wig; brown sleep eyes with molded lashes. 7½in (19.1cm).
NOTE: Other Indian dolls have been made that were called Hiawatha, a common name for Indian dolls. For example, Louis Amberg and Son made a Hiawatha doll in composition in the early 20th century.

HICKOK, WILD BILL. American frontier marshal. Born 1837 as James Butler Hickok; died 1876. Wild Bill Hickok was known as a great marksman in his encounters with outlaws, but he was gunned down in Deadwood, South Dakota. Guy Madison played Hickok in a television series from 1951 to 1957. Many films have also been made of his exploits.

DOLLS:
1. WILD BILL HICKOK. Mego, No. 1364, 1973. All-vinyl and fully-jointed. Made in Hong Kong. 7½in (19.1cm).
2. WILD BILL HICKOK. Excel Toy Corp., 1974. All-vinyl and fully-jointed. Made in Hong Kong. 9¼in (23.6cm).
3. WILD BILL HICKOK. Durham Ind., Inc., No. 3020, 1975. All-vinyl and fully-jointed. Molded clothing, except hat. Made in Hong Kong. 8in (20.3cm).
4. WILD BILL HICKOK. Carolina Enterprises, Inc., 1978. All-vinyl and fully-jointed. Made in Hong Kong. 4¼in (10.9cm).

HOBSON, RICHMOND PEARSON. American naval officer. Born 1870; died 1937. During the Spanish-American War in 1898 Hobson gained notice with his effort to sink the *Merrimac* to block Santiago harbor in Cuba.

DOLLS:
1. RICHMOND PEARSON HOBSON. Made in Germany. 13⅜in (33.9cm). *Illustration 457.*
SEE: SPANISH-AMERICAN WAR HEROES.

Illustration 457. 13⅜in (33.9cm) RICHMOND PEARSON HOBSON, manufacturer unknown, circa 1900-1910. Bisque head; jointed composition body. Painted hair, moustache and eyes. Part of a series of six officers from the Spanish-American War. Made in Germany. *Courtesy of the Margaret Woodbury Strong Museum.*

HOLDER, GEOFFREY. Actor, choreographer, director. Born in Trinidad, West Indies, on August 1, 1930. Holder made his debut in the United States with his own dance company in 1953. He appeared in several Broadway plays and received two Tony Awards for "The Wiz" in 1977 (director and costume design). Holder also appeared in several films. In *Annie* (1982) he played Punjab.

DOLLS:
1. PUNJAB. Knickerbocker Toy Co., Inc., No. 3866, 1982. All-vinyl and fully-jointed with painted features. Copyright by Columbia Pictures Industries, Inc. 7in (17.8cm).

SEE: ANNIE.

HOOD, DARLA. Actress. Born 1931; died 1979. From 1935 to 1942 Darla Hood appeared in 132 "Our Gang" comedy films. The "leading lady" of the Gang sang and provided the "love interest" for Alfalfa. She also appeared in some feature films before retiring at age 14. Later she sang jingles for some TV commercials and did bit parts in movies.

DOLLS:
1. DARLA from OUR GANG. Mego, No. 61600/4, 1975. 6in (15.2cm). *Illustrations 458* and *459*.

SEE: OUR GANG.

HOPE, BOB. Actor, comedian. Born Leslie Townes Hope on May 29, 1903, in England. Hope, a wisecracking comedian, has been a major name in the entertainment industry for 45 years. He spent years in vaudeville and musical comedy before establishing himself as a star in films during the 1940s. In his late 70s, Hope continues to appear on television regularly, delivering lines written by a staff of gag writers. He won special Academy Awards in 1940, 1944, 1952, 1959 and 1965, not for any acting ability, but for his humanitarian endeavors and contributions to the motion picture industry. Hope made annual Christmas tours overseas to entertain the troops for years. He wrote several humorous books about his career and his travels. He is supposed to be the richest entertainer who ever lived, as his wealth is estimated at between $400 million and $700 million, coming from investments including real estate, oil and gas wells, horseracing, a broadcasting company and the Cleveland Indians baseball team. He grew up in Cleveland, Ohio, arriving there from England with his parents at age four.

DOLLS:
1. BOB HOPE. Zany Toys, Inc., 1952. Hand puppet with a vinyl head with painted features.
2. BOB HOPE. Peggy Nisbet, No. P764, 1970s. Made in England. 7½in (19.1cm). *Illustration 460*.

Illustration 458. DARLA HOOD, MICKEY GUBITOSI and PORKY LEE from "Our Gang." *Jean Canaday Collection.*

Illustration 460. 7½in (19.1cm) BOB HOPE in *Road to Morocco* (1942) by Peggy Nisbet, No. P764, 1970s. All-hard plastic and jointed only at the arms. Painted hair and features. Made in England. *Photograph Courtesy of House of Nisbet.*

Illustration 459. 6in (15.2cm) DARLA HOOD from "Our Gang" by Mego, No. 61600/4, 1975. All-vinyl and fully-jointed. Rooted dark brown hair. Copyright by Metro-Goldwyn-Mayer, Inc. *Jean Canaday Collection.*

HOSKINS, ALLEN CLAYTON. Actor. Born 1920; died 1980. Hoskins played pigtailed Farina for 11 years in the "Our Gang" comedies and retired from the movies when he was 15. He then studied for a Certificate as a Psychiatric Technician and became the director for a workshop for a psychiatric agency near San Francisco, California, to help youngsters with drug problems.

DOLLS: SEE OUR GANG.

HORSE, MICHAEL. Actor. Michael Horse played Tonto in the 1981 film *The Legend of the Long Ranger.*
DOLLS: SEE THE LONE RANGER.

HOWARD, CATHERINE. Queen of England. Born circa 1521; died 1542. Thomas Howard, the Duke of Norfolk supported the marriage of his niece, Anne Boleyn, to Henry VIII and later presided at her trial and execution for immoral conduct. Henry's fifth wife, Catherine Howard, was also a niece of Thomas Howard. She, too, was accused of immoral conduct a year after her marriage in 1540, a charge to which she confessed. She was beheaded primarily to rid Henry of the influence of the Howard family.
DOLLS:
  1. CATHERINE HOWARD.   Peggy Nisbet, No. H221, 1970s. Plastic "collectors' doll." Made in England. About 7½in (19.1cm). Part of a series of Henry VIII and his six wives, "The Tudors, Standard Series." Companion dolls are Henry VIII, No.H218; Katherine (sic) of Aragon, No. H219; Jane Seymour, No. H220; Anne of Cleves, No. H222; Catherine Parr, No. H223; and Anne Boleyn, No. H217.
  2. CATHERINE HOWARD.   Peggy Nisbet, No. P606, 1970s. Plastic "collectors' doll." Made in England. about 7½in (19.1cm). Part of a series of Henry VIII and his six wives, "Portrait Series." Companion dolls are Henry VIII, No. P653; Catherine of Aragon, No. P602; Jane Seymour, No. P604; Anne of Cleves, No. P605; Catherine Parr, No. P607; and Anne Boleyn, No. P603.
  3. CATHERINE HOWARD.   Peggy Nisbet, No. M935. Inch-to-the-foot miniature, 1970s. Plastic "collectors' doll." Made in England. Companion dolls in this "Historical Series" are Henry VIII, No. M930; Catherine of Aragon, No. M931; Jane Seymour, No. M933; Anne of Cleves, No. M934; Catherine Parr, No. M936; and Anne Boleyn, No. M932.

HOWARD, RON (RONNY).   Actor. Born March 1, 1954. Ronny Howard's professional debut was at age two in a stage production of "The Seven Year Itch." His first screen appearance was in 1959, and he played child roles for several years. On television he was Opie

in "The Andy Griffith Show" on CBS-TV from October 1960 to September 1968 and Richie Cunningham on "Happy Days" on ABC-TV beginning in January 1974. His most memorable screen role was in George Lucas' *American Graffiti* in 1973. By the late 1970s he had turned to directing and producing as well as acting. His younger brother, Clint Howard, was also a juvenile performer in films and television.
DOLLS:
  1. RICHIE.   Mego, No. 63001/1, 1976. Made in Hong Kong. 8in (20.3cm). *Illustration 461.*
SEE: HAPPY DAYS.

HOWES, SALLY ANN.   Actress, singer. Born July 20, 1930, in London, England. Sally Ann Howes began her screen career as a child performer in the 1940s. As an adult she appeared on stage, television and in motion pictures in both Britain and the United States. She was Truly Scrumptious in the 1968 musical film *Chitty Chitty Bang Bang.*
DOLLS:
  1. CHITTY CHITTY BANG BANG.   TRULY SCRUMPTIOUS.   Mattel, 1968. All-vinyl; jointed head with rooted blonde hair; blue painted eyes. 2¼in (5.8cm). Came in a set with Mr. Potts (Dick Van Dyke), Jeremy (Adrian Hall) and Jemima (Heather Ripley).
  2. TRULY SCRUMPTIOUS.   Mattel, No. 1107, 1968. Made in Japan. 11½in (29.2cm). *Illustrations 462 and 463.*

Illustration 462. 11½in (29.2cm) SALLY ANN HOWES as *Talking Truly Scrumptious* from *Chitty Chitty Bang Bang* by Mattel, No. 1107, 1968. All-vinyl and fully-jointed. Rooted blonde hair; painted blue eyes with attached lashes. Copyright by Gledrose Prod., Ltd. and Warfield Prod. Ltd. Made in Japan. This is a variation on the Barbie doll. *Ted Menten Collection. Photograph by Ted Menten.*

Illustration 461. 8in (20.3cm) RON HOWARD as *Richie* from "Happy Days" by Mego, No. 63001/1, 1976. All-vinyl and fully-jointed with painted hair and eyes. Head marked: " © 1976 PARAMOUNT // PICTURES CORP." Back marked: " © MEGO CORP. 1974 // REG U.S. PAT OFF // PAT PENDING // HONG KONG."

182

Illustration 463. SALLY ANN HOWES as *Truly Scrumptious. Ted Menten Collection. Photograph by Ted Menten.*

HUBBEL, ELAINE DANIELE. Elaine Daniele Hubbel played Kathy Jo Elliott, the baby daughter of Betty Jo, on "Petticoat Junction" on CBS-TV (September 1963 to September 1970) during the later part of the program's run.

DOLLS:
1. KATHY JO. Remco, 1969. All-vinyl and fully-jointed. Molded hair; painted eyes; open mouth nurser. Copyright by Wayfilms. This is he same doll used for *My Three Sons.* (See Todd Triplets.) 9in (22.9cm).

HUNTER, GLENN. Actor. Born 1897; died 1945. Glenn Hunter played handsome, humorous country bumpkins in films during the 1920s. His greatest role was in *Merton of the Movies* in 1924.

DOLLS:
1. GLENN HUNTER as he appeared in *Merton of the Movies.* Particulars not known.

HUNTER, KIM. Actress. Born Janet Cole on November 12, 1922, in Detroit, Michigan. Kim Hunter made an impressive screen debut in 1943 in the thriller *The Seventh Victim,* but her parts after that were minor ones. She went to England to appear in movies and returned to the United States in 1947 when she won the part of Stella Kowalski in "A Streetcar Named Desire" on Broadway. She won the Best Supporting Actress Academy Award for repeating the part in the 1951 film. She was then black-listed by the film industry for several years for alleged Communist sympathies, and her later roles did not live up to her early promise. She was Zira in *Planet of the Apes,* 1968, *Beneath the Planet of the Apes,* 1970, and *Escape from the Planet of the Apes,* 1971.

DOLLS:
1. ZIRA. Mego, No. 1963, 1974. All-vinyl and fully-jointed. Painted hair and features. Made in Hong Kong. 8in (20.3cm).
SEE: PLANET OF THE APES.

HURST, RICK. Actor. Born in Houston, Texas, on January 1, (?). Hurst has played many "southern types" in films and on television. He was Cleaver, a convict, in "On the Rocks" on ABC-TV from September 1975 to May 1976. In "The Dukes of Hazzard" he has been Cletus since January 1979 for CBS-TV.

DOLLS:
1. CLETUS. Mego, No. 09010/6, 1982. All-vinyl and fully-jointed. Painted features and clothing. Copyright by Warner Bros., Inc. Made in Hong Kong. 3¾in (9.6cm).
SEE: DUKES OF HAZZARD, THE.

HUXLEY, RICK. Musician. Rick Huxley played guitar and banjo with the group The Dave Clark Five from 1964 to 1973.
DOLLS: SEE THE DAVE CLARK FIVE.

J

JACKSON, KATE. Actress. Born October 29, 1948. Kate Jackson achieved her greatest popularity playing Sabrina Duncan on ABC-TV's "Charlie's Angels" from September 1976, when the series began, until the end of the 1978-1979 season when she left the show. Before this assignment she has also been in the cast of "Dark Shadows" and "The Rookies." In 1979 she starred with her husband, Andrew Stevens, in the television pilot "Topper." Both the projected series and the marriage failed.

DOLLS:
1. SABRINA STARRING KATE JACKSON. Hasbro, No. 4861, 1977. Made in Hong Kong. 8½in (21.6cm). *Illustration 464.*
2. KATE JACKSON. Mattel, No. 2495, 1978. Made in Korea. 11½in (29.2cm). *Illustration 465.*
SEE: CHARLIE'S ANGELS.

Illustration 464. 8½in (21.6cm). KATE JACKSON as *Sabrina* from "Charlie's Angels" by Hasbro, No. 4861, 1977. All-vinyl and fully-jointed. Rooted dark brown hair; painted brown eyes. Copyright by Spelling-Goldberg Productions. Made in Hong Kong. *Shirley Buchholz Collection.*

Illustration 465. 11½in (29.2cm) KATE JACKSON, one of "TV's Star Women," by Mattel, No. 2495, 1978. All-vinyl and fully-jointed. Rooted long dark brown hair and painted brown eyes. Copyright by C & D Enterprises. Made in Korea.

JACKSON, SARAH. First Lady during the Administration of President Andrew Jackson (1829-1837). Sarah Jackson was the wife of Andrew Jackson's adopted son, whose mother, Rachel Robards, had divorced her husband to marry Jackson. Rachel died on December 22, 1828, after her husband's election and before his inauguration as the seventh President of the United States.

DOLLS:
1. SARAH JACKSON. Madame Alexander, No. 1507, 1979. Plastic and vinyl. 14in (35.6cm).
SEE: FIRST LADIES.

JACKSON, SHERRY. Actress. Born Sharon Diane Jackson on February 15, 1947. Sherry Jackson was Terry Williams on television's "Make Room for Daddy" from 1953 to 1964 and "Make Room for Granddaddy" during the 1970-1971 season. She appeared in guest roles in other television programs and was the lead in the pilot show "Brenda Starr, Reporter" in 1979, but her adult career was never successful.

DOLLS:
1. SHERRY. Effanbee, circa 1955. Vinyl head with rooted saran hair in pigtails; hard plastic body. A walking doll. 19in (48.3cm).

JACOBS, LAWRENCE-HILTON. Actor. Born September 4, 1953. Lawrence-Hilton Jacobs played Frederick, "Freddie, Boom Boom" Washington on "Welcome Back, Kotter" on ABC-TV from 1975 to 1979. He was also in the miniseries "Roots" in 1977.

DOLLS:
1. WASHINGTON from WELCOME BACK, KOTTER. Mattel, No. 9773, 1976. Made in Taiwan. 9¼in (23.6cm). *Illustration 466*.
SEE: WELCOME BACK, KOTTER.

Illustration 466. 9¼in (23.6cm) LAWRENCE-HILTON JACOBS as Freddie "Boom Boom" *Washington* from "Welcome Back, Kotter" by Mattel, No. 9773, 1976. All-vinyl and fully-jointed with painted hair and features. Copyright by the Wolper Organization, Inc. and the Komack Company, Inc. Made in Taiwan. *Shirley Buchholz Collection*.

JAMES BOND. Sexy super spy James Bond, Agent 007, was the fictional creation of novelist Ian Fleming. The first film version of the James Bond novels, *Dr. No,* came to the screen in 1962 and was not very successful upon its initial release. The thriller soon caught on with audiences and began one of the most successful and durable film series in the history of the movies. Relatively unknown Sean Connery was chosen to play Bond. He repeated the part in *From Russia With Love* (1963), *Goldfinger* (1964), *Thunderball* (1965) and *You Only Live Twice* (1967). Then Connery refused to do the part any longer. In *On Her Majesty's Secret Service* (1969) Bond was played by George Lazenby. The Lazenby Bond was not as successful at the box office as the previous entries in the series so Connery was given one million dollars to return as Bond in *Diamonds Are Forever* (1971). Then the role was taken over by Roger Moore who was Bond in *Live and Let Die* (1973), *The Man With the Golden Gun* (1974), *The Spy Who Loved Me* (1977) and *Moonraker* (1979). The rumor persists that Sean Connery will return to the role.

Dolls were made of SEAN CONNERY from *Thunderball,* HAROLD SAKATA as *Oddjob* from *Goldfinger,* and from *Moonraker* ROGER MOORE as *Bond* , LOIS CHILES as *Holly,* MICHAEL LONSDALE as *Drax* and RICHARD KIEL as *Jaws.*

JAMES, JESSE. American outlaw. Born 1847; died 1882. Jesse and his brother, Frank, became leaders of a gang which robbed and murdered throughout most of the central states. Jesse and his family were from Missouri, and they favored the Southern cause during the Civil War. They suffered from the Union forces because of this so Jesse became a Confederate informer when he was 15. He joined the guerilla forces of W. C. Quantrill and after the group surrendered, James was shot and wounded. He became a fugitive and was declared an outlaw from 1866 until his death. Two members of his group killed him to collect the $10,000 "dead or alive" reward offered by the governor of Missouri.

DOLLS:
1. JESSE JAMES. Excel Toy Corp., 1974. All-vinyl and fully-jointed. Made in Hong Kong. 9¼in (23.6cm).
2. JESSE JAMES. Carolina Enterprises, Inc., No. 0102/0160, 1978. Made in Hong Kong. 4¼in (10.9cm). *Illustration 467.*

Illustration 467. 4¼in (10.9cm) JESSE JAMES by Empire Toys, No. 0102/0160, 1978. All-vinyl and fully-jointed with painted features and clothing. Copyright by Carolina Enterprises, Inc. Made in Hong Kong.

JEFFERSON, THOMAS. Third President of the United States (1801-1809). Born 1743; died 1826. Jefferson was the author of the Declaration of Independence, a member of the Virginia Legislature, Minister to France, Secretary of State, Vice President and became President in 1800 when he was elected by the House of Representatives because no candidate had obtained a majority of the Electoral Vote. He became the first President to be inaugurated in Washington, the city he had helped to plan. Notable achievements of his first administration were the Louisiana Purchase and the Lewis and Clark Expedition. After he retired to his home, Monticello, in 1809, he founded the University of Virginia and continued as a scientist, architect, philosopher and statesman. He and John Adams, his chief

opponent in the election of 1800, both died on July 4, 1826, the 50th Anniversary of the proclamation of the Declaration of Independence.

DOLLS:
1. THOMAS JEFFERSON. Peggy Nisbet, No. P723, 1970s. All-plastic "collectors' doll." Made in England. About 8in (20.3cm).
2. THOMAS JEFFERSON. Made for the S. S. Kresge Company, 1976. A "Hero of the American Revolution." Made in Hong Kong. 7½in (19.1cm). *Illustration 468.*

Illustration 468. 7½in (19.1cm) THOMAS JEFFERSON manufactured for the S.S. Kresge Company, 1976. Vinyl head with painted hair and features. Fully-jointed plastic body with swivel waist. Marked on back: "MADE IN // HONG KONG." *Shirley Buchholz Collection.*

JOAN OF ARC. French saint and national heroine of the Hundred Years War. Born circa 1412; died 1431. When she was quite young Joan heard the "voices" of St. Michael, St. Catherine and St. Margaret who begged her to aid the dauphin of France, the future Charles VII, to gain his throne from which he was being kept by the English, who were trying to conquer France. In 1429 Joan adopted male attire, which she was to keep until her death. She was given troops and they lifted the Seige of Orléans which cleared the area of the English. She stood beside Charles when he was crowned king. In 1430 Joan was captured by the Burgundians and sold to the English. She was tried by a church court for heresy and sorcery and was condemned to be burned at the stake. She was rehabilitated in a new trial in 1456, 25 years after her death, and was canonized by the church in 1920.

DOLLS:
1. JOAN OF ARC. Peggy Nisbet, No. P795, 1970s. All-plastic "collectors' doll." Made in England. About 7½in (19.1cm).

JOHN XXIII. Pope of the Roman Catholic Church. Born Angelo Roncalli in Italy in 1881; died 1963. In 1904 Roncalli was ordained a priest. During World War I he served as a sergeant in the medical corps. After the war he filled various administrative capacities for the Vatican in Bulgaria, Turkey, Greece and France. In 1958 he was elected as a compromise candidate for the Papacy, because it was thought he would be a caretaker pontif because of his years. When he became pope he quickly dispelled this idea with his internationalizing of the College of Cardinals and his travels. In 1962 he opened the Second Vatican Council, the first in 100 years, whose aim it was to modernize the Catholic Church. His successor, Pope Paul VI, initiated proceedings so that he can become a saint. (This can not occur until 50 years after his death.)

DOLLS:
1. POPE JOHN XXIII. Peggy Nisbet, No. P797, 1970s. Plastic "collectors' doll." Made in England. About 8in (20.3cm).

JOHN PAUL II. Pope of the Roman Catholic Church. Born Karol Wojtyla in Wadowiche, Poland, May 18, 1920. On October 16, 1978, he was elected as the first non-Italian pope in 456 years to succeed Pope John Paul I. John Paul I died on September 28, 1978, after serving as Pope for only 34 days.

DOLLS:
1. POPE JOHN PAUL II. Peggy Nisbet, 1980. All-plastic "collector's doll." Wears white and gold papal vestments. Made in England. About 8in (20.3cm).

JOHNNY, the PHILIP MORRIS PAGEBOY. SEE: ROVENTINI, JOHNNY.

JOHNSON, LYNDON B(AINES). The 36th President of the United States (1963-1969). Born August 27, 1908; died January 22, 1973. As a United States Democratic Senator from Texas Johnson became a highly successful majority leader. As Vice President he succeeded the assassinated President Kennedy in November 1963. As President he exercised his political skill in passing legislation in the areas of civil rights, tax reduction, antipoverty programs and conservation. He escalated American involvement in South Vietnam and anti-Vietnam War sentiment caused him to decide not to seek renomination in 1968.

DOLLS:
1. LYNDON B. JOHNSON. Remco, No 1815, 1964. Made in USA. 5¾in (14.7cm). *Illustration 469.* See also *Illustration 470.* Barry Goldwater is a companion doll.

Illustration 470. 16in (40.6cm) LYNDON B. JOHNSON by Remco. There is a possibility that the vinyl head was inserted on the plastic body as a "put-together," although the fit is perfect. (See *Illustration 469.*) The vinyl head is marked: "126 // REMCO IND. INC. // 1964." The lower torso is marked: "DR. // JOHN // LITTLECHAP // ® // REMCO INDUSTRIES // © 1964." The jacket of the black tuxedo is labeled similarly as Dr. John Littlechap. (The Littlechap Family of dolls is part of a series.)

Illustration 469. 5¾in (14.7cm) LYNDON B. JOHNSON by Remco, No. 1815, 1964. All-vinyl with a jointed head and a one-piece body. Plastic hat. The features and the clothing are painted. This was a tie-in for the 1964 presidential elections, in which the President was the winning candidate. Barry Goldwater, the Republican candidate, was also issued using the same concept. Made in USA. *Shirley Buchholz Collection.*

JOLSON, AL. Singer; actor. Born Asa Yoelson in St. Petersburg, Russia, May 26, 1886; died 1950. From his childhood in America Jolson was a noted singer, first in a synagogue, then in a circus, and later as a black-faced vaudeville entertainer. Before long he became America's most popular recording artist. In 1926 he sang three songs in a Warner Brothers experimental short film *April Showers.* The following year he made motion picture history by starring in the world's first talking feature film *The Jazz Singer.* His popularity declined until two films, loosely based on his life, *The Jolson Story* (1946) and *Jolson Sings Again* (1949) were released. Larry Parks played Jolson, but he dubbed his own singing. He died of a heart attack shortly after returning from Korea where he was entertaining the American troops.

DOLLS:
1. AL JOLSON. Maker unknown, early 1930s. Rubber head with painted features in "black-face." Open mouth with painted teeth. Cloth body with leather hands. Dressed in a white shirt and black suit. 19in (48.2cm).

JONES, ANISSA. Actress. Born 1958; died 1976. Anissa Jones played cute Buffy Davis, who had a doll named Mrs. Beasley, on the CBS-TV show "Family Affair" from September 1966 to September 1971. She also appeared in the Elvis Presley film *The Trouble With Girls* (1969). She was found dead at age 18 from a drug overdose.

DOLLS:
1. BUFFY AND MRS. BEASLEY. Mattel, No. 3577, 1967. 6¼in (15.9cm). *Illustrations 471* and *472*.
2. TALKING BUFFY AND MRS. BEASLEY. Mattel, No. 3107, 1969. 10½in (26.7cm). *Illustration 471* and *473*.

Illustration 471. 10½in (26.7cm) ANISSA JONES as *Buffy* from "Family Affair" with 6¼in (15.9cm) *Buffy*, both by Mattel. See *Illustrations 472* and *473*.

Illustration 472. 6¼in (15.9cm) ANISSA JONES as *Buffy* from "Family Affair" by Mattel, No. 3577, 1967. All-vinyl with a one-piece body that has wire inside for posing positions. The vinyl head has rooted blonde hair and painted blue eyes. Marked on lower back: " © 1965 // MATTEL INC. // JAPAN // 25." Arm tag: "Buffy // © 1967 Family Affair Company." *Shirley Buchholz Collection.*

Illustration 473. 10½in (26.7cm) ANISSA JONES as *Buffy* from "Family Affair" by Mattel, No. 3107, 1969. Vinyl head with rooted blonde hair; painted blue eyes. Pull string in plastic torso for talking mechanism. Vinyl arms and legs. Lower back marked: " © 1967 MATTEL, INC. // U.S. & FOR. // PATS. PEND. // MEXICO." Dress tag: " © 1968 Mattel Inc. // Made in Hong Kong."

JONES, BEN. Actor. Ben Jones has played Cooter on "The Dukes of Hazzard" on CBS-TV since the show began in January 1979.

DOLLS:
1. COOTER. Mego, No. 09010/7, 1982. All-vinyl and fully-jointed. Painted hair and features. Copyright by Warner Bros., Inc. Made in Hong Kong. 3¾in (9.6cm).

SEE: DUKES OF HAZZARD, THE.

JONES, CAROLYN. Actress. Born April 28, 1929. Carolyn Jones was a versatile and popular screen actress during the 1950s. In 1951 she was nominated for a Supporting Actress Academy Award for *The Bachelor Party*. Her widest popularity came from playing Morticia on NBC-TV's "The Addams Family" from September 1964 to September 1966. In October 1977 the original cast was reunited for a special Halloween episode of the series.

DOLLS:
1. THE ADDAMS FAMILY, MORTICIA. Remco, 1964. Vinyl head with rooted black hair; one-piece hard plastic body. Copyright by Filmways TV Prod., Inc. 5in (12.7cm).
2. THE ADDAMS FAMILY HAND PUPPET. MORTICIA. Ideal, 1964. Vinyl head with painted features; remainder is a glove with a lithographed body.

JONES, DAVY. Singer; actor. Born David Jones in Manchester, England, December 30, 1946. Davy Jones was one of the Monkees, a prefabricated vocal group, who had their own television show from September of 1966 to August of 1968 on NBC-TV. During this time the Monkees were very popular with young people and had a number of hit records. Jones tried to re-form the group with Micky Dolenz, another member of the band, in 1975 but the project failed.

DOLLS:
1. DAVY JONES. A "Show Biz Baby" by Hasbro, No. 8802, 1967. Made in Hong Kong. 4in (10.2cm). *Illustration 475.*
2. DAVY JONES. Remco, circa 1975. Made in Hong Kong. 5in (12.7cm). *Illustration 476.*
3. MONKEES HAND PUPPET. Mattel, No. 5373, 1977. 10½in (26.7cm).

SEE: THE MONKEES.

Illustration 476. 5in (12.7cm) DAVY JONES of the Monkees singing group, a finger puppet by Remco, circa 1975. Vinyl head with rooted black hair and painted eyes. Moveable vinyl arms. The legs are cloth pants for finger manipu-Head marked: "2." Back marked: " © 1970 // REMCO // IND. INC. // HARRISON, N.J. // PAT. PEND. // HONG KONG."

Illustration 474. Davy Jones from the Monkees' first record album cover, 1966.

JONES, JOHN PAUL. American naval hero. Born in Scotland in 1747; died 1792. During the American Revolution Jones was a privateer who harassed British shipping from ports in France. He later served in the Russian navy.

DOLLS:
1. JOHN PAUL JONES. Made for the S.S. Kresge Company, 1976. A "Hero of the American Revolution." Made in Hong Kong. 7½in (19.1cm). *Illustration 477.*

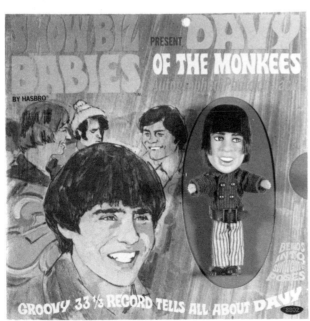

Illustration 475. 4in (10.2cm) DAVY JONES of the Monkees, a "Show Biz Baby" by Hasbro, No. 8802, 1967. All-vinyl; jointed only at the head; wired vinyl "poseable" body. Rooted dark brown hair; painted brown eyes. Attached to a 33 1/3 rpm record cover. Copyright by Raybert Productions, Inc. and a Trademark of Screen Gems, Inc. Made in Hong Kong. *Wanda Lodwick Collection.*

Illustration 477. 7½in (19.1cm) JOHN PAUL JONES manufactured for the S.S. Kresge Company, 1976. Vinyl head with painted hair and features. Fully-jointed plastic body with swivel waist. Marked on back: "MADE IN // HONG KONG." *Shirley Buchholz Collection.*

JONES, SPIKE. Musician. Born Lindley Armstrong Jones on December 14, 1911; died 1965. Spike Jones' musical style was to create zany variations of currently popular songs. He used odd instruments, such as a washboard or a fog horn, to achieve wierd sound effects. Spike Jones and his singer wife, Helen Grayco, along with Spike's City Slicker Band, presented their musical mayhem on several variety shows on television during the 1950s. "The Spike Jones Show" was a comedy variety program that was used as a fill-in and summer replacement from 1954 to 1961.

DOLLS:
1. SPIKE JONES. Hand puppet by Zany Toys, Inc., 1952. Vinyl head with painted features; cloth body.

JOSEPH. (CHIEF JOSEPH). American Indian leader. Born circa 1840; died 1904. Chief Joseph's Indian name was Hinmatonyalatkit, and he was a chief of the Nez Percé. The tribe refused to recognize land cessions made to the United States in 1863 so Joseph attempted to lead it to Canada, traveling 1600 miles through Idaho and Montana before surrendering in 1877.

DOLLS:
1. CHIEF JOSEPH. Hallmark, No. 400DT113-4, 1979. Made in Taiwan. 7in (17.8cm). *Illustrations 478* and *479*.

Illustration 478. 7in (17.8cm) CHIEF JOSEPH by Hallmark, No. 400DT113-4, 1979. All-cloth. Sewn body joints with printed features and clothing. Made in Taiwan. *Shirley Buchholz Collection.*

Illustration 479. CHIEF JOSEPH by Hallmark. *Shirley Buchholz Collection.*

K

KAPLAN, GABRIEL (GABE). Comedian, actor. Born March 31, 1945. Kaplan began in show business as a stand-up comic. From September 1975 to August 1979 he played Gabe Kotter in "Welcome Back, Kotter" on ABC-TV. The show was based on Kaplan's real-life experiences as a Brooklyn high school student, although on the series he was the teacher of the "unteachable" students. "Welcome Back, Kotter" made John Travolta a star. Kaplan had very modest success in his film *Fast Break* in 1979 and returned to television in the fall of 1980 in the short-lived comedy "Lewis and Clark."

DOLLS:
1. MR. KOTTER from WELCOME BACK, KOTTER. Mattel, No. 9770, 1976. Made in Taiwan. 9¼in (23.6cm). *Illustration 480.*
SEE: WELCOME BACK, KOTTER.

Illustration 480. 9¼in (23.6cm) GABRIEL KAPLAN as *Mr. Kotter* from "Welcome Back, Kotter" by Mattel, No. 9770, 1976. All-vinyl and fully-jointed with painted hair and features. Copyright by the Wolper Organization, Inc. and the Komack Company, Inc. Made in Taiwan.

KARATH, KYM. Child actress. Kym Karath played Gretl in *The Sound of Music* in 1965.

DOLLS:
1. GRETL. Madame Alexander, No. 1000, 1965. All-hard plastic with dark wig. 8in (20.3cm).
2. GRETL. Madame Alexander, No. 1101, 1965-1970. Vinyl head with rooted blonde hair; vinyl and plastic body. 12in (30.5cm). *Illustration 481.*
3. GRETL. Madame Alexander, 1966. Same doll as No. 2 dressed in the sailor school outfit.
4. GRETL. Madame Alexander, No. 0801, 1971-1973. All-hard plastic with blonde wig. With or without bending knees. 7½in (19.1cm). *Illustration 482.*
SEE: SOUND OF MUSIC, THE.

Illustration 481. 12in (30.5cm) KYM KARATH as *Gretl* from *The Sound of Music* by Madame Alexander, No. 1101, 1967-1970. Vinyl with rooted blonde hair; blue sleep eyes with lashes. Head marked: "ALEXANDER // 19©64." *Jean Canaday Collection*.

KARLOFF, BORIS. Actor. Born William Henry Pratt November 23, 1887, in England; died 1969. In 1909 Karloff emigrated to Canada and worked as a farmhand. He joined a touring company and was in stage parts until 1916 when he made his first film. He did not gain much recognition in his 40 silent films. His career picked up momentum in 1931 when he was cast as the Monster in *Frankenstein*, a role turned down by Bela Lugosi. During the 1930s he was the lead in other horror films such as *The Mask of Fu Manchu, The Mummy, The Ghoul, The Bride of Frankenstein* and *The Son of Frankenstein*. Karloff appeared in more than 140 films, one of which even had his name in the title—*Abbott and Costello Meet the Killer—Boris Karloff*. In person Karloff was a mild-mannered gentleman, but he will always be remembered as a monster or a deranged scientist.

DOLLS:
1. FRANKENSTEIN. Mego Corp., No. 1900, 1974. All-vinyl and fully-jointed. Made in Hong Kong. 8in (20.3cm).
2. THE MUMMY. Mego Corp., No. 1903, 1974. All-vinyl and fully-jointed. Made in Hong Kong. 8in (20.3cm).
3. OFFICIAL UNIVERSAL STUDIOS' THE FRANKEN-STEIN MONSTER. Remco, No. 751, 1980. All-vinyl and fully-jointed. Made in Hong Kong. 8in (20.3cm).
4. OFFICIAL UNIVERSAL STUDIOS' THE MUMMY. Remco, No. 753, 1980. All-vinyl and fully-jointed. Made in Hong Kong. 8in (20.3cm). (20.3cm).
5. THE FRANKENSTEIN MONSTER. Remco, 1980. All-vinyl and fully-jointed. Copyright by Universal City Studios, Inc. Made in Hong Kong. 4in (10.2cm).
6. THE MUMMY. Remco, 1980. All-vinyl and fully-jointed. Copyright by Universal City Studios, Inc. Made in Hong Kong. 4in (10.2cm).

Illustration 482. 7½in (19.1cm) KYM KARATH as *Gretl* from *The Sound of Music* by Madame Alexander, No. 801, 1971. All-hard plastic and fully-jointed, including bending knees. Blonde wig; blue sleep eyes with molded lashes. Back marked: "ALEX."

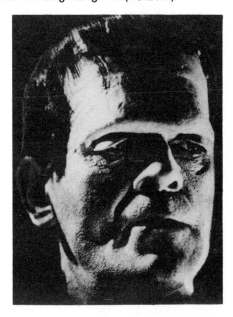

Illustration 483. Boris Karloff made up for his part as Frankenstein's monster.

KATHARINE or KATHERINE OF ARAGON. SEE: CATHERINE OF ARAGON.

KATT, WILLIAM. Actor. Born 1955. William Katt is the son of actor Bill Williams (real name, William Katt) and actress Barbara Hale. Katt entered films in the 1970s and appeared in a variety of roles. In *Butch and Sundance, the Early Days* (1979) he was The Sundance Kid, a part that Robert Redford played ten years earlier. In 1981 he began his own television show as "The Greatest American Hero."

DOLLS:
1. THE SUNDANCE KID. Kenner, No. 53020, 1979. 4in (10.2cm). *Illustration 485.*
2. RALPH. Mego, No. 22010, 1982. All-vinyl and fully-jointed. Painted yellow hair, features and clothing. Comes in a set called "The Greatest American Hero Free-Wheeling Convertible Bug With Ralph and Bill." Copyright by Stephen J. Connell Production.* 3¾in (9.6cm).
3. RALPH. Mego, Series No. 22001, 1982. All-vinyl and fully-jointed. Painted yellow hair; painted features. Copyright by Stephen J. Connell Productions.* 8in (20.3cm).

SEE: GREATEST AMERICAN HERO, THE.

*So stated in the Mego catalog. The television show is produced by Stephen J. Cannell Productions.

Illustration 484. WILLIAM KATT.

Illustration 485. 4in (10.2cm) WILLIAM KATT as *The Sundance Kid* from *Butch and Sundance The Early Days* by Kenner, No. 53030, 1979. All-vinyl and fully-jointed. Painted features and clothing. Copyright by Twentieth Century-Fox Film Corporation. Made in Hong Kong.

KAYE, DANNY. Actor. Born David Daniel Kaminski on January 18, 1913. Kaye made his Broadway debut in 1939 after performing for years in vaudeville and nightclubs. In 1944 he made his first film and enjoyed enormous popularity in the movies until the late 1950s. From 1963 to 1967 he had a TV variety program, "The Danny Kaye Show." In recent years he has devoted much of his time on behalf of UNICEF, entertaining children in developing countries.

DOLLS:
1. DANNY KAYE IN HANS CHRISTIAN ANDERSEN. Peggy Nisbet, No. P763, 1970s. All-plastic "collectors' doll." Made in England. About 8in (20.3cm).

KEESHAN, BOB (ROBERT). TV personality. Born June 27, 1927. Keeshan was Clarabell Hornblow, the clown on "Howdy Doody" on NBC-TV from 1947 to 1952. As Clarabell, Keeshan did not speak, but provided his comments with a horn. After he left the show Bob Nicholson and then Lou Anderson played the part of Clarabell. Since 1955 on CBS-TV he has been the creator/producer/star of "Captain Kangaroo," the longest running network program on television. As Captain Kangaroo, Bob Keeshan explains the adult world to children through cartoons, stories, songs and sketches. In 1982 he began doing this at 6:30 AM so CBS could move its news program up earlier to remain more competitive in the news ratings.

Illustration 486. 21in (53.3cm) BOB KEESHAN as *Captain Kangaroo* by Baby Barry Toy, late 1950s. Vinyl head and hands; stuffed cloth body. Painted gray hair and moustache; blue set-in glass eyes. The black vinyl feet are part of the body construction. Marked on the neck: " © // B.B." Tag on clothing: "EXCLUSIVE LICENSEE // BABY BARRY // TOY N.Y.C." Reverse of Tag: "CAPTAIN // KANGAROO." *Wanda Lodwick Collection.*

DOLLS:
1. to 3.
CLARABELL. Madame Alexander, 1951. All-stuffed cloth and fully-jointed with applied features. 20in (50.8cm), 29in (73.7cm) and 42in (101.6cm).
4. CLARABELL. Peter Puppet Playthings Inc., 1953. Puppet on strings with a composition head that has painted features and a moving mouth, composition hands and feet and a flat wooden section for the torso. No markings. Designed by Raye Copelan and Copyrighted by Bob Smith. 15½in (39.4cm).
5. CLARABELL. Manufacturer unknown, 1953. Vinyl head; cotton cloth body; celluloid moving eyes. 12in (30.5cm).
6. CAPTAIN KANGAROO. Baby Barry Toy, late 1950s. 21in (53.3cm). *Illustration 486.*
7. CAPTAIN KANGAROO. Mattel, No. 5334, 1967. 20in (50.8cm). *Illustration 487.*
NOTE: In 1954 Ideal Toy Corporation mada a *Clarabell* with a mask face and cloth body in sizes of 16in (40.6cm) and 20in (50.8cm).

Illustration 487. 20in (50.8cm) BOB KEESHAN as *Captain Kangaroo* by Mattel, No. 5334, 1967. All-cloth with a talking mechanism inside. Printed features and clothing with attached extra clothing. Tag marked: "© ROBERT KEESHAN // ASSOCIATES, INC. // ALL RIGHTS RESERVED // © MATTEL, INC." *Wanda Lodwick Collection.*

KEITH, RICHARD. Child performer. Richard Keith played Little Ricky on "I Love Lucy" during the 1956-1957 television season. It was a national event when Lucy Ricardo gave birth to Little Ricky on the television show the same night that Lucille Ball gave birth to her second child, Desiderio Alberto Arnaz IV. Desi Arnaz, Jr. was born January 19, 1953; so was Little Ricky.
DOLLS:
1. LITTLE RICKY. (RICKY JR.). Zany Toys, Inc., 1953. About 8in (20.3cm). *Illustration 488.*
2. LITTLE RICKY. (RICKY JR.). American Character, 1953. 20½in (52.1cm). *Illustration 489* and *490.*

Illustration 488. About 8in (20.3cm) RICHARD KEITH as *Little Ricky* (*Ricky, Jr.*), a puppet doll from "I Love Lucy" by Zany Toys, Inc., 1953. Vinyl head, hands and feet attached to a blanket and pajamas. Painted brown hair; painted blue eyes. Tag on blanket: "I AM // RICKY, JR. // © LUCILLE BALL // AND DESI ARNAZ." *Wanda Lodwick Collection.*

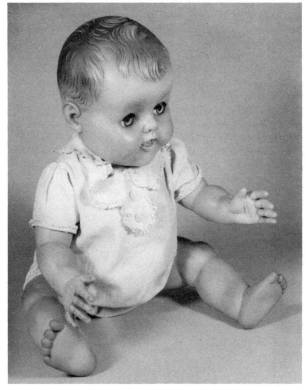

Illustration 489. 20½in (52.1cm) RICHARD KEITH as *Little Ricky* (*Ricky, Jr.*) from "I Love Lucy" by American Character, 1953. Stuffed vinyl head; vinyl fully-jointed body. Molded and painted brown hair; blue sleep eyes with lashes; open mouth for nursing. Head marked: "AMER. CHAR. DOL." The original rompers are missing a matching belt with "Ricky Jr." embroidered across the front in script. *Wanda Lodwick Collection.*

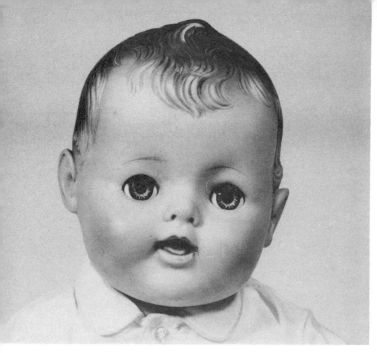

Illustration 490. 20½in (52.1cm) RICHARD KEITH as *Little Ricky* (*Ricky, Jr.*) by American Character, 1953. *Jean Canaday Collection*.

KELLEY, DeFOREST. Actor. Born January 20, 1920. Since the 1950s Kelley has played many parts in films and on television, mostly as "heavies." He was McCoy in the legendary NBC-TV series "Star Trek" from September 1966 to September 1969 and played the part again in the film *Star Trek the Motion Picture* in 1979.

DOLLS:
1. DR. McCOY (BONES). Mego, No. 51200/3, 1974. Made in Hong Kong. 8in (20.3cm). *Illustration 491*.
2. DR. McCOY. Mego, No. 91200/6, 1979. Made in Hong Kong. 3¾in (9.6cm). *Illustration 492*.

SEE: STAR TREK.

Illustration 491. 8in (20.3cm) DeFOREST KELLEY as *Dr. McCoy* (*Bones*) from "Star Trek" by Mego, No. 51200/3, 1974. All-vinyl and fully-jointed. Painted hair and features. Copyright by Paramount Pictures Corporation. Made in Hong Kong. *Penny Caswell Collection*.

Illustration 492. 3¾in (9.6cm) DeFOREST KELLEY as *Dr. McCoy* from *Star Trek The Motion Picture* by Mego, No. 91200/6, 1979. All-vinyl and fully-jointed. Painted features and clothing. Copyright by Paramount Pictures Corporation. Made in Hong Kong.

KELLY, EMMETT. Clown. Born December 8, 1898; died March 28, 1979. Beginning in 1931 Kelly was a full-time circus clown, and his character was always "Wearie Willie." Willie never spoke and he never laughed. He wore a battered hat and tattered clothes. His nose was red, he needed a shave and his mouth was turned down at the corners. He was poignant and amusing at the same time. Kelly was Willie in several different circuses until 1956 when he left Ringling Brothers, Barnum and Bailey over a labor dispute. He had appeared in the films *The Fat Man* (1951) as a clown who was a murderer and in *The Greatest Show on Earth* (1952) as Willie. During his last years he made nightclub and television appearances.

DOLLS:
1. EMMETT KELLY. Baby Barry Toy, No. 713, late 1950s. 13¼in (33.7cm). *Illustration 493*.
2. EMMETT KELLY. Baby Barry Toy, late 1950s. 21½in (54.6cm). *Illustration 494*.
3. EMMETT KELLY. Baby Barry Toy, late 1950s. Vinyl head with rooted hair; glass inset eyes. (This is basically the same doll as No. 2.) The nose lights up with a small light bulb powered by two penlite batteries that fit into an opening in the back of the head. Head marked: "B & B." 20½in (52.1cm).
4. EMMETT KELLY. Juro, 1970s. 29in (73.7cm). *Illustration 495*.

Kelly, Emmett

Illustration 494. 21½in (54.6cm) EMMETT KELLY as *Willie the Clown* by Baby Barry Toy, late 1950s. Vinyl head and hands; stuffed cloth body. Rooted fringe of brown hair; green set-in eyes. Wire inside arms and legs for changing positions. The shoes are felt and are sewn on. (Other identical dolls have brown eyes and the colors of the hat and the clothing can differ.) Clothing tag: "EXCLUSIVE LICENSEE // BABY BARRY // TOY N.Y.C." Reverse of tag: "EMMETT KELLY'S // WILLIE THE CLOWN." *Wanda Lodwick Collection.*

ABOVE: *Illustration 493.* 13¼in (33.7cm) EMMETT KELLY by Baby Barry Toy, No. 713, late 1950s. All-vinyl. The head is jointed; the body is one-piece. Molded black hat; painted black hair and features. Brown vinyl shoes. Head marked: "B.B." Tag on jacket: "Exclusive Licensee // Baby Barry // Toy - N.Y.C."

RIGHT: *Illustration 495.* 29in (73.7cm) EMMETT KELLY as a *Willie the Clown* "dummy" by Juro, 1970s. Vinyl head with painted hat molded to head; painted features; string makes mouth "talk;" vinyl hands; remainder is stuffed cloth. Marked on neck: "EMMETT KELLY // TRADE MARK // WILLIE THE CLOWN // JURO NOVELTY CO. INC. // 2." *Wanda Lodwick Collection.*

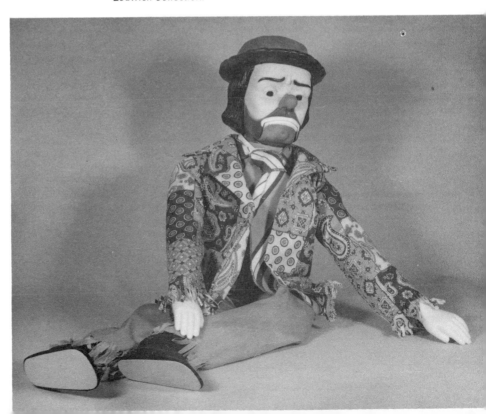

KELLY, EMMETT, JR. The son of famed clown Emmett Kelly performed in an act similar to his father's Wearie Willie.

DOLLS:
1. EMMETT KELLY, JR. Horsman, 1979. Vinyl head with painted features and a moving mouth. Cloth stuffed body. Dressed similar to Emmett Kelly. 24in (61cm).

KENNEDY, CAROLINE. Celebrity. Born November 27, 1957. Caroline is the daughter of President John F. Kennedy and Jacqueline Bouvier Kennedy Onassis. She lives in New York, New York, with three friends and is a research assistant in the film and TV department of the Metropolitan Museum of Art.

DOLLS:
All of the CAROLINE dolls are by Madame Alexander. They were not advertised as "Caroline Kennedy," but the meaning was obvious. They are 15in (38.1cm). All-vinyl and fully-jointed. Rooted blonde hair with a side-part; blue sleep eyes with lashes.
1. No. 4290, 1961. Dressed in a dotted swiss dress with a taffeta petticoat and flowered tricot panties.
2. No. 4930, 1961. Dressed in a three-piece play suit of corduroy.
3. No. 4925, 1961. Dressed in an organdy party dress.
4. No. 1305, 1962. Dressed in a check cotton dress with a white organdy collar.
5. No. 1312, 1962. Dressed in riding clothes with high boots.
6. No. 1310, 1962. Lace trimmed organdy dress with embroidery.
Note: In both 1961 and 1962, Caroline had "an extensive assortment of outfits." In 1962, the name "Caroline" was registered as a trademark by Madame Alexander.

KENNEDY, JACQUELINE BOUVIER. (JACQUELINE KENNEDY ONASSIS). Celebrity. Born July 28, 1929. In 1953 she married the future president John F. Kennedy. As First Lady she planned and conducted the restoration of the White House décor. She was greatly admired by people all over the world until she married Greek shipping tycoon Aristotle Onassis in 1968, five years after the assassination of her first husband. When Onassis died in 1975 she fought for and received 26 million dollars from his estate. In recent years she has worked as an editor for publishing houses.

DOLLS:
The following JACQUELINE dolls are by Madame Alexander. They were not advertised as "Jacqueline Kennedy," but like the companion doll, Caroline, the likeness was obvious to the celebrity. In 1962, the name "Jacqueline" was registered as a trademark for dolls by Madame Alexander. In 1962 many extra outfits could be purchased for both sizes of the Jacqueline doll.
1. No. 2218, 1961. Dressed in a "three-piece brocade short coat costume." Vinyl and plastic and fully-jointed. Dark wig; brown sleep eyes with lashes. 21in (53.3cm).
2. No. 2130, 1962. Dressed in a silver and white brocade evening gown. 21in (53.3cm). Same basic doll as No. 1.

3. No. 2125, 1962. 21in (53.3cm). *Illustration 496.* Same doll as No. 1.
4. No. 2140, 1962. Dressed in a floor length ball gown with a full length lined evening coat of satin. 21in (53.3cm). Same doll as No. 1.
5. No. 2117, 1962. Dressed in riding clothes. 21in (53.3cm). Same doll as No. 1.
6. No. 865, 1962. Wore slacks, sweater with matching hat and a leather jacket. All-plastic and fully-jointed, including at the knees. Dark brown wig; brown sleep eyes with molded lashes. 10in (25.4cm).
7. No. 885, 1962. 10in (25.4cm). *Illustrations 497* and *498.*
8. No. 886, 1962. Satin evening gown with a full length matching stole. 10in (25.4cm). Same basic doll as No. 6 above.
9. No. 894. Wore a two-piece suit with a lined jacket and matching hat. Nylon blouse. 10in (25.4cm). Same doll as No. 6.
10. No. 895, 1962. Wore a long coat over a matching sheath dress. 10in (25.4cm). Same doll as No. 6.
11. JACQUELINE KENNEDY. Peggy Nisbet, No. P718, 1970s. All-plastic "collectors' doll." Wears a white silk dress like Mrs. Kennedy wore to President Kennedy's Inaugural Ball in 1961. John F. Kennedy, No. P717, is a companion doll. Made in England. About 7½in (19.1cm).

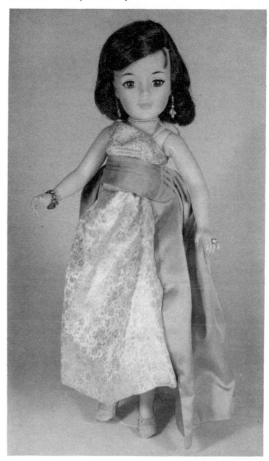

Illustration 496. 21in (53.3cm) JACQUELINE KENNEDY by Madame Alexander, No. 2125, 1962. Vinyl with rooted dark brown hair. Head marked: "ALEXANDER // 19 © 61. The gown is brocade with satin side panels. She also wears a pearl necklace, earrings and a ring. *Fran's Dolls.*

Illustration 497. 10in (25.4cm) JACQUELINE KENNEDY by Madame Alexander, No. 885, 1962. All-hard plastic and fully-jointed. Very dark brown wig; brown sleep eyes with lashes. The ball gown is pink satin. *Ted Menten Collection. Photograph by Ted Menten.*

Illustration 499. 21in (53.3cm) *Bride* by Madame Alexander, No. 2151, 1965. This is the same doll that was used for *Jacqueline* in 1961-1962. Vinyl with rooted dark brown hair. Head marked: "ALEXANDER // 19©61." *Fran's Dolls.*

Illustration 498. Close-up of 10in (25.4cm) JACQUELINE KENNEDY. *Ted Menten Collection. Photograph by Ted Menten.*

KENNEDY, JOHN (FITZGERALD). United States President. Born May 29, 1917; died November 22, 1963. After serving in World War II, Kennedy entered Democratic politics. He was a Representative from Massachusetts from 1947 to 1953; a Senator from Massachusetts from 1953 to 1960; and the 35th President from 1961 to 1963. He was the first Roman Catholic to be elected President. During his short term he took responsibility for the Bay of Pigs invasion of Cuba; started the Alliance for Progress with Latin America; began the Peace Corps; forced the USSR to remove missiles from Cuba; and negotiated a limited test-ban treaty. He was assassinated in Dallas, Texas, by Lee Harvey Oswald.

DOLLS:
1. JOHN F. KENNEDY. Shackman, No. 4700, early 1960s. Hand puppet with a vinyl head with painted features. The cloth body is not stuffed and is for hand insertion. Nikita Khrushchev, No. 4701, is a companion piece. Made in Japan. 13½in (34.3cm).
2. JOHN F. KENNEDY. Kamar, early 1960s. Seated in a rocking chair. Made in Japan. 10½in (26.7cm). *Illustration 500.*
3. KENNEDY. Maker unknown, early 1960s. Made in Japan. 7in (17.8cm). *Illustration 501.*
4. JOHN F. KENNEDY. Peggy Nisbet, No. P717, 1970s. All-plastic "collectors' doll." Jacqueline Kennedy, No. P718, is a companion doll. Made in England. About 8in (20.3cm).

Illustration 500. 10½in (26.7cm) JOHN F. KENNEDY by Kamar, early 1960s. (The doll is in a seated position and is attached to the rocking chair.) Vinyl head, half-arms, shoes and socks. Cardboard body with wire armatures for the arms and legs. Painted hair and features. Label on the trousers: "TRADE MARK // TKR // FANCY DOLL // JAPAN." *Fran's Dolls.*

Illustration 501. 7in (17.8cm) JOHN F. KENNEDY, a bobble-head made in Japan in the 1960s. Composition over plaster, painted all black with green highlights. The only mark is a sticker on the bottom reading, "JAPAN." *Phyllis Houston Collection.*

KEPPEL, ALICE. Mistress of Edward VII of England. In the late 1890s Mrs. Alice Keppel, who was at least 30 years his junior, became King Edward's last long-term lover. The affair lasted for 12 years, during which time both Mr. Keppel and Queen Alexandra fully accepted the situation. When the King was dying of bronchitis at age 68 in 1910, Mrs. Keppel was the first person the Queen notified to rush to his bedside.

DOLLS:
1. HON. ALICE KEPPEL. Peggy Nisbet, No. P787, 1970s. All-plastic "collectors' doll." Two other mistresses of Edward VII are companion dolls: Countess of Warwick (Lady Brooke), No. P786, and Lillie Langtry, No. P788. Made in England. About 7½in (19.1cm).

KHAMBATTA, PERSIS. Model; actress. Born October 2, 1950, in Bombay, India. When she was 13 Persis Khambatta was discovered by a photographer in Bombay. She became a model and at age 16 was elected Miss India in a beauty contest and became her country's entry in the Miss Universe Pageant. She then appeared in five Indian films and at age 17 left for London. In England she was a model and appeared in several films. Then she came to the United States where she again worked as a model and an actress. In 1979 she was chosen to play in *Star Trek the Motion Picture* in a role which required her to shave off all her hair.

DOLLS:
1. ILIA. Mego, No. 91200/4, 1979. Made in Hong Kong. 3¾in (9.6cm). *Illustration 502.*
2. ILIA. Mego, No. 91210/4, 1979. Made in Hong Kong. 13in (33cm). *Illustration 503.*
SEE: STAR TREK.

Illustration 502. 3¾in (9.6cm) PERSIS KHAMBATTA as *Ilia* from *Star Trek* by Mego, No. 91200/4, 1979. All-vinyl and fully-jointed. Painted features and clothing. Copyright by Paramount Pictures Corporation. Made in Hong Kong.

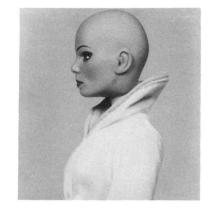

Illustration 503. 13in (33cm) PERSIS KHAMBATTA as *Ilia* from the movie *Star Trek* by Mego, No. 91210/4, 1979. All-vinyl and fully-jointed, including twist waist. Bald head; painted features. Head marked: "© PPC." Marked on buttock: " © MEGO CORP. 1975 // MADE IN HONG KONG." *Penny Caswell Collection.*

KHRUSHCHEV, NIKITA. Soviet communist leader. Born April 17, 1894; died September 11, 1971. Khrushchev was First Secretary for the Soviet Communist Party from 1953 to 1964 and Premier from 1958 to 1964. He initiated a policy to revert from the brutal policies of Joseph Stalin and a plan for peaceful coexistence with the Western powers. He was removed from power for his failure in agricultural production in Russia and the increasingly bitter struggle with Communist China.

DOLLS:
1. PREMIER NIKITA KHRUSHCHEV. Shackman, No. 4701, 1960s. Made in Japan. President Kennedy, No. 4700, is a companion piece. *Illustration 504.*

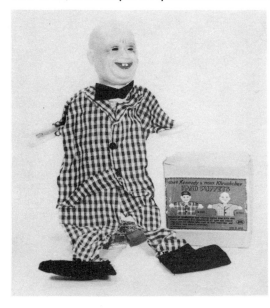

Illustration 504. 13½in (34.3cm) NIKITA KHRUSCHCHEV hand puppet made in Japan by Shackman, No. 4701, early 1960s. Vinyl head with painted features; cloth suit for hand insertion. The head is not marked.

KIEL, RICHARD. Actor. Born 1939. By age 12 Kiel had reached his present height—seven feet, two inches. He weighs about 330 pounds and wears a size 16 EEE shoe. His most memorable role in movies was as the gigantic Jaws in the James Bond films *The Spy Who Loved Me* (1977) and *Moonraker* (1979).

DOLLS:
1. JAWS. Mego, No. 96004, 1979. Vinyl head; plastic body; fully-jointed. Copyright by Eon Productions, Ltd. Made in Hong Kong. 12½in (31.8cm).
SEE: JAMES BOND.

KISS. KISS is a rock group begun in New York, New York, in 1973. The band is famous for its bizarre Kabuki makeup, but it became the most popular group in American, Japan and many other nations during the late 1970s. The original members of the group were ACE FREHLEY on guitar, PAUL STANLEY on guitar, PETER CRISS (CRISCOULA) on drums and GENE SIMMONS (EUGENE KLEIN) on vocals. In 1980 Peter left the group and was replaced by Eric Carr. The best KISS record album was *Destroyer* in 1976.

Illustration 505. KISS. The box is for Gene. From left to right: Gene (Eugene Klein), Ace (Paul Daniel Frehley), Peter (Peter George John Criscoula) and Paul (Paul Stanley).

Illustration 506. KISS dolls. From left to right: *Gene, Ace, Peter* and *Paul. Penny Caswell Collection.*

KLEIN, EUGENE (GENE SIMMONS). Singer, musician. Born August 25, 1949. Gene is a member of the rock band KISS. He was Cher's lover for a time after her final divorce from Gregg Allman.
DOLLS:
1. GENE. Mego, No. 88000/2, 1978. Made in Hong Kong. 12½in (31.8cm). *Illustration 507.*
SEE: KISS.

Illustration 507. 12½in (31.8cm) EUGENE KLEIN (GENE SIMMONS), *Gene* of KISS, by Mego, No. 88000/2, 1978. All-vinyl and fully-jointed. Rooted hair and painted features and makeup. Head marked: " © 1978 AUCOIN // MGMT. INC." Back marked: " © MEGO CORP. 1977 // MADE IN HONG KONG." Copyright by Aucoin Management, Inc. by agreement with KISS, a partnership. *Penny Caswell Collection.*

KNIEVEL, EVEL. Stunt motorcyclist. Born Robert Craig Knievel October 17, 1938. Knievel is famous for his attempted skycyle jump of the Snake River Canyon in Idaho in 1974. He was played by George Hamilton in the biographical movie *Evel Knievel* in 1972, and he appeared as himself in a terrible film, *Viva Knievel!* in 1977.
DOLLS:
1. EVEL KNIEVEL. Ideal, No. 3400-9, 1972. Made in Hong Kong. 7in (17.8cm) *Illustration 508.*
2. EVEL KNIEVEL. Ideal, No. 3401-7, 1972. The same doll as the above, dressed in a white outfit.
3. EVEL KNIEVEL. Ideal, No. 3402-5, 1972. The same doll as in No. 1, dressed in a blue outfit.
The Evel Knievel dolls also had a "Scramble Van," No. 3408-2, and a "Stuntcycle," No. 3407-4, both from Ideal in 1972.

Illustration 508. 7in (17.8cm) EVEL KNIEVEL by Ideal, No. 3400-9, 1972. All-vinyl and fully-jointed. Painted light brown hair; painted black eyes. The doll wears a red uniform and comes with a safety helmet and swagger stick. Made in Hong Kong.

Illustration 509. 5½in (14cm) ROBBIE KNIEVEL by Ideal, No. 3456-1, 1976. All-vinyl with a wired body for posing. Painted hair and features. No marks.

KNIEVEL, ROBBIE. Child stunt motorcyclist. Robbie is the son of Evel Knievel.
DOLLS:
1. ROBBIE KNIEVEL. Ideal, No. 3456-1, 1976. 5½in (14cm) *Illustration 509.*

KOPELL, BERNIE. Actor. Born in New York, New York, on June 21, 1933. Kopell was onscreen after 1965 in films. He appeared on many television shows and was a regular on the following: "Bewitched," ABC-TV, September 1964 to July 1972; "Get Smart," NBC-TV, September 1965 to September 1969 and CBS-TV, September 1969 to September 1970 as Conrad Siegfried, the head of K.O.A.S.; "That Girl," ABC-TV, September 1966 to September 1971 (early episodes only); "The Doris Day Show," CBS-TV, September 1968 to September 1973; "Needles and Pins," NBC-TV, September to December 1973; "When Things Were Rotten," ABC-TV, September to December 1975; "Greatest Heroes of the Bible," NBC-TV, November 1978. On "Love American Style," ABC-TV, September 1969 to January 1974, he was a regular in blackout sequences. In early 1977 he was in two pilot films for "The Love Boat" on ABC-TV as Adam "Doc" Bricker, and he continued the role on a regular basis beginning in September 1977.

DOLLS:
1. "DOC" from THE LOVE BOAT. Mego, No. 23005/3, 1982. All-vinyl and fully-jointed. Painted hair and features. Molded glasses and clothing. Copyright by Aaron Spelling Productions, Inc. Made in Hong Kong. 3¾in (9.6cm).
SEE: LOVE BOAT, THE.

KORNMAN, MARY. Actress. Born 1917; died 1973. Mary Kornman was Mary in the original *Our Gang* silent film comedies beginning in 1923. After 1930 she appeared in 15 of *The Boy Friends* series of short comedies with Mickey Daniels, also from the *Our Gang* series. She retired from the movies in 1938 to become a housewife.

DOLLS: SEE: OUR GANG.

L

LACEY, RONALD. English character actor. Ronald Lacey played Toht in the film *Raiders of the Lost Ark* (1981).

DOLLS:
1. TOHT. Kenner, Series, No. 46010, 1982. All-vinyl and fully-jointed. Painted features and clothing with a vinyl hat and cape. Copyright by Lucasfilm Ltd. About 4in (10.2cm).
SEE: RAIDERS OF THE LOST ARK.

LADD, CHERYL. Actress, singer. Born Cheryl Stoppelmoor on July 2, 1951. The name Ladd comes from Cheryl's first marriage to David Ladd, the son of actor Alan Ladd. She is best known for playing Kris Munroe, the sister of Jill (played by Farrah Fawcett) on "Charlie's Angels" on ABC-TV from the fall season of 1977 through re-runs in the summer of 1981. Kris came on the show when Jill left to pursue a racing career in Europe.

DOLLS:
1. KRIS STARRING CHERYL LADD. Hasbro, No. 4850, 1977. Made in Hong Kong. 8½in (21.6cm). *Illustration 510.*
2. CHERYL LADD. Mattel, No. 2494, 1978. Made in Korea. 11½in (29.2cm). *Illustration 511.*
SEE: CHARLIE'S ANGELS.

Illustration 510. 8½in (21.6cm) CHERYL LADD as *Kris* from "Charlie's Angels" by Hasbro, No. 4850, 1977. All-vinyl and fully-jointed. Rooted blonde hair; painted brown eyes. Copyright by Spelling-Goldberg Productions. Made in Hong Kong.

Illustration 511. 11½in (29.2cm) CHERYL LADD, one of "TV's Star Women" by Mattel, No. 2494, 1978. All-vinyl and fully-jointed. Rooted blonde hair; painted green eyes. No marks on head. Back marked: "© MATTEL INC. // 1966 // 15 KOREA." Copyright 1978 by C & D Enterprises. Made in Korea.

LAFAYETTE (or LA FAYETTE), MARIE JOSEPH PAUL YVES ROCH GILBERT du MOTIER, MARQUIS de. French general and statesman. Born 1757; died 1834. The Marquis de Lafayette is considered a hero of the American Revolution because, despite opposition from the French government, he sailed to America in 1777 to join Washington's army. Congress made him a Major General. He returned to France in 1779 and was vital in securing the French aid that made the difference at Yorktown in 1781, which caused the British to surrender. Lafayette was later active in the French Revolution of 1792. During 1824-1825 he toured the United States and was received everywhere as a legendary hero.

DOLLS:
1. MARQUIS De LAFAYETTE. A "Hero of the American Revolution," made for the S. S. Kresge Company, 1976. Made in Hong Kong. 7½in (19.1cm). *Illustration 512.*

Illustration 512. 7½in (19.1cm) MARQUIS De LAFAYETTE manufactured for the S.S. Kresge Company, 1976. Vinyl head with painted hair and features. Fully-jointed plastic body with swivel waist. Marked on back: "MADE IN // HONG KONG." *Shirley Buchholz Collection.*

LAFFITE (or LAFITTE), JEAN. Privateer. Born circa 1780; died circa 1825. Laffite was a French pirate who led a band of ruffians and smugglers which operated out of the United States to prey on Spanish shipping off the coast of Louisiana and Texas. During the War of 1812 he aided the United States in the Battle of New Orleans, which lasted about 20 minutes and during which some 2,000 British and 12 Americans were killed.

DOLLS:
1. JEAN LAFITTE. Mego, No. 54000/3, 1975. All-vinyl and fully-jointed. Painted hair and features. Made in Hong Kong. 8in (20.3cm).

LAHR, BERT. Actor. Born Irving Lahrheim in 1895; died 1967. Lahr was a popular comic in vaudeville, burlesque, the legitimate stage and motion pictures. His most memorable role was as the Cowardly Lion in *The Wizard of Oz* in 1939.

DOLLS:
1. COWARDLY LION from THE WIZARD OF OZ. Mego, No. 51500/3, 1974. Made in Hong Kong. 7½in (19.1cm). *Illustration 513.*

2. COWARDLY LION from THE WIZARD OF OZ. Mego, No. 59038, 1974. Vinyl head; cloth body. Copyright 1974 by MGM, Inc. Made in Hong Kong. 15in (38.1cm).
SEE: WIZARD OF OZ, THE.

Illustration 513. 7½in (19.1cm) BERT LAHR as the *Cowardly Lion* from *The Wizard of Oz* by Mego, No. 51500/3, 1974. All-vinyl and fully-jointed. Painted head molded as a lion's features. Copyright by Metro-Goldwyn-Mayer, Inc. Made in Hong Kong. *Shirley Buchholz Collection.*

LANDAU, MARTIN. Actor. Born 1925 or 1931. Landau appeared on stage, on TV and in the movies, mostly in character parts. He and his wife, Barbara Bain, were in "Mission: Impossible" on CBS-TV from September of 1966 to the end of the 1968-1969 season when they left over a contract dispute. They later teamed for "Space: 1999," a syndicated show begun in 1975.

DOLLS:
1. COMMANDER KOENIG from SPACE: 1999. Mattel, No. 9542, 1975. Made in Taiwan. 8¾in (22.3cm). *Illustration 514.*
SEE: SPACE: 1999.

Illustration 514. 8¾in (22.3cm) MARTIN LANDAU as *Commander Koenig* from "Space: 1999" by Mattel, No. 9542, 1975. All-vinyl and fully-jointed. Painted hair and features. Copyright 1973 by ATV Licensing Limited; copyright 1975 by Mattel, Inc. Made in Taiwan. *Shirley Buchholz Collection.*

LANDER, DAVID L. Actor. Born June 22, ?. Lander teamed with Michael McKean to form the comedy group The Credibility Gap and toured the United States for four years. McKean and Lander later became Lenny and Squiggy on "Laverne and Shirley" on ABC-TV, beginning in January 1976. Lander, as Squiggy, is the short, chubby one of the pair.

DOLLS:
1. LENNY AND SQUIGGY from LAVERNE AND SHIRLEY. Mego, No. 86500/2, 1977. Made in Hong Kong. 12in (30.5cm). *Illustration 515.*

SEE: LAVERNE AND SHIRLEY.

Illustration 515. 12in (30.5cm) DAVID L. LANDER as *Squiggy* from "Laverne and Shirley" by Mego, No. 86500/2, 1977. (This doll came as a set with Michael McKean as *Lenny.*) All-vinyl and fully-jointed. Painted black hair and painted blue eyes. Copyright by Paramount Pictures Corporation. Made in Hong Kong.

LANDON, MICHAEL. Actor, writer, director, producer. Born Eugene Maurice Orowitz on October 31, 1936 or 1937. Landon made his motion picture debut in 1957 playing the title role in *I Was a Teenage Werewolf.* (The film was not as bad as the title indicates.) He later played Little Joe Cartwright on NBC-TV's "Bonanza" for almost 14 years (September 1959 to January 1973) and has been Charles Ingalls on NBC-TV's "Little House on the Prairie" for eight years (beginning in September 1974). Landon is also producer of "Little House," and he writes and directs many of the scripts.

DOLLS:
1. LITTLE JOE OF THE CARTWRIGHT FAMILY. Fully-jointed "action figure" by American Character, 1965. Plastic. Painted and molded hair, features and clothing. Lorne Greene as Ben Cartwright and Dan Blocker as Hoss Cartwright are companion dolls. See *Illustration 117.* 8in (20.3cm).

LANE, HARRIET JOHNSTON. First Lady. Born May 9, 1830; died July 3, 1903. Harriet Lane was the niece of James Buchanan, the only unmarried President of the United States. She was his hostess at his home, Wheatlands, in Pennsylvania and later when he was the American Minister in London, England. Buchanan served only one term as President, 1857-1861. In 1866 Harriet Lane married wealthy Henry Elliott Johnston. Her fine art collection was donated as a memorial to Johns Hopkins Hospital, where it is exhibited in the Harriet Lane Wing.

DOLLS:
1. HARRIET LANE. Madame Alexander, No. 1516, 1982. All-vinyl and fully-jointed. Rooted blonde hair. Dressed in a white satin moire gown. Part of the third six First Ladies Series. 14in (35.6cm).

SEE: FIRST LADIES, THE.

LANE, LUPINO. Actor, director. Born Henry Lane in London, England, in 1892; died 1959. Comic Lupino Lane was the brother of screen actor Wallace Lupino-Lane and a cousin of film comedian Stanley Lupino, the father of actress Ida Lupino. Lane entered films in 1915 in British shorts and gained fame and popularity in numerous Hollywood shorts and features during the 1920s. In one film he played at least 25 different roles. He returned to British films in 1930 but retired by World War II.

DOLLS:
1. LUPINO LANE. Dean's Rag Book Company, 1937. Cloth doll in the "True-to-Life" design, which is printed features on cloth that is molded to a stiffened buckram backing. Made in England.

LANGE, TED. Actor. Born January 5, ?. Before beginning his role as Issac Washington, the bartender, on two pilot films of "The Love Boat" and the regular series on ABC-TV beginning in September 1977, Lange was in two other television series on ABC-TV. He was in "That's My Mama" from September 1974 to December 1975 and "Mr. T and Tina" during September and October 1976.

DOLLS:
1. ISAAC from THE LOVE BOAT. Mego, No. 23005/4, 1982. All-vinyl and fully-jointed. Painted hair and features. Molded clothing. Copyright by Aaron Spelling Productions, Inc. Made in Hong Kong. 3¾in (9.6cm).

SEE: LOVE BOAT, THE.

LANGTRY, LILLIE. Actress and famous beauty. Born Emilie Charlotte Le Breton on the British isle of Jersey in 1853; died 1929. Lillie Langtry was called "The Jersey Lily," and sex was the most serious business of her life. She escaped Jersey by marrying a wealthy man, Edward Langtry. She was five feet, eight inches tall and perfectly proportioned; she had thick red-gold hair; her complexion was flawless. She was considered the greatest beauty of her day. Lillie posed for the most famous artists of the time and became a stage actress in 1881. While playing in America, Texas Judge Roy Bean had Langtry, Texas, named for her. In 1897 Mr. Langtry died broke in an insane asylum. Two years later Lillie married a baron, Hugo de Bathe, which made her Lady de Bathe. Still, her best friends were important men, one of whom was the Prince of Wales, later to become King Edward VII. The Prince ended their intimate relationship when Lillie playfully slipped an ice cube down his back while partying. When Lillie was 60 years old and still a great beauty, she made a film for Famous Players (later Paramount Pictures).

DOLLS:
1. LILLIE LANGTRY. Peggy Nisbet, No. P714, 1970s. Plastic "collectors' doll." Made in England. About 7½in (19.1cm).
2. LILLIE LANGTRY. Peggy Nisbet, No. P788, late 1970s. Plastic "collectors' doll." Part of a series of the mistresses of King Edward VII that includes Countess of Warwick (Lady Brooke), No. P786, and Hon. Alice Keppel, No. P787. Made in England. About 7½in (19.1cm).

LANSBURY, ANGELA. Actress. Born October 16, 1925, in London, England. Lansbury began training for the stage in childhood and was signed by MGM to a long-term contract in 1943. For her first role, in *Gaslight* (1944), she was nominated for a Best Supporting Actress Oscar. She received two more nominations for the Academy Award but was playing mothers and aunts while still in her early thirties. Angela Lansbury was always highly respected within the acting profession and was popular with the public, but as a motion picture actress she never became a "star." Her greatest career triumph came on Broadway in musicals. She received a Tony Award for "Mame" (1966) and "Sweeny Todd" (1979) as Best Actress in a Musical.

DOLLS:
1. MISS PRICE from BEDKNOBS AND BROOMSTICKS. Horsman, 1971. Made in Hong Kong. 6¼in (15.9cm). *Illustration 516.*

Illustration 516. 6¼in (15.9cm) ANGELA LANSBURY as *Miss Price* from *Bedknobs and Broomsticks* by Horsman, 1971. All-vinyl; jointed only at the head. Rooted blonde hair; painted blue eyes with long inset lashes. Head marked: "HONG KONG." This doll came with a metal bed that was battery operated to "fly" (move around on a smooth surface).

LARSEN, KEITH. Actor. Born June 17, 1926. Larsen played leading men in "B" films during the 1950s. He was in four television series, each role lasting less than a year: "The Hunter" during 1954; "Brave Eagle" as the lead from September 1955 to June 1956; "Northwesst Passage" from September 1958 to September 1959; and "The Aquanauts" from September 1960 to September 1961.

DOLLS:
1. BRAVE EAGLE AND HIS HORSE, "WHITE CLOUD." Hartland Plastics, Inc., No. 812, circa 1958. All-plastic. Made in Hartland, Wisconsin. Copyright by Roy Rogers Enterprises. About 8in (20.3cm).

LAUDER, (SIR) HARRY. Scottish entertainer. Born August 4, 1870; died 1950. Sir Harry Lauder appeared in five British films and was a star of British music hall and American vaudeville. He was known for his droll recitations while dressed in a traditional kilt.

DOLLS:
1. SIR HARRY LAUDER. Made in Germany, early 1950s. 6¼in (15.9cm). *Illustration 517.*

Illustration 517. 6¼in (15.9cm) SIR HARRY LAUDER, early 1950s. Papier-mâché-composition head and hands with cup molded to right hand. The lower torso is a spring covered with oilcloth that emits a loud squeak and moves the cup to the mouth when pressed down. Painted features with bright green eyes. The hat and the clothing are glued in place. Stamped on the bottom of the cardboard feet: "MADE IN // WESTERN GERMANY." *Ted Tarr Collection.*

LAUREL, STAN. Actor. Born Arthur Stanley Jefferson in England in 1890; died 1965. Laurel made his stage debut at age 16 in Glasgow, Scotland, and for several years played in both drama and comedy. In 1910 and in 1912 he was Charlie Chaplin's understudy for American tours. After the second tour ended he remained in the United States and entered American vaudeville, billed as Stan Laurel. He then made 76 films before teaming with Oliver Hardy in 1926. (Both comedians had appeared in a two-reel short, *Lucky Dog,* in 1917, but not as a team.) Laurel's screen character was established as a clown who wore clothing that was too large for him, and he added this to his characterization with witty mannerisms when he joined with Hardy. Laurel was the "skinny one" and the funnier one. He created most of the team's comedy routines. After Hardy's death in 1957 he was inconsolable and never performed again.

DOLLS: SEE: LAUREL AND HARDY.

LAUREL AND HARDY. Laurel and Hardy were the most successful comedy team in motion picture history. The pair appeared together after 1927 in more than 100 films, 27 of them features. Their comedy depended more on situation than on plot and more on physical and facial expression than on dialogue. In most of their parts they constantly got into trouble because of their stupidity. Laurel was the "skinny one," Hardy the "fat one," and this contrast in appearance was always worked into their routines. They stopped making films in 1945 after the big studios no longer gave them complete control over production. Then they toured Britain in a revue, made a disasterous film that was a French-Italian co-production and toured Britain again in 1954. Laurel resolved never to perform again after the death of Hardy in 1957, but he continued to write comedy material. The memory of Laurel and Hardy has been kept alive over the years by a series of compilation films of their work together and by television showings of their short films, particularly during the early 1960s.

DOLLS:

1. LAUREL AND HARDY. Lakeside Toys, 1960s. One-piece vinyl with molded and painted features and clothing. Made in Japan. Laurel is 5¾in (14.7cm); Hardy is 4¾in (12.2cm).
2. LAUREL AND HARDY. Dell, 1962. One-piece vinyl with molded and painted features and clothing. Hardy, *Illustration 519*, 7½in (19.1cm).
3. LAUREL AND HARDY. Knickerbocker, 1960s. Made in Japan. Laurel, 9½in (24.2cm); Hardy, 8½in (21.6cm). *Illustrations 520* and *521*.
4. LAUREL AND HARDY. Finger puppets; maker unknown. Laurel, 2⅞in (7.3cm); Hardy, 2⅝in (6.7cm). *Illustration 522*.
5. LAUREL AND HARDY. Berman & Anderson, Inc., 1975. Made in Hong Kong. Each is 13in (33cm). *Illustration 523*.
6. LAUREL AND HARDY FROM THE MUSIC BOX. Peggy Nisbet, No. P756 and No. P757, late 1970s. Made in England. 7½in (19.1cm). *Illustration 524*.
7. LAUREL AND HARDY. Circa 1981, made in Taiwan. Laurel, 21in (53.3cm); Hardy, 18½in (47cm). *Illustration 525*.

Illustration 519. 7½in (19.1cm) OLIVER HARDY by Dell, 1962. One-piece vinyl except for hat, which pops up when squeezed. Painted features and clothing. Marked on back: "DELL // © LARRY HARMON PICTURES CORP. 1962 // OLIVER HARDY." *Wanda Lodwick Collection.*

Illustration 518. Stan Laurel and Oliver Hardy.

Illustration 520. 9½in (24.2cm) STAN LAUREL "Bend-Em" by Knickerbocker, 1960s. Vinyl head with a molded hat; cloth body over a wire frame. Head marked: "© LARRY HARMON PICTURES // CORP. // JAPAN."

Illustration 521. 8½in (21.6cm) OLIVER HARDY by Knickerbocker, 1960s. Vinyl head with painted features and molded hat. Cloth body with wire inside for "posing." Tag: "OLIVER HARDY // TM // BEND-EM // © LARRY HARMON PICTURES CORP." Made in Japan.

Illustration 522. LAUREL and HARDY finger puppets, maker unknown, 1972. All-vinyl with painted features, hats and clothing. STAN LAUREL is 2⅞in (7.3cm) and OLIVER HARDY is 2⅝in (6.7cm). The backs are marked: "© 1972 // LARRY HARMON // PICTURES CORP." *Shirley Buchholz Collection.*

Illustration 523. 13in (33cm) OLIVER HARDY and STAN LAUREL by Berman & Anderson, Inc., 1975. All-vinyl and fully-jointed. Molded hats; painted features. Oliver is standing on a plastic box that is battery operated to play records, like the one he holds in his right hand. The records are Laurel and Hardy singing. Each doll is marked on the foot: " © 1975 // BERMAN & ANDERSON, INC. // MADE IN HONG KONG." Tags on the clothing read: "LARRY HARMON PICTURES CORPORATION // MADE IN HONG KONG." *Jean Canaday Collection.*

Illustration 524. 8in (20.3cm) OLIVER HARDY, No. P757, and STAN LAUREL, No. P756, by Peggy Nisbet from *The Music Box* (a 1932 short), late 1970s. All-hard plastic and jointed only at the arms. Painted hair and features. Made in England. Copyright 1978 by Larry Harman (sic) Picture Corp. *Photograph Courtesy of House of Nisbet.*

Illustration 525. LAUREL and HARDY. Both dolls were made in Taiwan and sold in 1981. They have porcelain heads with molded black hats, porcelain lower arms and shoes and stuffed cloth bodies. The simple suits are cotton shirts with black flannel jackets and gray flannel pants. No markings appear on the dolls and the original boxes list no manufacturer or importer. The boxes describe them as "Fine Porcelain Dolls," which they are not. OLIVER HARDY is on the left. He is 18½in (47cm). STAN LAUREL is on the right. He is 21in (53.3cm). Both dolls have painted gray hair and painted blue eyes.

LAURIE, PIPER. Actress. Born Rosetta Jacobs on January 22, 1932. Piper Laurie began at Universal as a "starlet" and played ingenue parts, many of them in Tony Curtis pictures, during the 1950s. By the early 1960s she had become a respected dramatic actress, and she earned an Academy Award nomination for her Best Actress part in *The Hustler* (1961) and a Best Supporting Actress nomination for her role as the fierce mother in *Carrie* (1976).

DOLLS:
1. PIPER LAURIE. Madame Alexander, circa 1950. All-hard plastic and fully-jointed. Bright red wig with center part; blue sleep eyes with lashes. Dressed in a long gown. 14in (35.6cm). (This doll is not confirmed with original advertising.)

LAVERNE AND SHIRLEY.   "Laverne and Shirley" is a television situation comedy about two pretty girls who work and room together. The show was a spin-off from "Happy Days," in which the girls appeared briefly. The theme song from "Laverne and Shirley"—"Making Our Dreams Come True," was a hit record in 1976 by Cyndi Grecco, who sings it on the show at the opening. Penny Marshall plays Laverne DeFazio, the realistic one, and Cindy Williams plays Shirley Feeney, the romantic one. In the cast is also the comedy team of Michael McKean, who plays their friend Lenny Kosnoski, and David L. Lander, as his buddy Squiggy. Mego made four dolls depicting these characters. PENNY MARSHALL as *Laverne* and CINDY WILLIAMS as *Shirley* were packaged as a set; DAVID L. LANDER as *Squiggy* and MICHAEL McKEAN as *Lenny* were packaged as another set. See entries under each celebrity.

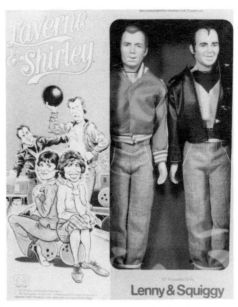

Illustration 527. 12in (30.5cm) *Lenny and Squiggy* from "Laverne and Shirley" by Mego, No. 86500/2, 1977. Made in Hong Kong. See DAVID L. LANDER and MICHAEL McKEAN.

LEARNED, MICHAEL.   Actress. Born April 9, 1939. At first billed as "Miss Michael Learned," she appeared on several television programs in guest roles. She played Olivia Walton, the mother, when "The Waltons" began on CBS-TV as a series in September of 1972. For her role in this series she won an Emmy Award in 1973, 1974 and 1976. By 1981 she was the lead in her own show, "Nurse."

DOLLS:
1. MOM AND POP from THE WALTONS.   Mego, No. 56000/2, 1975. 8in (20.3cm). *Illustration 528.*
SEE: WALTONS, THE.

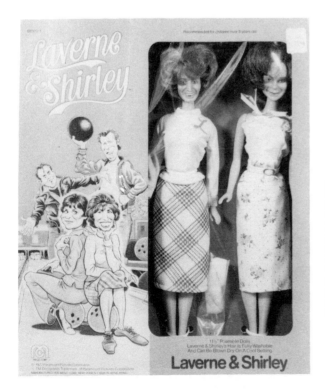

Illustration 526. 11½in (29.2cm) *Laverne and Shirley* by Mego, No. 86500/1, 1977. Made in Hong Kong. See PENNY MARSHALL and CINDY WILLIAMS.

Illustration 528. 8in (20.3cm) MICHAEL LEARNED as *Mom*, Olivia Walton, from "The Waltons" by Mego, No. 56000/2, 1975. All-vinyl and fully-jointed. Rooted blonde hair; painted brown eyes. *Pop* (see RALPH WAITE) was part of a packaged pair of dolls. Head marked: "© 1974 // LORIMAR INC." *Penny Caswell Collection.*

LEE, PINKY. Comic. Born Pincus Leff in 1916. Pinky Lee began as a comic in burlesque and by the 1940s was appearing in motion pictures. He later became one of the first television stars. In 1949 he was in the variety show "Hollywood Premier;" in 1950 he was the stage-hand in the situation comedy "The Pinky Lee Show" on NBC-TV; from November 1951 to April 1953 he was in the situation comedy "Those Two," also on NBC-TV. His greatest success came from his appearances on various Saturday morning children's shows from 1954 to 1957, in which he entertained in his familiar suits with wild patterned designs.

DOLLS:
1. PINKY LEE. Stern Toy, 1950s. 9in (22.9cm). *Illustration 529.*
2. PINKY LEE. Juro (Eegee), 1950s. 25in (64.8cm). *Illustration 530.*

Illustration 529. 9in (22.9cm) PINKY LEE, manufacturer unknown, early 1950s. All-vinyl. Head is on a long-stemmed neck and is re-movable. Painted features and molded, painted clothing with a black and white check suit. Marked on feet: "PINKY LEE // ENT. // © A STERN // TOY."

Illustration 531. 6in (15.2cm) PORKY LEE as *Porky* from *Our Gang* by Mego, No. 61600/6, 1975. All-vinyl and fully-jointed. Painted brown hair and brown eyes; molded cap. Head marked: "© 1975 // MGM INC." Back marked: "© MEGO CORP. 1975 // REG. U.S. PAT. OFF. // PAT. PENDING // HONG KONG."

Illustration 530. 25in (64.8cm) PINKY LEE by Juro (Eegee), circa early 1950s. Vinyl head with molded hat; cloth body; composition hands. Painted features; open/closed mouth with painted teeth. Tag on jacket: "Pinky Lee // NBC-TV." Head marked: "A // JURO // CELEBRITY // PRODUCT." *Billie Jo Phillips Collection.*

LEE, PORKY. Child actor. Born Eugene Lee in 1933. Porky Lee appeared in 42 *Our Gang* comedies during the 1930s. He was hired for the part of Porky because of his resemblance to Spanky. He began in the series playing Spanky's brother. When Lee left the series, he left show business and became a teacher in his native Texas.

DOLLS:
1. PORKY from OUR GANG. Mego, No. 61600/6, 1975. Made in Hong Kong. 6in (15.2cm). *Illustration 531.*

SEE: OUR GANG.

LEE, ROBERT E. General-in-Chief of the Confederate armies during the American Civil War. Born 1807; died 1870. Although Lee loved the Union and the army, he remained loyal to the state of Virginia when it seceded from the Union in 1861. Lee is generally conceded to be the greatest military mind of his time, but his enemy was one that always had more resources. He took full blame for the failure of the Gettysburg Campaign, the last chance the South had to place itself in a bargaining position. On April 9, 1865, he surrendered to Grant at Appomattox Courthouse in southern Virginia, ending the Confederacy. After the war he became the president of Washington (now Washington and Lee) College. He is still idolized by the South.

DOLLS:

1. GENERAL ROBERT E. LEE AND HIS FAMOUS HORSE, "TRAVELER." Hartland Plastics, Inc., No. 808, circa 1958. Plastic. Made in Hartland, Wisconsin. About 8in (20.3cm).
2. GEN. ROBERT E. LEE. Excel Toy Corp., 1974. All-vinyl and fully-jointed. Painted hair and features. Made in Hong Kong. 9¾in (24.9cm).

LEICESTER, ROBERT DUDLEY, EARL OF. English courtier and favorite of Queen Elizabeth I. Born circa 1532; died 1588. Leicester was involved in the plot to place Lady Jane Grey upon the throne of England (1553) but he was later pardoned. Queen Elizabeth considered marrying him at one time. Leicester was a patron of letters and the drama and his acting company was the first to be granted a royal patent.

DOLLS:

1. EARL OF LEICESTER. Peggy Nisbet, No. P809, early 1980s. Plastic "collectors' doll." Made in England. About 8in (20.3cm).

LEIGH, VIVIEN. Actress. Born Vivian Mary Hartley in India in 1913; died 1967. One of the greatest beauties ever to appear in films, Vivien Leigh made her debut in British movies in 1934. The impact that she created in *Fire Over England* (1937) with her future husband, Laurence Olivier, is what led to her gaining the most importance role in screen history, that of Scarlett O'Hara in *Gone With the Wind.* Much attention is still given to the fact that for two years hundreds of actresses tested for the part in the "intensive search" by David O. Selznick for the perfect Scarlett. Almost every actress who ever appeared in a film, or who had aspirations to, was "considered." It made great news copy when Vivien Leigh was "presented" to Selznick on December 10, 1938, as he watched the filming of the burning of Atlanta, ending the two year "search." William Pratt in *Scarlett Fever* (Macmillian Publishing Co., 1977) tells that Selznick *never* wanted a famous actress to dominate what he wanted to be a "Selznick film." The records show that Miss Leigh was under consideration for Scarlett in early 1938 (when many famous ladies were still "testing") and that she had made a "secret trip" to New York earlier to meet Selznick, who had been impressed with her work in *Fire Over England.* Miss Leigh, herself, claimed that she knew that she would be Scarlett right after she read the book in 1936. Anyhow, the publicity engendered by the search for the perfect Scarlett only increased interest in the project of filming Margaret Mitchell's novel of the Civil War, and Vivien Leigh *was* perfect as Scarlett. She won an Academy Award for this and for playing a very faded version of Scarlett in *A Streetcar Named Desire* in 1951. During the later stages of her career Miss Leigh was plagued with health problems, both physical and mental, supposedly brought on by her being unable to cope with the fact that she was "aging."

DOLLS:

The Madame Alexander dolls of Scarlett O'Hara, No. 1 through No. 33, all represent Vivien Leigh, although the Alexander Doll Company is supposed to have produced some dolls before Vivien Leigh was cast in the film. The first advertisement for a Scarlett O'Hara doll was in *Playthings* in August 1940 (*Illustration 532.*)

1. to 5.
   1940. All-composition and fully-jointed. Black wig; green (and other colors) sleep eyes. Various costumes. Sizes of 11in (27.9cm), 14in (35.6cm), 16in (40.6cm), 18in (45.7cm), 21in (53.3cm).
6. Circa 1950. All-hard plastic and fully-jointed. Black wig; sleep eyes. Various costumes. 14in (35.6cm).
7. No. 485, 1955. All-hard plastic. Wearing a print gown. 7½in (19.1cm).
8. No. 631, 1956. All-hard plastic. Wears a print gown. 8in (20.3cm).
9. No. 431, 1957. Same as No. 8 in an organdy gown.
10. No. 2240, 1961. All-hard plastic using the "Cissy" head mold. Wears a blue taffeta gown. 21in (53.3cm).
11. No. 1256, 1963. All-hard plastic using the "Lissy" doll. Green taffeta gown. 12in (30.5cm).

Illustration 532. Vivien Leigh from *Gone With the Wind.* Alexander Doll Company advertisement on the back cover of *Playthings,* August 1940.

Illustration 533. 9in (22.9cm) VIVIEN LEIGH as *Scarlett O'Hara* from *Gone With the Wind* by Madame Alexander, No. 1174, No. 1180, or No. 1181, 1968-1973. All-hard plastic and fully-jointed, including knees. Dark brown wig. This is the "Cissette" doll with bright green eyes and blue eye shadow. Bright green taffeta gown with matching bonnet, labeled as "Scarlett." Back marked: "MME // ALEXANDER." *Wanda Lodwick Collection.*

Illustration 534. VIVIEN LEIGH as *Scarlett. Wanda Lodwick Collection.*

12. No. 1760, 1963. All-hard plastic using the "Elise" head mold. Pale blue organdy gown. 18in (45.7cm).
13. No. 785, 1965. All-hard plastic. White taffeta gown. 8in (20.3cm).
14. No. 2152, 1965. All-vinyl using the "Jacqueline" doll. Green satin gown. 21in (53.3cm).
15. No. 725, 1966-1972. All-hard plastic. Green print cotton gowns in various patterns. 8in (20.3cm).
16. No. 2061, 1966. All-vinyl using the "Coco" doll. White gown. 21in (53.3cm).
17. No. 2174, 1967. All-vinyl using the "Jacqueline" doll. Green taffeta gown. 21in (53.3cm).
18. No. 1174, 1968-1969. All-hard plastic using the "Cissette" doll and called a "Portrette." Green taffeta gown. 9in (22.9cm). *Illustrations 533* and *534.*
19. No. 1490, 1968-1973. All-vinyl using the "Mary Ann" doll. White organdy gown. 14in (35.6cm).
20. No. 1495, 1968. Same as the above doll in a printed dress.
21. No. 2180, 1968. All-vinyl using the "Jacqueline" doll. Print and white gown. 21in (53.3cm). *Illustrations 535* and *536.*
22. No. 2190, 1969. Same as No. 17 above. 21in (53.3cm).
23. No. 1181, 1970-1972. All-hard plastic using the "Cissette" doll. Green taffeta gown. 9in (22.9cm). *Illustrations 533* and *534.*
24. No. 2180, 1970. All-vinyl using the "Jacqueline" doll. Green taffeta gown. 21in (53.3cm).
25. No. 0725, 1973. All-hard plastic. Called "Scarlet." White organdy gown. 8in (20.3cm).

Illustration 535. 21in (53.3cm) VIVIEN LEIGH as *Scarlett* by Madame Alexander, No. 2180, 1968. All-vinyl and fully-jointed. Dark wig; green sleep eyes with lashes. The dress is muslin with yellow flower print. The hat is natural straw with ribbons for ties. Many collectors feel that this version of Scarlett O'Hara is attired in the most authentic movie costume and that the doll's hair style most closely resembles that of Vivien Leigh in the film. *Ted Menten Collection. Photograph by Ted Menten.*

26. No. 1180, 1973. Same as No. 23. 9in (22.9cm). *Illustrations 533* and *534*.
27. No. 425, 1974-1981. Also called "Scarlet." Same as No. 25 above. 8in (20.3cm).
28. No. 1590, 1974-1981. Same as No. 19 above. 14in (35.6cm).
29. No. 2292, 1975. All-vinyl using the "Jacqueline" doll. Green taffeta gown. 21in (53.3cm).
30. No. 2295, 1976. Same as No. 29 above. 21in (53.3cm).
31. No. 2296, 1977. Same as No. 29 above. 21in (53.3cm).
32. No. 2210, 1978. Same as No. 29 above in a satin print gown. 21in (53.3cm).
33. No. 2240, 1979-1981. Same as No. 29 above in a green velvet gown. 21in (53.3cm).
34. VIVIEN LEIGH AS SCARLET (sic) O'HARA IN GONE WITH THE WIND. Peggy Nisbet, No. P751, late 1970s. Plastic "collectors' doll." Copyright 1939 by David O. Selznick; renewed 1967 M.G.M. Clark Gable as Rhett, No. P750 is a companion doll. Made in England. About 7½in (19.1cm).
35. SCARLETT. Madame Alexander, No. 1385, 1981. Vinyl head with rooted hair; hard plastic body that is fully-jointed. Wears a green taffeta gown with a bustle-length jacket. Rhett, No. 1380, is a companion doll. 12in (30.5cm).
36. VIVIEN LEIGH. Ann Parker, 1982. Plastic "collectors' doll," attached to a stand. Painted features; mohair wig. Made in England. About 11in (27.9cm).

Illustration 536. 21in (53.3cm) VIVIEN LEIGH as *Scarlett. Ted Menten Collection. Photograph by Ted Menten.*

LENARD, MARK. Actor. Lenard played support parts in films after 1966. He was in the television series "Here Comes the Brides" from September 1968 to September 1970. During the fall of 1974 he played Urko on the short-lived television version of "Planet of the Apes." In 1979 he was the Klingon Captain in *Star Trek the Motion Picture*.

DOLLS:
1. GENERAL URKO from PLANET OF THE APES. Mego, No. 50900/8, 1975. All-vinyl and fully-jointed with painted and molded ape features. Copyright by Twentieth Century-Fox Film Corporation. Made in Hong Kong. 7½in (19.1cm).
2. KLINGON. Mego, No. 91200/7, 1979. All-vinyl and fully-jointed with painted hair, features and clothing. Copyright by Paramount Pictures Corporation. Made in Hong Kong. 3¾in (9.6cm).
3. KLINGON COMMANDER. Mego, No. 91210/5, 1979. All-vinyl and fully-jointed with painted features. Copyright by Paramount Pictures Corporation. Made in Hong Kong. 12½in (31.8cm).

SEE: PLANET OF THE APES and STAR TREK.

LENNON, JOHN. Singer, musician, songwriter. Born October 9, 1940; died December 8, 1980. While still in school, Lennon formed a singing group, The Quarrymen. Later when he became part of The Beatles he combined with Paul McCartney to become one of the most successful songwriting teams in the history of entertainment. After he married Yoko Ono in 1969 the Beatles began to come apart as a group, and he recorded with Ono. After the breakup of The Beatles, Lennon had some successful recordings but during the last half of

Illustration 537. 4½in (11.5cm) JOHN LENNON by Remco, No. 1801, 1964. All-vinyl. Only the head is jointed. Rooted black hair; painted features. Head marked: "44." Bottom of foot marked: "U.C. BY BEATLES INC. // © // NEWS // ENT. LTD. // 1964." *Shirley Buchholz Collection.*

the 1970s he went into semi-retirement and stayed at home as a "house husband" to raise his son by Ono. He believed that the first five years of a child's life are the most important and because of his wealth could afford to devote all of his time to his son. In 1980 Lennon returned to recording his music and was planning to revive his entertainment career when he was gunned down at the door of his apartment house in New York, New York, by John Hinkley, a deranged young man who had admired him.

DOLLS:
1. JOHN LENNON—THE BOB'N HEAD BEATLES. Car Mascots, Inc., 1964. Papier-mâché and plaster "nodder." Made in Japan. 7¾in (19.8cm).
2. JOHN LENNON—THE BOB'N HEAD BEATLES. Same as the above in all-plastic, 1964. 4in (10.2cm).
3. JOHN LENNON—THE OFFICIAL BEATLES. Remco, No. 1801, 1964. 4½in (11.5cm). *Illustration 537.*
4. JOHN LENNON. Pelham Puppets, 1965. See THE BEATLES for Illustration.
5. JOHN LENNON. Made in Hong Kong, 1981. All-vinyl with painted hair and features. Holds microphone and stands on a "stage" that is a battery operated radio. 8in (20.3cm).
SEE: BEATLES, THE

LEWIS, AL. Actor. Born Al Meister on April 30, 1923. Lewis played character parts in movies after 1964 but became better known for his television roles. He was in the comedy "Car 54, Where Are You" on NBC-TV from September 1961 to September 1963. And he is even better remembered for playing Grandpa Munster in another situation comedy, "The Munsters" on CBS-TV from September 1964 to September 1966.

DOLLS:
1. GRAMPA (sic) MUNSTER. Remco, No. 1821, 1964. Made in USA. 4¾in (12.2cm). *Illustration 538.*
SEE: THE MUNSTERS.

Illustration 538. 4¾in (12.2cm) AL LEWIS as *Grampa* from "The Munsters" by Remco, No. 1821, 1964. Vinyl head. One-piece body of plastic. Rooted black and white hair; green skin tones; painted features. Head marked: "27." Back marked: "GRAMPA // MUNSTER // THE MUNSTERS // © 1964 KARO-VUE // PROD." Made in USA. *Phyllis Houston Collection.*

LEWIS, JERRY. Actor, director, producer. Born Joseph Levitch on March 16, 1926. From the age of five Lewis performed in resort hotels with his parents' singing act. In 1946 he joined with another entertainer who called himself Dean Martin. By the end of the 1940s Martin and Lewis were the most popular comedy team in America. They made their motion picture debut in 1949 in *My Friend Irma.* They appeared in 16 more films before splitting in 1956. Jerry Lewis then began producing and directing a series of films in which he starred. In the United States these films were considered very silly but in France they elevated him to a cult hero. Lewis appeared on many television shows with and without Dean Martin and was the star of "The Jerry Lewis Show" on ABC-TV from September to December 1963 and on NBC-TV from September 1967 to May 1969. In the 1970s his name was used for a chain of movie theaters.

DOLLS:
1. DEAN MARTIN-JERRY LEWIS PUPPET. National Mask and Puppet Corp., 1952. Vinyl head with a cloth body. Painted features. One face of the head is Jerry Lewis; reversed it is Dean Martin.
SEE: MARTIN, DEAN.

LEWIS, SHARI. Puppeteer, ventriloquist. Born Shari Hurwitz January 17, 1934. Shari Lewis and her puppet creation, Lamb Chop, have entertained children on television since the early 1950s. Her shows were "Facts 'N' Fun" (1953), "Shari and Her Friends" (1954), "Shariland" (1957), "Hi, Mom" (1957-1959), "The Shari Lewis Show" (1960-1963), and "The Shari Show" (1975). Another version of "The Shari Lewis Show" was also presented on British television. She has recorded several record albums for children.

Illustration 539. 12in (30.5cm) SHARI LEWIS by Madame Alexander, No. 1430, 1959. All-hard plastic and fully-jointed. Auburn wig; brown sleep eyes with lashes; high heel feet. Gold lace, lined "short evening gown," labeled "Shari." *Ted Menten Collection. Photograph by Ted Menten.*

DOLLS:

The Shari Lewis dolls are by Madame Alexander. They are all-hard plastic and are fully-jointed with high heeled feet. They were produced in 1959 and had a head mold that was not used for other Alexander dolls, a rarity for this company.

1. No. 1430. 12in (30.5cm). *Illustrations 539* and *540*.
2. No. 2430. 21in (53.3cm). A larger version of the above doll and costume (gold lace evening gown).
3. No. 1433. 12in (30.5cm). The same doll as No. 1, wearing a green satin skirt and a rayon jersey blouse.
4. No. 2433. 21in (53.3cm). A larger version of the above doll and costume. *Illustration 541*.
5. No. 1440. 12in (30.5cm). Wears a "theater costume of heavy slipper satin..." and a lined coat.
6. No. 2440. 21in (30.5cm). A larger version of the above doll and costume.

LINCOLN, ABRAHAM. 16th President of the United States. Born 1809; died 1865. Lincoln was born in a log cabin in Kentucky and was mostly self-schooled. The story of his youthful love affair with Ann Rutledge is now discredited, but it illustrates the romanticism always associated with Lincoln. He was a United States Representative from Illinois from 1847 to 1849 and lost his bid for a Senate seat to Stephen A. Douglas in 1858. In 1860 he was elected as the first Republican President. Although he regarded slavery as a great injustice, Lincoln was not an abolitionist. His election caused the secession of the South, as he was opposed to the extension of slavery, and this brought on the Civil War. Lincoln was determined to preserve the Federal Union "even if I have to free the slaves to do it." (Direct quote from Lincoln.) His famous Emancipation Proclamation is not what freed the slaves. (The 13th Amendment to the American Constitution did this after his death.) The Proclamation showed the moral tone of his Administration, but it was a military, political and diplomatic move and only applied to slaves in the seceeded areas. Lincoln's assassination by John Wilkes Booth on April 14, 1865, ruined the South's chance for a peaceful reconciliation with the rest of the country and brought on the harsh measures of Reconstruction. Lincoln will always be a symbol of American democracy.

DOLLS:

1. ABRAHAM LINCOLN. Fun World, 1976. All-vinyl with painted hair and features. Made in Hong Kong. 8½in (20.3cm).
2. ABRAHAM LINCOLN. Peggy Nisbet, No. P715, 1970s. Plastic "collectors' doll." Mary Lincoln, No. P716, is a companion doll. Made in England. About 8in (20.3cm).

LINCOLN, MARY TODD. Wife of President Abraham Lincoln. Born 1818; died 1882. Mary Todd Lincoln has always been the victim of unkind comments, and her personality did nothing to create an alternative impression. One of the reasons for her unpopularity was that she was from the South. Her stern disposition was in part caused by the fact that three of her four sons died while they were children.

Illustration 540. 12in (30.5cm) SHARI LEWIS. *Ted Menten Collection. Photograph by Ted Menten.*

Illustration 541. 21in (53.3cm) SHARI LEWIS by Madame Alexander, No. 2433, 1959. All-hard plastic and fully-jointed with high heel feet. Auburn wig; brown sleep eyes with lashes. Head marked: "ALEXANDER." The green satin skirt is worn with a rayon blouse tagged "Shari." *Fran's Dolls.*

DOLLS:
1. MARY LINCOLN. Peggy Nisbet, No. P716, 1970s. Plastic "collectors' doll." Abraham Lincoln, No. P715, is a companion doll. Made in England. About 7½in (19.1cm).
2. MARY TODD LINCOLN. Madame Alexander, No. 1517, 1982. Vinyl and plastic and fully-jointed. Rooted brown hair pulled to the side in a long curl. She wears a purple cotton velveteen gown. Part of the third six First Ladies Series.
SEE: FIRST LADIES, THE.

LIND, JENNY. Soprano singer. Born Johanna Maria Lind in 1820; died 1887. Jenny Lind began as an opera singer in her native Sweden but became internationally famous after her tour of the United States with P.T. Barnum from 1850 to 1852. Because she was the greatest coloratura soprano of her time, she was known as "the Swedish nightingale."

DOLLS:
Many china head dolls are called Jenny Lind, but most collectors feel that this is because of the hair style. *Playthings* reported in October 1938 that "the Jenny Lind doll exhibited at the First National Doll Show (1938)...dates back to 1855." There is still no proof for this claim.
1. JENNY LIND. Madame Alexander, No. 1171, 1969. 10½in (26.7cm). *Illustrations 542* and *544*.
2. JENNY LIND. Madame Alexander, No. 2191, 1969. All-vinyl "Portrait" using the "Jacqueline" doll. 21in (53.3cm).
3. JENNY LIND. Madame Alexander, No. 1491, 1970. 14in (35.6cm). *Illustrations 543* and *544*.
4. JENNY LIND AND HER LISTENING CAT. Madame Alexander, No. 1470, 1970-1971. 14in (35.6cm). *Illustration 545*.

5. JENNY LIND. Madame Alexander, No. 2181, 1970. The same as doll No. 2 with lace trim on the gown. 21in (53.3cm).
6. JENNY LIND. Madame Alexander, No. 1184, 1970. The same doll as No. 1 with lace added to the dress. 10½in (26.7cm).

Illustration 543. 14in (35.6cm) JENNY LIND by Madame Alexander, No. 1491, 1970. Vinyl head and arms; plastic torso and legs. Rooted light blonde hair. The gown is pink satin, trimmed in lace. *Ted Menten Collection. Photograph by Ted Menten.*

Illustration 542. 10½in (26.7cm) JENNY LIND by Madame Alexander, No. 1171, 1969. All-hard plastic and fully-jointed. Blonde wig; blue sleep eyes with molded lashes. (This is the standard *Cissette* doll.) The long sleeved satin gown is pink. *Ted Menten Collection. Photograph by Ted Menten.*

Illustration 544. 10½in (26.7cm), No. 1171, and 14in (35.6cm), No. 1491, JENNY LIND dolls by Madame Alexander. *Ted Menten Collection. Photograph by Ted Menten.*

Illustration 545. 14in (35.6cm) JENNY LIND and her *Listening Cat* by Madame Alexander, No. 1470, 1970-1971. Vinyl head and arms; plastic torso and legs. Rooted blonde hair; blue sleep eyes with lashes. The dress is blue cotton with white flowers. *Ted Menten Collection. Photograph by Ted Menten.*

LINDBERGH, CHARLES A., JR. Aviator. Born 1902; died 1974. "Lucky Lindy" became America's greatest hero in 1927 when he flew nonstop alone over the Atlantic from New York to Paris, France, in 1927. He gained immense public sympathy in 1932 when his infant son was kidnapped and murdered. Because of this he and his family moved to England in 1935. He resigned from his army reserve commission because of the criticism of his anti-war speeches before World War II. (He admired Adolph Hitler.) His wife, Anne Morrow Lindbergh, wrote several books, many of them extolling his virtues.

DOLLS:
1. OUR LINDY. Regal Doll Co., 1928. 33in (83.8cm). *Illustrations 546* and *547*.

Illustration 546. 33in (83.8cm) CHARLES A. LINDBERGH, JR., *Our Lindy*, by Regal Doll Co., 1928. Composition shoulder plate head; stuffed cloth body. Painted dark blonde hair; painted blue eyes; open/closed mouth with molded and painted teeth. The khaki colored suit has fur trim on the collar. Advertisement from *Playthings*, June 1928.

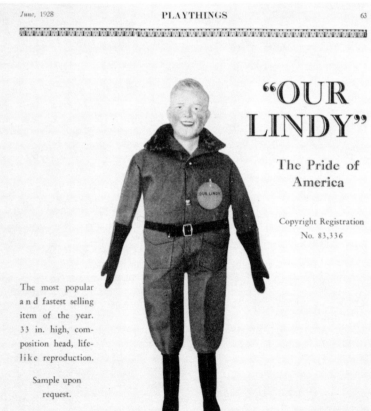

Illustration 547. Close-up of CHARLES A. LINDBERGH, JR. by Regal. The shoulder plate is marked: " © REGAL DOLL CO. // "SCULP" E. PERRUGGI // 1928." *Ruth E. Fisher Collection. Photograph by John Schoonmaker.*

LIPSON, JOHN. Actor. Lipson played Vultan in the 1936 serial *Flash Gordon.*
SEE: FLASH GORDON.
DOLLS:
1. VULTAN from FLASH GORDON. Mattel, No. 1532, 1980. All-vinyl and fully-jointed. Painted hair, features and clothing. Molded wings on back. Copyright by King Features Syndicate, Inc. Made in Hong Kong. 3¾in (9.6cm).
SEE: FLASH GORDON.

LLOYD, CHRISTOPHER. Actor. Born October 22, 1938. Christopher Lloyd has acted on Broadway, in films and on television. He is a regular on ABC-TV's "Taxi," having joined the show in its second season in the fall of 1979. On "Taxi" Lloyd is the rumpled and obviously-on-drugs Reverend Jim. In 1981 he played Butch Cavendish in *The Legend of the Lone Ranger,* the new movie version of the early television favorite.
DOLLS:
1. BUTCH CAVENDISH. Gabriel, No. 31632, 1981. Made in Hong Kong. 3¾in (9.6cm). *Illustration 548.*
SEE: LONE RANGER, THE.

Illustration 548. 3¾in (9.6cm) CHRISTOPHER LLOYD as *Butch Cavendish* from *The Legend of the Long Ranger* by Gabriel, No. 31632, 1981. All-vinyl and fully-jointed with painted features and clothing. The hat is molded to the head. Copyright by Lone Ranger Television, Inc. Made in Hong Kong.

LLOYD, HAROLD. Actor. Born April 20, 1893; died 1971. In 1912 Lloyd made his film debut for the Edison Company playing a near-naked Indian. In 1914 film maker Hal Roach hired him for a series of one-reel comedies. Roach and Lloyd made more than 100 short comedies in 1916-1917 based on the character Lonesome Luke. This was patterned after Charlie Chaplin, but the films were very successful. In 1917 Lloyd and Roach developed another comic character, Everyman. This was an average young man in glasses who went through funny and dangerous situations which he overcame by persistence and luck. Lloyd became the highest paid actor in Hollywood. Even though he lost part of his right hand in a stunt explosion in 1920, Lloyd continued to perform dangerous sequences for his comedies, like hanging from the dial of a clock atop a skyscraper. After sound came to films, Lloyd's brand of comedy was less popular. In the 1960s he issued compilation films of his old comedies, earning fame from a new generation of filmgoers. When Lloyd died of cancer at age 77 he left five million dollars to his heirs and his fabulous estate (the best in Hollywood) to be used as a motion picture museum. The neighbors fussed about the project, and the 44-room mansion was auctioned off and leveled and the vast grounds were turned into lots by a developer.
DOLLS:
1. HAROLD LLOYD. Maker unknown, circa late 1920s/early 1930s. Lithographed cloth. Belt buckle in front is stamped: "H.L." On the back it is "autographed:" "Yours for Happiness, Harold Lloyd." See color section for photograph.
2. LLOYD DOLL. Maker unknown, 1934. All-celluloid with jointed arms only. Painted in bright colors. 3¾in (9.6cm).

LOCKWOOD, GARY. Actor. Born John Gary Yusolfsky in 1937. Lockwood began his career as a stuntman and a stand-in for Anthony Perkins. He began playing parts in films in 1960. On television he was in "Follow the Sun" on ABC from September 1961 to September 1962 and "The Lieutenant" on NBC from September 1963 to September 1964. He was Dan Holland in the Disney film *The Black Hole* (1979).

DOLLS:
1. CAPTAIN DAN HOLLAND from THE BLACK HOLE. Mego, No. 95010/2, 1979. All-vinyl and fully-jointed with painted hair, features and clothing. Copyright by Walt Disney Productions. Made in Hong Kong. 3¾in (9.6cm).
2. CAPTAIN DAN HOLLAND from THE BLACK HOLE. Mego, No. 95005/5, 1979. Made in Hong Kong. 12¼in (31.2cm). *Illustration 549.*

SEE: THE BLACK HOLE.

Illustration 549. 12¼in (31.2cm) GARY LOCKWOOD as *Captain Dan Holland* from *The Black Hole* by Mego, No. 95005/5, 1979. All-vinyl and fully-jointed. Painted black hair and painted brown eyes. Head marked: "© WALT DISNEY // PRODUCTIONS 1979." Back marked: "© MEGO CORP. 1977 // MADE IN HONG KONG."

LONE RANGER, THE. The Lone Ranger, created by George W. Trendle and Fran Striker, began as a classic radio series in 1933 and two years later also became a comic strip. On September 15, 1949, "The Lone Ranger" came to television. There were 182 half-hour films produced. (Some sources list 221 episodes.) They ran on prime-time until 1957 and on Saturday afternoons until 1961. In 1966 another version of The Lone Ranger came to Saturday morning television as an animated cartoon.

The first episode of the filmed television show told the reason why the Texas Ranger became "lone:" Six Texas Rangers were after a gang of desperados who ambushed the rangers and thought that all were left for dead. One of them, John Reid, crawled into a cave and was nursed back to health by Tonto, a friendly Indian. The two promised to avenge the deaths of the other five Texas Rangers. John Reid donned a mask so that the killers would not know who he was. He supported himself with the proceeds of a silver mine, from which came his silver bullets, and traveled around with Tonto to avenge wrongdoings. The Lone Ranger never killed anyone; he let the bad guys do themselves in. The programs always began with the "William Tell Overture" by Rossini (composed in 1829).

Tonto was always played on television and in two feature films by Jay Silverheels. The Lone Ranger was played by Clayton Moore from 1949 to 1952 and from 1954 to 1957. John Hart was in the part from 1952 to 1954. Moore also played the Lone Ranger in two films.

JAY SILVERHEELS was born in 1919 and died in 1980. He was a Mohawk Indian born in Ontario, Canada. He played Tonto in all of the Lone Ranger episodes on television and in the films *The Lone Ranger* (1956) and *The Lone Ranger and the Lost City of Gold* (1958). He also played Indians in other feature films.

JOHN HART entered the movies in 1938 and still plays character parts. On the television program "The Greatest American Hero" he played himself and himself as the Lone Ranger in the fall of 1981. In the 1981 film *The Legend of the Lone Ranger* he had a small part as Lucas Striker.

CLAYTON MOORE was born in 1914. After a career as a circus acrobat and a male model, he entered films in 1938. He was mostly in serials and low-budget action pictures. He also repeated his television part in *The Lone Ranger* (1956) and *The Lone Ranger and the Lost City of Gold* (1958) for the movie versions. The Wrather Corporation, who controls the rights to the character, had to have a court order to restrain Moore from appearing in public in a mask as The Lone Ranger for endorsement purposes in 1980, at which time the new film version of the story was being prepared. Moore was promised a small part in this film as a condition for not appearing in public as The Lone Ranger, but he refused the role.

DOLLS:
Examples of Lone Ranger and Tonto dolls are shown in *Illustrations 550, 551, 553, 554, 555, 556* and *557* but these are not celebrity dolls as they do not represent any of the above-mentioned actors. Only the following are celebrity dolls. The Lone Ranger, because of the date, would most likely be CLAYTON MOORE; JAY SILVER-HEELS is Tonto.
1. THE LONE RANGER AND "SILVER." Hartland Plastics, Inc., No. 801, 1955. All-plastic. Made in Hartland, Wisconsin. About 8in (20.3cm).
2. TONTO AND "SCOUT." Hartland Plastics, Inc., No. 805, 1955. All-plastic. Made in Hartland, Wisconsin. About 8in (20.3cm).

Except for the Lone Ranger and Tonto dolls from Hartland Plastics, the only dolls that are celebrity dolls are those from Gabriel in 1981. The 1981 film version of the popular radio and television episodes, *The Legend of the Lone Ranger*, was declared a disaster by the critics but even *The New York Times* admitted, "There's a certain magic to the Lone Ranger story that not even this listless version has been able to erase." In anticipation of a success, Gabriel received a license from Wrather Productions (Lone Ranger Television, Inc.) to produce a line of dolls and horses based on the characters in this film. They are KLINTON SPILSBURY as *The Lone Ranger*, MICHAEL HORSE as *Tonto*, CHRISTOPHER LLOYD as *Butch Cavendish*, TED FLICKER as *Buffalo Bill Cody* and LINCOLN TATE as *General George Custer*. See also entries under the above celebrities.

Lone Ranger

Illustration 550. 20½in (52.1cm) *Lone Ranger* by Dollcraft Novelty Co., 1938. Composition head and hands; cloth body; composition molded shoes. Tag on clothing: "Copyright T.L.R. Co., Inc." Printed on pants: "T // L.R. // INC." The manufacture of this doll would have coincided with the popularity of the radio shows and the comic strips. *Billie Jo Phillips Collection.*

Illustration 551. 20½in (52.1cm) *Tonto* by Dollcraft Novelty Co., 1938. Composition head and hands; wooden feet; cloth body. Painted hair and features. Suede clothing with leather moccasins. Tag: "Copyright T.L.R. Co., Inc." Printed on pants: "L.R. // INC. // THE LONE RANGER'S PAL." This is a companion doll to the *Lone Ranger* in *Illustration 550. Billie Jo Phillips Collection.*

Illustration 553. 30in (76.2cm) *Lone Ranger* by Mollye (International Doll Co.), 1950s. Hard plastic head. Blue sleep eyes with lashes; open mouth with two teeth and felt tongue. Early vinyl arms and legs. Cloth body. Wears blue shirt and neck scarf; brown pants; leatherette holster with a plastic gun; brown boots. No marks on the doll. Tag on shirt: "Created by // *Mollye* // International // Doll Co. // Phila, Pa." Neck scarf, hat band and original box read: "LONE RANGER." Picture on scarf copyright by T.L.R., INC. This is a boy doll dressed in a "Lone Ranger" cowboy suit, not a Lone Ranger doll.

Illustration 552. Clayton Moore as the Lone Ranger and Jay Silverheels as Tonto, 1950s.

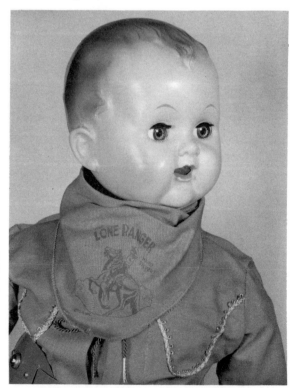

Illustration 554. Lone Ranger by Mollye.

Illustration 555. 10½in (26.7cm) *Lone Ranger* hand puppet. Vinyl molded head with plastic hat. Vinyl glove for hand manipulation. Printed on front: "THE LONE RANGER // © 1966 BY WRATHER CORPORATION." This item was manufactured at the time the Lone Ranger was a cartoon show on television.

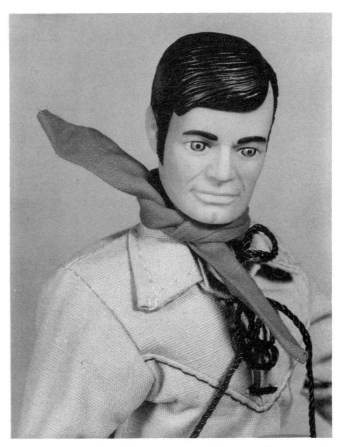

Illustration 557. 9¾in (24.9cm) *Lone Ranger* by Gabriel.

Illustration 556. 9¾in (24.9cm) *Lone Ranger* by Gabriel, No. 23620, 1975. Vinyl head with painted hair and eyes; plastic jointed body. Back marked: " © 1973 LONE RANGER // TEL. INC. // MADE IN HONG KONG // FOR GABRIEL IND., INC." Copyright by Lone Ranger Television, Inc. This doll does not resemble any of the actors who played the Lone Ranger, and was manufactured to coincide with the television animated cartoon program.

Illustration 558. Klinton Spilsbury, the star of *The Legend of the Ranger*, 1981.

Illustration 561. 3¾in (9.6cm) MICHAEL HORSE as *Tonto* from *The Legend of the Lone Ranger* by Gabriel, No. 31631, 1981. All-vinyl with painted features and clothing. Copyright 1980 by Lone Ranger Television, Inc. Made in Hong Kong.

LONSDALE, MICHAEL (or MICHEL). Actor. Born in Paris, France, in 1931. After he gained acting experience on the stage in Paris, Lonsdale entered films playing in many international productions. In *Moonraker* (1979), from the British James Bond series, he was Hugo Drax.

DOLLS:
1. DRAX from MOONRAKER. Mego, No. 96002, 1979. Made in Hong Kong. 12½in (31.8cm). *Illustrations 562* and *563.*
SEE: JAMES BOND.

Illustration 559. 3¾in (9.6cm) KLINTON SPILSBURY as *The Lone Ranger* by Gabriel, No. 31630, 1981. All-vinyl with painted features and clothing. Copyright 1980 by Lone Ranger Television, Inc. The manufacture of this doll coincided with the 1981 movie production. Note how much the painting resembles Klinton Spilsbury. Made in Hong Kong.

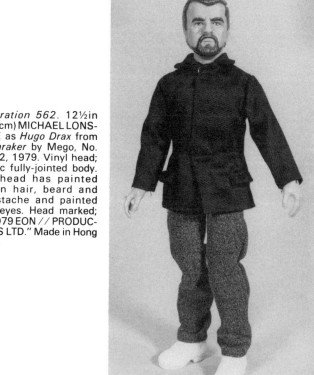

Illustration 562. 12½in (31.8cm) MICHAEL LONSDALE as *Hugo Drax* from *Moonraker* by Mego, No. 96002, 1979. Vinyl head; plastic fully-jointed body. The head has painted brown hair, beard and moustache and painted blue eyes. Head marked; "© 1979 EON // PRODUCTIONS LTD." Made in Hong Kong.

Illustration 560. KLINTON SPILSBURY as the *Lone Ranger* riding his great white stallion *Silver* by Gabriel. *Silver* is No. 31635 and is 4½in (11.5cm) high. All-plastic. Jointed at the legs. Copyright 1980 by Lone Ranger Television, Inc. Made in Hong Kong.

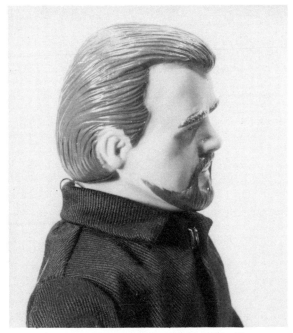

Illustration 563. MICHAEL LONSDALE by Mego.

LOUIS, JOE. Boxer. Born Joseph Louis Barrow 1914; died 1981. "The Brown Bomber" was the world heavyweight champ from 1937 to 1949, the longest record in boxing history. He defended his title 25 times and retired undefeated. His most publicized match was at Yankee Stadium in 1938 against Germany's Max Schmeling. It took Louis just 2:04 minutes to drop Hitler's favorite.
DOLLS:
  1. JOE LOUIS.   Maker unknown. Vinyl head; cloth body. 20in (50.8cm).

LOUIS XVI.   King of France (1774-1793). Born 1754; died 1793. Twenty year old Louis inherited an extravagant, corrupt, immoral and nearly bankrupt court from his grandfather, Louis XV, who had been king for almost 60 years. Louis' pleasure-loving queen, Marie Antoinette, added to his unpopularity as the ruler of France. Some historians contend that the excesses of Marie Antoinette were caused by her frustration of not being able to produce an heir, a duty expected of a queen. The reason for this was that lovemaking was physically very painful for Louis. After he underwent a simple operation, Marie Antoinette bore four children. By this time economic conditions in France were becoming intollerable for the people, and the money spent in aiding the Patriots' cause during the American Revolution further increased the problem. In 1789 when violence erupted throughout the country, Louis and his queen thought that the best course was to ignore it. Further bumbling and ineptness worsened conditions, and the royal family decided that they should flee the country for their safety as the revolution increased. They were captured at the border and the entire family was imprisoned in 1792 for treason. The National Convention, now the government, voted to execute the king because as long as he was alive the "Old Ways" might be restored, and he would also be an example to monarchs all over Europe who might oppose the changes in France. On January 21, 1793, Louis was led to the guillotine. He told the assembled mob: "Frenchmen, I

Illustration 564. 8in (20.3cm) KING LOUIS XVI, No. P458, and MARIE ANTOINETTE, No. P459, by Peggy Nisbet, 1970s. All-hard plastic and jointed only at the arms. Mohair wigs and painted features. Made in England. *Photograph Courtesy of House of Nisbet.*

die innocent; it is from the scaffold and near to appearing before God that I tell you so. I pardon my enemies. I desire that France..." His voice was drowned out as the head of Paris National Guard screamed, "*Tambours!*," and the drums beat loudly. The severed head of Louis XVI was displayed to the mobs and "all Frenchmen trod with a heavy step that day."

DOLLS:
1. KING LOUIS XVI. Peggy Nisbet, No. P458, late 1970s. Made in England. About 8in (20.3cm). *Illustration 564.*

THE LOVE BOAT. Television comedy series. The regular series on ABC-TV was preceeded by three pilot films. "The Love Boat" lasted two hours on September 17, 1976; "The Love Boat II" was two hours long on January 21, 1977; "The Love Boat III" was an hour on May 5, 1977. The series program premiered September 29, 1977. The setting for the show is on the *Pacific Princess*, an ocean liner. The regular cast and the guest cast each week board "The Love Boat" for a cruise (usually to Acapulco, Mexico) and search for romance. The regular cast is GAVIN MacLEOD as Captain Merrill Stubing; LAUREN TEWES as Julie McCoy, the cruise director; BERNIE KOPELL as Adam "Doc" Bricker, the physician; FRED GRANDY as Burl "Gopher" Smith, the yeoman purser; TED LANGE as Issac Washington, the bartender; and JILL WHELAN as Vicki Stubing, the captain's daughter. Grandy, Kopell and Lange were also in "The Love Boat II." The entire cast, except for Whelan, were seen in "The Love Boat III." See listings under the six celebrities.

LOW, JULIETTE. Founder of the Girl Scouts in the United States. Born 1860; died 1927. Mrs. Low was a native of Georgia, but she had lived in England and had helped to organize the Girl Guide troops there. The Girl Guides was the sister organization of the Boy Scouts of Great Britain. Low was the first president of the American Girl Scouts and at her death there were troops in every state and more than 140,000 members.

DOLLS:
1. JULIETTE LOW. Hallmark, No. 400DT114-3, 1979. Made in Taiwan. 6¾in (17.2cm). *Illustration 565.*

Illustration 565. 6¾in (17.2cm) JULIETTE LOW by Hallmark, No. 400DT114-3, 1979. Lithographed cloth. Stuffed and jointed. The skirt and the jacket are not formed to the body; the hat is. Made in Taiwan.

Illustration 565-A. The cast from TV's "The Love Boat" by Mego, 1982. From left to right: TED LANGE as *Issac,* BERNIE KOPELL as *"Doc,"* FRED GRANDY as *"Gopher,"* GAVIN MacLEOD as *Captain Stubing,* LAUREN TEWES as *Julie* and JILL WHELAN as *Vicki.* The adults are 3¾in (9.6cm); *Vicki* is 3½in (8.9cm). Copyright by Aaron Spelling Productions, Inc. From *Soar with the Eagles* (Mego catalog), 1982.

LUGOSI, BELA. Actor. Born Bela Blasko in Hungary in 1882; died 1956. Beginning in 1901 in Hungary Lugosi played leads on the stage and after 1915 in films. He became a communist leader after the collapse of the monarchy in 1918, but when the Leftists were defeated in 1919 he fled to Germany and later to the United States. He acted on the stage and achieved his greatest success with the play "Dracula" on Broadway in 1927. In 1931 he played the same part in the screen version and scared the beejabbers out of theater goers when they saw him as the vampire. For the rest of his acting career Lugosi portrayed a similar type of evil personage. In 1955 he committed himself to a state hospital for drug addiction. After his release he returned to the screen and announced plans for his fourth marriage, but he died shortly afterwards. He was buried with his Dracula cape.

DOLLS:
1. DRACULA. Mego, No. 1910, 1974. All-vinyl and fully-jointed. Painted and molded hair and features. Made in Hong Kong. 8in (20.3cm).
2. COUNT DRACULA. Remco, 1980. All-vinyl and fully-jointed with painted hair, features and clothing. Wears a vinyl cape. Copyright by Universal City Studios, Inc., Made in Hong Kong. 4in (9.6cm).
3. COUNT DRACULA. Remco, No. 752, 1980. All-vinyl and fully-jointed. Painted hair and features. Copyright by Universal City Studios, Inc. Made in Hong Kong. 8in (20.3cm).

LUKE, KEYE. Actor. Born in 1904 in China. Luke came to the United States as a child and entered films as an actor in 1934 after serving as a technical advisor on Hollywood movies with Chinese themes. He played orientals in many films and is best remembered as Charlie Chan's "Number One Son," Henry, in many films of the detective series. He also appeared in a number of *Dr. Kildare* films and was Kato, the Green Hornet's servant, in two serials. He was Master Po in flashbacks in ABC-TV's "Kung Fu" from October 1972 to June 1975.

DOLLS:
1. HENRY. Hand puppet by Ideal, 1973. Vinyl head with painted features. Printed body on glove portion of puppet. Warner Oland as Charlie Chan is a companion piece.

LUPTON, JOHN. Actor. Born August 22, ?. Lupton made his Broadway debut with Mae West in "Diamond Lil" in the late 1940s and came to Hollywood to begin work in films in 1951. He played Tom Jeffords on the ABC-TV western series "Broken Arrow" from September 1956 to September 1958. The television show was based on the 1950 movie *Broken Arrow*, from the novel *Blood Brother*. Cochise, the Apache chief, was Jefford's "blood brother."

DOLLS:
1. TOM JEFFORDS FROM BROKEN ARROW. Hartland Plastics, Inc., No. 821, circa 1958. All-plastic with an Appaloosa stallion. Made in Hartland, Wisconsin. About 8in (20.3cm).

LYNLEY, CAROL. Actress. Born Carol Lee in 1942. Carol Lynley began her professional life as a teen-age model. She started in films as an adolescent and later in motion pictures and on television was an attractive leading lady. In 1965 she was in one of the awful versions of the life of Jean Harlow, playing the legendary star of the 1930s.

DOLLS:
1. and 2.
CAROL LYNLEY. Johana Gast Anderton in *More Twentieth Century Dolls* (1974) cites that Tops in Toys advertised a Carol Lynley doll in sizes of 18in (45.7cm) and 30in (76.2cm) in 1960.

M

M*A*S*H. Television situation comedy. On September 17, 1972, "M*A*S*H" came to television. This was during the time that a large part of the American population was polarized against the war in Viet Nam. The anti-war comedy, set in Korea, became popular very quickly. The cast of characters in the series were all members of the 4077th Mobile Army Surgical Hospital stationed behind the lines. Their job was to treat the wounded and save the dying. There have been many cast changes in the show but the most enduring actors are ALAN ALDA as Hawkeye, an intellectual prankster; MIKE FARRELL as B.J., a replacement for Wayne Rogers, the original co-star and roommate of Hawkeye; DAVID OGDEN STIERS as Winchester, an aristocratic Bostonian who replaced Larry Linville as Major Burns; LORETTA SWIT as Major Margaret Houlihan, called Hot Lips in the early years of the show; JAMIE FARR as Klinger, who dressed in women's clothing when he joined the show in the fall of 1973 but dropped this act when it did not bring about the desired discharge he wanted; HARRY MORGAN as Colonel Sherman Potter, who replaced McLean Stevenson as the head of the M*A*S*H unit in the fall of 1975; and WILLIAM CHRISTOPHER as Father Mulcahy, a Catholic chaplain. The television series was inspired by the popular film *M*A*S*H* (1970), which was based on the novel written by a doctor who had served in Korea. The doctor used the name Richard Hooker in writing so as not to compromise his medical standing with his insights and revelations. There are dolls of the seven characters cited above. In about 1976 Mego produced dolls representing Alan Alda and Loretta Swit for F. W. Woolworth. In 1982 a new company, Tristar International, Ltd., made dolls of all seven characters.

MacARTHUR, DOUGLAS. United States Army officer. Born 1880; died 1964. After graduating from West Point with some of the highest honors ever bestowed there, MacArthur made the Army his career. In World War I he commanded the 42nd Division. From 1919 to 1922 he returned to West Point as a Superintendent. Prior to World War II he was the Army Chief of Staff and the military advisor to the Philippines. He retired in 1937, but was recalled in 1941. After Japan took over the Philippines he was made Supreme Allied Commander of the south west Pacific and in 1944-1945 he liberated the islands, telling the populace, "People of the Philippines, I have returned." After 1945 he was commander of the occupational forces in Japan. From 1950 to 1951 he was Commander in Chief of the United Nations military forces in Korea. President Harry S. Truman dismissed MacArthur from his last position, because he publicaly challenged Truman's conduct of the war. He returned to the United States to a hero's welcome, announcing, "Old soldiers never die, they just fade away." This line was turned into a hit record.

DOLLS:
1. GENERAL DOUGLAS MacARTHUR. Freundlich Novelty Corporation, 1940s. 18in (45.7cm). *Illustration 566*.
2. GEN. DOUGLAS MacARTHUR. Excel Toy Corp., 1974. All-vinyl and fully-jointed with painted hair and features. Made in Hong Kong. 9¾in (24.9cm).

MacDONALD, FLORA. Scottish Jacobite heroine. Born 1722; died 1790. When Charles Edward Stuart (Bonnie Prince Charlie) landed in Scotland in 1745 to stir up a rebellion to have his father, James, placed on the throne of the United Kingdom, Flora MacDonald aided the cause. James Stuart was the son of King James II of England, who in 1688 was forced to give up his line of succession because his wife was Catholic. This brought on the Jacobite rebellion to restore the Stuarts to the throne. 2000 Highlanders joined Bonnie Prince Charlie, but he was defeated and forced into exile again. It was Flora MacDonald who dressed the Prince as a servant girl so he could escape to France undetected by English soldiers.

DOLLS:
1. FLORA MacDONALD. Peggy Nisbet, No. H224, 1970s. Plastic "collectors' doll." Made in England. About 7½in (19.1cm).
2. FLORA MacDONALD. Peggy Nisbet, No. P719, 1970s. Plastic "collectors' doll." This doll, unlike No. 1., is supposed to be a portrait of Flora MacDonald. Made in England. About 7½in (19.1cm).

MacGREGOR, ROBERT. SEE: ROB ROY.

MacLEOD, GAVIN. Actor. Born February 28, 1931. MacLeod appeared in movies after 1958. He played Murray Slaughter, the writer, on "The Mary Tyler Moore Show" on CBS-TV for seven years—September 1970 to September 1977. During February 1980 he was in the miniseries "Scruples" on CBS-TV. His most recent long-term role is as Merrill Stubing, the captain of "The Love Boat" on ABC-TV, beginning in September 1977. He was in "The Love Boat III," an hour pilot for the series in May 1977. Gavin MacLeod is a collector of Kewpie dolls.

DOLLS:
1. CAPTAIN STUBING of THE LOVE BOAT. Mego, No. 23005/1, 1982. All-vinyl and fully-jointed. Painted fringe of gray hair; painted features. Molded clothing. Copyright by Aaron Spelling Productions, Inc. Made in Hong Kong. 3¾in (9.6cm).
SEE: LOVE BOAT, THE.

MADISON, DOLLY (or DOLLEY). Wife of James Madison, the 4th President of the United States. Born 1768; died 1849. Dolly Madison acted as White House Hostess for President Jefferson and for her husband during his two terms (1809-1817). Mrs. Madison was noted for "the magnificence of her entertaining as well as for charm, tact and grace." Right before the British burned the White House in September 1814, Dolly cut the portrait of George Washington out of its frame and hid it on her person as she escaped.

DOLLS:
Many unmarked china head dolls that were made in Germany during the late 19th and early 20th centuries are called "Dolly (or Dolley) Madison." They have painted black hair with a more elaborate hairdo than usual for a china head and painted blue eyes. This name

OPPOSITE PAGE: Illustration 566. 18in (45.7cm) GENERAL DOUGLAS MacARTHUR by Freundlich Novelty Corporation, 1940s. All-composition with jointed arms and legs only. The hat is molded with the head; painted features with black eyes. No markings. The original paper tag also tells that the General is "The Man of the Hour." *Jean Pritchard Collection.*

refers to a "type" rather than the fact that the doll represents Dolly (Dolley) Madison.

1. DOLLEY MADISON. Madame Alexander, No. 1504, 1976-1978. All-vinyl and fully-jointed. Rooted brown hair; brown sleep eyes with lashes. Dressed in a satin and silver floral dress.
SEE: FIRST LADIES.

MAJORS, LEE. Actor. Born April 23, 1939, 1940 or 1942. Majors attended college on a football scholarship but turned down offers to play professionally so he could go to Hollywood and try to break into the movies, according to his "official" press biographies. Majors was not quite handsome or talented, but he was persistent. He acted in some films in the 1960s and played tight-panted cowboys in two television series. They were "The Big Valley" from September 1965 to May 1969 and "The Virginian" during the 1970-1971 (the 11th and last) season. On "Owen Marshall, Counsler At Law," from September 1971 to August 1974, he was a young lawyer. He finally gained stardom with his own series, "The Six Million Dollar Man," which lasted from January 1974 to March 1978. In the fall of 1981 he returned to television, much aged, as "The Fall Guy," playing a stunt man, reportedly at a greatly reduced salary. His second wife was actress Farrah Fawcett.

DOLLS:
1. THE BIONIC MAN. THE SIX MILLION DOLLAR MAN. Kenner, No. 65030, 1977. 13in (33cm). *Illustrations 567* and *568*. Richard Anderson as Oscar Goldman, No. 65100, and Lindsay Wagner, No. 65810, as the Bionic Woman are companion dolls.

Illustration 567. 13in (33cm) LEE MAJORS as *Colonel Steve Austin, the Bionic Man,* from "The Six Million Dollar Man" by Kenner, No. 65030, 1977. All-vinyl and fully-jointed. Painted blonde hair; painted blue right eye. The left eye is a "bionic eye," a secret eye with a lens that permits viewing from the back of the doll's head. Back marked: " CHARACTER // © UNIVERSAL CITY STUDIOS, INC. 1973 // ALL RIGHTS RESERVED." *Penny Caswell Collection.*

Illustration 568. LEE MAJORS by Kenner. *Penny Caswell Collection.*

Illustration 569. The Mamas and the Papas, circa 1965. At the top is Cass Elliot. In front, from left to right, Denny Doherty, Michelle Phillips and John Phillips.

THE MAMAS AND THE PAPAS. "The first genuine hippy band" was organized in 1965 by John Phillips. The Mamas were CASS ELLIOTT and MICHELLE PHILLIPS; the Papas were JOHN PHILLIPS and DENNY DOHERTY. The vocal harmonies of the group were heard on four huge hit records in 1966—"California Dreamin'," "Monday, Monday," "I Saw Her Again" and "Words of Love." In 1968 the group began coming apart along with the marriage of John and Michelle Phillips. In 1981,

Illustration 570. THE MAMAS AND THE PAPAS, "Show Biz Babies" by Hasbro, 1967. From left to right: DENNY DOHERTY, No. 8806, JOHN PHILLIPS, No. 8807, MICHELLE PHILLIPS, No. 8808, and CASS ELLIOT, No. 8809. All-vinyl with jointed heads. Painted features; rooted hair; open mouths with molded teeth. Each doll is about 4½in (11.5cm). They are attached to a 33-1/3 rpm record that "tells all about" the singer. Copyright by Dunhill Records, Inc. Made in Hong Kong.

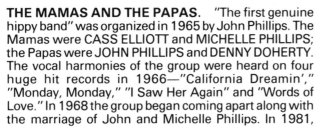

after a five-year cocaine and heroine binge, John Phillips re-formed the group with his daughter Mackenzie Phillips, who had been "on the trip" with him (for which she was fired from her part in the television show "One Day At a Time"). The other members of the new band are Denny Doherty, the other original Papa, and Elaine "Spanky" McFarlane. See also the individual original Mamas and Papas.

DOLLS:
1. THE MAMAS AND THE PAPAS. "Show Biz Babies." Hasbro, 1967. DENNY, No. 8806; JOHN, No. 8807; MICHELLE, No. 8808; CASS, No. 8809. Made in Hong Kong. 4½in (11.5cm). *Illustration 570.*

MANTLE, MICKEY. Baseball player. Born October 20, 1931. As a New York Yankees outfielder-first baseman, Mantle hit 536 career home runs. He hit a record 18 World Series home runs. In 1974 he was inducted into the Baseball Hall of Fame.

DOLLS:
1. MICKEY MANTLE. Nodder. Made in Japan, circa 1960s. All-composition with painted and molded features and hat. Wears Yankees uniform and has a fascimilie autograph on the base. 7in (17.8cm).

MANTOOTH, RANDOLPH. Actor. Born September 19, 1945. Mantooth, who early in his career claimed Indian blood, played Paramedic John Gage on "Emergency" on NBC-TV from January 1972 to September 1977. During 1978 he was on the series "Operation Petticoat."

DOLLS:
1. JOHN from EMERGENCY. L.J.N. Toys Ltd., No. 6166, 1975. Made in Hong Kong. 7¾in (19.8cm). Kevin Tighe as Roy is a companion doll. *Illustrations 571 and 572.*
2. JOHN from EMERGENCY. L.J.N. Toys Ltd., No. 6102, 1976. Made in Hong Kong. 7½in (19.1cm). Kevin Tighe as Roy is a companion doll. *Illustration 573.*

Illustration 572. RANDOLPH MANTOOTH by L.J.N. Toys.

Illustration 571. 7¾in (19.8cm) RANDOLPH MANTOOTH as John from "Emergency" by L.J.N. Toys Ltd., Item No. 6166, 1975. All-vinyl and fully-jointed with painted black hair and eyes. L.J.N. Toys dolls are blow-molded vinyl and are very light weight with poor delineation of the features. Copyright by Universal City Studios, Inc. Made in Hong Kong.

Illustration 573. 7½in (19.1cm) RANDOLPH MANTOOTH as *John* from "Emergency" by L.J.N. Toys Ltd., No. 6102, 1976. All-vinyl and fully-jointed. Painted hair and features. Copyright 1973 by Emergency Productions. Made in Hong Kong.

MARGARET. Saint and Queen of Scotland. Margaret was the queen of King Malcom III of Scotland. She promoted church reform and founded new monastaries. Her husband was killed in 1093 and she died later that year leaving three sons, Edgar, Alexander and David, all of whom became kings of Scotland. Margaret was canonized in 1250.

DOLLS:
1. ST. MARGARET, QUEEN OF SCOTLAND. Peggy Nisbet, No. P800, 1979. Plastic "collectors' doll." Made in England. About 7½in (19.1cm).

MARGARET OF ANJOU. Queen Consort of King Henry VI of England. Born circa 1430; died 1482. Henry VI was rather inept as a ruler and Margaret dominated court policy, causing her unpopularity in England. The struggle between the King's supporters and the followers of Richard, the Duke of York, led to the War of the Roses in 1455. The King and Queen were captured by the York faction in 1471. Henry died in the Tower shortly afterwards and Margaret returned to her native France, where she died in poverty.

DOLLS:
1. MARGARET OF ANJOU. Peggy Nisbet, No. P256, early 1980s. Plastic "collectors' doll." Made in England. About 7½in (19.1cm).

MARGARET ROSE. British princess. Born at Glamis Castle, Scotland, August 21, 1930. Her father was later King George VI; her mother is Queen Elizabeth, the Queen Mother; her sister is Queen Elizabeth II. In 1937,

when their father became king, Princess Margaret Rose and her older sister Elizabeth became child celebrities in whom the public was interested. Margaret Rose was the "rebel" of the sisters and was involved in some love affairs of which her family did not approve. In 1960 she married photographer Anthony Armstrong-Jones who did have some social connections. He then became the Earl of Snowden. Her children are David, the Viscount Linley, born 1961, and Lady Sarah, born 1964. She scandalized her family again in the 1970s by living on a commune, divorcing her husband and taking up with younger lovers.

DOLLS:
1. H.R.H. PRINCESS MARGARET ROSE. Chad Valley, circa 1938. Made in England. 17in (43.2cm). *Illustration 574.*
2. PRINCESS MARGARET ROSE. Liberty of London, circa 1938. All-cloth with painted and stitched features. This is from the "Coronation Group" and includes dolls of George VI, Queen Elizabeth, Mary, the Queen Mother and Princess Elizabeth. Made in England. About 6in (15.2cm).
3. MARGARET ROSE. Madame Alexander, circa 1952. 14in (25.6cm). *Illustration 575.*
4. MARGARET ROSE. Madame Alexander, No. 5023, circa 1952. 21in (53.3cm). *Illustration 576.*
5. PRINCESS MARGARET ROSE. Madame Alexander, No. 2020B, 1953. All-plastic and fully-jointed. Wears a "court gown of bluish faille taffeta." Part of the "Beaux Arts Creations" group. 18in (45.7cm).

Illustration 576. 21in (53.3cm) PRINCESS MARGARET ROSE by Madame Alexander, circa 1952. All-hard plastic and fully-jointed. Blonde mohair wig; blue sleep eyes. The dress is pink with white trim and is tagged: "MARGARET ROSE." The head is marked: "A.L." *Fran's Dolls.*

OPPOSITE PAGE. Illustration 574. 17in (43.2cm) H.R.H. PRINCESS MARGARET ROSE by Chad Valley, circa 1938. Jointed cloth doll Pressed felt head with a light brown mohair wig and blue glass inset eyes. The body is velveteen and is stuffed. Pink felt coat and hat over a pink print dress. Tag on right foot: "HYGENIC TOYS // MADE IN ENGLAND BY // CHAD VALLEY CO. LTD." Dress labeled in front: "MADE IN ENGLAND." *Edna Tinker Collection. Photograph by Jane Buchholz.*

Illustration 575. 14in (35.6cm) MARGARET ROSE by Madame Alexander, circa 1952. All-hard plastic and fully-jointed. Blonde mohair wig; blue sleep eyes with lashes. The gown is pink rayon organdy over a rayon taffeta slip. The doll is not marked. The gown is tagged "Margaret Rose." *Dolls & Stuff—Ginny's Antiques.*

6. H.R.H. PRINCESS MARGARET. Peggy Nisbet, No. P417, 1979. Plastic "collectors' doll." Made in England. About 7½in (19.1cm).
7. PRINCESS MARGARET ROSE. Tower Treasures Limited, 1979. Bisque head with painted features and a synthetic wig; bisque limbs, stuffed cloth body. Wears labeled cotton dress and straw hat. Princess Elizabeth is a companion doll. Made in England. 15in (38.1cm).

MARGARITA TERESA.   Infanta of Spain. Born 1651; died 1673. The Infanta Margarita, the daughter of King Philip IV of Spain, was married at the age of 15 to Emperor Leopold of Austria. As a child, she was the subject of two masterpieces by Spanish artist Diego Valazquez which are in the Prado in Madrid, Spain. "The Infanta Margarita Teresa" was painted about 1654; "Las Meninas" (The Maids of Honor) was painted about 1656.

DOLLS:
1. THE INFANTA MARGARITA. Doll Classics by Al Trattner, 1982. Made in Delaware. 12in (30.5cm). *Illustration 576-A.*

Illustration 576-A. 12in (30.5cm) INFANTA MARGARITA TERESA by Doll Classics by Al Trattner, 1982. All-bisque and fully-jointed. Blonde wig; brown glass eyes; pierced nostrils. Dressed in gold metallic brocade. A limited edition of 1500 dolls. Made in Delaware. Based on the painting "The Infanta Margarita Teresa" by Diego Valazquez, circa 1654. Head marked: "Doll Classics // by // Al Trattner // © 1982 // DMS // SCD // 1-82." *Photograph Courtesy of Al Trattner.*

MARIA THERESA. Empress of the Holy Roman Empire (1745-1765); Queen of Bohemia and Hungary (1740-1780). Born 1717; died 1780. In 1713 Maria Theresa succeeded to all Hapsburg lands. Her father, Emperor Charles VI, formulated the Pragmatic Sanction so that a woman could inherit where there was no male

heir, and the rulers of most European countries reluctantly went along with the plan. Later Maria Theresa had to defend her rights in The War of the Austrian Succession (1740-1748) and The Seven Years War (1756-1763) so that she could hold her throne. As a ruler, she was very popular and during her reign, Vienna became the musical capital of the world because of composers like Gluck and Mozart. She was also a model wife and mother and had sixteen children, the most famous of whom was Queen Marie Antoinette of France.

DOLLS:
1. MARIA-TERESA.   Lenci, No. 252, 1925. All-felt and fully-jointed. Painted features; mohair wig. Wears cotton and felt clothing. Mozart, No. 253, is a companion doll. Made in Italy. 20in (50.8cm).

MARIE ANTOINETTE.   Queen of France. Born 1755; died 1793. Marie Antoinette was the consort of Louis XVI and the daughter of Holy Roman Emperor Francis I and Maria Theresa. Finding the young Louis of France inadequate as a husband, Marie Antoinette threw herself into a life of pleasure and extravagance. As France's economic woes increased, the Queen became more unpopular. She never said "Let them eat cake" during the bread famine, but it illustrates what the citizens of France thought of her. After the birth of her first son, Louis (1781-1789), she became more responsible. In 1792 the King and Queen, the Princess Royale and the Dauphin Louis were imprisoned when the leaders of the French Revolution determined that their bumbling was the cause of France's problems. In 1793 Marie Antoinette, age 38, looked like an old woman as she was led to the guillotine after spending more than a year in prison under terrible conditions. Like Louis before her, she faced her execution calmly. Any faults that Marie Antoinette may have had should be expiated by the brutality of her time in prison, the pleasure her jailers took in informing her how they were abusing her eight year old son who was kept apart from her, and the unfairness of her trial. The Dauphin Louis (considered Louis XVII after the execution of Louis XVI in January 1793) died in prison in 1795 at age 10. Madame Royale died in 1851 at age 73.

DOLLS:
Many cheaply constructed dolls and many "souvenir dolls" represent Queen Marie Antoinette of France. These are not considered here.
1. MARIE ANTOINETTE.   Peggy Nisbet, No. H215, 1970s. Plastic "collectors' doll." This is from a series called "The French Court" and includes Madame du Barry, No. H271, and Madame Pompadour, No. H227. Made in England. About 7½in (19.1cm).
2. MARIE ANTOINETTE.   Peggy Nisbet, No. P459, 1970s. Plastic "collectors' doll." King Louis XVI, No. P458, is a companion doll. Made in England. About 7½in (19.1cm). *Illustration 564.*

MARIN DOLLS. José Marín Verdugo of southern Spain began making dolls in 1929, and his dolls are still in production. The first dolls were made of fired clay and they represented folkloric "types," dressed in regional Spanish costumes. Over the years hundreds of different models have been added to the line. The dolls are now made of vinyl and plastic. They are dressed in regional costumes as real Spanish bullfighters, and many of them also represent other well-known persons, particularly entertainers from Spain. Like the dolls from most doll companies, a single model is used for various completed dolls. One of the loveliest dolls produced by Marín was Jacqueline Kennedy as a widow, dressed in black, which was a real "portrait doll" in a limited edition. The dolls are all marked with a paper label attached to the clothing. As most of the celebrities portrayed in doll form are not well-known outside of Spain and are not easily available in the United States, the Marín dolls shown in *Illustrations 577* through *581* are included to show samples of the production of this company. More information on the Marin dolls is found in *Collectible Dolls in National Costume* (Hobby House Press, 1977) by the author.

Illustration 579. 10¼in (26.1cm) Flamenco dancer JUAN MONTIJO by Marín, No. 485, circa 1960s. All-heavy vinyl; jointed at the arms. Black wig; painted features. Marked with a paper tag, as all the Marin dolls are. Made in Spain.

Illustration 577. 9¾in (24.9cm) Flamenco dancers NIÑA ALCAZABA, No. 411, and ANTONIO ARACENA, No. 408, by Marín, circa 1960s. All-heavy vinyl and jointed at the arms. Black wigs; painted features. Marked with a paper tag that carries on the front: "MARIN // (picture of a girl) // CHICLANA // (ESPAÑA) // MADE IN SPAIN." The two dancers performed in nightclubs in Spain.

Illustration 580. 11½in (29.2cm) DIEGO PUERTA by Marín, late 1960s. All-heavy vinyl; jointed at the arms. Black wig; painted features. The *traje de luces* (suit of lights) is bright red satin and is trimmed with gold braid. The *muleta* (red flanned cape) is held in place with a plastic sword. The bull is also from Marin. Made in Spain.

LEFT: *Illustration 578.* 9¾in (24.9cm) NIÑA ALCAZABA by Marin.

RIGHT: *Illustration 581.* 11½in (29.2cm) DIEGO PUERTA with a post card from Spain that is a reproduction of a poster for a bullfight in the Plaza de Toros of Madrid.

MARIS, ROGER. Baseball player. Born Roger Eugene Maris, September 19, 1934, in Hibbing, Minnesota. Maris was a New York Yankee outfielder from 1960 to 1966. He hit a record 61 home runs in 1961.

DOLLS:
1. ROGER MARIS. Nodder. 1960. Made in Japan. 4¾in (12.2cm). *Illustration 582.*

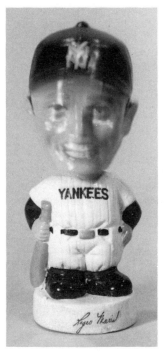

Illustration 582. 4¾in (12.2cm) ROGER MARIS, a "bobble-head," or "nodder," made in Japan in the 1960s. Composition over plaster with painted features and clothing. Photographed while "bobbing." *Phyllis Houston Collection.*

MARLOWE, MARION. Singer. Born March 7, 1929. From 1950 to 1955 soprano Marion Marlowe sang on the CBS-TV show "Arthur Godfrey and His Friends." She was fired in 1955 along with singers Haleloke and the Mariners. This came after Godfrey fired several other regulars on the program. Marion Marlowe's offense to Godfrey was that she became engaged to his producer, Larry Puck, which infuriated him. After Godfrey fired her, Marlowe signed an exclusive contract with Ed Sullivan. She is now retired from show business.

DOLLS:
1. to 3.
    MARION MARLOWE. Valentine Dolls, Inc., 1954. Vinyl head with rooted dark hair; "beauty spot" on the right cheek. The body is fully-jointed hard plastic and the doll is a walker. The gown, designed by Marion Marlowe, is an "all over lace formal on taffeta, trimmed with exquisite antique brocade." Sizes of 18in (45.7cm), 22in (55.9cm) and 25in (63.5cm).

MARSHALL, PENNY. Actress. Born October 15, 1942, in the Bronx, New York. Penny Marshall began as an actress on television in the 1950s. By the 1960s she was appearing in supporting roles on both television and in films. She was a semi-regular in the television series "The Odd Couple" from 1971 to 1975 and was in "Paul Sands in Friends and Lovers" from September 1974 to January 1975. Since January 27, 1976, she has played Laverne in the top-rated comedy series "Laverne and Shirley." Her second husband is actor Rob ("All in the Family") Reiner, the son of actor-director Carl Reiner.

DOLLS:
1. LAVERNE AND SHIRLEY. Mego, No. 86500/1, 1977. Made in Hong Kong. 11½in (29.2cm). *Illustration 584.*
SEE: LAVERNE AND SHIRLEY.

Illustration 583. Penny Marshall and Cindy Williams.

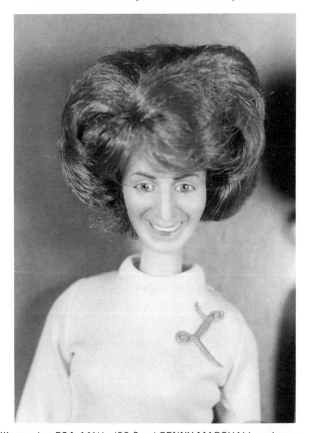

Illustration 584. 11½in (29.2cm) PENNY MARSHALL as *Laverne* from "Laverne and Shirley" by Mego, No. 86500/1, 1977. (The doll came in a set with Cindy Williams as *Shirley.*) All-vinyl and fully-jointed. Rooted reddish-brown hair; green painted eyes. Head marked: " © PARAMOUNT // PICT. CORP." Back marked: " © MEGO OF HONG KONG // 1977 // MADE IN HONG KONG." *Shirley Buchholz Collection.*

MARTIN, DEAN. Actor, singer. Born Dino Paul Crocetti on June 7, 1917, in Steubenville, Ohio. Dean Martin began his professional career as a singer and joined with comedian Jerry Lewis in 1946. The team enjoyed great popularity but they split in 1956. Dean Martin appeared on many television shows with and without Jerry Lewis and had his own program, "The Dean Martin Show," on NBC-TV from September 1965 to May 1974. He was in many films, including the Matt Helm series of spoofs, in which he played a James Bond-type adventurer.

DOLLS:
1. DEAN MARTIN-JERRY LEWIS PUPPET. National Mask and Puppet Corp., 1952. Vinyl head with a cloth body. Painted features. One side of the head is Jerry Lewis; the reverse is Dean Martin.
SEE: LEWIS, JERRY.

MARTIN, LORI. Actress. Young Lori Martin played Velvet Brown on the television program "National Velvet" on NBC-TV from September 1960 to September 1962. Apparently she was unknown before this time and has not been heard from since.

DOLLS:
1. NATIONAL VELVET/LORI MARTIN. Ideal, 1961. 36in (91.4cm). *Illustrations 585* and *586.*

Illustration 586. LORI MARTIN. *Barbara DeVault Collection.*

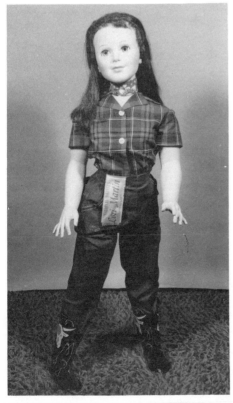

Illustration 585. 36in (91.4cm) LORI MARTIN as *Velvet Brown* from "National Velvet" by Ideal, 1961. Vinyl head with rooted dark brown hair; the remainder is plastic. Fully-jointed with a twist waist and twist ankles. Blue sleep eyes with lashes. The original boots are made of vinyl. Head marked: "METRO GOLDWYN MAYER INC. // MFG BY // IDEAL TOY CORP. // 38." Back marked: " © IDEAL TOY CORP. // G-38." The cloth tag also tells that the character is copyrighted by Metro, Goldwyn Mayer Inc. Note: Some Lori Martin dolls measure 38in (96.5cm). *Barbara DeVault Collection.*

MARTIN, MARY. Singer, actress. Born December 1, 1913, in Texas. During the 1930s and the 1940s Mary Martin appeared in a number of films that were not of the first class. She became more successful on Broadway playing Nellie Forbush in "South Pacific" (played by Mitzi Gaynor in the movie); the title role in "Peter Pan," which she repeated many times for television; Maria in "The Sound of Music" (played by Julie Andrews in the movie); and others. Her son is actor Larry Hagman, J.R. of "Dallas."

DOLLS:
1. MARY MARTIN. Madame Alexander, 1949. All-hard plastic and fully-jointed. Curly caracul wig; sleep eyes (usually brown, can be blue) with lashes. Dressed in a white sailor suit from "South Pacific" with her name embroidered on the top. 14-14½in (35.6cm-36.9cm).
2. MARY MARTIN. Madame Alexander, 1950. All-hard plastic and fully-jointed. Caracul wig; sleep eyes with lashes. Dressed in a long white gown from "South Pacific" for the "Some Enchanted Evening" number. 14in (35.6cm).
3. MARY MARTIN. Madame Alexander, 1950. Same as the above in the 17in (43.2cm) size. *Illustration 587.*

Illustration 587. 17in (43.2cm) MARY MARTIN from "South Pacific" by Madame Alexander, 1950. All-hard plastic and fully-jointed. Blonde caracul wig; blue sleep eyes with lashes. The evening gown is white. *Ted Menten Collection. Photograph by Ted Menten.*

MARX, GROUCHO. Comedian. Born Julius Henry Marx 1890; died 1977. The five Marx Brothers were encouraged to enter show business by their mother. In vaudeville Harpo, Groucho, Zeppo, Chico and Gummo were a singing act. When they switched to comedy they became more successful. The Marx Brothers made several slapstick comedy films together from 1929 to 1950. Character actress Margaret Dumont was the foil of their hilarious pranks in several of these movies. Groucho also appeared in other films until 1968 and authored several autobiographical books that drew from his comedy material. With an ever-present cigar in his hand, Groucho hosted the quiz/audience participation show "You Bet Your Life" on NBC-TV from October 1950 to September 1961. Before he died Groucho was senile and frail and was involved with a much younger woman, which led to a fight over his estate.

DOLLS:
1. GROUCHO MARX hand puppet.   Ralph A. Freundlich, Inc., 1939. Details unknown; advertised in *Playthings,* April, 1939. Harpo Marx hand puppet advertised as a companion piece.
2. GROUCHO MARX.   La Nina, circa 1979. Made in Barcelona, Spain. 22in (55.9cm). *Illustration 588.*
3. GROUCHO MARX.   Juro (Eegee), No. 30, 1981. 30in (76.2cm). *Illustration 589.*

Illustration 588. 22in (55.9cm) GROUCHO MARX by La Nina, circa 1979. All-stuffed cloth. Black yarn hair, button eyes, appliqued moustache. Wears a tuxedo with a coat of black felt with long tails; black felt shoes; wire rimmed glasses; felt cigar attached to mouth. Made in Barcelona, Spain.

Illustration 589. 30in (76.2cm) GROUCHO MARX ventriloquist doll by Juro (a division of Eegee, Goldberger Doll Mfg. Co., Inc.), No. 30, 1981. Vinyl head and hands; stuffed cloth body. Painted black hair and painted brown eyes. The mouth operates from an elastic cord at the back of the head. Head marked: "GROUCHO MARX // © EEGEE CO. INC."

MARX, HARPO. Comedian. Born Adolph, but known as Arthur, Marx 1888; died 1964. When the Marx Brothers became a comedy team the character Harpo devised was one who never spoke a line. He acted his parts out in pantomine. With his brothers he appeared in a number of classic comedies and also acted without them in other films. In 1961 his autobiography, *Harpo Speaks!,* was published. With his curly blonde wig, his top hat, his harp and the way he chased girls in the Marx Brothers movies, many critics insist that he was the most inventive of the group.

DOLLS:
1. HARPO MARX hand puppet. Ralph A. Freundlich, Inc., 1939. Details unknown; advertised in *Playthings,* April 1939. Groucho Marx hand puppet advertised as a companion piece.

MARY I ("BLOODY MARY"). Queen of England from 1553 to 1558. Born 1516; died 1558. Mary was the daughter of Henry VIII and Catherine of Aragon. After her parents' divorce, Mary was forced to declare herself illegitimate and to renounce the Catholic Church. When Henry VIII died his son, Edward VI, became king. When Edward died a brief claim was placed on the throne by Lady Jane Grey. Then Mary became legitimate again and was crowned Queen. She was hated because of her unpopular alliance with Catholic Spain with her marriage to Philip II, the reestablishment of Papal authority and her persecution of Protestants. For this she earned the name "Bloody Mary." It shows the strength of Protestantism in England, as Mary only persecuted about 300 Protestants, as compared with the thousands of Catholics later dispatched by her stepsister, Elizabeth I.

DOLLS:
1. QUEEN MARY I (BLOODY MARY). Peggy Nisbet, No. P454, 1970s. Plastic "collectors' doll." Made in England. About 7½in (19.1cm).

MARY II. Queen of England from 1689 to 1694. Born 1662; died 1694. Mary was the daughter of Anne Hyde and King James II of England, and she was raised as a Protestant. When James married a second wife, the Catholic Mary Modena of France, after the death of Anne Hyde, a son was born and he was baptized Catholic. This led to the Glorious Revolution of 1688 during which James and his new family were driven into exile in France because of the threat that the Catholic son, James Stuart, might one day be King. In 1677 Mary had married William of Orange, a Protestant Dutch prince. To insure that England remain Protestant, William and Mary were invited to become King and Queen of England. At the same time Parliament passed a law declaring that no Catholic could ever sit on the throne of England. The problem never arose again.

DOLLS:
1. QUEEN MARY II. Peggy Nisbet, No. P452, 1970s. King William III (William of Orange), No. P453, is a companion doll. Made in England. 7½in (19.1cm). *Illustration 590.*

Illustration 590. 7½in (19.1cm) QUEEN MARY II, No. P452, and KING WILLIAM III, No. P453, by Peggy Nisbet, 1970s. All-hard plastic and jointed only at the arms. Mohair wigs and painted features. Made in England. *Photograph Courtesy of House of Nisbet.*

MARY. Queen consort of George V and mother of Edward VIII and George VI of Great Britain. Born 1867; died 1953. As Princess Mary of Teck, she married the eldest son of Edward VII in 1893. Their reign (1910-1936) was dominated by World War I. It is said that Mary never forgave her son, Edward VIII, for marrying Mrs. Simpson, which caused his abdication, and that she always refused to "receive" Mrs. Simpson, who became the Duchess of Windsor.

DOLLS:
1. QUEEN MARY. Liberty of London, circa 1938. All-cloth with stitched and painted features. Part of the "Coronation Group" which includes George VI, Queen Elizabeth, Princess Elizabeth and Princess Margaret Rose. Made in England. 9in (22.9cm).
2. QUEEN MARY CONSORT OF KING GEORGE V. Peggy Nisbet, No. P710, 1970s. Plastic "collectors doll," dressed in State Robes. Part of the series called "The House of Windsor, Portrait Series," which includes King George V, No. P709, and King Edward VIII, Duke of Windsor, No. P711. Made in England. About 7½in (19.1cm).
3. QUEEN MOTHER MARY. Tower Treasures, 1980. Bone china head and limbs; white simulated leather body. Mohair wig; painted features. Limited edition of 790 dolls. Made in England. 8in (20.3cm).

MARY QUEEN OF SCOTS. Born 1542; died 1587. Mary was the only child of James V of Scotland and Mary of Guise. Her mother sent her to France as a child, and she married King Francis II in 1558 when she was 16. He died two years later and she returned to Scotland, where she became Queen in 1561. She was attacked by John Knox for her refusal to abandon Catholicism, but her charm and her intelligence made her rather popular. In 1565 she married her cousin, Lord Darnley, to reinforce her claim on the throne of England.

Mary despised her husband because of his weak nature, and he joined a plot of Protestants who wanted her murdered. (Lord Darnley was having an affair with one of Mary's advisors.) Mary escaped to loyal nobles and her son was born soon after. Then she fell in love with the Earl of Bothwell, who was suspected of murdering her husband. Bothwell was acquitted and Mary married him. Scotland was outraged so Mary abdicated and fled to England. Queen Elizabeth, her cousin, welcomed her but imprisoned her. In prison Mary became involved in plots with the English Catholics, the French and the Spanish, most of them dealing with her claim on the throne of England. (This supposed that Elizabeth was illigitimate and had no right to the throne.) Mary was tried for treason and beheaded in 1587. In her later years Mary was deeply religious, and she withstood the trial and the execution with great dignity. (Her calm manner and her willingness to assist the executioner unnerved him so much that his first blow split her head open instead of severing it.) She probably was guilty of entering the plot to have Elizabeth killed, and Elizabeth knew that her throne would never be secure as long as her cousin, Mary, was alive. When Elizabeth died in 1603 Mary's son became King James I of England. He was already King James VI of Scotland, so this united the two kingdoms.

DOLLS:
1. MARY QUEEN OF SCOTS. Peggy Nisbet, No. H209, 1970s. Plastic "collectors' doll," dressed in Fotheringay Costume. Made in England. About 7½in (19.1cm).
2. MARY QUEEN OF SCOTS. Peggy Nisbet, No. P608, 1970s. Plastic "collectors' doll," dressed in Wedding Dress. Made in England. About 7½in (19.1cm).
3. MARY, QUEEN OF SCOTS. Tower Treasures, 1979. Bone china head and limbs; white simulated leather body. Mohair wig; painted features. Made in England. 8in (20.3cm).

MAYHEW, PETER. Actor. Mayhew played Chewbacca in *Star Wars* in 1977 and *The Empire Strikes Back* in 1980.
DOLLS:
1. CHEWBACCA. Kenner, No. 38210, 1978. All-vinyl and fully-jointed figure with modeling that resembles an ape. Made in Hong Kong. 4¼in (10.9cm).
2. CHEWBACCA. Kenner, No. 38600, 1978. All-plastic and fully-jointed figure with modeling that resembles an ape. Made in Hong Kong. 15in (38.1cm).
SEE: STAR WARS.

McARDLE, ANDREA. Actress. Born in Philadelphia, Pennsylvania, on November 5, 1963. In 1977 Andrea McArdle dazzled audiences and critics with her portrayal of the lead in the Broadway hit musical play "Annie." She received a Tony nomination for her singing and dancing, but lost to Dorothy Louden who was also in the play. After Andrea McArdle grew out of the role she left the cast of "Annie." In the biographical film for television *Rainbow* (1978) she played the young Judy Garland.

DOLLS:
1. ANNIE AND HER DOG SANDY FROM THE HIT MUSICAL. Knickerbocker Toy Co., No. 3851, 1977. Made in Taiwan. 15in (38.1cm). *Illustration 590-A.*
SEE: ANNIE.

Illustration 590-A. 15in (38.1cm) ANDREA McARDLE as *Annie* from the Broadway play by Knickerbocker Toy Co., No. 3851, 1977. All-cloth with jointed arms and legs. Orange yarn hair, painted features. Removable dress; shoes and socks sewn in place. Copyright by the *Chicago Tribune.* Made in Taiwan. Sandy, in the dress pocket, is 1½in (3.8cm) and is plush with appliqued features.

McCALLUM, DAVID. Actor. Born 1933 in Glasgow, Scotland. McCallum began his show business career as a child playing classical music on the oboe but became an actor and entered British films in the late 1950s. By the 1960s he settled in Hollywood and appeared in

Illustration 591. 12¼in (31.2cm) DAVID McCALLUM as *Ilia Kuryakin* from "The Man from U.N.C.L.E." by Gilbert, 1965. All-vinyl with painted hair and features. Head marked with illegible symbols. *Shirley Buchholz Collection.*

American movies. His greatest popularity came from playing the blonde Russian secret agent Ilya Kuryakin on "The Man From U.N.C.L.E." on NBC-TV from September 1964 to January 1968.

DOLLS:
1. ILYA KURYAKIN from THE MAN FROM U.N.C.L.E. Gilbert, 1965. Robert Vaughn as Napoleon Solo is a companion doll. 12¼in (31.2cm). *Illustration 591*.

McCARTHY, NEIL. Actor. English supporting actor Neil McCarthy has been in films since the 1960s. In *Clash of the Titans* (1981) he played Calibos.

DOLLS:
1. CALIBOS from CLASH OF THE TITANS. Mattel, No. 3270, 1981. Made in the Phillipines. 4in (10.2cm). *Illustration 592*.
SEE: CLASH OF THE TITANS.

Illustration 592. 4in (10.2cm) NEIL McCARTHY as *Calibos* from *Clash of the Titans* by Mattel, No. 3270, 1981. All-vinyl and fully-jointed. Painted hair, features and clothing; attached horns and tail. Copyright by Metro-Goldwyn-Mayer Film Co. Made in the Philippines.

McCARTNEY, PAUL. Singer, musician, songwriter. Born June 18, 1942, in Liverpool, England. McCartney was the most successful of the solo Beatles. After the celebrated breakup of the Beatles, he formed a touring ensemble called Wings in 1971. Wings consisted of his wife Linda, Denny Laine, Denny Seiwell and Henry McCullough. Wings is still the name of McCartney's touring group, but Laine is the only permanent member. In 1980 Paul McCartney spent several well-publicized days in jail in Japan for the possession of marijuana.

DOLLS:
1. THE BOB'N HEAD BEATLES. Car Mascots, Inc., 1964. Made in Japan. 7¾in (19.8cm). *Illustration 593*.
2. THE BOB'N HEAD BEATLES. 1964. Nodders like the above doll, in hard plastic. 4in (10.2cm).
3. PAUL McCARTNEY. Remco, No. 1803, 1964. 4⅞in (12.4cm). *Illustration 594*.

4. PAUL McCARTNEY. Pelham Puppets, 1965. Strung marionette. Composition head and hands; wooden feet; jointed wooden segments for the body. Black fur wig; painted features. Made in England. About 13in (33cm). See *Illustration 107*.
SEE: BEATLES, THE

Illustration 593. 7¾in (19.8cm) PAUL McCARTNEY "nodder," or "bobble head," made in Japan by Car Mascots, Inc., 1964. Papier-mâché head with painted features; painted plaster body attached to a base.

Illustration 594. 4⅞in (12.4cm) PAUL McCARTNEY of the Beatles by Remco, No. 1803, 1964. Vinyl head on a plastic body. Rooted dark brown hair; painted features. Head marked: "86." Body marked: "THE // BEATLES // T.M. // LIC. BY SELTAEB INC. // © NEWS ENT. LTD. 1964." (The guitar is missing.) *Wanda Lodwick Collection.*

Illustration 595. 10in (25.4cm) PAUL McCART-NEY bubble bath bottle (*not a doll*) from Colgate-Palmolive, 1965. The bottle is plastic; the head is firm, but thin plastic. Painted features. The bottom is marked: " © 1965 NEWS ENTERPRISES LTD. // COL-GATE-PALMOLIVE CO. // NEW YORK, N.Y. // IMCO // 11 fl. oz." *Fran's Dolls.*

McDOWALL, RODDY. Actor. Born Roderick Andrew Anthony Jude McDowall on September 17, 1928, in London, England. Roddy McDowall began as a child actor in British films in the late 1930s. During the Blitz of 1940 he was evacuated to Hollywood and won even more popularity as a juvenile actor in such films as *How Green Was My Valley* (1941) and *Lassie Come Home* (1942). By the 1950s he was playing a broad range of adult roles on the stage, television and in films. In the 1968 film *Planet of the Apes* he played Cornelius; in the 1974 television show "Planet of the Apes" he played Galen. Roddy McDowall is also a highly respected portrait photographer and a collector of old motion pictures.

Illustration 597. 6in (15.2cm) "SPANKY" Mc-FARLAND from *Our Gang* by Mego, No. 61600/2, 1975. All-vinyl and fully-jointed. Painted brown hair with molded beanie. Copyright by Metro-Goldwyn-Mayer Inc. *Wanda Lodwick Collection.*

Illustration 596. 8in (20.3cm) RODDY McDOWALL as *Cornelius* from *Planet of the Apes* by Mego, No. 1961, 1974. All-vinyl and fully-jointed. Painted hair and features. Head marked: " © APJAC PROD. INC. & // 20th CENTURY—FOX FILM CORP. 1974." Back marked: " © MEGO CORP. // REG. U.S. PAT. OFF. // PAT. PENDING // HONG KONG // MCMLXXI."

DOLLS:
1. CORNELIUS from PLANET OF THE APES. Mego, No. 1961, 1974. Made in Hong Kong. 8in (20.3cm). *Illustration 596.*
2. GALEN from PLANET OF THE APES. Mego, No. 50900/6, 1975. All-vinyl and fully-jointed. The head is molded to look like an ape, like doll No. 1. Made in Hong Kong. 8in (20.3cm).
SEE: PLANET OF THE APES.

McFARLAND, SPANKY. Child actor. Born George Robert Phillips McFarland in Dallas, Texas, on October 2, 1928. Spanky appeared in 95 *Our Gang* comedies in 11 years. He was hired to replace Joe Cobb as the fat boy. He also appeared in other films until 1944, when he returned to Texas to work in nonacting jobs. He was not in the 1974 film *Moonrunners,* although there was a Spanky McFarland listed in the cast. He also had nothing to do with the 1960s rock group called Spanky and Our Gang. Spanky's brother, Tom, was also in the *Our Gang* comedies, but he seldom had any lines.
DOLLS:
1. SPANKY from OUR GANG. Mego, No. 61600/2, 1975. 6in (15.2cm). *Illustration 597.*
SEE: OUR GANG.

McKEAN, MICHAEL. Actor, musician, songwriter. Born October 17, ?. McKean joined with David L. Lander to form the comedy group The Credibility Gap and toured for four years. They have played Lenny and Squiggy on ABC-TV's "Laverne and Shirley" since January 27, 1976, when the show began. McKean also acted in other television programs and in some feature films.

DOLLS:
1. LENNY AND SQUIGGY from LAVERNE AND SHIRLEY. Mego, No. 86500/2, 1977. Made in Hong Kong. 12in (30.5cm). *Illustration 598.*

SEE: LAVERNE AND SHIRLEY.

Illustration 598. 12in (30.5cm) MICHAEL McKEAN as *Lenny* from "Laverne and Shirley" by Mego, No. 86500/2, 1977. (This doll came in a set with David L. Lander as Squiggy, which see.) All-vinyl and fully-jointed. Painted brown hair and painted blue eyes. Copyright by Paramount Pictures Corporation. Made in Hong Kong.

McKEEN, SUNNY. Child actor. Died at age eight in 1933. As a baby, Sunny McKeen played Baby Snookums in the two-reel silent comedy series *The Newlyweds and Their Baby* in the late 1920s. Ethlyne Clair and Syd Saylor were the bumbling young parents. By age four Sunny was earning over $15,000 a year in his own comedy series.

DOLLS:
1. SNOOKUMS. Madame Hendren, circa 1928. Composition head and arms; cloth body. Painted hair and features; open-closed mouth with painted teeth. About 12in (30.5cm). (See Loraine Burdick: *Child Star Dolls and Toys Revised*, Quest-Eridon Books, 1977.)

McKINLEY, WILLIAM. President of the United States from 1897 to 1901. Born 1843; died 1901. As a Republican United States Representative from Ohio (1877-1891) McKinley sponsored the highly-protective McKinley Tariff Act. The skill of his good friend, millionaire Mark Hanna of Cleveland, Ohio, got him elected Presi-

dent in 1896. It was the flexible conscience of McKinley that made the United States a world power. At the beginning of his Administration, as troubles were developing in the Spanish colony of Cuba, he said that forced annexation was a "criminal aggression." After a brief and successful war in which the United States gained the Philippine Islands, he credited it to "the hand of Almighty God." Then he signed a bill to annex Hawaii and supported the Open Door policy in China. He was reelected to a second term in 1900 but while attending the Pan American Exposition in Buffalo, New York, on September 6, 1901, he was shot by Leon Czolgosz, an anarchist. He died on September 14, 1901, with Mark Hanna holding his hand.

DOLLS:
1. WILLIAM McKINLEY. Manufacturer unknown; made in Germany, 1900 to 1910. 15in (38.1cm). *Illustration 599.*

SEE: SPANISH-AMERICAN WAR HEROES.

McNELLIS, MAGGI. Television personality. Born June 1, 1917. Maggi McNellis was one of early television's most ubiquitous personalities and guests. She was a hostess on "Crystal Room" during August and September of 1948; her own show, "Maggi's Private Wire," ran from April to July 1949; she was a moderator on "Leave It To the Girls" from April 1949 to March 1954; and she was a team captain for the charades program "Say It With Acting" from January 1951 to February 1952.

DOLLS:
1. MAGGI McNELLIS. A "Juro Celebrity Doll" by Goldberger Doll Manufacturing Co., Inc., 1952. Details not known.

McNICHOL, KRISTY. Actress. Born September 9, 1963, in Los Angeles, California. Kristy began playing child roles on television and in films, managed by a mother who was determined that she would become a star. In 1977 and 1979 she won Emmy Awards for her part as Buddy on "Family" (ABC-TV, March and April 1976; September 1976 and May 1979; December 1979 to March 1980). Her brother, Jimmy, born 1961, who is prettier than Kristy, has had the same career direction.

DOLLS:
1. KRISTY McNICHOL AS BUDDY. Mattel, No. 1013, 1978. Made in the Phillipines. 9¼in (23.6cm). *Illustrations 600* and *601.*
2. KRISTY McNICHOL. Mego, No. 86400, 1978. Made in Hong Kong. 9½in (24.2cm). *Illustration 602.*

OPPOSITE PAGE: Illustration 599. 15in (38.1cm) WILLIAM McKINLEY, manufacturer unknown, 1900 to 1910. Bisque head; jointed composition body. Painted hair and features. Part of a series of six officers from the Spanish-American War. Made in Germany. *Courtesy of the Margaret Woodbury Strong Museum.*

Illustration 600. 9¼in (23.6cm) KRISTY McNICHOL as *Buddy* from "Family" by Mattel, No. 1013, 1978. All-vinyl and fully-jointed, including twist waist. Rooted dark brown hair; painted brown eyes; painted teeth. The original package also included a jacket, cap, skirt and sandals. Head marked: " © 1978 // SPELLING-GOLDBERG // PROD." Made in the Philippines.

Illustration 602. 9½in (24.2cm) KRISTY McNICHOL by Mego, No. 86400, 1978. All-vinyl with rooted dark brown hair and painted eyes. Head marked: "© MEGO CORP. // MADE IN HONG KONG." Back marked: "© 1977 MEGO CORP. // MADE IN HONG KONG." Copyright by Mego Corp; licensed by Armon/Halpren Attractions.

MELLER, RAQUEL. Spanish singer. Born 1888; died 1962. Raquel Meller is most famous for the 1926 French version of *Carmen*, a production designed especially for her. With a great deal of fanfare, she was brought to Hollywood to star in *The Oppressed* in 1929. She impressed neither moviegoers nor the critics. She returned to Europe, where she was very popular, to make films and to sing in nightclubs.

DOLLS:
1. RAQUEL MELLER. Lenci, 1925, No. 263. Felt head on a felt shoulder plate; muslin body. Painted features; mohair wig. Made in Italy. 28in (70cm). (See Dorothy S. Coleman: *Lenci Dolls, Fabulous Figures of Felt*, Hobby House Press, 1977, page 65.)
2. RAQUEL MELLER. Manufacturer unknown; made in France, circa 1927. 10½in (26.7cm). *Illustration 603.*

Illustration 601. KRISTY McNICHOL by Mattel.

Illustration 603. 10½in (26.7cm) RAQUEL MELLER, made in France circa 1927. Imitation molded felt head; cloth body with slim proportions. Black silk floss wig; brown painted eyes. The costume is a well-known stage outfit of Raquel Meller: Silk dress and shawl, white silk net stockings and high heeled black slippers which lace up the legs. Tag sewn to left leg: "MADE IN FRANCE." *Coleman Collection.*

MELVILLE, SAM. Actor. Born in Utah, August 20, 1940. Melville acted in films and on television, beginning in the 1960s. He played Officer Mike Danko on ABC-TV's "The Rookies" from September 1972 to July 1976.

DOLLS:
1. MIKE from THE ROOKIES. L.J.N. Toys, Ltd., No. 6101, 1976. Made in Hong Kong. 7½in (19.1cm). *Illustration 604*.

SEE: THE ROOKIES.

Illustration 605. 14in (35.6cm) HEATHER MENZIES as *Louisa* from *The Sound of Music* by Madame Alexander, 1965-1970. Vinyl with rooted blonde hair; black eyes. Head marked: "ALEXANDER // 19 © 65." *Jean Canaday Collection.*

Illustration 604. 7½in (19.1cm) SAM MELVILLE as *Mike* from "The Rookies" by L.J.N. Toys Ltd., No. 6101, 1976. All-vinyl and fully-jointed. Painted hair and features. Copyright 1973 by Spelling-Goldberg Productions. Made in Hong Kong.

MENZIES, HEATHER. Actress. Born in Toronto, Ontario, Canada, December 3, 1949. Heather Menzies debuted on the screen as Louisa in *The Sound of Music* in 1965. Later she acted in various films and television programs. She was in the 11 episodes of "Logan's Run" in the fall of 1977. In "Vega$," starring Robert Urich, she played various roles. Heather Menzies is married to Robert Urich, who was born in Totonto, Ohio. (See also ROBERT URICH.)

DOLLS:
1. LOUISA. Madame Alexander, No. 1004, 1965. All-hard plastic; fully-jointed. Part of the all-8in (20.3cm) Sound of Music set.
2. LOUISA. Madame Alexander, No. 1404, 1965-1970. Part of the large set of Sound of Music dolls, using the "Mary Ann" doll. 14in (35.6cm). *Illustrations 605* and *606*.
3. LOUISA. Madame Alexander, 1966. Same as the above only dressed in the sailor/school outfit.
4. LOUISA. Madame Alexander, No. 1104, 1971. Part of the small set of Sound of Music dolls. 9in (22.9cm). *Illustration 607*.

SEE: SOUND OF MUSIC, THE.

Illustration 606. 14in (35.6cm) HEATHER MENZIES as *Louisa* from *The Sound of Music* by Madame Alexander, 1965-1970. This is the same doll as *Illustration 605*, except that the skirt is pink instead of flowered. The shoes are replacements. *Fran's Dolls.*

Illustration 607. 9in (22.9cm) HEATHER MENZIES as *Louisa* from *The Sound of Music* by Madame Alexander, No. 1104, 1971. All-hard plastic and fully-jointed, including bending knees. Dark blonde wig; blue sleep eyes with molded lashes and blue eye shadow. Back marked: "MME // ALEXANDER."

Illustration 608. 4in (10.2cm) CHARLES MIDDLETON as *Ming* from *Flash Gordon The Greatest Adventure of All* by Mattel, No. 1526, 1980. All-vinyl and fully-jointed. Painted features and clothing. Copyright by King Features Syndicate, Inc. Made in Hong Kong.

MEREDITH, BURGESS. Actor; director. Born November 16, 1908, in Cleveland, Ohio. Meredith has been one of the most talented actors of the American stage and screen. His first film role was in 1936. During 1966 and 1967 he was the villain known as "The Penguin" on television's "Batman" as a guest star. His third wife (1944-1949) was actress Paulette Goddard, who had recently left Charlie Chaplin.

DOLLS:
1. PENGUIN. Mego, No. 1350, 1974. All-vinyl and fully-jointed. Part of the "Arch Enemy" series of the characters from "Batman." Made in Hong Kong. 8in (20.3cm).

MIDDLETON, CHARLES. Actor. Born 1879; died 1949. Middleton became a carnival and circus performer while in his teens. He then appeared in vaudeville, on the stage, and entered films in the late 1920s. He played character parts in more than 100 films but is best remembered as Ming the Merciless in the Flash Gordon serials in the 1930s.

DOLLS:
1. MING from FLASH GORDON. Mattel, No. 1526, 1980. Made in Hong Kong. 4in (10.2cm). *Illustration 608*.
SEE: FLASH GORDON.

MILLS, HAYLEY. Actress. Born April 18, 1946, in London, England. Hayley is the daughter of actor John Mills and his novelist-playright wife Mary Hayley Bell and is the younger sister of actress Juliet Mills. Hayley made an impressive screen debut playing a witness to a murder by actor Horst Buchholz in one of the most exciting films ever made, *Tiger Bay*, 1959. She won awards for this part and then was signed to a contract by Walt Disney. For her performance in *Pollyanna* (1960) she won a special Academy Award. She continued to play innocent children and adolescents in other Disney productions until she changed her image by appearing nude in the film *The Family Way* (1967) and moving in with producer-director Roy Boulting, who was 33 years older. They married in 1971 and later divorced.

DOLLS:
1. POLLYANNA. Uneeda, 1960. All-vinyl and fully-jointed. Rooted light blonde hair; sleep eyes with lashes; high heeled feet. Dressed in a checked cotton dress with matching pantalettes and a straw hat. Came in a trunk with extra clothing. Copyright by Walt Disney Productions. 10½in (26.7cm). (See *Illustration 36* for a similar doll.)
2. POLLYANNA. Uneeda, 1960. Same description as the above doll with non-removable molded shoes. 17in (43.2cm).
3. POLLYANNA. Uneeda, 1960. Same description as the No. 1 doll. 31in (78.7cm).
4. POLLYANNA. Uneeda, 1960. Same description as the No. 1 doll. 35in (88.9cm).

MILNE, CHRISTOPHER ROBIN. Protagonist of the Winnie-the-Pooh tales; writer. Born August 21, 1920. British writer A.A. Milne said in his autobiography (1939) that he and his wife chose to call their son Christopher and Robin, "names wasted on him who called himself Billy Moon as soon as he could talk, and has been Moon to his family and friends ever since." A.A. Milne wrote humorous verses, essays and plays from 1906 until 1924. None of these ventures were terribly successful. In 1924 *When We Were Very Young* was published. This was a collection of verses about Milne's only son, and is some of the best verses about children ever written. All of this was surpassed by two books about Christopher Robin and his toy animals— *Winnie-the-Pooh* (1926) and *The House at Pooh Corner* (1928), which have become children's classics. Christopher Robin (or Moon) was never terribly excited about his part in these books. As an adult he donated his original Winnie-the-Pooh teddy bear to a museum, glad to be rid of it. Winnie-the-Pooh achieved popularity with a new generation of children when Walt Disney released an animated film of his adventures in 1964.

DOLLS:
1. CHRISTOPHER ROBIN. Horsman, 1964. 11in (27.9cm). *Illustration 609*.
2. CHRISTOPHER ROBIN. Maker unknown, 1964. Vinyl head with painted hair and features; stuffed cloth body. His name is printed in script across the front of the shirt. Copyright by Walt Disney Productions. 19in (48.3cm).
3. CHRISTOPHER ROBIN. Gund, circa 1964. All-cloth. Copyright by Walt Disney Productions. 16in (40.6cm).
4. CHRISTOPHER ROBIN. Anne Wilkinson Designs, Ltd., No. 81CMACTOY, 1982. All-cloth and fully-jointed. Yellow yarn wig; painted features. Dressed in "mackintosh, sou'wester and wellies." Made in Cheltenham, Glouscestershire, Great Britain. 21¾in (55.3cm).

Illustration 609. 11in (27.9cm) CHRISTOPHER ROBIN MILNE with *Winnie-the-Pooh* by Horsman, 1964. Christopher Robin is all-vinyl and fully-jointed. Rooted blonde hair; painted features. Head marked: "7 // HORSMAN DOLLS INC. // 66111." Winnie-the-Pooh is 3½in (8.9cm) and is all-vinyl with a jointed head and jointed arms. The back is marked: "HORSMAN DOLLS INC. // © 1964 // WINNIE THE POOH // © 1964 DISNEY PROD. // 7." The record in the background is on the Disneyland label and is from 1965. *Jean Canaday Collection*.

5. CHRISTOPHER ROBIN. Anne Wilkinson Designs, Ltd., No. 81CHRISTOY, 1982. Same doll as the above, dressed in summer clothes, removable sun hat and sandals.

MIMIEUX, YVETTE. Actress. Born in Los Angeles, California, on January 8, 1939. Highly versatile Yvette Minieux has, besides being an actress, become involved in art, poetry, music, the dance and a wide variety of business interests. She appeared on the stage, in films and on television since 1960. In the 1979 film by Walt Disney's studios, *The Black Hole*, she was Dr. Kate McRae.

DOLLS:
1. DR. KATE McRAE from THE BLACK HOLE. Mego, No. 95010/5, 1979. Made in Hong Kong. 3¾in (9.6cm). *Illustration 610*.
2. DR. KATE McRAE from THE BLACK HOLE. Mego, 1979. All-vinyl and fully-jointed. Made in Hong Kong. Copyright by Walt Disney Productions. 12in (31.8cm).

SEE: BLACK HOLE, THE.

Illustration 610. 3¾in (9.6cm) YVETTE MIMIEUX as *Dr. Kate McRae* from *The Black Hole* by Mego, No. 95010/5, 1979. All-vinyl and fully-jointed. Painted hair, features and clothing. Copyright by Walt Disney Productions. Made in Hong Kong.

MIRANDA, CARMEN. Singer, dancer, actress. Born Maria do Carmo Miranda da Cunha on February 9, 1909, near Lisbon, Portugal; died 1955. As a child Carmen moved with her parents from Portugal to its former colony, Brazil. She sang on the radio as a youngster and became a popular recording star in Brazil. In 1939 she was brought to Broadway and later signed to a film contract by Twentieth Century-Fox. She was billed as the "Brazilian Bombshell" and tried to live up to the title with her staccato singing and her frantic dancing. She appeared in musical films for Fox during the 1940s, usually in specialty numbers. She dressed in flamboyant costumes with enormous headgear decorated with all sorts of fruit and wore high, platform

Miranda, Carmen

shoes. Dynamic Carmen lost her film contract when moralistic pressure groups united behind her. They, and studio head Darryl F. Zanuck, were outraged when it was discovered by low-angle camera shots that what was suspected was true: she did not wear undergarments under her provocative dancing costumes! Carmen Miranda died of a heart attack at 46 after performing a volatile number for a television show. Those who knew her claimed that Carmen Miranda was a real lady and when her body was flown home to Brazil, it was a cause for national mourning.

DOLLS:

There are no dolls that were actually sold as "Carmen Miranda" dolls. The Madame Alexander dolls were called only "Carmen," but the tie-in was obvious, as there was no one else like her.

1. to 6. Madame Alexander, 1941-1942. All-composition. Black mohair wigs. The catalog description called the dolls "Carmen, dressed in a Pan-American or Bahaan (sic) costume." No other dolls in foreign, or folk costumes, were advertised in the catalog.

1. 7in(17.8cm). No. 7A. Jointed arms and legs. Painted brown eyes. Back marked: "MME // ALEXANDER."
2. 9in (22.9cm). No. 9A. Fully-jointed. Painted brown eyes. *Illustrations 612* and *613.*
3. 11in (27.9cm). No. 11A. Fully-jointed. *Illustration 614.*
4. 15in (38.1cm). No. 15A. Fully-jointed.
5. 18in (45.7cm). No. 18A. *Illustration 615.*
6. 22in (55.9cm). No. 22A. Fully-jointed.

Dolls made by Dream World were also dressed in various Carmen Miranda costumes. Unmarked, circa late 1940s. 11in (27.9cm). Examples are seen in *Illustration 616.*

Illustration 617 shows that the Virga doll had a specific name. This 7¼in (18.5cm) plastic doll is typical of "cheap" costume or souvenir dolls and is not a highly desirable collectible.

Illustration 612. 9in (22.9cm) CARMEN MIRANDA by Madame Alexander, 1941-1942. All-composition and fully-jointed. The Alexander catalog described this doll as *Carmen*, "dressed in a Pan-American or Bahaan (sic) costume." Carmen dolls, as all buyers would know, tied into the popularity of movie star Carmen Miranda. The black mohair wig is in a chignon at the neck. The painted eyes are brown. The outfit is tagged "Carmen" but it has lost the headdress, earrings, jewelry and hose. The side-snap shoes are red. Back marked: "MME. ALEXANDER // NEW YORK."

Illustration 611. Carmen Miranda in *That Night in Rio*, 1941.

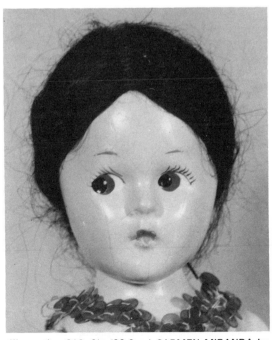

Illustration 613. 9in (22.9cm) CARMEN MIRANDA by Madame Alexander.

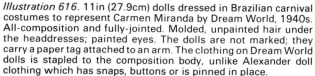

Illustration 614. 11in (27.9cm) CARMEN MIRANDA by Madame Alexander, circa 1942. All-composition and fully-jointed. Black mohair wig; blue sleep eyes with lashes and eye shadow. The doll is not marked. The dress is tagged only "Carmen" with the Alexander label. *Fran's Dolls.*

Illustration 616. 11in (27.9cm) dolls dressed in Brazilian carnival costumes to represent Carmen Miranda by Dream World, 1940s. All-composition and fully-jointed. Molded, unpainted hair under the headdresses; painted eyes. The dolls are not marked; they carry a paper tag attached to an arm. The clothing on Dream World dolls is stapled to the composition body, unlike Alexander doll clothing which has snaps, buttons or is pinned in place.

Illustration 617. 7¼in (18.5cm) costume doll that is not Carmen Miranda. This is *Del Rio* by Virga, No. 442, early 1950s. All-plastic with jointed arms only. Painted brown eyes; no hair under headdress. The original box is light pink with "Virga" printed all over it in blue.

Illustration 615. 18in (45.7cm) CARMEN MIRANDA by Madame Alexander, No. 18-A, circa 1942. All-composition and fully-jointed. Black mohair wig; blue sleep eyes with lashes. The earrings are attached to the headdress. Head marked: "ALEX-ANDER." Dress tagged "Carmen." *Shirley Buchholz Collection.*

MONKEES, THE. The Monkees were America's first totally prefabricated vocal group, put together by rock entrepreneur Don Kirshner in answer to the Beatles in 1965. The group was DAVY JONES on vocals, MIKE NESMITH on guitar and vocals, PETER TORK on bass and vocals, MICKY DOLENZ on drums and vocals. The records of the Monkees became quick hits. In 1966 alone they recorded "Daydream Believer," "Last Train to Clarksville," "I'm a Believer" and "Shades of Grey." From September 1966 to August 1968 "The Monkees" was a television show. The Monkees, like the Beatles, were unconventional and their program, like the Beatles films, utilized surrealistic film techniques with fast and slow motion and distorted focus, comic film inserts, one-liners and non sequiturs. All of this was delivered at a frantic pace and showed the rock quartet in all sorts of bizarre situations. After the group disbanded in 1969 Mike Nesmith was the only one to continue in music. In 1975 Jones and Dolenz tried to re-form the Monkees but failed.

DOLLS:
1. MONKEES hand puppet. Mattel, No. 5373, 1967. Made in Hong Kong. 10½in (26.7cm). *Illustration 619.*
2. THE MONKEES, "Show Biz Babies." Hasbro, 1967. PETER, No. 8801; DAVY, No. 8802; MICKY, No. 8803, MIKE, No. 8804. Made in Hong Kong. 4in (10.2cm). *Illustration 620.*
3. CLEVER FINGER DOLLS. Remco, circa 1975. 5in (12.7cm). DAVY and MICKY only. *Illustration 621.*

Illustration 619. MONKEES hand puppet by Mattel, No. 5373, 1967. The cloth glove with a talker mechanism is 10½in (26.7cm) and the vinyl heads with painted hair and features average 2½in (6.4cm) high. From left to right the Monkees are: Micky Dolenz, Davy Jones, Mike Nesmith and Peter Tork. The cloth tag tells that the Monkees are copyrighted by Raybert Productions, Inc. and the trademark is owned by Screen Gems, Inc. Made in Hong Kong. *Shirley Buchholz Collection.*

Illustration 618. MONKEES playing cards. Copyright 1966 by Raybert Productions Inc. The logo on the reverse of the cards appears on all Monkees collectibles, including the dolls and puppets. *Peter Bransky Collection.*

Illustration 620. THE MONKEES, "Show Biz Babies" by Hasbro, 1967. each is 4in (10.2cm). From left to right: MICKY DOLENZ, No. 8803; PETER TORK, No. 8801, DAVY JONES, No. 8802; and MIKE NESMITH, No. 8804. All-vinyl with jointed heads and wired bodies that bend "into swinging poses." Rooted brown hair; painted brown eyes; open mouths with molded teeth. Each doll came attached to a 33-1/3 rpm record that "tells all about" the star. Copyright by Raybert Productions, Inc. Trademark of Screen Gems, Inc. Made in Hong Kong.

Illustration 621. 5in (12.7cm) DAVY JONES and MICKY DOLENZ of the Monkees in a set of two finger puppets that were packaged on a cardboard backing with a shrink wrap covering. Remco, circa 1975. The set is called only "Clever Finger Dolls." It was marketed at the time when Jones and Dolenz tried to re-form the Monkees. The finger puppets are the same design as *Adventure Boy*, No. 3171, from Remco in 1970. See the listings under each celebrity for a description of the dolls.

MONROE, ELIZABETH. Wife of President James Monroe. Born 1769; died 1830. James Monroe was the 5th President of the United States and his two terms (1917-1825) were known as the "Era of Good Feelings" because of the relative peace and prosperity of the times. When Elizabeth Kortright Monroe died in 1830, she was survived by her husband and their two daughters.

DOLLS:
1. ELIZABETH MONROE. Madame Alexander, No. 1505, 1976-1978. All-vinyl and fully-jointed. Rooted auburn hair; blue sleep eyes with lashes. Dressed in a rose and brocade gown. 14in (35.6cm).
SEE: FIRST LADIES, THE.

MONTGOMERY, BABY PEGGY. SEE: BABY PEGGY.

MONTGOMERY, ELIZABETH. Actress. Born April 15, 1933. Elizabeth Montgomery is the daughter of actor Robert Montgomery. She has acted in films and on television in many "TV movies." From September 1964 to July 1972 Montgomery played Samantha, a "pretty, young witch" on "Bewitched" for ABC-TV. She was also Serena, Samantha's "mischevious look-alike cousin."
DOLLS:
1. SAMANTHA, THE WITCH. Ideal, 1965. 12in (30.5cm). *Illustration 622.*

Illustration 622. 12in (30.5cm) ELIZABETH MONTGOMERY as *Samantha, the Witch* from "Bewitched" by Ideal, 1965. Vinyl head, arms and legs; plastic torso. Rooted blonde hair; painted brown eyes with eye shadow. The costume is bright red with various colors of metalic glitter applied to it; the high-heel shoes are also red. Head marked: "© 1965 // IDEAL TOY CORP. // W12-3." Right hip marked: " © 1965 // IDEAL // 1 M-12." Samantha is missing her broom. This is the same doll as Ideal's *Glamour Misty.*

MOORE, CLAYTON. SEE: LONE RANGER, THE.

MOORE, ROGER. Actor. Born October 14, 1928, in London, England. Moore has been a leading man in British and American films and TV since the late 1940s. On television he was in the series "Ivanhoe," a British syndication, 1957; "The Alaskans," from October 1959 to September 1960 on ABC-TV; "Maverick," for ABC-TV during the 1960-1961 season; "The Saint," on NBC-TV from May 1967 to September 1969; and "The Persuaders," September 1971 to June 1972 on ABC-TV. Moore's big break came in 1973 when he began to play super-hero James Bond in the movies.
DOLLS:
1. JAMES BOND from MOONRAKER. Mego, No. 96001, 1979. Made in Hong Kong. 12½in (31.8cm). *Illustration 623.*
SEE: JAMES BOND.

Illustration 623. 12½in (31.8cm) ROGER MOORE as *James Bond* from *Moonraker* by Mego, No. 96001, 1979. All-vinyl and fully-jointed. Painted brown hair and painted blue eyes. The modeling is so precise that the doll even has Roger Moore's mole on the face. Dark skin tones. Head marked: " © 1979 EON // PRODUCTIONS LTD." Back marked: " © MEGO CORP 1977 // MADE IN HONG KONG." Copyright by Eon Productions, Ltd. and Gilrose Publications, Ltd.

MORGAN, HARRY (HENRY). Actor. Born Harry Bratsburg on April 10, 1915. He was once known as Henry Morgan but this caused confusion because of the other Henry Morgan, the cynical TV comedian. Harry Morgan has played many character parts on stage, in films and on television since the 1940s. He had a regular role in eight different television shows. They are "December Bride," CBS, October 1954 to April 1961; Pete in "Pete and Gladys," CBS, September 1960 to September 1962; a member of the repertory company of "The Richard Boone Show" on NBC from September 1963 to September 1964; "Kentucky Jones" on NBC, September 1964 to September 1965; Officer Bill Gannon on "Dragnet" from 1967 to 1970 (The NBC show ran from January 1952 to September 1970); "The D.A.," NBC from September 1971 to January 1972; "Hec Ramsey," NBC from October 1972 to August 1974; and as Colonel Potter on "M*A*S*H," CBS since the fall of 1975, replacing McLean Stevenson as Colonel Blake.

DOLLS:
1. COL. POTTER (COLONEL SHERMAN POTTER). Tristar International, Ltd., Series No. 4100, 1982. All-vinyl and fully-jointed. Painted features and clothing. Made in Hong Kong. 3¾in (9.6cm).
SEE: M*A*S*H.

MORSE, BARRY. Actor. Born in England in 1919. Morse has played character parts in many films and on television. On ABC-TV's "The Fugitive," September 1963 to August 1967, Morse played Lt. Gerard who persued the doctor played by David Janssen. On "Space: 1999," syndicated in 1975, he was Professor Victor Bergman.

DOLLS:
1. PROFESSOR BERGMAN from SPACE: 1999. Mattel, No. 9543, 1975. Made in Taiwan. 8¾in (22.3cm). *Illustration 624.*
SEE: SPACE: 1999.

Illustration 624. 8¾in (22.3cm) BARRY MORSE as *Professor Bergman* from "Space: 1999" by Mattel, No. 9543, 1975. All-vinyl and fully-jointed. Painted hair and features. Copyright 1973 by ATV Licensing Limited; Copyright 1975 by Mattel, Inc. Made in Taiwan. *Shirley Buchholz Collection.*

MOST, DONNY. Actor. Born August 8, 1953. Donny Most played juveniles on television and in films. He was Ralph Malph, Richie's friend, on "Happy Days" on ABC-TV when the show began in January 1974.

DOLLS:
1. RALPH from HAPPY DAYS. Mego, No. 63001/3, 1976. Made in Hong Kong. 8in (20.3cm). *Illustration 625.*
SEE: HAPPY DAYS.

Illustration 625. 8in (20.3cm) DONNY MOST as *Ralph* from "Happy Days" by Mego, No. 63001/3, 1976. All-vinyl and fully-jointed with painted hair and eyes. Head marked: " © 1976 PARAMOUNT // PICTURES CORP." Back marked: " © MEGO CORP. 1974 // REG. U.S. PAT. OFF. // PAT. PENDING // HONG KONG." Copyright by Paramount Pictures Corporation.

MOUNTBATTEN, LOUIS, 1st EARL MOUNTBATTEN OF BURMA. British admiral. Born 1900; died 1979. Mountbatten was the last living great-grandson of Queen Victoria and the uncle of Prince Philip of England. During World War II he directed commando raids on Norway and France and the Allied operations against the Japanese in Burma. He was the last British Viceroy of India. He became the NATO commander in the Mediterranean in 1952, Britian's Admiral of the Fleet in 1956, and Britain's Chief of Defense in 1959. Lord Mountbatten was widely admired in Britain. In September 1979 he was killed by a bomb planted by the IRA (Irish Republican Army) in a fishing boat off the coast of Ireland. The Ulster Freedom Fighters, a Protestant organization, warned that it would avenge the death of Mountbatten and others who had been murdered by the IRA and showed journalists a list of almost 100 IRA members who were targeted for killing. Lord Mountbatten's state funeral was the largest ever staged in England for a national hero.

DOLLS:
1. LORD MOUNTBATTEN OF BURMA. Peggy Nisbet, No. P424, 1979. Made in England. About 8in (20.3cm). *Illustration 626.*

Illustration 626. 8in (20.3cm). LORD MOUNT-BATTEN OF BURMA by Peggy Nisbet, No. P424, 1979. All-hard plastic; jointed only at the arms. Painted hair and features. Made in England. *Photograph Courtesy of House of Nisbet.*

MOZART, WOLFGANG AMADEUS. Musician; composer. Born in Salzburg, Austria, 1756; died 1791. Leopold Mozart, the court musician to the Archbishop of Salzburg, trained his son in music. At the age of five the child was composing minuets and other pieces and was proficient on both the harpsichord and the violin. He toured Europe in concert from 1762 at age six, until 1781, playing the pianoforte. He tried to secure a suitable position in Austria and finally in 1787 was appointed court composer and imperial court musician to succeed Gluck. He wrote in all forms—Masses and other church music; vocal music; instrumental pieces; chamber music; sonatas; concertos; operas; and symphonies. He died in poverty in Vienna at age 35. He was buried the next day in a ceremony attended only by the grave digger.

DOLLS:
1. MOZART. Lenci, 1925-1926, No. 253. All-felt and fully-jointed. Maria-Teresa, No. 252, is a companion doll. 20in (50.8cm).
2. MOZART. Lenci, late 1920s; early 1930s. Made in Italy. 14in (35.6cm). *Illustrations 628* and *629.*

Illustration 627. Detail from the painting "Mozart Singing His Requiem" by Thomas W. Shields, 1882. The invalid composer is seated. Of the "Requiem," a Mass for the dead, Mozart said, "I well know that I am writing this 'Requiem' for myself." It was uncompleted when he died.

Illustration 628. 14in (35.6cm) MOZART as the child prodigy by Lenci, late 1920s/early 1930s. Stiffened felt; fully-jointed. Blonde mohair wig; painted brown eyes with pale green shading underneath. The clothing with the exception of the cotton ruffle at the neck is all of felt. The flared waist coat is a pale green, lined in lavender. The breeches are lavender and so is the three-cornered hat under his left arm. Beneath the coat he wears a tan vest trimmed with flowers and six buttons. The shoes are the same shade of green as the jacket. The stockings are ribbed cotton. Stitched to the back of the coat are two cardboard tags. The first reads: "PRODVZIONE // ORIGNALE // LENCI (in script)." The second tag reads: "LENCI (in script) DI E. SCAVINI // TURIN (ITALY) // MADE IN ITALY // N MOZART (handwritten in pencil)." Patent and date information is also included with the second tag.

OPPOSITE PAGE: Illustration 629. MOZART by Lenci.

MULLENS (MULLINS), PRISCILLA. SEE: ALDEN, PRISCILLA.

THE MUNSTERS. This was a situation comedy on CBS-TV from September 24, 1964, to September 1, 1966. The Munsters considered themselves an everyday, normal American family. The neighbors saw something else: Herman, played by FRED GWYNNE, was seven feet tall and looked like Frankenstein's monster. His wife Lily, played by YVONNE DeCARLO looked like a vampire. Their son Eddie, played by Butch Patrick, was turning into, or out of, a werewolf. Grandpa, played by AL LEWIS, looked like Count Dracula, and he could change himself into a bat if the situation warranted it. The family members were friendly monsters, all looking for a better state in life. See entries under each celebrity. Of the dolls that were made of the characters from The Munsters, Herman, Lily and Grandpa are a set from Remco in 1964 and as hand puppets in 1965. See the individual celebrities and *Illustration 630*.

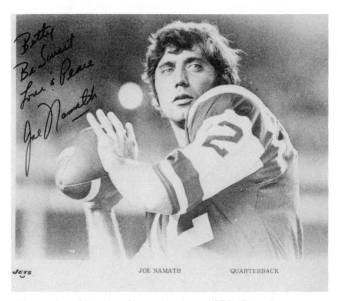

Illustration 631. Joe Namath, circa 1970. The picture was autographed to Bette Ann Axe.

Illustration 630. Three-piece set of *The Munsters* hand puppets from the *Montgomery Ward Talk of the Town Christmas Catalog 1965*. The catalog description says that, "the heads are precisely molded of vinyl. Hand fits easily into sleeve-type, cloth bodies. Even small children can manipulate them." Grandpa, Lily and Herman Munster were played by Al Lewis, Yvonne DeCarlo and Fred Gwynne.

N

NAMATH, JOE. Football player; actor. Born May 31, 1943, in Beaver Falls, Pennsylvania. "Broadway Joe" was a quarterback with the New York Jets from 1965 to 1977 and for the Los Angeles Rams from 1977 to 1978. In 1967 he passed for a record of 4007 yards. In 1969 he led the Jets to a Super Bowl victory. After 1970 Namath acted in several films. Recently he has been singing and dancing in musicals in summer stock.

DOLLS:
1. BROADWAY JOE NAMATH. Mego, 1970. Made in Hong Kong. 12in (30.5cm). *Illustration 632, 633, 634*.

Illustration 632. 12in (30.5cm) JOE NAMATH by Mego, 1970. Soft vinyl head; remainder hard vinyl. Painted hair and features. Fully-jointed. Back marked: "BROADWAY JOE" TM // © MEGO CORP. MCMLXX // MADE IN HONG KONG." *Lee Jenkins Collection*. (Note: Joe Namath personally autographed the original box for Lee Jenkins.)

Illustration 633. JOE NAMATH in one of his extra outfits by Mego. The suede suit with the flared-leg pants is very typical of the 1970s.

NARANJO, IVAN. Actor. Naranjo played Lone Wolf in a few episodes of "How the West Was Won," which was on ABC-TV in 1978 from February to May and during July and August. He later supplied the voice for Tonto in the animated cartoon version of "The Lone Ranger," which premiered on CBS-TV in September 1980.

DOLLS:

1. LONE WOLF from HOW THE WEST WAS WON. Mattel, No. 2369, 1978. James Arness as Zeb Macahan, No. 2367, is a companion doll. Made in Hong Kong. 9½in (24.2cm). *Illustrations 635* and *636.*

Illustration 635. 9½in (24.2cm) IVAN NARANJO as *Lone Wolf* from "How the West Was Won" by Mattel, No. 2369, 1978. All-vinyl and fully-jointed. Rooted dark brown hair; painted black eyes. Head marked: " © 1978 MATTEL INC." Back marked: " © 1971 MATTEL, INC. // HONG KONG US & // FOREIGN PATENTED." (This is the *Big Jim* body by Mattel.) Copyright by MGM, Inc. *Shirley Buchholz Collection.*

Illustration 634. JOE NAMATH by Mego.

Illustration 636. IVAN NARANJO by Mattel. *Shirley Buchholz Collection.*

NASSER, GAMAL ABDEL. Egyptian leader. Born January 15, 1918; died September 28, 1970. Nasser was the first President of Egypt, 1956-1958, and the first President of the United Arab Republic, 1958-1970. He was the symbol of Arab nationalism and of Arab unity. It was Nasser who led the coup d'etat against King Farouk in 1952, ending the Egyptian monarchy. As President, Nasser began construction on the Aswan Dam, forced Britain to evacuate the Suez Canal in 1956, accepted Soviet aid and arms and lost the war with Israel in 1967, in which Israel gained the Sinai Peninsula.

DOLLS:
1. NASSER. People Toys for Animals, 1969. One-piece vinyl with molded and painted features and clothing. This doll was meant to be a dog squeek toy. The original box called it a "People toy for animals and/or people; for Sinai Sit-ins." Back marked: NASH-ON-NASSER//© 1969 ROSENEL."

NAUGHTON, JAMES. Actor. Born December 6, 1945. Naughton appeared in films beginning in the 1970s. On television he was in "Faraday and Company," part of the "NBC Mystery Movie," from September 1973 to August 1974. He was Peter Burke in the 13 episodes of "Planet of the Apes" on CBS-TV in the fall of 1974.

DOLLS:
1. PETER BURKE. Mego, No. 50902, 1975. Made in Hong Kong. 7¾in (19.8cm). *Illustration 637.*
SEE: PLANET OF THE APES.

Illustration 637. 7¾in (19.8cm) JAMES NAUGHTON as *Peter Burke* from "Planet of the Apes" by Mego, No. 50902, 1975. All-vinyl and fully-jointed. Painted brown hair and painted brown eyes. Head marked: "© 1974 MEGO CORP." Made in Hong Kong.

NEEDHAM, HAL. Stuntman, stunt coordinator, second unit director, director. Born March 6, 1931, in Memphis, Tennessee. From 1956 to 1976 Needham was a stunt man for dangerous sequences in films and television shows. He also directed other stunt performers. He later became an acting director also. On television he appeared in Specials that featured stunt performances.

DOLLS:
1. HAL NEEDHAM. THE STUNTMAN. Gabriel, No. 37422, 1977. Some components made in Hong Kong. 7½in (19.1cm). *Illustration 639.*

Illustration 638. Hal Needham from original box of the doll.

Illustration 639. 7½in (19.1cm) HAL NEEDHAM by Gabriel, No. 37422, 1977. Soft vinyl head and hands; the rest is heavy vinyl. Painted hair and features; molded clothing and boots. He also wears a suede cloth vest and a vinyl hat, holster and gun. Spring action in the arms. Comes with an "Air-Ram Launcher" so that Hal can tumble, roll, leap and fly. There are also two cardboard cowboys for him to perform stunts with. No marks. Copyright by Hal Needham and Gabriel. Some components made in Hong Kong.

NEFERTITI (also NOFRETETE, NEPRETITI, NEPH-RETITI). Egyptian queen of the XVIII Dynasty. Nefertiti's husband was the Pharoah Akhenaton (or Ikhnaton), from circa 1375 B.C. to circa 1385 B.C. Akhenaton attempted to unify political, social and artistic life under monotheism, centered around the one god Aton. The priests opposed him, leading to his downfall, but his time was one of the greatest periods of Egyptian art in which painting and sculpture were more realistic. The portrait bust of Nefertiti from circa 1360 B.C. is a familiar treasure of ancient art. There is some evidence that around 1367 B.C. the beautiful Nefertiti fell from favor and lived in retirement afterwards.

DOLLS:
1. NEFERTITI. Peggy Nisbet, No. P1003, 1980. Plastic "collectors' doll." Made in England. 8in (20.3cm).

NELSON, HORATIO, VISCOUNT NELSON. English naval hero. Born 1758; died 1805. In 1798 Nelson's destruction of the French fleet ended Napoleon's plan to conquer eastern Europe. Later Nelson went to Sicily to assist the King and he prolonged his stay in Naples because Emma Hamilton, his mistress, was staying there. In 1805, again combatting Napoleon, he destroyed the combined French and Spanish fleet off Cape Trafalger on the coast of Spain. He was killed in action during the battle.

DOLLS:
1. LORD NELSON. Peggy Nisbet, No. P462, 1970s. Lady Hamilton, No. P463, is a companion doll. Made in England. About 8in (20.3cm). *Illustration 640.*
2. NELSON. Ann Parker, late 1970s. All-plastic "collectors' doll," affixed to a wooden base. Gray wig; painted features. About 11in (27.9cm).

Illustration 640. 8in (20.3cm) LORD NELSON, No. P462, and LADY HAMILTON, No. P463, by Peggy Nisbet, 1970s. All-hard plastic and jointed only at the arms. Mohair wigs and painted features. Made in England. *Photograph Courtesy of House of Nisbet.*

NESMITH, MIKE. Musician, songwriter, actor. Born December 30, 1942, in Houston, Texas. Mike Nesmith was the only true musician of the group The Monkees when it was formed in 1965 as a performing group and a television act on a series show. In 1970, after the demise of The Monkees, Nesmith put together a new group and cut an album that had a hit single, "Joanne." He has had critical success as a musician but the public is not interested. As a Monkee, he was known as "Wool Hat."

DOLLS:
1. MONKEES hand puppet. Mattel, No. 5373, 1967. Cloth glove with talking mechanism; vinyl heads with painted hair and features attached to top. Copyright by Raybert Productions, Inc. Made in Hong Kong. 10½in (26.7cm).
2. MIKE, a "Show Biz Baby." Hasbro, No. 8804, 1967. Made in Hong Kong. 4in (10.2cm). *Illustration 642.*

Illustration 641. Mike Nesmith from the Monkee's first album cover, 1966.

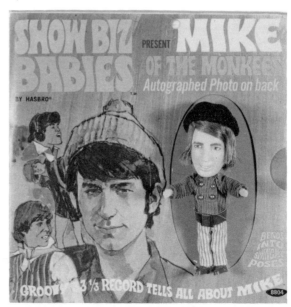

Illustration 642. 4in (10.2cm) MIKE NESMITH of the Monkees, a "Show Biz Baby" by Hasbro, No. 8804, 1967. All-vinyl; jointed only at the head; wired vinyl body that is "poseable." Rooted light brown hair; painted brown eyes. Attached to a record cover. Copyright by Raybert Productions, Inc. and a Trademark of Screen Gems, Inc. Made in Hong Kong. *Wanda Lodwick Collection.*

NEVILLE (or NEVILL), ANNE.   Consort of Richard III of England (1483-1485). Born 1456; died 1485. When the future Richard III married Anne Neville, the younger daughter of Richard Neville, the Earl of Warwick, he secured a claim to half of the vast Neville inheritance. Anne and Richard had a son, Edward, who died in 1484. Anne died in March and Richard III was killed in battle in August of 1485. See RICHARD III for his colorful life.

DOLLS:
1. LADY ANNE NEVILL.   Peggy Nisbet, No. P457, 1970s. Plastic "collectors' doll." King Richard III, No. P456, is a companion doll. Made in England. About 7½in (19.1cm).

NICHOLAS II.   Last Russian Czar. Born 1868; died 1918. Nicholas staunchly upheld the autocratic principal while the seeds of revolution were growing in Russia. In 1904-1905 Russia was involved in a war with Japan. The problem was solved to the benefit of Japan and the humiliation of Russia by the arbitration of President Theodore Roosevelt. This caused economic problems in Russia and because of that the workers in St. Petersburg, the capital, tried to petition the Czar by a peaceful demonstration in front of the Winter Palace. The Czar's troops fired on the marchers. This brought on a general strike. Nicholas still refused to liberalize the government and bring needed reforms. During World War I he personally led the army, leaving Empress Alexandra Feodorovna in charge of the government. She was already under the influence of the "holy man" Rasputin, who promised to cure their son, the heir Aleksei, of hemophilia. In March 1917 Nicholas was forced to abdicate by the Bolshevik revolutionary government. The royal family was imprisoned at Tsarskoe Selo Palace, then at Tobolsk and finally in Ekaterinburg. On the night of July 16-17, 1918, the Czar, the Empress and their five children were all shot to death by the Bolsheviks in the cellar of a house in the Russian Asian city Ekaterinburg, now called Sverdlovsk.

DOLLS:
1. TSAR NICHOLAS II.   Peggy Nisbet, No. P792, 1970s. Plastic "collectors' doll." Tsaritsa Alexandra, No. P791, is a companion doll. Made in England. About 8in (20.3cm).

NICHOLS, NICHELLE.   Actress. Born December 28, circa 1935. Nichelle Nichols began her career as a singer and dancer in nightclubs and then progressed to the stage and motion pictures. She was Lt. Uhura on "Star Trek" on NBC-TV from September 1966 to September 1969 and repeated her part in *Star Trek the Motion Picture* in 1979. After the demise of the television series, Nichols continued her interest in space travel and was appointed to the board of directors of the National Space Institute. She was asked to help in a campaign to recruit women and minorities as possible future astronauts. In recognition of her achievements in aiding the Space Program she was selected as the recipient of the Woman of the Year, Friend of Space Award for 1979, an honor bestowed by the National Society of Aerospace Education. She is now working on a novel and a stage musical. The subject of these projects is outer space.

DOLLS:
1. LT. UHURA.   Mego, No. 51200/4, 1974. Made in Hong Kong. 8in (20.3cm). *Illustration 643*.
SEE: STAR TREK.

Illustration 643. 8in (20.3cm) NICHELLE NICHOLS as *Lt. Uhura* from "Star Trek" by Mego, No. 51200/4, 1974. All-vinyl and fully-jointed. Rooted black hair; painted eyes. Copyright by Paramount Pictures Corporation. Made in Hong Kong. *Penny Caswell Collection*.

NICHOLSON, BOBBY (BOB).   Actor. Born circa 1918. Nicholson played Clarabell the Clown on "Howdy Doody" after Bob Keeshan left the role. Dolls of Clarabell were still made, but it is difficult to assign them to a celebrity, as others also played the part of Clarabell. SEE: BOB SMITH.

NIGHTINGALE, FLORENCE.   English hospital administrator and reformer of nurses' training. Born 1820; died 1910. In 1844 Florence Nightingale began visiting hospitals and studying their methods of training nurses. During the Crimean War (1854) she organized a hospital unit of 38 nurses and against bitter opposition became one of the first women to aid the wounded on the battlefield. In 1860, based on her studies and experiences, she founded a training school for nurses in St. Thomas Hospital in London, England. This was the beginning of modern nursing as a career for women. Florence Nightingale is known as "The Lady of the Lamp."

DOLLS:
1. FLORENCE NIGHTINGALE.   Ann Parker, 1970s. Plastic "collectors' doll," affixed to a wooden base. Made in England. About 11in (27.9cm).
2. FLORENCE NIGHTINGALE.   Effanbee, No. 1155, 1977-1978. Vinyl and plastic; fully jointed. Rooted blonde hair; blue sleep eyes with lashes. Dressed in a long blue gown with a white apron over it. 11in (27.9cm).

NIMOY, LEONARD. Actor. Born March 26, 1931. Nimoy trained at the Pasadena Playhouse and then played supporting roles in movies and on television after 1951. He will always be identified with the role of Mr. Spock, the pointed-eared half-human and half-Vulcan officer of the *USS Enterprise* of "Star Trek." He was Mr. Spock on the television show from September 1966 to September 1969. He was also on "Mission: Impossible" from 1969 to 1971, replacing Martin Landau who left the show. He continued with his acting career and also produced two books that are a combination of his poetry and photography. In 1976 he became the host-narrator of "In Search Of...," a syndicated documentary on television that seeks answers for some of the mysteries of everyday life (ghosts, myths and such) and "The Coral Jungle," a documentary of life in the seas, also in syndication. In 1979 he reprised his role as Mr. Spock for *Star Trek the Motion Picture*.

DOLLS:
1. MR. SPOCK. Mego, No. 51200/2, 1974. Made in Hong Kong. 8in (20.3cm). *Illustration 645.*
2. MR. SPOCK. Mego, No. 91200/2, 1979. Made in Hong Kong. 3¾in (9.6cm). *Illustration 646.*
3. MR. SPOCK. Mego, No. 91210/2, 1979. Made in Hong Kong. 12½in (31.8cm). *Illustration 647.*
4. MR. SPOCK. Knickerbocker, No. 0598, 1979. Made in Haiti and USA. 13in (33cm). *Illustration 648.*

SEE: STAR TREK.

Illustration 646. 3¾in (9.6cm) LEONARD NIMOY as *Mr. Spock* from *Star Trek the Motion Picture* by Mego, No. 91200/2, 1979. All-vinyl with painted features and clothing. Copyright by Paramount Pictures Corporation. Made in Hong Kong.

Illustration 644. Leonard Nimoy as Mr. Spock and William Shatner as Capt. James T. Kirk from "Star Trek," circa 1967.

Illustration 645. 8in (20.3cm) LEONARD NIMOY as *Mr. Spock* from "Star Trek" by Mego, No. 51200/2, 1974. All-vinyl and fully-jointed. Painted hair and features. Copyright by Paramount Pictures Corporation. Made in Hong Kong. *Penny Caswell Collection.*

Illustration 647. 12½in (31.8cm) LEONARD NIMOY as *Mr. Spock* from *Star Trek the Motion Picture* by Mego, No. 91210/2, 1979. All-vinyl and fully-jointed. Painted hair and features. Head marked: "© PPC." Back marked: "© MEGO CORP. 1977 // MADE IN HONG KONG." *Penny Caswell Collection.*

Illustration 649. 8in (20.3cm) MRS. PEGGY NISBET, Silver Anniversary Doll, Limited Edition of 1978, No. P1001. All-hard plastic with a mohair wig and painted features. The doll wears a red formal with a matching velvet cloak. Made in England. *Photograph Courtesy of House of Nisbet.*

NORTON-TAYLOR, JUDY. Actress. Born in Santa Monica, California, January 1, 1958. Judy Norton-Taylor has played Mary Ellen on "The Waltons" since the series began on September 14, 1972.

DOLLS:
1. JOHNBOY and ELLEN from THE WALTONS. Mego, No. 56000/1, 1975. Made in Hong Kong. 7½in (19.1cm). *Illustration 650.*

SEE: WALTONS, THE

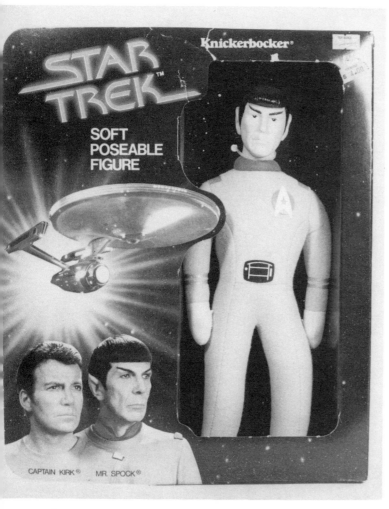

Illustration 648. 13in (33cm) LEONARD NIMOY as *Mr. Spock* from "Star Trek" by Knickerbocker, No. 0598, 1979. Jointed vinyl head with painted features; stuffed cloth body. Head marked: "© 1979 P.P.C. // K.T.C." Sewn in Haiti; finished in USA.

NISBET, PEGGY. Dollmaker. Mrs. Peggy Nisbet began making dolls in England in 1953. Her husband, her son and her daughter assisted her. This was the beginning of Peggy Nisbet Limited, now a major doll company. The dolls are dressed as historical and modern personages, British regional costumes, doll house dolls and others. If the number of a Nisbet doll is preceded by a "P" the doll is a portrait; otherwise the dolls are from standard molds. At present, Allison Wilson, Mrs. Nisbet's daughter, is in charge of production and Jack Wilson, her son-in-law, is Chairman and Managing Director of the company. Mrs. Nisbet is in charge of design and research. In 1978 Mrs. Nisbet celebrated her 25th Anniversary as a doll maker and to commmorate this event made a doll of herself. The Mrs. Peggy Nisbet doll was a "Limited Edition" model and each doll was signed by its creator. (No catalogs from the company tell how "limited" the edition was.) Mrs. Nisbet is the only commercial doll maker to have marketed a doll of herself.

DOLLS:
1. MRS. PEGGY NISBET (SILVER ANNIVERSARY DOLL). Peggy Nisbet, No. P1001, 1978. Made in England. 8in (20.3cm). *Illustration 649.*

Illustration 650. 7½in (19.1cm) JUDY NORTON-TAYLOR as *Ellen* (Mary Ellen) from "The Waltons" by Mego, No. 56000/1, 1975. All-vinyl and fully-jointed. Rooted blonde hair; painted features. Head marked: "© 1974 // LORIMAR INC." This doll is part of a set with Richard Thomas as John Boy. Made in Hong Kong. *Shirley Buchholz Collection.*

O

OAKLEY, ANNIE. Markswoman. Born Phoebe Anne Oakley Mozee, August 13, 1860, in Patterson Township, Ohio; died November 3, 1926. In 1885 Annie Oakley, an expert markswoman wih a rifle and shotgun, joined Buffalo Bill's Wild West Show. Her ability to hit the target every time was never equalled by anyone and she was the show's star attraction for 17 years. Annie Oakley was the subject of the musical play and film *Annie Get Your Gun*.

DOLLS:
1. to 4.
   ANNIE OAKLEY.   American Character, 1954. All-hard plastic and fully-jointed. Blonde saran wig; blue sleep eyes with lashes. Wears a cowgirl outfit with a fringed shirt; a holster with two guns; cowgirl boots. "Annie Oakley" is embroidered across the front of the skirt. These are the *Sweet Sue* dolls and are usually unmarked.
5. ANNIE OAKLEY.   Maker unknown, 1954. All-plastic with a jointed head and jointed arms. Blonde mohair wig; sleep eyes. These are cheap plastic dolls dressed in cowgirl costumes. 7½in (19.1cm).
6. ANNIE OAKLEY.   Excel Toy Corp., 1974. All-vinyl and fully-jointed. Painted yellow hair; painted features. Made in Hong Kong. 9¼in (23.6cm).
7. ANNIE OAKLEY.   Hallmark, No. 400DT113-3, 1979. Made in Taiwan. 7in (17.8cm). *Illustration 651*.

SEE: DAVIS, GAIL.

Illustration 651. 7in (17.8cm) ANNIE OAKLEY by Hallmark, No. 400DT113-3, 1979. All-cloth with printed features and clothing. Sewn body joints. Made in Taiwan. *Shirley Buchholz Collection*.

O'BRIAN, HUGH. Born Hugh Charles Krampe (or Krampke) on April 19, 1925. O'Brian entered films in 1950, but he is best remembered for his roles in television shows. From September 1955 to September 1961 he played the lead on "The Life and Legend of Wyatt Earp" on ABC-TV. Beginning in September 1972 he was in "Search" which lasted for a year on NBC-TV. O'Brian also acted in guest roles on many other television programs beginning in 1951 and he still does, looking about the same as ever. His name is often listed as "O'Brien."

DOLLS:
1. MARSHALL WYATT EARP from THE LIFE AND LEGEND OF WYATT EARP.   Hartland Plastics, Inc., No. 709, circa 1958. All-plastic with jointed arms; painted hair and features; painted clothing; removable hat. Made in Hartland, Wisconsin. 8in (20.3cm).

O'BRIEN, MARGARET. Actress. Born Angela Maxine O'Brien on January 15, 1937. Margaret O'Brien was considered by critics and movie audiences as the greatest child performer of the 1940s. Her range and her delivery were superb. When she cried it was for real. After *Meet Me in St. Louis* in 1944 she was given a Special Academy Award for her performances. Her contemporaries had another version of her. In her autobiography, actress Mary Astor, who was in several Margaret O'Brien films, called her "appalling" and said that she "could cry at the drop of a cue, with apparently no emotion drain whatsoever." Mary Astor said that during the filming of *Little Women*, in which she played Marmee, Margaret O'Brien would look at her "as though she were planning something very unpleasant." To prove her acting ability to Director George Cukor, Margaret O'Brien told him, "When I'm having a row with my mother, I break off to smile very sweetly to anyone who passes, then back to the row." James Robert Parish reported in *The MGM Stock Company* (Bonanza, 1972) that when Margaret was 12 her mother remarried. Margaret insisted on going along for the honeymoon. She sat up all night in an adjoining room howling as loudly as possible. Margaret got the desired results: the honeymoon and the marriage were spoiled. After Margaret O'Brien grew out of childhood her acting was inadequate, mostly because of her weak voice. She appeared in a few roles as an ingenue and faded out of sight. When she turned 21 she came into an estate reportedly valued at $200,000 to one million dollars from her childhood earnings at MGM. She was married from 1959 to 1968 to an advertising art director and when the marriage ended went to Lima, Peru, where she appeared in two films based on Edgar Allan Poe tales. She then hosted a soap opera on television in Peru and married a wealthy Peruvian business man. The couple came back to California in 1972 and Margaret O'Brien, now a plump and matronly-looking type, appeared in "Marcus Welby, M.D." with Robert Young, who was her co-star in her first major movie role, *Journey for Margaret* in 1942. She appeared in other television programs and in summer stock and in 1974 married a Scandinavian steel executive.

DOLLS:

All the Margaret O'Brien dolls were made by Madame Alexander. None are marked "Margaret O'Brien." The original clothing is labeled "Alexander" or "Madame Alexander" and does not include "Margaret O'Brien," which causes "faking" of dolls by adding a proper wig and appropriate clothing. Original advertising in Sears catalogs called the dolls a "Genuine Margaret O'Brien Doll."

1. 14in (35.6cm). 1946. All-composition and fully-jointed. Various shades of mohair wigs, usually brown or dark red, with a center part, long braids drawn up in loops and bangs. The dresses vary in style, color and design. Compare *Illustrations 656* and *658*.

2. 18in (45.7cm). 1946. Same description as the above. Examples are seen in *Illustrations 659* and *660.*

3. 21in (53.3cm). 1946. Same description as No. 1. Examples are seen in *Illustrations 661, 662* and *663.*

4. 14in (25.6cm). 1947. All-hard plastic and fully-jointed. This doll is similar in modeling to the composition examples and is called the "Margaret" head mold from Alexander. The costumes are also similar to the dolls from 1946. Hard plastic Margaret O'Brien dolls are much more scarce than composition ones are. See color section for an Illustration.

5. 18in (45.7cm). 1947. Same description as No. 4 above.

6. 21in (53.3cm). 1947. Same description as No. 4. The marking "A.L." may be an Alexander marking on the first hard plastic dolls from the company. See *Illustration 664* for an example.

Illustration 654. Margaret O'Brien, circa 1947.

Illustration 652. Margaret O'Brien and Jimmy Durante in *Music for Millions,* 1944.

Illustration 653. Margaret O'Brien, *Motion Picture Magazine,* February, 1945.

Illustration 655. Copyright, 1947, Whitman Publishing Co.

Illustration 656. Margaret O'Brien doll from original advertising, circa 1946.

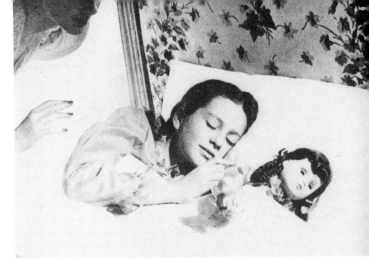

Illustration 657. Pepperell sheet ad, late 1940s, showing a Madame Alexander Margaret O'Brien doll.

Illustration 658. 14in (35.6cm) MARGARET O'BRIEN by Madame Alexander, 1946. All-composition and fully-jointed. Brown mohair wig; blue sleep eyes with lashes. The costume is not original. Head marked: "ALEXANDER." *Marge Meisinger Collection*.

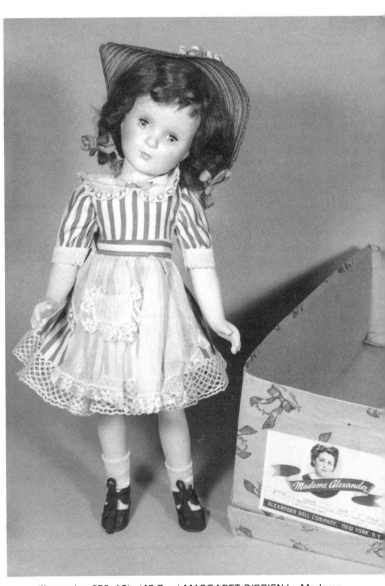

Illustration 659. 18in (45.7cm) MARGARET O'BRIEN by Madame Alexander, 1946. All-composition and fully-jointed. Dark red mohair wig; blue sleep eyes with lashes; eye shadow. Head marked: "MME ALEXANDER." Back marked: "ALEXANDER." Dress labeled: "MADAME // ALEXANDER // NEW YORK U.S.A." The original box makes no reference to Margaret O'Brien. *Wanda Lodwick Collection*.

Illustration 662. 21in (53.3cm) MARGARET O'BRIEN by Madame Alexander, 1946. All-composition and fully-jointed. Brown sleep eyes with lashes; brown mohair wig. The costume is replaced. Head and back marked: "ALEXANDER." *Barbara DeVault Collection.*

Illustration 660. 18in (45.7cm) MARGARET O'BRIEN by Madame Alexander, 1946. All-composition and fully-jointed. Brown mohair wig; blue sleep eyes with lashes. The dress is of heavy cotton and is labeled. Head and back marked: "ALEXANDER."

Illustration 661. 21in (53.3cm) MARGARET O'BRIEN by Madame Alexander, 1946. All-composition and fully-jointed. Reddish-brown mohair wig; green sleep eyes with lashes. Labeled dress. Replaced shoes. *Wanda Lodwick Collection.*

Illustration 663. 21in (53.3cm) MARGARET O'BRIEN by Madame Alexander, 1946. All-composition and fully-jointed. Dark reddish-brown mohair wig; blue sleep eyes with lashes. Head and back marked: "ALEXANDER." The tagged dress has an attached apron. *Jean Canaday Collection.*

Illustration 666. 12¼in (31.2cm) TIM O'CONNOR as *Dr. Huer* from "Buck Rogers in the 25th Century" by Mego, No. 85001/6, 1979. All-vinyl and fully-jointed. Painted gray hair; painted brown eyes. Head marked: " © 1978 ROBERT // C. DILLE." Back marked: " © MEGO CORP. 1977 // MADE IN HONG KONG."

Illustration 664. 21in (53.3cm) MARGARET O'BRIEN, probably by Madame Alexander, 1947. All-hard plastic and fully-jointed. Blue sleep eyes. The modeling on this doll is identical to the so-called "Margaret-face" Alexander dolls. The clothing and the wig are replacements. The head is marked: "A.L." *Barbara DeVault Collection.*

O'CONNOR, TIM. Actor. Veteran character actor Tim O'Connor is a familar face on television in supporting roles. He was in the cast of "Peyton Place" from 1965 to 1968. On "Buck Rogers in the 25th Century" he played Dr. Huer, the earth scientist, in the first version of the show on NBC-TV from September 1979 to September 1980. He has also appeared on television in at least seven pilot films, proposals for other series shows.

DOLLS:
1. DR. HUER. Mego, No. 85000/9, 1979. Made in Hong Kong. 3¾in (9.6cm). *Illustration 665.*
2. DR. HUER. Mego, No. 85001/6, 1979. Made in Hong Kong. 12¼in (31.2cm). *Illustration 666.*

SEE: BUCK ROGERS IN THE 25th CENTURY.

Illustration 665. 3¾in (9.6cm) TIM O'CONNOR as *Dr. Huer* from "Buck Rogers in the 25th Century" by Mego, No. 85000/9, 1979. All-vinyl and fully-jointed. Painted hair, features and clothing. Copyright by Robert C. Dille. Made in Hong Kong.

OLAND, WARNER. Actor. Born Werner Ohlund in Sweden in 1880; died 1938. Warner Oland began his career in the theater and entered films in 1912. He played many character parts and became typecast as an Oriental. He was "Charlie Chan" in 16 films of that series from 1931 until his death. The part was then taken over by Sidney Toler (22 films), Roland Winters (six films), J. Carrol Naish (39 TV films), and Ross Martin (one TV feature). In 1972 the series became a cartoon show for children with Keye Luke, who had been Charlie Chan's "Number One Son" so often in the 1930s, as the voice of Charlie Chan.

DOLLS:
1. CHARLIE CHAN. Glove doll, or puppet. Ideal, 1973. Vinyl head with painted features and a molded hat. Vinyl glove portion for hand insertion. Keye Luke as Henry is a companion doll. (These dolls tie into the cartoon series from the 1970s, but use the characters from the 1930s.)

O'LOUGHLIN, GERALD S. Actor. Born December 23, 1921. O'Loughlin acted on Broadway, in films and on television. On TV he was in the series programs "The Doctors," "Lassiter," "The Storefront Lawyers," "Men at Law," "The Rookies" (as Lt. Edward Ryker on ABC-TV from September 1972 to September 1976), "Roots: The Next Generation," and "Blind Ambition." He was also in the miniseries "Wheels" and "Woman in White" in 1979 and "Sparrow," a pilot film in 1978.

DOLLS:
1. LT. RYKER from THE ROOKIES. L.J.N. Toys Ltd., No. 6101, 1976. All-vinyl and fully-jointed. Painted hair and features. Made in Hong Kong. 7½in (19.1cm).

SEE: THE ROOKIES.

ONASSIS, JACQUELINE BOUVIER KENNEDY.
SEE: KENNEDY, JACQUELINE.

O'NEAL, TATUM. Actress. Born November 5, 1963. Tatum O'Neal is the daughter of actor Ryan O'Neal and actress Johanna Moore. She was the youngest person ever to win an Academy Award. Her Best Supporting Actress Oscar was for her memorable portrayal as Addie Pray, a nine-year-old cussing and cigarette-smoking con artist in *Paper Moon* (1973), her first film. For *The Bad News Bears* in 1976 she received a salary of $350,000 and 9 percent of the profits, becoming the highest-paid child performer in the history of the movies. She was Velvet Brown in *International Velvet* in 1978, a role and film that could be described as "bad news."

DOLLS:
1. INTERNATIONAL VELVET. Kenner, No. 44000, 1978. Made in Hong Kong, Taiwan, Korea and Macao. 11½in (29.2cm). *Illustration 668*.

Illustration 667. Tatum O'Neal in *International Velvet*, 1978.

Illustration 668. 11½in (29.2cm) TATUM O'NEAL as *Sarah Velvet Brown* from *International Velvet* by Kenner, No. 44000, 1978. All-vinyl and fully-jointed. Rooted long blonde hair; painted blue eyes. Head marked: "HONG KONG // © 1976 U.C.S.I." Marked on back below jointed waist: " © 1978 G.M.F.G.I. KENNER PROD. // CINCINNATI, OHIO 45202 // MADE IN HONG KONG." Copyright by Metro-Goldwyn-Mayer, Inc. The box tells that different parts of the doll and her accessories were made in Hong Kong, Taiwan, Korea and Macao "as labeled herein."

O'NEIL, KITTY. Stunt woman. Born in Corpus Christi, Texas, on March 24, 1946. Tiny Kitty O'Neil was born deaf. She performed in stunt sequences in many films and TV shows. She set 26 world records on land, two on water and one on water skis. She won the Women's World Land Speed Record, with a top speed of 618 miles an hour. She was the first stunt woman to perform a 180 foot high fall and a 90 foot high fall while on fire. She has won many achievement awards from institutes for the deaf and other handicapped. Stockard Channing played Kitty O'Neil in a television biographical film, *Silent Victory* in 1979.

DOLLS:
1. KITTY O'NEIL. Mattel, No. 2247, 1978. Made in Taiwan. 11½in (29.2cm). *Illustration 669*.

Illustration 669. 11½in (29.2cm) KITTY O'NEIL, one of "TV's Star Women," by Mattel, No. 2247, 1978. All-vinyl and fully-jointed. Rooted dark brown hair; painted blue eyes. Copyright by Rocket Kat, Inc. and C & D Enterprises. Made in Taiwan.

ONTKEAN, MICHAEL. Actor. Born January 24, 1946. Michael Ontkean has acted in films since the 1970s. On television he played Officer William Gillis on "The Rookies," for ABC-TV from September 1972 to June 1974, when he left the series to concentrate on motion pictures.

DOLLS:
1. WILLIE from THE ROOKIES. L.J.N. Toys Ltd., No. 6101, 1976. Made in Hong Kong. 7½in (19.1cm). *Illustration 671*.
SEE: THE ROOKIES.

Illustration 670. Michael Ontkean in *Willie and Phil*, 1980.

Illustration 672. 12in (30.5cm) BOBBY ORR by Regal Toy Ltd., 1975. All-vinyl and fully-jointed, including waist. Painted brown hair and painted black eyes. Head marked: "©REGAL CAN-75." Costume tagged: "BOBBY ORR // REGAL TOY LIMITED. Made in Hong Kong for Canadian distribution.

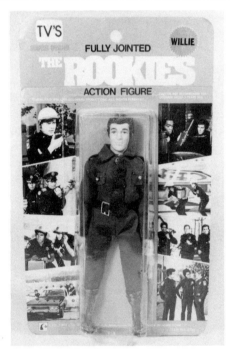

Illustration 671. 7½in (19.1cm) MICHAEL ONTKEAN as *Willie* from "The Rookies" by L.J.N. Toys Ltd., No. 6101, 1976. All-vinyl and fully-jointed. Painted hair and features. Copyright 1973 by Spelling-Goldberg Productions. Made in Hong Kong.

ORR, BOBBY. Hockey player. Born March 20, 1948, in Parry Sound, Ontario, Canada. Bobby Orr was a defenseman with the Boston Bruins from 1967 to 1976 and with the Chicago Black Hawks from 1977 to 1979. In 1967 he was named National Hockey League Rookie of the Year. In 1970 and in 1975 he was the NHL leading scorer, the first defenseman to achieve this record. From 1968 to 1975 he was on the NHL all-star team and each year he won the coveted Norris Trophy as best defenseman. In 1975 he scored 46 goals, an unequaled record. His career in hockey was shortened by five knee operations.

DOLLS:
1. BOBBY ORR. Regal Toy Ltd., 1975. Made in Hong Kong for the Canadian market. 12in (30.5cm). *Illustrations 672* and *673*.

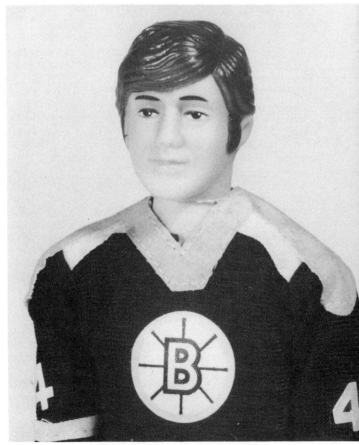

Illustration 673. BOBBY ORR by Regal.

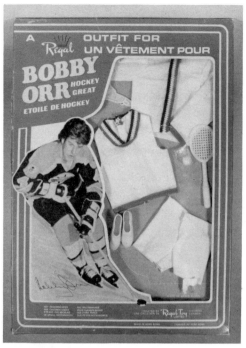

Illustration 674. One of the extra clothing outfit packages for the Bobby Orr doll by Regal.

Illustration 675. Marie and Donny Osmond.

THE OSMONDS. Family of entertainers from Ogden, Utah. The Osmonds came to television on a regular basis on "The Andy Williams Show," which appeared on NBC-TV from July 1958 to July 1971. Williams discovered the older boys performing at Disneyland, and they were first seen on his show on December 20, 1962, singing "I'm a Ding Dong Daddy from Dumas" and "Side by Side." The Osmond Brothers were billed as a "youthful barbershop hormony quartet" and they were Alan, Wayne, Merrill and Jay. Six-year-old Donny made his debut on the show on December 10, 1963. The Osmonds stayed with Andy Williams until the end of the show's run. Donny and his sister, Marie, had their own variety show, "Donny and Marie," from January 1976 to May 1978 and from September 1978 to January 1979. The Osmond Brothers also performed on this show, as did the youngest brother, Jimmy. "The Osmond Family Show" was on television from January to March and during May of 1979 and featured all of the above members in variety acts. In December 1979 "Marie" was a pilot show that never developed into a series. Again in December 1980 and January 1981 "Marie" was a variety program that aired four times. Two other brothers, Virl and Tom, were also involved in the production of the Osmond's various shows. In 1973 Jimmy Osmond, the youngest member of the family, had two hit records in Britain and at age nine was the youngest performer ever to top the British charts. This makes Jimmy the most successful Osmond as a recording artist. In early 1980 the Osmonds all flew to England for what was announced as their "last tour together." The fan turnout was so slight in some cities that free tickets were distributed for Osmond concerts. In Britain this was credited to the fact that tickets cost $28.00 each, to cover the expenses of 126 people in the Osmond entourage, including 32 members of the Osmond family. The Osmonds blamed their failure on a "lack of advance publicity" when they cancelled the tour.

Illustration 676. THE OSMONDS by Mattel. From left to right: 11¾in (29.9cm) MARIE, No. 9768, 1976. All-vinyl and fully-jointed. Rooted brown hair; painted brown eyes; open smiling mouth with painted teeth. Microphone attached to right hand. Copyright 1976 by Osbro Productions, Inc. Marked on hip: "© MATTEL INC. // 1966 // 12 // KOREA." 10in (25.4cm) JIMMY, No. 2200, 1978. All-vinyl and fully-jointed. Painted brown hair; painted brown eyes; freckles; open smiling mouth with painted teeth; microphone attached to left hand. Copyright by Osbro Productions, Inc. Marked on lower back: "2200 -2109 2 // © MATTEL INC. // 1969 // TAIWAN." 11¾in (29.9cm) DONNY, No. 9767, 1976. All-vinyl and fully-jointed. Painted brown hair; painted brown eyes; smiling open mouth with painted teeth; microphone attached to left hand. Copyright by Osbro Productions, Inc. Marked on lower back: "1088 - 0500 4 // © MATTEL // INC. 1968 // HONG KONG.

OSMOND, DONNY. Entertainer. Born Donald Clark Osmond on December 9, 1957. In early 1982 Donny prepared for his Broadway musical "Little Johnny Jones," a George M. Cohan play from 1903. See also THE OSMONDS.
DOLLS:
1. DONNY OSMOND. Mattel, No. 9767, 1976. Made in Hong Kong. 11¾in (29.9cm). Marie Osmond, No. 9768, is a companion doll. *Illustrations 676* and *677.*
2. DONNY OSMOND. Marionette. Maker unknown, 1978. Marie Osmond is a companion piece. 11½in (29.2cm).

Illustration 677. DONNY OSMOND by Mattel.

OSMOND, JIMMY. Entertainer. Born James Arthur Osmond on April 16, 1963. See THE OSMONDS.
DOLLS:
1. JIMMY OSMOND. Mattel, No. 2200, 1978. Made in Taiwan. 10in (25.4cm). *Illustrations 676* and *678.*

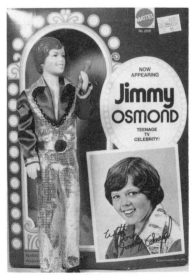

Illustration 678. JIMMY OSMOND by Mattel.

OSMOND, MARIE. Entertainer. Born October 13, 1959. See THE OSMONDS.
DOLLS:
1. MARIE OSMOND. Mattel, No. 9768, 1976. Made in Korea. 11¾in (29.9cm). Donny Osmond, No. 9767, is a companion doll. *Illustration 676.*
2. MARIE OSMOND. Marionette. Maker unknown, 1978. Donny Osmond is a companion doll. 11½in (29.2cm).
3. MARIE OSMOND. Mattel, No. 9826, 1976. Made in USA. 30in (76.2cm). *Illustration 679.*

Illustration 679. 30in (76.2cm) MARIE OSMOND, a "Modeling Doll" by Mattel, No. 9826, 1976. Vinyl head; fully-jointed plastic body. Rooted dark brown hair; painted brown eyes; smiling mouth. A bra and panties are molded into the body construction. The stand is also original with the doll. Marked vertically at the neck: " © OSBRO PROD. / / 1976 / / U.S.A." *Wanda Lodwick Collection.*

OSORIO DE ZUÑIGA, (DON) MANUEL. Subject of a painting by the Spanish artist Francisco Goya. Don Manuel Osorio de Zuñiga was the son of the Count of Altamira of Spain. His portrait was painted by Goya in 1784. The painting is now in the Metropolitan Museum in New York, New York, and is popularly known as "The Red Boy."
DOLLS:
1. RED BOY. Madame Alexander, No. 740, 1972-1973. All-hard plastic and fully-jointed with bending knees. Dark brown wig; brown sleep eyes with molded lashes. 7½in (19.1cm).
2. RED BOY. Madame Alexander, No. 440, 1974 to present. Same as the above without bending knees. 7½in (19.1cm). *Illustration 681.*
3. DON MANUEL OSORIO DE ZUÑIGA. Doll Classics by Al Trattner, 1982. Made in Delaware. 12in (30.5cm). *Illustration 681-A.*

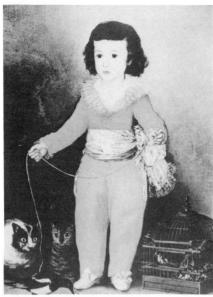

Illustration 680. Don Manuel Osorio de Zúñiga, popularly known as "The Red Boy," painted by Francisco Goya in 1784. In *The World of Goya (1746-1828)* published by Time-Life Books, 1968, author Richard Schickel describes the effect of this work: Goya "captured the gravity of childhood, and he has suggested as well, the inevitable ending of its innocence. The boy holds a bird by a string, and three cats, their eyes gleaming avidly, stare fixedly at the creature, ready to pounce—symbols of the terrors of the world which will all too soon spring from the shadows and introduce the child to the anxieties and dread of adulthood."

Illustration 681-A. 12in (30.5cm) DON MANUEL OSORIO DE ZUÑIGA by Doll Classics by Al Trattner, 1982. All-bisque and fully-jointed. Brown wig; brown glass eyes; pierced nostrils. Red velvet suit with gold sash belt. A limited edition of 1500 dolls. Made in Delaware. Based on the painting by Francisco Goya. Head marked: "Doll Classics // by // Al Trattner // © 1982 // DMS // SCD // 1-82." *Photograph Courtesy of Al Trattner.*

Illustration 681. 7½in (19.1cm) "Red Boy," DON MANUEL OSORIO DE ZUÑIGA, the son of the Count of Altamira, inspired by the painting of the Spanish artist Francisco Goya, by Madame Alexander, No. 440, 1975. All-hard plastic and fully-jointed. Dark brown synthetic wig; brown sleep eyes with lashes. Back marked: "ALEXANDER."

OUR GANG. A long-running (1924-1944) series of slapstick comedy shorts featuring a company of child actors. Producer, director, screen writer Hal Roach assembled the juvenile cast for the *Our Gang* comedies, emphasizing "types" rather than acting experience. Many talented youngsters appeared in the *Our Gang* comedies. The most important child stars of the comedies in the 1920s were ALLEN CLAYTON HOSKINS as Farina, JACKIE DAVID as Jackie, MARY KORNMAN as Mary, MICKEY DANIELS as Freckles and JOE COBB as Fatty. Another important "actor" was Pete, the dog with a black circle around his right eye. During the sound era (the 1930s and the 1940s) important players were DARLA HOOD, PORKY LEE, BUCKWHEAT THOMAS, ALFALFA SWITZER, SPANKY McFARLAND and MICKEY GUBITOSI (later billed as Bobby Blake and then Robert Blake). Other children who were in the series were Jean Darling, Jackie Cooper, Norman "Chubby" Chaney, Bobby "Wheezer" Hutchins, Matthew "Stymie" Beard, Dickie Moore and Scotty Beckett. All of the *Our Gang* comedies were "shorts," lasting less than a half hour, with the exception of *General Spanky*, a feature-length film released in 1936. In 1938 Hal Roach sold the rights to the series to MGM, who then produced the shorts until 1944. In 1955 about 100 of the Hal Roach shorts were sold to television, but they had to be called "The Little Rascals" because the rights to the title "Our Gang" belonged to MGM. During the 1970s *Our Gang* short films from MGM were also on syndicated television. The players above in capitals were made as dolls. Those from the 1920s were made by Sayco in 1926; those from the 1930s and the 1940s were made by Mego in 1975. In 1975 Mego also made a Clubhouse with a scooter, and a Rowboat and Orange Crate Cart to go with the dolls. See also listings under the individual performers in capitals.

DOLLS:
Set 1.

OUR GANG DANCING COMEDY DOLLS. Sayco (Schoen & Yondorf Co., Inc.), 1926. Sold individually or as a set. The characters were ALLEN CLAYTON HOSKINS as *Farina*, JACKIE DAVID as Jackie, MARY KORNMAN as Mary, MICKEY DANIELS as Freckles and JOE COBB as Fatty. *Illustration 682.*

Set 2.

OUR GANG. Mego, 1975. Made in Hong Kong. 6in (15.2cm). The characters were ALFALFA SWITZER, No. 61600/1; SPANKY McFARLAND, No. 61600/2; BUCKWHEAT THOMAS, No. 61600/3; DARLA HOOD, No. 61600/4; MICKEY GUBITOSI, No. 61600/5; PORKY LEE, No. 61600/6. For Illustrations see individual celebrity.

Illustration 683. Our Gang calendar cover, 1941. From left to right: Buckwheat, Mickey, Darla, Alfalfa and Porky.

Illustration 682. OUR GANG "Dancing Comedy Dolls" by Sayco from a *Playthings* advertisement, April 1926. The dolls probably have composition heads with painted features and composition lower arms; stuffed cloth bodies. The dolls are, from left to right: ALLEN CLAYTON HOSKINS as *Farina*, JACKIE DAVID as *Jackie,* MARY KORNMAN as *Mary*, MICKEY DANIELS as *Freckles* and JOE COBB as *Fatty.*

Illustration 684. Our Gang from 1975 Mego package. From left to right: Porky, Buckwheat, Alfalfa, Darla, Spanky and Mickey.

P

PAHLAVI (or PAHLEVI), FARAH. Empress of Iran. Born Farah Diba on October 14, 1938. In December 1959 Farah Diba married the Shah of Iran. She was the daughter of an Iranian army officer and had studied architecture in Paris, France, before her marriage. The Shah's marriage to his second wife, Soraya, was dissolved in April 1958 because Soraya could not produce an heir to the throne. On October 31, 1960, Farah gave birth to a son, thus insuring the survival of the Pahlavi line. After the death of the deposed Shah in 1980 Empress Farah remained in Egypt under the protection of the government.

DOLLS:

1. EMPRESS FARAH OF IRAN. Peggy Nisbet, No. P465, late 1970s. Plastic "collectors' doll." Shah Mohammed Reza Pahlav (sic) of Iran, No. P464, is a companion doll. Made in England. 7½in (19.1cm). *Illustration 685.*

PAHLAVI (or PAHLEVI), MOHAMMED REZA. Shah of Iran, 1941-1979. Born October 26, 1919, in Teheran, Persia (now Iran); died July 27, 1980, near Cairo, Egypt. In 1925, after a revolution, Reza Khan took over the government of Persia. In 1926 he was crowned amid great public enthusiasm as Reza Shah Pahlavi with the right of succession to his heirs. Iran became the official name of the country in 1935. In 1941 Reza Shah abdicated in favor of his eldest son Mohammed Reza Pahlavi. The new Shah followed a course of rapid industrialization that led to unrest and his eventual overthrow. On October 26, 1967, Pahlavi had himself crowned Shahanshah (Shah of Shahs) and crowned his wife Shahbanou, or Empress, the first since Iran embraced Islam in the 600s. The Shah claimed to have waited 26 years for his coronation because he first wanted to strengthen his country, improve the lives of the people and father a male heir. The coronation ceremony cost many million of dollars. During the 1970s political opposition to the Shah's domination of Iran was not tolerated, causing the rise of the Muslim extremists who took over in 1979, forcing the Shah and his family into exile. During his last year he lived in Egypt, Mexico, the United States, Panama, and Egypt again, where he died of cancer, while 52 Americans were still being held hostage in Iran.

DOLLS:
1. SHAH MOHAMMED REZA PAHLAV OF IRAN. Peggy Nisbet, No. P464, late 1970s. Plastic "collectors' doll." Empress Farah of Iran, No. P465, is a companion doll. Made in England. About 8in (20.3cm). *Illustration 685.*

Illustration 685. 8in (20.3cm) SHAH MOHAMMED REZA PAHLAV (sic), No. P464, and EMPRESS FARAH OF IRAN, No. P465, by Peggy Nisbet, late 1970s. All-hard plastic and jointed only at the arms. The Shah has molded hair and painted features; the Empress has a mohair wig and painted features. Made in England. *Photograph Courtesy of House of Nisbet.*

PALILLO, RON. Actor. Born Ronald G. Palillo April 2, 1954. Palillo played one of Mr. Kotter's "Sweat Hogs," Arnold Horshack, on "Welcome Back, Kotter" on ABC-TV from September 1975 to August 1979.

DOLLS:
1. HORSHACK from WELCOME BACK, KOTTER. Mattel, No. 9771, 1976. Made in Taiwan. 9¼in (23.6cm). *Illustration 686.*
SEE: WELCOME BACK, KOTTER.

Illustration 686. 9¼in (23.6cm) RON PALILLO as *Arnold Horshack* from "Welcome Back, Kotter" by Mattel, No. 9771, 1976. All-vinyl and fully-jointed with painted hair and features. Copyright by the Wolper Organization, Inc. and the Komack Company, Inc. Made in Taiwan. *Shirley Buchholz Collection.*

PARKER, FESS. Actor. Born August 16, 1926, in Fort Worth, Texas. Parker played rugged, handsome leading men in films and on television. His first movies were in 1952. Parker became a big star playing Davy Crockett on the "Walt Disney" anthology series on television. The three original Crockett episodes were "Davy Crockett, Indian Fighter" (December 15, 1954), "Davy Crockett Goes to Congress" (January 26, 1955), and "Davy Crockett at the Alamo" (February 23, 1955). Crockett was killed at the Alamo, but because of the popularity of this portion of the "Walt Disney" show, Parker played him in several more episodes. "The Ballad of Davy Crockett" was the Number One Record of 1955 by Bill Hayes, although Parker had also recorded the song. This all led to a national Davy Crockett craze, and Crockett coonskin caps and other merchandise sold like crazy. Fess Parker also starred on television in "Mr. Smith Goes to Washington," based on the 1939 James Stewart movie. This series only lasted from September 1962 to March 1963. "Daniel Boone" was more successful. Fess Parker played the frontier hero from September 1964 to August 1970 on NBC-TV.

DOLLS:
1. FESS PARKER AS DANIEL BOONE. Remco, 1964. 5in (12.7cm). *Illustration 687.*

Illustration 687. 5in (12.7cm) FESS PARKER as *Daniel Boone* by Remco, 1964. Vinyl jointed head with painted brown hair and painted black eyes. One-piece heavy vinyl body. Head marked: "32." Body marked: "© AMERICAN // TRADITION CO. // 1964." *Phyllis Houston Collection.*

PARR, CATHERINE. Queen Consort of Henry VIII of England. Born 1512; died 1548. Catherine Parr was the sixth and last wife of Henry VIII. After Henry died in 1547 she married Baron Seymour of Sudeley.

DOLLS:

Note: The six wives of King Henry VIII were (in order) Catherine of Aragon, Anne Boleyn, Jane Seymour, Anne of Cleves, Catherine Howard and Catherine Parr.

1. CATHERINE PARR. Peggy Nisbet, No. P607, 1970s. Plastic "collectors' doll," part of a series of Henry VIII and his six wives, "Henry VIII, Portrait Series." Costume from contemporary portraits in the National Gallery, London. Made in England. 7½in (19.1cm).
2. CATHERINE PARR. Peggy Nisbet, No. H223, 1970s. Plastic "collectors' doll," part of a series of Henry VIII and his six wives, "Henry VIII, Standard Series." The costume is an accurate reproduction of the clothing worn by Catherine. Made in England. 7½in (19.1cm).
3. CATHERINE PARR. Peggy Nisbet, No. M936, 1979. Plastic "collectors' doll," part of a series of Henry VIII and his six wives, "Henry VIII, Historical Series." Made in England. Inch-to-the-foot miniature.

PARTON, DOLLY. Singer, actress. Born January 19, 1946 (?) in Tennessee. Very buxom Dolly Parton became one of country music's top singers and songwriters, but turned her back on Nashville to become a pop singer and an actress. Dolly's songs were inspired by her life as a poor child in a large mountain family. Her first success was in her teaming with top country singer Porter Wagoner. In 1974 she had her first solo hit single, "Jolene," and by 1977 was the top female country star, but she began to change her image with television over-exposure. In December 1980 Parton's first film, *Nine to Five* was released.

DOLLS:

1. DOLLY PARTON. Goldberger, No. DP12, 1978. Made in Hong Kong. 11½in (29.2cm). *Illustrations 689* and *690*.

Illustration 689. 11½in (29.2cm) DOLLY PARTON by Goldberger, No. DP12, 1978. All-vinyl and fully-jointed. Rooted light blonde hair; painted dark blue eyes; very pale complexion. Head marked: "DOLLY PARTON // © EEGEE CO. // HONG KONG." (No dates are given on the doll or on the package.)

Illustration 690. DOLLY PARTON by Goldberger.

Illustration 688. Dolly Parton.

PATTERSON, MARTHA JOHNSON. First Lady. Born October 25, 1828; died July 10, 1901. When Andrew Johnson became President of the United States in 1865 after the assassination of Abraham Lincoln, his wife was too ill to assume the obligations of a First Lady. Their daughter, Mrs. Patterson, took her place. Mrs. Patterson also presided over the renovation of the White House, which had suffered neglect during the Lincoln years. When Johnson's term ended in 1869, Mrs. Patterson returned to her home in Tennessee.

DOLLS:
1. MARTHA JOHNSON PATTERSON. Madame Alexander, No. 1518, 1982. Vinyl and plastic and fully-jointed. Rooted blonde hair pulled to one side and gathered into a long curl. She wears a pink, blue and gold brocade gown. Part of the third six First Ladies series. 14in (35.6cm).
SEE: FIRST LADIES, THE.

PATTON, GEORGE ("OLD BLOOD AND GUTS"). United States army officer. Born November 11, 1885; died December 21, 1945. In 1942-1943 Patton led the American army in North Africa against the Nazis. In 1943 he led the 7th Army in its assault on Sicily. He then caused a furor on the home front by slapping an American GI and cursing others in a field hospital in Sicily. In 1943 he led the invasion of German-occupied Europe. Because of his wild political statements about what should be done with Germans and Russians, he was relieved of his command in 1945.

DOLLS:
1. GEN. GEORGE S. PATTON, JR. Excel Toy Corp., 1974. Made in Hong Kong. 9¾in (24.9cm). *Illustration 691*.

Illustration 691. 9¾in (24.9cm) GENERAL GEORGE S. PATTON, JR. by Excel Toy Corp., 1974. All-vinyl and fully-jointed, including extra joints at the elbow, wrists, knees and ankles. Made in Hong Kong. *Fran's Dolls.*

PAVLOVA, ANNA MATVEYEVNA. Russian ballerina. Born January 31, 1882; died January 23, 1931. Pavlova was with the Maryinsky Theater after 1899 and was its prima ballerina from 1906 to 1913. In 1909 she went on tour with the Ballet Russes and made her American debut at the Metropolitan Opera. Her most famous dancing role was as *The Dying Swan*. In 1916 she starred in the film *The Dumb Girl of Portici*. In 1935 *The Immortal Swan* was released. This feature film was a composite of various short films of her dances made years earlier. Pavlova's most important dancing partner was the troubled Vaslav Nijinsky.

DOLLS:
1. PAVLOVA. Effanbee, No. 1156, 1977-1978. All-vinyl and fully-jointed with rooted hair and sleep eyes. 11in (27.9cm).
2. PAVLOVA. Effanbee, No. 1185, 1979. Same as the above. 11in (27.9cm). *Illustration 692*.

Illustration 692. 11in (27.9cm) "Historical Collection" dolls by Effanbee from the 1978 catalog. Top row, from left to right: DAVY CROCKETT, FLORENCE NIGHTINGALE, CLEOPATRA. Front row, from left to right: BETSY ROSS, PAVLOVA, POCAHONTAS. All-vinyl and fully-jointed with rooted hair and sleep eyes.

PAYNE, JOHN. Actor. Born May 23, 1912, in Roanoke, Virginia. Payne was popular in musical films of the 1940s, playing opposite Alice Faye and Betty Grable. By the 1950s he had switched to western and action films. When western series were the vogue on television, he played Vint Bonner in "The Restless Gun" from September 1957 to September 1959. In 1973 he teamed again with Alice Faye for the stage musical revival "Good News." He was married to actresses Anne Shirley and Gloria De Haven.

DOLLS:
1. VINT BONNER from THE RESTLESS GUN. Hartland Plastics, Inc., No. 765, 1958. All-plastic; jointed at the arms. Painted hair and features; painted clothing. Made in Hartland, Wisconsin. 8in (20.3cm).

PAYTON, DENIS. Musician. English-born Denis Payton played guitar, reeds and saxaphone with the group The Dave Clark Five from 1964 to 1973.

DOLLS: SEE: DAVE CLARK FIVE, THE.

PEARY, MARIE AHNIGHITO. Daughter of polar explorer Robert E. Peary. Born September 12, 1893, in Greenland; deceased. Ahnighito Peary was known as the "Snow Baby" because she was supposed to have been the first white child born north of the Arctic Circle. She became famous because of books written about her in the early 20th century, during which time her father was conducting explorations in the arctic region. After pictures appeared in newspapers of Ahnighito dressed in fur parkas, this style of winter wear became popular for children. As an adult she organized her father's writings and records, and she led an expedition to the Arctic to erect a monument in his memory in 1932. (See Johana Gast Anderton, *More Twentieth Century Dolls*, 1974, pp. 1027-1028.)

DOLLS:
Various dolls with bisque heads and dressed in a fur costume are thought to represent Marie Ahnighito Peary. *Illustration 693* is an example. In September 1909 *Playthings* carried an advertisement from The Strobel & Wilken Co. calling a similar doll an "Eskimo Doll."

Illustration 693. 12in (30.5cm) *Snow Baby,* thought to represent MARIE AHNIGHITO PEARY, the daughter of arctic explorer Robert E. Peary, early 20th century. Bisque head on a five-piece jointed composition body. Inset glass eyes; open mouth with teeth; rabbit fur glued on head and body to form snow suit. In *The Collector's Encyclopedia of Dolls* by the Colemans (Crown Publishers, Inc., 1977, page 367) reference is made to dressed dolls by Gebruder Kraus (Kraus Brothers) that were advertised from 1907 to 1911. This may be a doll from that German firm. She is incised on the head:

GK
✕
W
MADE IN GERMANY
103. 13/0
DEP
Shirley Buchholz Collection.

PEARY, ROBERT E(DWIN). Arctic explorer; discoverer of the North Pole. Born in Cresson, Pennsylvania, on May 6, 1856; died February 29, 1920. In 1886 Peary began exploring Greenland and he returned in 1891 with his wife, and began an expedition during which he discovered that Greenland was an island. During the 1890s Peary made several trips to northern Greenland and in 1898 told of his plan to reach the North Pole. On April 6, 1909, Peary arrived at the North Pole, accompanied by an aide and four Eskimos. F.A. Cook

claimed to have accomplished this feat a year earlier when Peary announced that he had completed his goal. Cook's claims were generally discredited later, but this spoiled the triumph of years of work by Peary.

DOLLS:
1. PEARY. An advertisement in *Playthings,* September 1909, shows dolls from The Strobel & Wilken Co. with pictures of "Peary, Cook and Eskimo dolls." The doll of Peary seems to have a head with an applied moustache and is dressed in a fur jacket and fur pants. Skis are strapped to the feet. The doll was probably made in Germany.

PERKINS, ANTHONY. Actor. Born April 4, 1932. Perkins is the son of actor Osgood Perkins. He began acting in summer stock at age 15 and at age 21 made his film debut. For *Friendly Persuasion,* 1956, he earned an Academy Award nomination for best supporting actor. His most memorable performance was as Norman Bates, the psychopathic motel keeper in Alfred Hitchcock's *Psycho,* 1960. After this success he acted in many international productions, such as *The Black Hole,* 1979.

DOLLS:
1. DR. ALEX DURANT from THE BLACK HOLE. Mego, No. 95010, 1979. Made in Hong Kong. 3¾in (9.6cm). *Illustrations 694* and *695.*
2. DR. ALEX DURANT from THE BLACK HOLE. Mego, 1979. All-vinyl and fully-jointed with painted hair and features. Made in Hong Kong. 12½in (31.8cm).

SEE: THE BLACK HOLE.

Illustration 694. 3¾in (9.6cm) ANTHONY PERKINS as *Dr. Alex Durant* from *The Black Hole* by Mego, No. 95010, 1979. All-vinyl and fully-jointed with painted features and clothing. Copyright by Walt Disney Productions. Made in Hong Kong.

Illustration 695. 3¾in (9.6cm) ANTHONY PERKINS by Mego.

PERREAU, GIGI. Actress. Born Ghislaine Elizabeth Marie Thérèse Perreau-Saussine on February 6, 1941, in Los Angeles, California, to French parents who fled the Nazis in Paris. During the 1940s and 1950s she was a successful child star in films but she was not able to maintain her popularity as an adult player. Her brother was child performer Peter Miles.

DOLLS:
1. GIGI PERREAU. Goldberger Doll Manufacturing Co., Inc., 1952. Vinyl head with dark dynel wig; plastic fully-jointed body. 20in (50.9cm).

PERRY, ROD. Actor. Rod Perry played Sgt. David "Deacon" Kay on ABC-TV's "S.W.A.T." from February 1975 to July 1976.

DOLLS:
1. DEACON from S.W.A.T. L.J.N. Toys Ltd., No. 6600, 1975. Made in Hong Kong. 7½in (19.1cm). *Illustration 696.*
2. DEACON from S.W.A.T. L.J.N. Toys Ltd., No. 6850, 1976. All-vinyl and fully-jointed. Painted hair and features. Made in Hong Kong. 7½in (19.1cm).
SEE: S.W.A.T.

PERSHING, JOHN. American general. Born 1860; died 1948. Pershing commanded the American army against the raids of the Mexican revolutionary Pancho Villa in the southwest of the United States before World War I. During the First World War he was commander-in-chief of the American Expeditionary Forces in Europe.

DOLLS:
1. GEN. JOHN J. PERSHING. Excel Toy Corp., 1974. All-vinyl and fully-jointed with painted hair and features. Made in Hong Kong. 9¾in (24.9cm).

PETRIE, HAY. Actor. Born 1895; died 1948. Petrie was a Scottish character actor who specialized in playing bizarre and grotesque characters in films after 1930. In *The Thief of Bagdad* (1940) he was the Astrologer.

DOLLS:
1. ASTROLOGER from THE THIEF OF BAGDAD. Molly-'es, No. 1100, 1940. All-cloth with a felt mask face. Gray mohair wig and applied moustache; painted blue eyes. Wears a turban and Arabian style clothing. Marked with a paper tag. 18in (45.7cm).

PHILIP II. King of Spain. Born 1527; died 1598. When Philip's father, Charles V, abdicated his throne and retired in 1556, Philip became King of Spain, Naples and Sicily. He had already received the Low Countries, Franche-Comté and Milan. When his first wife, Mary I of Portugal, died he married Mary I of England. He left England after Mary's death but sought to marry her half-sister Elizabeth I. During his time Spain became the most powerful nation in Europe because of the wealth coming from the New World and the control exerted by the Spanish Inquistion, which maintained the alliance between the throne and the Church. In 1580, he seized the throne of Portugal when Henry I died without issue. The Netherlands were trying to become free of Spain and were aided by English pirates financed by Queen Elizabeth. To end sea rivalry, Philip sent the Invincible Spanish Armada of 124 ships and 124,000 men to conquer England in 1588. The destruction of the Armada cost Spain its position as the strongest power on earth. Philip's chief colonial conquest was that of the Philippine Islands. His fourth wife, Anne of Austria, gave birth to the future Philip III. Philip II spent his last years concentrating on religious fanaticism.

DOLLS:
1. KING PHILIP II OF SPAIN. Peggy Nisbet, No. P455, 1970s. Plastic "collectors' doll." Queen Mary I (Bloody Mary), No. P454, is a companion doll. Made in England. About 8in (20.3cm).

PHILIP (PRINCE PHILIP MOUNTBATTEN, DUKE OF EDINBURGH). Prince Philip is the husband of Queen Elizabeth II of Great Britain. Born on the islands of Corfu, June 10, 1921. Philip descended from the kings of Russia, Greece, Denmark and England. He was born

Illustration 696. 7½in (19.1cm) ROD PERRY as *Deacon* from "S.W.A.T." by L.J.N. Toys Ltd., No. 6600, 1975. (The same mold from 1976 is No. 6850.) All-vinyl and fully-jointed with painted hair and features. Copyright by Spelling-Goldberg Productions. Made in Hong Kong.

Prince Philip of Greece of a German family. In 1947 he became engaged to Princess Elizabeth of England as Lieutenant Philip Mountbatten of the Royal Navy and also became a British citizen. On November 20, 1947, he married Princess Elizabeth in Westminister Abbey and was created Duke of Edinburgh. He is involved with international wildlife conservation groups.

DOLLS:
1. PRINCE PHILIP. Madame Alexander, circa 1953. 17¾in (45.2cm). *Illustration 697.*
NOTE: The identity of this doll has not been confirmed with original advertising; it may be simply a "groom."
2. H.R.H. PRINCE PHILIP (IN GARTER ROBES). Peggy Nisbet, No. P403, 1970s. Plastic "collectors' doll," Queen Elizabeth II, No. P401, and H.R.H. Prince Charles, No. P402, are companion dolls in the same robes. Made in England. About 8in (20.3cm).
3. H.R.H. PRINCE PHILIP, DUKE OF EDINBURGH. Peggy Nisbet, No. P416, late 1970s. Plastic "collectors' doll." H.M. Queen Elizabeth II in State Robes, No. P400, is a companion doll. Made in England. About 8in (20.3cm).

Illustration 697. 17¾in (45.2cm) PRINCE PHILIP by Madame Alexander, circa 1953. (This identification is not confirmed by advertising; the doll may simply be a "groom.") All-hard plastic and fully-jointed. Dark brown saran wig; brown sleep eyes with lashes. The doll is not marked. The shirt is labeled "Madame Alexander." The wrist tag also cites: "FASHION ACADEMY AWARD." *Irene Trittschuh Collection.*

PHILLIPS, JOHN. Singer, musician, producer. Born circa 1935. John Phillips formed the group The Mamas and the Papas in 1965 as an extension of his involvement with folk music in New York, New York. In 1968 the group disbanded when his marriage with Michelle Phillips broke up. In 1967 he helped stage the Monterey Pop Festival, which launched the careers of Janis Joplin, Jimi Hendrix and The Who. He later became a producer of both records and films. He is the father of actress Mackenzie Phillips.

DOLLS:
1. JOHN PHILLIPS of THE MAMAS AND THE PAPAS. A "Show Biz Baby" by Hasbro, No. 8807, 1967. Made in Hong Kong. 4in (10.2cm). *Illustration 698.*
SEE: THE MAMAS AND THE PAPAS.

Illustration 698. 4in (10.2cm) JOHN PHILLIPS, one of the "Show Biz Babies" by Hasbro, No. 8807, 1967. All-vinyl with a jointed head. The body "bends into swinging poses." Rooted brown hair; painted blue eyes; open-closed mouth with molded teeth; painted brown beard and moustache. Copyright by Dunhill Records, Inc. Made in Hong Kong. Came attached to a 33 1/3rpm record that "tells all about John."

PHILLIPS, MARK. Husband of Princess Anne of Great Britain. Born 1948. On November 14, 1973, Lieutenant Mark Phillips of the Queen's Dragoon Guards married Princess Anne in Westminister Abbey. He, like Anne, is a horseman and takes part in competitive riding.

DOLLS:
1. LIEUT. MARK PHILLIPS OF THE QUEEN'S DRAGOON GUARDS. Peggy Nisbet, No. P407, 1970s. Plastic "collectors' doll." Made in England. About 8in (20.3cm).

PHILLIPS, MICHELLE. Singer, actress. Born Holly Michelle Gilliam on April 6, 1944. Michelle Phillips was married to John Phillips when he formed the group the Mamas and the Papas in 1965. After her divorce from John, Michelle launched an acting career. In 1977 she played Natacha Rambova to Rudolf Nureyev's *Valentino*. She also appears on television shows in guest roles.

DOLLS:
1. MICHELLE PHILLIPS of THE MAMAS AND THE PAPAS. A "Show Biz Baby" by Hasbro, No. 8808, 1967. Made in Hong Kong. 4½in (11.5cm). *Illustration 699.*
SEE: THE MAMAS AND THE PAPAS.

Illustration 699. 4½in (11.5cm) MICHELLE PHILLIPS, one of the "Show Biz Babies" by Hasbro, No. 8808, 1967. This member of the Mamas and the Papas group has a vinyl head with rooted blonde hair; painted blue eyes; open-closed mouth with molded teeth. Body is one-piece vinyl with wire inside for posing. Back marked: "© 1967 // HASBRO ® // HONG KONG."

PICKFORD, MARY. Actress. Born Gladys Mary Smith in Toronto, Ontario, Canada, on April 8, 1893; died May 29, 1979. After acting on the stage, Mary Pickford began her screen career in 1909. She was the first movie star to have her name in marquee lights. After two years of work for studio executive Adolph Zukor she told him, "You know, Mr. Zukor, for years I've dreamed of making $20,000 a year before I was twenty. And I'll be twenty very soon now." Zukor paid what Pickford demanded. He also paid when she demanded $100,000 a year and when she demanded half a million. (Griffith and Mayer, *The Movies,* Simon and Schuster, 1957; 1970.) For 23 years Mary Pickford was the queen of the silent screen and for 14 years she was the most famous woman in the world. She played little girls until she was well in her 30s. She was in such successes as *Poor Little Rich Girl, The Little Princess, Pollyanna, Little Annie Rooney,* and *Rebecca of Sunnybrook Farm,* all silent films. She only made four talking films, none of which were as popular, and retired after starring in *Secrets* in 1932, her 194th movie. In 1920, at which time she was known as "America's Sweetheart," she founded the United Artists company with Charlie Chaplin and Douglas Fairbanks so they could produce their own films. The next year she married Fairbanks and they lived in "Pickfair," where they entertained royalty from around the world. The marriage ended because of an indiscretion by Fairbanks and she married Buddy Rogers, 11 years her junior. She helped to establish the Academy of Motion Pictures Arts and Sciences and the Motion Picture Relief Fund. After her death of a massive stroke, Rogers put the fabulous "Pickfair" up for sale and auctioned off all of Mary Pickford's mementos.
DOLLS:
There are no dolls of Mary Pickford for which actual confirmation exists. A doll was made during the 1920s by Lenci in felt and cloth that resembles Mary Pickford. The *Little Annie Rooney* doll by Cameo, in all-composition with painted features and long yellow braids is thought to represent Mary Pickford from the 1925 film.

PIERCE, JAMES. Actor. Born August 8, 1910. "Big Jim" Pierce entered films in 1923 after playing football at Indiana University. He was Tarzan in the 1927 film *Tarzan and the Golden Lion,* produced by Joseph P. Kennedy, a film which is now "lost." He also played Tarzan on radio for five years, beginning in 1932. On radio Jane was played by Joan Burroughs, the daughter of Tarzan's creator Edgar Rice Burroughs, whom Pierce met while he was making *Tarzan and the Golden Lion.* They were married in 1928. Pierce played King Thun in the 1936 serial *Flash Gordon* and later appeared in action and western films. In the 1940s he retired from acting to pursue a career in real estate.
DOLLS:
1. THUN, THE LION MAN from FLASH GORDON. Mattel, No. 1528, 1980. Made in Hong Kong. 3¾in (10.2cm). *Illustration 700.*
SEE: FLASH GORDON.

Illustration 700. 3¾in (9.6cm) JAMES PIERCE as *Thun, the Lion Man,* from *Flash Gordon The Greatest Adventure of All* by Mattel, No. 1528, 1980. All-vinyl and painted features and clothing. Copyright 1979 by King Features Syndicate, Inc. Made in Hong Kong.

PIERCE, JANE. First Lady. Born Jane Means Appleton on March 12, 1806; died December 2, 1863. Mrs. Pierce's tenure as White House hostess during her husband Franklin Pierce's single term, 1853-1857, was not a happy one. Shortly after Pierce's election their only surviving son was killed in a train wreck. Mrs. Pierce did not arrive in Washington until after the inauguration and gladly left for the Pierce home in New Hampshire at the end of her husband's term.
DOLLS:
1. JANE PIERCE. Madame Alexander, No. 1515, 1982. Vinyl and plastic and fully-jointed. Rooted blonde hair. She wears a black net gown lined with black taffeta. Part of the third six First Ladies series. 14in (35.6cm).
SEE: FIRST LADIES, THE.

PIGOTT-SMITH, TIM.   Actor. Tim Pigott-Smith played Thallo in the 1981 film *Clash of the Titans.*

DOLLS:
1. THALLO from CLASH OF THE TITANS.   Mattel, No. 3267, 1981. Made in Philippines. 4in (10.2cm). *Illustration 701.*

SEE: CLASH OF THE TITANS.

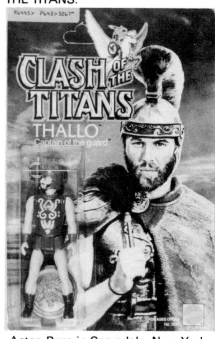

Illustration 701. 4in (10.2cm) TIM PIGOTT-SMITH as *Thallo* from *Clash of the Titans* by Mattel, No. 3267, 1981. All-vinyl and fully-jointed. Painted features with molded and painted helmet and clothing. Copyright 1980 by Metro-Goldwyn-Mayer Film Co. Made in Philippines.

PINE, ROBERT.   Actor. Born in Scarsdale, New York, July 10, 1941. Pine has appeared in many films since the 1960s. He was a regular in two police series on television. From February to July of 1976 he played Inspector Larry Johnson on "Bert D'Angelo/Superstar" on ABC-TV. Beginning in September 1977 he played Sgt. Joe Getraer on "CHiPs." on NBC-TV.

DOLLS:
1. SARGE from CHIPS.   Mego, No. 08010/3, 1981. Made in Hong Kong. 3¾in (9.6cm). *Illustration 702.*
2. SARGE from CHIPS.   Mego, No. 87500/3, 1981. Made in Hong Kong. 8in (20.3cm). *Illustration 703.*

SEE: CHIPS.

Illustration 702. 3¾in (9.6cm) ROBERT PINE as *Sarge* from "CHiPs" by Mego, No. 08010/3, 1981. All-vinyl with painted features and clothing. Copyright 1977 by Metro-Goldwyn-Mayer Film Co. Made in Hong Kong.

Illustration 703. 8in (20.3cm) ROBERT PINE as *Sarge* from "CHiPs" by Mego, No. 87500/3, 1981. All-vinyl and fully-jointed. Painted brown and gray hair; painted brown eyes; painted teeth. Original package includes helmet and decals. Head not marked. Copyright 1977 by Metro-Goldwyn-Mayer Film Co. Made in Hong Kong.

PITCHER, MOLLY. (MARY McCAULEY).   American Revolutionary War heroine. Born October 13, 1754; died January 22, 1832. Molly Pitcher earned her legendary name from carrying water to the soldiers at the Battle of Monmouth in 1778. She also fired a cannon during the battle.

DOLLS:
1. MOLLY PITCHER.   Peggy Nisbet, No. H292, 1970s. Plastic "collectors' doll." Made in England. About 7½in (19.1cm).
2. MOLLY PITCHER.   Hallmark, No. 400DT114-5, 1979. Made in Taiwan. 6¾in (17.2cm). *Illustration 704.*

Illustration 704. 6¾in (17.2cm) MOLLY PITCHER by Hallmark, No. 400DT114-5, 1979. All-cloth with printed features and clothing. Sewn joints in arms and legs. Made in Taiwan.

PLANET OF THE APES. *Planet of the Apes* was a film with four sequels and also two television programs. The several dolls sold as "Planet of the Apes" represent characters from the film and characters from the TV series. Apparently when the TV series was announced Mego made a set of five dolls based on the film. Then when the TV show was cast another set of five dolls was made. They are all sorted out below.

PLANET OF THE APES. 1978 film starring Charlton Heston, Roddy McDowall, Kim Hunter, Maurice Evans, James Whitemore and Linda Harrison. Based on the novel *Monkey World* by Pierre Boulle. This is a science-fiction adventure in which astronaut Heston finds himself in a future world where the apes are the masters and the humans are the slaves. The makeup for the characters who played the apes was created by John Chambers and it took hours to apply. The sequels to the film were *Beneath the Planet of the Apes* (1969), *Escape From the Planet of the Apes* (1971), *Conquest of the Planet of the Apes* (1972), and *Battle For the Planet of the Apes* (1973).

DOLLS:
Mego, 1974. 8in (20.3cm). Copyright 1967 by APJAC Productions, Inc. and Twentieth Century-Fox Film Corporation.
RODDY McDOWALL as Cornelius, No. 1961
MAURICE EVANS as Dr. Zaius, No. 1962
KIM HUNTER as Zira, No. 1963
Soldier Ape, No. 1964; *Illustration 707*
Astronaut, No. 1965

PLANET OF THE APES. CBS-TV Science-Fiction series, September 13, 1974 to December 27, 1974, starring Roddy McDowall, Ron Harper, James Naughton, Mark Lenard and Booth Coleman. The plot of this series was similar to the 1968 film. Two astronauts find themselves trapped in a civilization of the future in which the orangutangs are the ruling class, the gorillas are the military class and the humans are the slaves. The TV episodes dealt with the astronauts' adventures as hunted fugitives. In 1975 there was another TV series based on *Planet of the Apes* that was a children's cartoon show.

DOLLS:
MEGO, 1975. 8in (20.3cm). General Ursus was copyrighted in 1967; the others were copyrighted in 1975 by Twentieth Century-Fox Film Corporation.
RODDY McDOWALL as Galen, No. 50900/6
MARK LENARD as General Urko, No. 50900/8
JAMES NAUGHTON as Peter Burke, No. 50900/9 *Illustration 705*.
RON HARPER as Alan Virdon, No. 50900/0; *Illustration 705*.
General Ursus, No. 50900/7
See also *Illustrations 706* through *708*.

ABOVE: *Illustration 706*. PLANET OF THE APES dolls and toys from *J C Penney Christmas 1974* catalog.

Illustration 707. 8in (20.3cm) *Soldier Ape* from *Planet of the Apes* by Mego, No. 1964, 1974. All-vinyl and fully-jointed. Painted hair and features. Head marked: "© APJAC PRODUCTIONS INC & // 20th CENTURY—FOX FILM CORP. 1974."

Illustration 705. RON HARPER and JAMES NAUGHTON from "Planet of the Apes," the television show. See listings under the celebrities.

Illustration 708. "PLANET OF THE APES" showing the doll characters and accessories from the TV show.

POCAHONTAS. Daughter of Indian chief Powhatan. Born circa 1595; died 1617. In 1608 Captain John Smith was placed in charge of the colony of Jamestown to impose strict military discipline because the venture was failing after its first year. Smith reported that he was saved from execution by the Indians by the intercession of a beautiful dusky maiden, Pocahontas. Before he had come to Virginia he had been captured by the Turks in Hungary, where he reported that a beautiful fair-haired maiden had rescued him. Both of these rescues are generally discredited. Pocahontas, whose Indian name was Matoaka, did marry a member of the Jamestown Company, John Rolfe. She converted to Christianity and was christened Rebecca. Her marriage helped to bring

about peaceful relations between the Indians and the English in Virginia.

DOLLS:
1. POCHAHONTAS (sic). Excel Toy Corp., 1974. All-vinyl and fully-jointed with painted hair and features. Made in Hong Kong. 9¼in (23.6cm).
2. POCAHANTAS (sic). Madame Alexander, No. 721, 1967-1970. 7½in (19.1cm). *Illustration 709*.
3. POCAHONTAS. Effanbee, No. 1157, 1977-1978. All-vinyl and fully-jointed. Rooted hair; brown sleep eyes with lashes. 11in (27.9cm).
4. POCAHONTAS. Peggy Nisbet, No. P825, early 1980s. Plastic "collectors' doll." Made in England. About 7½in (19.1cm).

POLK, SARAH. Wife of the 11th President of the United States, James K. Polk. Born Sarah Childress in 1803; died 1891. She married Polk on January 1, 1824 while he was a state representative in Tennessee. The social prominence of Mrs. Polk's family and her fame as a hostess were assets to her husband when he developed further political ambitions. Polk became President in 1845 and at 49 was the youngest man ever elected up to that time. (Polk was born in 1795; he died in 1849.) Polk was elected on a platform of Manifest Destiny, or expansion of the United States. As President he managed the War with Mexico, which as an end result almost doubled the size of the country. Polk died two months after he left office. Mrs. Polk maintained Polk Place in Nashville, Tennessee, as a shrine to her husband's memory for more than 40 years.

DOLLS:
1. SARAH POLK. Madame Alexander, No. 1511, 1979. All-vinyl and fully-jointed. Rooted auburn wig with curls on top; sleep eyes with lashes. Wears blue taffeta gown trimmed in lace. Part of the "First Ladies" set. 14in (35.6cm).
SEE: FIRST LADIES.

POMPADOUR, JEANNE ANTOINETTE POISSON, MARQUISE DE. Mistress of King Louis XV of France from 1745 until her death. Born December 29, 1721; died April 15, 1764. Madame Pompadour was born of a humble family and she used her beauty, intelligence and ambition to improve her state in life. By the time of her death she was the actual ruler of France. Her foreign policy created the alliance with Austria, which later brought Marie Antoinette to France. In about 1751 her physical liaison with Louis XV ended but she continued as his friend and advisor. Her status at court was made secure with her appointment as lady-in-waiting to the queen in 1756. Madame Pompadour was a lavish patron of artists and writers and she helped to make Paris the cultural center of Europe.

DOLLS:
1. MADAME POMPADOUR. Lenci, No. 165/16, 1927. Felt and cloth. Made in Italy. 27½in (69.9cm).
2. MADAME POMPADOUR. Madame Alexander, No. 2197, 1970. 21in (53.3cm). *Illustration 710*.
3. MADAME POMPADOUR. Peggy Nisbet, No. H227, 1970s. Plastic "collectors' doll." Painted features; high white wig. Made in England. About 7½in (19.1cm).
4. MADAME POMPADOUR. Anili, 1981. Designed

Illustration 709. 7½in (19.1cm) POCAHANTAS (sic) by Madame Alexander, No. 721, 1967. All-hard plastic and fully-jointed. Dark skin tones; dark brown synthetic wig; brown sleep eyes. The costume is a copy of the original by Patricia Gardner. Back marked: "ALEX."

by Lenci and made in Italy. 23in (43.2cm). *Illustration 711.*

NOTE: There are also many inexpensive dolls and souvenir dolls that are called Madame Pompadour, as well as composition dolls with high white wigs that may represent her.

Illustration 710. 21in (53.3cm) MADAME POMPADOUR by Madame Alexander, No. 2197, 1970. All-vinyl and fully-jointed. Rooted blonde hair; blue sleep eyes with lashes. Pink satin gown. *Dolls & Stuff– Ginny's Antiques.*

Illustration 711. 23in (43.2cm) MADAME POMPADOUR by Anili and designed by Lenci® 1981. Stiffened felt and fully-jointed. Blonde synthetic wig; painted blue eyes. Made in Italy. *Shirley Buchholz Collection.*

PORTSMOUTH, LOUISE RENEE de KEROULLE, DUCHESS OF. French mistress of King Charles II of England. Born 1649; died 1734. The Duchess of Portsmouth exerted great influence in England in favor of France after 1671. She was hated in England so she returned to France after the death of Charles in 1685.

DOLLS:
1. DUCHESS OF PORTSMOUTH. Peggy Nisbet, No. LE86, 1970s. Part of a "Special Collectors' Set" of plastic dolls with painted features and mohair wigs. The group includes King Charles II, No. LE83 and his other two "favorite mistresses," Nell Gwyn, No. LE84, and the Countess of Castlemaine, No. LE85. Made in England. About 7½in (19.1cm). See *Illustration 188.*

POTTER, BEATRIX. Writer; illustrator. Born in London, England, July 6, 1866; died December 22, 1943. When Beatrix Potter was 27 and still living with her strict parents, she began sending illustrated letters to the sick child of her former governess. She amused him with stories of animals who dressed like people. This was the basis for *The Tale of Peter Rabbit*, which she published herself in 1902. She eventually found a publisher who brought out 25 of her books. Beatrix Potter's stories were about animals and about nature and, although written for children, they were not sentimental. At times they were macabre and squemish. In her later years Beatrix Potter's eyesight diminished so her final stories and illustrations are not her best. Her animal characters, like Peter Rabbit, Benjamin Bunny, Jemima Puddle-Duck and Mrs. Tiggy-Winkle, have become classic characterizations in literature.

DOLLS:
1. BEATRIX POTTER. Ann Parker, late 1970s. Made in England. 10¾in (27.4cm). *Illustration 712.*

Illustration 712. 10¾in (27.4cm) BEATRIX POTTER by Ann Parker, late 1970s. All-hard plastic and permanently affixed to a base. The facial features are painted; the wig is mohair. The rabbit is covered with imitation fur. Tagged with the Ann Parker label. *Shirley Buchholz Collection.*

PRESLEY, ELVIS. Singer, actor. Born January 8, 1935 in Tupelo, Mississippi; died August 16, 1977 in Memphis, Tennessee. Elvis Presley was considered "an international legendry performer" although he never performed outside the United States, except for some sequences in his movie *G.I. Blues*, which was filmed in Germany in 1960 while he was still in the army. Elvis Presley caused mass hysteria among young people and mass condemnation from older people when he first appeared on television in 1956. His "pelvic gyrations" were considered so terrible that he was only filmed from the waist up for his celebrated guest spots on "The Ed Sullivan Show" because he had disturbed parents and religious leaders with his earlier act. Compared with today's standards for rock performers on television he was *very* mild. Elvis Presley's style of music was right for the times. His manager, Colonel Tom Parker, promoted him well, causing Presley to become the highest earning performer in history. All of Elvis' early records for RCA Victor were Number One hits. From 1956 to 1958 he made four movies of respectable quality. Then he was drafted into the army for two years. His records continued to be released to insure the survival of his popularity. From 1960 to 1969 he made 27 films, all of them tailor-made vehicles for his talents. The critics hated these films but they brought in $150 million. His last two films were documentaries of his concerts. During the late 1960s Elvis made rare personal appearances, but by the 1970s he was a headliner in Las Vegas, retaining his ardent fans and bringing in new ones. At the height of his second career success Presley began having weight problems and mental problems. The weight problems were caused by his addiction to "junk food;" the mental problems were caused by worry over losing his looks and a dependency on an enormous variety of stimulant and depressant pills. He died of a minor heart ailment, allegedly aggravated by the drug problem. During his lifetime Elvis Presley sold more records than any other recording artist. After his death sales of Presley record albums increased even more. Elvis Presley is the single most important performer in the history of rock and roll music.

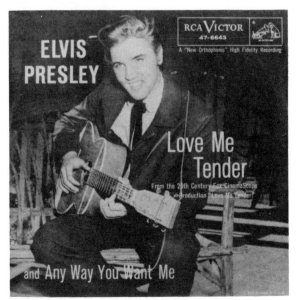

Illustration 713. Elvis Presley 45rpm record cover from his first movie, *Love Me Tender*, September 1956.

DOLLS:
1. ELVIS PRESLEY. Maker unknown, 1957. Vinyl head; vinyl "magic skin" body. Painted and molded hair; painted blue eyes; open-closed mouth with painted teeth. Head marked: "1957 EPE." See color section for Illustration.
2. ELVIS PRESLEY, THE MEMORIAL OF RADIO. Made in Hong Kong, circa 1978. 8in (20.3cm). *Illustration 714.*

Illustration 714. 8in (20.3cm) ELVIS PRESLEY, "The Memorial of Radio," made in Hong Kong, circa 1978. Vinyl jointed head, arms, wrists and torso to the waist. Plastic one-piece lower torso and legs with molded black boots. Painted dark brown hair; painted blue eyes. The costume is a gaudy pink shirt with metallic threads through the material; bright brocade jacket; a belt of gold and black braid; silver lamé pants. There are holes in the feet to attach the doll to the AM radio. No company wanted to claim manufacture on the original box.

PRESTON, WADE. Actor. Wade Preston played a handsome young government undercover agent, Christopher Colt, in the western adventure "Colt .45" on ABC-TV from October 1957 until 1959-1960. (The show ended in September 1960.) Preston walked out of his show shortly after it began, demanding more money, and was eventually replaced by Donald May, who played his cousin more and more often until he was the star of the show. After 1963 Preston made several western films in Italy, where he took up residence. The films were seldom shown in the United States but they earned a fortune for Preston.

DOLLS:
1. CHRISTOPHER COLT OF COLT .45. Hartland Plastics, Inc., No. 761, circa 1958. All-plastic with jointed arms. Painted hair and features; painted and molded clothing. Made in Hartland, Wisconsin. 8in (20.3cm).

PROWSE, DAVID. Actor. David Prowse played Lord Darth Vader in *Star Wars* in 1977 and *The Empire Strikes Back* in 1980. The voice for Darth Vader was supplied by actor James Earl Jones.

DOLLS:
1. DARTH VADER. Kenner, No. 38230, 1978. All-vinyl and fully-jointed with painted costume. Made in Hong Kong. 4¼in (10.9cm).
2. DARTH VADER. Kenner, No. 38610, 1978. Plastic and vinyl and fully-jointed. Black molded costume. Made in Hong Kong. 15in (38.1cm).
SEE: STAR WARS.

PURVIS, JACK. Jack Purvis was Chief Jawa in *Star Wars* in 1977 and Chief Ugnaught in the second *Star Wars* film, *The Empire Strikes Back* in 1980.
DOLLS:
1. JAWA. Kenner, No. 38270, 1978. All-vinyl and fully-jointed with molded features. Made in Hong Kong. 2¼in (5.8cm).
2. JAWA. Kenner, No. 39350, 1978. Vinyl and plastic and fully-jointed with molded features. Made in Hong Kong. 15in (38.1cm).
3. UGNAUGHT. Kenner, No. 39319, 1981. All-vinyl and fully-jointed. Molded and painted features and clothing with a cloth vest. Made in Hong Kong. About 4in (10.2cm).
SEE: STAR WARS.

PYLE, DENVER. Actor. Born May 11, 1920. Pyle is a character actor who has played in many films and TV series, most of them Westerns. He was a regular in "The Andy Griffith Show," CBS-TV from October 1960 to September 1968; "The Doris Day Show," as Doris' father, on CBS-TV from September 1968 to September 1969, when the format of the program changed; "Karen," ABC-TV from January to June 1975; "The Life and Times of Grizzly Adams," NBC-TV from February 1977 to July 1978 with a final show on December 19, 1978; and as Uncle Jesse on "The Dukes of Hazzard" on CBS-TV since January 1979.
DOLLS:
1. UNCLE JESSE. Mego, No. 09010/6, 1982. Made in Hong Kong. All-vinyl and fully-jointed. Copyright by Warner Bros., Inc. 3¾in (9.6cm).
SEE: DUKES OF HAZZARD, THE.

Q

QUIGLEY, JUANITA. Child actress, originally billed as Baby Jane. Born June 24, 1931. Juanita Quigley performed in pictures from 1933 to 1936 as Baby Jane and from 1936 to 1944 as Juanita Quigley. David Ragan in *Who's Who in Hollywood* (Arlington House Publishers, 76) states that "as a youngster, she was a bright-eyed, precocious doll, with her hair in bangs and a phenomenal I.Q." When she was 18, Juanita Quigley ended her film career and entered college. In 1951, shortly before her 20th birthday, she entered a convent and was a nun and teacher. Thirteen years later she left the convent, later married, and continued teaching.
DOLLS:
1. BABY JANE. Madame Alexander, 1935. 17in (43.2cm). *Illustrations 716 and 717.*

Illustration 716. 17in (43.2cm) JUANITA QUIGLEY (BABY JANE) by Madame Alexander, 1935. All-composition and fully-jointed. Auburn mohair wig; brown sleep eyes with lashes; open mouth with teeth and a tongue. Head marked: "BABY-JANE // REG // MME ALEXANDER." The costume is not original. This doll was Madame Alexander's answer to Ideal's Shirley Temple. Neither the performer nor the doll were ever as popular as Shirley Temple or Shirley Temple dolls; however, this is one of the better portrait dolls from Alexander. *Betty Shriver Collection.*

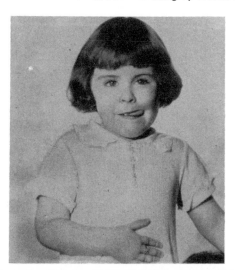

Illustration 715. Juanita Quigley (Baby Jane), 1935.

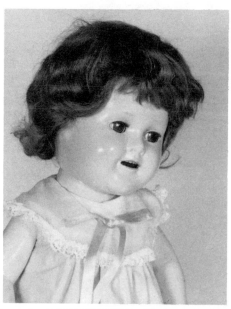

Illustration 717. BABY JANE by Madame Alexander.

QUINN, AILEEN. Juvenile actress. Born 1973. Aileen Quinn from Yardley, Pennsylvania, was discovered during a "world-wide talent search" in which 8,000 little girls were tested for the lead in the 1982 film *Annie*. Aileen Quinn is a gifted young performer and advance promotional material for the film credited her with being "the best little singer and dancer since Shirley Temple in the 1930s."

DOLLS:
1. ANNIE. Knickerbocker Toy Co., Inc., No. 3856, 1982. 6in (15.2cm). Six different Annie fashions were made for the doll. *Illustration 717-B.*
2. ANNIE TOTE'N DOLL. Knickerbocker Toy Co., Inc., No. 3854, 1982. A cotton tote bag with a 6in (15.2cm) all-cloth doll in the front pocket. Bright red yarn hair and printed features and clothing.
3. ANNIE. Knickerbocker Toy Co., Inc., No. 3851, 1982. All-cloth with jointed arms and legs. Bright red yarn hair, printed features. Bright red dress; white socks that are sewn to the feet and shoes. A plush dog, Sandy, is in the dress pocket. This is the same doll that was used for "Annie and Her Dog Sandy from the Hit Musical," *Illustration 309-A.* 16in (40.6cm).
4. ANNIE. Knickerbocker Toy Co., Inc., No. 3852, 1982. Same as the above in 23½in (59.7cm).

NOTE: For 1982 Knickerbocker produced a line of merchandise called "The World of Annie." This line includes the above dolls; dolls of the "Annie Co-Stars;" Annie Limousine (a 1929 Duesenberg); Annie Mansion (a doll house); a plush Sandy; Annie wig; Annie locket; and Annie Miniatures, character figures of the players in the film *Annie*.
SEE: ANNIE.

Illustration 717-B. 6in (15.2cm) AILEEN QUINN as *Annie* from *Annie* by Knickerbocker Toy Co., Inc., No. 3856, 1982. All-vinyl and fully-jointed. Rooted bright red hair; painted freckles across the nose; open-closed mouth. From *The World of Annie* (catalog) by Knickerbocker.

R

RAIDERS OF THE LOST ARK. A film released in 1981. George Lucas, who wrote *Star Wars* and *The Empire Strikes Back* also wrote *Raiders of the Lost Ark* as a story for the screen. (Lucas also directed *Star Wars* and was the executive producer of *The Empire Strikes Back* and *Raiders of the Lost Ark*.) Lucas described his story ideas for *Raiders* as a series of sagas that would detail the experience of an adventurer, archeologist, Indiana Jones. Indiana was involved in mortal adventures and also "otherworldly" events as he sought hidden treasures. (Derek Taylor: *The Making of Raiders of the Lost Ark*, Ballantine Books, 1981.) The film was released in the summer of 1981 and by January of 1982 was the fifth highest grossing film in history. (*Star Wars* and *The Empire Strikes Back* are in first and second place.) *Raiders* was nominated for an Academy Award as the Best Film of 1981. Lucas said in 1981 that if *Raiders* was successful there would be sequels in the high-adventure series that draws its inspiration from the Saturday afternoon serials of the 1930s and 1940s. HARRISON FORD, the star of the *Star Wars* films, played the hero, Indiana Jones, who carried a 10 foot bull whip that gave him super powers. Other characters from the film who were made as dolls by Kenner are RONALD LACEY as *Toht*, KAREN ALLEN as *Marion Ravenwood*, TERRY RICHARDS as the *Cairo Swordsman* (Arab Swordsman in the film), and PAUL FREEMAN as *Belloq*. The "action figure" series is called "The Adventures of Indiana Jones." See listings under each performer and *Illustration 717-C*.

Illustration 717-A. Aileen Quinn with 6in (15.2cm) *Annie* doll. *Photograph Courtesy of Knickerbocker Toy Co., Inc.*

Illustration 717-C. "The Adventures of Indiana Jones Action Figures" from *Raiders of the Lost Ark* by Kenner, 1982. From left to right: HARRISON FORD as *Indiana*, RONALD LACEY as *Toht* and TERRY RICHARDS as the *Cairo Swordsman*, all about 4¾in (12.2cm). At the right: KAREN ALLEN as *Marion Ravenwood*, about 4in (10.2cm). *Photograph Courtesy of Kenner Products.*

RALEGH (or RALEIGH), ELIZABETH. Wife of English explorer Sir Walter Ralegh. Lady Elizabeth Throckmorton was a lady-in-waiting to Queen Elizabeth of England. Sometime in 1591 she and Sir Walter Ralegh were secretly married. After the birth of the couple's first of three children in 1592 they were taken to the Tower as prisoners, presumably because of Queen Elizabeth's fury over having been betrayed. Sir Walter Ralegh secured their release from prison by turning over to the Queen the wealth his sailors had captured from a Portuguese ship.

DOLLS:
1. LADY ELIZABETH RALEIGH. Peggy Nisbet, No. P654, 1970s. Plastic "collectors' doll." Sir Walter Raleigh, No. P695, is a companion doll. Made in England. About 7½in (19.1cm).

RALEGH (or RALEIGH), WALTER. English statesman; explorer; writer. Born circa 1552; died 1618. Sir Walter Ralegh was a favorite friend of Queen Elizabeth of England. Although he never set foot in North America he planned and financed the first English colony, Roanoke Island off the coast of North Carolina, in 1584. Ralegh introduced the use of tobacco to England, and reportedly the growing of potatoes. As a writer, he was associated with a group who gained a reputation for "atheism." He fell from favor with Queen Elizabeth when he married Elizabeth Throckmorton Ralegh but his real problems came about when James I took the

throne in 1603. Under James he was accused of conspiring to aid England's rival, Spain, and he spent 13 years confined to the Tower. In 1616 he was released from prison and led an expedition to South America. Again he was accused of conspiring with Spain and was brought back to the Tower, where he was beheaded on October 29, 1618, under the original sentence of treason.

DOLLS:
1. SIR WALTER RALEIGH. Peggy Nisbet, No. P695, 1970s. Plastic "collectors' doll." Lady Elizabeth Raleigh, No. P654, is a companion doll. Made in England. About 8in (20.3cm).

RAND, SALLY. Actress, fan dancer. Born Helen Gould Beck on April 12, 1903; died August 31, 1979. Sally Rand played in many silent films but she was a has-been by the sound era. At the Chicago World's Fair in 1933 she took a job as a chorus girl. She performed a sensational fan dance that got her arrested and launched her new career. When she was well into her 70s she was still doing her fan dance for appreciative audiences all over the United States.

DOLLS:
1. FAN DANCER. Manufacturer unknown, 1936. Made of composition in one-piece construction. Called "The sensation of A Century of Progress" (the name of the Chicago Fair). Fans made of feathers cover the body portions. Painted and molded features and hair. 12in (30.5cm).

Note: Celluloid dolls covered with bright feathers became popular carnival prizes after Sally Rand became the hit of the Chicago World's Fair in 1933. These dolls have molded, waved hair and come in many different sizes.

RANDOLPH, MARTHA WASHINGTON JEFFERSON. Daughter of President Thomas Jefferson. Born September 27, 1772; died October 10, 1836. Thomas Jefferson was the 3rd President of the United States from 1801 to 1809. While he presided from the White House several prominent ladies, most notably Dolly Madison, acted as his official hostess, as he was a widower. Jefferson's daughter, Martha, also filled this role.

DOLLS:
1. MARTHA RANDOLPH. Madame Alexander, No. 1503, 1976-1978. All-vinyl and fully-jointed. Rooted blonde hair in an upsweep style. Dressed in a gown of ivory lace over pink taffeta, a black cape and a wide band across the head. 14in (35.6cm).
2. MARTHA JEFFERSON RANDOLPH. Peggy Nisbet, No. P724, 1976. Plastic "collectors' doll." Thomas Jefferson, No. P723, is a companion doll. Made in England. About 7½in (19.1cm).
3. MARTHA JEFFERSON RANDOLPH. Crafted Heirlooms, designed by Sandy Williams, 1981. Made in Cumberland, Maryland. 12in (30.5cm). *Illustration 718.*

SEE: FIRST LADIES.

Illustration 718. 12in (30.5cm) MARTHA JEFFERSON RANDOLPH from the First Ladies Collection by Crafted Heirlooms, designed by Sandy Williams, 1981. All-cloth, hand-screened in white bleached muslin. Jefferson's daughter is wearing an Empire-style dress, a long paisley shawl. (Martha Washington and Abigail Adams are part of a set of three.) Made in Cumberland, Maryland.

REAGAN, NANCY (NANCY DAVIS). Actress; wife of President Ronald Reagan. Born Anne Frances Robbins on July 6, 1921. During the 1950s Nancy Davis worked as an actress in Hollywood. In 1957 she appeared in *Hellcats of the Navy* with her husband, Ronald Reagan, whom she had married in 1952. The following year she retired from films to aid her husband in his political pursuits.

DOLLS:
1. NANCY REAGAN. Peggy Nisbet, No. P737, 1982. Plastic "collectors' doll," dressed in inaugural gown. A "limited edition of under 2000." Ronald Reagan, No. P736, is a companion doll. Made in England. About 7½in (19.1cm). *Illustration 718-A.*

Illustration 718-A. NANCY REAGAN with RONALD REAGAN from *Illustration 719.* 7½in (19.1cm) NANCY REAGAN by Peggy Nisbet, No. P737, 1982. Plastic with jointed arms. Dark blonde mohair wig. Dressed in a white gown and coat like Mrs. Reagan wore to the Inauguration Ball on January 20, 1981. Made in England. *Photograph Courtesy of House of Nisbet.*

REAGAN, RONALD. Actor; Governor of California; President of the United States. Born February 6, 1911 in Tampico, Illinois. Reagan began his professional career as a sports announcer and went to Hollywood in the 1930s to work as an actor in movies. Most of his films were "programmers," or second-rate features. His best performances were in *King's Row* (1942) and *The Hasty Heart* (1950). He was the host of two anthology series on television—"General Electric Theater" from 1954 to 1962 and "Death Valley Days" from 1964 to 1967. He was the president of the Screen Actors Guild from 1947 to 1952 and again in 1959. Politically, Reagan had always been a staunch liberal Democrat but he became a "champion of conservativism" in 1962 when he became a Republican. In 1966 he began his eight-year term as Governor of California. In the 1976 presidential primaries he narrowly lost to Gerald Ford. In 1980 he defeated incumbent President Jimmy Carter. His Inauguration on January 20, 1981 was the most memorable in American History, as that was the day the 52 American hostages were freed in Iran after 444 days.

DOLLS:
1. RONALD REAGAN. Peggy Nisbet, No. P736, 1981. Nancy Reagan is a companion doll. Made in England. 8½in (21.6cm). *Illustrations 718-A, 719* and *720.*
2. RONALD REAGAN (AT "THE WESTERN WHITE HOUSE" RANCHO DEL CIELO IN SANTA BARBARA, CALIFORNIA). Peggy Nisbet, No. P738, 1982. Made in England. 8in (20.3cm). *Illustration 720-A.*

Illustration 719. 8½in (21.6cm) RONALD REAGAN by Peggy Nisbet, No. P736, 1981. All-hard plastic; jointed only at the arms. Painted dark brown hair; blue painted eyes. This example is No. 653 of a "Signed Introductory Limited Edition of 1,000 dolls." Made in England. Nancy Reagan is a companion doll.

Illustration 720. RONALD REAGAN by Peggy Nisbet.

Illustration 720-A. 8in (20.3cm) RONALD REAGAN by Peggy Nisbet, No. P738, 1982. Plastic with jointed arms. Painted hair and eyes. Made in England. *Photograph Courtesy of House of Nisbet.*

REEVE, CHRISTOPHER. Actor. Born September 25, 1952. After appearing on Broadway, a soap opera on television ("Love of Life") and in a film (*Gray Lady Down*). Christopher Reeve was chosen for the title role in the multi-million dollar production *Superman,* released in 1978. He repeated the part in *Superman II* in 1981 and further productions are planned. (Christopher Reeve is not related to George Reeves, who played Superman on television during the 1950s.)

DOLLS:
1. SUPERMAN. Madel, S.A., No. 1300, 1979. Made in Spain. 6½in (16.5cm). *Illustration 722*.
SEE: SUPERMAN.

Illustration 721. Christopher Reeve as Superman, 1978.

Illustration 722. 6½in (16.5cm) CHRISTOPHER REEVE as *Superman* by Madel, S.A., No. 1300, 1979. All-vinyl and fully-jointed. Painted hair and features. No marks. Copyright by DC Comics, Inc. Made in Spain. Note that the original box calls attention to *Superman the Movie*. The movie logo is used; the end flaps show scenes from the film. This doll is used for "Madelman," a popular action figure in Spain that comes in various sports outfits and as military characters. It is interesting to note that the original carton is licensed for Superman, as the doll does not bear much resemblance to Christopher Reeve.

REVERE, PAUL. American Revolutionary patriot. Born 1735; died 1818. Revere was a silversmith, a designer and a printer in Boston. He took part in the Boston Tea Party and in many of the radical demonstrations that led up to the Revolution. He is remembered for his ride on horseback on April 18, 1775, when he warned the Massachusetts countryside of the advance of British soldiers who were on their way to Concord to destroy the arms the patriots had secreted there.

DOLLS:
1. PAUL REVERE. Excel Toy Corp., 1974. All-vinyl and fully-jointed. Painted hair and features. Made in Hong Kong. 9¾in (24.9cm).
2. PAUL REVERE. Made for the S.S. Kresge Company, 1976. Made in Hong Kong. 7½in (19.1cm). *Illustration 723*.
3. PAUL REVERE. Effanbee, No. 1151, 1976. 11in (27.9cm). *Illustration 724*.
4. PAUL REVERE. Peggy Nisbet, No. P704, late 1970s. Plastic "collectors' doll." Made in England. About 7½in (19.1cm).

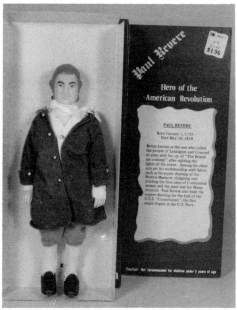

Illustration 723. 7½in (19.1cm) PAUL REVERE manufactured for S.S. Kresge Company, 1976. Vinyl head with painted hair and features. Fully-jointed plastic body with swivel waist. Marked on back: "MADE IN // HONG KONG." *Shirley Buchholz Collection.*

RICHARD III. King of England. Born October 2, 1452; died August 22, 1485. Richard III's reputation as a horrible monster comes from the play by Shakespeare and was based on Tudor propaganda. There is no evidence to support the allegation that he was a hunchback. In 1471 he did not stab to death the son of Queen Margaret, as the Tudors reported, but he probably was implicated in the murder of Henry VI. When Richard's brother Edward IV died in 1483 he was named protector for the young Edward V. In June of 1483 he was proclaimed King because of the charges that Edward V was illigitimate, as his father had had a marriage contract with another lady before he married the young king's mother. Edward and his young brother Richard were taken to the Tower and in August 1483 they disappeared. It is most likely that they were murdered by their uncle's orders so that his claim on the throne would be secure. Edward then concentrated on building the economy of England and preserving order. In 1485 Henry Tudor (later Henry VII) gathered support against Richard and met him in battle at Bosworth Field. Richard was killed and his naked and bloody body was thrown across a horse and hauled to the church of the Greyfriers in Leicester where it was buried without honors.

DOLLS:
1. KING RICHARD III. Peggy Nisbet, No. P456, late 1970s. Plastic "collectors' doll." Made in England. About 8in (20.3cm).

RICHARDS, TERRY. Actor. Richards played a minor but important part near the end of *Raiders of the Lost Ark* as the Arab Swordsman.

DOLLS:
1. CAIRO SWORDSMAN. Kenner, Series No. 46010, 1982. All-vinyl and fully-jointed. Painted features. Wears a fabric robe. Copyright by Lucasfilm Ltd. About 3in (9.6cm).
SEE: RAIDERS OF THE LOST ARK.

Illustration 724. 11in (27.9cm) PAUL REVERE by Effanbee, No. 1151, 1976. Vinyl head and arms; plastic legs and torso. Rooted brown hair; brown sleep eyes with molded lashes. Head marked: "EFFANBEE // ©1976 // 1176." *Phyllis Houston.*

RIPLEY, HEATHER. Child performer. Heather Ripley played Jemima in the film *Chitty Chitty Bang Bang* in 1968.

DOLLS:
1. JEMIMA from CHITTY CHITTY BANG BANG. Mattel, 1968. All-vinyl with a jointed head. Companion dolls are Adrian Hall as Jeremy, Dick Van Dyke as Mr. Potts and Sally Ann Howes as Truly Scrumptious. Made in Hong Kong. 1¼in (3.2cm).

RIPPY, RODNEY ALLEN. Child performer. Born 1968. Rodney Allen Rippy was a cute little boy who appeared on television commercials and programs in the early 1970s.

DOLLS:
1. RODNEY ALLEN RIPPY. Shindana Toys, 1973. Made in Taiwan and USA. 16in (40.6cm). *Illustration 725.*

Illustration 725. 16in (40.6cm) Talking RODNEY ALLEN RIPPY by Shindana Toys, 1973. All-cloth with printed features and clothing. Jointed arms and legs. Copyright by Target Marketing, Inc. and Shindana Toys, Division of Operation Bootstrap, Inc. Made in Taiwan and USA.

ROBERTSON, DALE. Actor. Born Dayle Robertson on July 14, 1923. After 1949 Robertson appeared in many action and western films. He was the star of two western series entries on television. From March 1957 to September 1962 he was Jim Hardie of "Tales of Wells Fargo" on NBC-TV. He was the star of "The Iron Horse" on ABC-TV from September 1967 to January 1968.

DOLLS:
1. JIM HARDIE FROM TALES OF WELLS FARGO. Hartland Plastics, Inc., No. 764, circa 1958. Plastic with jointed arms. Painted hair, features and clothing. Made in Hartland, Wisconsin. 8in (20.3cm).

ROBEY, GEORGE. British music hall comedian. Born George Edward Wade in 1869; died 1954. In the silent era in films Robey, who was billed as "the prime minister of mirth," appeared in comedy farces. He later appeared in character roles. He was knighted by the Crown.

DOLLS:
1. GEORGE ROBEY. Dean's Rag Book Company, 1923. All-cloth with an applied mask face in the "Tru-to-Life" design. Dressed in a jacket, pants and a bowler hat. Made in England. 14½in (36.9cm).

ROBINSON, JACKIE. Baseball player. Born Jack Roosevelt Robinson on January 31, 1919; died October 24, 1972. In 1947 Jackie Robinson became the first black player with the major leagues when he joined the Brooklyn Dodgers. In 1949 he was the National League's leading batter and was named the league's Most Valuable Player. His lifetime batting average was .311. In 1962 he was inducted into the Baseball Hall of Fame. After he retired from baseball in 1956 he became a civil-rights activist. In 1950 he played himself in the film *The Jackie Robinson Story*, which told of the racial issues involved in his baseball career.

DOLLS:
1. JACKIE ROBINSON. Allied-Grand Manufacturing Co., Inc., 1950. 13in (33cm). *Illustration 726.*

Illustration 726. 13in (33cm) JACKIE ROBINSON, Allied-Grand Doll Manufacturing Co., Inc., circa 1950. All-composition and fully-jointed. Molded, painted black hair; painted features. The Brooklyn Dodgers uniform is gray with a blue jacket and cap. Originally came with a ball, a wooden bat (made by Hillerich S. Bradsby & Co.) and a Jackie Robinson comic book. *Patricia N. Schoonmaker Collection. Photograph by John Schoonmaker.*

ROB ROY. Scottish freebooter. Born Robert Campbell MacGregor in 1671; died 1734. In Gaelic his name meant "Red Rob" and he became famous by Sir Walter Scott's novel *Rob Roy,* which told of his adventures as an outlaw.

DOLLS:
1. ROB ROY. Peggy Nisbet, No. P799, 1979. Plastic "collectors' doll." Made in England. About 8in (20.3cm).

ROGERS, ROY. Actor, singer. Born Leonard Slye on November 5, 1912, in Cincinnati, Ohio. In the early 1930s Slye went to California and changed his name to Dick Weston. He formed a singing group, The Sons of the Pioneers, and they appeared on the radio and in films. By 1942, as Roy Rogers, he had replaced Gene Autry as "The King of the Cowboys." He made dozens of western films for Republic Studios until 1951, appearing often with his wife, Dale Evans. His horse Trigger (now stuffed and in his museum) was billed as "the smartest horse in the movies." In the 1950s Rogers also branched out into TV production, marketing of western products, cattle raising, thoroughbred horse raising, real estate, rodeo shows and a chain of resturants. In 1975 he returned to the screen for *Mackintosh and T.J.* Roy Rogers and Dale Evans were on two television series shows. "The Roy Rogers Show" was a western from December 1951 to June 1957. "The Roy Rogers and Dale Evans Show" was a musical variety series from September to December 1962. Roy and Dale still occasionally sing on television.

DOLLS:
1. ROY ROGERS. Dolls of Hollywood, 1948. All cloth with painted features. Dale Evans is a companion doll. 17in (43.2cm).
2. ROY ROGERS. Duchess Doll Corp., 1948. All-plastic and fully-jointed. Sleep eyes; mohair wig. **Dale Evans is a companion doll. 7in (17.8cm).**

Illustration 727. 6½in (16.5cm) ROY ROGERS bobble head, 1962. Papier-mâché. The head is attached to a wire spring to make it "bobble" when moved. Painted features; molded hat. Marked on bottom. "EXCLUSIVE LICENSE RIGHTS // © 1962 JAPAN." Shirley Buchholz Collection.

3. ROY ROGERS. Ideal, 1949. Stuffed vinyl head with painted hair and features; cloth body with vinyl hands. 25in (63.5cm).
4. ROY ROGERS. Zany Toys, Inc., 1952. Hand puppet with a viny head with painted features. Dale Evans is a companion doll.
5. ROY ROGERS. Nancy Ann Storybook Dolls, Inc., circa 1955. All-plastic and fully-jointed. Painted brown hair; sleep eyes with molded lashes. Dale Evans is a companion doll. 8in (20.3cm).
6. ROY ROGERS, KING OF THE COWBOYS and TRIGGER. Hartland Plastics, Inc., No. 806, 1955. Plastic doll with plastic horse. Dale Evans, No. 802, is a companion doll. Made in Hartland, Wisconsin. About 8in (20.3cm).
7. ROY ROGERS. Bobble head doll, made in Japan, 1962. 6½in (16.5cm). *Illustration 727.*

ROGERS, WILL. Rustic comedian; political commenter. Born November 4, 1879, in Indian Territory (now Oklahoma); died 1935. Rogers began his career in Wild West shows and by 1917 he was a star of the Ziegfeld Follies. After 1918 he acted in movies, but gained his greatest popularity after the advent of sound in films. He also appeared on radio and in newspaper columns, commenting on the political situation. (He was instrumental in the election of Franklin D. Roosevelt in 1932.) He was killed in a plane crash in Alaska with aviator Wiley Post. Will Rogers, Jr. portrayed his father in the films *Look for the Silver Lining* (1949), *The Story of Will Rogers* (1952) and *The Eddie Cantor Story* (1953.)

DOLLS:
1. WILL ROGERS. Peggy Nisbet, No. P730, late 1970s. Plastic "collectors' doll." Made in England. About 8in (20.3cm).

ROMERO, CESAR. Actor. Born February 15, 1907, in New York, New York, of Cuban parents. Romero was a ballroom, nightclub and stage dancer before entering motion pictures. In films he played "Latin lover" parts and later character roles. During 1939 and 1940 he played the Cisco Kid in several films. From January 1966 to March 1968 he was the arch villian The Joker on "Batman" on ABC-TV on a semi-regular basis.

DOLLS:
1. JOKER. Mego, No. 1351, 1974. All-vinyl and fully-jointed. Painted hair and features. Part of the set "World Greatest Super Heroes 'Arch Enemy' Series" from "Batman." Made in Hong Kong. 8in (20.3cm).

THE ROOKIES. Police series on ABC-Television. First telecast September 11, 1972; last telecast July 6, 1976. The basis for the programs was that three young rookie cops had learned tactics that were in opposition to those of a veteran officer who was their superior. The Rookies used more modern and humane methods of law enforcement; the older officer was "old fashioned." The young officers were Terry Webster, played by GEORG STANFORD BROWN; Willie Gillis, played by MICHAEL ONTKEAN; and Mike Danko, played by SAM MELVILLE. GERALD S. O'LOUGHLIN was Lt. Eddie Ryker. Mike's wife, Jill, was played by Kate Jackson. From 1974 to

1976 Willie was replaced by BRUCE FAIRBURN as Officer Chris Owens. Dolls were made of the five male characters of the series by L.J.N. Toys Ltd. in 1976. All of the dolls are No. 6101 and the names on the packages are *Terry, Willie, Mike, Chris* and *Lt. Ryker*. See entries under the names of the five celebrities who played them.

ROOSEVELT, ANNA ELEANOR ROOSEVELT. First Lady; writer, lecturer. Born October 11, 1884; died November 7, 1962. Her maiden name was Roosevelt, and she was the favorite niece of Theodore Roosevelt and a distant cousin of Franklin D. Roosevelt. As the wife of President Franklin D. Roosevelt she was called "The First Lady of the World." Mrs. Roosevelt worked for social betterment as a lecturer, a newspaper columnist and a world-wide traveler. She wrote several books about her political ideas and her experiences. She was a United States delegate to the United Nations from 1945 to 1952 and in 1946 she was named Chairman of the Commission of Human Rights.

DOLLS:
1. ELEANOR ROOSEVELT. Peggy Nisbet, No. P726, 1970s. Plastic "collectors' doll." Franklin D. Roosevelt, No. P725, is a companion doll. Made in England. About 7½in (19.1cm).

ROOSEVELT, EDITH. Wife of President Theodore Roosevelt. Born Edith Kermit Carow on August 6, 1861; died September 30, 1948. Theodore Roosevelt's first wife, Alice Lee Roosevelt, died in 1884 and in 1886 he married Edith Kermit Carow. The second Mrs. Roosevelt was First Lady during Theodore Roosevelt's two terms as President, 1901 to 1909.

DOLLS:
1. EDITH ROOSEVELT. Peggy Nisbet, No. P732, 1970s. Theodore Roosevelt, No. P731, is a companion doll. Made in England. About 7½in (19.1cm). *Illustration 729.*

ROOSEVELT, FRANKLIN D(ELANO). President of the United States. Born January 30, 1882; died April 12, 1945. Franklin D. Roosevelt had the same political background as his 5th cousin, President Theodore Roosevelt—Assistant Secretary of the Navy (1913-1920) and Vice Presidential Candidate (1920). In 1921 Franklin D. Roosevelt was striken with polio, which left him permanently crippled. He was inaugurated President at the height of the Depression (1933) and promptly declared a "Bank Holiday," or closing, to end the "run" on banks. His New Deal Programs provided relief and employment with the establishment of government agencies to revive the economy. He was reelected in 1936, and again in 1940 for an unprecedented third term because of the crisis that developed in Europe in 1939, causing World War II. In 1944, during which time the United States was involved in the War in both Europe and in the Pacific, he was elected a fourth time. Shortly before his death he took part in international conferences that decided the fate of the post-war world. Roosevelt's character, his policies and his achievements are still hotly argued by those who disagreed with him.

DOLLS:
1. FRANKLIN D. ROOSEVELT. Peggy Nisbet, No. P725, 1970s. Plastic "collectors' doll." Eleanor Roosevelt, No. P726, is a companion doll. Made in England. About 8in (20.3cm).

ROOSEVELT, THEODORE. President of the United States from 1901 to 1909. Born October 27, 1858; died 1919. Roosevelt first came to public prominence when he organized the Rough Riders to fight the Spanish in Cuba in 1898. When William McKinley died from gunshop wounds afflicted by an assassin in 1901 Roosevelt, as his Vice President, became the youngest President in American history. His policies favored "trust busting," conservation of natural resources and "Big Stick" diplomacy in Latin America to protect American interests. In 1908 Roosevelt retired to hunt wild animals in Africa and handpicked William Howard Taft to succeed him, but the two men soon became political rivals. Roosevelt announced in 1912 that he was "as strong as a bull moose" and formed the Progressive Party when the Republicans would not nominate him for President again. He and Taft were defeated at the polls by Woodrow Wilson, the Democrat's candidate.

DOLLS:
1. TED. Elms & Sellon (selling agents), 1909. Cloth, printed on heavy art ticking; cloth clothing. Part of a set called "Jungle Subjects" that included Jocko, a monkey; a giraffe; and Jumbo the Elephant. Advertised in *Playthings,* September 1909.

Illustration 728. 9in (22.9cm) THEODORE ROOSEVELT by Schoenhut, circa 1910. All-wood with painted features and fully-jointed. The helmet is also wood and is removable. *Mary K. Dahl Collection. Photograph by Fay Rodolfos.*

2. TEDDY ROOSEVELT. Palmer Cox, circa 1909. Appears to be papier-mâché and cloth. See cover of *Doll News*, Fall 1981.
3. THEODORE ROOSEVELT. Schoenhut, circa 1910. 9in (22.9cm). *Illustration 728*.
4. LT. COL. THEODORE ROOSEVELT. Excel Toy Corp., 1974. All-vinyl and fully-jointed. Painted hair and features; wears glasses. Made in Hong Kong. 9¾in (24.9cm).
5. THEODORE ROOSEVELT. Peggy Nisbet, No. P731, late 1970s. Edith Roosevelt, No. P732, is a companion doll. Made in England. About 8in (20.3cm). *Illustration 729*.

Illustration 729. About 8in (20.3cm) THEODORE ROOSEVELT, No. P731, and EDITH ROOSEVELT, No. P732, by Peggy Nisbet, 1970s. All-hard plastic and jointed only at the arms. He has molded hair and painted features; she has a mohair wig with painted features. Made in England. *Photograph Courtesy of House of Nisbet.*

ROSS, BETSY. Seamstress. Born Elizabeth Griscom on January 1, 1752; died 1836. The story that Betsy Ross designated the first American flag to George Washington's specifications is generally discredited. However, researcher Sally Hile (*Personality Doll Houses*, privately published, n.d.) sets forth evidence that Mrs. Betsy Ross was commissioned to create the flag in 1776 and was paid for doing the job in 1777. Hile tells that Betsy married three times and that she "remained alive and alert to age 84."

DOLLS:
1. BETSY ROSS. Madame Alexander, No. 731, 1967-1974. All-hard plastic and fully-jointed. Dark brown wig; sleep eyes with molded lashes. Carries tiny American flag. 7½in (19.1cm).
2. BETSY ROSS. Madame Alexander, No. 431, 1975 to present. Same as the above. 7½in (19.1cm).
3. BETSY ROSS. Effanbee, No. 1152, 1976-1978. 11in (27.9cm). *Illustration 730*.

4. BETSY ROSS. Peggy Nisbet, No. H226, circa 1976. Plastic "collectors' doll." Made in England. About 7½in (19.1cm).
5. BETSY ROSS. Hallmark, No. 250DT900-4, 1979. Called "Betsey Ross" on tag. Made in Taiwan. 7in (17.8cm). *Illustration 731*.

Illustration 730. 11in (27.9cm) BETSY ROSS by Effanbee, No. 1152, 1976. Vinyl head and arms; plastic legs and torso. Rooted blonde hair; blue sleep eyes with molded lashes. Head marked: "EFFANBEE // © 1976 // 1176." *Phyllis Houston.*

Illustration 731. 7in (17.8cm) BETSY ROSS by Hallmark, No. 250DT900-4, 1979. All-cloth with sewn joints in arms and legs. Printed features and clothing. Made in Taiwan. (The tag on the doll spells the name as *Betsey.*) *Rosemarye Bunting Collection.*

ROSS, DIANA. Singer, actress. Born March 26, 1944, in Detroit, Michigan. In 1960 Diana Ross and her friends, Mary Wilson and Florence Ballard, won a high school singing contest billed as The Primettes. Berry Gordy, Jr., an executive with Motown Records, spotted the girls and signed them to a recording contract later. The Supremes recorded a dozen Number One hit records within five years, beginning in 1962. In 1967 Florence Ballard left the group (and later died a drug addict on welfare) and was replaced by Cindy Birdsong. Diana Ross left the Supremes in 1969 and began an equally successful solo career. In 1972 Ross played blues singer Billie Holiday in *Lady Sings the Blues* and won an Academy Award Nomination for her acting. Her second film, *Mahagony* in 1975, was less successful and her third film *The Wiz* was a musical version of *The Wizard of Oz* and a complete flop. In *The Wiz* Diana Ross was cast as Dorothy, a young school teacher. It seemed rather silly that she should be frightened by strange creatures when she went into the city. But this did not hurt the career of Diana Ross, which is still in high gear.

DOLLS:
1. DIANA ROSS OF THE SUPREMES. Ideal, No. 0920-9, 1969. 19in (48.3cm). *Illustration 733* and *734.*
2. DIANA ROSS. Mego, No. 76000, 1977. Made in Hong Kong. 12¼in (31.2cm). *Illustrations 735* and *736.*

Illustration 732. Diana Ross.

Illustration 734. DIANA ROSS by Ideal. *Lee Jenkins Collection.*

Illustration 733. 19in (48.3cm) DIANA ROSS by Ideal, No. 0920-9, 1969. All-vinyl and fully-jointed. Rooted black hair; dark brown sleep eyes with lashes. Copyright by Motown Inc. *Jean Canaday Collection.*

Illustration 735. 12¼in (31.2cm) DIANA ROSS by Mego, No. 76000, 1977. All-vinyl and fully-jointed. Rooted black hair; painted brown eyes with long attached lashes. Head marked: "©MOTOWN // RECORD CORPORATION." Made in Hong Kong. *Shirley Buchholz Collection.*

Illustration 736. DIANA ROSS by Mego. *Shirley Buchholz Collection.*

ROVENTINI, JOHNNY. Living trademark for Philip Morris cigarettes. Born circa 1910. Johnny Roventini was a midget working as a page boy in the lobby of the Hotel New Yorker in Manhattan in 1933 when an advertising man impressed upon the president of the Philip Morris Company that he would be perfect as a

Illustration 737. Johnny, the Philip Morris page boy, in an advertisement that appeared in *The Saturday Evening Post,* May 21, 1938.

living trademark for Philip Morris cigarettes. The cigarette company was already using a page boy as its trademark, so Johnny was hired and did promotional work until the mid 1950s. He was presented in all visual advertising and on radio and early television yelled out his famous advice, "Call for Phil-lip More-rees." At last report, Johnny is retired and living in Brooklyn, New York.

DOLLS:
1. PAGE BOY. Maker unknown, circa 1943. Composition head; felt hands; cloth stuffed body. Painted hair and features; open-closed mouth with painted tongue and teeth. Felt page boy hat. 15in (38.1cm).
2. PAGE BOY. Maker unknown, circa 1943. Composition head; stuffed cloth body. Painted hair and features; closed mouth. The page boy cap is molded to the head. 11in (27.9cm).
3. BELLBOY. I.B. Wolfset, No. 100B, 1943. Composition head; cloth glove for body. 9½in (24.2cm). *Illustration 738.*

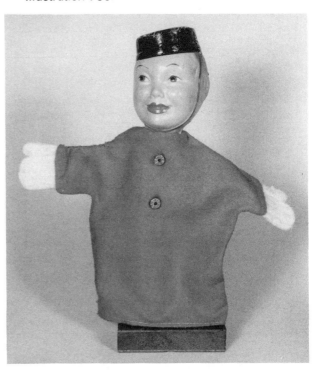

Illustration 738. 9½in (24.2cm) glove doll inspired by JOHNNY (ROVENTINI), the Philip Morris page boy, by I.B. Wolfset, No. 100B, 1943. Although advertised only as a *Bellboy,* this is the most famous real person made as an advertising doll. The composition head measures 4¼in (10.9cm). The features are painted; the eyes are blue and the hair is brown. This type of doll, or hand puppet, was rather common in the late 1930s and the early 1940s. In 1938 Ideal made a Charlie McCarthy using a similar concept, calling the item a "hand doll." In 1938 Crown Toys made a *Dopey* from *Snow White and the Seven Dwarfs* and in 1939 a *Pinocchio,* calling them "glove dolls." These other dolls also had composition heads with painted features.

ROXANNE. Actress. Born Delores Rosedale in Minneapolis, Minnesota. Roxanne was a staturesque blonde assistant to Bud Collyer on the CBS-TV show "Beat the Clock" from 1950 to 1955. At first on the game show Roxanne was a silent display of considerable physical attributes; later she was more articulate. This led to some movie roles in the 1950s. She left "Beat the Clock" to have a baby and was replaced by Beverly Bentley.

DOLLS:
1. to 3.
   ROXANNE. Valentine Doll Co., 1952. All-vinyl. Head has a blonde wig and sleep eyes. Body is possibly one-piece "magic skin" vinyl. "Roxanne" is embroidered across the skirt. Sizes of 17in (43.2cm), 19in (48.3cm) and 22in (55.9cm).
4. to 6.
   ROXANNE. Maker unknown, 1953. All-hard plastic walker; fully-jointed. Blonde saran wig in bangs; sleep eyes with lashes. Came with a camera on a strap around the neck. Sizes of 16in (40.6cm), 18in (45.7cm) and 22in (55.9cm). 18in (45.7cm) size marked on the head: "180."

RUNCIE, ROBERT ALEXANDER KENNEDY, THE MOST REVEREND ARCHBISHOP OF CANTERBURY. Born October 2, 1921. Runcie was ordained as an Anglican (Church of England) priest in 1951, after having served as a chaplain in World War II. He became the Archbishop of Canterbury in February 1980. On July 29, 1981, the Archbishop of Canterbury, "the primate of all England," married Lady Diana Spencer to Prince Charles in St. Paul's Cathedral in London, England.

DOLLS:
1. ARCHBISHOP OF CANTERBURY. Peggy Nisbet, No. P429, 1982. "Royal Wedding Commemorative Doll." Plastic, with jointed arms; wears wire spectacles. Made in England. About 8in (20.3cm).

RUNYON, CHARLES M. Television clown. Loraine Burdick reports in *Adult Star Dolls and Toys, Book 2* that Runyon was a Los Angeles TV star who played Chucko the Clown on a children's program in the mid-1950s. Chucko the Clown also made personal appearances.

DOLLS:
1. CHUCKO THE CLOWN. Hollywood Doll Mfg. Co., 1955. All-hard plastic and fully-jointed. Painted clown features. Dressed in a clown costume. 8½in (21.6cm).

RUSSELL, JOHN. Actor. Born January 8, 1921. John Russell was in many movies after 1937. On television he was Marshal Dan Troop on "The Lawman" on ABC-TV from October 1958 to October 1962. Peter Brown played his deputy, Johnny McKay.

Illustration 739. John Russell as Marshal Dan Troop and Peter Brown as Deputy Johnny McKay from "The Lawman."

DOLLS:
1. DAN TROOP FROM LAWMAN. Hartland Plastics, Inc., number not known, 1958. Plastic with jointed arms. Peter Brown as Johnny McKay, No. 768, is a companion doll. Made in Hartland, Wisconsin. 8in (20.3cm).

RUTH, GEORGE HERMAN (BABE RUTH). Baseball player. Born February 6, 1895; died August 16, 1948. Babe Ruth was crude, vulgar and uncouth and he had excessive appetites. He was also the greatest baseball player up to his time, the first to become internationally famous. Publicity and the art of sham and his cooperation with his fans made him a great American hero. His other nicknames were "The Bambino" and "The Sultan of Swat." He played with the Boston Red Sox from 1914 to 1919; with the New York Yankees from 1920 to 1934; with the Boston Braves in 1935. He held over 50 baseball records when he retired. He had 714 career home runs, including the most in one season (60 in 1927); a lifetime batting average of .342; played in ten World Series games; led the American League in runs brought in. He was elected into the Baseball Hall of Fame in 1936. Because of his tremendous popularity Babe Ruth appeared in three silent films, *Headin' Home, Babe Comes Home* and *Speedy.* In the last he played himself as "The Babe." In *The Babe Ruth Story*, 1948, William Bendix played Babe Ruth as a great hero, further adding to his legend.

DOLLS:
1. BABE RUTH. Hallmark, No. 400DT113-5, 1979. Made in Taiwan. 7in (17.8cm). *Illustration 741.*

Illustration 740. Babe Ruth holding four-year-old C. Kenneth Clark, Jr., March 1934. *Photograph by Alton Norris.*

Illustration 741. 7in (17.8cm) BABE RUTH by Hallmark, No. 400DT113-5, 1979. All-cloth. Sewn body joints with printed features and clothing. Made in Taiwan. *Shirley Buchholz Collection.*

S

S.W.A.T. Television police story series. "S.W.A.T." was telecast on ABC-TV from February 24, 1975, to June 26, 1976. S.W.A.T. stands for Special Weapons and Tactics. The show was inspired by real-life SWAT teams that were formed around the United States in response to the riots in many cities during the late 1960s. On the TV show the SWAT team handled violent situations that the regular police were afraid to tackle. The members of the team were all veterans from Vietnam and they were trained for urban combat. Their captain tried to hold the more eager members of the team back, but their tactics were usually to blast their way into trouble with whatever weapons it took to do the job. STEVE FORREST played "Hondo" Harrelson, the leader. The other members of the SWAT team were ROD PERRY as David "Deacon" McKay, ROBERT URICH as Jim Street, MARK SHERA as Dominic Luca, and JAMES COLEMAN as T.J. McCabe. The show was criticized because of the disproportionate amount of violence that is featured, causing its cancellation. See entries under each celebrity.

DOLLS:
L.J.N. toys issued five dolls in 1975, using No. 6600 for each doll. In 1976 the five dolls were marketed in a different package and the number was 6850 for each doll. The names for the dolls are *Hondo, Deacon, Street, Luca* and *McCabe.* See celebrity listings for each doll under the celebrity.

SABU. Actor. Born Sabu Dastagir, sometime in 1924 in India; died December 2, 1963. Director Robert Flaherty discovered Sabu when he was 12 and was playing around the elephant stables of the Maharajah of Mysore. Flaherty was searching for a boy to cast in the British film *Elephant Boy* (1937), based on a story by Rudyard Kipling. For several years Sabu specialized in playing the part of an exotic boy. He was cast in many films that were Arabian Nights adventure tales. The best remembered of these is *The Thief of Bagdad* in 1940, in which he essayed the title role. Sabu died of a heart attack at 39.

DOLLS:
1. SABU. Molly-'es, circa 1940. 15in (38.1cm). *Illustrations 743* and *744.*

Illustration 742. Sabu and Maria Montez in *Arabian Nights 1942.*

OPPOSITE PAGE: *Illustration 743.* 15in (38.1cm) SABU by Molly-'es, circa 1940. All-composition and fully-jointed with brown skin tones. Painted black eyes. Note the Asian modeling of the face, which is highly unusual for the time period in doll manufacture. Sabu wears a pink velvet vest, silk pants and turban with an attached "jewel" and gold shoes. The doll is not marked. The cardboard tag has "Sabu" penciled in and tells that he was "inspired by Alexander Korda's 'Thief of Bagdad.'"

Illustration 745. 8in (20.3cm) ANWAR SADAT by Peggy Nisbet, No. P830, 1982. Plastic with jointed arms. Painted hair and features with dark skin tones. Made in England. *Photograph Courtesy of the House of Nisbet.*

Illustration 744. SABU by Molly-'es.

SADAT, ANWAR (MOHAMED ANWAR EL-SADAT).

Egyptian leader. Born December 25, 1918; died October 6, 1981. Anwar Sadat was a highly respected world leader and he was at the height of his prestige when he was gunned-down by assassins who were Muslim religious fanatics. During the 1940s he served time in prison for anti-government activities. In 1952 he helped to overthrow King Farouk. He served in governmental positions under President Nasser and became President of Egypt in 1970. During his long term Sadat tried to develop Egypt, as Nasser had done, although he established his firm control over the government at the same time. He ousted the Soviet advisers and technicians in 1972. After several wars between Egypt and Israel, Sadat traveled to Israel to promote peace between the two nations and in 1977 he signed a peace agreement with Israel.

DOLLS:
1. PRES. ANWAR SADAT. Peggy Nisbet, No. P830, 1982. Made in England. 8in (20.3cm). *Illustration 745.*

SAKATA, HAROLD.

Actor. In the James Bond film *Goldfinger*, 1964, Sakata was Oddjob, a massively built oriental who dressed in a morning suit and top hat. Oddjob's hat was a deadly weapon. When he cast it at a victim it could sever his head. During the climax of *Goldfinger*, Oddjob throws Bond (Sean Connery) around a vault at Fort Knox and when Bond flings gold bars at Oddjob, they bounce off his chest. Oddjob was electrocuted when he attempted to retrieve his hat which he had thrown at Bond, who ducked causing it to become embedded in a row of protective bars that were electrified.

DOLLS:
1. HAROLD SAKATA AS ODDJOB IN "GOLDFINGER." Gilbert, No. 16012, 1965. All-vinyl and fully-jointed. Painted hair and features. Copyright by Gilrose Productions, Ltd., Danjaq, S.A. and A.C. Gilbert Co. Made in Portugal. 10½in (26.7cm).

SEE: JAMES BOND.

SALES, SOUPY.

Comedian. Born Milton Hines on January 8, 1926. On television Soupy Sales was seen in a number of children's shows over the years. He had his own prime-time program during July and August of 1955 and from January to April of 1962. His most frequently used comic routine was pie throwing. He was also a panelist on game shows and he appeared in two films during the 1960s.

DOLLS:
1. SOUPY SALES. Ideal, 1965. Vinyl head; jointed cloth body. Flocked black hair; painted blue eyes. Wears a bow tie and a red sweat shirt. Head marked: " © 1965 // IDEAL TOY CORP. // SOUPY SALES — WMC. // H9." 23in (58.4cm).
2. SOUPY SALES. Knickerbocker, 1966. Made in Japan. 13in (33cm). *Illustrations 746* and *747*.

Illustration 746. 13in (33cm) SOUPY SALES by Knickerbocker, 1966. Vinyl head with molded and painted hair and features. Stuffed cloth body that is a corduroy jacket and pants. The felt collar is made to the shirt; the bow tie is glued in place. Copyright by Soupy Sales, W.M.C. Head marked: " © 1966 KNICK // JAPAN."

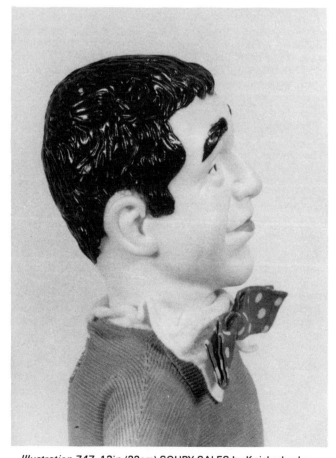

Illustration 747. 13in (33cm) SOUPY SALES by Knickerbocker.

SAMPSON, WILLIAM THOMAS. American naval officer. Born 1840; died 1902. Sampson commanded the North Atlantic squadron during the Spanish-American War in 1898. He designed the plans for the Battle of Santiago, but the credit for the victory went to W.S. Schley (which see).

DOLLS:
1. WILLIAM THOMAS SAMPSON. Manufacturer unknown, circa 1900 to 1910. Made in Germany. 15in (38.1cm). *Illustration 748.*

SEE: SPANISH-AMERICAN WAR HEROES.

Illustration 748. 15in (38.1cm) WILLIAM THOMAS SAMPSON, manufacturer unknown, 1900 to 1910. Bisque head on a jointed composition body. Painted hair, moustache, beard and eyes. Part of a series of six officers from the Spanish-American War. Made in Germany. *Courtesy of the Margaret Woodbury Strong Museum.*

SANDERS, (COLONEL) HARLAND. Fast foods magnate. Born September 9, 1890; died December 16, 1980. Sanders dropped out of school in the sixth grade and worked at a number of jobs. In 1930 he settled in Corbin, Kentucky, and built a motel and restaurant. He developed a recipe for quick-cooked chicken that became Kentucky Fried Chicken with its "11 herbs and spices." By 1960 there were 400 franchises for the restaurant chain and Sanders royalty payment was a nickle for each chicken used. In 1964 Sanders sold his business to future governor of Kentucky John Y. Brown, Jr. Brown sold the Kentucky Fried Chicken restaurants to Heublin Inc. in 1971 for a stock transaction valued at $250 million. The Colonel, who used an honorary title bestowed by the state of Kentucky, sued the company in 1974, claiming that it was misusing his image and that the recipe "tasted like wallpaper paste." He got $1 million in an out-of-court settlement. Sanders held onto his franchises in Canada at the time of the initial sale and later donated them to charity there. Colonel Sanders, dressed in his familiar white suit, continued to promote his recipe until a year before he died of lukemia.

DOLLS:
1. COLONEL SANDERS. Maker unknown, 1960s. Plastic nodder, molded to a base. Holds a bucket of fried chicken. Back marked: "KENTUCKY FRIED CHICKEN." 7in (17.8cm).

SAVALAS, TELLY. Actor. Born January 21, 1924. Savalas' first career after serving in the army in World War II was as a newsman for ABC. After 1960 he became an actor, and usually portrayed despicable villains. His greatest popularity came from playing "Kojak," a detective, on CBS-TV from October 1973 to April 1978. His brother, George Savalas, was also a detective on the show during the first two years.

DOLLS:
1. KOJAK. Excel Toy Corp., No. 550, 1976. Made in Hong Kong. 8in (20.3cm). *Illustration 749*.

SCHELL, MAXIMILIAN. Actor, director, producer, screenwriter. Born April 8, 1930, in Vienna, Austria. In 1938 Schell fled to Switzerland with his family to escape the Nazis. His sisters, Maria and Edith, and his brother, Karl, also became actors in international productions. Maximilian Schell first acted on the stage and later in films. He earned an Academy Award for playing the defense attorney in *Judgment at Nuremberg* (1961). Although he was handsome and talented, the award did nothing for his acting career. He later turned to directing, producing and writing for films, as well as acting.

DOLLS:
1. DR. HANS REINHARDT. Mego, No. 95010/1, 1979. Made in Hong Kong. 3¾in (9.6cm). *Illustration 750*.
2. DR. HANS REINHARDT. Mego, No. 95005, 1979. All-vinyl and fully-jointed. Painted hair and features. Made in Hong Kong. 12½in (31.8cm).
SEE: BLACK HOLE, THE.

Illustration 750. 3¾in (9.6cm) MAXIMILIAN SCHELL as *Dr. Hans Reinhardt* from *The Black Hole* by Mego, No. 95010/1. All-vinyl and fully-jointed. Painted hair and features; painted red clothing. Copyright 1979 by Walt Disney Productions. Made in Hong Kong.

Illustration 749. 8in (20.3cm) TELLY SAVALAS as *Kojak* by Excel Toy Corp., No. 550, 1976. All-vinyl and fully-jointed. The vinyl head is balloon-thin and has painted brown eyes. Back marked: " © 1976 UNIVERSAL // CITY STUDIOS, INC. // © 1976 EXCEL TOY CORP. // MADE IN HONG KONG." The clothing is also of a very cheap construction. Plastic accessories, a gun and holster, a hat, a cigar and lollipops came with the doll.

SCHLEY, WINFIELD SCOTT. American naval officer. Born 1839; died 1911. Schley was in command at the Battle of Santiago in the Spanish-American War. A controversy over credit for the victory arose between him and William Thomas Sampson, the commander of the fleet.

DOLLS:
1. WINFIELD SCOTT SCHLEY. Manufacturer unknown, circa 1900 to 1910. Made in Germany. 8⅛in (20.6cm). *Illustration 751*.
SEE: SPANISH-AMERICAN WAR HEROES.

Illustration 751. 8⅛in (20.6cm) WINFIELD SCOTT SCHLEY, manufacturer unknown, 1900 to 1910. Bisque head; jointed composition body. Painted hair, moustache and beard; fixed glass eyes. Part of a series of six officers from the Spanish-American War. Made in Germany. *Courtesy of the Margaret Woodbury Strong Museum.*

Illustration 752. John Schneider.

Illustration 753. 3¾in (9.6cm) JOHN SCHNEIDER as *Bo* from "The Dukes of Hazzard" by Mego, No. 09060, 1981. (Part of a set with a car and TOM WOPAT as *Luke*. See THE DUKES OF HAZZARD.) All-vinyl and fully-jointed. Painted yellow hair; molded clothing. Note the two different head modelings, especially the changes in the hair, of the two figures. Backs marked: "© WB 1980 // MADE IN HONG KONG."

SCHNEIDER, JOHN. Actor, singer. Born April 8, circa 1953 in Mt. Kisco, New York. John Schneider began his career as a model and later became an actor in films and on television. He began playing Bo Duke on "The Dukes of Hazzard" on CBS-TV on January 26, 1979. In 1981 he recorded some hit records.

DOLLS:
1. BO from THE DUKES OF HAZZARD. Mego, No. 09060, 1981. Part of a set with a car and TOM WOPAT as Luke. Came with two different head molds. Also given as a premium by Mego, which could be ordered with a slip from the purchase of the car, "The General Lee," when sold separately. Made in Hong Kong. 3¾in (9.6cm). *Illustration 753.*
2. BO from THE DUKES OF HAZZARD. Mego, No. 09050/1, 1981. Made in Hong Kong. 8in (20.3cm). *Illustrations 754 and 755.*
3. BO from THE DUKES OF HAZZARD. Mego, No. 09010/1, 1982. This is the same doll as No. 1, packaged individually.

SEE: DUKES OF HAZZARD, THE.

Illustration 754. 8in (20.3cm) JOHN SCHNEIDER as *Bo* from "The Dukes of Hazzard" by Mego, No. 09050/1, 1981. All-vinyl and fully-jointed. Painted yellow hair and painted blue eyes. Head marked: "© WARNER BROS., // INC. 1980." Back marked: "© MEGO CORP. 1974 // REG U.S. PAT OFF // PAT PENDING // HONG KONG."

Illustration 755. 8in (20.3cm) JOHN SCHNEIDER as *Bo* by Mego.

SCOTT, BARBARA ANN. Ice skater. Born in Ottawa, Canada, on May 9, 1928. By age ten Barbara Ann Scott was an award-winning skater. At age 11 she won the Canadian Junior Championship and was taken to tea by Sonja Henie. In 1940 she was the runner-up of the Canadian Senior Ladies Championship. In 1941, 1942, 1944, 1945 and 1946 she took first place in this competition. In 1947 she won the Women's European Figure Skating Championship and a gold medal at the Winter Olympics. In 1948 she turned professional. Part of the proceeds from her earnings went to a fund to aid crippled and under-privileged children. The profits from the sale of the Barbara Ann Scott doll also went to this fund.

DOLLS:
1. BARBARA ANN SCOTT. Reliable Doll, 1949. Made in Canada. 15in (38.1cm). *Illustration 757.*

Illustration 756. Barbara Ann Scott.

Illustration 757. 15in (38.1cm) BARBARA ANN SCOTT by Reliable Doll, 1949. All-composition and fully-jointed. Golden brown mohair wig; blue sleep eyes with lashes; open mouth with teeth. The skating costume is pink net with applied silver glitter over a satin underskirt and is trimmed with marabou feathers. The head is marked: "RELIABLE DOLL // MADE IN CANADA." *Celina Carroll.*

SEATON, MARY. Lady-in-Waiting to Mary Queen of Scots. Mary Seaton and Mary Fleming accompanied Mary of Scotland to France. When her husband, the King of France, died in 1560 they returned to Scotland with the Queen.

DOLLS:
1. MARY SEATON. Peggy Nisbet, No. H247, 1970s. Plastic "collectors' doll." Mary Fleming, No. H248, is a companion doll. Made in England. 7½in (19.1cm).

SELLECCA, CONNIE. Actress. Born circa 1952. Connie Sellecca is an especially beautiful brunette actress who was in two short-lived television programs before playing Pam on "The Greatest American Hero" on ABC beginning in March 1981. Her earlier shows were "Flying High" on CBS from September 1978 to January 1979 and "Beyond Westworld," three episodes on CBS in March 1980. She is married to actor Gil Gerard.

DOLLS:
1. PAM. Mego, Series No. 22001, 1982. All-vinyl and fully-jointed. Rooted long dark hair. Dressed in a sweater and jeans. Copyright by Stephen J. Connell Productions.* 8in (20.3cm).
SEE: THE GREATEST AMERICAN HERO.

*So stated in the Mego catalog. The television show is produced by Stephen J. Cannell Productions.

SEYMOUR, JANE. Third queen of Henry VIII of England. Born circa 1509; died 1537. Jane Seymour's insistence on marriage to Henry was the cause of the trial of Anne Boleyn. Jane died shortly after the birth of her son, the future Edward VI.
DOLLS:
NOTE: The wives of Henry VIII, in order, are Catherine of Aragon, Anne Boleyn, Jane Seymour, Anne of Cleves, Catherine Howard and Catherine Parr.
  1. JANE SEYMOUR. Peggy Nisbet, No. H220, 1970s. Plastic "collectors' doll." Part of a series of Henry VIII and his six wives, Standard Series. The costume is an accurate reproduction of clothing worn by Jane Seymour. Made in England. About 7½in (19.1cm).
  2. JANE SEYMOUR. Peggy Nisbet, No. P604, 1970s. Plastic "collectors' doll." Part of a series of Henry VIII and his six wives, Portrait Series. Based on a contemporary portrait. Made in England. About 7½in (19.1cm).
  3. JANE SEYMOUR. Peggy Nisbet, No. M933, 1970s. Inch-to-the-foot miniatures in the Historical Series. Part of a series of Henry VIII and his six wives. Made in England.
SEE: HENRY VIII.

SHAKESPEARE (also SHAKSPERE and SHAK-SPEARE), WILLIAM. English poet and dramatist. Born 1564; died 1616. Very little is known about the life of William Shakespeare, the most important figure in English literature. He was certainly well educated. He may have been a schoolteacher. He married Anne Hathaway and the couple may have had three children. He went to London and became interested in the theater. His first play was produced in about 1589. It was either *The Comedy of Errors* or the first part of *Henry VI.* He continued to produce a steady stream of works until he retired to Stratford-on-Avon in about 1610 with a fortune. Many scholars dispute the authorship of the plays attributed to Shakespeare and the exact chronology is not certain. Regardless of this, the plays attributed to William Shakespeare are considered among the greatest ever written. Even without the plays, he would be remembered for his sonnets, dedicated to a W.H.
DOLLS:
  1. WILLIAM SHAKESPEARE. Peggy Nisbet, No. P617, 1970s. Plastic "collectors' doll." Made in England. About 8in (20.3cm).

SHANKS, DON. Actor. Don Shanks played Nakuma, the blood brother of Grizzly Adams on NBC-TV's "The Life and Times of Grizzly Adams," which was seen from February 1977 to July 1978.
DOLLS:
  1. NAKOMA. (sic). Mattel, No. 2381, 1978. Don Haggarty as Grizzly Adams, No. 2377, is a companion doll. Made in Hong Kong. 9½in (24.2cm). *Illustrations 758* and *759.*

Illustration 758. 9½in (24.2cm) DON SHANKS as *Nakuma (Nakoma* on package) from "The Life and Times of Grizzly Adams" by Mattel, No. 2381, 1978. All-vinyl and fully-jointed. Rooted black hair in braids; painted features and "war paint." Head marked: " © MATTEL INC." Lower back marked: " © 1971 MATTEL INC. // HONG KONG US & // FOREIGN PATENTED." (This is the *Big Jim* body from Mattel.) Copyright by Schick Sunn Classic Productions, Inc. *Shirley Buchholz Collection.*

Illustration 759. DON SHANKS by Mattel. *Shirley Buchholz Collection.*

SHANNON, FRANK. Actor. Died in 1959 at the age of 84. Shannon played Dr. Zarkov, the scientist who built the rocket ships in the Flash Gordon serials in the 1930s. He sent Flash, Dale Arden and himself to the planet Mongo in *Flash Gordon* (1936), to Mars in *Flash Gordon's Trip to Mars* (1938), and to Frigia in *Flash Gordon Conquers the Universe* (1940). Frank Shannon had been in films in the silent era, and he continued in films after the Flash Gordon series ended.

DOLLS:
1. DR. ZARKOV. Mattel, No. 1529, 1980. Made in Hong Kong. 4in (10.2cm). *Illustration 760.*
SEE: FLASH GORDON.

Illustration 760. 4in (10.2cm) FRANK SHANNON as *Dr. Zarkov* from *Flash Gordon The Greatest Adventure of All* by Mattel, No. 1529, 1980. All-vinyl and fully-jointed with painted features and clothing. Copyright by King Features Syndicate, Inc. Made in Hong Kong.

SHATNER, WILLIAM. Actor. Born in Montreal, Quebec, Canada, on March 22, 1931. Shatner's first film role was as a juvenile in *The Brothers Karamazov* in 1958. He also acted on Broadway, on television and in other movies. He will always be identified with the role of Captain Kirk, which he played on "Star Trek" on NBC-TV from September 1966 to September 1969 and in *Star Trek the Motion Picture* in 1979. Between the "Star Trek" assignments Shatner had another TV series, "The Barbary Coast" on ABC-TV from September 1975 to January 1976.

DOLLS:
1. CAPTAIN KIRK. Mego, No. 51200/1, 1974. Made in Hong Kong. 8in (20.3cm). *Illustration 761.*
2. CAPT. KIRK. Mego, No. 91200/1, 1979. Made in Hong Kong. 3¾in (9.6cm). *Illustration 762.*
3. CAPTAIN JAMES KIRK. Mego, No. 91210/1, 1979. Made in Hong Kong. 12½in (31.8cm). *Illustration 763.*
4. CAPTAIN KIRK. Knickerbocker, No. 0599, 1980. Made in Haiti and USA. 13in (33cm). *Illustrations 764 and 765.*
SEE: STAR TREK.

Illustration 761. 8in (20.3cm) WILLIAM SHATNER as *Captain Kirk* of "Star Trek" by Mego, No. 51200/1, 1974. All-vinyl and fully-jointed. Painted hair and features. Copyright by Paramount Pictures Corporation. Made in Hong Kong. *Penny Caswell Collection.*

Illustration 762. 3¾in (9.6cm) WILLIAM SHATNER as *Captain Kirk* of "Star Trek" by Mego, No. 91200/1, 1979. All-vinyl and fully-jointed. Painted hair and features. Copyright by Paramount Pictures Corporation. Made in Hong Kong.

Illustration 763. 12½in (31.8cm) WILLIAM SHATNER as *Captain James Kirk* from the movie *Star Trek* by Mego, No. 91210/1, 1979. All-vinyl and fully-jointed. Painted hair and features. Head marked: "© PPC." Back marked: "© MEGO CORP. 1977 // MADE IN HONG KONG." *Penny Caswell Collection.*

SHENTALL, SUSAN. Actress. Before her retirement from acting, the only important role Susan Shentall had was in the British film *Romeo and Juliet* in 1954. Laurence Harvey played Romeo.

DOLLS:
1. JULIET from ROMEO AND JULIET. Madame Alexander, No. 473, 1955. Laurence Harvey as Romeo, No. 474, is a companion doll. 7¾in (19.8cm). *Illustration 766.*

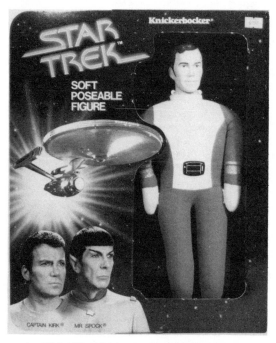

Illustration 764. 13in (33cm) WILLIAM SHATNER as *Captain Kirk* from *Star Trek* by Knickerbocker, No. 0599, 1980. Vinyl head with painted hair and features. Cloth body with velcro on hands to make them stick together. Head marked: "© 1979 P.P.C. // K.T.C." Copyright by Paramount Pictures Corporation. Sewn in Haiti; finished in USA.

Illustration 766. 7¾in (19.8cm) SUSAN SHENTALL as *Juliet* from *Romeo and Juliet* by Madame Alexander, No. 473, 1955. All-hard plastic and fully-jointed. Straight leg walker. Blonde synthetic wig; blue sleep eyes with molded lashes. Back marked: "ALEX." Cream brocade dress and cape trimmed in dark pink velvet and gold braid. *Patricia Gardner Collection.*

SHERA, MARK. Actor. Born Mark Shapiro on July 10, 1949. Shera was a regular on two television series. He was Dominic Luca on "S.W.A.T." from February 1975 to July 1976 on ABC-TV. On Buddy Ebsen's "Barnaby Jones," CBS-TV, January 1973 to September 1980, he played Jedediah Romano (J.R.) Jones from the fall of 1976 until the end of the series.

DOLLS:
1. LUCA from S.W.A.T. L.J.N. Toys, Ltd., No. 6600, 1975. All-vinyl and fully-jointed. Painted hair and features. Made in Hong Kong. 7½in (19.1cm).
2. LUCA from S.W.A.T. L.J.N. Toys, Ltd., No. 6850, 1976. Made in Hong Kong. 7½in (19.1cm). *Illustration 767.*
SEE: S.W.A.T.

Illustration 768. Brooke Shields and Calvin Klein on the cover of *People Weekly,* January 18, 1982.

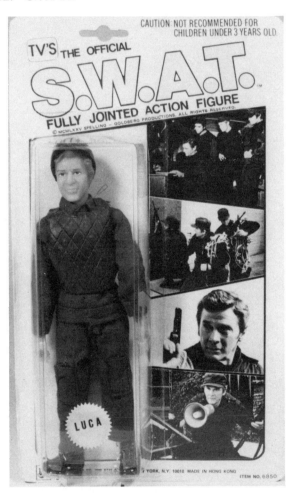

Illustration 767. 7½in (19.1cm) MARK SHERA as *Luca* from "S.W.A.T." by L.J.N. Toys Ltd., No. 6850, 1976. All-vinyl and fully-jointed with painted hair and features. Copyright 1975 by Spelling-Goldberg Productions. Made in Hong Kong.

SHIELDS, BROOKE. Model, actress. Born May 31, 1965. Brooke Shields was a model from the time she was a baby. Her most famous endorsement was for Calvin Klein jeans in the early 1980s. She became a movie star playing a 12-year-old prostitute in *Pretty Baby* in 1978.

DOLLS:
1. BROOKE SHIELDS. L.J.N. Toys, No. 8833, 1982. Made in Hong Kong. 11½in (29.2cm). *Illustrations 769 and 770.*

Illustration 769. 11½in (29.2cm) BROOKE SHIELDS by L.J.N. Toys, No. 8833, 1982. All-vinyl and fully-jointed. Rooted dark brown hair. Painted blue eyes. Designed by Karyn Weiss; head sculpted by Ken Sheller. According to advance publicity for the doll each purchaser received a special gift—" a star-shaped ring containing strawberry-flavored lip gloss and a picture of Brooke signed 'with love, Brooke Shields'." The doll also has Brooke Shields fashion accessories and a "Glamour Center." This doll, unlike other celebrity dolls from L.J.N. Toys, is a quality product. Brooke Shields received a reported one million dollars for the rights to produce the doll and L.J.N. Toys promised one million dollars in advertisements. Brooke was seen with the doll on "The Johnny Carson Show" on television and in *Time* magazine in February 1982. The Brooke Shields doll is made in Hong Kong. *Photograph by Sharon Kent for L.J.N. Toys.*

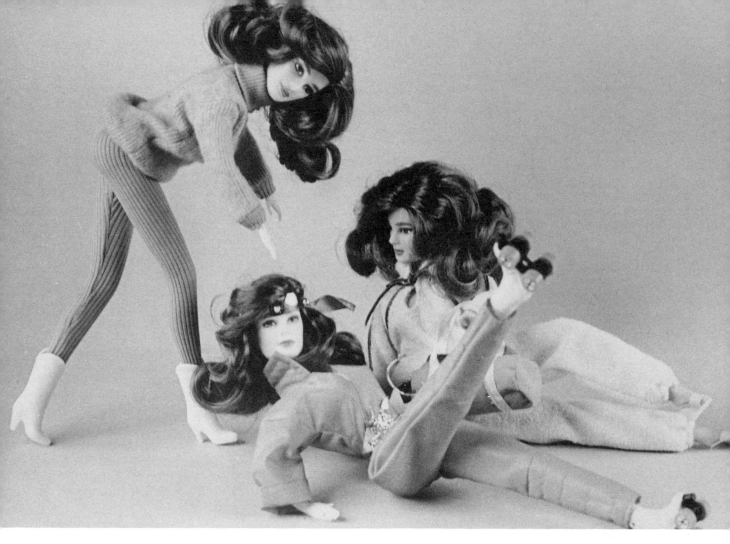

Illustration 770. BROOKE SHIELDS by L.J.N. Toys. *Photograph by Sharon Kent for L.J.N. Toys.*

SHIRLEY, ANNE. Actress. Born Dawn Evelyeen Paris in New York on April 17, 1918. Anne Shirley is still one of the loveliest and most gracious stars ever to appear in motion pictures. She began her career as an actress and model when she was about 18 months old to support her mother. Before her fourth birthday she was playing child parts in movies, mostly under the name Dawn O'Day. (She was also billed as Lenn Fondre and Lindley Dawn.) Her first film was probably *The Spanish Dancer,* released in 1923. Dawn O'Day was in about 50 films, playing such roles as the younger Jean Arthur, Madge Bellamy, Frances Dee, Ann Dvorak, Janet Gaynor, Mryna Loy, Barbara Stanwyck and Fay Wray, which in itself sets a record. As she grew older, work in films became increasingly difficult to obtain. Another break came in 1934 when she was "discovered" and given the lead in *Anne of Green Gables* for RKO Studios. She took the name Anne Shirley, the name of the girl in the film. She played top roles in almost 40 more films before retiring at 26 after *Murder, My Sweet* in 1945. As the daughter in *Stella Dallas,* 1937, her acting was honored with an Academy Award nomination as best supporting actress. From 1937 to 1943 she was married to actor John Payne, by whom she has a daughter, Julie, who became an actress. In 1949 she married greatly admired screenwriter Charles Lederer, by whom she has a son, Daniel. Anne Shirley Lederer kept active in her "retirement," living in California in two beautiful homes. In early 1976 Charles Lederer died suddenly. He, like Anne Shirley, will always be remembered by those who love the movies.

DOLLS:
1. ANNE SHIRLEY.   Effanbee, circa 1934. This is the Mary Lee doll. All-composition and fully-jointed. Red wig in pigtails; sleep eyes with lashes. Head marked: " © MARY LEE." Back marked: "EFFANBEE // PATSY-JOAN." Identified with a paper tag that reads: "I am Anne Shirley. Inspired by Anne Shirley in RKO Pictures 'Anne of Green Gables.' An Effanbee Durable Doll." 16½in (41.9cm).
2. ANNE SHIRLEY.   Effanbee, circa 1934. This is the Patricia Kin doll. All-composition and fully-jointed. Red or reddish-blonde human hair wig in pigtails; blue tin sleep eyes with lashes. Head marked: "EFFANBEE // PATRICIA KIN." Back marked: "EFFANBEE // PATSY JR. // DOLL." 11½in (29.2cm). *Illustrations 774 and 775.*
3. ANNE SHIRLEY.   Effanbee, circa 1934. This is the Patricia doll. All-composition and fully-jointed. Reddish mohair wig in pigtails; sleep eyes with lashes. Back marked: EFFANBEE // "PATRICIA." 14½in (36.9cm). *Illustration 776.*
4. ANNE SHIRLEY.   Effanbee, circa 1935 to 1940. All-composition and fully-jointed. Human hair or mohair wigs; sleep eyes with lashes. Back marked: "EFFANBEE // ANNE-SHIRLEY." 15in (38.1cm). *Illustration 777.*

NOTE: During the late 1930s Effanbee used dolls marked "ANNE-SHIRLEY" for many characters, such as Snow White, the American Children series, the Historical

Dolls series, an ice skater and a wedding party set. Examples are seen in *Illustrations 778, 779, 780, 781* and *782.*

In the early 1940s Effanbee used dolls marked "ANNE-SHIRLEY" for characters in the Little Lady series. Examples are seen in *Illustrations 783, 784, 785, 786, 787* and *788.*

From the mid to late 1940s Effanbee used dolls with the Anne Shirley modeling, but marked only "EFFANBEE // U.S.A." for the Little Lady series. Examples are seen in *Illustrations 789, 790, 791, 792* and *793.*

Probably all dolls that truly represent ANNE SHIRLEY should be dressed as Anne of Green Gables from the 1934 film. They should have long braids and a short, little girl dress.

NOTE: In the 1939 Effanbee catalog a 9in (22.9cm) Anne Shirley was advertised. Details not known.

Illustration 773. Anne Shirley, circa 1940. *Courtesy of Cleveland Public Library.*

Illustration 774. 11½in (29.2cm) *Patricia Kin* as ANNE SHIRLEY of *Anne of Green Gables* by Effanbee, circa 1934. All-composition and fully-jointed. Reddish-blonde human hair wig; blue tin sleep eyes with lashes. The all-original out-fit is blue cotton with a white sleeveless blouse sewn to the pleated skirt; cotton panties of the same blue also attached; a matching bolero jacket with attached white collar; and a matching felt hat. The blue ribbon used on the hat is also trim for the bow tie of the jacket and for the ribbons in the pigtails. Black oilcloth shoes and white rayon socks. Head marked: "EFFANBEE // PATRICIA KIN." Body marked: "EFFANBEE // PATSY JR. // DOLL." Effanbee metal heart bracelet on wrist. This is probably one of the first dolls that was used by Effanbee to represent Anne Shirley, the leading character from the 1934 film. *Ursula Mertz Collection. Photograph by Linda Mertz.*

Illustration 771. Anne Shirley when she was acting under the name Dawn O'Day, circa 1923.

Illustration 772. O.P. Heggie, Anne Shirley and Helen Westley from *Anne of Green Gables,* an RKO Picture, 1934.

Illustration 775. Patricia Kin ANNE SHIRLEY by Effanbee. *Ursula Mertz Collection. Photograph by Linda Mertz.*

Illustration 776. 14½in (36.9cm) *Patricia* as ANNE SHIRLEY from *Anne of Green Gables* by Effanbee, circa 1934. All-composition and fully-jointed. Red mohair wig in pigtails; brown sleep eyes with lashes. The ribbons in the hair are not original. Back marked: "EFFANBEE // "PATRICIA"." *Patricia Slabe Collection.*

Illustration 778. 17⅛in (43.5cm) girl from the *American Children* series by Effanbee, 1939. (These dolls had such names as Barbara Lou and Barbara Joan.) All-composition except for the hard rubber arms; fully-jointed. Blonde human hair wig; open mouth with teeth; brown sleep eyes with lashes. She wears her metal heart bracelet and the dress and shoes may be original. Back marked: "EFFANBEE // ANNE-SHIRLEY."

Illustration 777. 15in (38.1cm) ANNE SHIRLEY by Effanbee, circa 1935 to 1940. All-composition and fully-jointed. Brown sleep eyes with lashes. The wig and the costume are replacements, but they are appropriate for the doll. Back marked: "EFFANBEE // ANNE-SHIRLEY."

Illustration 779. 14½in (36.9cm) *Snow White from Grimm's Fairy Tales* by Effanbee, circa 1939. All-composition and fully-jointed. Blonde human hair wig; green sleep eyes with lashes; open mouth with teeth. The gown is pink taffeta trimmed in maroon. She wears both a metal heart bracelet and a cardboard tag. Head marked: "EFFANBEE." Back marked: EFFANBEE // ANNE-SHIRLEY."

Illustration 780. 15in (38.1cm) *Historical Dolls* by Effanbee, circa 1939. All-composition and fully-jointed. Dark brown human hair wigs; painted blue eyes. The doll on the left appears to be all-original, but there is no reference to this costume, which is a brown and white dress over a long slip. Like all of the *Historical Dolls* she wears long hose that are held in place at the top with adhesive tape. The lady on the right represents the *Monroe Doctrine—1816* Period. Her costume is a long skirt with an over-dress. The stripes and trim are bright red. Both dolls are marked on the backs: EFFANBEE // ANN-SHIRLEY."

Illustration 781. 14½in (36.9cm) Ice Skater, using the Anne Shirley mold, by Effanbee, early 1940s. All-composition except for hard rubber arms; fully-jointed. Blonde human hair wig; blue sleep eyes with lashes; closed mouth. The skating costume is white satin trimmed with marabou feathers. Back marked: "EFFANBEE // ANNE-SHIRLEY."

Illustration 782. 15in (38.1cm) Flower Girl, using the Anne Shirley mold, by Effanbee, circa early 1940s. All-composition and fully-jointed. Blonde human hair wig; blue sleep eyes with lashes. She wears a pink net dress over pink taffeta with matching pantaloons. Back marked: "EFFANBEE // ANNE-SHIRLEY."

Illustration 783. Boxed *Little Lady* puzzle by Effanbee, circa 1943. These *Little Lady* dolls are marked "ANNE-SHIRLEY" and are often confused with the true Anne Shirley doll, which came earlier.

Illustration 784. 21in (53.3cm) *Anne Shirley* or *Little Lady* by Effanbee, probably early 1940s. All-composition and fully-jointed. Bright red human hair wig; blue sleep eyes with lashes. Black lace bolero over a long white satin gown; gold sandals. Back marked: "EFFANBEE // ANNE-SHIRLEY."

Illustration 786. 14in (35.6cm) girl doll that uses an Anne Shirley head and body by Effanbee, circa early 1940s. All-composition and fully-jointed. Note that the arms, with magnets in the palms, are not the usual Anne Shirley mold. The blonde human hair wig is not in the original set, as it is not sewed for braids; brown sleep eyes with lashes. Back marked: "EFFANBEE // ANNE-SHIRLEY."

Illustration 787. 20in (50.8cm) *Anne Shirley/Little Lady* by Effanbee. All-composition, except for the hard rubber arms, and fully-jointed. Dark brown human hair wig; brown sleep eyes with lashes. The rayon dressing gown is worn over a bra and panties. The body of this doll is of a thinner proportion than the ones in *Illustrations 784* and *785.* Head marked: "EFFANBEE // U.S.A." Back marked: "EFFANBEE // ANNE-SHIRLEY."

Illustration 785. 21in (53.3cm) *Anne Shirley* or *Little Lady* by Effanbee, early 1940s. All-composition, except for hard rubber arms, and fully-jointed. Blonde human hair wig; replaced blue eyes. The hands of the hard rubber arms have magnets inserted in the palms for holding metal objects. The blue and white organdy dress is labeled with a logo like the metal heart bracelet; blue trimmed socks; blue shoes. Back marked: "EFFANBEE // ANNE-SHIRLEY."

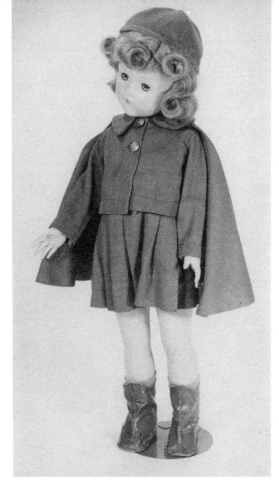

Illustration 790. Close-up of the *Little Lady* from *Illustration 789*.

Illustration 788. 20½in (52.1cm) *Little Lady* as a Navy Nurse with the Anne Shirley head modeling by Effanbee, 1942 or 1943. All-composition, except for the hard rubber arms, and fully-jointed. (A similar doll is pictured in the upper right in the Effanbee Little Lady puzzle, *Illustration 783*.) Blonde human hair wig; blue sleep eyes with lashes. The costume is dark blue; the boots are red. Head marked: "EFFANBEE // U.S.A." Back marked: "EFFANBEE // ANNE-SHIRLEY."

Illustration 789. 17½in (44.5cm) *Little Lady* with the Anne Shirley head modeling by Effanbee, No. 8500, mid 1940s. All-composition and fully-jointed. Blonde yarn wig; brown sleep eyes with lashes. The original box also included a plastic comb for the yarn wig, which was utilized during World War II, supposedly because of supply shortages of wig material. Head and back marked: "EFFANBEE // U.S.A."

Illustration 791. 17½in (44.5cm) *Little Lady* with the Anne Shirley head modeling as a majorette by Effanbee, late 1940s. All-composition and fully-jointed. Dark red mohair wig; blue sleep eyes with lashes; painted red fingernails. The white boots are not original. Head and back marked: "EFFANBEE // U.S.A."

Illustration 792. 18in (45.7cm) *Little Lady* with the Anne Shirley head modeling by Effanbee, 1940s. All-composition, except for the hard rubber arms; fully-jointed. Blonde human hair wig with braids intertwined at the nape of the neck; brown sleep eyes with lashes. The gown is an Effanbee design but is not original to the doll. Head and back marked: "EFFANBEE // U.S.A."

Illustration 793. 27in (68.6cm) *Little Lady Gibson Girl* by Effanbee, late 1940s. This is the largest of the *Anne Shirley/Little Lady* dolls. All-composition and fully-jointed. Dark brown human hair wig; brown sleep eyes with lashes. The blouse is white organdy and the skirt and matching parasol are taffeta. The head is marked: "EFFANBEE."

SIGSBEE, CHARLES DWIGHT. United States admiral. Born January 16, 1845; died July 19, 1923. Sigsbee was the commander of the *U.S.S. Maine* when it was sunk at Havana harbor in 1898. "Remember the Maine" became the slogan for the Spanish-American War that followed. There is no evidence to prove that Spain blew up the *Maine,* in which 260 American men were killed. This was most likely caused by an internal explosion. But in 1898 the public and the government were itching for an excuse to go to war.

DOLLS:
1. CHARLES DWIGHT SIGSBEE. Maker unknown, circa 1900 to 1910. Made in Germany. About 15in (38.1cm). *Illustration 794.*
SEE: SPANISH-AMERICAN WAR HEROES.

Illustration 794. About 15in (38.1cm) CHARLES DWIGHT SIGSBEE, manufacturer unknown, 1900-1910. Bisque head; jointed composition body. Painted hair, moustache and eyes. Part of a series of six officers from the Spanish-American War. Made in Germany. *Courtesy of the Margaret Woodbury Strong Museum.*

SILLA, FELIX. Midget performer. Felix Silla has had various roles in television shows. From September 1964 to September 1966 he was Cousin Itt in "The Addams Family" on ABC-TV. He also appeared in that part in the reunion show on October 30, 1977, when the Addams Family celebrated its favorite holiday—Halloween. Silla played life-size Sid and Marty Krofft puppets on two television shows between September 1969 and August 1974—"H.R. Pufnstuf" and "Lidsville." He was a regular on "The Sonny and Cher Show" on

CBS from February 1976 to March 1977. In "Buck Rogers in the 25th Century," NBC-TV, September 1979 to September 1980, he was the little robot Twiki. Twiki's voice was supplied by Mel Blanc, the man of many voices in children's cartoons. Silla as Twiki also appeared in the re-vamped show, "Buck Rogers" on NBC-TV from January to September 1981 and he seemed to be using his own voice.

DOLLS:
1. TWIKI from BUCK ROGERS IN THE 25TH CENTURY. Mego, No. 85000/2, 1979. Made in Hong Kong. 2½in (6.4cm). *Illustration 795.*
2. TWIKI from BUCK ROGERS IN THE 25TH CENTURY. Mego, No. 85016, 1979. Made in Hong Kong. 7½in (17.8cm). *Illustration 796.*

SEE: BUCK ROGERS IN THE 25TH CENTURY.

SILVA, HENRY.   Actor. Born in New York City, New York, in 1928 of Puerto Rican parents. Beginning in the 1950s Silva played a wide variety of character parts in films. He is beady-eyed and high-cheekboned so he was cast as Indians, Mexicans, Orientals, sadists and wierd villains.

DOLLS:
1. KILLER KANE from BUCK ROGERS IN THE 25TH CENTURY. Mego, No. 85000/4, 1979. Made in Hong Kong. 3 ¾in (9.6cm). *Illustration 797.*
2. KILLER KANE from BUCK ROGERS IN THE 25TH CENTURY. Mego, No. 85001/3, 1979. All-vinyl and fully-jointed. Painted hair and features. Copyright by Robert C. Dille. Made in Hong Kong. 12½in (31.8cm).

SEE: BUCK ROGERS IN THE 25TH CENTURY.

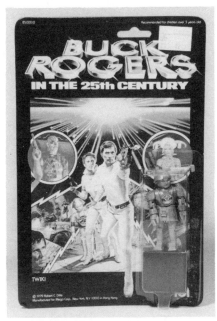

Illustration 795. 2½in (6.4cm) FELIX SILLA as *Twiki* from "Buck Rogers in the 25th Century" by Mego, No. 85000/2, 1979. vinyl and fully-jointed robot. Copyright by Robert C. Dille. Made in Hong Kong.

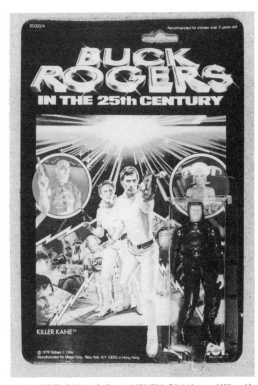

Illustration 797. 3¾in (9.6cm) HENRY SILVA as *Killer Kane* from "Buck Rogers in the 25th Century" by Mego, No. 85000/4, 1979. All-vinyl and fully-jointed. Painted hair, features and clothing. Copyright by Robert C. Dille. Made in Hong Kong.

Illustration 796. 7in (17.8cm) FELIX SILLA as *Twiki* from "Buck Rogers in the 25th Century" by Mego, No. 85016, 1979. All-plastic and fully-jointed. The only color is gray except for a decal in the center of the chest. A key-wind mechanism makes the robot walk. Back marked: " © 1978 ROBERT C. DILLE." Made in Hong Kong.

SILVERHEELS, JAY.   SEE: LONE RANGER, THE.

SIMMONS, GENE.   SEE: KLEIN, EUGENE.

SIMMONS, RICHARD.   Actor. Born 1918. Simmons was onscreen from 1942. On television he was "Sergeant Preston of the Yukon" on CBS-TV from September 1955 to September 1958. The series told tales about an officer of the Royal Northwest Mounted Police who dealt single-handedly with lawbreakers in the Canadian northwest, aided by his dog, Yukon King.

DOLLS:
1. SERGEANT WILLIAM PRESTON. Hartland Plastics, Inc., No. 804, 1958. Plastic; jointed at the arms. Painted features and clothing. Made in Hartland, Wisconsin. About 8in (20.3cm).

SIMMS, LU ANN. Singer. Born 1932. Lu Ann Simms sang on "Arthur Godfrey and His Friends" on CBS-TV from 1952 to 1955.

DOLLS:
1. LU ANN SIMMS. Roberta Doll Co., Inc., circa 1953. 18in (45.7cm). *Illustration 798.*
2. LU ANN SIMMS. Roberta Doll Co., Inc., No. 122, circa 1953. 21in (53.3cm). *Illustrations 798* and *799.*

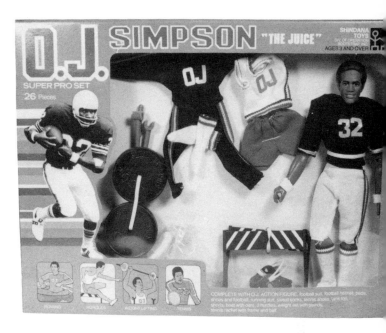

Illustration 800. 9½in (24.2cm) O.J. SIMPSON Super Pro Set by Shindana Toys, No. 9005, 1975. All-vinyl and fully-jointed with painted hair and features. Twenty-six pieces of sports equipment are included with the doll. Head marked: "SHINDANA TOYS // © 1975." Copyright by O.J. Simpson Enterprises Inc. Made in Hong Kong.

Illustration 799. 21in (53.3cm) LU ANN SIMMS by Roberta Doll Co., showing the pony tail hairdo.

SIMPSON, O.J. Football player; newscaster; actor. Orenthal James Simpson was born in San Francisco, California, on July 9, 1947. Simpson, called "The Juice," was a running back with the Buffalo Bills from 1969 to 1977 and with the San Francisco 49ers from 1978 to 1979. He had a National Football League record of rushing for 2003 yards. He was named Most Valuable Player in 1973. As an actor he appeared in action films, like *The Towering Inferno* in 1974. He is also seen on television commercials for Hertz car rentals.

DOLLS:
1. O.J. SIMPSON. Shindana Toys, No. 9005, 1975. Made in Hong Kong. 9 ½in (24.2cm). *Illustrations 800* and *801.*

OPPOSITE PAGE: Illustration 798. 21in (53.3cm) LU ANN SIMMS "Walking Doll" by Roberta Doll Co., Inc., No. 122, and 18in (45.7cm) LU ANN SIMMS, also a walker by Roberta, circa 1953. Both dolls are all-hard plastic and fully-jointed. They have dark brown Saran wigs; blue sleep eyes with lashes; open mouths with four teeth and a felt tongue. The cotton pique dresses are maize trimmed with green ric-rac. The black vinyl shoes on the larger doll are marked: "FAIRY-LAND TOY PROD.// NO. 3 // MADE IN U.S.A.;" the smaller doll's black vinyl shoes are marked: "CINDERELLA // NO. 2 // WILKINSON & GROSS." The larger doll is marked on the head and back: "210;" the smaller is marked only on the head: "180." The smaller doll carries a green vinyl purse that contains rubber hair curlers.

Illustration 801. O.J. SIMPSON by Shindana.

SITTING BULL. Hunkpapa Sioux Indian leader and medicine man. Born Tatanka Iyotake in South Dakota, circa 1831; died December 15, 1890. Sitting Bull organized the Indian resistance that led to the Battle of Little Bighorn in 1876. He took no part in the fighting. He only "made medicine." He was driven into Canada in 1876 by Nelson Appleton Miles, the American army general who waged wars with the Western Indians. Sitting Bull later traveled with Buffalo Bill's Wild West Show. He was a leader in the Ghost Dance agitation leading to the Battle of Wounded Knee in 1890.

DOLLS:
1. SITTING BULL. Mego, No. 1365, 1973. All-vinyl and fully-jointed. Painted hair and features. Made in Hong Kong. 7½in (19.1cm).
2. SITTING BULL. Peggy Nisbet, No. P824, early 1980s. Plastic "collectors' doll." Made in England. 8in (20.3cm).

SMITH, BUFFALO BOB. Television personality. Born Robert E. Smith, November 27, 1918. Buffalo Bob was the host of "Howdy Doody" and the voice for Howdy. "Howdy Doody" was one of the first popular children's shows on television. It debuted on December 27, 1947, on NBC-TV and was seen until September 24, 1960, totaling 2,543 shows. As a show for children, "Howdy Doody" did not pretend to have any educational value. It was to entertain and children loved it. Howdy Doody himself is now a legendary American folk hero. He and his twin brother, Double Doody, were born in Texas on December 27, 1941, and they lived on a ranch for six years. Then their rich uncle Doody died and left the twins some property in New York City, New York. Double wanted to remain in Texas but Howdy saw his chance to fulfill his dream of operating a circus. When NBC wanted to purchase Howdy's land for a television studio, a deal was made for NBC to construct a circus for Howdy on the grounds. Bob Smith, called Buffalo Bob because he was from Buffalo, New York, was appointed as Howdy's guardian and he helped Howdy operate the circus. Then NBC gave Howdy his own television show and brought in a "Peanut Gallery" of children to enjoy it. The show was about a circus troupe that tried to perform against the wishes of Phineas T. Bluster, a mean old man whose main interest in life was to prevent people from having fun. Some of the characters on the show were puppets and others were human performers. Clarabell Hornblow, the mute clown, was played by Bob Keeshan (who was later Captain Kangaroo) and then by Bob Nicholson, followed by Lou Anderson. Among the live performers were also Arlene Dalton as the Story Princess and Judy Tyler as Princess Summerfall-Winterspring. The most important puppets were Howdy; Phineas T. Bluster, who was 70 years old and "as spry as a pup;" Heidi Doody, Howdy's cousin; the Flubadub, the main circus attraction; and Dilly Dally, who could wiggle his ears. In 1976 "The New Howdy Doody Show" was made for syndicated television, but it did not last long.

DOLLS:
1. BUFFALO BOB. Manufacturer unknown, circa early 1950s. 17½in (44.5cm). *Illustration 803.* This doll's identity is not confirmed with original advertising.

Illustration 802. Bobby Nicholson as Clarabel, Howdy Doody, Judy Tyler as Princess Summerfall-Winterspring and Buffalo Bob Smith, 1953.

Illustration 803. 17½in (44.5cm) BUFFALO BOB SMITH, manufacturer unknown, 1950s. Stuffed vinyl head; hard plastic body with jointed arms and legs to the ankles. Molded, painted dark brown hair; blue sleep eyes with lashes; open-closed mouth with molded tongue; dimples in the cheeks. The doll "walks" with a key-wind mechanism. The plastic shoes have metal soles with inset rollers that causes the walking action when wound. Head marked: "A E." The fringed shirt and pants are made of dark brown felt. *Janet Butler Collection.*

SMITH, JACLYN. Actress. Born October 26, 1947. Smith played Kelly Garrett on "Charlie's Angels" on ABC-TV from September 1976 to September 1981. She was also in a biographical television film about the life of Jacqueline Kennedy Onassis in 1981. She was briefly married to actor Dennis Cole.

DOLLS:
1. KELLY STARRING JACLYN SMITH. Hasbro, No. 4862, 1977. Made in Hong Kong. 8½in (21.6cm). *Illustration 804.*

SEE: CHARLIE'S ANGELS.

Illustration 804. 8½in (21.6cm) JACLYN SMITH as *Kelly* from "Charlie's Angels" by Hasbro, No. 4862, 1977. All-vinyl and fully-jointed. Rooted dark brown hair; painted brown eyes. Copyright by Spelling-Goldberg Productions. Made in Hong Kong. *Shirley Buchholz Collection.*

SMITH, MIKE. Performer. Smith had studied classical music since he was about four years old. From 1964 to 1970 he was a member of the group The Dave Clark Five.

DOLLS: SEE: DAVE CLARK FIVE, THE.

SOMERS, SUZANNE. Actress. Born Suzanne Marie Mahoney on October 16, 1946. Somers played Christmas "Chrissy" Snow on "Three's Company" on ABC-TV from 1977 until the 1980-1981 season. The comedy was provided by misunderstandings and double entendres among three platonic friends, a male and two females, who shared an apartment for economic reasons. The program was top-rated so Somers decided that she was the cause of this and went on strike for a raise of several thousand dollars per episode in 1981. The producers concluded that they could do without her expensive services and proved themselves right. After Somers left the series, the high ratings for "Three's Company" held and the rest of the cast were reportedly happier than ever.

DOLLS:
1. SUZANNE SOMERS. Mego, No. 76300, 1978. Made in Hong Kong. 12¼in (31.2cm). *Illustration 806.*

Illustration 805. Suzanne Somers.

Illustration 806. 12¼in (31.2cm) SUZANNE SOMERS as *Chrissy* of "Three's Company" by Mego, No. 76300, 1978. All-vinyl and fully-jointed. Rooted blonde hair; painted blue eyes with long attached lashes; dark skin tones. Head marked: "© THREE'S // COMPANY." Made in Hong Kong.

SOUL, DAVID. Actor, singer. Born David Solberg on August 28, 1943. David Soul became a leading man in films and on television shows in the 1970s. He was a regular on "Here Come the Brides" on ABC-TV from September 1968 to September 1970. In February 1974 he replaced Lee Majors on "Owen Marshall: Counselor At Law," but the show ended in August 1974. Soul became a superstar playing Detective Ken "Hutch" Hutchinson on "Starsky and Hutch" on ABC-TV from September 1975 to August 1979. He appeared on many other television programs in both dramatic parts and as a singer.

DOLLS:
1. HUTCH from STARSKY AND HUTCH. Mego, No. 62800/2, 1976. Made in Hong Kong. 7½in (19.1cm). *Illustration 808*.
SEE: STARSKY AND HUTCH.

Illustration 807. David Soul.

Illustration 808. DAVID SOUL as *Hutch* and PAUL MICHAEL GLASER as *Starsky* by Mego, 1976. Both dolls are 7½in (19.1cm) and are all-vinyl; fully-jointed, including waists. DAVID SOUL as *Hutch*, No. 62800/2, has painted yellow hair; PAUL MICHAEL GLASER as *Starsky*, No. 62800/1, has painted black hair. Copyright by Spelling-Goldberg Productions. Made in Hong Kong.

THE SOUND OF MUSIC.   Musical film, 1965. The inspiration for this movie was Maria Augusta Von Trapp (born January 26, 1905), who organized the Trapp Family Singers and toured the world after fleeing from the Nazis in Austria in 1939. In 1956 the singing act ended and Mrs. Von Trapp settled in Vermont and managed the Trapp Family Lodge from 1962 until it burned to the ground in 1980. Rogers and Hammerstein romanticized the Von Trapp's flight from Austria for Broadway in 1959 and Mary Martin starred in "The Sound of Music" as Maria. In 1965 Julie Andrews became a world-wide superstar by playing a spunky Maria and singing several songs in the film *The Sound of Music*. The musical had a simple story, sumptuous Austrian locations, a romantic time period and the public loved it. *The Sound of Music* is the Number Nine all-time box office champion, earning $79,748,000 in rentals in the United States and Canada by the end of 1981.

DOLLS:
Madame Alexander made dolls that are named "Sound of Music" on the clothing tags. In the booklet attached to the arms of the dolls attention is called to "Twentieth Century-Fox presents a Robert Wise Production *The Sound of Music*." The booklet also states that the dolls are "The musical Trapp family as they (sic) appeared in the motion picture, in the Austrian costumes of the period." The performers from the film in doll form are JULIE ANDREWS as *Maria*, CHARMAIN CARR as *Liesl*, ANGELA CARTWRIGHT as *Brigitta*, DUANE CHASE as *Kurt*, NICHOLAS HAMMOND as *Friedrich*, KYM KARATH as *Gretl*, HEATHER MENZIES as *Louisa* and DEBBIE TURNER as *Marta*. See entry under each performer. The various sets of Sound of Music dolls are as follows.

DOLL SETS by Madame Alexander:
Set 1.
        All-8in (20.3cm).   1965. All-hard plastic and fully-jointed. Gretl, No. 1000; Friedrich, No. 1001; Marta, No. 1002; Brigitta, No. 1003; Louisa, No. 1004; Liesl, No. 1005; Maria, No. 1006.
Set 2.
        Large Set.   1965-1966. Gretl, No. 1101; Marta, No. 1102; Friedrich, No. 1007—All use the 11in (27.9cm) "Janie" mold doll. Brigitta, No. 1403; Louisa, No. 1404; Liesl, No. 1405—All use the 14in (35.6cm) "Mary Ann" mold doll. Maria, No. 1706, is the 17in (43.2cm) "Polly" mold doll.

Illustration 809. Julie Andrews and children from *The Sound of Music*, 1965.

Set 3.

Large Set. 1966. All are dressed in the regular Tyrolean costumes. Gretl, Marta and Friedrich are the same as Set No. 2 above. Louisa and Liesl are the same as Set No. 2 above. Brigitta is 12in (30.5cm) and uses the "Lissy" mold doll. She is all-hard plastic and fully-jointed. Maria, No. 1706, is 17in (43.2cm) and uses the "Elise" doll mold.

Set 4.

Large Set. 1966. All the children are dressed in sailor school outfits. Maria is dressed in the Tyrolean outfit. Marta and Gretl are the same dolls as Set No. 2 above. Liesl and Louisa are the same dolls as Set No. 2 above. Brigitta is the same as Set No. 3 above. Maria is the same as Set No. 3 above. There is no Friedrich with this set. The seventh doll is Kurt. Kurt is 12in (30.5cm) and is the "Smarty" doll mold.

Set 5.

Large Set. 1967-1970. The children are all the same as Set No. 2 above. Maria is the same as Set No. 3 above.

Set 6.

Small Set. 1971-1973. Gretl, No. 801; Marta, No. 802; Friedrich, No. 807—all are 7½in (19.1cm) and are all-hard plastic and fully-jointed, with or without bending knees. Brigitta, No. 1103; Louisa, No. 1104; Liesl, No. 1105 are 9in (22.9cm) and are all-hard plastic and fully-jointed. Maria, No. 1206 is 12in (30.5cm) and uses the "Nancy Drew" doll mold. This set is dressed in Tyrolean costumes.

Review of SOUND OF MUSIC dolls by Celebrity:

KYM KARATH. *Gretl.* Set 1, 8in (20.3cm); Set 2, 3, 4 and 5, 11in (27.9cm), "Janie" doll mold; Set 6, 7½in (19.1cm).

NICHOLAS HAMMOND. *Friedrich.* Set 1, 8in (20.3cm); Set 2, 3 and 5, 11in (27.9cm), "Janie" doll mold; Set 6, 7½in (19.1cm).

DEBBIE TURNER. *Marta.* Set 1, 8in (20.3cm); Set 2, 3, 4 and 5, 11in (27.9cm), "Janie" doll mold; Set 6, 7½in (19.1cm).

ANGELA CARTWRIGHT. *Brigitta.* Set 1, 8in (20.3cm); Set 2 and 5, 14in (35.6cm) "Mary Ann" doll mold; Set 3 and 4, "Lissy" doll mold; Set 6, 9in (22.9cm).

HEATHER MENZIES. *Louisa.* Set 1, 8in (20.3cm); Set 2, 3, 4 and 5, 14in (35.6cm) "Mary Ann" doll mold; Set 6, 9in (22.9cm).

CHARMAIN CARR. *Liesl.* Set 1, 8in (20.3cm); Set 2, 3, 4 and 5, 14in (35.6cm) "Mary Ann" doll mold; Set 6, 9in (22.9cm).

DUANE CHASE. *Kurt.* Set 5, 12in (30.5cm) "Smarty" doll mold.

JULIE ANDREWS. *Maria.* Set 1, 8in (20.3cm); Set 2, 17in (43.2cm) "Polly" doll mold; Set 3, 4 and 5, 17in (43.2cm) "Elise" doll mold; Set 6, 12in (30.5cm) "Nancy Drew" doll mold.

Illustration 810. Large set of SOUND OF MUSIC dolls (Set No. 2), 1967-1970. Back row, from left to right: *Brigitta* (ANGELA CARTWRIGHT), *Maria* (JULIE ANDREWS), *Liesl* (CHARMAIN CARR), *Gretl* (KYM KARATH). Front row, from left to right: *Marta* (DEBBIE TURNER), *Friedrich* (NICHOLAS HAMMOND), *Louisa* (HEATHER MENZIES). *Jean Canaday Collection.*

SPACE ACADEMY.   Science fiction television series. "Space Academy" on CBS-TV from September 1977 to September 1979 told about the exploits of the Nova Blue Team in the year 3732. This was a group of youthful cadets who trained in a man-made planet in space. The mentor of the cadets, Professor Issac Gampu, was played by JONATHAN HARRIS. The cadets were RIC CARROTT as Chris Gentry, BRIAN TOCHI as Tee Gar Soom (Tiger), Pamela Ferdin as Laura Gentry and Maggie Cooper as Cadet Adrian. Young ERIC GREENE played Loki, the alien ally of the group. See entries under the four male players.

Illustration 811. "Space Academy" dolls from left to right: RIC CARROTT as *Chris Gentry,* ERIC GREENE as *Loki,* BRIAN TOCHI as *Tee Gar Soom* and JONATHAN HARRIS as *Isaac Gampu. Penny Caswell Collection.*

SPACE: 1999.   Science fiction television series. The premise of this series on syndicated television beginning in 1975 was that 300 men and women were working on the moon in the year 1999, acting as look-outs for invaders from space. A radioactive blast sent the moon away from Earth orbit and the earthlings struggled to find another planet in outer space to which the moon could affix itself. The leading players in the series were MARTIN LANDAU as Commander John Koenig, BARBARA BAIN as Dr. Helena Russell and BARRY MORSE as Professor Victor Bergman. See entries under these actors.

SPANISH-AMERICAN WAR HEROES.   A series of six dolls depicting five naval officers of the war of 1898 and President McKinley. The dolls date from circa 1900 to 1910 and are found individually in many private collections. The only known complete collection is in the Margaret Woodbury Strong Museum in Rochester, New York. The dolls represent GEORGE DEWEY, RICHMOND PEARSON HOBSON, WILLIAM McKINLEY, WILLIAM THOMAS SAMPSON, WINFIELD SCOTT SCHLEY and CHARLES DWIGHT SIGSBEE. See each gentleman.

SPENCER, LADY DIANA.   SEE: DIANA, PRINCESS.

SPILSBURY, KLINTON.   Actor. Born 1951 or 1956. In 1981 Spilsbury starred in *The Legend of the Lone Ranger* in the title role. He was picked for the part because he is unusually handsome, but during production it became apparent that he had not had sufficient training for film work. To compound problems, his speaking voice was "unsuitable" (high pitched?) and it had to be dubbed by another actor after the film was completed. The 1981 movie had a poor reception and was listed as one of the worst films of the year by reviewers.

DOLLS: SEE LONE RANGER, THE.

STALIN, JOSEPH.   Soviet political leader. Born Iosif Vissarionovich Dzhugashvili on December 21, 1879; died March 5, 1953. He called himself Stalin ("made of steel") after joining the revolutionary movement in Russia. Stalin was born the son of a shoemaker and he became a Marxist while studying to become a priest. He was expelled from the seminary in 1899 and he joined the Bolsheviks. In 1917, after the October Revolution, he alligned himself with Lenin. He was active in the Civil War of 1918-1920 and was elected General Secretary of the Communist Party in 1922. Lenin died in 1924 and by 1927 Stalin was rid of his rivals—Trotsky and Zinoviev—and was the dictator of the Soviet Union, although he held no formal public office until 1941. In 1928 he began the Five Year Plan to industrialize

Illustration 812. 11in (27.9cm) JOSEPH STALIN, probably a souvenir from the Soviet Union from the 1930s to the 1950s. Plaster head, hands and feet; stuffed cloth body. The doll seems to be commercially made and he wears a beige suit of wool felt. The features are painted. No markings on the doll. (This information, which is not very reliable, is based on the fact that the doll came from a collection of "souvenir dolls" from various European countries and the other dolls in the collection date from the 1930s to the 1950s.)

Russia, during which time millions of people were put to death as he began "to build Socialism in one country." When Hitler attacked Russia in 1941 Stalin also assumed military leadership of the country. At the conferences with Churchill and Roosevelt at the end of World War II, Stalin showed how skillful he was as a diplomat when he gained concessions for the Soviet Union in Eastern Europe. When the Nazis were defeated in 1945 Stalin signaled Communist leaders throughout the world that cooperation between Communists and Capitalists had ended. Stalin continued to rule with an iron hand until his death.

DOLLS:
1. JOSEPH STALIN.   Maker unknown, circa 1930s-1950s. 11in (27.9cm). *Illustration 812*.

STANLEY, PAUL. Musician. Born Stanley Eisen on January 20, 1952. Paul is a member of the band KISS and he has a black star painted over and around his right eye.

DOLLS:
1. PAUL of KISS.   Mego, No. 88000/1, 1978. Made in Hong Kong. 12½in (31.8cm). *Illustration 813*.
SEE: KISS

Illustration 813. 12½in (31.8cm) PAUL STANLEY, Paul of KISS, by Mego, No. 88000/1, 1978. All-vinyl and fully-jointed. Rooted black hair and painted features and makeup. Head marked: "© 1978 AUCOIN // MGMT. INC." Back marked: "© MEGO CORP. 1977 // MADE IN HONG KONG." Copyright by Aucoin Management, Inc. by agreement with KISS, a partnership. *Penny Caswell Collection.*

STAR TREK. A legendary television science fiction series; a movie with a proposed sequel. "Star Trek" was on ABC-TV as a regular series from September 8, 1966, to September 2, 1969, and has been seen in re-runs ever since. It was the first TV series of its type to have well-written and serious scripts. It followed the ad-

ventures of the crew aboard the *U.S.S. Enterprise* some 200 years in the future and charted their experiences as they explored new worlds in space. The travelers on "Star Trek" encountered strange life forms and were constantly troubled by two alien races, the Klingons and Romulans. NBC cancelled the program because advertisers came to the conclusion that its following consisted of children and teenagers, making sponsoring the show unprofitable. A fanatical cult following of the show developed and fans tried to get it back on network television. Annual Star Trek conventions were held in the United States and England beginning in 1972. From 1973 to 1975 an animated cartoon version of "Star Trek" was on Saturday morning television. Because of the demand for "Star Trek" shows and the conventions, the show was to return to television in 1976. This plan was turned into a major motion picture instead and the original cast of "Star Trek" was reunited ten years after the television series was cancelled. In 1979 *Star Trek* (also called *Star Trek the Motion Picture*) was released. By the end of 1980 it was already Number 17 of all-time film rental champions, having taken in 56 million dollars.

DOLLS:
During the time of the animated cartoon show "Star Trek" (1974) Mego Corp. made a set of dolls of the original television program cast. The dolls are 8in (20.3cm) and they were made in Hong Kong.
No. 51200/1   WILLIAM SHATNER as *Captain Kirk*
No. 51200/2   LEONARD NIMOY as *Mr. Spock*
No. 51200/3   DeFOREST KELLEY as *Dr. McCoy (Bones)*
No. 51200/4   NICHELLE NICHOLAS as *Lt. Uhura*
No. 51200/5   JAMES DOOHAN as *Mr. Scott* (Scottie)
No. 51200/6   MICHAEL ANSARA as *Klingon*
In 1979 Mego Corp. had two sets of dolls using the characters from *Star Trek the Motion Picture*. All of the dolls were made in Hong Kong. The dolls from the smaller set are 3¾in (9.6cm); the dolls from the larger set are 12½in (31.8cm).

Illustration 814. Large Mego STAR TREK characters from 1979. From left to right: WILLIAM SHATNER as *Captain James Kirk*, PERSIS KHAMBATTA as *Ilia* and LEONARD NIMOY as *Mr. Spock*. *Penny Caswell Collection.*

Small set from 1979:
No. 91200/1 WILLIAM SHATNER as *Capt. Kirk*
No. 91200/2 LEONARD NIMOY as *Mr. Spock*
No. 91200/3 STEPHEN COLLINS as *Decker*
No. 91200/4 PERSIS KHAMBATTA as *Ilia*
No. 91200/5 JAMES DOOHAN as *Scotty*
No. 91200/6 DeFOREST KELLEY as *Dr. McCoy*
No. 91200/7 MARK LENARD as *Klingon*
No. 91200/8 *Zaranite*
No. 91200/9 *Betelgeusian*
No. 91201/1 *Acturian*
No. 91201/2 *Megarite*
No. 91201/3 *Rigellian*
Large set from 1979:
No. 91210/1 WILLIAM SHATNER as *Captain James Kirk*
No. 91210/2 LEONARD NIMOY as *Mr. Spock*
No. 91210/3 STEPHEN COLLINS as *Decker*
No. 91210/4 PERSIS KHAMBATTA as *Ilia*
No. 91210/5 MARK LENARD as *Klingon Commander*
No. 91210/6 Acturian
In 1980 Knickerbocker marketed dolls of two of the celebrities from *Star Trek the Motion Picture.* They are 13in (33cm) and were made in Haiti and USA.
No. 0598 LEONARD NIMOY as *Mr. Spock*
No. 0599 WILLIAM SHATNER as *Captain Kirk*

STAR WARS. Motion picture, 1977; sequel, *The Empire Strikes Back*, 1980. George Lucas (born 1945), a former racecar driver, directed his first feature film *American Graffiti* in 1973. The financial success of this film led to Lucas' next project, *Star Wars. Star Wars* is a science-fiction thriller that was nominated for 10 Academy Awards, including best picture, best director, best original screenplay and best editing (by Lucas' wife, Marcia). The phenomenal success of *Star Wars* led to a sequel, *The Empire Strikes Back* (also called *Star Wars II),* released in 1980, with more films in the series planned. By the end of 1981 *Star Wars* was the Number One motion picture box office champion of all time, having earned $185,138,000. *The Empire Strikes Back* was Number Two, having earned $134,209,000. These statistics are based on rental earnings in the United States and Canada alone. The receipts are indeed impressive when compared with *The Sound of Music* (1965), which earned $79,748,000 and is Number Nine and *Gone With the Wind* (1939), which is Number Twelve with $76,700,000, considering that these highly acclaimed and popular films have been re-issued several times. Toy and doll merchandise tie-ins from *Star Wars* were still leading items for Toy Fair 1982.

The cast of *Star Wars* in whose image a doll or figure was made follows:
MARK HAMILL   Luke Skywalker
HARRISON FORD   Han Solo
CARRIE FISHER   Princess Leia Organa
ALEC GUINNESS   Ben (Obi-Wan) Kenobi
ANTHONY DANIELS   See Threepio (C3PO)
KENNY BAKER   Artoo-Detoo (R2D2)
PETER MAYHEW   Chewbacca
DAVID PROWSE   Lord Darth Vader
JACK PURVIS   Chief Jawa
Additional cast from *The Empire Strikes Back* in whose image a doll or figure was made:
BILLY DEE WILLIAMS   Lando Calrissian
JEREMY BULLOCH   Boba Fett
JACK PURVIS   Chief Ugnaught

Illustration 815. Large STAR WARS figures by Kenner. From left to right: HARRISON FORD as *Han Solo,* PETER MAYHEW as Chewbaca, CARRIE FISHER as *Princess Leia Organa,* MARK HAMILL as *Luke Skywalker,* Stormtrooper, KENNY BAKER as *Artoo-Detoo* (R2D2) (in front), ALEC GUINNESS as *Ben* (Obi-Wan) *Kenobi,* ANTHONY DANIELS as *See Threepio* (C3PO), DAVID PROWSE as *Lord Darth Vader,* JACK PURVIS as *Chief Jawa* (in front), and JEREMY BULLOCH as *Boba Fett. Bobby Lodwick Collection.*

The complete listing of all STAR WARS dolls and figures:
Large STAR WARS dolls by Kenner. Made in Hong Kong 1978.

Princess Leia Organa	No. 38070	11¼in (28.6cm)
Luke Skywalker	No. 38080	11¾in (29.9cm)
R2-D2 (Radio Controlled)	No. 38430	8in (20.3cm)
Chewbacca	No. 38600	15in (38.1cm)
Darth Vader	No. 38610	15in (38.1cm)
C-3PO	No. 38620	12in (30.5cm)
R2-D2	No. 38630	7½in (19.1cm)

Illustration 816. Small STAR WARS figures with the "Millenium Falcon" spaceship, all by Kenner. Figures, from left to right: HARRISON FORD as *Han Solo, Greedo,* PETER MAYHEW as *Chewbacca,* JEREMY BULLOCK as *Boba Fett,* CARRIE FISHER as *Princess Leia Organa,* MARK HAMILL as *Luke Skywalker X-Wing Pilot* and *Luke, Sand People,* ALEC GUINNESS as *Ben* (Obi-Wan) *Kenobi,* JACK PURVIS as *Chief Jawa,* KENNY BAKER as *Artoo-Detoo* (R2D2), *Death Squad Commander,* ANTHONY DANIELS as *See Threepio (C3PO), R5D4, Death Star Droid, Snaggletooth, Sand People, Hammerhead, Walrus Man,* and DAVID PROWSE as *Lord Darth Vader. Bobby Lodwick Collection.*

1979:

Boba Fett	No. 39140	13¼in (33.3cm)
Han Solo	No. 39170	12in (30.5cm)
Stormtrooper	No. 39180	12in (30.5cm)
Ben (Obi-Wan) Kenobi	No. 39340	12in (30.5cm)
Jawa	No. 39350	8¼in (20.6cm)
IG-88	No. 39960	15in (38.1cm)

Set #1 small STAR WARS figures by Kenner. Made in Hong Kong. 1978. 12 figures.

Luke Skywalker	No. 38180	3¾in (9.6cm)
Princess Leia Organa	No. 38190	3½in (8.9cm)
R2-D2	No. 38200	2¼in (5.4cm)
Chewbacca	No. 38210	4¼in (10.9cm)
C-3PO	No. 38220	3¾in (9.6cm)
Darth Vader	No. 38230	4¼in (10.9cm)
Stormtrooper	No. 38240	3¼in (8.3cm)
Ben (Obi-Wan) Kenobi	No. 38250	3¼in (8.3cm)
Han Solo	No. 38260	3¾in (9.6cm)
Jawa	No. 38270	2¼in (5.4cm)
Sand People	No. 38280	3¾in (9.6cm)
Death Squad Commander	No. 38290	3¾in (9.6cm)

Set #2 small STAR WARS figures by Kenner. Made in Hong Kong. 1979. 21 figures. Packaged as STAR WARS THE EMPIRE STRIKES BACK. Series No. 39710
12 figures from Set #1 and:

Princess Leia Organa in Bespin Gown	3½in (8.9cm)
Luke Skywalker in Bespin Fatigues	3¾in (9.6cm)
IG-88	4½in (11.5cm)
Bespin Security Guard	3⅞in (9.8cm)
Han Solo in Hoth Battle Gear	3¾in (9.6cm)
Imperial Snow Stormtrooper	3⅞in (9.8cm)
Lando Calrissian	3¾in (9.6cm)
Bossk	3¾in (9.6cm)
FX-7	3⅜in (8.5cm)
Rebel Snow Soldier	3¾in (9.6cm)

Set #3 small STAR WARS figures by Kenner. Made in Hong Kong. 1980. 30 figures. Packaged as STAR WARS THE EMPIRE STRIKES BACK. Series No. 38899
21 figures from Set #1 and Set #2 and:

Greedo	3¾in (9.6cm)
R5-D4	2½in (6.4cm)
Hammerhead	4in (10.2cm)
Power Droid	2¼in (5.4cm)
Death Star Droid	3¾in (9.6cm)
Walrus Man	3¾in (9.6cm)
Snaggletooth	2⅞in (7.3cm)
Luke Skywalker X-Wing Pilot	3¾in (9.6cm)
Boba Fett	3¾in (9.6cm)

Set #4 small STAR WARS figures by Kenner. Made in Hong Kong. 1981. 41 figures. Packaged as STAR WARS THE EMPIRE STRIKES BACK. Series No. 69360.
30 figures from Set #1, Set #2, Set #3 and:
Star Destroyer Commander
Yoda
Rebel Commander
Leia Organa in Hoth Outfit
Ugnaught
Lobot
2-1B
Han Solo in Bespin Outfit
At-At Driver
Imperial Commander
Dengar (Bounty Hunter)

Set #5 small STAR WARS FIGURES by Kenner. Made in Hong Kong. 1982. 47 figures. Packaged as STAR

WARS THE EMPIRE STRIKES BACK. Series No. 69570 and No. 69590
41 figures from Set #1, Set #2, Set #3, Set #4, except for two discontinued figures:
R2-D2
C-3PO
New figures for 1982:
Imperial TIE Fighter Pilot
Zuckuss
Luke Skywalker (Hoth Battle Gear)
At-At Commander
Artoo-Detoo (R2-D2) with Sensorscope
See-Threepio (C-3PO) with removable limbs and carrying basket
Cloud Car Pilot
Bespin Security Guard (new)
Also free with five proofs of purchase:
4LOM

STARR, BELLE. Outlaw. Born Myra Belle Shirley on February 5, 1848 in Carthage, Missouri; died February 3, 1889. Belle Starr had a checkered career as a hard-living, hard-loving woman. She led a band of cattle rustlers and horse thieves that made regular raids on Oklahoma ranches. She was a friend of Jesse James.
DOLLS:
1. BELLE STARR. Excel Toy Corp., No. 300, 1974. Made in Hong Kong. 9¼in (23.6cm). *Illustration 817.*

Illustration 817. 9¼in (23.6cm) BELLE STARR from the "Legends of the West" series by Excel Toy Corp., No. 300, 1974. All-vinyl and fully-jointed. Molded brown hair in a bun style; painted brown eyes. Head marked: " © EXCEL TOY CORP. // HONG KONG."

STARR, RINGO. Musician; actor. Born Richard Starkey on July 7, 1940, in Liverpool, England. After the celebrated break-up of the Beatles in 1971 Ringo Starr continued to record as a solo act. His work, although interesting, was not as well received as that of Lennon, McCarthy or Harrison. He also essayed some off-beat roles in films beginning in the 1970s.

Illustration 818. 4½in (11.5cm) RINGO STARR by Remco, No. 1802, 1964. All-vinyl. Only the head is jointed; rooted black hair; painted features. Head marked: "223." Back marked: "THE // BEATLES // TM." *Shirley Buchholz Collection.*

DOLLS:
1. THE BOB'N HEAD BEATLES. Car Mascots, Inc., 1964. Papier-mâché and plaster "nodders." Made in Japan. 7in (17.8cm).
2. THE BOB'N HEAD BEATLES. Same as the above in all-plastic. 1964. 4in (10.2cm).
3. RINGO STARR. Remco, No. 1802, 1964. 4½in (11.5cm) or 4¾in (12.2cm). *Illustrations 818* and *819.*
4. THE BEATLES. Pelham Puppets. Composition head and hands; wooden feet; jointed wooden segments for body. Black fur wig; painted features. Stamped on wooden cross bars: "MADE IN ENGLAND" and "PELHAM PUPPETS." About 13in (33cm). *Illustration 107.*
SEE: THE BEATLES.

STARSKY AND HUTCH. Police series on ABC-TV from September 10, 1975, to August 28, 1979. Detective Dave Starsky, played by PAUL MICHAEL GLASER, and Detective Ken "Hutch" Hutchinson, played by DAVID SOUL, were two plainclothes cops who were very close friends. Starsky was the "street-wise" one; Hutch was the better educated one. Together they chased after pimps, dope pushers, muggers and various other hoodlums in a bright red 1974 Ford Torino. Their quick-tempered boss, Captain Dobey, was played by BERNIE HAMILTON. ANTONIO FARGAS as Huggy Bear was their flamboyant informant. The show was highly popular for a few years, but lost favor because of the high degree of violence it showed. Mego made dolls of the four main characters and one of "Chopper," a villain, to go with the set.

Illustration 819. 4¾in (12.2cm) RINGO STARR of the Beatles by Remco, No. 1802, 1964. This is a slight variation from the doll in *Illustration 818.* The head is marked: "108." *Wanda Lodwick Collection.*

Illustration 820. From STARSKY AND HUTCH package: Paul Michael Glaser, David Soul, Bernie Hamilton, "Chopper," and Antonio Fargas.

STEVENSON, PARKER. Actor. Born Richard Stevenson Parker on June 4, 1952. Parker Stevenson debuted in films as a sensitive young student in *A Separate Peace* in 1972, very effectively playing the part of a boy of about 15. On television he played Frank Hardy on ABC-TV's "The Hardy Boys Mysteries" from January 1977 to January 1979 and from June to August 1979. Shaun Cassidy played his brother, Joe.

DOLLS:
1. PARKER STEVENSON AS FRANK HARDY. Kenner, No. 45020, 1978. Shaun Cassidy as Joe Hardy, No. 45000, is a companion doll. Made in Hong Kong. 12in (30.5cm). *Illustration 822.*

Illustration 821. Parker Stevenson.

Illustration 822. 12in (30.5cm) PARKER STEVENSON as *Frank Hardy* from "The Hardy Boys" by Kenner, No. 45020, 1978. All-vinyl and fully-jointed. Painted dark brown hair and brown eyes. Head marked: "© 1978 U.C.S.I." The two-way radio has a panel for writing "secret messages." Copyright by Universal City Studios, Inc. Made in Hong Kong.

STEWART, JAMES. Actor. Born May 20, 1908, in Indiana, Pennsylvania. Stewart has been a box office star since the mid 1930s. He won an Academy Award for *The Philadelphia Story* in 1940. He began in films playing romantic leads but over the years has changed to character parts, talking more slowly with each role. On television he played a lawyer in "Hawkins" on CBS-TV from October 1973 to September 1974.

DOLLS:
1. BUTTONS THE CLOWN from THE GREATEST SHOW ON EARTH. Maker unknown, circa 1952. 6in (15.2cm). *Illustration 824.*

Illustration 823. James Stewart (left) and Emmett Kelly in *The Greatest Show on Earth,* 1952.

Illustration 824. 6in (15.2cm) JAMES STEWART as *Buttons, the Clown* from Cecil B. DeMille's *The Greatest Show on Earth,* maker unknown, circa 1952. Early vinyl with wire inside for "posing." Painted features with molded hat; felt clothing. Bottom of left foot marked:

Paramount

Wanda Lodwick Collection.

STIERS, DAVID OGDEN. Actor. Born October 31, 1942. Stiers has acted on Broadway, in movies and on television. For CBS-TV he was in "Doc" from September to October 1976. On "M*A*S*H" he has played pompous Bostonian Major Charles Emerson Winchester III since the 1977 season began.

DOLLS:
1. WINCHESTER (MAJOR CHARLES EMERSON WINCHESTER III). Tristar International, Ltd., Series No. 4100, 1982. All-vinyl and fully-jointed. Painted and molded features and clothing. Made in Hong Kong. 3¾in (9.6cm).

SEE: M*A*S*H.

STILLWELL, JOSEPH. American general. Born March 19, 1883; died October 12, 1946. Stillwell commanded the United States forces in the China-Burma-India theater during World War II. He also served as Chief of Staff to Chinese President Chiang Kai-Shek. Stillwell's disagreement with Chiang over the role of Chinese forces led to his being relieved of his command by President Roosevelt. He later commanded the 10th Army on Okinawa. Stillwell was nicknamed "Vinegar Joe."

DOLLS:
1. GEN. JOSEPH W. STILLWELL. Excel Toy Corp., 1974. All-vinyl and fully-jointed with painted hair and features. Made in Hong Kong. 9¾in (24.9cm).

STIMSON, SARA. Child actress. Born in Texas in 1973. Sara Stimson won the coveted role of Little Miss Marker in the 1980 film *Little Miss Marker*. She did fine in the role but was unfavorably compared with Shirley Temple who was in the original in 1934. The story was

also made as *Sorrowful Jones* in 1949 and as *40 Pounds of Trouble* in 1963. The cast of the 1980 film also included Walter Matthau, Julie Andrews and Tony Curtis, but as entertainment it was a total bummer.

DOLLS:
1. SARA STIMSON AS LITTLE MISS MARKER. Ideal, No. 1382-1, 1980. Made in Hong Kong. 11½in (29.2cm). *Illustration 825*.

STUART (or STEWART), ARABELLA. Cousin of James I of England. Born 1575; died 1615. Arabella secretly married William Seymour, who was the heir to the throne of Henry VIII by his will. The couple was sent to prison after the death of Henry VIII, but they escaped. In 1611 Arabella was recaptured and she died insane in the Tower.

DOLLS:
1. ARABELLA STUART. Tower Treasures (Peggy Nisbet), 1977. Made in England. 15in (38.1cm). *Illustrations 826* and *827*.

Illustration 825. 11½in (29.2cm) SARA STIMSON as *Little Miss Marker* by Ideal, No. 1382-1, 1980. All-vinyl and fully-jointed. Rooted dark brown hair and painted brown eyes. This doll has a rather large head for the body proportions and is not a quality finished product. There was supposed to be a new 1980 Shirley Temple in the same size with the same body. (See SHIRLEY TEMPLE, *Illustration 895*.) Head marked: "© 1979 // UNIV. STUDIOS // H-330 // HONG KONG P." Copyright 1980 by Universal City Studios, Inc.

Illustration 826. 15in (38.1cm) ARABELLA STUART by Tower Treasures, 1977. Bisque head, hands and feet; cloth body. Painted gray eyes; brown mohair wig. Cloth label in underslip: "NISBET 1977." The tiny doll is cloth with a wooden head and has a mohair wig. The Arabella Stuart doll is based on a portrait painted when she was 23 months old. Made in England. *Shirley Buchholz Collection*.

Illustration 827. ARABELLA STUART by Tower Treasures. *Shirley Buchholz Collection.*

STUART (or STEWART), CHARLES EDWARD. "BONNIE PRINCE CHARLIE."

Claimant to the throne of England. Born 1720; died 1788. James Stuart, called the Old Pretender, was the son of King James II of England after he married the Catholic Mary Modena. The Catholic marriage caused the Glorious Revolution, followed by the Act of Settlement. The Stuarts were driven into exile and all male descendents were excluded from succession to the throne. King Louis XIV of France took James in as a pensioner and his defendants, the Jacobites, hailed him as James VIII of Scotland and James III of England. His son, Charles Edward Stuart, affectionately called Bonnie Prince Charlie by his supporters and the Young Pretender by his detractors, returned secretly to England and was involved in many plots to restore James Stuart to the throne. After Prince Charles' final defeat he escaped back to France. He was later expelled from France and he died in Rome. He was married to Louise Stoberg Gedern. Bonnie Prince Charlie was the subject of much English and Scottish poetry.

DOLLS:
1. CHARLES EDWARD STUART (BONNIE PRINCE CHARLIE). Peggy Nisbet, No. H210 in 1976 catalog; No. P210 in 1979 catalog. Plastic "collectors' doll." White mohair wig; painted features. Dressed in Scottish kilt. Made in England. About 8in (20.3cm). (A prefix "P" in a Peggy Nisbet doll number denotes a portrait doll; a prefix "H" designates a doll from a standard mold. The doll is probably not a portrait.)

SUPERMAN. Fictional hero. The adventures of Superman have been related in many popular forms. He was born far out in space on the planet Krypton. Krypton was drawing closer to the Sun and was going to be destroyed. A scientist, Jor-El, and his wife planned to escape with their baby Kal-El. The couple constructed a small experimental rocket ship but before they could enlarge their design, the planet began to explode. They put their baby in the rocket and sent him towards Earth, which they knew was inhabited. The baby landed in Smallville, USA, and a childless couple, the Kents, took him in. They kept the boy's amazing abilities a secret. His powers included super strength, super breath, super speed, the ability to fly, X-ray vision, telescopic vision, microscopic vision, super memory, super hearing and super thinking. When the boy, called Clark, was 25 his mother urged him to use his powers to benefit mankind. Clark Kent moved to Metropolis and obtained a job as a reporter for *The Daily Planet*. "Mild-mannered Clark Kent" retained his disguise and turned into Superman when there was crime to fight and villains to catch.

The story of Superman evolved out of the magazine *Science Fiction*. In 1938 writer Jerry Siegel and artist Joe Schuster introduced the character to D.C. Publications' *Action Comics*. This led to a *Superman magazine*.

In the 1940s *Superman* was a radio program and Bud Collyer (of "Beat the Clock") was heard as Superman and Clark Kent. In the late 1940s an animated cartoon version of the story was produced for theaters by Paramount Pictures. In 1948 Columbia Pictures produced a 15-episode serial version starring Kirk Alyn as

Illustration 828. 12½in (31.8cm) *Superman* by Mego, No. 87001, circa 1978. All-vinyl and fully-jointed. Painted black hair and painted blue eyes. Head marked: " © D C COMICS INC. // 733 // 1977." Back marked: " © 1978 MEGO CORP. // MADE IN HONG KONG." This doll looks very much like Christopher Reeve (which see) who played the part of Superman in the 1978 film, but Christopher Reeve also looks very much like the cartoon conception of Superman. The doll should be considered a "comic character," as all copyright information pertains to the comic book, rather than to the motion picture. (The body of the doll was used on other Mego dolls, such as Gil Gerard as Buck Rogers, which see.)

"The Man of Steel." In 1950 Columbia Pictures produced the first feature-length film, *Atom Man vs. Superman,* also starring Alyn. In 1951 Lippert Pictures starred George Reeves in *Superman and the Mole Men.* This last picture became the basis for the television series starring George Reeves, syndicated in 1953. In the Kirk Alyn film Lois Lane was played by Noel Neill and Jimmy Olsen by Tommy Bond. In the George Reeves television show Lois was played by Phyllis Coates and then by Noel Neill. Jimmy was Jack Larson.

Various animated cartoon versions of Superman were also on television. Among them were "The New Adventures of Superman" on CBS-TV from September 1966 to September 1967, in which Bud Collyer was heard as Clark and Superman; "The Superman-Aquaman Hour" on CBS-TV from September 1967 to September 1968 "The Batman-Superman Hour" on CBS-TV from September 1968 to September 1969; and "The Superfriends," which premiered on September 1973.

In 1978 *Superman: The Movie* was released. This was the most profitable movie ever made by Warner Bros. Studio in its 58 year history. The budget for the film topped $40 million and by the end of 1981 it earned $82,500,000 in the United States and Canada (The Number Eight box office champ). The first actor signed was Marlon Brando, as Jor-El, who earned $3,000,000 for nine days' work. Christopher Reeve, a young stage actor, was chosen for the lead. He was perfect for the role and looked just like the comic book drawings. Reeve embarked on a strenuous physical fitness program after he was signed to build his body up to the right proportions. Mario Puzo, the best-selling author of *The Godfather*, was paid $350,000, plus 5 per cent of the gross to write the script. Canadian actress Margot Kidder got the part of Lois Lane. In 1981 *Superman II* was one of the highest grossing films of the year. When *Superman: The Movie* was shown on television on February 7 and 8, 1982, it became one of the most watched four hours ever on television.

Illustration 830. 12½in (31.8cm) *General Zod Of The Phantom Zone* by Mego, No. 87003/3, 1978. Vinyl head; plastic, fully-jointed body. The vinyl head has painted features with graying hair and green eyes. Head marked: " © D.C. COMICS INC. // 1977." Terrence Stamp played General Zod in *Superman.* Made in Hong Kong.

Illustration 829. 12½in (31.8cm) *Lex Luthor* by Mego, No. 87003/2, 1978. Vinyl head; plastic body. Painted blue eyes. Head marked: " © D.C. COMICS INC. // 1977." Gene Hackman played Lex Luthor in the film. Made in Hong Kong.

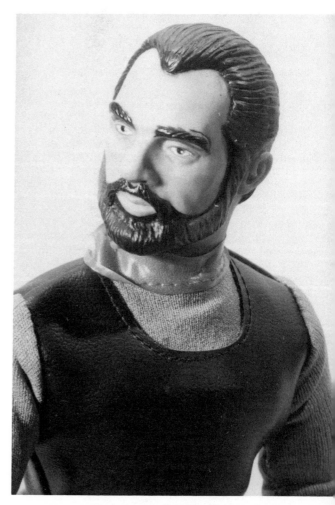

Illustration 831. General Zod from *Superman.*

Superman was the inspiration for other comics, films and television shows, including Batman, Spiderman, Doc Savage, The Six Million Dollar Man, and most recently, The Greatest American Hero. The producers of ABC-TV's "The Greatest American Hero," a comic farce starring William Katt, were taken to court by the copyright owners to Superman. The Superman people lost their case.

DOLLS:

Many different versions of Superman dolls have been made by several different manufacturers, particularly since the early 1970s. All of these dolls give credit to D.C. Comics as the copyright holder. A series of "Superman" dolls was manufactured by Mego Corp. in 1977. These include *Superman, General Zod, Lex Luthor* and *Jor-El*, all of whom were characters in the 1978 film. These dolls resemble the actors from the film, especially Christopher Reeve as Superman, but this is a tie-in released at the right time, rather than actual celebrity dolls. Christopher Reeve looks very much like the comic conception of Superman, which can cause this belief. The *Jor-El* doll does not look at all like Marlon Brando, except for hair color. See *Illustrations 828, 829, 830, 831* and *832*. The *only* doll that has a direct tie-in to *Superman: The Movie* was made in Spain. See CHRISTOPHER REEVE.

Illustration 832. 12½in (31.8cm) *Jor-el* from *Superman* by Mego, No. 87003/1, 1978. All-vinyl and fully-jointed with painted hair and features. Copyright by D C Comics. Made in Hong Kong. Marlon Brando played this part in *Superman*.

SWIT, LORETTA. Actress. Born November 4, 1937. Loretta Swit appeared in films, on Broadway and on many television shows. The role that she is most identified with is that of Major Margaret "Hot Lips" Houlihan on "M*A*S*H." She began the part on September 17, 1972, and won an Emmy Award for the role in 1980.

DOLLS:

1. M*A*S*H NURSE. Distributed by F.W. Woolworth Co., circa 1976. Alan Alda is a companion doll. Made in Hong Kong. 8½in (21.6cm). *Illustration 833.*
2. HOT LIPS (MAJOR MARGARET HOULIHAN). Tristar International, Ltd., Series No. 4100, 1982. All-vinyl and fully-jointed. Painted hair, features and clothing. Made in Hong Kong. 3¾in (9.6cm).

SEE: M*A*S*H.

Illustration 833. 8½in (21.6cm) LORETTA SWIT as a nurse from "M*A*S*H," made for F.W. Woolworth Co., circa 1976. All-vinyl with molded yellow hair. Copyright 1969 by Aspen Productions, Inc. and Twentieth Century-Fox Productions. Made in Hong Kong.

SWITZER, CARL "ALFALFA." Actor. Born August 8, 1927; died January 21, 1959. Alfalfa Switzer was in the *Our Gang* comedies from 1935 until 1942. His last film was *The Defiant Ones* in 1958. Alfalfa's trademarks were his squeaky singing voice, his bug eyes and his waxed cowlick, and he was loaded with personality and talent. After the *Our Gang* comedies ended, Carl Switzer was in other films and on the Roy Rogers television show as a semi-regular. By 1958 the former child star was plagued with a series of problems. He tried suicide; was arrested for stealing Christmas trees in Sequoia National Park in California; and claimed to have been shot by an unknown assailant. On the evening of January 21, 1959, he got into a fight with a former friend in a bar in North Hollywood, California, demanding the return of a 50 dollar loan. The two men struggled and a pistol was fired into Switzer's abdomen. He died instantly.

DOLLS:

1. ALFALFA from OUR GANG. Mego, No. 61600/1, 1975. Made in Hong Kong. 6in (15.2cm). *Illustration 835.*

SEE: OUR GANG.

T

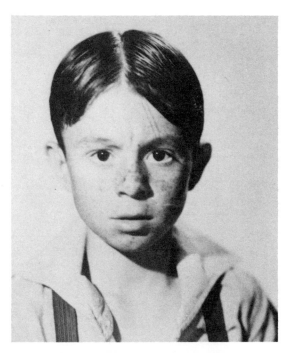

Illustration 834. Carl "Alfalfa" Switzer.

Illustration 835. 6in (15.2cm) CARL "ALFALFA" SWITZER of "Our Gang" by Mego, No. 61600/1, 1975. All-vinyl and fully-jointed. Painted red hair; freckles. Copyright by Metro-Goldwyn-Mayer Inc. Made in Hong Kong. *Wanda Lodwick Collection*.

TABATHA. Character on two television series played by many actresses. The ABC-TV fantasy situation comedy "Bewitched" starred Elizabeth Montgomery as a modern witch and was on from January 1966 to July 1972; "Tabitha" was on ABC-TV from September 1977 to January 1978. All dolls, toys, games, books and other licensed merchandise for the character call her "Tabatha." Tabitha was born on "Bewitched" on January 13, 1966. As a baby she was played by Cynthia Black and then by twins Heidi and Laura Gentry, followed by Julie and Tamar Young. For the 1967 season twins Erin and Diane Murphy played the part of Tabitha. After the 1968-1969 season Tabitha was played only by Erin Murphy. In the show "Tabitha," the lead was played by Liberty Williams, and her age was jumped forward to make her a young adult witch.

DOLLS:
1. TABATHA from BEWITCHED. Ideal, 1965. All-vinyl and fully-jointed. Rooted blonde hair; painted blue eyes; closed mouth. Head marked: " © 1965 // SCREEN GEMS, INC. // IDEAL TOY CORP. // T.A. 18-6 // H-25." 11½in (29.2cm).

TATE, LINCOLN. Actor. Lincoln Tate played General George Custer in the 1981 film *The Legend of the Lone Ranger*.

DOLLS:
1. GENERAL GEORGE CUSTER from THE LEGEND OF THE LONE RANGER. Gabriel, No. 31633, 1981. Made in Hong Kong. 4in (10.2cm). *Illustration 836*.

SEE: LONE RANGER, THE.

Illustration 836. 4in (10.2cm) LINCOLN TATE as *General George Armstrong Custer* from *The Legend of the Lone Ranger* by Gabriel, No. 31633, 1981. All-vinyl and fully-jointed. Painted yellow hair, beard and moustache. The hat is molded to the head. Marked on the back: " © 1980 // HONG KONG."

TAYLOR, ELIZABETH. Actress. Born February 27, 1932, in London, England, of American parents. Elizabeth Taylor was born beautiful; she was always a great actress; she married frequently. Her parents brought her to the United States in 1939 and she made her first movie in 1942—a comedy with Alfalfa Switzer called *There's One Born Every Minute*. The next year she signed a long-term contract with MGM and went from child actress to ingenue to superstar. Her first Academy Award was for *Butterfield 8* in 1960 and it is generally conceded that she won this award because of the sympathy engendered by her almost dying during voting time for the awards. Her second Oscar was for playing a shrew in *Who's Afraid of Virginia Woolf* in 1966. Taylor's most publicized movie was *Cleopatra* (1963) because it was the most expensive film made and because of her headline-making romance with co-star Richard Burton. Her husbands have been (so far) 1.) Conrad "Nicky" Hilton, Jr. for a few months in 1950; 2.) British actor Michael Wilding from 1952 to 1957; 3.) Mike Todd from 1957 to his death in a private airplane in 1958; 4.) Eddie Fisher from 1959 to 1964; 5.) British star Richard Burton from 1964 to 1973; 6.) Richard Burton from 1975 to 1976; 7.) John Warner, a United States Senator from Virginia, from 1976 to 1981, when they separated.

DOLLS:
1. ELIZABETH TAYLOR IN FATHER OF THE BRIDE. Peggy Nisbet, No. P758, 1970s. Made in England. About 7½in (19.1cm). *Illustration 837*.
2. ELIZABETH TAYLOR IN THE BLUE BIRD. Horsman, No. 9921, 1976. Made in USA. 11½in (29.2cm). *Illustration 839* and *840*.

Illustration 838. Elizabeth Taylor with Todd Lookinland and Patsy Kensit in *The Blue Bird*, 1976.

Illustration 839. 11½in (29.2cm) ELIZABETH TAYLOR from *The Blue Bird* by Horsman, No. 9921, 1976. Vinyl head; plastic body. Rooted black hair; painted blue eyes. This is the same doll as was used for Mary Poppins (See: JULIE ANDREWS), and was designed by Irene Szor. Made in USA.

Illustration 837. 7½in (19.1cm) ELIZABETH TAYLOR in *Father of the Bride* (1950) by Peggy Nisbet, No. P758, 1970s. All-hard plastic and jointed at the arms. Mohair wig and painted features. Copyright 1950 by Loew's (sic). Made in England. *Photograph Courtesy of House of Nisbet.*

Illustration 840. ELIZABETH TAYLOR by Horsman.

Illustration 841. Shirley Temple as *Little Miss Marker*, 1934.

TEMPLE, SHIRLEY. Actress; politician. Born April 23, 1928. It is a familiar story how Shirley Temple entered films in 1932 to play in a series of short comedies called *Baby Burlesks*. By 1936 she was the Number One Box Office Star, a position she held until 1939 when she fell to fifth place. After 1940 her career went into a sharp decline until it fizzled out by 1950. Shirley Temple was the most famous child in the history of the world and in the 1930s she was the seventh highest paid person in the United States. In 1935 she received a Special Academy Award "in grateful recognition of her outstanding contribution to screen entertainment during 1934." Shirley Temple was the best thing that happened during the Depression, and she created an industry with endorsements of dolls and every other product imaginable. With her 50 golden curls, she was the cutest little performer ever in the movies. As an ingenue her acting ability was not very good and she retired from films in 1950 after her marriage to businessman Charles Black. She attempted an acting comeback in 1958 that was not successful. Her show, "Shirley Temple's Storybook," was 16 Specials on ABC-TV during 1958 and a series that was on every third Monday during 1959. From September 1960 to September 1961 on NBC-TV she had a weekly series called "The Shirley Temple Show." She only acted occasionally in these stories, which were mostly fairy tales for children. A revival of her old films was more popular television fare. In the late 1960s she entered Republican Party politics and unsuccessfully tried to get elected as a Congresswoman from California. In 1968 President Nixon appointed her as a representative to the United Nations. From 1974 to 1976 she served as the United States Ambassador to Ghana, a Nixon appointment. She was the first ambassador to Africa to ever learn an African language—Ashanti. In 1976 she became the United States Chief of Protocol, an appointment by President Ford, and she planned the inauguration of Jimmy Carter. She campaigned vigorously for the elections of Gerald Ford in 1976 and Ronald Reagan in 1980.

The feature films of Shirley Temple:

1932　The Red-Haired Alibi
1933　To the Last Man
　　　Out All Night
1934　Carolina
　　　Mandalay
　　　Stand Up and Cheer
　　　Now I'll Tell
　　　Change of Heart
　　　Little Miss Marker
　　　Baby Take a Bow
　　　Now and Forever
　　　Bright Eyes
1935　The Little Colonel
　　　Our Little Girl
　　　Curly Top
　　　The Littlest Rebel
1936　Captain January
　　　Poor Little Rich Girl
　　　Dimples
　　　Stowaway

1937　Wee Willie Winkie
　　　Heidi
1938　Rebecca of Sunnybrook Farm
　　　Little Miss Broadway
　　　Just Around the Corner
1939　The Little Princess
　　　Susannah of the Mounties
1940　The Blue Bird
　　　Young People
1941　Kathleen
1942　Miss Annie Rooney
1944　Since You Went Away
1945　I'll Be Seeing You
　　　Kiss and Tell
1947　Honeymoon
　　　The Bachelor and the Bobbysoxer
　　　That Hagen Girl
1948　Fort Apache
1949　Mr. Belvedere Goes To College
　　　Adventure in Baltimore (Baltimore Adventure)
　　　The Story of Seabiscuit
　　　A Kiss for Corliss

Illustration 842. One of the first advertisements for the Shirley Temple dolls, *Sears 1934 Christmas Catalog.*

Illustration 843. 9 in (22.9cm) SHIRLEY TEMPLE by Ideal, circa 1934. All-composition and fully-jointed. Painted, molded curly brown hair; painted blue eyes. Marked on the back: " e // IDEAL DOLL." All the clothing is replaced. This is one of the rarest of all the Ideal composition Shirley Temple dolls, if indeed it was originally intended to be she. *Marge Meisinger Collection.*

Temple's picture and a facimile signature." Stores were already planning promotions for the dolls by staging contests for little Shirley Temple look-alikes. The first dolls came in four sizes and retailed for $3, $5, $6 and $7. The company was so confident of success with the new doll that it did not hand out any samples to retailers, as had been the custom among doll manufacturers for many years.

Ideal heavily promoted SHIRLEY TEMPLE dolls and their accessories from 1935 through 1937. In 1936 a contest that was part of "one of the largest national promotions ever undertaken by any doll or toy manufacturer" (*Playthings,* November 1936) was launched to advertise SHIRLEY TEMPLE dolls. The contest was an announcement that appeared in 14,000,000 Sunday newspapers' comic sections along with an ad for the dolls. More than 11,000 cash and merchandise prizes were supposed to go to the winners of the contest. The first ten prizes were Scotch Terrier puppies that were like Shirley's dog, Corky. The other prizes were Shirley Temple merchandise, such as doll buggies, shoes and coats. To enter the contest, little girls had to present

Illustration 844. 11 in (27.9cm) SHIRLEY TEMPLE in composition by Ideal. Head marked: "SHIRLEY TEMPLE." Body marked: "SHIRLEY TEMPLE // 11." *Fran's Dolls.*

SHIRLEY TEMPLE DOLLS

The most popular celebrity doll ever was the SHIRLEY TEMPLE doll by the Ideal Novelty & Toy Company (later called the Ideal Toy Corporation). It was also the most copied and imitated doll.

Ideal was granted the first commercial license to use Shirley Temple's name. The SHIRLEY TEMPLE doll first came on the market in full force in time for Christmas of 1934. By the fall of 1934 Ideal was announcing in trade publications that "so many orders are already in hand that orders will be filled in the order received." Ideal secured the rights to manufacture a SHIRLEY TEMPLE doll from the Fox Film Corporation (later merged as Twentieth Century-Fox), who had the little actress under exclusive contract, but this was done with "the authorization of the parents of Shirley Temple." The first ads by Ideal told that the dolls were dressed in "authentic Shirley Temple costumes, and to each doll is fastened a beautiful celluloid button bearing Shirley

themselves to a doll dealer who would provide them with the contest forms. The application blank showed SHIRLEY TEMPLE dolls dressed in six different costumes. The child had to place the costumes in the order in which she found them the most appealing and come up with reasons for wanting to have her own SHIRLEY TEMPLE doll. The contest was rather cruel because the entire object was to increase the desire of little girls to own SHIRLEY TEMPLE dolls. Stores liked the plan because the contest form could not be mailed in, but had to be returned to the doll counter where an elaborate SHIRLEY TEMPLE doll display was set up, further stimulating the little girl's desire.

In January of 1937 *Playthings* reported that Ben Michtom, the son of the founder of the Ideal Novelty & Toy Company, had just returned from a promotional trip throughout the country. The purpose of the journey was to "acquaint the public with the Shirley Temple Doll Contest." While Mr. Michtom was in Hollywood he met Shirley Temple and her parents on the set of the Twentieth Century-Fox film *Stowaway*. Mr. Michtom "found Shirley to be an alert, intelligent, unspoiled and thoroughly likable youngster, and a finished actress in spite of the fact that she is not seven." (Shirley Temple was actually going on eight; this was during the period when the studio "lied" about her age.) Ben Michtom posed with Shirley and her 11-week-old Pekinese puppy, Chin Chin, and later related in the most laudatory terms his interview with her. He also reported:

> She is a real little girl with determination and acting ability possessed by few adults. *Stowaway* is her best picture, a really fine piece of work that will undoubtedly further increase Shirley's margin as the leading box office attraction of the motion picture screen.

Mr. Michtom's enthusiasm was certainly tempered by the lucrative contracts that he possessed.

Ideal's composition child dolls eventually came in 12 sizes. The baby doll, based on Shirley Temple at age two, was introduced in the summer of 1935. She came in six sizes. Special editions of the dolls came packed in a wardrobe trunk with extra costumes. Separate outfits were available for the dolls by early 1936. One of the most interesting of these was a reproduction of the "Cape Cod Slicker," a raincoat like the one Shirley wore in the film *Captain January*. One of the more unusual and desirable versions of the doll was the cowgirl costume in the spring of 1936. This was first called the *Official Doll of the Texas Centennial* and later the *Shirley Temple Texas Ranger Doll*. And no wonder so many of the composition SHIRLEY TEMPLE dolls are found with messy hair today. In 1937 Ideal sold all the dolls with "a generous supply of hair curlers and full instructions" for "keeping Shirley curly." Ads proclaimed that "the genuine Shirley Temple Doll is the *only* doll with *enough* hair—and *good enough hair*—to be waved, curled and dressed in all the latest styles."

Special advertising promotions for the dolls were held to coincide with Shirley Temple's birthday—April 23—and for other events such as Children's Day (the second Sunday in June, originally a holiday begun by the Protestant Churches in the United States) and the traditional present-giving holidays. Each of these occasions became a national merchandising event.

Right from the beginning Ideal had problems with other doll companies who wanted to take part in the market created by the most successful play doll created up to that time. It has been reported in print many times that Madame Alexander was opposed to marketing the SHIRLEY TEMPLE doll for this reason:

> I always thought Shirley Temple was extremely talented, but about the time she became a child star I had been quoted in a newspaper interview that I disapproved of commercializing on a child's efforts. Because I could not go against what I had said, I did not make the doll.

Only Ideal had the rights to produce Shirley Temple dolls. Yet in March of 1935 Madame Alexander presented "the only authentic 'Little Colonel' doll." All advertising cited the fact that Alexander's permission to produce the doll came from the holders of the copyrights of the children's books based on the character. The dolls look very similar in appearance to the SHIRLEY TEMPLE doll by Ideal. *Wards 1935 Christmas Catalog* shows these dolls in various costumes. An interesting feature of the *Little Colonel* dolls is that they have wigs that look like a SHIRLEY TEMPLE doll wig, forehead curl and all. Alexander advertising cited the fact that "the book has been a juvenile classic for innumerable years and is a tremendous seller today" and most important of all, that *"the film* appeals to adults and juveniles alike." All of this coincided with Shirley Temple's 1935 Fox release *The Little Colonel*.

Illustration 845. 13in (33cm) composition SHIRLEY TEMPLE. The dress has the NRA label. Head marked: "SHIRLEY TEMPLE // 13." Body marked only: "SHIRLEY TEMPLE." *Fran's Dolls.*

In March of 1935, the same month in which the *Little Colonel* ad appeared in *Playthings,* Ideal carried an "Important Notice" with the SHIRLEY TEMPLE doll ad. It stated:

> We are the only doll manufacturer authorized by the parents of Shirley Temple and by Fox Film Corporation to put out 'Shirley Temple' dolls, dresses and accessories.
>
> The manufacturer or sale of any imitation 'Shirley Temple' dolls will be vigorously prosecuted.
>
> The sale of imitation 'Shirley Temple' dolls is a misdemeanor in New York State in addition to civil rights throughout the country. 'Shirley Temple' is our registered trademark.

All of this was during the time that Alexander was making Dionne Quintuplet dolls. The Dionne Quintuplets, the most exploited children of the era, were made in doll form by Madame Alexander beginning in 1935. By November of 1935 Alexander carried ads in *Playthings* warning about infringements against its rights to produce Dionne Quintuplet dolls. (See DIONNE QUINTUPLET Dolls.)

In July of 1936, the E. Goldberger Doll Company (Eegee) introduced *Miss Charming* and *Baby Charming.* The Goldberger *Miss Charming* in all the ads looks just like a SHIRLEY TEMPLE doll with a wig and dress style that is much the same. Here is a description of the dolls from *Playthings* in September of 1936:

LITTLE MISS CHARMING—The doll that everybody loves! This beautifully dressed doll has moving eyes with lashes, a gorgeous head of well set blonde hair, and shiny white teeth showing through her laughing mouth. She stands 17 inches tall and wears a cute celluloid button bearing her name and picture. A pretty ribbon and two golden clips adorn her hair. She is fully dressed, with white shoes and jeweled buckles. A fine assortment of dress styles is available. Placed in a strong, attractive box... Little Miss Charming Dolls are available in all popular sizes from 12 to 27 inches high. 'Baby Charming,' a companion line—consists of a complete assortment of baby dolls with and without wigs.

The entire description seems like one for SHIRLEY TEMPLE dolls. Goldberger and Alexander were not the only infringers of Ideal's SHIRLEY TEMPLE. Almost every doll company had a similar doll.

In the August 1936 *Playthings* along with the advertisement for SHIRLEY TEMPLE dolls by the Ideal Novelty & Toy Company this notice appeared:

WARNING!

We have recently settled a lawsuit in Common Pleas Court of Philadelphia County *by securing a perpetual injunction.* An injunction was issued perpetually restraining the defendant 'from using in connection or in association with any doll not manufactured by plaintiff, Ideal Novelty & Toy Company, its successors or assigns, the trade name 'Shirley Temple' or any deceptive simulation thereof, or the name 'Shirley' or any deceptive simulation thereof, or the picture of actress 'Shirley Temple;' or from selling or causing to be offered for sale dolls not manufactured and sold by the plaintiff which are deceptively similar in appearance, dress and get-up to the doll of the plaintiff known as 'Shirley Temple' dolls, etc.

It is the intention of Ideal Novelty & Toy Company to proceed vigorously against any other infringers.

Illustration 847. 13in (33cm) SHIRLEY TEMPLE in composition. The costume is original; the wig is a replacement. The white cup is of unknown date. *Wanda Lodwick Collection.*

Illustration 848. 15in (38.1cm) composition SHIRLEY TEMPLE. The dress is probably not original. The doll is marked in an unusual way for a Shirley Temple. Head marked: "60 // SHIRLEY TEMPLE." *Wanda Lodwick Collection.*

OPPOSITE PAGE: Illustration 846. 13in (33cm) SHIRLEY TEMPLE in composition. The original dress is red. Fully marked. *Fran's Dolls.*

Illustration 849. 16in (40.6cm) SHIRLEY TEMPLE by Ideal in composition. Head marked like *Figure 1*. The pleated dancing dress is pale pink.

Over the years many dolls were made who took their inspiration directly from the SHIRLEY TEMPLE dolls by Ideal. The largest variety came during the late 1930s in composition. Many of these SHIRLEY TEMPLE look-alikes have fooled the unwary. Enthusiastic sellers have been known to take any old composition doll with a blonde wig and put it in a flea market with a big sign on it proclaiming that it is an "unmarked SHIRLEY TEMPLE doll" with a price on it that is higher than the genuine article would bring. The original SHIRLEY TEMPLE doll always has the name "SHIRLEY TEMPLE" on it. Authentic SHIRLEY TEMPLE dolls have been verified with no markings, but one should be cautious in considering them the "real thing" if they have no original clothing, and particularly if they do not have an original SHIRLEY TEMPLE wig.

After 1939 when Shirley Temple declined sharply as a film attraction, Ideal stopped promoting and producing the dolls, using the molds for other characters like *Snow White*. (These dolls have "SHIRLEY TEMPLE" markings.) Some molds were sold to companies who tooled out the Shirley Temple name; other molds appear to have been copied.

Even the vinyl SHIRLEY TEMPLE dolls by Ideal in the 1950s were copied by other doll manufacturers. Another terrible violation of Ideal's design is the *Shirley* doll from Taiwan (*Illustration 894*) in porcelain and sold in a kit.

See *Illustrations 873, 874, 875, 876* and *878* for all-composition Shirley Temple look-alike dolls. See *Illustration 889* for a vinyl Shirley Temple look-alike doll.
DOLLS:
1. 9in (22.9cm) by Ideal, circa 1934. All-composition and fully-jointed. Molded hair, closed mouth. *Illustration 843*.
2. to 11.
   Made by Ideal from 1934 to about 1939. All-composition and fully-jointed. Dark blonde wigs of mohair (Some are human hair.); sleep eyes with lashes (usually a greenish shade); open mouth with upper teeth and a tongue (usually felt; sometimes metal). Marked on head and/or back. These dolls came dressed in a wide variety of costumes, most of them from Shirley Temple films.
2. 11in (27.9cm). *Illustration 844*.
3. 13in (33cm). *Illustrations 845, 846* and *847*.
4. 15in (38.1cm). *Illustration 848*.
5. 16in (40.6cm). *Illustration 849*.
6. 17in (43.2cm). *Illustration 850*.
7. 18in (45.7cm). *Illustrations 851, 852, 853, 854,* and *855*.
8. 20in (50.8cm). *Illustrations 856* and *857*.
9. 22in (55.9cm). *Illustrations 858, 859, 860* and *861*.
10. 25in (63.5cm).
11. 27in (68.6cm). *Illustrations 862, 863, 864* and *865*.
12. to 17.
    SHIRLEY TEMPLE BABY by Ideal, 1935. Composition head, arms and lower legs. Stuffed cloth body. Blonde mohair wigs or molded hair; green sleep eyes that are usually "flirty;" open mouth with two upper and three lower teeth.
12. 14in (35.6cm).
13. 16in (40.6cm). *Illustration 866*.
14. 18in (45.7cm).
15. 20in (50.8cm). *Illustrations 867* and *868*.
16. 25in (63.5cm).
17. 27in (68.6cm).
    Some of the foreign-made SHIRLEY TEMPLE dolls from the 1930s.
18. 18in (45.7cm) by Reliable. All-composition and fully-jointed. This doll looks like the 18in (45.7cm) doll by Ideal. Marked: "RELIABLE // MADE IN CANADA." Circa 1936.
19. Chad Valley. Cloth SHIRLEY TEMPLE dolls. Made in England, circa 1936.
20. Allwin. Cloth dolls. Made in England, circa 1936. *Illustration 869*.
21. Lenci. All-felt with a mohair wig. Made in Italy, 1930s. 32in (81cm).
    Wears a dress similar to those from the film *The Little Colonel*.
22. Manufacturer unknown. Made in Germany, 1930s. Painted bisque; papier-mâché body. 15in (38.1cm). *Illustration 870*.
23. Manufacturer unknown. Made in Germany, 1930s. Painted bisque. 4in (10.2cm). *Illustration 871*.

OPPOSITE PAGE: Illustration 850. 17in (43.2cm) SHIRLEY TEMPLE in composition. The dress is white with red dots. Head marked like *Figure 1*. Back marked "SHIRLEY TEMPLE // 17." *Fran's Dolls*.

Illustration 852. 18in (45.7cm) SHIRLEY TEMPLE. The labeled dress has a blue background in the print design. Head and body marked: SHIRLEY TEMPLE // 18." *Fran's Dolls.*

24. Manufacturer unknown.   Made in Japan, 1930s. All-bisque. 6½in (16.5cm). *Illustration 872.*
25. Manufacturer unknown.   Made in Japan, 1930s. All-composition. 7½in (19.1cm). *Illustration 871.*
26. There is an all-hard plastic doll marked "SHIRLEY TEMPLE" from about 1950, reportedly made by Ideal and so marked. It is about 15in (38.1cm) and the modeling is similar to the composition doll from the 1930s.

OPPOSITE PAGE: Illustration 851. 18in (45.7cm) SHIRLEY TEMPLE in composition by Ideal. Head marked like *Figure 1.* The dress is pale yellow.

Illustration 853. 18in (45.7cm) composition SHIRLEY TEMPLE. The pale green dress is tagged. Head marked like *Figure 1.* Back marked: "SHIRLEY TEMPLE // 18." *Fran's Dolls.*

27. to 31.
    Ideal. 1957 to 1960. All-vinyl and fully-jointed. Rooted dark blonde hair; hazel sleep eyes with lashes. All sizes are dressed in a variety of costumes and extra clothing could also be purchased. The clothing is labeled.
27. 12in (30.5cm). *Illustrations 880, 881* and *882.*
28. 15in (38.1cm). *Illustrations 883* and *884.*
29. 17in (43.2cm). With regular sleep eyes and with "flirty" sleep eyes. *Illustrations 885* and *886.*
30. 19in (48.3cm). With regular sleep eyes and with "flirty" sleep eyes. *Illustration 887.*
31. 35in (88.9cm). With jointed or unjointed wrists. *Illustration 888.*
32. Ideal. 1972. Special doll made for Mongomery Ward's 100th Anniversary. Made in Hong Kong. 14in (35.6cm). *Illustration 890.*
33. Ideal. 1973. All-vinyl and fully-jointed with stationary eyes. Very soft hair texture. *Illustration 891.*
34. Ideal. 1973. All-vinyl and fully-jointed with stationary eyes. Coarser hair texture than No. 33. *Illustrations 892* and *893.*

35. to 40.
   Ideal. 1982. All-vinyl and fully-jointed. 8in (20.3cm) in six models. See *Illustration 898*.
40. to 46.
   Ideal. 1982. All-vinyl and fully-jointed. 12in (30.5cm) in six models. See *Illustration 898*.

FIGURE 1.
   Head mark: Back mark:

Illustration 856. 20in (50.8cm) composition SHIRLEY TEMPLE. The original dress is white. Head marked like *Figure 1*. Body unmarked. *Fran's Dolls.*

Illustration 855. 18in (45.7cm) SHIRLEY TEMPLE in composition. The polka dot dress is red with white dots. The shoes and socks are replaced. Head and back marked: "SHIRLEY TEMPLE // 18."

OPPOSITE PAGE: Illustration 854. 18in (45.7cm) composition SHIRLEY TEMPLE dolls in labeled dresses. The sailor dress is dark blue; the pleated dancing dress is pink. *Wanda Lodwick Collection.*

Illustration 857. 20in (50.8cm) SHIRLEY TEMPLE in composition by Ideal. The cotton dress is red with white stars and has the NRA label. Head marked like *Figure 1*. *Wanda Lodwick Collection.*

Illustration 858. 22in (55.9cm) SHIRLEY TEMPLE by Ideal in all-composition, 1937. This very rare original, tagged costume is based on the dream sequence in the film *Heidi*, in which Heidi danced and sang as a Dutch girl. The apron is separate. The hat is white organdy. The wig is also seldom seen on an original composition Shirley Temple doll. It is dark blonde mohair in a center part with bangs and long pigtails gathered up in loops. The cotton stockings are also original, as are the hand-carved wood shoes that are rather thin and fit well on the foot. Head marked: "SHIRLEY TEMPLE." Back marked: SHIRLEY TEMPLE (curved pattern) // 22." *Patricia Slabe Collection.*

OPPOSITE PAGE: Illustration 859. 22in (55.9cm) SHIRLEY TEMPLE from *Heidi*. *Patricia Slabe Collection.*

Illustration 860. 22in (55.9cm) composition SHIRLEY TEMPLE. This dress is from *Bright Eyes*, 1934; the pin is an original one. Head and back marked like *Figure 1*. *Fran's Dolls.*

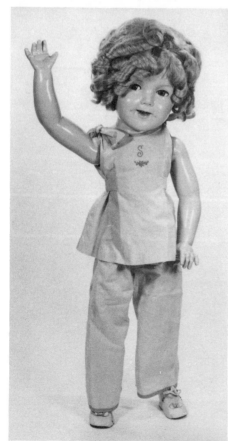

Illustration 861. 22in (55.9cm) composition SHIRLEY TEMPLES in replaced costumes. *Wanda Lodwick Collection.*

Illustration 862. 27in (68.6cm) composition SHIRLEY TEMPLE. Hazel flirty eyes; metal tongue. The hair is in the original set. Replacement costume. Head marked like *Figure 1*. Back marked: "SHIRLEY TEMPLE." *Wanda Lodwick Collection.*

Illustration 863. Close-up of 27in (68.6cm) SHIRLEY TEMPLE from *Illustration 862. Wanda Lodwick Collection.*

Illustration 864. 27in (68.6cm) SHIRLEY TEMPLE with flirty eyes. The dress is white with gold print. Head marked like *Figure 1*. Body marked: "SHIRLEY TEMPLE." *Fran's Dolls.*

Illustration 865. 27in (68.6cm) Composition SHIRLEY TEMPLE with flirty eyes. The dress is white with red dots. Marked like *Figure 1. Fran's Dolls.*

Illustration 867. 20in (50.8cm) SHIRLEY TEMPLE baby by Ideal, 1935. The head, arms and legs are composition; the body is stuffed cloth. Head marked: "SHIRLEY TEMPLE." *Fran's Dolls*.

Illustration 868. 20in (50.8cm) SHIRLEY TEMPLE baby by Ideal, 1935. Composition head on a shoulder plate; composition arms and legs; stuffed cloth body. Flirty sleep eyes with lashes; two upper teeth and three lower teeth. Head marked: "SHIRLEY TEMPLE." *Barbara DeVault Collection*.

OPPOSITE PAGE: Illustration 866. 16in (40.6cm) SHIRLEY TEMPLE baby by Ideal 1935. Composition head, arms and lower legs. Cloth stuffed body. Blonde mohair wig; green flirty eyes; two upper and three lower teeth. Head marked: "SHIRLEY TEMPLE." The original outfit is a pink organdy dress under a pink rayon coat and hat; white leather booties. The pin is also original. *Betty Shriver Collection*.

SHIRLEY TEMPLE DOLLS "THE WORLD'S DARLING" IN 18 CHARACTER STUDIES

These life-like Dolls are charming reproductions of "The World's Darling" and are giving thousands of delighted children great pleasure in all parts of the Country.

A "Shirley Temple" Doll is always a favourite birthday present and there are 18 different character studies from which to choose. Write to Allwins who are the sole British makers for illustrated list.

PRICES RANGE FROM 10/6 to 32/6
•
OBTAINABLE FROM LEADING STORES AND TOY DEALERS THROUGHOUT GREAT BRITAIN
•
THE ONLY AUTHORISED BRITISH REPRODUCTION OF "THE WORLD'S DARLING"—AND MADE SOLELY BY:—

RICHARDS SON & ALLWIN, LTD., GREAT BRIDGE, TIPTON, STAFFS.

Illustration 869. Advertisement from *Film Pictorial*, a British magazine, August 1, 1936. Very little is known about the Allwin Shirley Temple dolls. They appear to have been made from cloth.

Illustration 871. Foreign-made SHIRLEY TEMPLE dolls, circa late 1930s. The larger doll is 7½in (19.1cm) in a papier-mâché type of composition over plaster. Fully-jointed, including the head. Painted and molded light brown curls; painted blue eyes; smiling mouth with painted teeth; dimples in the cheeks. Stamped on the torso: "JAPAN." The smaller doll is painted all-bisque and is 4in (10.2cm). Only the arms and the legs are jointed. Painted and molded light brown curls; painted black eyes; closed mouth. The painted shoes have heels. Incised at the neck: "GERMANY // 5649." Neither doll is in an original costume.

Illustration 870. 15in (38.1cm) SHIRLEY TEMPLE (?) from Germany, 1930s. Painted bisque socket head with an open crown; five-piece papier-mâché body. Dark blonde mohair wig; blue glass sleep eyes without lashes; painted lower lashes; upper teeth in the open mouth. The costume is a replacement. Head marked: "T // GERMANY // A // 1." *Betty Shriver Collection.*

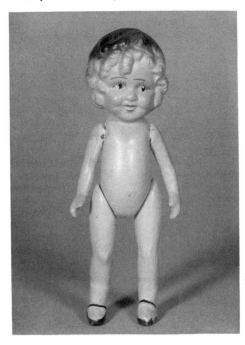

Illustration 872. 6½in (16.5cm) all-bisque SHIRLEY TEMPLE from Japan, circa 1930s. Jointed only at the arms and legs. Molded hair; painted blue eyes. Back incised: "MADE IN // JAPAN // ST22." *Wanda Lodwick Collection.*

Illustration 874. 17in (45.7cm) all-composition Shirley Temple look-alike, circa 1936. This doll is probably Goldberger's *Miss Charming.* Dark blonde mohair wig in a "Shirley Temple" set, although it has been redone; blue tin sleep eyes with lashes; open mouth with teeth; dimples in the cheeks. There are no markings on the doll.

Illustration 873. 16in (40.6cm) "Shirley Temple type" from an unknown manufacturer, circa 1930s. She is very unusual in that she is all-hard rubber, which has the appearance of composition. Effanbee used this material for the arms of the Anne Shirley dolls and for the head of Dy-Dee Baby. She has a dark blonde human hair wig, brown tin sleep eyes with lashes, and an open mouth with teeth and dimples in the cheeks. All of this is similar to the design of Ideal's Shirley Temple dolls; the quality is like Effanbee dolls from the late 1930s. The dress is pale blue organdy with pink trim. The shoes and socks are like those found on original Shirley Temple dolls. The doll is not marked.

Illustration 875. Shirley Temple look-alike from *Illustration 874.*

Illustration 876. 28in (71.1cm) *Miss Charming* by Eegee (Goldberger), circa 1937. Composition shoulder-plate head, arms and legs; stuffed cloth body. Blue tin sleep eyes with lashes; open mouth with six teeth. The wig is replaced, as is the costume. The head and the back of each leg is marked, at the top: "E.G."

Illustration 878. 14in (35.6cm) *Bright Star* by Horsman from the late 1930s. This is a "knock-off" of Ideal's Shirley Temple doll. All-composition and fully-jointed. Blonde mohair wig; blue tin sleep eyes; open mouth with four teeth. The organdy dress is white with red flowers and is trimmed in red. The doll is unmarked. The tag in front shows a doll that looks like the Shirley Temple doll and it reads: "HORSMAN'S // BRIGHT STAR // 'With eyes that shine // and hair so fine'." The second tag showing that she was probably a salesman's sample carries the information: "REGAL DOLL CORPORATION // HORSMAN DOLLS, INC. // TRENTON, N.J. // Style No. 526."

Illustration 877. Button that was on the *Miss Charming* doll by Eegee (Goldberger).

Illustration 879. Shirley Temple, circa 1957, with a vinyl Shirley Temple doll from that year on the left and a composition Shirley Temple doll from about 1935 on the right.

Illustration 880. 12in (30.5cm) SHIRLEY TEMPLE dolls from the late 1950s. All-vinyl and fully-jointed. Rooted dark blonde hair; hazel sleep eyes with molded lashes. Head and back marked: "IDEAL DOLL // ST-12. On the left is the costume from *Wee Willie Winkie;* on the right is *Rebecca of Sunnybrook Farm.*

Illustration 881. 12in (30.5cm) SHIRLEY TEMPLE dolls from the late 1950s in original costumes that were sold in boxed sets. (None of the shoes are original.) *Wanda Lodwick Collection.*

Illustration 882. 12in (30.5cm) SHIRLEY TEMPLE dolls from the late 1950s. These outfits were sold in boxes sets and are all labeled by Ideal. *Fran's Dolls.*

Illustration 885. 17in (43.2cm) SHIRLEY TEMPLE by Ideal, late 1950s. All-vinyl and fully-jointed. Rooted dark blonde hair; hazel "flirty" eyes with lashes. Head marked: "IDEAL DOLL // ST-17-1." Back marked: "IDEAL DOLL // ST-17." The dress is rose and is labeled.

Illustration 883. 15in (38.1cm) SHIRLEY TEMPLE by Ideal, late 1950s. All-vinyl and fully-jointed. Rooted dark blonde wig; hazel sleep eyes with lashes. Head marked: "IDEAL DOLL // ST-15-N." Back marked: "IDEAL DOLL // ST-15." Note the Shirley Temple script pin. *Wanda Lodwick Collection*.

Illustration 884. 15in (38.1cm) SHIRLEY TEMPLE from the late 1950s dressed as *Heidi* with her original "autographed" purse.

Illustration 886. 17in (43.2cm) SHIRLEY TEMPLE by Ideal, late 1950s. She carries her original "autographed" purse. *Wanda Lodwick Collection*.

Illustration 887. 19in (48.3cm) and 17in (43.2cm) SHIRLEY TEMPLES from the late 1950s in original labeled dresses. Both dolls have flirty eyes. The shoes on both dolls are replacements. The 19in (48.3cm) doll is marked on the head: "IDEAL DOLL // ST-19-1." The back is marked: "IDEAL DOLL // ST-19." *Fran's Dolls*.

Illustration 888. 35in (88.9cm) SHIRLEY TEMPLE by Ideal from about 1960. Note that this doll has jointed wrists. Other versions have the Patty Play Pal body with unjointed wrists. Head marked: "IDEAL DOLL // ST-35-38-2." Back marked: "IDEAL // 35-5." *Wanda Lodwick Collection*.

Illustration 889. 19in (48.3cm) Shirley Temple look-alike, called *Little Miss Movie Star*, late 1950s to early 1960s. All-vinyl and fully-jointed. Rooted dark blonde hair; blue sleep eyes with lashes; open mouth with painted teeth; dimples. This doll seems like it was made from the mold of the 19in (48.3cm) 1957 Ideal doll. The body is the same; the head is of a lighter weight vinyl but the hair is identical. Production savings were made with less careful facial detail painting and the lack of inset teeth. Back marked: "19 // S // A E // 195." Left arm marked at the joint: "19." Legs marked at the joints: "19 ST." The replacement costume is a Madame Alexander accessory.

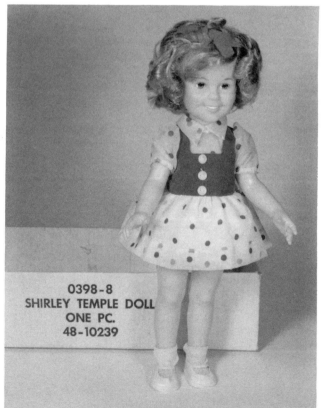

Illustration 890. 14in (35.6cm) SHIRLEY TEMPLE by Ideal, made for Montgomery Wards 100th Anniversary in 1972. All-vinyl and fully-jointed. Rooted dark blonde hair; hazel sleep eyes with lashes; open mouth with teeth; dimples. Everything is original including the bobby pins in the hair and the white vinyl shoes. Head marked: "HONG KONG // IDEAL DOLL // ST-15-N." Back marked: "IDEAL ST 15 // HONG KONG." Dress labeled "MADE IN HONG KONG."

Illustration 892. 16¾in (42.6cm) SHIRLEY TEMPLE by Ideal, No. 3P-0572, 1973. All-vinyl and fully-jointed. Rooted dark blonde hair; fixed hazel eyes with lashes; open mouth with painted teeth; dimples. Head marked: "© 1972 // IDEAL TOY CORP. // ST-14-H-213." Back marked: " IDEAL // © 1972 // 2-M-5534."

Illustration 891. 16¼in (41.3cm) SHIRLEY TEMPLE by Ideal, 1973. All-vinyl and fully-jointed. Rooted dark blonde hair; hazel fixed eyes. This doll is wearing a variation of the "coin dot" dress and was sold in a plain carton by Montgomery Ward as shown. Head marked: "© 1972 // IDEAL TOY // ST-14-H-213." Back marked: " © 1972 // IDEAL TOY CORP. // ST-14-B-38." *Fran's Dolls.*

Illustration 893. 16¾in (42.6cm) SHIRLEY TEMPLE dolls by Ideal, 1973. These dolls are wearing the four "authentic" movie costumes that were available separately for the dolls. From left to right, they are: *Heidi, Captain January, The Little Colonel* and *Rebecca of Sunnybrook Farm. Wanda Lodwick Collection.*

Illustration 894. 15½in (38.1cm) Shirley Temple copy by Albert E. Price, Inc., No. 9048, 1978. All-porcelain with painted blue eyes; open-closed mouth. This direct copy of the composition Shirley Temple mold by Ideal was made in Taiwan. The original box calls this "Hello Dolly // Porcelain // Do-It-Yourself Kit // Shirley Doll." The synthetic wig defies description. *Fran's Dolls.*

Illustration 895. The 11½in (29.2cm) Ideal SHIRLEY TEMPLE doll that never was. It was reported in *New York* (Magazine) on November 10, 1980, that Shirley Temple Black "kicked up a fuss after the Ideal Toy Company (sic) planned to market, side by side, two dolls—one representing Shirley Temple in her 'Little Miss Marker' role and the other modeled on Sara Stimson, who played the part.." in the 1980 version of the film. Shirley Temple was quoted as having said that *she* was Little Miss Marker, not Sara Stimson. The illustration is from the 1980 Ideal Toy Corporation catalog. The 1980 film version of *Little Miss Marker* (the fourth filming of the story) was such a bomb that it was not widely distributed. The small packaged Shirley Temple doll pictured above the larger Shirley Temple doll's head is an even different version in facial modeling and body construction. It is also less pretty. Shirley Temple probably "kicked up a fuss" because the doll is such an inferior product.

Illustration 897. Shirley Temple in *The Littlest Rebel*, 1935.

Illustration 896. Shirley Temple and unknown player from *The Little Colonel*, 1935.

Illustration 898. SHIRLEY TEMPLE by Ideal, 1982. All-vinyl and fully-jointed. Rooted dark blonde nylon hair; hazel sleep eyes with lashes. There are six dolls in two sizes each—8in (20.3cm) and 12in (30.5cm)—dressed in costumes from Shirley Temple's movies. Top row, left to right, *Heidi* and *Stand Up and Cheer.* Front row, left to right: *The Little Colonel, Stowaway, Captain January,* and *The Littlest Rebel.* The dolls were announced to be made only during 1982. Photograph Courtesy of Ideal Toy Corporation.

TENNILLE, TONI. Singer. Born Cathryn Antoinette Tennille in Montgomery, Alabama, May 8, 1943. Toni Tennille co-wrote the rock-ecology musical "Mother Earth" for which Daryl Dragon was hired as a pianist. Dragon worked between tours of the Beach Boys group in which he was in the band. Tennille joined the group until she and Dragon were married and they formed the team "The Captain and Tennille." Their hit record "Love Will Keep Us Together" won a Grammy Award in 1975. They had a television show—"The Captain and Tennille"—on ABC-TV from September 1976 to March 1977. Toni Tennille also had her own syndicated variety show on television in 1980.

DOLLS:
1. TONI TENNILLE. Mego, No. 75000, 1977. Daryl Dragon, No. 75001, is a companion doll. Made in Hong Kong. 12¼in (31.2cm). *Illustrations 899* and *899-A.*

Illustration 899. 12¼in (31.2cm) TONI TENNILLE of The Captain and Tennille by Mego, No. 75000, 1977. All-vinyl and fully-jointed, including twist waist. Rooted brown hair; painted brown eyes with long lashes. Head marked: " © MOONLIGHT & // MAGNOLIAS INC." Made in Hong Kong. *Shirley Buchholz Collection.*

Illustration 899-A. TONI TENNILLE by Mego. *Shirley Buchholz Collection.*

TEWES, LAUREN. Actress. Born in Trafford, Pennsylvania, on October 26, (?). Lauren Tewes has played cruise director Julie McCoy on "The Love Boat" since September 1977. She was also in the part for the pilot film "The Love Boat III" in May 1977.

DOLLS:
1. JULIE from THE LOVE BOAT. Mego, No. 23005 /2, 1982. Made in Hong Kong. 3¾in (9.6cm). *Illustration 899-B.*

SEE: LOVE BOAT, THE.

Illustration 899-B. 3¾in (9.6cm) LAUREN TEWES as *Julie* from "The Love Boat" by Mego, No. 23005/2, 1982. All-vinyl and fully-jointed. Painted red hair; painted blue eyes. Painted and molded clothing, and a vinyl skirt. Copyright by Aaron Spelling Productions, Inc. Made in Hong Kong. On the left is JILL WHELAN as *Vicki* from the same series, No. 23005/6. She is 3¼in (8.3cm) and her description is the same.

THATCHER, MARGARET. Prime Minister of the United Kingdom. Born October 13, 1925. Mrs. Thatcher was elected on May 3, 1979, and she took office the following day. She was the first woman to hold this position. She is known as "The Iron Butterfly" because of her determination to cut government spending.

DOLLS:
1. PRIME MINISTER MRS. MARGARET THATCHER. Peggy Nisbet, No. P822, 1979. Made in England. 7½in (19.1cm). *Illustration 900.*

Illustration 900. 7½in (19.1cm) PRIME MINISTER MRS. MARGARET THATCHER by Peggy Nisbet, No. P822, 1979. All-hard plastic with jointed arms. Painted hair and features. Made in England. Foot stamped: " May 3, 1979." (This was the date of Mrs. Thatcher's victory.) *Photograph Courtesy of House of Nisbet.*

THOMAS, BILLY "BUCKWHEAT." Actor. Born William Henry Thomas, Jr. in 1931; died October 10, 1980. Buckwheat joined the cast of *Our Gang* when he was three years old, earning $40 a week. Buckwheat had a load of pigtails on his head like Farina and for a while his sex was the subject of speculation, as some little girls had also played the part. After appearing in 89 movies Thomas worked as a film technician for Technicolor for more than 20 years. He died of natural causes.

DOLLS:
1. BUCKWHEAT. Mego, No. 61600 /3, 1975. Made in Hong Kong. 6in (15.2cm). *Illustration 901*.
See: Our Gang.

Illustration 901. 6in (15.2cm) BILLY THOMAS as *Buckwheat* from "Our Gang" by Mego, No. 61600/3, 1975. All-vinyl and fully-jointed. Painted black kinky hair. Copyright by Metro-Goldwyn-Mayer Inc. Made in Hong Kong. *Wanda Lodwick Collection*.

THOMAS, MARLO. Actress. Born Margaret Julia Thomas on Novembr 21, 1937. Marlo Thomas broke into show business because of the influence of her father, Danny Thomas. After plastic surgery to reduce the size of her nose she became a perky performer in movies and on television. Her comedy show "That Girl" on ABC-TV lasted from September 1966 to September 1971, a very successful run. She is married to talk show host Phil Donahue.

DOLLS:
1. THAT GIRL—MARLO. Madame Alexander, No. 1789, 1967. All-vinyl and fully-jointed. Rooted dark brown hair; black pupilless sleep eyes with lashes. Dressed in a blue and green jersey shift dress, white stockings and high white boots. 17in (43.2cm).
2. THAT GIRL—MARLO. Madame Alexander, No. 1793, 1967. Dressed in a red velvet gown. 17in (43.2cm). *Illustrations 902* and *903*.

Illustration 902. 17in (43.2cm) MARLO THOMAS by Madame Alexander, No. 1793, 1967. Vinyl head with rooted dark brown hair, black pupilless eyes; vinyl arms and plastic legs and torso. Head marked: "ALEXANDER // 19© 66." Reproduction dress by Pamela K's Doll Fashions.

Illustration 903. MARLO THOMAS by Madame Alexander.

THOMAS, RICHARD. Actor. Born June 13, 1951. Richard Thomas was onscreen from 1969 playing juveniles and young villains. He is famous for playing John Boy on "The Waltons" on CBS-TV from September 1972 to August 1981. He appeared only occasionally during the later part of the show, as he was trying to change his acting image. In August 1981 Thomas' wife gave birth to identical triplet girls. The couple already had a son.

DOLLS:
1. JOHNBOY and ELLEN from THE WALTONS. Mego, No. 56000/1, 1975. Made in Hong Kong. 7½in (19.1cm).
SEE: WALTONS, THE.

Illustration 904. 7½in (19.1cm) RICHARD THOMAS as *John Boy Walton* from "The Waltons" by Mego, No. 56000/1, 1975. All-vinyl and fully-articulated, as are all Mego dolls of this size with extra joints at the elbows, knees, hands, feet and waist. Painted hair and features, including Richard Thomas' mole. Head marked: " © 1974 LORIMAR // PROD. INC." Back marked: " © MEGO CORP. 1974 // REG. U.S. PAT. OFF. // PAT. PENDING // HONG KONG." *Shirley Buchholz Collection.*

TIGHE, KEVIN. Actor. Born August 13, 1944. Tighe is the son of character actor Harry Shannon. He entered the movies in the 1960s. His most popular part was as Fireman Roy DeSoto on NBC-TV's "Emergency" from January 1972 to September 1977. Two more episodes of the series aired in June and July 1979. Tighe's voice was heard as Roy DeSoto in the animated cartoon version of the show, called "Emergency Plus Four" from September 1973 to September 1976.

DOLLS:
1. ROY from EMERGENCY. L.J.N. Toys, Ltd., 1975. All-vinyl and fully-jointed with painted hair and features. John, No. 6166, is a companion doll. Came packaged with "Action Accessories." Made in Hong Kong. 7½in (19.1cm).
2. ROY from EMERGENCY. L.J.N. Toys, Ltd.,1976. All-vinyl and fully-jointed with painted hair and features. John, No. 6102, is a companion doll. Made in Hong Kong. 7½in (19.1cm).

TIU, GINNY. Child performer. Born circa 1954. Ginny Tiu was a cute little Chinese girl who was part of a family singing act that got some television spots in the 1960s. She was also in an Elvis Presley film, *It Happened At the World's Fair* in 1963.

DOLLS:
1. GINNY TIU. Maker unknown, 1960s. 14½in (36.9cm). *Illustration 905.*

Illustration 905. 14½in (36.9cm) GINNY TIU, maker unknown, 1960s. All-vinyl and fully-jointed. Rooted dark brown hair; painted eyes; open mouth with painted teeth. The heavy vinyl body is like the mold of the late 1950s Shirley Temple dolls by Ideal. The hair should be in two long braids. Head marked: "K-7." Lower back marked: "15-5." *Wanda Lodwick Collection.*

TOCHI, BRIAN. Juvenile actor. Brian Tochi played Tee Gar Soom, called "Tiger," on "Space Academy" on CBS-TV from September 1977 to September 1979.

DOLLS:
1. TEE GAR SOOM (TIGER). Aviva Toy Company, No. 100, 1978. Made in Hong Kong. 8½in (21.6cm). *Illustration 906.*
SEE: SPACE ACADEMY.

Illustration 906. 8½in (21.6cm) BRIAN TOCHI as *Tee Gar Soom (Tiger)* from "Space Academy" by Aviva Toy Company for F.W. Woolworth Co., No. 100, 1978. All-vinyl and fully-jointed. Painted black hair and eyes. Lower back marked: "© 1978 // FILMATION ASSOCIATES // ALL RIGHTS RESERVED // MADE IN HONG KONG // PAT. PEND." *Penny Caswell Collection.*

TODD TRIPLETS. JOSEPH, MICHAEL and DANIEL TODD. Child performers. Born circa 1968. From 1970 to 1972 the boys played on "My Three Sons" on CBS-TV. Joseph was Steve Douglas, Jr., Michael was Charley Douglas and Daniel was Robbie Douglas II.
DOLLS:
1. MY THREE SONS. Remco, No. 3312, 1969. 9½in (24.2cm). *Illustration 907.*

Illustration 907. 9½in (24.2cm) JOSEPH, MICHAEL and DANIEL TODD as *Steve Douglas, Jr., Charley Douglas* and *Robbie Douglas II* from "My Three Sons" by Remco, No. 3312, 1969. All-vinyl and fully-jointed. Molded hair; painted blue eyes; open mouths for nursing. Heads marked: "REMCO IND. INC. // 19 © 69 // 18." Backs marked: "REMCO IND. INC. // © 1969." Note: On the original box the names of the babies are Steve, Robbie and Charles. Copyright by Columbia Broadcasting System, Inc. *Jean Canaday Collection.*

TORK, PETER. Musician. Born February 13, 1944, in Washington, D.C. Peter Tork was part of the prefabricated rock group The Monkees. From September 1966 to August 1968 he was on the television series "The Monkees." Tork tried to keep active in the entertainment business after the demise of the band in 1968, but this only lasted about another year.
DOLLS:
1. MONKEES hand puppet. Mattel, No. 5373, 1967. Cloth glove portion with "talking" mechanism; vinyl heads. Made in Hong Kong. 10½in (26.7cm). *Illustration 619.*
2. PETER of THE MONKEES. A "Show Biz Baby." Hasbro, No. 8801, 1967. Made in Hong Kong. 4in (10.2cm). *Illustration 909.*

SEE: MONKEES, THE.

Illustration 908. Peter Tork from the Monkee's first album cover, 1966.

Illustration 909. 4in (10.2cm) PETER TORK of the Monkees, a "Show Biz Baby" by Hasbro, No. 8801, 1967. All-vinyl; jointed only at the head; wired vinyl poseable body. Rooted dark blonde hair; painted brown eyes. Attached to a 33-1/3rpm record cover. Copyright by Raybert Productions, Inc. and a Trademark of Screen Gems, Inc. Made in Hong Kong. *Wanda Lodwick Collection.*

TRAVOLTA, JOHN. Actor, singer, dancer. Born in Englewood, New Jersey, on February 18, 1954. John Travolta became a superstar from playing dim-witted Vinnie Barbarino on "Welcome Back, Kotter" on ABC-TV from September 1975 to August 1979. His career began at age 16 when he dropped out of school to appear in commercials and off-Broadway productions. He went to Hollywood and had small parts on television shows. Then he joined a touring company of the play "Grease" and later starred in this musical on Broadway. After his success on "Kotter" he made some films and some hit records. He was the star of two of the biggest movie hits of the 1970s—*Saturday Night Fever* in 1977 and *Grease* in 1978. It remains to be seen if his superstar status will hold.

DOLLS:
1. BARBARINO. Mattel, No. 9772, 1976. Made in Taiwan. 9in (22.9cm). *Illustration 911*.
2. BARBARINO. Gabriel, No. 78938, 1977. 5in (12.7cm). *Illustration 912*.
3. JOHN TRAVOLTA. Chemtoy, No. 610, 1977. Made in Hong Kong. 11¼in (28.6cm). *Illustrations 913* and *914*.

SEE: WELCOME BACK, KOTTER.

Illustration 912. 5in (12.7cm) JOHN TRAVOLTA as *Barbarino* from "Welcome Back Kotter" by Gabriel, No. 78938, 1977. Bendable vinyl figure on a skateboard that has a metal chassis. Copyright 1977 by the Wolper Organization, Inc. and the Komack Co., Inc.

Illustration 910. John Travolta.

Illustration 911. 9in (22.9cm) JOHN TRAVOLTA as *Barbarino* from "Welcome Back Kotter" by Mattel, No. 9772, 1976. All-vinyl and fully-jointed. Painted black hair and painted blue eyes. Copyright by the Wolper Organization, Inc. and the Komack Company. Made in Taiwan.

Illustration 913. 11¼in (28.6cm) JOHN TRAVOLTA by Chemtoy, No. 610, 1977. All-vinyl and fully-jointed. Painted black hair and painted blue eyes. Head marked: "43 // HONG KONG." Copyright by John Travolta T.M. Licensed by Meryl Corey Enterprises Ltd.

OPPOSITE PAGE: Illustration 914. JOHN TRAVOLTA by Chemtoy.

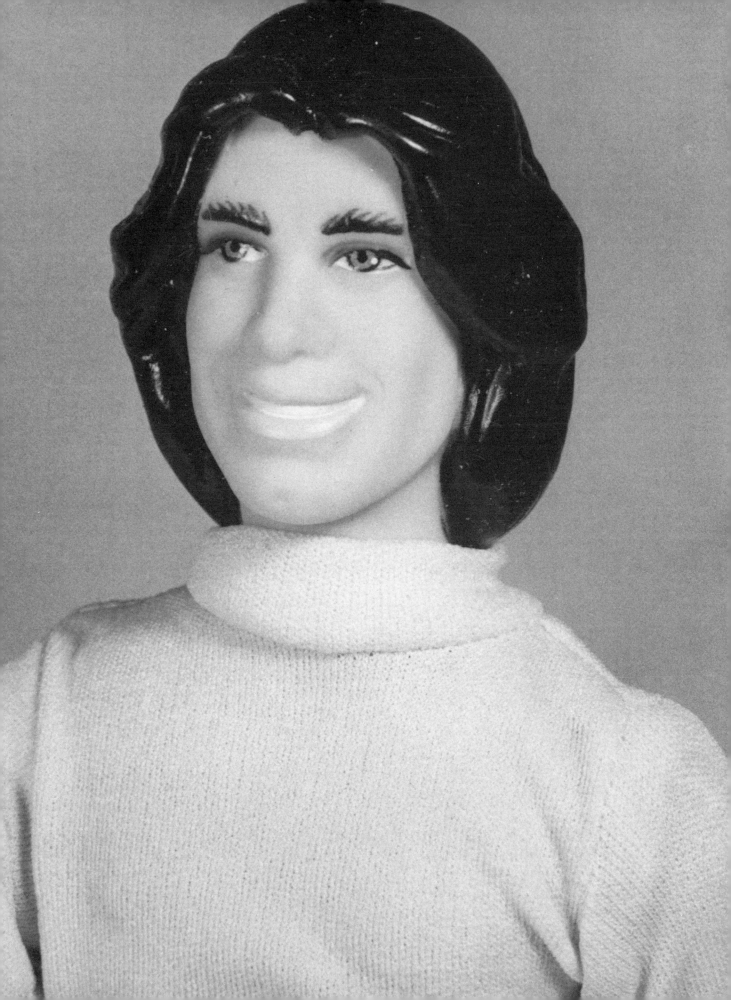

TRUMAN, BESS. First Lady. Born Elizabeth Virginia Wallace on February 13, 1885; died October 18, 1982. In 1919 Bess married future President Harry S. Truman. They had a daughter, Margaret, who for a time attempted a show business career. After President Truman's death in 1972, Mrs. Truman continued to live in their home in Independence, Missouri.

DOLLS:
1. ELIZABETH (BESS) TRUMAN. Peggy Nisbet, No. P734, 1970s. Plastic "collectors' doll." Harry S. Truman, No. P733, is a companion doll. Made in England. About 7½in (19.1cm).

TRUMAN, HARRY S. President of the United States. Born in Lamar, Missouri, on May 8, 1884; died in Independence, Missouri, on December 26, 1972. Truman was a United States Senator from Missouri from 1935 to 1945. When Franklin D. Roosevelt died in 1945, Truman, as his Vice President, became President. The "Truman Doctrine" of 1947, aimed at curbing Communism, brought on the Cold War with the Soviet Union. In 1948 Truman won a surprising victory over his opponent, Thomas E. Dewey, the Republican candidate for the Presidency. In June 1950 Truman sent American troops to Korea to resist Communist aggression. Also in 1950 he ordered development of the hydrogen bomb. In 1951 his dismissal of General Douglas MacArthur caused considerable furor. He declined to run for President again in 1952. In 1957 the Harry S. Truman Library, housing the papers and mementos of his Presidency, opened in Independence, Missouri.

DOLLS:
1. HARRY S. TRUMAN. Peggy Nisbet, No. P733, 1970s. Plastic "collectors' doll." Elizabeth (Bess) Truman, No. P734, is a companion doll. Made in England. About 8in (20.3cm).

TURNER, DEBBIE. Child actress. Debbie Turner played Marta in the 1965 film *The Sound of Music*.

DOLLS:
1. MARTA from THE SOUND OF MUSIC. Madame Alexander, No. 1002, 1965. All-hard plastic and fully-jointed. Dark brown wig. 8in (20.3cm).
2. MARTA from THE SOUND OF MUSIC. Madame Alexander, No. 1102, 1965-1970. All-vinyl and fully-jointed. Rooted dark brown hair. This is the "Janie" doll mold. 11in (27.9cm).
3. MARTA from THE SOUND OF MUSIC. Madame Alexander, 1966. Same as No. 2 above except that she is dressed in the sailor school dress.
4. MARTA from THE SOUND OF MUSIC. Madame Alexander, No. 802, 1971-1973. 7½in (19.1cm). *Illustration 915.*
SEE: SOUND OF MUSIC, THE.

TUTANKHAMEN. Pharaoh of Ancient Egypt. Born circa 1371 B.C.; died circa 1350 B.C. Tutankhamen was the son-in-law of the Pharaoh Akhenaton, and he revised Akhenaton's policy of the worship of one god and returned Egypt to its traditional ways. He became pharaoh when he was about ten-years-old and he married a girl of 12. He died when he was about 19. In 1922 his underground tomb was discovered by Howard Carter and the Earl of Carnarvon. This was the only important tomb in the Valley of the Kings that had not been plundered over the years and it yielded a wealth of treasures. It remains the world's most exciting archeological discovery and is the best source for studying the quality of life in Ancient Egypt. Thousands of valuable objects came from the tomb, including toys from the young pharaoh's childhood. In the late 1970s many of the treasures of Tutankhamen were featured in a traveling exhibition all over the United States, drawing an audience of millions.

DOLLS:
1. KING TUTANKHAMEN. Peggy Nisbet, No. P1002, 1980. Plastic "collectors' doll." Made in England. About 8in (20.3cm).

TWAIN, MARK. (SAMUEL LONGHORN CLEMENS). American humorist and writer. Born November 30, 1835, in Florida, Missouri; died April 21, 1910. He grew up in Hannibal, Missouri, and was a pilot on the Mississippi River from 1857 until the Civil War (1861). He took his pen name from the leadsman's call "mark twain," which meant two fathoms depth sounded. His first attention as a writer came from his humorous short story "The Celebrated Jumping Frog of Calaveras County" in 1865. He married in 1870 and settled in New York and later Connecticut. His great classic novels, *The Adventures of Tom Sawyer* (published in 1876) and *The Adventures of Huckleberry Finn* (published in 1884), are based on his boyhood experiences. By 1893 he was heavily in debt from unsound investments so he traveled around the world lecturing. He was saddened by the deaths of two daughters and his wife and his last works are bitterly pessimistic.

DOLLS:
1. MARK TWAIN. Hallmark, No. 400DT114-1, 1979. Made in Taiwan. 6¾in (17.2cm). *Illustration 916.*

Illustration 915. 7½in (19.1cm) DEBBIE TURNER as *Marta* from *The Sound of Music* by Madame Alexander, No. 0802, 1971. All-hard plastic and fully-jointed. Dark brown wig; blue sleep eyes with molded lashes. Back marked: "ALEX."

Illustration 916. 6¾in (17.2cm) MARK TWAIN by Hallmark, No. 400DT114-1, 1979. All-cloth with sewn joints at the legs and arms. Printed features and clothing with a cloth coat. Made in Taiwan.

TWIGGY. Model; actress. Born Leslie Hornby in London, England, on September 19, 1949. By the late 1960s the funky Twiggy was internationally famous as a very thin fashion model who made popular the designs from Carnaby Street in London, which featured the micro mini skirt. Her first movie was *The Boy Friend* (1971) in a part that Julie Andrews did on Broadway.

DOLLS:
1. TWIGGY. Mattel, No. 1185, 1967-1968. Made in Japan. 10¾in (27.4cm). *Illustration 917.*

Illustration 917. 10¾in (27.4cm) TWIGGY by Mattel, No. 1185, 1967. Vinyl head, arms and legs; plastic torso. Fully-jointed with a twist waist. Rooted light blonde hair; painted blue eyes with long lashes. Marked on the right hip: "©1966 // MATTEL, INC. // U.S. PATENTED // U.S. PAT. PEND. // MADE IN // JAPAN. Marked on left hip: "5." *Lee Jenkins Collection.*

TYLER, JUDY. Actress. Born circa 1933; died July 3, 1957. Beautiful and vivacious brunette Judy Tyler played Princess Summerfall-Winterspring on NBC-TV's "Howdy Doody" for three years during the 1950s. She co-starred with Elvis Presley in his best film, *Jailhouse Rock* in 1957. Right after completing her part in the film, Judy Tyler and her husband were killed in a car accident in Wyoming. Gregory Lafayette, her husband of less than four months, was driving the car.

DOLLS:
1. PRINCESS SUMMERFALL-WINTERSPRING. Peter Puppet Playthings, Inc., 1953. 14½in (36.9cm). This puppet was part of a series that included Howdy Doody, Dilly Dally, Flubadub, Mr. Bluster and Clarabell. *Illustration 918.*
SEE: SMITH, BUFFALO BOB.

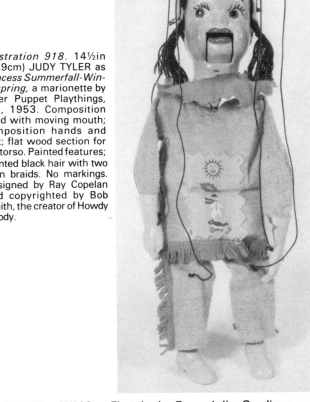

Illustration 918. 14½in (36.9cm) JUDY TYLER as *Princess Summerfall-Winterspring,* a marionette by Peter Puppet Playthings, Inc., 1953. Composition head with moving mouth; composition hands and feet; flat wood section for the torso. Painted features; painted black hair with two yarn braids. No markings. Designed by Ray Copelan and copyrighted by Bob Smith, the creator of Howdy Doody.

TYLER, JULIA. First Lady. Born Julia Gardiner on May 4, 1820; died 1889. In 1844 she married John Tyler (1790-1862), who had become the 10th President of the United States on April 4, 1841, when William Henry Harrison died. Tyler was the first Vice President to become President while in office and the only President to be expelled by his party, the Whigs. Tyler died before he could take his seat in the Congress of the Confederacy.

DOLLS:
1. JULIA TYLER. Madame Alexander, No. 1510, 1979. All-vinyl and fully-jointed. Rooted dark hair in an upsweep. Her costume is a white ruffled dress with flowers in the trim. 14in (35.6cm).
SEE: FIRST LADIES, THE.

U

UGGAMS, LESLIE. Singer, actress. Born May 25, 1943. Leslie Uggams began her professional singing career at age five and two years later made her television debut on one of Johnny Oleson's talent shows. She then sang on many radio and TV shows. She was considered a Mitch Miller "discovery" and was featured on "Sing Along with Mitch" on NBC-TV from January 1961 to September 1966. She had her own show, "The Leslie Uggams Show" on CBS-TV from September to December 1969. She also appeared on many other variety and game shows as a guest and host. In 1977 she was in the large cast of "Roots" and in 1979 "Backstairs at the White House," both of which were a miniseries on television. Leslie Uggams won a Tony Award for her part in the 1968 Broadway musical "Hallelujah Baby."

DOLLS:
In 1965 Madame Alexander registered the name "Leslie" as a trademark for dolls. The Alexander Doll Company catalogs referred to this doll as [a] "Negro." Like the Carmen (Miranda), Jacqueline and Caroline (Kennedy) dolls, the Leslie does not propose to be the famous celebrity, but again the inspiration is apparent. The LESLIE doll is all-vinyl and fully-jointed. She has rooted black hair and brown sleep eyes with lashes. The arms and legs can be bent at the elbows and the knees for the doll to be "posed in many desired positions." 17in (43.2cm).

1. No. 1615. 1965. Dressed in a "green and white striped cotton dress."
2. No. 1624. 1965. Dressed in "white cotton lace short formal."
3. No. 1632. 1965. Dressed in a "petal pink formal gown."
4. No. 1651. 1965. Dressed in a "yellow permanent pleated bouffant gown."
5. No. 1620. 1966. Dressed in a "cotton dress with lace."
6. No. 1630. 1966. Ballerina. *Illustration 919*.
7. No. 1650. 1966; 1968-1969. Formal dress.
8. No. 1660. 1966; 1968-1969. Bride.
9. No. 1635. 1967. Ballerina.
10. No. 1655. 1967. Formal gown.
11. No. 1695. 1967. Bride.
12. No. 1640. 1968-1969. Ballerina.
13. No. 1645. 1970. Ballerina.
14. No. 1655. 1970. Formal.
15. No. 1665. 1970. Bride.
16. No. 1615. 1971. Ballerina.
17. No. 1625. 1971. Formal.
18. No. 1635. 1971. Bride.

URICH, ROBERT. Actor. Born December 19, 1946, in Toronto, Ohio. Robert Urich has acted in theatrical films, television films and on many television shows. He was in "Bob & Carol & Ted & Alice" on ABC-TV from September to November 1973 and in the pilot show "The Specialist" on NBC-TV in January 1975. Then he was Officer James Street on ABC-TV's "S.W.A.T." from February 1975 to June 1976 and September 1976 to April 1977. Next came "Tabitha" from September 1977 to January 1978 on ABC-TV. His biggest break came from playing tennis pro and hired boy friend Peter Campbell on "Soap" during the show's first season (1977-1978). Peter Campbell was bludgeoned, stabbed, drowned and shot in a bathtub by four different people. Actually, he had already died from slipping on a bar of

Illustration 919. 17in (43.2cm) *Leslie Ballerina* that represents LESLIE UGGAMS by Madame Alexander, No. 1630, 1966. Vinyl head with rooted dark brown hair; brown sleep eyes with lashes. Fully-jointed body with vinyl arms and plastic legs and torso. Head marked: "ALEX-ANDER//19©66." Reproduction costume by Pamela K's Doll Fashions.

Illustration 920. Robert Urich on the cover of *TV Guide,* October 14, 1978.

soap. This part led to Urich's playing hard-boiled detective Dan Tanna on "Vega$" on ABC-TV from September 1978 to September 1981. Robert Urich is married to Heather Menzies (which see) from Toronto, Ontario, Canada.

DOLLS:
1. STREET from S.W.A.T. L.J.N. Toys, Ltd., No. 6600, 1975. All-vinyl and fully-jointed with painted hair and features. Made in Hong Kong. 7½in (19.1cm). *Illustrations 921* and *922*.
2. STREET from S.W.A.T. L.J.N. Toys, Ltd., No. 6850, 1976. Same doll as the above in a different package. Made in Hong Kong. 7½in (19.1cm).

SEE: S.W.A.T.

Illustration 921. 7½in (19.1cm) ROBERT URICH as *Street* from "S.W.A.T." by L.J.N. Toys Ltd., No. 6850, 1976. All-vinyl and fully-jointed with painted hair and features. Copyright by Spelling-Goldberg Productions. Made in Hong Kong.

Illustration 922. ROBERT URICH as *Street* from "S.W.A.T." The back is marked with the L.J.N. clown logo and: "LJN TOYS LTD // HONG KONG // ALL RIGHTS RESERVED."

V

VALENTINO, RUDOLPH. Born Rodolfo Alfonso Raffaello Pierre Filibert Guglielmi de Valentina d'Antonguolla on May 6, 1895, in Castellaneta, Italy; died August 23, 1926. Valentino's film career only lasted about seven years but he became the first great male sex symbol in American films. He came to the United States as a teenager and by 1921 was elevated to major stardom after having worked as a taxi dancer, an exhibition dancer and as a screen actor in minor parts. The influential screenwriter June Mathis insisted that he be given the lead as Julio in the important Metro film *The Four Horsemen of the Apocalpyse*. The film was a smash box office success. When *The Shiek* was released in 1921 women who viewed the film fainted in theaters and created a demand for Arab motifs in fashion and interior design. Valentino's popularity rose with the release of *Blood and Sand* in 1922. He married two protégés of the scandalous Russian actress Nazimova. The first brief marriage was to actress Jean Acker and led to divorce and to a jail sentence because he married his second wife, actress and designer Natasha Rambova (born Winifred Shaunessy), before the divorce decree had become final. Rambova took full charge of his career and almost ruined it. As a condition for Valentino's employment, after he went on a strike against Famous Players-Lasky Studios, Rambova was denied entrance to the sets of his films. Her response was to leave Valentino and file for divorce. (Most of Valentino's biographers report that neither of his marriages was consumated.) While he was promoting

Illustration 923. Rudolph Valentino, circa 1925. The photograph was personally autographed in green ink by Valentino.

his last film, *The Son of the Shiek*, Valentino was striken with a perforated ulcer in New York, New York. He died at age 31. His funeral caused riots because of the thousands of fans who wanted a last glimpse of "the great lover." There were even reports of suicides by those who "could not live without Rudy." Polish screen actress, Pola Negri, claiming to be his financée, offered to restage her fainting spells for the photographers at the funeral. Valentino fan clubs and cults continued to grow after his death. For years a "mysterious lady in black" visited his crypt and laid a single rose beside it on the day of his death. Valentino is buried in Hollywood in the family crypt of June Mathis, the important writer who insisted that he be cast in *The Four Horsemen of the Apocalypse*. Anthony Dexter portrayed Valentino in a film biography in 1951; Franco Nero essayed the role for television in 1976; Rudolf Nureyev took the part in a 1977 film. None of these ventures was able to explain the influence that Rudolph Valentino had on women in the 1920s.

DOLLS:
1. RUDOLPH VALENTINO.   Made in Germany, circa early 1920s. 22½in (57.2cm). *Illustration 925* and *926.*
2. RUDOLPH VALENTINO.   Lenci, circa late 1920s. Made in Italy. About 29in (73.7cm). *Illustrations 928* and *929.*

Illustration 926. RUDOLPH VALENTINO doll from Germany. The bandana is silk. (Compare the costume with *Illustration 924*.)

Illustration 924. Rudolph Valentino in *Blood and Sand*, 1922.

OPPOSITE PAGE: Illustration 925. 22½in (57.2cm) RUDOLPH VALENTINO, made in Germany, circa 1922. Papier-mâché head; stuffed cloth body with elongated limbs. Black mohair wig; painted features. The costume is from the film *Blood and Sand*, 1922. It is a soft cotton shirt with tiny buttons, a black velvet vest trimmed with gold beads and black velvet trousers that have gold stenciling on them. The leatherette shoes have high heels. The doll is not marked.

Illustration 927. Rudolph Valentino as *The Shiek*. 4in (10.2cm) diameter "Beauty Box" by Canco. A paper label inside the lid says that the candy contents were from the Fred W. Schraff Company of Chicago, Illinois.

Illustration 928. 29in (73.7cm) RUDOLPH VALENTINO by Lenci, 1920s. All-felt with a brown mohair wig and painted brown eyes. The bright-colored felt costume and the leather boots are from the film *The Shiek* (1921) or *The Son of the Shiek* (1926). *Margaret Ashbrook Collection. Photograph by John Schoonmaker.*

VAN BUREN, ANGELICA. Hostess for President Martin Van Buren. Van Buren was the eighth President of the United States, 1837 to 1841. His wife, Hannah Hoes, had died of tuberculosis in 1819 and he never remarried. In 1838 Van Buren's eldest son, Abraham, married and his wife acted as White House hostess for the President.

DOLLS:
1. ANGELICA VAN BUREN. Madame Alexander, No. 1508, 1979. All-vinyl and fully-jointed. Rooted dark wig with top curls and long curls on the neck. She wears a blue velvet gown trimmed in lace. 14in (35.6cm).
SEE: FIRST LADIES, THE.

VAN DYKE, DICK. Actor. Born December 13, 1925. By the 1960s Dick Van Dyke was a star of Broadway, Hollywood and network television shows. His first film, a repeat of his musical role on stage, was *Bye Bye Birdie*, 1963. He starred in several films, among them the musicals *Mary Poppins*, 1964, and *Chitty Chitty Bang Bang*, 1968. On television he was the host for "CBS Cartoon Theater" from June to September 1956, a

regular on "The Andy Williams Show" on ABC-TV during 1958, and the emcee for "Laugh Line" on NBC-TV from April to June 1959. He was also on "Pantomine Quiz" on ABC-TV during the 1958-1959 season. His greatest success was "The Dick Van Dyke Show" with Mary Tyler Moore on CBS-TV from October 1961 to September 1966. He won three successive Emmy Awards for this (1964-1966). He later returned with "The New Dick Van Dyke Show" on CBS-TV from September 1971 to September 1974, followed by a variety show on NBC-TV, "Van Dyke and Company" from September to December 1976. His last part as a regular was on "The Carol Burnett Show" on CBS-TV in 1977.

DOLLS:
1. MR. POTTS from CHITTY CHITTY BANG BANG. Mattel, 1968. All-vinyl with a jointed head. Companion dolls are Adrian Hall as Jeremy, Heather Ripley as Jemima and Sally Ann Howes as Truly Scrumptious. Made in Hong Kong. 2in (5.1cm).
2. MR. POTTS from CHITTY CHITTY BANG BANG. Mattel, No. 5235, 1969. Made in Mexico. 22½in (57.2cm). *Illustration 930.*

Illustration 930. 22½in (57.2cm) DICK VAN DYKE as *Mr. Potts* from *Chitty Chitty Bang Bang* by Mattel, No. 5235, 1969. All-cloth with printed features and attached clothing. Pull ring in the side activates a talking mechanism. Copyright by Gilrose Productions. Ltd. and Warfield Production, Inc. Made in Mexico.

OPPOSITE PAGE: Illustration 929. 29in (73.7cm) RUDOLPH VALENTINO by Lenci, 1920s. This is another variation of the doll from *Illustration 928,* wearing a burnoose on the head. *Betty Kilgore Collection. Photograph by Betty Kilgore.*

VAUGHN, ROBERT. Actor. Born November 22, 1932. Vaughn entered films in 1957 and continued his college education at the same time. He holds a Ph. D. degree in political science. He received a supporting actor Oscar nomination for his role in *The Young Philadelphians*, 1959. On television he was in "The Lieutenant" on ABC-TV from September 1963 to September 1964. His greatest success was as superagent Napoleon Solo on "The Man From U.N.C.L.E." on NBC-TV from September 1964 to January 1968. In 1972 he published the highly praised book *Only Victims*, an account of the Hollywood purges of the 1950s because of alleged Communist activity.

DOLLS:
1. NAPOLEON SOLO, THE MAN FROM U.N.C.L.E. Gilbert, No. 16120, 1965. David McCallum as Ilya Kuryakin is a companion doll. Made in Hong Kong, Japan and USA. 12½in (31.8cm). *Illustration 931* and *932.*

Illustration 932. ROBERT VAUGHN as *Napoleon Solo* by Gilbert.

Illustration 931. 12½in (31.8cm) ROBERT VAUGHN as *Napoleon Solo*, "The Man from U.N.C.L.E.," by Gilbert, No. 16120, 1965. Vinyl head with painted hair and features; heavy vinyl arms; plastic legs and torso. The right arm has a spring mechanism that raises and fires a cap pistol, like the James Bond from Gilbert. Head marked: "K 4 5." Lower torso marked: "2." Copyright by Metro-Goldwyn-Mayer, Inc. Made in Hong Kong, Japan and USA.

VICTORIA, EMPRESS OF GERMANY (EMPRESS FREDERICK). Wife of Frederick III, King of Prussia and Emperor of Germany. Born 1840; died 1901. Victoria, the daughter of Queen Victoria of England, married crown prince Frederick in 1858. She excelled her husband in intelligence and brought him in contact with English liberalism. The couple waited for 30 years before Frederick acceded the throne in 1888, and he then died after only three months. Victoria was known as "Empress Frederick" after his death.

DOLLS:
1. VICTORIA, PRINCESS ROYAL AND EMPRESS OF GERMANY. Peggy Nisbet, No. P789, 1970s. Plastic "collectors' doll." Kaiser Frederick III, No. P790, is a companion doll. Made in England. 7½in (19.1cm).

VICTORIA. Queen of England (1837-1901) and Empress of India (1876-1901). Born May 24, 1819, in London, England; died January 22, 1901. Queen Victoria reigned longer than any monarch in English history and the term "Victorian" will always be used to describe her times and her view of life. Victoria was the last constitutional monarch of England who was able to exercise personal control over the government. Her prime ministers and advisers tried not to let her know that her power was not absolute. In 1839 she proposed marriage to her cousin Prince Albert of Saxe-Coburg, whom she loved very deeply. They were married on February 10, 1840. When the nine children of the couple were married it created alliances with the royal houses of Russia, Germany, Greece, Denmark and Romania. When Albert died in 1861 Victoria went into seclusion for three years. Prime Minister Benjamin

Disraeli encouraged her to emerge from her private grief. The previous Prime Minister, William Gladstone, also dominated the latter part of her reign. The Diamond Jubilee of her reign in 1897 was a state event that proved her great popularity. Victoria's long reign saw England's culture change because of the Industrial Revolution, humanitarian reform, and aggressive Imperialism, primarily in Africa and India. All of the kings and queens of England since Victoria's death have been her direct descendants. (Edward VII, George V, Edward VIII, George VI and Elizabeth II). Queen Victoria was the epitome of a royal personage.

DOLLS:
1. QUEEN VICTORIA. Liberty of London, circa 1941. All-cloth and fully-jointed. Stitched and painted features. Made in England. About 8¼in (21cm).
2. QUEEN VICTORIA (STATE ROBES). Peggy Nisbet, No. P708, 1970s. Plastic "collectors' doll." (This is the older model with a proportionately larger head.) Made in England. About 7½in (19.1cm).
3. QUEEN VICTORIA (WIDOW). Peggy Nisbet, No. P610, 1970s. Plastic "collectors' doll." Made in England. 7½in (19.1cm).
4. QUEEN VICTORIA. Ann Parker, late 1970s. Plastic "collectors' doll," affixed to a wooden base. Dressed in a black gown. Made in England. About 10in (25.4cm).
5. QUEEN VICTORIA. Robin and Nell Dale, 1977. Made in England. 7⅞in (20cm). *Illustration 933.*
6. ROYAL VICTORIAN CHRISTENING. Peggy Nisbet Special Collectors Set No. 20, 1982. Limited edition of 500 sets. Queen Victoria is dressed in lavender, No. LE98; Prince Albert, No. LE99; Nanny holding the Future King (Edward VII), No. LE100. Made in England. About 7½in (19.1cm).

VILLIERS, BARBARA (COUNTESS OF CASTLE-MAINE). Mistress of King Charles II (reigned 1660 to 1685) of England.

DOLLS:
1. COUNTESS OF CASTLEMAINE (BARBARA VILLIERS). Peggy Nisbet, No. LE85 from Special Collectors Set No. 15, King Charles II, the Merry Monarch, and Three of his Favourite Mistresses. Limited edition of 500 sets. King Charles II, No. LE83, Nell Gwynn, No. LE84, and Duchess of Portsmouth, No. LE86, are part of the set. Plastic with jointed arms. Made in England. 7½in (19.1cm).
SEE: CHARLES II.

W

WAGNER, LINDSAY. Actress. Born June 22, 1949. Before becoming successful on television, Wagner sang with a rock group and made her film debut in 1973. For ABC-TV she portrayed Jaime Sommers, the Bionic Woman, first as a recurring role on "The Six Million Dollar Man" from January 1974 to March 1978 and on her own show, a spin-off of this, "The Bionic Woman" from January 1976 to May 1977 and September 1977 to September 1978.

DOLLS:
1. THE BIONIC WOMAN. Kenner, No. 65810, 1978. Made in Hong Kong. 12½in (31.8cm). *Illustration 934.*

Illustration 933. 7⅞in (20cm) QUEEN VICTORIA by Robin and Nell Dale, 1977. The figure is a turned wooden dowel with jointed arms. The skin tones are natural wood; the clothing is painted. From the Silver Jubilee Collection, Bank House Farm, Holme Mills, Holme, Carnforth, Lancashire, England. Marked on the bottom: "QUEEN VICTORIA BY ROBIN AND NELL DALE // ENGLAND // SILVER // JUBILEE // 1977." *Rosemarye Bunting Collection.*

Illustration 934. 12½in (31.8cm) LINDSAY WAGNER as "The Bionic Woman" by Kenner, No. 65810, 1978. All-vinyl and fully-jointed with "bionic modules" in her right arm, both legs and her ears. Rooted blonde hair; painted olive eyes. The character is copyrighted by Universal City Studios, Inc. Made in Hong Kong.

WAITE, RALPH. Actor. Born June 22, 1928. Waite holds a degree in Divinity from Yale University. He acted in films but his most known role comes from having played John Walton, the father of the family, on CBS-TV's "The Waltons" from September 1972 to August 1981. On February 22, 1982 he repeated his part for the TV movie *A Wedding on Walton's Mountain*.

DOLLS:
1. MOM and POP from THE WALTONS. Mego, No. 56000/2, 1975. Made in Hong Kong. 8in (20.3cm). *Illustration 935*.

SEE: WALTONS, THE.

Illustration 935. 8in (20.3cm) RALPH WAITE as *Pop, John Walton*, from "The Waltons" by Mego, No. 56000/2, 1975. All-vinyl and fully-jointed. Painted brown hair and painted blue eyes. Head marked: " © 1974 LORIMAR // PROD. INC." Made in Hong Kong. *Penny Caswell Collection*.

WALKER, CLINT. Actor. Born May 30, 1927. Muscular and virile leading man, Clint Walker, broke into films in the mid 1950s. He became a superstar by playing the title role in ABC-TV's "Cheyenne" from September 1955 to September 1963. It was based on the 1947 movie of the same title. Cheyenne Brodie was a western adventurer in the days after the Civil War. He was 6'7" (or 6'5", or 6'8", depending on the press release). He drifted from job to job, encountering all sorts of adventures. Walker attempted another series for ABC-TV, playing a cop in Alaska on "Kodiak," but the show only lasted four episodes in September and October 1974.

DOLLS:
1. CHEYENNE. Hartland Plastics, Inc., No. 818, 1958. All-plastic with jointed arms. Painted hair, features and clothing. Came with a "big bay horse." Copyright by Warner Bros. Made in Hartland, Wisconsin. About 8in (20.3cm).

Illustration 936. Clint Walker on an arcade card, late 1950s.

WALKER, JIMMIE. Actor. Born June 25, 1949. Walker acted in films and on television. His best known role was as James "J. J." Evans, Jr. on "Good Times" on CBS-TV from February 1974 to August 1979. He was also in the six episodes of "B.A.D. Cats" on ABC-TV during January and February 1980.

DOLLS:
1. DYN-O-MITE J.J. Shindana, No. 1045, 1975. Made in Taiwan. 15in (38.1cm). *Illustration 937* and *938*.
2. TALKING DYN-O-MITE J.J. Shindana, 1975. 21in (53.3cm). Sewn skin made in Taiwan; doll made in USA. *Illustration 939*.

Illustration 937. 15in (38.1cm) JIMMIE WALKER as *J.J.* from "Good Times" by Shindana, No. 1045, 1975. Vinyl head with painted features. Floppy cloth body. Head marked: " © 1975 // SHINDANA TOYS." Copyright by Tandem Productions Inc. Made in Taiwan.

Illustration 938. 15in
(38.1cm) JIMMIE WALKER
by Shindana.

Illustration 939. 21in (53.3cm) JIMMIE WALKER as *"Talking"* J.J.
from "Good Times" by Shindana, 1975. All-printed cloth. Sewn
skin made in Taiwan; doll made in USA. The pull ring makes J.J.
say phrases like his famous reaction, "Dyn-o-mite!" Tag: "©1975
// TANDEM // PRODUCTIONS // INC. // SHINDANA TOYS."

WALTONS, THE. Television drama series on CBS from September 14, 1972, to August 13, 1981. The show was created by author Earl Hamner, Jr., who also narrated, and was based on his reminiscences of his childhood in the South during the Depression. The series began as a television film *The Homecoming* on CBS on December 19, 1971, starring Patricia Neal and Andrew Duggan as Olivia and John Walton. Until RICHARD THOMAS left the series after the 1976-1977 season everything was seen through the eyes of his character, John Boy, the oldest son who wanted to be a novelist. "The Waltons" always concentrated on family life and did not feature sex, violence, action or adventure. The show was never popular in large cities but was a big hit in rural and middle America, and it did so well in the television ratings that it forced Flip Wilson's show off the air. "The Waltons" lasted for so long that there were many cast changes. MICHAEL LEARNED played Olivia Walton until the 1980 season; ELLEN CORBY was Grandma except during the time that the actress was recovering from a stroke; WILL GEER was Grandpa until his death in 1978. RALPH WAITE as John Walton and JUDY NORTON-TAYLOR as Mary Ellen remained through the entire show. The other Walton children were David W. Harper as Jim-Bob, Kami Cotler as Elizabeth, Jon Walmsley as Jason, Mary Elizabeth McDonough as Erin and Eric Scott as Ben. John Ritter (later of "Three's Company") was Rev. Matthew Fordwick from 1972 to 1977. On February 22, 1982, Erin was married in the special TV movie *A Wedding on Walton's Mountain,* reuniting all of the cast except for Thomas, Learned and Geer.

DOLLS:

In 1975 Mego made doll of the Waltons in sets of two to a package. They were RICHARD THOMAS and JUDY NORTON-TAYLOR; MICHAEL LEARNED and RALPH WAITE; and ELLEN CORBY and WILL GEER. See also entries under these celebrities and *Illustrations 940, 941,* and *942.*

Illustration 940. 8in (20.3cm) THE WALTONS— *Johnboy* and *Ellen* (sic) by Mego, No. 56000/1, 1975. See RICHARD THOMAS and JUDY NORTON-TAY-LOR. *Shirley Buchholz Collection.*

Illustration 941. 8in (20.3cm) THE WALTONS— *Mom* and *Pop* by Mego, No. 56000/2, 1975. See MICHAEL LEARNED and RALPH WAITE. *Penny Caswell Collection.*

Illustration 942. 8in (20.3cm) THE WALTONS—*Grandma* and *Grandpa* by Mego, No. 56000/3, 1975. See ELLEN CORBY and WILL GEER. *Penny Caswell Collection.*

WARD, BURT. Actor. Born Burt John Gervais, Jr. on July 6, 1945. Ward is best known for playing Dick Grayson, who disguised himself as Robin on "Batman" on ABC-TV from January 1966 to March 1968. Ward came under heavy attack from the Catholic Legion of Decency because of the fit of his costume and several adjustments were required. He later traveled around the country and appeared at sales events dressed as Robin. He did the voice of Robin for the animated cartoon version of the series, "The New Adventures of Batman" on CBS-TV from February 1977 to February 1978.

DOLLS:
1. ROBIN. Mego, No. 51302, 1973. All-vinyl and fully-jointed. Made in Hong Kong. 7¾in (19.8cm).
Note: This doll's production did not coincide with the television shows and, although it looks like Ward, it is really a comic character doll. See also WEST, ADAM.

WASHINGTON, GEORGE. First President of the United States; Commander of the Continental Army in the American Revolution; called The Father of His Country. Born February 22, 1732 (February 11, old style calendar); died December 14, 1799. Washington first gained public notice in 1753 by acting as a spy for the governor of Virginia in the Ohio country. He was a leader in the French and Indian War that developed from this activity. He married the widow Martha Dandridge Custis on January 6, 1759, and later settled down on his plantation, Mount Vernon. On June 15, 1775, he was named by unanimous decision of the Continental Congress to lead the armed forces in the rebellion against Great Britain. He was Commander-in-Chief during the Battles of Long Island, Brandywine, Germantown, Trenton and Princeton. His winter at Valley Forge (1777-1778) made the town's name synonymous with hardship and suffering (most of it was propaganda). On October 19, 1781, he accepted the surrender of Cornwallis at Yorktown. His two elections (1788 and 1792) were unanimous and unopposed. In 1796 he refused a third term and retired again to Mount Vernon. After Washington's death, "Parson" Mason Weems wrote and sold a book about Washington that went through 29 editions. These books tell the many legends about the character of George Washington, (e.g., the tale of the cherry tree). The entire United States went into mourning when Washington died. John Marshall told the House of Representatives that he was "first in war, first in peace, and first in the hearts of his countrymen."

DOLLS:
1. GEORGE WASHINGTON. Chase, 1921. Stockinet and cloth. Head has painted features in oils. Designed and made by Martha J. Chase of Pawtucket, Rhode Island. 25in (63.5cm).
2. GEORGE WASHINGTON. Maker unknown, circa 1930s. Martha Washington is a companion doll. Made in Japan. 7in (17.8cm). *Illustration 943.*
3. GEORGE WASHINGTON. Norah Wellings, date unknown. All-felt. Hair is white embroidery floss; painted features. Dressed in felt and silk colonial costume. Martha Washington is a companion doll. Made in England. 24in (61cm).
4. GEORGE WASHINGTON. Effanbee, circa 1940s. Martha Washington is a companion doll. 9½in (24.2cm). *Illustration 944.*
5. GEORGE WASHINGTON AND HIS WARHORSE "AJAX." Hartland Plastics, Inc., No. 815, 1958. Plastic with jointed arms. Made in Hartland, Wisconsin. About 8in (20.3cm).
6. GEN. GEORGE WASHINGTON. Excel Toy Corp., 1974. All-vinyl and fully-jointed. Made in Hong Kong. 9¾in (24.9cm).
7. GEORGE WASHINGTON. Made for the S. S. Kresge Company, 1976. A "Hero of the American Revolution." Made in Hong Kong. 7½in (19.1cm). *Illustration 945.*
8. GENERAL GEORGE WASHINGTON. Peggy Nisbet, No. P702, 1970s. Plastic "collectors' doll." Martha Washington, No. P703, is a companion doll. Made in England. About 8in (20.3cm).
9. GEORGE WASHINGTON. Ann Parker, late 1970s. Plastic "collectors' doll," attached to a wood base. Martha Washington is a companion doll. Made in England. About 11in (27.9cm).

Illustration 943. 7in (17.8cm) GEORGE and MARTHA WASH-INGTON from Japan, circa 1930s. All-celluloid; jointed at the arms. Painted features with white hair and blue eyes; brightly painted clothing. Embossed on the backs: "⊕// JAPAN." *Shirley Buchholz Collection.*

10. GEORGE WASHINGTON. Hallmark, No. 250DT 900-6, 1979. Made in Taiwan. 7in (17.8cm). *Illustration 946.*
11. GEORGE WASHINGTON. United States Historical Society, 1982. Made in USA. 12in (30.5cm). *Illustration 947.*

Illustration 946. 7in (17.8cm) GEORGE WASHINGTON by Hallmark, No. 250DT900-6, 1979. All-cloth with printed features and clothing. Sewn joints in the arms and legs. Made in Taiwan. *Shirley Buchholz Collection.*

Illustration 945. 7½in (19.1cm) GEORGE WASHINGTON manufactured for the S.S. Kresge Company, 1976. Vinyl head with painted hair and features. Fully-jointed plastic body with swivel waist. Marked on back: "MADE IN // HONG KONG." *Shirley Buchholz Collection.*

OPPOSITE PAGE: Illustration 944. 9½in (24.2cm) GEORGE and MARTHA WASHINGTON by Effanbee, circa early 1940s. These dolls are the standard Patsyette in all-composition and are fully-jointed. White mohair wigs over molded hair. George has painted brown eyes; Martha's are blue. Marked on the back: "EFFANBEE // PATSYETTE DOLL." The clothing is felt and organdy.

WASHINGTON, MARTHA DANDRIDGE. Wife of George Washington. Born June 21, 1731; died 1802. Mrs. Washington served as hostess for her husband from the Executive Mansion in New York and later in Philadelphia, which were the nation's capitals at the time. She was the wealthy widow of Daniel Parke Custis when she married Washington in 1759. She was famous for her great common sense, her charm and her graciousness. It was her custom to be seated when receiving guests.

DOLLS:
1. MARTHA WASHINGTON. Made in Japan, circa 1930s. 7in (17.8cm). *Illustration 943*, with George Washington, a companion doll.
2. MARTHA WASHINGTON. Norah Wellings, date unknown. All-felt. Hair is white embroidery floss. Painted features. Dressed in a silk and felt colonial costume. George Washington is a companion doll. Made in England. 24in (61cm).

3. MARTHA WASHINGTON. Effanbee, circa 1940s. 9½in (24.2cm). *Illustration 944*, with George Washington, a companion doll.
4. MARTHA WASHINGTON. Peggy Nisbet, No. P703, 1970s. Plastic "collectors' doll." George Washington, No. P702, is a companion doll. Made in England. 7½in (19.1cm).
5. MARTHA WASHINGTON. Effanbee, No.1153, 1976. 11in (27.9cm). *Illustration 948*.
6. MARTHA WASHINGTON. Madame Alexander, No. 1501, 1976-1978. Vinyl and plastic and fully-jointed. Rooted blonde curls; blue sleep eyes with lashes. Dressed in long gown with matching dust cap. 14in (35.6cm).
7. MARTHA WASHINGTON. Hallmark, No. 250DT900-5, 1979. Made in Taiwan. 7in (17.8cm). *Illustration 949*.
8. MARTHA WASHINGTON. Ann Parker, 1979. Plastic "collectors' doll," attached to a wood base. Made in England. About 10in (25.4cm).
9. MARTHA WASHINGTON. Crafted Heirlooms; designed by Sandy Williams, 1981. Made in Cumberland, Maryland. *Illustration 950*.

NOTE: Martha Washington is a common theme for souvenir dolls, cheaply made plastic dolls and even quality dolls, so others exist.
SEE: FIRST LADIES, THE.

Illustration 948. 11in (27.9cm) MARTHA WASHINGTON by Effanbee, No. 1153, 1976. Vinyl head and arms; plastic legs and torso. Rooted blonde hair; blue sleep eyes with molded lashes. Blue taffeta dress. Head marked: "EFFANBEE // © 1976 // 1176." *Phyllis Houston Collection.*

OPPOSITE PAGE: Illustration 947. 12in (30.5cm) GEORGE WASHINGTON by the United States Historical Society, 1982. Porcelain head and hands; plastic body. Gray wig. The military costume is authentic. A limited edition doll. Made in USA. *Photograph Courtesy of the United States Historical Society.*

Illustration 949. 7in (17.8cm) MARTHA WASHINGTON by Hallmark, No. 250DT900-5, 1979. All-cloth with sewn joints in the arms and legs. Printed features and clothing. Made in Taiwan. *Rosemarye Bunting Collection.*

Illustration 950. 12in (30.5cm) MARTHA WASHINGTON by Crafted Heirlooms, designed by Sandy Williams, 1981. All-cloth, hand-screened in white bleached muslin. Martha wears a salmon pink faille gown. (Abigail Adams and Martha Randolph are part of a set of three First Ladies.) Made in Cumberland, Maryland.

WAYNE, JOHN. Actor. Born Marion Michael Morrison on May 26, 1907, in Winterset, Iowa; died June 11, 1979. Called "Duke." Wayne began his long film career in 1928 and appeared in about 250 films. After playing in routine westerns for years he became a star with his part as the Ringo Kid in *Stagecoach* in 1939. His last film was *The Shootist* in 1976. He received an Academy Award for *True Grit* in 1969. John Wayne was identified with two genres of roles—the cowboy and the soldier. He was a superpatriot, a fundamentalist and a superhawk. He made the Vietnam War a personal crusade. His 1968 film *The Green Berets* was a tribute to American involvement there. He was widely admired because of the courage with which he faced his last years as he was dying with cancer. In 1963 he had a lung removed; in 1978 he had open-heart surgery; in 1979 he had his stomach removed. He was carried to the 1979 Oscar ceremonies in Hollywood in a stretcher. Immediately before presenting an award he was lifted to his feet and was returned home by ambulance after making a well-received presentation. The audience was not aware of this. He died within weeks. A Congressional Medal was struck in his honor.

DOLLS:
1. JOHN WAYNE. Effanbee, 1981. 17in (43.2cm). *Illustrations 952* and *953*.
2. JOHN WAYNE. Manufacturer unknown, No. 228, 1981. Made in Hong Kong. 9½in (24.2cm). *Illustration 954*.
3. JOHN WAYNE. Effanbee, No. 2981, 1982. 18in (45.7cm). *Illustration 955*.

Illustration 951. John Wayne in the 1930s.

OPPOSITE PAGE: Illustration 952. 17in (43.2cm) 1981 JOHN WAYNE Commemorative Doll by Effanbee. All-vinyl and fully-jointed. Painted features and blue eyes. Head and back marked: "WAYNE // ENT. // 19 © 81." The doll also has a felt cowboy hat and a plastic rifle.

Illustration 954. 9½in (24.2cm) JOHN WAYNE, manufacturer unknown, Model 228, 1981. Vinyl head and arms; plastic body. Jointed at head, arms and waist. Painted black hair and painted black eyes. The base is a Solid State AM radio. No markings on doll. Radio marked: "HONG KONG." This doll is similar to the Elvis Presley and John Lennon dolls that stand on a radio.

Illustration 953. 1981 JOHN WAYNE by Effanbee. Note the modeling that resembles wood carving. Although not a John Wayne fan, the author considers this the most outstanding design rendition that Effanbee ever produced.

OPPOSITE PAGE: Illustration 955. 18in (45.7cm) JOHN WAYNE by Effanbee, No. 2981, 1982. All-vinyl and fully-jointed. Painted blue eyes; painted hair. This is the second John Wayne doll of the "Legend Series" and he is dressed as a cavalry soldier. *Photograph Courtesy of Effanbee Doll Company.*

WELCOME BACK, KOTTER. Situation comedy on ABC-TV. First telecast on September 9, 1975; last telecast on August 3, 1979. In "Welcome Back, Kotter" GABRIEL KAPLAN played Kotter, a Brooklyn teacher who returned to the inner-city school from which he graduated to teach a tough class of remedial students. The group with which Kotter worked called themselves the "Sweathogs." They were all streetwise but outcasts as academic students. They were JOHN TRAVOLTA as Vinnie Barbarino, ROBERT HEGYES as Juan Luis Pedro Phillipo de Huevos Epstein, LAWRENCE—HILTON JACOBS as Freddie "Boom Boom" Washington and RON PALILLO as Arnold Horshack. By 1978 Kaplan was only seen occasionally on the series. The most important development to the career of any person connected with the series is that it made a superstar of John Travolta. Mattel made a series of five dolls of the principals from the series in 1976; Chemtoy and Gabriel also made dolls of John Travolta in 1977. See entries under each celebrity.

Illustration 956. The cast of "Welcome Back, Kotter" in 1975. From left to right: John Travolta as Vinnie Barbarino, Ron Palillo as Arnold Horshack, Gabriel Kaplan as Gabe Kotter, Robert Hegyes (standing) as Juan Luis Pedro Phillipo de Heuvos Epstein, and Lawrence-Hilton Jacobs as Freddie "Boom Boom" Washington.

OPPOSITE PAGE: Illustration 958. 11in (27.9cm) DUKE OF WELLINGTON by Ann Parker, late 1970s. All-hard plastic and permanently affixed to a wooden base. The facial features are painted; the hair is mohair. Tagged with Ann Parker label. Made in England. *Shirley Buchholz Collection.*

WELLER, PETER. Actor. Peter Weller played U.S. Marshall Joe LeFors in the 1979 film *Butch and Sundance: The Early Days.*

DOLLS:
1. MARSHALL JOE LeFORS from BUTCH AND SUNDANCE: THE EARLY DAYS. Kenner, No. 53050, 1979. Made in Hong Kong. *Illustration 957*.

Illustration 957. 4in (10.2cm) PETER WELLER as *Marshall Joe LeFors* from *Butch and Sundance: The Early Days* by Kenner, No. 53050, 1979. All-vinyl and fully-jointed. Painted hair; hat molded to head; painted features. Copyright by Twentieth Century-Fox Film Corporation. Made in Hong Kong.

WELLINGTON, ARTHUR WELLESLEY, 1st DUKE OF. British soldier and statesman. Born 1769; died 1852. From 1796 to 1805 Wellington fought for Britain in India; from 1809 to 1813 he was the commander of the Peninsular War, and drove the French out of Spain; in June of 1815 at Waterloo in southern Belgium he caused the final defeat of Napoleon. From 1828 to 1830 he was the British Prime Minister and he secured passage of the Catholic Emancipation Bill, which he had previously opposed. In 1842 he was made Commander-in-Chief for life.

DOLLS:
1. THE DUKE OF WELLINGTON. Ann Parker, late 1970s. Made in England. *Illustration 958*.

WEST, ADAM. Actor. Born William Anderson on September 19, 1928. West's career in films was never an important one but he made a great impression with his acting on television. During the 1961-1962 season on TV he was on "The Detectives Starring Robert Taylor" on NBC-TV. He became a huge hit playing Bruce Wayne, who disguised himself as Batman on "Batman" on ABC-TV from January 1966 to March 1968. Later he did the voice for Batman on the animated cartoon version, "The New Adventures of Batman" on CBS-TV from February 1977 to February 1978. He still appears in films and television roles in supporting parts.

DOLLS:
1. BATMAN.   Mego, No. 51301, 1973. All-vinyl and fully-jointed. Made in Hong Kong. 7¾in (19.8cm).
Note: Although this doll resembles Adam West, its production did not coincide with the television shows. It is actually a comic character doll. Burt Ward played Robin, which see.

Illustration 959. Burt Ward as Robin and Adam West as Batman from "Batman," 1966.

WEST, MAE.   Actress; playright. Born August 17, 1892; died November 22, 1980. The Brooklyn-born sex symbol began her stage career at age five. She felt by 1926 that she could write her own plays and produced "Sex" on Broadway. For this she spent 10 days in prison on Welfare Island, insisting that she could not live without vital necessities—silk underwear. Her greatest Broadway success was "Diamond Lil" in 1928, which she also wrote. Her witty lines were frequently quoted and phrases like, "It's better to be looked over than over-looked" and "Too much of a good thing can be wonderful," became public domain. Miss West's popularity as a star was based on her ability to parody her own image. She was in her 40s when she made her first film for Paramount and was an instant success, although the titles of films had to be changed to please the censors. "Diamond Lil" became *She Done Him Wrong* (1933) on the screen and saved Paramount Pictures from bankruptcy during the Depression. By 1939 the novelty had worn off when she was signed by Universal to appear with W.C. Fields in *My Little Chickadee*. She wrote her own script and Fields wrote his and the end result was a mess. After another film in 1943 she returned to Broadway. In 1947 she took "Diamond Lil" on tour of England and the United States for several years. In 1954, at age 62, she formed a nightclub act in which she was surrounded by musclemen. This lasted for three years. In 1970, at age 78, she made a comeback film, *Myra Breckenridge*, of which the only decent thing that can be said is that Mae West was in it. Her last film was *Sextette*, in 1978, based on her own material. At age 85 she again played a hard-living and hard-loving woman. Her autobiography, *Goodness Had Nothing To Do With It*, (1959), can not be all true but it is full of her funny lines, like "I always say, keep a diary and one day it will keep you," "I used to be Snow White but I drifted," and "A man in the house is worth two in the street." Mae West was unique and she made herself a legend all her life.

DOLLS:
1. MAE WEST.   Effanbee, No. 1982, 1982. 18in (45.7cm). *Illustration 961.*

OPPOSITE PAGE: Illustration 961. 18in (45.7cm) MAE WEST by Effanbee, No. 1982, 1982. All-vinyl and fully-jointed. Rooted light blonde hair; painted blue eyes. Mae is dressed in a form-fitting black taffeta gown with a matching black hat. The hat is trimmed in marabou feathers that match the gray boa over her shoulders. She carries a walking stick. This doll, from Effanbee's "Legend Series," was produced only in 1982. *Photograph Courtesy of Effanbee Doll Company.*

Illustration 960. Mae West in the 1940s.

WHELAN, JILL. Juvenile actress. Born about 1967. In March and April 1979 she was in the five episodes of "Friends" on ABC-TV. In 1979 at age 12 or 13 she joined the cast of "The Love Boat" to play Vicki, the daughter of the captain.

DOLLS:
1. VICKI from THE LOVE BOAT. Mego, No. 23005/6, 1982. Made in Hong Kong. 3¼in (8.3cm). *Illustration 962.*

SEE: LOVE BOAT, THE.

Illustration 962. 3¼in (8.3cm) JILL WHELAN as *Vicki* from "The Love Boat" by Mego, No. 23005/6, 1982. All-vinyl and fully-jointed. Painted red hair; painted blue eyes. Molded and painted clothing and a vinyl skirt. Copyright by Aaron Spelling Productions, Inc. Made in Hong Kong.

WILCOX, LARRY. Actor. Born August 8, 1948. Wilcox was in the syndicated television version of "Lassie" in 1972. He later became a top star by playing Officer Jon Baker on NBC-TV's "CHiPs" beginning in September 1977.

DOLLS:
1. JON from CHiPs. Mego, No. 08010/2, 1981. Made in Hong Kong. 3¾in (9.6cm). *Illustration 963.*
2. JON from CHiPs. Mego, No. 87500/1, 1981. Made in Hong Kong. 8in (20.3cm). *Illustration 964.*

SEE: CHiPs

Illustration 963. 3¾in (9.6cm) LARRY WILCOX as *Jon* from "CHiPs" by Mego, No. 08010/2, 1981. All-vinyl and fully-jointed. Painted yellow hair and painted uniform. Copyright 1977 by Metro-Goldwyn-Mayer Film Co. Made in Hong Kong.

Illustration 964. 8in (20.3cm) LARRY WILCOX as *Jon* from "CHiPs" by Mego, No. 87500/1, 1981. All-vinyl and fully-jointed with painted yellow hair. Copyright 1977 by MGM, Inc. Made in Hong Kong.

WILLIAM III. King of England, Scotland and Ireland from 1689 to 1702. Born 1650; died 1702. William was the son of William II of Orange and he married Mary, the Protestant daughter of King James II of England. In 1689 William helped The Glorious Revolution along and prevented bloodshed by allowing James II to escape to France. He became King William III and his wife Queen Mary II. This all came about because of the issue raised when James II had his first-born son, to a second wife, baptized a Catholic. As a condition for taking the throne, Parliament gained more power over the monarchy. During William's time England began a series of wars with France that lasted until 1815 and in the United States were the French and Indian War, The Revolution and the War of 1812. In Ireland William continued the ruthless policy of confiscating land to give it to English favorites. The problem of a permanent national debt also began at this time. After the death of Mary (1694), William's popularity diminished even more.
DOLLS:
1. KING WILLIAM III (WILLIAM OF ORANGE). Peggy Nisbet, No. P453, 1970s. Plastic "collectors' doll." Queen Mary II, No. P452, is a companion doll. Made in England. 8in (20.3cm). See MARY II for Illustration.

WILLIAMS, ANSON. Actor. Born Anson William Heimlick on September 25, 1949. Williams was in the cast of "The Paul Lynde Show" on ABC-TV from September 1972 to September 1973. In January 1974 he began playing Warren "Potsie" Webber on "Happy Days" on ABC-TV.
DOLLS:
1. POTSY. Mego, No. 63001/2, 1976. Made in Hong Kong. 8in (20.3cm). *Illustration 965.*
SEE: HAPPY DAYS.

Illustration 965. 8in (20.3cm) ANSON WILLIAMS as *Potsy* from "Happy Days" by Mego, No. 63001/2, 1976. All-vinyl and fully-jointed with painted hair and eyes. Head marked: " © 1976 PARAMOUNT // PICTURES CORP." Back marked: " © MEGO CORP. 1974 // REG. U.S.-PAT OFF // PAT PENDING // HONG KONG." Copyright by Paramount Pictures Corporation.

WILLIAMS, BILLY DEE. Actor. Born April 6, 1937, in New York, New York. Billy Dee Williams made his Broadway debut at age seven in "The Firebrand." As an adult he appeared in plays, films and on television. In *The Empire Strikes Back* (1980) he was Lando Calrissian.

1. LANDO CALRISSIAN. Kenner, No. 39800, 1980. Made in Hong Kong. 4in (10.2cm). *Illustration 966.*
SEE: STAR WARS.

Williams, Billy Dee

Illustration 966. 4in (10.2cm) BILLY DEE WILLIAMS as *Lando Calrissian* from *The Empire Strikes Back* by Kenner, No. 39800, 1980. All-vinyl and fully-jointed. Painted hair and features. The cape is gray vinyl. Marked on the back of the left leg: "© 1980 L.F.L. // HONG KONG."

Illustration 967. 11½in (29.2cm) CINDY WILLIAMS as *Shirley* from "Laverne and Shirley" by Mego, No. 86500/1, 1977. All-vinyl and fully-jointed. Rooted dark brown hair; painted blue eyes. Head marked: " © PARAMOUNT // PICT. CORP." Back marked: " © MEGO OF HONG KONG // 1977 // MADE IN HONG KONG." *Shirley Buchholz Collection.*

WILLIAMS, CINDY. Actress. Born Cynthia Jane Williams on August 22, 1948. Cindy Williams was in the popular film *American Graffiti* (1973) which became the basis for the TV show "Happy Days," beginning in January 1974. She appeared in this show as Shirley Feeney and continued the part in the spin-off "Laverne and Shirley" on ABC-TV beginning in January 1976. It became the most popular show on television.

DOLLS:
1. LAVERNE AND SHIRLEY. Mego, No. 86500/1, 1977. Part of a set with Penny Marshall as Laverne. Made in Hong Kong. 11½in (29.2cm). *Illustration 967.*

SEE: LAVERNE AND SHIRLEY.

WILLIAMS, GUY. Actor. Born January 14, 1924. Williams had acting assignments in films since the early 1950s. Later, on television, he was in leading roles. From October 1957 to October 1959 he was Don Diego de la Vega (Zorro) in ABC-TV's "Zorro." From September 1965 to September 1968 he was the father of the family who was "Lost in Space" on CBS-TV.

DOLLS:
1. ZORRO. Gund, circa 1958. 10in (25.4cm). *Illustration 968.*

Illustration 969. 4in (10.2cm) ROBIN WILLIAMS as *Mork from Ork* from "Mork and Mindy" with his egg space ship by Mattel, No. 1275, 1979. All-vinyl and fully-jointed doll with molded clothing. Back marked: " © 1979 PPC // HONG KONG." Copyright by Paramount Pictures Corporation.

Illustration 968. 10in (25.4cm) GUY WILLIAMS as *Zorro* by Gund, circa 1958. Vinyl head with painted blue eyes and painted black hair. Cloth glove for puppet action. Head marked: " © W.D.P." Tagged: "Walt Disney Character."

WILLIAMS, ROBIN. Actor. Born July 21, 1952. Robin Williams began his show business career as a comedian in nightclubs. On television he was in the revised version of "Laugh-In" on NBC-TV from September 1977 to February 1978. He played Mork from the planet Ork on "Mork and Mindy" on ABC-TV from the time the show premiered on September 14, 1978. Pam Dawber played Mindy. This entry was a huge success during its first year on television and declined sharply in the ratings afterwards. In 1980 Williams played the lead in the film *Popeye*.

DOLLS:
1. MORK.   Mattel, No. 1275, 1979. Made in Hong Kong. 4in (10.2cm). *Illustration 969*.
2. MORK.   Mattel, No. 1276, 1979. Made in Taiwan. 9in (22.9cm). *Illustration 970*.
3. TALKING MORK.   Mattel, No. 1279, 1979. Made in Taiwan. 16in (40.6cm). *Illustration 971*.

Illustration 970. 9in (22.9cm) ROBIN WILLIAMS as *Mork* from "Mork and Mindy" by Mattel, No. 1276, 1979. All-vinyl and fully-jointed. Painted hair and features. Head marked: " © 1979 PPC TAIWAN." Back marked: " © 1973 // MATTEL INC. // TAIWAN." Back pack has talking mechanism that says eight of Mork's phrases, like "Na no na no." Copyright by Paramount Pictures Corporation.

WILSON, FLIP. Comic actor. Born Clerow Wilson on December 8, 1933. Comic performer Flip Wilson was the first black person to gain stardom with his own variety show on television. "The Flip Wilson Show" on NBC-TV from September 1970 to June 1974 was the Number Two rated show on television for its first two years. Wilson played a stock collection of characters, including sassy Geraldine Jones, a swinging, liberated woman who had a jealous boyfriend named "Killer." Flip's most famous comic line was "The Devil made me do it!"

DOLLS:
1. FLIP WILSON. Shindana, early 1970s. Made in Taiwan and USA. *Illustrations 972, 973* and *974.*

Illustration 971. 16in (40.6cm) Talking ROBIN WILLIAMS as *Mork* from "Mork and Mindy" by Mattel, No. 1279, 1979. All-cloth with printed features and clothing. Copyright by Paramount Pictures Corporation. Made in Taiwan. *Rosemarye Bunting Collection.*

Illustrations 972, 973 and *974.* 15in (38.1cm) FLIP WILSON as himself and as *Geraldine Jones* by Shindana, early 1970s. All-cloth "talking doll" that is printed differently on the two sides to create both characters. A pull ring causes the doll to say Flip's lines, like "The Devil made me buy this dress" and "Don't touch me—you don't know me that well." Made in Taiwan and USA. Copyright by Street Corner Productions, Inc. *Wanda Lodwick Collection.*

WINDSOR, BESSIE WALLIS WARFIELD, DUCHESS OF. American-born English duchess. Born June 19, 1894. Before she became the Duchess of Windsor she had been Mrs. Simpson; previous to that she had been Mrs. Spencer. In 1936 Edward VIII of England abdicated his throne because of his friendship with Mrs. Simpson. The problem of her two previous marriages caused the most traumatic period for British royalty in modern times. The couple was married on June 3, 1937, and they never lived in England again. As far as English royalty was concerned, Edward's wife had no share in his royal rank and she was never "received."

DOLLS:
1. MRS. WALLIS SIMPSON, DUCHESS OF WINDSOR. Peggy Nisbet, No. P419, 1970s. Plastic "collectors' doll." Edward VIII, Duke of Windsor, No. P418, is a companion doll. Made in England. 7½in (19.1cm).

WINKLER, HENRY. Actor. Born October 30, 1946. After graduating from Yale, Winkler acted on radio and in TV commercials. In January 1974 he began playing Arthur "Fonzie" Fonzarelli on "Happy Days" for ABC-TV. At first on "Happy Days" leather-jacketed Fonzie was a supporting player part but the immense popularity of the character caused Winkler's part to be enlarged and he became a superstar. He appeared in several motion pictures without Fonzie's greased hair. None of them was successful.

DOLLS:
1. FONZIE. Mego, No. 63000, 1976. Made in Hong Kong. 8in (20.3cm). *Illustrations 975* and *976*.
2. THE FONZ. Samet and Wells, Inc., No. SW1000, 1976. Made in Taiwan. 16½in (44.5cm). *Illustration 977*.
SEE: HAPPY DAYS.

Illustration 977. 16½in (44.5cm) HENRY WINKLER as *The Fonz* from "Happy Days" by Samet and Wells Inc., No. SW1000, 1976. All-cloth with printed clothing and features. Copyright by Paramount Pictures Corporation. Made in Taiwan.

Illustration 975. 8in (20.3cm) HENRY WINKLER as *Fonzie* from "Happy Days" by Mego, No. 63000, 1976. All-vinyl and fully-jointed with painted hair and features. Copyright by Paramount Pictures Corporation. Made in Hong Kong.

WISEMAN, JOSEPH. Actor. Born May, 1918 in Montreal, Quebec, Canada. Wiseman acted on the stage and entered motion picture work in the 1950s in character parts. His most memorable role was as the sinister Dr. No in the first James Bond film, *Dr. No* (1962). On television he played the villianous Draco in the early episodes of "Buck Rogers in the 25th Century," which began September 27, 1979, on ABC-TV.
DOLLS:
1. DRACO. Mego, No. 85000/5, 1979. Made in Hong Kong. 3¾in (9.6cm). *Illustration 978.*
2. DRACO. Mego, No. 85001/4, 1979. All-vinyl and fully-jointed. Painted hair and features. Made in Hong Kong. 12½in (31.8cm).
SEE: BUCK ROGERS IN THE 25TH CENTURY.

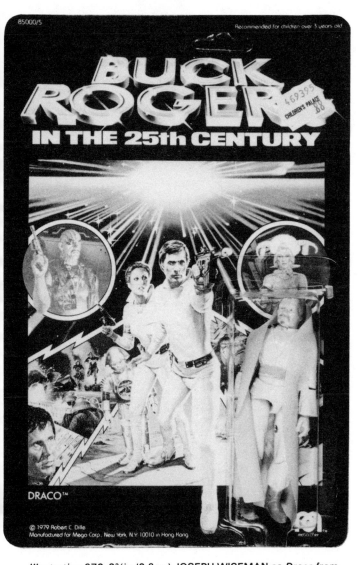

Illustration 978. 3¾in (9.6cm) JOSEPH WISEMAN as *Draco* from "Buck Rogers in the 25th Century" by Mego, No. 85000/5, 1979. All-vinyl and fully-jointed. Painted gray hair and painted brown eyes; painted clothing. Copyright by Robert C. Dille. Made in Hong Kong.

WITHERS, JANE. Actress. Born April 12, 1926, in Atlanta, Georgia. Jane Withers was a child performer from age four and she entered films at age six. Her first important part was when she was mean to little Shirley Temple in *Bright Eyes* in 1934. (Her character wanted a machine gun for Christmas.) During the next few years she went from tomboy to junior miss to young leading lady. In 1938 she was Number Eight at the Box Office. Her parts gradually became fewer and she retired to raise a family after 1947. In 1956 she had a character part in *Giant* and another in 1964 in *Captain Newman, M.D.* In 1963 she began a 12-year stint as Josephine, the down-to-earth plumber, pitching Comet cleanser in television commercials. Jane Withers is immensely likable and she is devoutly religious. She is dedicated to helping the Hollywood Museum become a reality by collecting memorabilia from old movie sets. She also has a fabulous doll collection which she has shown on television.

DOLLS:
All Jane Withers dolls were made by Madame Alexander in 1937. They are all-composition and fully-jointed. The wig is usually mohair and is a dark red color; the eyes are usually brown and have lashes. The dolls are not marked but they are easily identifiable. The dress is labeled and a gold-colored metal pin spelling "Jane Withers" in script was attached to the bodice.
1. to 4.
Closed mouth. Sizes of 13in (33cm), 15in (38.1cm), 17in (43.2cm), and 20in (50.8cm). *Illustrations 981, 982,* and *983.*
5. to 7.
Open mouth with upper teeth and a felt tongue. Sizes of 15in (38.1cm), 17in (43.2cm), and 20in (50.8cm). *Illustrations 984* and *985.*

Illustration 979. Jane Withers, 1937.

OPPOSITE PAGE: Illustration 976. HENRY WINKLER by Mego.

Jane Withers

FASHIONED CLOTHES

CUT-OUT DOLL BOOK

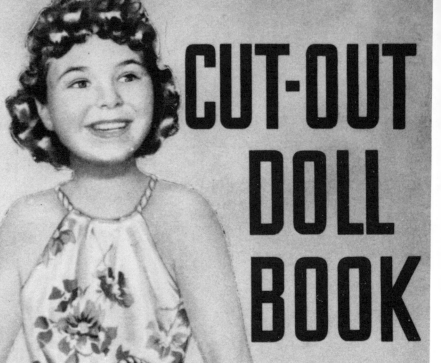

"Sketched from Life by AVIS MAC*"*

AGAIN, Mme. ALEXANDER, Famous Doll Designer, Scores a Hit!

JANE WITHERS' DOLLS—1937's BIG HIT!

Jane Withers

NEW! $2.25 13½ Inch

Alexander Sensation
In 4 Adorable Sizes

The lovable imp of the movies created into a laughing, **adorable human looking doll.** And not one bit of her bubbling enthusiasm, warming smile, saucy spirit has been lost in the process —a new triumph for the world famous designer. Head turns and tilts. Soft combination "brown ringlets and bangs" mohair wig. "Go-to-sleep" eyes. Curly lashes. Teeth and tiny tongue. (49 V 3350 has closed mouth, no teeth or tongue.) **De Luxe composition,** inside jointed arms, long slim legs. Lace trimmed dress, cute hat with saucy, turned brim. Lace undies, rayon socks, snap buckle shoes complete the **prettiest doll of the year.** "Gold plated" name pin and Jane Withers photo included.

SIDE VIEW

13½ In. Tall	15 In. Tall	17 In. Tall	20 In. Tall
Shpg. wt., 1 lb. 4 oz.	Shpg. wt., 1 lb. 12 oz.	Shpg. wt., 2 lbs.	Shpg. wt., 2 lbs. 8 oz.
49 V 3350	49 V 3351	49 V 3352	49 V 3353
$2.25	$2.69	$3.59	$4.59

Illustration 981. JANE WITHERS by Madame Alexander, 1937. *Sears 1937 Christmas Book.*

RIGHT: Illustration 983. 13in (33cm) JANE WITHERS by Madame Alexander, 1937. All-composition and fully-jointed. The original dark red-brown mohair wig is sparse; blue sleep eyes with lashes; closed mouth. The original dress is tagged: "JANE WITHERS // ALL RIGHTS RESERVED // MADAME ALEXANDER, N.Y." The shoes and socks are replaced. *Jean Canaday Collection.*

OPPOSITE PAGE: Illustration 980. Jane Withers paper doll book by Avis Mac, 1938. Copyright by the Whitman Publishing Co. *Marge Meisinger Collection.*

Illustration 982. 13in (33cm) JANE WITHERS by Madame Alexander, 1937. All-composition and fully-jointed. Reddish mohair wig; brown sleep eyes with lashes; closed mouth. The original dress is tagged and is a pale blue with darker blue flowers. *Connie Chase Collection.*

Illustration 984. 15in (38.1cm) JANE WITHERS by Madame Alexander, 1937. All-composition and fully-jointed. Dark red mohair wig; green sleep eyes with lashes; open mouth with four teeth. Doll not marked. Dress labeled: "JANE WITHERS // ALL RIGHTS RESERVED // MADAME ALEXANDER, N.Y." The bow in the hair is not original. *Wanda Lodwick Collection.*

THE WIZARD OF OZ. Motion picture from MGM. 1939 was one of Hollywood's best years and many films that are now considered classics were released that year. It was the year of *Gone With the Wind, Stagecoach, Mr. Smith Goes to Washington, Wuthering Heights, Of Mice and Men, Gunga Din, The Hunchback of Notre Dame* and another remake of *Beau Geste.* Bette Davis had four big hits—*Dark Victory, Juarez, The Old Maid* and *The Private Lives of Elizabeth and Essex.* Ingrid Bergman arrived in Hollywood to make *Intermezzo.* And JUDY GARLAND became a star by playing Dorothy in *The Wizard of Oz. The Wizard of Oz* has never been off release since 1939, unlike any other film. Fox refused to lend Shirley Temple for the lead part, a very fortunate break for MGM. The direction and production values were outstanding. The film was a dreamlike adventure and it called for a talent of Garland's proportions to make it work. Judy Garland's singing of "Over the Rainbow" alone makes the film worth watching—time and again. The rest of the cast was perfect also. JACK HALEY was the Tin Man, RAY BOLGER the Scarecrow, BERT LAHR the Cowardly Lion, FRANK MORGAN was the Wizard of Oz, BILLIE BURKE was Glinda, the Good Witch, and MARGARET HAMILTON was the Wicked Witch of the West. In many respects *The Wizard of Oz* is the single most successful television program in history. The film was first shown on TV on November 3, 1956, and almost every year since. It has never received a rating lower than 20.2 and usually has more than a 40 share. See each celebrity cited above for dolls.

Illustration 986. Judy Garland, Jack Haley and Ray Bolger from *The Wizard of Oz,* 1939.

OPPOSITE PAGE: Illustration 985. 20in (50.8cm) JANE WITHERS by Madame Alexander, 1937. All-composition and fully-jointed. Dark reddish-brown mohair wig; green sleep eyes with lashes; open mouth with teeth. The dress is blue; the hat is pink. Wears the "Jane Withers" script pin. The doll is not marked. *Fran's Dolls.*

WOLSEY, THOMAS. English statesman and prelate, lord chancellor, archbishop of York, cardinal of the Roman Catholic Church. Born circa 1472; died 1530. Wolsey rose rapidly in public life and gained favor with Henry VIII. By 1514 he virtually controlled English domestic and foreign policy. Twice he failed to be elected for the papacy but he lived lavishly in several private palaces in England. His ruin was caused by Henry's desire to be rid of Catherine of Aragon so he could marry Anne Boleyn. Wolsey presided at Catherine's annulment trial and in the end was stripped of all his honors except as archbishop. He was arrested for treason but died en route to the Tower. Wolsey's political and diplomatic skill was largely responsible for England becoming a first-rate world power in the 16th century.

1. CARDINAL WOLSEY. Peggy Nisbet, No. LE93, 1980. 8in (20.3cm). King Henry VIII, No. LE91, and Catherine of Aragon, No. LE92, are part of a set of three dolls. Made in England. *Illustration 987*.

Illustration 987. Special Collectors' Set No. 17, limited to the sale of 500 sets, by Peggy Nisbet, 1980. CARDINAL WOLSEY, No. LE93, and KING HENRY VIII, No. LE91 are 8in (20.3cm). CATHERINE OF ARAGON, No. LE92, is 7½in (19.1cm). All-hard plastic with jointed arms. Made in England. *Photograph Courtesy of House of Nisbet.*

WOPAT, TOM. Actor. Born September 9, 1951. In 1977 Wopat went to New York and soon landed a role on Broadway. He later went to Los Angeles, California, and tested along with about 100 other handsome, dark-haired young men to play in "The Dukes of Hazzard" with blonde John Schneider. The TV show began on CBS-TV in January 1979 and is a silly comedy about car chases and simple-minded rural southern characters, but it is also highly entertaining and it has made Tom Wopat a highly visible star.

DOLLS:
1. LUKE. Mego, No. 09060, 1981. Part of a set with a car and John Schneider as Bo. Came with two different head molds. Also given as a premium by Mego, which could be ordered with a slip from the purchase of the car, "The General Lee." Made in Hong Kong. 3¾in (9.6cm).
2. LUKE. Mego, No. 09050/2, 1981. Made in Hong Kong. 8in (20.3cm). *Illustrations 989* and *990*.
3. LUKE. Mego, No. 09010/2, 1982. This is the same doll as No. 1, packaged individually.
SEE: DUKES OF HAZZARD, THE.

Illustration 988. Tom Wopat.

Illustration 990. TOM WOPAT as *Luke* by Mego.

Illustration 989. 8in (20.3cm) TOM WOPAT as *Luke* from "The Dukes of Hazzard" by Mego, No. 09050/2, 1981. All-vinyl and fully-jointed. Painted dark brown hair and painted blue eyes. Head marked: " © WARNER BROS., // INC. 1980." Back marked: " © MEGO CORP. 1974 // REG U.S. PAT OFF // PAT PENDING // HONG KONG."

Bibliography
General Reference

Agan, Patrick. *Is That Who I Think It Is? Vol. I.* New York: Ace Books, 1974.

_____. *Is That Who I Think It Is? Vol. 2.* New York: Ace Books, 1975.

_____. *Is That Who I Think It Is? Vol. 3.* New York: Ace Books, 1976.

Allen, Don. *The World of Film and Filmmakers.* New York: Crown Publishers, Inc., 1979.

Anger, Kenneth. *Hollywood Babylon.* San Francisco: Straight Arrow Books, 1975.

Bane, Michael. *Who's Who In Rock.* New York: Facts on File, Inc., 1981.

Basinger, Jeanine. *Shirley Temple.* New York: Pyramid Publications, 1975.

Baxter, John. *King Vidor.* New York: Monarch Press, 1976.

Benziger Brothers, Inc. *Little Pictorial Lives of the Saints.* New York: Benziger Brothers, Inc., 1878.

Berman, Connie. *The Shaun Cassidy Scrapbook.* New York: Sunridge Press, 1978.

Bland, Alexander. *The Nureyev Image.* New York: New York Times Books, 1976.

Blum, Daniel. *A New Pictorial History of the Talkies.* New York: G. P. Putnam's Sons, 1968.

Bodeen, DeWitt. *More From Hollywood.* South Brunswick and New York: A. S. Barnes and Company, 1977.

Botham, Noel, and Donnelly, Peter. *Valentino the Love God.* New York: Ace Books, 1976.

Bowser, James W. *Starring Elvis.* New York: Dell Publishing Co., Inc., 1956, 1957, 1958, 1961, 1962, 1963, 1964, 1965, 1969 and 1977.

Brode, Douglas. *The Films of the Fifties.* Secaucus, New Jersey: The Citadel Press, 1976.

Brooks, Tim, and Marsh, Earle. *The Complete Directory of Prime Time Network TV Shows 1946—Present.* New York: Ballantine Books, 1979.

Bronaugh, Robert Brett. *The Celebrity Birthday Book.* Middle Village, New York: Jonathan David Publishers, Inc., 1981.

Brosnan, John. *James Bond in the Cinema.* (Second Edition). San Diego: A. S. Barnes & Co., Inc., 1981.

Brown, Dale and the Editors of Time-Life Books. *The World of Velázquez.* New York: Time-Life Books, 1969.

Brown, Les. *The New York Times Encyclopedia of Television.* New York: New York Times, 1977.

Bruno, Michael. *Venus in Hollywood.* New York: Lyle Stuart, Inc., 1970.

Bruns, Bill, and Clarkson, Rich. *Montreal '76 The Games of the XXI Olympiad.* Island Heritage Limited, 1976.

Burdick, Loraine. *The Shirley Temple Scrapbook.* Middle Village, New York: Jonathan David Publishers, 1975.

Canaday, John. *The Lives of the Painters* (4 Volumes). New York: W. W. Norton & Company, Inc., 1969.

Capra, Frank. *The Name Above the Title.* New York: The Macmillan Company, 1971.

Carroll, David. *The Matinee Idols.* New York: Galahad Books, 1972.

Casson, Lionel. *Ancient Egypt.* New York: Time-Life Books, 1965.

Coulson, John. *The Saints: A Concise Biographical Dictionary.* New York: Hawthorn Books, Inc., 1958.

Crumbaker, Marge, and Tucker, Gabe. *Up and Down with Elvis Presley.* New York: G. P. Putnam's Sons, 1981.

Current Biography. Various Editions. New York: H.W. Wilson Company, various years.

Dimmitt, Richard Bertrand. *A Title Guide to the Talkies.* New York: The Scarecrow Press, Inc., 1965.

Dunning, John. *Tune In Yesterday.* Englewood Cliffs, New Jersey: Prentice-Hall, Inc., 1976.

Druxman, Michael B. *Charlton Heston.* New York: Pyramid Publications, 1976.

_____. *Make It Again, Sam, A Survey of Movie Remakes.* South Brunswick and New York: A. S. Barnes and Company, 1975.

_____. *One Good Film Deserves Another, A Pictorial Survey of the Film Sequels.* South Brunswick and New York: A. S. Barnes and Co., 1977.

Eames, John Douglas. *The MGM Story.* New York: Crown Publishers Inc., 1975.

Edwards, Anne. *Vivien Leigh—A Biography.* New York: Simon and Schuster, 1977.

Erens, Patricia. *The Films of Shirley Maclaine.* South Brunswick and New York: A. S. Barnes and Co., 1978.

Essoe, Gabe. *Tarzan of the Movies.* New York: The Citadel Press, 1968.

Finch, John A., and Elby, Paula A. *Close-Ups from the Jorafin Collection from the Golden Age of the*

Silent Cinema. South Brunswick and New York: A. S. Barnes and Co., 1978.

Fitzgerald, Michael G. *Universal Pictures—A Panoramic History in Words, Pictures and Filmographics.* New Rochelle, New York: Arlington House Publishers, 1977.

Flamini, Roland. *Scarlett, Rhett, and a Cast of Thousands—The Filming of Gone With the Wind.* New York: Macmillan Publishing Co., Inc., 1975.

Foster, Alan Dean. *Clash of the Titans.* New York: Warner Books, 1981.

Fredrik, Nathalie. *Hollywood and the Academy Awards.* Beverly Hills, California: Hollywood Awards Publications, 1969.

Gish, Lillian. *Dorothy and Lillian Gish.* New York: Macmillan, 1973.

Goldwyn, Samuel. *Behind the Screen.* New York: George H. Doran Company, 1923.

Gray, Andy. *Great Pop Stars.* London, New York, Sydney, Toronto: Hamlyn Publishing Group Ltd., 1973.

Griffith, Richard, and Mayer, Arthur. *The Movies.* New York: Simon and Schuster, 1957.

Halliwell, Leslie. *The Filmgoer's Companion* (Sixth Edition). New York: Hill and Wang, 1965.

_____. *Mountain of Dreams: The Golden Years of Paramount Pictures.* New York: Stonehill Publishing Company, 1976.

_____. *Halliwell's Film Guide.* New York: Charles Scribner's Sons, 1977; 1979.

Harbinson, W. A. *The Illustrated Elvis.* New York: Grossett & Dunlap, 1975.

Harmetz, Aljean. *The Making of the Wizard of Oz.* New York: Alfred A. Knopf, Inc., 1977.

Harris, Jay S. *TV Guide the First 25 Years.* New York: Simon and Schuster, 1978.

Higham, Charles, and Greenberg, Joel. *Hollywood in the Forties.* New York: Paperback Library, 1968.

Hill, Randal C. *The Official Price Guide to Collectible Rock Records.* Orlando, Florida: House of Collectibles, 1979.

Hirsch, Foster. *Elizabeth Taylor.* New York: Pyramid Publications, 1973.

Hirschhorn, Clive. *The Warner Bros. Story.* New York: Crown Publishers, Inc., 1979.

Hogarth, Burne. *Tarzan of the Apes.* New York: Watson-Guptil Publications, 1972.

Hudson, Peggy. *The Television Scene.* New York, Toronto, London, Sydney, Auckland, Tokyo. Scholastic Book Services, 1972.

_____. *TV 72.* New York, Toronto, London, Auckland, Sydney, Tokyo, 1971.

Jones, Ken D., McClure, Arthur F., and Twomey, Alfred E. *Character People—The Stalwarts of the Cinema.* South Brunswick and New York: A. S. Barnes and Co., 1976.

Kaplan, Mike. *Variety International Showbusiness Reference.* New York and London: Garland Publishing, Inc., 1981.

Katz, Emphriam. *The Film Encyclopedia.* New York: Thomas Y. Crowell, 1979.

Keylin, Arleen. *Hollywood Album 2—Lives and Deaths of Hollywood Stars from the Pages of the New York Times.* New York: Arno Press, 1979.

Knight, Arthur. *The New York Times Directory of the Film.* New York: Arno Press, 1974.

La Fay, Howard. *The Vikings.* Washington, D. C.: The National Geographic Society, 1972.

Lamparski, Richard. *Whatever Became of...? Vol. III.* New York: reprint by Ace Books, 1970.

_____. *Whatever Became of...? The New Fourth Series.* New York, Toronto and London: reprint by Bantam Books, 1973.

_____. *Whatever Became of...? Fifth Series.* New York: Crown Publishers, Inc., 1974.

_____. *Whatever Became of...? 1st Giant Annual.* New York, Toronto, London: reprint by Bantam Books, 1976.

Lane, Hana Umlauf. *The World Almanac Book of Who.* New York: World Almanac Publications, 1980.

Levin, Martin. *Hollywood and the Great Fan Magazines.* New York: Arbor House, 1970.

Lichter, Paul. *Elvis in Hollywood.* New York: Simon and Schuster, 1975.

Maltin, Leonard, and Bann, Richard W. *Our Gang—The Life & Times of the Little Rascals.* New York: Crown Publishers, Inc., 1977.

Maltin, Leonard. *TV Movies.* All editions from 1969 to 1982. New York, Signet Book, 1969 to 1982.

Malone, Michael. *Heroes of Eros.* New York: E. P. Dutton, 1979.

Manuell, Roger. *Love Goddesses of the Movies.* New York: Crescent Books, 1975.

Marquis Who's Who in America. Chicago, Illinois: A. N. Marquis Company, various years.

Massie, Robert K. *Nicholas and Alexandra.* New York: Antheneum Publishers, 1967.

McClure, F., and Jones, Ken D. *Star Quality—Screen Actors from the Golden Age of Films.* South Brunswick and New York: A. S. Barnes and Company, 1974.

McColm, Bruce, and Payne, Doug. *Where Have They Gone? Rock 'N' Roll Stars.* New York: Grossett & Dunlap, 1979.

Michael, Paul. *The Academy Awards: A Pictorial History.* New York: Bonanza Books, 1964.

Miller, Don. *Hollywood Corral.* New York: Popular Library, 1976.

Miller, Jim, and Kingsbury, Robert. *The Rolling Stone's Illustrated History of Rock & Roll.* New York: Rolling Stone Press; Random House, 1976.

Munshower, Suzanne. *The John Travolta Scrapbook.* New York: Sunridge Press, 1976.

Nite, Norm, and Clark, Dick. *Rock On: The Solid Gold Years.* New York: Popular Library, 1974.

Oberfirst, Robert. *Rudolph Valentino the Man Behind the Myth.* New York: The Citadel Press, 1962.

Parish, James Robert. *Actors' Television Credits 1950-1972*. Metuchen, New Jersey: The Scarecrow Press, Ltd., 1973.

_____. *The Elvis Presley Scrapbook*. New York: Ballantine Books, 1975.

_____. *Great Child Stars*. New York; Ace Books, 1976.

_____. *Hollywood Character Actors*. New Rochelle, New York: Arlington House Publishers, 1978.

_____, and Bowers, Ronald L. *The MGM Stock Company: The Golden Era*. New York: Bonanza Books, 1972.

_____. *The Paramount Pretties*. Castle Books, 1972.

_____. *The RKO Gals*. New Rochelle, New York: Arlington House Publishers, 1974.

_____, and Stanke, Don E. *The Swashbucklers*. New Rochelle, New York: Arlington House Publishers, 1976.

Porges, Irwin. *Edgar Rice Burroughs—The Man Who Created Tarzan*. Provo, Utah: Brigham Young University Press, 1975.

Pratt, William. *Scarlett Fever—The Ultimate Pictorial Treasury of Gone With the Wind*. New York: Macmillan Publishing Co., Inc., 1977.

Prideaux, Tom. *Life Goes to the Movies*. New York: Time-Life Books, 1975.

Quirk, Lawrence J. *The Great Romantic Films*. Secaucus, New Jersey: The Citadel Press, 1974.

Ragan, David. *Who's Who in Hollywood*. New Rochelle, New York: Arlington House Publishers, 1976.

Ringgold, Gene. *The Films of Rita Hayworth: The Legend & Career of a Love Goddess*. Secaucus, New Jersey: The Citadel Press, 1974.

Ringgold, Gene, and Bodeen, DeWitt. *The Films of Cecil B. DeMille*. New York: The Citadel Press, 1969.

Rovin, Jeff. *The Films of Charlton Heston*. Secaucus, New Jersey: The Citadel Press, 1977.

Russell, Maggi. *The Shaun Cassidy Story*. Paradise Press, Inc., 1978.

St. Johns, Adela Rogers. *Love Laughter and Tears*. Garden City, New York: Doubleday & Company, Inc., 1978.

Salinger, Margaretta. *Diego Valazquez*. New York: Harry N. Abrams, Publishers, n.d.

Scagnetti, Jack. *The Intimate Life of Rudolph Valentino*. Middle Village, New York: Jonathan David Publishers, Inc., 1975.

Scheuer, Steven H. *The Television Annual 1978-79*. New York: Macmillan Publishing Co., Inc., 1979.

Schickel, Richard, and the Editors of Time-Life Books. *The World of Goya*. New York: Time-Life Books, 1968.

Sheed, Wilfrid. *Muhammad Ali*. New York and Scarborough, Ontario: New American Library, 1975.

Shipman, David. *The Great Movie Stars—The Golden Years*. New York: Bonanza Books, 1970.

_____. *The Great Movie Stars—The International Years*. New York: Hill and Wang, 1972.

Shulman, Irving. *Harlow an Intimate Biography*. New York: Dell Publishing Co., Inc., 1964.

_____. *Valentino*. New York: Pocket Books, 1967.

Silke, James R. *Here's Looking at You, Kid* Boston and Toronto: Little, Brown and Company, 1976.

Smithsonian Institution, The. *Portraits of the American Stage, 1771-1971*. Washington: Smithsonisn Institution Press, 1971.

Stallings, Penny, with Mandelbaum, Howard. *Flesh and Fantasy*. New York: St. Martin's Press, 1978.

Steinberg, Cobbett S. *Film Facts*. New York: Facts on File, Inc., 1980.

Stuart, Ray. *Immortals of the Screen*. New York: Bonanza Books, 1965.

Swann, Thomas Burnett. *The Heroine or the Horse—Leading Ladies in Republic's Films*. South Brunswick and New York: A. S. Barnes and Company, 1977.

Tatham, Dick. *Elvis*. Secaucus, New Jersey: Chartwell Books, Inc., 1976.

Taylor, Derek. *The Making of Raiders of the Lost Ark*. New York: Ballantine Books, 1981.

Terrace, Vincent. *The Complete Encyclopedia of Television Programs, 1947-1976*. (Volume I and Volume II.) South Brunswick and New York: A. S. Barnes & Co., Inc., 1976.

_____. *Television 1970-1980*. San Diego: A. S. Barnes & Company, Inc., 1981.

Thomas, Tony. *The Films of Ronald Reagan*. Secaucus, New Jersey: Citadel Press, 1980.

Troutman, Philip. *Velazquez*. London: Spring Art Books, 1965, 1966.

Truett, Randle Bond. *The First Ladies in Fashion*. New York: Hastings House Publishers, 1954; 1970.

Vance, Malcom. *Tara Revisited*. New York: Award Books, 1976.

Vermilyn, Jerry, and Ricci, Mark. *The Films of Elizabeth Taylor*. Secaucus, New Jersey: The Citadel Press, 1976.

Walker, Alexander. *Garbo a Portrait*. New York: Macmillan Publishing Co., Inc., 1980.

_____. *Rudolph Valentino*. New York: Stein and Day, 1976.

Wallace, Irving; Wallace, Amy; Wallechinsky, David; Wallace, Sylvia. *The Intimate Sex Lives of Famous People*. New York: Delacorte Press, 1981.

Warner, Jack, with Jennings, Dean. *My First Hundred Years in Hollywood: An Autobiography*. New York: Random House, 1964.

Weaver, John T. *Forty Years of Screen Credits—1929-1969*. Metuchen, New Jersey: Scarecrow Press, Inc., 1970

Wertheimer, Alfred. *Elvis '56 in the Beginning*. New York: Collier Books, 1979.

West, Mae. *Goodness Had Nothing To Do With It*. New York: Avon Book Division the Hearst Corporation, 1959.

Willis, John. *Screen World. Volumes 24, 25, 26, 27, 28, 29, 30, 31, 32*. New York: Crown Publishers Inc., 1973, 1974, 1975, 1976, 1977, 1978, 1979, 1980, 1981.

Windeler, Robert. *The Films of Shirley Temple*. Secaucus, New Jersey: Citadel Press, 1978.

Wlaschin, Ken. *The World's Great Movie Stars and Their Films*. New York: Harmony Books, 1979.

Woodward, W. E. Meet General Grant. Garden City, New York: Garden City Publishing Co., Inc., 1928.

Yesterday's Authors of Books for Children. Detroit: Gale Research Co., 1977.

Yorke, Ritchie. *The History of Rock 'n' Roll*. Toronto, New York, London, Sydney, Wellington: Methune/Two Continents, 1976.

Zmijewsky, Steven and Boris. *Elvis. The Films and Career of Elvis Presley*. Secaucus, New Jersey: Citadel Press, 1976.

Doll Reference

Anderton, Johana Gast. *Twentieth Century Dolls from Bisque to Vinyl*. North Kansas City, Missouri: The Trojan Press, 1971.

_____. *More Twentieth Century Dolls from Bisque to Vinyl*. North Kansas City, Missouri: Athena Publishing Co., 1974.

Angione, Genevieve, and Whorton, Judith. *All Dolls Are Collectible*. New York: Crown Publishers, Inc., 1977.

Axe, John. *Collectible Black Dolls*. Riverdale, Maryland: Hobby House Press, 1978.

_____. *Collectible Boy Dolls*. Riverdale, Maryland: Hobby House Press, 1977.

_____. *The Collectible Dionne Quintuplets*. Riverdale, Maryland: Hobby House Press, 1977.

_____. *Collectible Dolls in National Costume*. Riverdale, Maryland: Hobby House Press, 1977.

_____. *Collectible Patsy Dolls and Patsy-Types*. Riverdale, Maryland: Hobby House Press, 1978.

_____. *Collectible Sonja Henie*. Riverdale, Maryland: Hobby House Press, 1979.

_____. *Tammy and Dolls You Love to Dress*. Riverdale, Maryland: Hobby House Press, 1979.

Biggs, Marge. *Madame Alexander "Little People."* Privately Published, 1979.

Burdick, Loraine. *A Doll for Christmas or Any Time*. Puyallup, Washington: Quest Books, 1971.

_____. *Adult Star Dolls and Toys*. Book 1 and Book 2. Puyallup, Washington: Quest-Eridon Books, 1973 and 1981.

_____. *Child Star Dolls and Toys*. Puyallup, Washington: Quest-Eridon Books, 1968; 1977.

_____. *Shirley Dolls and Related Delights*. Puyallup, Washington: Quest Books, 1966.

Coleman, Dorothy S., Coleman, Elizabeth A., and Coleman, Evelyn J. *The Collector's Encyclopedia of Dolls*. New York: Crown Publishers, Inc., 1968.

Coleman, Dorothy S. *Lenci Dolls: Fabulous Figures of Felt*. Riverdale, Maryland: Hobby House Press, 1977.

Cooper, Marlowe. *Doll Home Library Series*. Vol. 12, Vol. 13 and Vol. 14. Privately published, 1973.

Desmonde, Kay. *All Color Book of Dolls*. London: Octopus Books Limited, 1974.

Ellenburg, M. Kelly. *Effanbee—The Dolls with the Golden Hearts*. North Kansas City, Missouri: The Trojan Press, 1973.

Foulke, Jan. *2nd Blue Book of Dolls and Values*. Riverdale, Maryland: Hobby House Press, 1976.

_____. *3rd Blue Book of Dolls and Values*. Riverdale, Maryland: Hobby House Press, 1978.

_____. *4th Blue Book of Dolls and Values*. Cumberland, Maryland: Hobby House Press, 1980.

_____. *Treasury of Madame Alexander Dolls*. Riverdale, Maryland: Hobby House Press, 1979.

Hille, Sally. *Personality Doll Houses*. Privately published, n.d.

Jacobson, Carol L. *A Sentimental Portrait of Dolls*. Privately published, 1973.

_____. *A Past & Present Portrait of Dolls*. Privately published, n.d.

_____. *A Very Special Portrait of Dolls*. Privately published, 1977.

Lutz, Nancie Anne. *Dolls—A Complete Bibliography*. Newport Beach, California: The Doll Works, 1981.

McKeon, Barbara Jo. *Rare & Hard to Find Madame Alexander Collector's Dolls*. Privately published, 1979.

Miller, Marjorie. *Nancy Ann Storybook Dolls*. Cumberland, Maryland: Hobby House Press, 1980.

Noble, John. *A Treasury of Beautiful Dolls*. New York: Weathervane Books, 1971.

Revi, Albert Christian, editor. *Spinning Wheel's Complete Book of Dolls*. New York: Galahad Books, 1949 to 1975.

Robinson, Joleen, and Sellers, Kay. *Advertising Dolls Identification & Value Guide*. Paducah, Kentucky: Collector Books, 1980.

Smith, Patricia R. *Madame Alexander Collector's Dolls*. Paducah, Kentucky: Collector Books, 1978.

_____. *Madame Alexander Collector's Dolls. Second Series*. Paducah, Kentucky: Collector Books, 1981.

_____. *Modern Collector's Dolls*. Paducah, Kentucky: Collector Books, 1973.

_____. *Modern Collector's Dolls. Second Series*. Paducah, Kentucky: Collector Books, 1975.

_____. *Modern Collector's Dolls. Third Series*. Paducah, Kentucky: Collector Books, 1976.

_____. *Modern Collector's Dolls. Fourth Series.* Paducah, Kentucky: Collector Books, 1979.

Stuecher, Mary. "The Shirley Temple Story" in *Shirley Temple Dolls and Collectibles* by Smith, Patricia R. Paducah, Kentucky: Collector Books, 1977.

Uhl, Marjorie V. Sturges. *Madame Alexander Dolls on Review.* Privately published, 1981.

United Federation of Doll Clubs, Inc. *Glossary.* United Federation of Doll Clubs, Inc., 1978.

Periodicals

(Various issues for each entry)

After Dark.

American Film Magazine of the Film & TV Arts.

The Antique Trader Weekly.

Celebrity Doll Journal.

Collectors United.

Doll Castle News.

Doll News.

Doll Reader.

Good Housekeeping.

Gossip.

Horizon.

Life.

Look.

Luxe.

Modern People.

Modern Screen.

Motion Picture.

National Geographic.

The National Glass, Pottery and Collectables Journal.

New York (Magazine).

Newsweek.

Parade.

People Weekly.

Playthings.

Popular TV.

Screen Stories.

16 Magazine.

Sunday News Magazine.

Super Teen.

Teen Bag.

Teen Beat.

Teen Beat's Super Stars.

Teen's Entertainment '80.

Tiger Beat.

Tiger Beat Star.

Time.

TV Guide.

TV Yearbook. (Various years)

US.

Variety.

Who's Who in Hollywood. (Various years from 1948 to 1964)

Who's Who in Movies. (Various years)

Who's Who in Television & Radio. (Various years)

Who's Who in TV. (Various years)

Newspapers

(Various dates for each entry)

Daily Signal. Huntington Park, California

Evening Independent. St. Petersburg, Florida

The Morning Call. Allentown, Pennsylvania

The New York Times.

The Youngstown Vindicator. Youngstown, Ohio

Manufacturer Catalogs

(Various years for each entry)

Aldens, Inc.

Alexander Doll Company, Inc.

American Character Dolls

Ann Parker Dolls

Anne Wilkinson Designs, Ltd.

Bea Skydell's Dolls & Friends

Dolls by Al Trattner

Effanbee Doll Corporation

FAO Schwarz

Ideal Toy Corporation

J. C. Penney, Inc.

Kenner Products

Knickerbocker Toy Co., Inc.

LJN Toys

Mark Farmer Co.

Mego Corp.

Montgomery Ward & Co., Inc.

Peggy Nisbet Limited

Sears, Roebuck and Co.

Shoppe Full of Dolls

Spiegel, Inc.

Standard Doll Co.

Tristar International, Ltd.

Under the Lilac

Addendum

A book of this scope takes a long time to complete. The author spent about five years compiling material that was based on hobbies and interests of a lifetime. Then the manuscript must spend some time in production and in preparation for printing. In the meantime, new celebrity dolls are appearing. Some are ones that were unknown to the author at the time the *Encyclopedia* was compiled; some are new dolls that have been released very recently; and others are dolls that were known only as prototypes and production models when photographs were obtained for inclusion in the book. As these words are being written many new celebrity dolls are being designed and prepared by various doll companies. Celebrity dolls are *the* dolls to collect!

Illustration 992. The original box for the *Chantal Goya* doll. This doll was made for distribution in France. Chantal Goya is a singer who is a favorite with children.

Illustration 991. 11½in (29.2cm) CHANTAL GOYÁ by Mattel of France, No. 8935-63, 1979. All-vinyl and fully-jointed with rooted dark brown hair. Head marked: "CHANTAL GOYA 1979 // TAIWAN."

Illustration 993. 9½in (24.2cm) BJÖRN ULVAEUS of the rock group ABBA by Matchbox, No. AB-104, 1978. All-vinyl and fully-jointed. Painted blonde hair; painted blue eyes. Marked on the buttock: "© HASBRO // U. S. PAT PEND // MADE IN // HONG KONG." ABBA from Sweden was very popular in Europe, where these dolls were distributed. There are also companion dolls of Benny Andersson, Anni-Frid Lyngstad-Fredriksson and Agnetha Ulvaeus, the other members of the group.

Illustration 994. 10in (25.4cm) RONALD REAGAN, the *Reaganomics Doll* by Dots Okay, 1982. All-cloth and printed in black and white. This is the "Supply Side;" the reverse is a sad looking character called "Demand Side." Tag: "Reagonomics Doll™ // DOTS OKAY ® // Annandale, VA 22003 // Copyright © 1982 // All rights reserved." Made in USA.

Illustration 996. 8in (20.3cm) and 12in (30.5cm) SHIRLEY TEMPLE by Ideal, late 1982. All-vinyl and fully-jointed. Rooted blonde hair; hazel sleep eyes with plastic lashes. The head of the 8in (20.3cm) doll is marked: "45904 // 4 // © 1982 // IDEAL TOY CORP. // ST-9-H371." The head of the 12in (30.5cm) doll is marked: "4560 // 8 // © 1982 // IDEAL TOY CORP. // ST-12-H368." The backs of both dolls are marked: " © IDEAL 1982 // HONG KONG." Compare these dolls with the prototype of the dolls in *Illustration 898*.

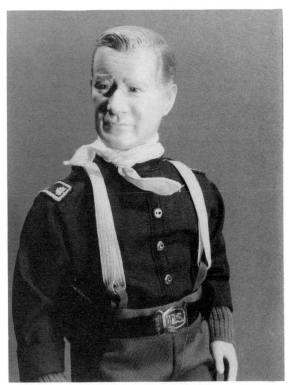

Illustration 995. AILEEN QUINN, 1982. On the left: 10in (25.4cm) "Annie Genuine Porcelain Doll. A true-to-life replica of 'ANNIE' Moviestar (sic), Aileen Quinn" by Applause (a division of Knickerbocker), No. 8904. Bisque shoulder plate head, arms and legs; cloth body. Orange wig; painted blue eyes. No marks on doll. Made in Taiwan. Red velveteen dress trimmed in white; black shoes. On the right: 10½in (26.7cm) "Movie Star Annie with party dress and shoes" by Knickerbocker, No. 3836. All-vinyl and fully-jointed. Rooted orange hair; painted blue eyes; open/closed mouth. Head marked: "MADE IN HONG KONG // © 1982 TRIBUNE COMPANY // SYNDICATE INC. // CPI INC. // MIDDLESEX, N.J. 08846 // H-17." Red and white dress; black vinyl shoes; wears *Annie* locket.

Illustration 997. 18in (45.7cm) JOHN WAYNE by Effanbee, No. 2981 1982. All-vinyl and fully-jointed. Painted hair; painted blue eyes. Head marked: "EFFANBEE // © 1982 // WAYNE ENT." Back marked: "EFFANBEE // ENT. // 19 © 81." Compare this photograph with the prototype doll in *Illustration 955*.

Illustration 998. 18in (45.7cm) MAE WEST by Effanbee, 1982. All-vinyl and fully-jointed. Rooted light blonde hair; painted blue eyes. Head and back marked: "© 1982 // EST. MAE WEST // effanbee." Compare this photograph with the prototype doll in *Illustration 961*.

Illustration 999. 18in (45.7cm) DIANA, THE PRINCESS OF WALES, the 1982 presentation of the Effanbee Limited Edition Doll Club. For full description and a photograph of the prototype doll see *Illustration 246-C*.

Illustration 1000. Royal Baby Boy Commemorative Set by House of Nisbet, "Hand Made in England," Limited Signature Edition Set No. 21, 1982. This is set No. 1672 and includes No. P1007, H.R.H. PRINCE CHARLES, THE PRINCE OF WALES; No. P1008(a), H.R.H. THE PRINCESS OF WALES; and No. P1008(b), PRINCE WILLIAM. PRINCE CHARLES is 8¼in (21cm), PRINCESS DIANA is 7¾in (19.8cm); PRINCE WILLIAM is 2⅝in (9.2cm). All-plastic. The two larger dolls are jointed at the arms only. This set of dolls was certainly in the conception stage long before Prince William's birth on 21 June 1982. The baby is dressed only in white. *Mary Lee Ruddell Collection.*

Index